OSCAR WARS

ALSO BY MICHAEL SCHULMAN

Her Again: Becoming Meryl Streep

OSCAR WARS

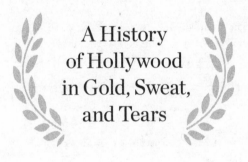

A History
of Hollywood
in Gold, Sweat,
and Tears

Michael Schulman

HARPER

An Imprint of HarperCollins*Publishers*

HarperCollins books may be purchased for educational, business, or sales promotional use. For information, please email the Special Markets Department at SPsales@harpercollins.com.

Portions of this book first appeared in *The New Yorker* and *Vanity Fair*.

FIRST EDITION

Designed by Nancy Singer

Library of Congress Cataloging-in-Publication Data has been applied for.

ISBN 978-0-06-285901-3

22 23 24 25 26 LBC 5 4 3 2 1

For my parents,
Nancy and Richard Schulman

*Let's get on with this farcical charade of vulgar
egotism and pomposity.*

—Bob Hope

CONTENTS

A Little Too Scared to Hope

The Oscars, it should be said at the start, are always getting it wrong. Twenty-four centuries after Euripides came in third place at the Athenian dramatic festival, *Brokeback Mountain* lost Best Picture to *Crash*, and the outcry will probably last another twenty-four centuries.

The ostensible purpose of the Academy Awards is to honor excellence in movies. But that lofty goal is what Alfred Hitchcock would have called a MacGuffin—the plot device that gets the real drama going. Each Oscar year is a suspense tale, a choose-your-own-adventure story. Like any good Hollywood screenplay, it has burgeoning conflict, a colorful cast of characters, and a few plot twists—all climaxing on a glittering stage, under the glare of the cameras and millions of viewers. Subplots ricochet down the ages with new players: the neglected masterpiece, the overreaching campaign, the breathless starlet. Elizabeth Taylor becomes Julia Roberts; *Citizen Kane* cross-fades into *Do the Right Thing*.

What *are* the Academy Awards, anyway? The answers vary. They're a vaunted tradition celebrating a great modern art form. They're an industry party—like a convention of landscapers, but with better outfits. They're the closest thing America has to royalty. They're the only thing forcing Hollywood to factor art into commerce. They're a marketing ploy propping up a multibillion-dollar business. They're a method, however dubious, of organizing movies into a canon. They're a game. They're a relic. They're a fashion show. They're a horse race. They're an orgy of self-congratulation by rich and famous people who think too highly of themselves. They're the Gay Super Bowl.

This book argues, in eleven installments, that they're something else, too. The Oscars are a battlefield where cultural forces collide and where the victors aren't always as clear as the names drawn from the envelopes. The red carpet runs through contested turf, but it can take years to see what the real battle lines were. An aesthetic sea change that sets the tone for a decade might be buried in the screenplay nominations. A political upheaval might be a whisper one year, a roar the next. Like Hollywood's greatest sagas—*Star Wars*, *The Godfather*—the Oscars often play out as a drama of generational conflict, as a new cohort shows up to displace the old. A young upstart may recur decades later as an industry heavyweight: the boyish Steven Spielberg who gets snubbed for *Jaws* becomes the establishment bigwig of *Saving Private Ryan*.

In recent years, the Oscars have become a conflict zone for issues of race, gender, and representation, high-profile signifiers of whose stories get told and whose don't. These reckonings are a long time coming. The #OscarsSoWhite campaign reached a crescendo in 2016, the same year America went through a political paroxysm steeped in racial animus. But #OscarsSoWhite grew out of a century's worth of absence, punctuated by lonely victories for such Black stars as Hattie McDaniel, Sidney Poitier, and Halle Berry. The next year, the Harvey Weinstein scandal took out one of the Oscars' most contentious players and tarnished Hollywood's self-enshrined mythos, but it echoed back to Harry Cohn's Oscar-encircled casting couch at Columbia Pictures.

In previous decades, Oscar wars were waged over different issues, but they were no less fraught. In the thirties, Hollywood's insurgent labor movement turned the Academy into Public Enemy No. 1, as workers boycotted the ceremony and nearly killed off the Oscars in their adolescence. In the fifties, the Academy bent to the paranoia of the House Un-American Activities Committee, forcing blacklisted screenwriters to hide behind false names—even as they won Oscars. In the late sixties, with the studio system crumbling and the generation gap wide open, the Oscars were besieged by young people with long hair and risqué tastes, as movies like *Easy Rider* heralded the arrival of the New Hollywood. In the nineties, an indie uprising brought in a rambunctious new crowd, led by a man who turned Oscar campaigning into a blood sport—when he wasn't doing far worse in the shadows.

If there's a common thread running through the decades of Oscar wars, it's power: who has it, who's straining to keep it, who's invading the golden citadel to snatch it. The Oscars are perpetually redrawing the bounds of the Hollywood establishment, pitting eminences against arrivistes, conventionalists against iconoclasts. As soon as the Academy Award was invented, people in Hollywood wanted it, because it created an organizing principle for power and prestige in a town whose hierarchy is always shifting beneath its denizens' feet. The statuette is a talisman that elicits powerful desires—for attention, for recognition, for clout—driving its suitors toward folly or excess or desperation. Art isn't meant to be ranked like a sports team or scored like a tennis match, but human nature drives us toward gamesmanship: we like watching people win or lose, and if given the chance, we want to win.

I started watching the Academy Awards in the early nineties, when Billy Crystal was the regular host and began each ceremony with a zingy comic medley. "And not an ounce of smut, / It ain't called *Howards Butt*! / They call it *Howards End*," he crooned in 1993, to the tune of "Hooray for Hollywood." I hadn't seen any of the Best Picture nominees, but to my adolescent brain, it was the height of comedy, the Olympus of schmaltz. As an adult, I organized office Oscar pools and memorized acceptance speeches. In 2016, as a writer at *The New Yorker*, I covered the Academy's tumultuous year in the wake of #OscarsSoWhite. Led by its first Black president, Cheryl Boone Isaacs, and its CEO, Dawn Hudson, the Academy was under fire for an initiative to recruit new, diverse members and demote others who had been inactive in the industry to "emeritus" status—a plan that had old-timers looking at their IMDb pages and panicking. The issue had cracked open Hollywood's fault lines of age and ideology, but, as I soon learned, it had all happened before. In 1970, the same year *Midnight Cowboy* became the first X-rated movie to win Best Picture, Academy president Gregory Peck had launched a similar plan to yank the membership into the present—and had also received rafts of angry letters. Now some of the hip, young talents of the New Hollywood were seasoned pros writing incensed op-eds in *The Hollywood Reporter*, howling against their perceived obsolescence.

In February 2017, I went to the Oscars for the first time. Sitting in the pressroom at the Loews Hollywood Hotel, where dozens of journalists from around the world sat at long tables, I watched the show on a monitor. Occasionally, the newly minted winners were shown in to answer questions. In the back of the room was a reference table where Academy librarians sat with thick binders. Toward the end of the night, the energy in the room flagged, as we lurched toward an inevitable Best Picture win for *La La Land*. When Faye Dunaway announced it as the winner, the reporters applauded warmly and wrapped up their stories.

Then all hell broke loose. On-screen, a *La La Land* producer was holding up a card that read that *Moonlight* had won. The pressroom let out a collective scream: something was actually *happening*. Journalists lined up at the reference table, which had been ignored most of the night, asking if anything like this had ever happened before. "I cannot think of a case where this has happened," one librarian said, frantically flipping through her binders. "There are times when people *thought* it happened."

After the show ended, I raced down the hall and took the elevator to the Governors Ball, the Academy's on-site afterparty. All anyone was talking about was the envelope mix-up. "When they said *Moonlight* really won, I thought they meant on an emotional level," one filmmaker said outside the station where winners get their statuettes engraved. "It's humiliating for everyone involved," his plus-one added. "What's more prestigious than the Oscars? The Nobel Prize?" I found Cheryl Boone Isaacs staring at her phone and asked what had gone through her mind. "Horror," she said. "I just thought, *What? WHAT?* I looked out and I saw a member of Pricewaterhouse coming on the stage, and I was like, *Oh, no, what—what's happening? What what WHAT? What could possibly . . . ?*

And then I just thought, *Oh, my God, how does this happen? How. Does. This. Happen?*" She sighed. "And it was such a wonderful show."

After a year in which the Academy had grappled with its own racial imbalance, the Best Picture debacle had supplied an explosive Hollywood ending. But other Oscar seasons had been just as eventful, just as full of hairpin turns. As I contemplated this book, I sifted through the ages for those Oscars years that told larger stories of cultural change and soon found myself back at the beginning, in the Hollywood of silent cinema, Charlie Chaplin, and Louis B. Mayer. The Oscars were originally an afterthought—an idea for "Awards of Merit" buried amid the newborn Academy's list of brainstorms in 1927. It wasn't until two years later that the first statuettes were handed out, in a ceremony that lasted around ten minutes. The airborne war epic *Wings* won the top prize, but the big story was off to the side: an honorary award for *The Jazz Singer*, a picture that sang, spoke, and upended the art form.

Over the decades, the Oscars grew to support a cottage industry of consultants, stylists, pundits, and prognosticators. Much like presidential politics, the Oscar race isn't as simple as voters checking a box; behind the scenes, it's driven by a vast, self-perpetuating machine. Where Washington has K Street lobbyists and pollsters, awards season has campaign strategists and "Oscarologists." Politicians kiss babies and eat pork chops on a stick at the Iowa State Fair; Oscar contenders pick at passed sashimi and answer endless questions about their process. Millions of dollars are spent. And what for? "Ego and bragging rights," executive Terry Press told me. "It's a town built on a rock-solid foundation of insecurity."

Caught in the cross fire are people: their thwarted ambitions, their artistic epiphanies, their messy collaborations, their dreams fulfilled or dashed. What follows is not the story of every Oscar year but a collection of tales, each representing a turning point for the Academy, for the movies, or for the culture at large. Some tales hinge on a single category, while others trace the trajectory of a decade. Some involve the most powerful Hollywood players of their era, while others are about the outsiders who stormed the palace gates.

From the beginning, the Academy Awards were freighted with outsize emotions. "There was more excitement than at a children's party when you played pin the tail on the donkey, and in a way it was not unlike the childhood game," Oscar-winning screenwriter Frances Marion wrote of those early years. "The participants found themselves blind-folded, a little too eager to win the prize, a little too scared to hope." As the Oscars approach their second century, the contenders are still eager, still scared, still hoping. But the blindfolds, sooner or later, come off.

OSCAR WARS

Second Anniversary and Awards Banquet
Academy of Motion Picture Arts and Sciences
BLOSSOM ROOM · ROOSEVELT HOTEL
HOLLYWOOD · MAY 16 1930

ONE

You Ain't Heard Nothin' Yet

1927–29

How Louis B. Mayer had a brainstorm over solitaire,
Mary Pickford tried to shed her girlish image, the
pictures started talking, and the Academy was born.

L ouis B. Mayer felt the cards thrum through his fingers. It was the
end of a yawning Sunday night—cigars, Napoleon brandy—and he
and the men had retired to the library. He flipped over one card, then
another. Across the room, his three guests idled from one topic to the
next: the weather, the price of sandlots in Los Angeles. Mayer feigned
absorption in his cards. He always played solitaire, according to one of
the men, director Fred Niblo, because it was "the only card game that
Mr. Mayer can play without taking a risk of having his guests lose their
money."

On January nights like this one, the breeze from the ocean would
waft in through the wrought-iron balcony and perfume the rooms of 625
Pacific Coast Highway. Sunday was the only day that Mayer opened his
new twenty-room villa in Santa Monica to outsiders. Typically, his wife
Margaret would serve a buffet supper, with sturgeon and Jewish deli food

imported from New York's Barney Greengrass. Drinks would follow, then perhaps a screening in the private projection room. Mayer had built the Spanish-style house the previous year, to satisfy Margaret's long-standing craving to live on the beach. But when the head of Metro-Goldwyn-Mayer wanted a beach house, he got it his own way. "When we need a set at the studio, we build it overnight," he reasoned, according to his daughter Irene. "We need a big village, we build it in weeks. Don't be at the mercy of those contractors. Don't start with the architects. With us, it's business, it gets done."

Mayer's head of design, Cedric Gibbons, whose sleek art deco interiors would leap off movie screens into homes across America, drew up plans. His production manager gathered a team of MGM laborers, who set up floodlights in the sand and worked in three shifts, day and night. Within six weeks, at a cost of $28,000, the Mayers had a new home, with a red-tile roof, bathrooms of onyx and marble, thick stucco walls to keep out the summer heat, and a pool that would fill up with ocean water when it stormed.

It was 1927, and the kings and queens of Hollywood were erecting mansions up and down Santa Monica's Gold Coast, trumpeting their arrival as America's nouveau-riche royalty. Down the road from Mayer, his protégé, Irving Thalberg, had taken up in a French Norman beach house. Douglas Fairbanks and Mary Pickford, Hollywood's reigning power couple, were about to set up nearby. Producer Jesse Lasky, of the mighty Famous Players-Lasky (the future Paramount), would be four doors down from them. As Lasky wrote his son that May, "[E]veryone is moving down to the beach and we are going to have a wonderful colony this summer."

Mayer flipped another card. He was less the King of Hearts than the King of Spades. "You are talking about the devil incarnate," Helen Hayes said of Mayer. "Not just evil, but the most evil man I have ever dealt with in my life. He was an untalented, mean, vicious, vindictive person." Actor Ralph Bellamy went farther: "Louis B. Mayer was a Jewish Hitler, a fascist. He had no feeling for any minority, including his own. No feeling for people, period." To others, Mayer was less a dictator than a monarch who ruled by fear. "His people respected him highly," one MGM writer said, "but he could destroy you with his pinkie and he damn well knew it." Director Marshall Neilan cracked that the "L.B." stood for "Lousy Bastard."

As a young man in Saint John, New Brunswick, Mayer had been a junk seller, dragging scrap metal from shipwrecks for his father, who had escaped anti-Semitic pogroms in eastern Europe. In 1907, Mayer refashioned a dingy theater in Massachusetts as the Orpheum, which he promised would feature "refined amusement." The public had become entranced by "the flickers," moving pictures that played in nickelodeons. Mayer knew that the real money was in "the business of making idols for the public to love and worship and to identify with." That business was increasingly out on "the Coast," where he set up Louis B. Mayer Productions. In 1924, theater chain owner Marcus Loew merged Mayer's studio with Metro Pictures and Goldwyn Pictures to form a Hollywood empire. MGM opened its doors in April 1924 with the pomp of a military parade, complete with planes showering flowers and a congratulatory telegram from President Calvin Coolidge.

Mayer now joined a cadre of Jewish moguls who had risen from poverty to the heights of America's fourth-largest industry. German-born Carl Laemmle had been a bookkeeper in Oshkosh, Wisconsin, before founding Universal. Adolph Zukor had come from a small Hungarian village and worked in penny arcades before starting Famous Players, which he would build into Paramount. Another Hungarian, Wilhelm Fuchs, became William Fox in America, where he sold soda pop and chimney black on his way to creating the Fox Film Corporation. And the Warner brothers—Harry, Albert, Sam, and Jack—were born to a Polish immigrant who worked as a cobbler in Baltimore before settling in Youngstown, Ohio, where his sons pooled funds to buy a movie projector.

Like any Hollywood plot, Mayer's origin story was subject to rewrites. He was born "Lazar Meir" in Ukraine in 1884. He claimed that his birth records were lost, so he took the Fourth of July as his birthday—though the actual date is the twelfth. Each Independence Day, production at MGM would halt so that Mayer's stable of stars, directors, cameramen, and commissary workers could picnic amid bunting and patriotic music. Were they celebrating America or their figurehead? Mayer saw himself as the embodiment of the American Dream, and his wholesome pictures would burnish that myth. "I worship good women, honorable men, and saintly mothers," he once told Frances Marion. During preproduction for *The Merry Widow*, in 1924, director Erich von Stroheim called Mae Murray's character a "whore," and Mayer slugged him—there were no "whores" at MGM.

As he shuffled his deck of cards, Mayer's instincts for idealism and acquisition of power were both at work. Like the men who had built his beach house, his guests that evening were in his employ. Across the room, Fred Niblo, who had directed Douglas Fairbanks in *The Three Musketeers*, cracked a joke about the cost sheet for *Ben-Hur*, the troubled MGM epic that Niblo had taken over in 1924 and turned into a $9.3-million hit. The two men chuckling at Niblo's self-deprecating jokes were Conrad Nagel and Fred Beetson. Nagel was a matinee idol with sensitive blue eyes and fair hair parted down the center. He'd arrived in Hollywood in 1920 and was typecast as the "Prince Consort," playing opposite stars like Gloria Swanson. Beetson had worked for the Republican National Committee under chairman William Harrison Hays, President Harding's postmaster general. Now Hays was running the new Motion Picture Producers and Distributors of America, known as the "Hays Office," charged with cleaning up Hollywood; Beetson was his secretary and treasurer.

The *Ben-Hur* war stories got Mayer's guests talking about a real battlefield. "Yes, we discussed the World War, and we were marveling what a wonderful thing war has been for pictures," Niblo recalled later. The men then "came to marvel at the fact that for the past five thousand years all nations, races, creeds, and colors have been warring one upon the other. They have all been trying to exterminate each other just because they didn't speak the same language, because they did not live as the other fellow did, because they did not understand each other."

"The cause of war," a voice piped in from the corner, "is hatred." It was Mayer. Three heads spun around. The cause of hatred, Mayer went on, was selfishness and suspicion. The cause of selfishness and suspicion was misunderstanding. And that meant that misunderstanding was responsible for more misery than all the plagues and natural disasters in human history. And it could all be solved, Mayer intoned in his noblest key, if all nations came together.

Here they were, in California, where sunlight flecked lemon groves and winter never arrived. And yet, Mayer opined, the industry they had built was embattled from within and without. Directors were suspicious of producers; producers were resentful of actors; Middle America thought of them all as godless heathens. "When the very wheels of industry paused as a result of the World War, our industry became a great institution, a great big industry here in California," Mayer went on. "And yet we have no effective organization." Sure, the Hays Office was keeping Hollywood in check and promoting its virtues. But what if Hollywood had its own League of Nations to bring harmony to its factions and speak as a united front?

His guests were struck momentarily dumb. "Great Scott!" Niblo finally said. "Why haven't you said anything about that before?"

"Because," Mayer replied, "I am a producer; because if I started it, everybody would be saying, 'I wonder what Mayer has up his sleeve.'"

Nagel, heeding the call, spoke up. "We will try," he said, "if you will agree to give us your cooperation."

Mayer shrugged. "Go ahead. I hope you will succeed." With that, his guests started planning. They would send out letters to some twenty-five of their colleagues, inviting them to a private dinner—say, at the Ambassador Hotel?

Mayer sat back, the King of Spades in his castle. Not for the first time, and not for the last, he held all the cards.

THERE ARE TWO STORIES ABOUT why the Academy of Motion Picture Arts and Sciences came to exist, and neither of them has to do with awards.

The first rests on the vision Mayer laid out that winter night: a utopian meeting of the minds that could promote "harmony" and advance the art of motion pictures. The other story is more cynical. By 1927, the movie business, once the bastard child of the "legitimate" stage, was a billion-dollar industry producing eight hundred features a year and employing 42,000 people. A hundred million people a week went to see movies at 25,000 theaters, and the studios that produced those movies, not counting the money they made from their associated theater chains, were worth some $65 million. But two threats kept the likes of Louis

B. Mayer up at night, each embodied by one of his guests that evening, Conrad Nagel and Fred Beetson.

Before coming to Hollywood, Nagel had been a Broadway actor and a soldier in Actors' Equity's 1919 battle for the right of theater workers to unionize. But Hollywood was a factory town, where men like Mayer could do what they wanted with their worker bees. The studio craftsmen had struggled for years to gain union recognition, but their creative counterparts had little interest, as Nagel, chairman of Equity's small West Coast outpost, knew well. The stars were well compensated, and the bit players, despite being subjected to seventeen-hour workdays and hazardous conditions, considered themselves stars-to-be. In November 1926, after studio mechanics threatened the "biggest strike in the history of the film industry," nine studios and five labor unions signed the Studio Basic Agreement, bringing the craftsmen's ten-year battle to unionize to a détente. But how long until the talent—actors, directors, even those persnickety writers—banded together? Mayer knew what unrestricted labor could get him: a sparkling new beach house in six weeks. Better to unite all these factions under the banner of "harmony." And given Nagel's involvement in Actors' Equity, it would be wise to keep him close.

Then there was Beetson, whose position at the Hays Office was the result of a long and agonizing sequence of events that nearly brought Hollywood to its knees. The loosening of mores after the war had boosted the movie industry, which fed the public more glamour, more extravagance, more sex. Small-town America was getting a taste of coastal values, and not everyone was pleased. After pushing for Prohibition, Christian-minded reformers who had successfully shuttered saloons eyed the pictures as America's chief corrupting influence. The movies were now subject to scissor-happy moralists. In Pennsylvania, one local body had cut scenes of a woman making baby clothes, "on the ground that children believe that babies are brought by the stork." Federal censorship was an existential threat to Hollywood, which increasingly became a byword for sin. Brother Wilbur F. Crafts, whose International Reform Bureau had helped push through Prohibition, proclaimed that the film industry was in the hands of "the devil and 500 non-Christian Jews."

A series of scandals in the early twenties gave the reformers all the ammunition they needed. There was the mysterious death of Olive Thomas, a former Ziegfeld girl who had moved to Hollywood and become the wife of Jack Pickford, the party-boy brother of virginal star Mary Pickford. In 1920, the couple sailed to Paris and checked into the Ritz, where Olive downed toxic mercury bichloride. Was it a suicide? Murder? Had poor Olive accidentally ingested cleaning supplies? Or the syphilis medication her husband had been prescribed by a French doctor? The papers breathlessly reported on the dead girl's "GAY REVELS IN UNDERWORLD OF PARIS."

Soon after came the arrest of Roscoe "Fatty" Arbuckle, one of Paramount's biggest stars, when a young starlet named Virginia Rappe died after visiting a Labor Day "orgy" in his hotel room. Overnight, Arbuckle's films were ripped from their projectors as ministers across the country denounced the portly star as a symbol of Hollywood debauchery. The papers—especially those belonging to William Randolph Hearst—ate up the scandal, and two deadlocked juries ensured that the salacious story dragged on for months. Arbuckle was eventually acquitted, but automaker Henry Ford laid the blame at the feet of Hollywood's moguls, warning of "the almost complete submergence of moviedom into the hands of Jews." The studio heads, more vulnerable than ever, came up with a solution: if you can't beat the referee, hire your own. Taking a cue from Major League Baseball, which had hired its first commissioner after the fixed 1919 World Series, the film chiefs offered Hays one hundred thousand dollars a year to be their movie "czar." But the scandals kept coming, including the murder of director William Desmond Taylor ("DEAD DIRECTOR VISITED QUEER PLACES!") and the death of morphine-addicted heartthrob Wallace Reid. Stars now found "morality clauses" written into their contracts; their private lives were public property, and they had better remain squeaky-clean.

Mayer had never pushed the envelope in his pictures, but now that the MGM merger had made him the biggest fish in the sea, he knew that the threat of government intervention anywhere was a threat to him. As the Jazz Age got jazzier, the movies (and their Jewish figureheads) remained convenient scapegoats. "Censorship of the films is a definite thing. The best that apparently can be anticipated just now is compromise," the *Los Angeles Times* wrote in July 1926, adding, "The motion picture has been caught in its youth and crippled." Hollywood had to strike back. At his beach house that night, Mayer rebranded the embattled picture industry in a single stroke. It was no longer a cesspool.

It was an Academy.

ON JANUARY 11, 1927, A group of handpicked VIPs gathered at the Ambassador Hotel on short notice. The hotel was six years old and already one of Hollywood's buzziest destinations; it housed the nightspot the Cocoanut Grove, where stars like Joan Crawford won Charleston competitions under indoor palm trees. Of the twenty-five summoned, Fred Niblo recalled, "we thought maybe at the most eight or ten perhaps would show up." But everyone came. Mayer outlined the idea for what the *Los Angeles Times* called "a cinema club." Membership, as the Academy's first official *Bulletin* would put it, would be open to anyone in the industry "who has accomplished distinguished work or acquired distinguished standing" and is "of good moral and personal standing." That left out Fatty Arbuckle.

Not everyone was sold. "I never in my life attended a meeting like that first meeting," director Frank Lloyd recalled, "where we all sat, with that rather cynical look—all of us, more or less—with the exception of the few who had conceived the idea, all of us wondering what the producer was doing in this thing." In other words, why was Mayer in charge? Was this a business ploy? But, as Lloyd and the others listened, "it slowly started to seep in that all politics, that any suggestion of the financial situation, was entirely wiped out, that it was a big 'get together' for our industry."

The founding members represented a cross section of Hollywood influence: producers (two Warner brothers, Harry and Jack), directors (Raoul Walsh, whose war drama *What Price Glory* was then in theaters), actors (movie cowboy Jack Holt, slapstick star Harold Lloyd), writers (Joseph W. Farnham, one of Hollywood's best intertitle writers, who had a sandwich named after him at the MGM commissary), and technicians (Roy Pomeroy, Paramount's wizard of technical effects). To these, Mayer had added a pair of lawyers—his own—plus Sid Grauman, who built movie palaces of Babylonian splendor and was about to top his Egyptian Theatre, with its glistening sphinx and sarcophagi, with the impending opening of Grauman's Chinese.

Most important, Mayer had secured the endorsement of Hollywood's reigning couple, Douglas Fairbanks and Mary Pickford. At forty-three, Fairbanks was the indefatigable swashbuckler of *The Mark of Zorro* and *The Three Musketeers*. Pickford, at thirty-four, was America's Sweetheart, with a cascade of curls that rendered her girlish beyond her years. Their wedding in 1920 had caused an international sensation, ballooning the power they had accrued as founders—along with Charlie Chaplin and D. W. Griffith—of United Artists in 1919. Securing them as Academy founders was a coup.

"At our first big 'get-together,'" Niblo remembered, "it was suggested Irving Thalberg be made President." At twenty-seven, Thalberg, whose storytelling acumen had made him an asset to MGM, was the youngest Academy founder. He was born with a heart defect, and doctors warned his parents that he wouldn't live long past thirty. As if trying to squeeze in a lifetime's career, Thalberg had joined Carl Laemmle's Universal as a teenager and was made general manager by age twenty, before Mayer lured him away to become his head of production. When the chance to be the Academy's first president came up, however, Thalberg declined, believing, according to Niblo, "that an actor should head the organization." The choice was obvious: Douglas Fairbanks.

Throughout the spring of 1927, the founders met in groups once or twice a week. Mayer chaired the "Plan and Scope" committee, where he could steer the ship while remaining out of sight. Fairbanks was the debonair chief ambassador. As they were readying to unleash their brainchild on to the world, Fairbanks sent a telegram to Cecil B. DeMille, who was in New York for the premiere of *The King of Kings*, saying that WE ARE NOW PREPARING FOR A BIG ORGANIZATION DINNER AND WOULD APPRECIATE IT IMMENSELY IF YOU WILL AUTHORIZE THE USE OF YOUR NAME AS ONE OF THE SPONSORS STOP. With DeMille on board, the now thirty-six founding members printed up a dainty manifesto, entitled "THE REASONS WHY"—bound with a sky-blue ribbon, as if announcing the birth of a baby boy—and mailed it out to the crème of Tinseltown. By "uniting into one body all branches of motion picture production," it promised, the Academy could "take aggressive action in meeting outside attacks that are unjust" and promote the "dignity and honor of the profession." Amid threats of walk-offs, it would "promote harmony and solidarity" and "reconcile any internal differences."

Wedged among the declarations was another proposal: to "encourage the improvement and advancement of the arts and sciences of our profession," the Academy would bestow "awards of merit for distinctive achievements."

HOURS BEFORE THE ACADEMY BANQUET on May 11, 1927, Mary Pickford hunched over a mess of papers. Words were crossed out and scribbled, paragraphs drafted and abandoned. Somehow the sentences weren't coming together.

She had stayed home all day at Pickfair, the Beverly Hills "cottage" Fairbanks had given her as a wedding gift. Pickfair was more than their home. It was Hollywood's White House, where Mary and Doug (as the world knew them) could host the likes of F. Scott Fitzgerald, Amelia Earhart, and the Duke of York. It was a palace fit for the King and Queen of Hearts: two wings containing twenty-five bedrooms, an oyster-shaped pool, tennis courts, rose gardens, stables, kennels, a cupid fountain, and a lodge housing fifteen servants. "This is a happy house," Mary would say. "This is a house that has never heard a cross word."

If any place could convince the world that Hollywood wasn't a Gomorrah of drug addicts, Jews, and nouveau-riche floozies, it was Pickfair, which had the dignity of a Newport mansion. Dinner there was followed by dancing—but "only the waltz or two-step," Mary cautioned. "We never 'jazz.'" As for smuggled booze, actress Miriam Cooper griped, you couldn't get "one lousy drop of wine."

Mary was Pickfair personified, as elegant and clean as a goblet of ice water. The reputation of the movies rested on her shoulders, along with her famous golden curls.

And yet, how close they had come to veering off a cliff.

When she met Doug, in 1915, both were married. Mary was already "America's Sweetheart," having joined Adolph Zukor's collection of

"Famous Players." Columnists extolled her as "the spirit of spring impris-
oned in a woman's body." Mary yearned to show her versatility, but the
public, Zukor observed, "demonstrated conclusively that she was wanted
complete with curls, puppies and a jam-smeared face and brave smile
while going through some of the worst adversity ever heaped upon a
young girl." Behind her childlike image, though, was a sharp business
sense; Chaplin would call her "Bank of America's Sweetheart."

Pickford and her first husband, Owen Moore, encountered the dashing Fairbanks on a getaway to a friend's mansion in Tarrytown. When
their hostess insisted they all go for a walk, Mary reached an ice-cold
stream and tentatively stepped on a log but found herself "immobile with
fright." Then Fairbanks emerged and carried her across—literally sweeping her off her feet. Mary was entranced by his "overwhelming dyna-
mism." But any whiff of an affair could have killed their careers. Doug
was a Boy Scout; she was "Little Mary." She and Doug were "discreet,
or thought they were," Zukor recalled. "In New York they sometimes
donned motorist's linen dusters and goggles and drove about, believing
themselves disguised. It was the sort of thing that appealed especially to
Doug's romanticism."

In 1919, when Pickford and Fairbanks joined Chaplin and Griffith
to form United Artists, MGM's Richard Rowland cracked, "The lunatics
have taken charge of the asylum." Mary was an anomaly—Hollywood's
first and only female mogul—but her affair with the now-divorced Doug
threatened to derail the whole thing. With tears in her eyes, she confided
to writer Adela Rogers St. Johns, "Adela, if I divorce Owen and marry
Douglas Fairbanks, will my people ever forgive me?" It would require all
Pickford's powers of spin. In 1920, she crossed the border to Nevada for
a quick divorce, telling reporters, "I have learned that I do not belong to
myself," and swearing never to remarry.

Three weeks later, she married Fairbanks.

The reaction, to the couple's shock, was jubilation. En route to
their honeymoon, Doug did handstands for the press as Mary cupped
her mouth in faux mortification. In London, their Rolls-Royce inched
through what Doug called "a lynch mob—except that it was smiling."
The screen had made them mythical, seemingly above public reproach.

And then Mary's brother had to muck it all up.

Jack Pickford had married Olive Thomas in 1916, and Mary had never much liked the girl; she saw Olive as a déclassé climber who would only drag down the Pickford name. And then, only months after Mary and Doug managed to finesse the public reaction to their marriage, her new sister-in-law had the nerve to die. The papers ran unseemly reports of Olive's debauchery and Jack's misadventures—why *did* he have mercury bichloride in his hotel room, again?

Mary vowed to protect her image. As St. Johns recalled, "It was as though Mary said, as had young Queen Victoria on coming to the throne, 'I will be good,' and meant, 'I will live up to what is expected of me, and be *here* as long as my people need me.'" But the problem, increasingly, was Mary herself. In her 1926 film *Sparrows*, she played a child in an orphan farm, with her hair in braided pigtails—and she was thirty-four. "A wild impulse would seize me," Pickford remembered, "to reach for the nearest shears and remove that blond chain around my neck." A jazzy, new kind of woman was emerging—women like Clara Bow and Louise Brooks— and long hair and virginity were out. Little Mary couldn't live forever.

With her public image resting on a knife's edge, it was time to draw a red line between the echelon she and Doug inhabited and the nether- world of Olive Thomas. Pickford had thrown herself into the planning meetings for the new Academy, sometimes hashing out points in smoke- clouded rooms until two in the morning. She joined the board—not as an actor, but as a producer, alongside Mayer. Of thirty-two meetings, she had not missed one as the group drew up its bylaws, applied for a charter, elected her husband president—presumably, it wasn't a woman's job— and made plans for the inaugural banquet, where, that night, she would get a few things off her chest.

But she was stymied. Doug would know what to do.

Fairbanks was at his United Artists bungalow, taking a poolside break from preparations for *The Gaucho*, in which he would play yet an- other swashbuckling rogue. (Pickford would have an uncredited cameo as—who else?—the Virgin Mary.) After a rejuvenating plunge, Fairbanks dipped into a steam bath in his private Turkish spa. Someone yelled that his wife was on the line. He threw on a bathrobe and headed out.

Just as he was saying hello, something behind him went *boom*. A heater had burst in the steam room. As flames licked the roof, Fairbanks, along with his seventeen-year-old son and director Herbert Brenon, sprayed fire extinguishers. By the time the firemen arrived, there was barely a spark left, and the three men were caked in soot. The papers would love this: Douglas Fairbanks, screen hero, saves the day.

But what about Mary? Doug rang her back at Pickfair to tell her that everything was fine. If she hadn't called at that very moment, he would have been blown to bits.

Mary breathed a sigh of relief. By a fluke of timing, the Academy had saved her husband's life. Could it protect her reputation, too?

"Ready, Doug?"

It was eight o'clock, and the toastmaster, Fred Niblo, was calling the evening to order. The new president of the Academy bounded to the dais and looked out over the crowd of Hollywood luminaries at the Biltmore Hotel's opulent Crystal Ballroom. Fairbanks quieted the ovation and then laid on the charm, telling a story about a friend who had collided his car with a truck. The burly truck driver had approached the car, "steaming with anger," but stopped short upon seeing who was in the passenger seat—boxer Jack Dempsey—and scurried away. "That was because Jack Dempsey's muscles were organized," Fairbanks quipped. "The object of this dinner tonight—is *organization!*"

In the audience were Mary Astor, Walter Wanger, Jack Warner, Gloria Swanson, and Ben-Hur himself, Ramon Novarro. As they feasted on lobster Eugénie and jumbo squash in Périgueux sauce, a succession of speakers echoed Fairbanks's boyish optimism—while also answering lingering doubts. "I have had a number of people with whom I have discussed the Academy say or imply that this proposition is controlled by the producers," writer Carey Wilson said. But he argued that the Academy would be governed by a fifteen-person board, with three representatives from each branch, which meant the producers could be easily outvoted.

United Artists president Joseph Schenck, in his speech, admitted that the Academy's name "doesn't appeal to me much. To my mind, it is all too lofty. But nevertheless, this Academy will certainly do away with lots of distrust, eliminate a major part of the dislike and all of the suspicion existing between the different members of one great organization." Conrad Nagel addressed the suspicion that the Academy would antagonize Actors' Equity. How could it, he said, when he himself was active in both? The Academy, he insisted, would signal "an era of cooperation and of partnership, of effort united in a common cause—the service of mankind."

No one was more utopian, though, than Cecil B. DeMille, who was back in Hollywood to see *The King of Kings* open the brand-new Chinese Theatre. "The world is more influenced by the little group in this room tonight," he told the Biltmore crowd, "than by any other power in the world. If you will give that a moment's thought, you will realize the tremendous potentialities of that. That cannot be taken too literally. That cannot be taken lightly. It is a very grave responsibility that rests upon us. Our ideals have got to be high. There was a little group like this that gathered in another little room and the result was the United States of America."

Spirits were high by the time the petits fours and coffee came out. After nine men spoke, Toastmaster Niblo quieted the crowd. "The next speaker, my friends, needs no introduction," he said. "But I would like to mention that just her name and her personality is a symbol for all that is fine and splendid and unselfish—*Mary*."

The audience rose to its feet as Pickford took the microphone. "With our influence, with our enthusiasm, and with our cooperation," she began, "this Academy should become a very powerful institution and second only in its importance to that of the motion picture industry itself." Then her tone shifted. "Too long have we submitted, without protest, to the interference of outsiders! We have been the recipients of spankings, as it were." Speaking as much about herself as the industry, she went on: "And we have come to the sudden realization that we are no longer the infant—that we have grown capable of self-government, of self-defense, and that we will fight for the protection of our good name against unjust accusations."

Losing her nerve for a moment, Pickford scanned her notes and smiled at Fairbanks. "Douglas got the easy end of this tonight," she said, to laughs. "Because I am little, they thought that it would be up to me tonight to take the belligerent stand. They said, 'Mary can do it!'" She steeled herself. Repeating the lesson she had learned during her divorce, she said, "Our lives do not belong to ourselves. We belong to each other. We are responsible for each other. And so, we must conduct ourselves accordingly. When one is injured, the whole industry is injured. We can't stop the world from talking; we are public characters. And since we cannot stop the world from talking, we must recognize our responsibility."

Over applause, she returned to the speaker's table and muttered to Fairbanks, "My, I went all to pieces."

It was up to Louis B. Mayer to bring back the peace and harmony, with a speech about how, together, they could "bring sunshine into the lives of the people in the industry."

All the press seemed to hear was one word: "spanking."

"Mary Pickford is tired of having the entire fraternity of movie players 'spanked' because of the moral turpitude of some," said the *New York Evening World*. The *Salt Lake City Telegram* ran the headline "AGAINST 'SPANKING.'" The magazine *The Film Spectator*, noting Pickford's "spirit of defiance," reported: "Industry Fashioning Weapon of Defence."

Whatever it was—idealism or defiance—the rollout worked. At the end of the night, 275 guests signed up to be Academy members, handing over $27,500 in initiation fees.

And there was no mention of awards.

HOLLYWOOD, MEANWHILE, WAS BUSY MAKING the movies that would win the first Academy Awards. Ten days after the banquet, as if to burnish the Academy's utopian vision, Charles Lindbergh touched down in Paris after his history-making solo transatlantic flight. In the crowd at Le Bourget Field was Adolph Zukor, who peered into the clouds as the *Spirit of St. Louis* glided down through the searchlights and landed, "soft as a feather," to euphoric cheers. Paramount had just held a sneak preview of *Wings*, its new wartime aviation adventure, and Lindbergh mania, Zukor knew, would only bolster the picture's appeal. He would need every ticket buyer he could get—thanks to its rambunctious young director, William "Wild Bill" Wellman, *Wings* had cost a head-spinning two million dollars.

The thirty-one-year-old Wellman had gotten his start in pictures from none other than Douglas Fairbanks, who spotted him playing minor-league ice hockey in Boston and suggested he try acting. In the Great War, Wellman had joined the French Foreign Legion as a fighter pilot and recorded three kills before getting shot down by the Germans. Fairbanks sent Wellman a cablegram: GREAT WORK BOY WE ARE PROUD OF YOU WHEN YOU GET HOME THERE IS A JOB WAITING FOR YOU.

Soon after the war, Fairbanks was hosting a posh polo party for the likes of Charlie Chaplin, Rudolph Valentino, and Fairbanks's then-secret lover, Mary Pickford. As guests lounged in the shade under umbrella tables, the roar of a silver SPAD going 132 miles per hour overhead interrupted their idyll. The ponies panicked as the aircraft landed nearby, and out of the cockpit leaped First Lieutenant Wellman. "Remember me, Mr. Fairbanks?" he asked, marching up to the host. "You said if I ever came to Hollywood, to look you up."

Fairbanks motioned over to Pickford. "Mary, I'd like you to meet Wild Bill Wellman. He's a helluva hockey player and a war hero."

"We've read about you," America's Sweetheart offered. "You have an unusual way of dropping by."

Wings made the Paramount brass nervous not just because of its no-name director, but because of its unknown leading men, Richard Arlen and the sweet-faced Charles "Buddy" Rogers. The only "name" in the picture belonged to Clara Bow, playing the girl next door. With her flame-red bob and sleepy-flirty eyes, Bow encapsulated the newfangled sex appeal of the Jazz Age flapper; by the time *Wings* came out, her role in the Paramount vehicle *It* had made her the first-ever "It" Girl, and she received twenty thousand fan letters a week. Completing the cast was Gary Cooper, in the small but crucial role of Cadet White. In his single scene, Cooper bites off a piece of chocolate, offers folksy wisdom ("Luck or no luck, when your time comes, you're going to get it!"), and promptly careens to his death in a training flight.

Producers had long ago concluded that there was "no kick in air stuff," and Wellman knew why. A Roman chariot circling an arena looked fantastic on-screen because its speed could be measured against the still background. But a shot of an airplane gliding across a clear sky looked dull. "You need something solid behind the planes," Wellman realized. "The clouds give you that, but against a blue sky, it's like a lot of goddam flies!" As Lasky observed with horror, "Wellman stubbornly refused to start shooting until there were clouds in the sky."

Wellman was far from the only director imagining new ways for the camera to float and dance. In September 1926, German expressionist F. W. Murnau began shooting his new film for Fox. In *Sunrise: A Song of Two Humans*, a country man's urban mistress ensnares him in a murder plot against his wife, played by Janet Gaynor; the married couple row into a lake, but instead of throwing his wife overboard, the man chases her into the city. Murnau concocted elaborate dolly maneuvers to follow the characters through forests and lakes. To create the bewitching big city, he made lavish sets in forced perspective. While shooting a restaurant scene, his cinematographer recalled, Murnau shot out a window looking downhill: "The people that you see across the street are all midgets dressed like normal people!"

When *Sunrise* wrapped in February 1927, Gaynor went to her dressing room, took off her wig, and went to work on Frank Borzage's *7th Heaven*, playing a downtrodden Parisian woman rescued by a handsome sewer cleaner. Rebuilding Paris on the Fox lot, Borzage pulled off a stunning sequence in which the pair ascend the spiral stairwell of the hero's building to reach his grotty seventh-floor "heaven." The nearly two-minute tour de force used an elevator scaffold and a system of ropes and pulleys to create a breathtaking illusion of ascendance.

At MGM, director King Vidor had something even more ambitious in mind. It was a story about an ordinary man facing ordinary milestones: birth, school, love, work, baby, bills. Pictures were the stuff of larger-than-life glamour—could he make one about someone who was perfectly average? Vidor considered naming it *One of the Mob*, but Irving Thalberg thought that sounded "too much like a capital-labor conflict" and renamed it *The Crowd*. To establish his hero's urban anonymity, Vidor imagined the camera rising up the edifice of an office tower, gliding in through a window, and finding the Everyman amid a sea of desks. To accomplish this near-impossible shot, he used miniatures, dissolves, and an overhead wire trolley. While the actors worked, Vidor had a live violinist and organ player set the mood. "Every set would have musicians," Conrad Nagel recalled. "These musicians would know a hundred to a hundred and fifty pieces of music, and they'd have a piece to go with whatever happened on the set."

Cinema may have been soundless, but it was bustling with invention and romance. It was a busy, moonstruck world whose inhabitants had little idea that its extinction had already begun.

THE NEWBORN ACADEMY SET UP temporary headquarters in a three-room office suite on Hollywood Boulevard "equipped with comfortable chairs for assembly purposes." Across the street was Grauman's Chinese Theatre, into whose cement sidewalk Mary Pickford and Douglas Fairbanks had recently pressed their hands and feet.

The organization had big plans. Nagel, elected chairman of the actors' branch, began work on a uniform contract for freelance players. The Conciliation Committee heard disputes. There were plans to assemble a research library. And there was a noontime lunch to get cracking on the "Awards of Merit," an idea championed by Academy secretary Frank Woods.

Mayer was ambivalent. Decades later, he would take credit for devising the awards as a means of manipulation: "I found that the best way to handle [artists] was to hang medals all over them. If I got them cups and awards they'd kill themselves to produce what I wanted. That's why the Academy Award was created." But, at the time, he imagined something far less grand. Nagel was given five hundred dollars to find some small way of honoring the actors. Columnist Louella Parsons suggested that they hand out scrolls, "like those things the city council hands out."

When Nagel brought up the idea of a banquet, Mayer blanched. "We're not going to spend that kind of money," he objected. Nagel recalled, "I considered it to be such a touchy subject that I appointed what I hoped would be a slow-moving committee to 'think about' some sort of honorariums. I told them to take their time about it."

But even that, along with the Academy's other well-laid plans, got swept aside by a full-blown crisis.

Adolph Zukor was convinced that something had to be done about profit-eating production costs. Zukor's own studio, Paramount, was the worst offender, thanks to lavish productions like *Wings*. The studios made a plan to institute a 10 to 25 percent pay cut for anyone making more than fifty dollars a week. The reaction was swift and furious, with *Variety* reporting "one of the most hectic weeks in the history of West Coast picture production, with a seething storm of protest waged from every studio, with threats of contract cancellations, walkouts and strikes." At one studio café, a sign for "COLD CUTS"—a potential reminder of the pay cuts—was replaced by one for "ASSORTED MEATS."

Suspicion of the Academy simmered. As one Hollywood correspondent recalled, "Those jerks in charge wanted it to seem like a labor union but to function as a company trust." Then the Academy did something surprising: it stopped the pay cut in its tracks. Despite Mayer's cheapness when it came to the Awards of Merit, he was never one for austerity: he was happy to throw money at pictures if that's what it took to make them beautiful. "The emergency could never have been anticipated when the Academy was in the process of organization last winter," its newsletter boasted, "but so well conceived was the plan on which the Academy was founded that it would seem to have been a providential instrument for this particular occasion."

Not everyone in Hollywood was so sure. *The Film Spectator* claimed that the real reason the producers had retreated from the pay cut was that a group of actors, led by Conrad Nagel, had demanded that Mayer open MGM's books for inspection. Under the headline "Academy Becomes Tool of Producers," which was fast becoming the common wisdom, the magazine ripped the new organization for its utopian talk of "harmony": "It is the kind of harmony that the cat felt while it was digesting the canary." Instead of generating goodwill, the Academy was accruing enemies.

Emboldened, Actors' Equity cofounder Frank Gillmore presided over a meeting of some eight hundred players, warning that the attempted pay cut was only one of the drastic measures the producers might try. The meeting ended with three hundred new Equity recruits, and Gillmore proposed a new standard contract, including a maximum forty-eight-hour work week. The producers roundly ignored Equity's proposal, instead throwing their weight behind the Academy, and

Fairbanks released a statement dripping with rosy talk of a "cooperative spirit." The message was clear: Hollywood wasn't big enough for both Equity and the Academy.

Equity's insurgency suffered a massive blow when Nagel—who, as an Equity *and* Academy official, was playing both sides of the war—released a statement announcing a change of heart and complete alignment with the Academy. Hours later, at a thousand-person Equity meeting, a stunned Gillmore looked on as Nagel claimed that it would be fruitless to "advance to the attack when the enemy extends the hand of friendship." Huddling actors whispered that the high-salaried stars had betrayed the rank and file, protecting their own interests by siding with the Academy. The next day, *Variety* reported that Gillmore had been "repulsed" back to New York, and that the Academy had "supplanted Equity."

Then there was the continuing censorship threat. At Will Hays's urging, a group that included Irving Thalberg drew up a list of rules, called the "Don'ts and Be Carefuls," which barred movies from showing sex, profanity, "ridicule of the clergy," or other vices. Mayer announced the list himself. The rules, naturally, would be self-enforced.

In November 1927, the bruised but victorious Academy moved its headquarters into the mezzanine of the Roosevelt Hotel. The "commodious, exclusive and convenient" quarters, as the Academy newsletter described them, included a lounge, an anteroom, a service kitchen, and a boardroom; dancing at the supper room downstairs was "conveniently possible."

Amid all this humming progress, the Academy made no mention of the most explosive event to take place in the motion picture business since its inception: the October 6 premiere of *The Jazz Singer*.

THE CONCEPT OF PUTTING SOUNDS to moving pictures was hardly new. As far back as 1891, Thomas Edison hoped to "throw upon a canvas a perfect picture of anybody, and reproduce his words." In 1913, eleven theaters premiered Edison's Kinetophone, with footage of a man smashing a plate and musicians playing "The Last Rose of Summer." But the novelty wore off fast, and *Variety* pronounced it "THE SENSATION THAT FAILED." By 1926, Edison himself had lost interest, saying, "Americans require a restful quiet in the moving picture theater, and for them talking from the lips of the figures on the screen destroys the illusion."

Western Electric, nevertheless, had been developing a sound-on-disc system that would become known as the Vitaphone. By the end of 1924, Paramount, MGM, and First National had seen demonstrations and shrugged. "Just a gimmick," sniffed Zukor. "A toy," concluded Mayer.

Sam Warner thought it was absolutely wonderful.

The brothers Warner were Hollywood underdogs, scraping by in the shadow of their counterparts at MGM and Paramount. Harry, the eldest, was the money-minded realist. Albert was the quiet one. Sam was the gregarious forward thinker who loved gadgets. And then there was Jack, whose job was vice president in charge of production but whose passions were partying, philandering, and tasteless humor. (He once told a woman waving to him, "Hiya, honey! Didja bring your douche bag?") Jack resented Harry's authority, while conservative Harry was appalled by Jack's womanizing and flash. "Sam was the bridge between them," recalled Darryl Zanuck, who joined Warner Bros. as a screenwriter and worked his way up to head of production. "What a boring guy Harry was. Jack was unreliable, but never boring."

The brothers' financial savior was a German shepherd rescued during the war from a bombed-out French dog kennel. Rin Tin Tin's first star vehicle, *Where the North Begins*, became a runaway hit in 1923. Overnight, "Rinty"—whom Jack nicknamed "Mortgage Lifter"—received thousands of fan letters and had his face on the side of dog biscuit containers. Eager for expansion, Warner Bros. started its own radio station, KFWB. (In the early days, Jack filled up airtime himself, under the pseudonym "Leon Zuardo.") While Sam was launching the station, a Western Electric representative invited him to see its latest experiment in synchronized sound. It was a simple demonstration, but Sam was beguiled. Weeks later, he asked Harry, who had been indifferent to talking pictures, to accompany him to Bell Labs in New York. Up on a screen came a man talking, and then a twelve-piece jazz orchestra. Harry, a music lover, perked up. "Now *that* is something," he whispered. He leaped up and checked behind the screen, to make sure there wasn't a hidden orchestra. "Think of the hundreds of small theater guys who can't afford an orchestra or any kind of an act," he exclaimed. "Or even a good piano player! What a gadget!"

"But don't forget," Sam nudged, "you can have actors talk, too."

"Who the hell wants to hear actors talk?"

Despite their conviction that he'd lost his mind, Sam was able to persuade the rest of the brothers to explore Vitaphone. In April 1926, Warner Bros. and Western Electric—which had failed to interest the higher-profile studios—announced their partnership. To showcase their secret weapon, the brothers decided to add an orchestral score to *Don Juan*, starring John Barrymore, promising a "new era in motion picture presentation" that would "thrill and startle the world." *Don Juan's* premiere, on August 6, 1926, did nearly that. It began with a filmed introduction from none other than Will Hays. The audience rustled as they heard the movie czar clear his throat on film. Then the lights dimmed, and the sound of the Philharmonic Orchestra playing the *Tannhäuser* overture filled the hall.

Among the startled audience was Hays himself, who watched his own speech in a daze: "I said to myself, 'A new miracle has been wrought and I have had a part of it,'" he recalled. The *New York Times* was similarly impressed, if limited in imagination, when it gushed, "The future of this new contrivance is boundless, for inhabitants of small and remote places will have the opportunity of listening to and seeing grand opera as it is given in New York." But there were still plenty of skeptics, including drama critic George Jean Nathan, who moaned that the device "will bring to the motion picture exactly the thing that the motion picture should have no use for, to wit, the human voice."

The West Coast finally woke up to what was happening when the new *Don Juan* opened at Grauman's Egyptian in October. (A silent version had been playing there for two months.) The crowd was studded with luminaries, among them Charlie Chaplin, Cecil B. DeMille, Greta Garbo, and even industry pariah Fatty Arbuckle. An exultant Jack Warner wired his brother Harry back east: WE ARE SPELLBOUND—ALL OTHER OPENINGS LIKE KINDERGARTEN IN COMPARISON WITH TONIGHT. NO USE TRYING TO TELL YOU HOW IT WENT OVER; MULTIPLY YOUR WILDEST IMAGINATION BY ONE THOUSAND—THAT'S IT.

The industry was wowed. Then it did nothing. *Don Juan* lasted only three weeks at the Egyptian, even as it reigned for nine months back in New York. The only other studio taking sound seriously was Fox, which had acquired a competing system, Movietone. In May, it premiered *7th Heaven* with a program of Movietone music and comedy shorts. The same day that Zukor was in Paris getting an autograph from Charles Lindbergh, Fox exhibited newsreel of the *Spirit of St. Louis* taking off in Long Island, with the accompanying vroom.

Warner Bros. busily added music to all its new releases, preceded by Vitaphone shorts of popular entertainers. The film *The Better 'Ole* featured a particularly crowd-pleasing curtain-raiser: Al Jolson singing in blackface. Born Asa Yoelson to a rabbi father, the Lithuanian Jolson was known nationwide for his spirited renditions of "Swanee" and "My Mammy"—performed with painted-on black skin and thick white lips. Gobsmacked by his intensity, playwright Samson Raphaelson wrote a short story about a Jewish singer who rebels against his cantor father to become a secular entertainer. In 1925, he turned it into a Broadway hit called *The Jazz Singer*. Warner Bros. paid fifty thousand dollars for the film rights. "I don't think it will make any money," Harry Warner said, "but it would be a good picture to do for the sake of religious tolerance, if nothing else."

The brothers, now constructing soundproof stages at their Sunset Boulevard studio, decided to make *The Jazz Singer* a Vitaphone picture. The plan was for Jolson to sing six songs in the film, including his signature "My Mammy." But, as shooting went on, sound engineer George Groves would recall, Jolson "insisted on ad-libbing in a couple of places. Sam Warner managed to persuade his brothers to leave the scenes in."

Sam knew they were risking half a million dollars on a film that could be played in only a handful of theaters. To add to his worries, he was suffering from sinus trouble stemming from abscessed teeth. In September, he checked himself into California Lutheran Hospital. In New York, his brothers Harry and Albert, who were preparing for *The Jazz Singer*'s East Coast premiere, dropped everything and boarded a train. They were inching through the Arizona desert when they received word that Sam had suffered a massive cerebral hemorrhage. Jack, meanwhile, was changing trains in Chicago when the doctors performed Sam's second emergency surgery.

They were all too late. Early on October 5, 1927, Sam Warner, the peacemaker and forward thinker, who had pushed past his brothers' apathy toward sound, died at forty.

The next day, *The Jazz Singer* premiered at the Warners' Theatre on Broadway. There were screams of laughter when the spectators heard Jolson's catchphrase, "You ain't heard nothin' yet!" At the end, there were chants for "Jolson! Jolson! Jolson!" The star emerged from the audience, climbed onstage, and announced, "I feel good."

Where previous sound efforts had provided a pleasant, passing jolt, the force of Jolson's stardom gave *The Jazz Singer* an emotional breakthrough to match the technological one. The film would also, finally, put Warner Bros. in league with the big studios. People were now swarming Warners' Theatre night after night, sending profits into the stratosphere. But the brothers felt numb. "A million dollars or not, the Jolson debut was an empty victory for us," Jack remembered. "When Sam died—and there is no doubt that *The Jazz Singer* killed him—something wonderful went out of our lives."

Back in Hollywood, the rival studios dipped their toes in the water. *Wings* was released in some theaters with sound effects, to simulate gunfire and whirring propellers. Fox released *Sunrise* with a Movietone score and sound effects, including church bells. But when *The Jazz Singer* opened on Hollywood Boulevard the last week of 1927, the crowd was hardly ecstatic. Sam Goldwyn's wife Frances recalled seeing "terror in all their faces," because the "game they had been playing for years was finally over." Riding home, Irving Thalberg assured his new wife, Norma Shearer, that "sound is a passing fancy. It won't last."

As 1928 BEGAN, HARRY AND Jack Warner announced that all their films would henceforth include Vitaphone. King Vidor was still juggling several possible endings for *The Crowd*—one artful, one ludicrously happy—perhaps in an effort to ward off Louis B. Mayer's disdain. Douglas Fairbanks was coasting off the success of *The Gaucho*. Fred Niblo was preparing to direct Conrad Nagel and Greta Garbo in *The*

Mysterious Lady. And the Academy was desperately trying to turn the page.

"We are in a manner placing our house in order before proceeding to larger and broader achievements," its New Year's Day *Bulletin* reported brightly. But its activities ranged from the grandiose to the pathetically modest. With Nagel's help, the Academy had wrapped up three months of "harmonious" work on a standard actors' contract, to the horror of Actors' Equity. Another subgroup was tackling government rules that prohibited pictures from using real money as props—putting currency on-screen was considered a form of counterfeit. And the Academy sheepishly admitted that its "wonderfully attractive quarters have been sadly neglected," an appeal that inspired Fred Beetson's wife to use it for bridge games.

A more significant goal was "improved relations with the public press," which, after the war with Equity, was increasingly hostile. The April 2 *Bulletin* opened with a statement entitled "What the Academy Means to Me," by Mary Pickford. "The Academy is the League of Nations of the Motion Picture Industry," she wrote. "It is our open forum where all branches can meet and discuss constructive problems with which each is confronted."

The past few months had been harrowing for America's Sweetheart. Her brother, Jack Pickford, was up to his usual no good. Alcohol and narcotics had tarnished his movie career, his second wife had divorced him, and he was in and out of hospitals for "breakdowns" or "severe colds," while Mary tried to keep the family name clean. As for talkies, she buried herself in denial; sound in film, she felt, was as unnecessary as "putting lip rouge on the Venus de Milo."

And something had irretrievably broken in her relationship with Doug.

The cause of the trouble—or, more likely, a symptom—was their most recent costars. Rumors swirled that the chemistry between Fairbanks and his nineteen-year-old screen partner in *The Gaucho*, "Mexican spitfire" Lupe Vélez, hadn't been confined to the cameras. Mary, meanwhile, had starred in what would be her last silent film, *My Best Girl*, playing a department store stock girl who falls for the boss's son, played by Charles

"Buddy" Rogers. Fresh off *Wings*, Rogers was hopelessly attracted to Pickford, who was twelve years his senior. The crew couldn't help noticing that they were spending quite a lot of time practicing their kissing scene.

The extent of both workplace flirtations is murky, but H. Bruce "Lucky" Humberstone, assistant director for both films, would claim that "everybody knew" that Fairbanks was "fooling around" with Vélez. Pickford possibly flaunted her chemistry with Rogers as payback for whatever gossip she was hearing about Fairbanks. It's not as if Mary and Doug were strangers to infidelity—that was what had brought them together—but the playful warmth with which the couple had carried out their public alliance started draining away.

On top of everything, Mary's mother, whom she considered "almost my very life," died of breast cancer. If something had been boiling inside Pickford, her mother's death unleashed it. "I was like a wild animal in the jungle," she remembered. In her haze, she announced the end of her film career. Fairbanks, perhaps sensing her self-destructive urge, dismissed his wife's decision as "idle street talk" and whisked her off to Europe. Their tour through Geneva, Cannes, Paris, and London inspired none of the frenzy of their honeymoon of eight years earlier. Pickford stayed inside, tending to headaches.

When they returned to New York, she made a simple decision with enormous consequences. One June day, she left Fairbanks behind at the Sherry-Netherland, walked into a salon on Fifth Avenue, and asked the hairdresser to cut off her signature mane of curls. "Are you sure you're not going to regret this step, Miss Pickford?" he asked.

"I'm quite sure."

She closed her eyes, and the nervous barber drew his shears. When Pickford looked down, her famous locks lay on the floor, all except for six little curls in her lap, which she kept as souvenirs. Little Mary, finally, was dead.

When she got back to the hotel room and took off her hat, Fairbanks turned pale and sank into a chair, weeping, "I never dreamt you'd do it."

Pickford felt a contradictory swirl of emotions. "I had suspected, and probably secretly wished, that Douglas would react the way he did," she recalled. She was less prepared for the avalanche of public criticism that followed. "You would have thought I had murdered someone," Pickford said, "and perhaps I had, but only to give her successor a chance to live."

HOLLYWOOD'S SUMMER OF PANIC WAS on. Executives frantically constructed soundstages. Adolph Zukor called a meeting at Paramount to discuss the fact that a second-tier studio like Warner Bros. was now making its first all-talking picture, *Lights of New York*. "And what have we got?" he berated his executives. "You don't know a goddamn thing about sound. A lot of dumbheads." As one *American Cinematographer* columnist observed that summer, "One cannot pick up a daily paper, walk along Hollywood Boulevard, attend a meeting of any kind or even sit at a table at Henry's" without "hearing a little matter of interest and a lot of nonsense on the 'talkies.'"

But there were still doubters. Jesse Lasky pointed to his wife's painting of trees blowing in the wind, installed over his desk at Paramount, and argued, "Do you have to hear the wind to appreciate the artist's intention?" Mayer was content to bide his time and let the lesser studios work out the kinks, so that MGM could sweep in with dialogue when it was good and ready. In the meantime, he added music and a few sound effects—laughs, whistles, and a single word, "Hello"—to a picture called *White Shadows in the South Seas*. But, when the film opened in New York in July 1928, the most notable sound was, for the first time, an opening roar from the studio's mascot, "Leo the Lion."

For the Academy, sound was the unforeseen crisis that would finally allow it to put its previous crises in the past. Suddenly, producers really *did* need to talk with technicians, and writers really *did* have questions for directors. In May, the Academy opened its Club Lounge to a series of meetings on voice and sound. The members were split. At one meeting, William deMille, brother of Cecil, said, "We are all groping, but out of this groping and discussions may come a new baby, resembling neither its father nor its mother, the stage and the silent drama." He was backed up by Sid Grauman, who announced that all the big theaters would soon be equipped for sound, forcing smaller ones to follow.

They were greeted with a raft of skeptics. Winifred Dunn, the story editor for Mary Pickford's *Sparrows*, cautioned against making talkies too "stagy." Jack Cunningham, who had written the Fairbanks vehicle *The Black Pirate*, wondered, presciently, how fans would react once "idolized players used their voices." DeMille suggested that new idols might emerge from the "charm" of speaking voices. He pointed to Shakespeare as the "original continuity writer," to which one attendee asked "what studio was employing this man Shakespeare."

The acting branch was, understandably, more unnerved than most. In July, some 125 of them gathered in the Academy rooms, where elocution professor Thomas C. Trueblood correctly predicted that talkies would be a leap forward for the standardization of English pronunciation. (This was likely of little comfort to screen actors who had not trained in elocution.) Dean Ray Immel, of the University of Southern California, used plaster models to explain the anatomy of the lungs, throat, and vocal apparatus. Nagel, the meeting's chairman, predicted that the talking picture might just be "a salvation for the industry. It will stir it up and jerk it out of the rut."

The Academy found renewed purpose that anxiety-ridden summer, playing both tutor and therapist to its panicked members. Having regained their footing, the board members finally got back to an idea that had been dropped "in the press of other business": the bestowal of Awards of Merit.

Not everyone in Hollywood was sold on the idea. In a letter to Academy secretary Frank Woods the previous November, Darryl Zanuck snarked that the awards were a terrific idea, because arguing about the winners would distract everyone from worrying about their salaries getting cut. Besides, he argued, wouldn't studio employees simply vote for their own stars? What would stop Warner Bros. from pushing Rin Tin Tin for Most Popular Player?

Nevertheless, by July 1928, the ground rules were laid out. The awards would cover films released between August 1, 1927, and August 1, 1928. Each branch of the Academy would have a panel of five judges, who would report their decisions to a central board. The eleven categories would cover acting (male and female), directing (comedy and drama), writing (original and adaptation), and technical achievements. The top prize would be split in two, one for "the most outstanding motion picture production, considering all elements that contribute to a picture's great-ness," and the other for "the most unique, artistic, worthy and original production without reference to cost or magnitude"—in other words, a big-budget blockbuster and a small art film. (The idea would recur ninety years later, when the Academy briefly considered adding an award for Outstanding Achievement in Popular Film.) Winners would receive a statuette, cast in bronze, that would be "a valued ornament for desk, table or mantel." Honorable mentions would be awarded with a diploma.

The nomination cards had scarcely been printed when the Awards of Merit ran into their first speed bump. The board had decided to omit sound pictures from competition, because they were "too recent." Meanwhile, a member of the "Titular Bishops," a band of high-profile intertitle card writers, including Paramount's Herman Mankiewicz and MGM's Joseph W. Farnham, wrote to "earnestly beg" that the Academy add an award for title writing. When the subject came up in a meeting, one board member cracked, "Include them, by all means. This may be their last chance." The ballots went out with a rider attached for the added category.

Nomination cards trickled in, but not enough for a consensus. Days before the August 15 deadline, the Academy was still exhorting its mem-bers to "DO IT NOW!" In the end, it received about a thousand nomina-tions spread over the twelve categories, from a membership that exceeded three hundred people. Despite Zanuck's fears, only one ballot included a nomination for Rin Tin Tin—signed by Jack Warner.

THE ARRIVAL OF SOUND, IRONICALLY, plunged movie sets into silence. No more directors shouting, "Slower on the dolly!" or "Now kiss him!" No more violin quartets setting the mood. As a young director at Columbia named Frank Capra would recall, "Suddenly, with sound we had to work in the silence of a tomb. When the red lights went on, everyone froze in his position—a cough or a belch would wreck the scene. It was like a quick switch from a bleacher seat at Ebbets Field to a box seat at a Wimbledon tennis match."

Cameras, once swooping and waltzing, were nailed to the floor. When Cecil B. DeMille started on his first talkie, *Dynamite*, he was dismayed to find that "You could not move the camera . . . Everything that the silent screen had done to bring the entertainment and the beauty . . . of action, was gone." The airborne adventure of *Wings*, the celestial climb of *7th Heaven*, the urban merry-go-round of *Sunrise*—they were all, temporarily, impossible. Actors now directed their lines into primitive microphones hidden in strategically placed lamps and houseplants. In one film, a hunchback walked in front of the actors during a scene. Inside his hump was a microphone, which he swung toward whoever was speaking.

The old hierarchies were topsy-turvy, with lowly soundmen elevated to all-knowing gods. Roy Pomeroy, Paramount's resident tech wizard, was put in charge of turning the silent film *Interference* into the studio's first all-talking picture. The overnight promotion went directly to Pomeroy's head—he insisted on casting approval and demanded exorbitant raises—and his career took a nosedive. Paramount directors were even more vexed by producer B. P. Schulberg's plan to import stage directors from New York, part of a buddy system in which Hollywood hands would oversee the cameras while the theater people handled dialogue. Screenwriters were similarly aggrieved by an influx of New York playwrights—what worked in silent film titles was often ridiculously florid when said aloud. Conrad Nagel, in *The Idle Rich*, now had to pull off such overwrought lines as "My, my, but it's good to see you again!"

No group was more conspicuously vulnerable than actors. On set, they nervously trilled their *r*'s, and Hollywood was overrun with elocution coaches. The silent players had every right to feel queasy; at one Academy meeting, as *Variety* not so delicately paraphrased it, Jack Warner declared that "screen actors without stage experience will shortly be relegated to the discard." At MGM, Louis B. Mayer and company mercilessly evaluated their players' voices. Aileen Pringle? "Sounds too ladylike to the human ear." Joan Crawford? "Has some stage experience, good dancer, and can sing." Some, like German star Emil Jannings, at Paramount, had the misfortune of having a foreign accent. "At the studio gates," Frances Marion recalled, "the incoming tide of actors with stage experience met the outgoing tide of actors who had lost the Battle of Sound. Life was very tense then, and only those who had invested their savings in stocks relaxed; the stock market was still on a spectacular rise."

Paramount's cast of *Wings* was alarmed. Richard Arlen had done stage work only once, and Gary Cooper had never done any. Buddy Rogers had what he described as a "corny Kansas accent." He recalled, "Dick and Coop and I made a pact to protect the one of us that we figured would turn out not to have a voice; the other two would give him a certain segment of our salaries until he could find something else to do." As for their costar Clara Bow, perhaps no voice could have lived up to her flapper exuberance. "All of us in pictures are so frightened," she confessed to a fan magazine. When she heard her Brooklyn-tinged accent on-screen, she screamed, "How can I play . . . with a voice like that?"

Then there was Douglas Fairbanks, newly elected to his second term as Academy president and readying *The Iron Mask*, a return to his *Three Musketeers* character, D'Artagnan. Fairbanks was no longer as spry as he used to be, and *The Iron Mask*, originally shot as a silent, would end with the dying D'Artagnan joining the ghosts of the fallen Musketeers as they march into the heavens. The film was nearly complete when Fairbanks returned to shoot a talking prologue, in which he slashes through a giant parchment and recites a musty verse about "Time's procession slow and vast." Fairbanks was a stage veteran, but when he finally heard the poem played back to him, the wax playback machine accelerated "just fast enough to give Doug a girlish falsetto," a soundman recalled. The actor turned "not pale, but green . . . I think Doug never really recovered from the shock of hearing that gibbering runaway version."

Mary Pickford was also disoriented. "Ladies and gentlemen, you catch me quite unawares," she said at one Academy meeting, having "just jumped into my first talking picture." The picture was *Coquette*, an adaptation of a Broadway melodrama. Pickford was gambling not only on an all-talking film but also on a new image, playing a wealthy flapper. When she first heard her voice test, she was aghast. "That's not me!" she said. "That's a pipsqueak voice. It's impossible. I sound like I'm twelve or thirteen. Oh, it's horrible."

Pickford gave *Coquette* every inch of theatrical training she had, which turned out to be way too much: heaving gasps, histrionic sobs. It was a performance delivered to the balcony—only, she wasn't on a Broadway stage. Still, audiences wanted to hear America's Sweetheart talk, and *Coquette* grossed a commanding $1.4 million—her biggest hit ever.

But, for both Mary and Doug, something had vanished. Douglas Fairbanks Jr. said of his father, "He didn't like sound pictures. He had a sense that his time of mime and ballet—and I use the phrase deliberately because he thought of silent films that way—were over." During *The Iron Mask*, the aging Musketeer said to art director Laurence Irving, "Let's go down and have a look at the soundstage." They sneaked in and saw "a ghastly sort of cave hung with blankets, no lights, the whole of the floor covered with serpentine wires and cables, and then these menacing microphones," Irving recalled.

Fairbanks grabbed Irving's arm and said, "Laurence, the romance of motion-picture making ends here."

AT THE SAME TIME, A new Hollywood icon was being born. Legend had it that Cedric Gibbons, MGM's design guru, sketched it on a napkin or a tablecloth. More likely, he used a piece of paper. He drew an "idealized male figure" with a Crusader's sword, which served as the Academy's insignia on printed material. In late 1928, the figure was handed off to sculptor George Stanley to transform into a three-dimensional work of art, which was then cast at the California Art Bronze Foundry: a twelve-inch-tall figurine standing atop a film reel, affixed to a Belgian marble base. By January 1929, the Academy touted the result as "an artistic and striking bronze statuette, with gold finish, on which will be inscribed the name of the winner."

The central board of judges met on Friday, February 15, and announced the winners of the first Awards of Merit in Monday morning's papers, along with twenty honorable mentions. There was no word on when the awards would be presented. Instead of the planned twelve awards, there were fifteen. *Sunrise* had two winning cinematographers, Karl Struss and Charles Rosher. The board had also decided to give two special prizes, one to Charlie Chaplin for *The Circus* and the other to Warner Bros. for *The Jazz Singer*, the dinosaur-killing asteroid that had "revolutionized the industry." The honorary award was an acknowledgment that talkies couldn't compete alongside silent films: they were a whole new art form.

For the first and only time, actors were awarded for multiple films. Emil Jannings won Best Actor for Paramount's *The Way of All Flesh* and *The Last Command*, and Janet Gaynor won Best Actress for Fox's *Sunrise*, *Street Angel*, and *7th Heaven*. *Sunrise* won Best Unique and Artistic Picture, though its director, F. W. Murnau, didn't even get an honorable mention. Neither did William Wellman, despite the fact that *Wings* won Outstanding Picture. Joseph W. Farnham, one of the Academy founders and a Titular Bishop, won the first and only award for Title Writing.

MGM's *The Crowd* got two honorable mentions, for King Vidor's direction and for Best Unique and Artistic Picture. For the rest of his life, Vidor would spin an intriguing tale about why the film lost to *Sunrise*. "Back then, there were five people who would end any kind of tie," he said. "They were Louis B. Mayer, Douglas Fairbanks, Joe Schenck, Mary Pickford, and Sid Grauman. They sat up all night and Sid Grauman called me up and said, 'I held out until five o'clock for *The Crowd*, but it didn't get it.' The reason was that Mayer did not want to vote for one of his own films." On another occasion, Vidor again named Mayer as the culprit but changed the motive: "It was his own picture, but it was unglamorous, against the studio's image."

Were the first Academy Awards rigged? Mayer did, indeed, dislike *The Crowd*, a drab cousin next to such sparkling entertainments as *The Broadway Melody*, MGM's new "ALL TALKING, ALL SINGING, ALL DANCING Dramatic Sensation," which grossed an astounding $4.3 million. And he was still careful about the appearance of self-interest. It's possible that Mayer put his thumb on the scale to avoid the appearance of collusion; MGM was conspicuously absent among the honorees, apart from the afterthought award for title writing. Yet, the Academy, in order to disprove any "favoritism or friendship," had disclosed the names of all the judges, none of whom was Mayer, Fairbanks, Pickford, or Schenck. Grauman did sit on the central board of judges, so he certainly could have been the one to call Vidor with the bad news. The most likely scenario is that *Sunrise*—one of the silent era's masterpieces—won fair and square and that Vidor's resentment had more to do with Mayer's general loathing of *The Crowd*.

Besides, Mayer had bigger problems than who won the Academy

Award: his perch at MGM was in mortal jeopardy. Marcus Loew, who ran MGM's parent company and who had remained his close ally, had died of a heart attack in 1927. His replacement was Nick Schenck—a "smiler with a knife," as one executive called him—whose distaste for Mayer was mutual. Later, another of Mayer's rivals, William Fox, secretly bought up 443,000 shares in Loew's Inc. from Loew's widow. Then he acquired Schenck's shares, plus another 227,000 on the open market. By the time his spending spree was done, Fox had spent fifty million dollars and controlled a little more than half of Loew's. Mayer found out about the incursion en route to Herbert Hoover's inauguration. Rumors floated that Schenck was preparing to oust Mayer and replace him with his brother, Joe, from United Artists. His rivals were closing in.

Zukor was officially informed that *Wings* had won the big prize in a letter from Academy secretary Frank Woods, reading, "This award consists of an artistic statuette of bronze and gold, and will be presented to you or your representative at an early date." Ten days later, he received another letter, saying that the prizes would be presented on May 16, at the Academy's Second Anniversary Dinner at the Roosevelt Hotel. "May we have your assurance by return mail that a representative of your company will be present?"

Zukor couldn't be bothered to travel from New York to pick up the trifle, so the Academy pitched a novel idea: What if Zukor accepted via a prerecorded talking film? This would affirm the Academy's forward thinking—but Zukor apparently wasn't eager to respond.

On May 10, with the ceremony days away, Woods sent a desperate telegram:

URGENTLY REQUEST YOU HAVE YOURSELF RECORDED ON TALKING FILM ACCEPTING ACADEMY AWARDS STOP THIS WILL BE FEATURE OF OUR DINNER AND ENTIRE ACADEMY CONSIDERS IT VERY IMPORTANT STOP

But Fairbanks had already been at Paramount's Long Island studio that morning, where he and Zukor filmed the prize handoff. Preserved in Zukor's papers are his notes for the first-ever Academy Award acceptance speech: "I am deeply impressed with the idea and purpose of the Academy Awards of Merit. The recognition of individual achievement is bound to be a great stimulus and inspiration to the persons engaged in production and to the whole industry. I hope that Paramount will be able to win the award next year, etc."

AMONG THE OTHER HONOREES WHO did not bother to show up were Charlie Chaplin ("cold feet") and Gloria Swanson, Best Actress runner-up for *Sadie Thompson*, who recalled, "I did not attend the Academy dinner, but in report it bore out all my feelings about awards and prizes." How could anyone compare her to Janet Gaynor? "Oranges and apples." Gerald Duffy, given honorable mention for writing the titles for *The Private Life of Helen of Troy*, had the best excuse: he had been dead for eleven months.

Emil Jannings, the inaugural Best Actor, was also absent. He arrived in Berlin the day of the awards, having picked up his statuette early. Zukor would deny that the forty-four-year-old Jannings was a casualty of talking pictures—after all, having a foreign accent didn't stop Greta Garbo. Nor would it hinder Jannings's new costar in *Der blaue Engel*, Marlene Dietrich. Nevertheless, his return to Germany was fateful. By the late thirties, Jannings was making Nazi propaganda films at the behest of Joseph Goebbels, who in 1941 awarded him the dubious distinction of "Artist of the State." After the war, when U.S. soldiers arrived at Jannings's home in Bavaria, the first thing he showed them, lore has it, was his gold-plated statuette.

For the 270 who did arrive at the Roosevelt Hotel on May 16, 1929, there was much to see. The evening began at seven, with a "talking picture entertainment" in the Academy lounge. Academy members, who were permitted to bring guests at five dollars per plate, were then shown through the arched doorways to the Blossom Room, lined with Spanish Colonial Revival stone columns and decorated with "soft lantern lights shedding rays and shadows on the brilliant gowns and gay blooms," the hotel's press release read. "Thirty-six tables with their scintillating glassware and long tapers, each table bearing a replica in waxed candy of the gold statuette award, filled the entire floor space of the room." As the guests sat down for a supper of consommé Célestine, fillet of sole sauté au beurre, half-broiled chicken on toast, string beans, and Long Branch potatoes, President Fairbanks rose to speak.

A week before his forty-fifth birthday, the swashbuckler was feeling his age. Not only had he killed off D'Artagnan, but he was now old enough to be a father-in-law: his nineteen-year-old son was engaged to Joan Crawford. "It is now two years since we gathered at our first dinner at the Biltmore hotel and organized the Academy," Fairbanks told the crowd. "We had many rosy dreams at that time, but like most dreams they were hazy. We felt, however, that we should get together and do things for the good of all the branches of motion-picture production. Some of our dreams did not come true, but as we look back we find that we have not been standing still."

The presentation of awards took no more than ten minutes. William deMille called up the winners, while Fairbanks handed out the statuettes and certificates. King Vidor was there to receive his honorable mention for directing *The Crowd*, but surely smarted to witness Louis B. Mayer accept the citation for best "unique and artistic picture"—two adjectives that summed up why the studio chief disdained *The Crowd*.

The Warner brothers were in New York, so Zanuck accepted the special prize for *The Jazz Singer* in honor of Sam Warner, "who first saw there was a possibility of making talking pictures," he said. Finally, the pièce de résistance: the Outstanding Picture award, for *Wings*. "I'd like to call up Mr. Adolph Zukor to accept this award for his company," de-Mille announced. A projector flickered, and the faces—and voices—of Fairbanks and Zukor appeared on a screen. The Academy had chosen the future, and it was sound.

Finally, deMille yielded the floor to Pickford, whose unglamorous job that night was to announce that the Motion Picture Relief Fund, which she had cofounded years earlier to support picture people who had fallen on hard times, was ending its association with the fund-raising group the Community Chest. A more intriguing speech came from one Mrs. Edward Jacobs, of the National Federation of Women's Clubs—the same pious churchgoers who had been the thorn in the industry's side through-out the decade. The Academy had slyly opened its screening room to the women's clubs to preview upcoming features, echoing Will Hays's strategy of keeping Hollywood's enemies close. "We are not censors," Mrs. Jacobs declared. "We boost the best and ignore the rest."

Vanilla and chocolate ice cream was served, and deMille brought up "one of the Academy's oldest and staunchest supporters," Louis B. Mayer. "When the Academy was first started," Mayer intoned, "it was my thought that there must be a closer understanding between the artistic and the business side of making pictures." He pointed out the dessert on the audience's plates, adorned with the names of famous movie palaces. "I can't say for sure, but if Sid Grauman got a Roxy"—Grauman's rival in Midtown Manhattan—"he ate it all and enjoyed it," he cracked. "I can vouch for Ben Schulberg, who enjoyed the MGM ice cream. You see, the Academy has done wonders in two years by making us all harmonious." As for the whispers against the Academy, Mayer said, disingenuously, "Personally I have not heard much of it."

The evening ended with a song from Al Jolson, who was now the biggest star in the world thanks to *The Jazz Singer* and its follow-up, *The Singing Fool*. "I notice they gave *The Jazz Singer* a statuette, but they didn't give me one," Jolson quipped. "I could use one; they look heavy, and I could use another paperweight." And then, a dig: "For the life of me, I can't see what Jack Warner would do with one of them. It can't say yes."

For the twenty-two-year-old Janet Gaynor, the highlight of the evening wasn't winning the first Best Actress award but meeting Douglas Fairbanks. "It was more like a private party than a big public ceremony," she recalled. "It wasn't open to anyone but Academy members, and as you danced, you saw the most important people in Hollywood whirling past you." Years after she won, Gaynor said, "It was nothing then like it is now. My agent didn't call me up the next day with an offer to double my salary; I didn't find a pile of scripts at my door. Photographers weren't camped on my front lawn. I just got up at 5:00 and drove off to the studio—as always."

Frances Marion, who won the writing award two years later, had a more acid assessment. In her memoir *Off with Their Heads!*, she recalled that "the little gold-washed statuette was thought, by skeptics and art lovers, a bit on the amateurish side. Still, I saw it as a perfect symbol of the picture business: a powerful athletic body clutching a gleaming sword with half of his head, that part which held his brains, completely sliced off."

THE FIRST ACADEMY AWARDS TURNED out to be an Irish wake for an art form that had reached its apotheosis and then vanished. By the second year of the awards, all the Outstanding Picture nominees had sound. MGM released its last silent film—*The Kiss*, starring Greta Garbo and Conrad Nagel—in November 1929. The once-grassy studio now had some two dozen soundstages, entombments of concrete. "Within two years," William deMille observed, "our little old Hollywood was gone and in its place stood a fair, new city, talking a new language, having different manners and customs, a more terrifying city full of strange faces, less friendly, more businesslike, twice as populous—and much more cruel."

But the twin crises that the Academy had been created to solve, censorship and labor organizing, didn't go away. Gloria Swanson's Academy honor for *Sadie Thompson* only drew more attention to the film's salacious source material, a W. Somerset Maugham story about a South Seas prostitute, and sound made the Hays Office's job even trickier, as actors now ad-libbed over their preapproved scripts. In the fall of 1929, Martin Quigley, the publisher of the *Motion Picture Herald* and an esteemed Catholic, drafted a strict set of censorship guidelines, called "Code to Govern the Making of Talking, Synchronized and Silent Motion Pictures." In February 1930, representatives from the five major studios unanimously agreed to adopt it as the new Production Code. It would take another four years—and the rise of a tougher enforcer than Hays, Joseph Breen—to make the Code stick, keeping the movies corseted and squeaky-clean for more than three decades. Sex would be expunged, moral standards would be upheld, and evil would always be punished by the final frame.

Actors' Equity, meanwhile, was clamoring at the gates. A month before the first Academy Awards, Equity's Frank Gillmore had promised to "invade" Hollywood studios. On June 5, he made a shock announcement: no Equity members would be allowed to appear in any sound picture without an all-union cast. The producers' association vowed to fight, saying it would honor only the Academy contract, while William Randolph

Hearst's papers bemoaned the "aggressive intrusion into the happy and harmonious situation existing in Los Angeles."

Undaunted, the Academy sent out ballots for the Second Annual Awards of Merit. But predictions of the Academy's demise became loud enough that secretary Frank Woods released a "refutation of statements freely bruited about Hollywood to the effect that if Equity should be able to impose Equity shop on the studios it would end the Academy." The infighting stretched on for eleven and a half summer weeks, during which Equity claimed to enlist more than two thousand new members. But its plans fizzled when stage star Ethel Barrymore, who had been instrumental in Equity since its formation, parachuted into Hollywood and publicly criticized Gillmore's tactics. *Variety* ran the headline "EQUITY BADLY WHIPPED," while the producers gloated that Equity had "invaded a healthy, wealthy and happy family and tried to perform an operation upon a healthy baby." By October, Equity was so fatigued with Hollywood that it rejected a plea from Nagel and forty-five others to form their own West Coast branch. There was talk, now, of a "body of screen actors independent of Equity." But the Academy, for the time being, had won.

FACING THE TWIN UNCERTAINTIES OF sound and middle age, Mary Pickford and Douglas Fairbanks played the biggest card they had: for the first time, they would star in a movie together. They chose *The Taming of the Shrew*. Mary sensed a "completely new Douglas, a Douglas who no longer cared apparently about me or my feelings." Pickford would show up for a nine-o'clock makeup call and wait until noon for Fairbanks to finish his morning ritual of sunbathing and calisthenics. When he arrived, his lines had to be chalked on a blackboard. Pickford was even more disappointed when the director, Sam Taylor, told her acting coach he wanted the "old Pickford tricks." "The making of that film was my finish," Pickford recalled. "My confidence was completely shattered, and I was never again at ease before the camera or microphone. All the assurance of *Coquette* was gone."

After witnessing the first Academy Awards, Pickford was now positioned to get a statuette of her own for *Coquette*. The next April, she accepted the second annual Best Actress award, for a performance that no one would claim to be her finest, kicking off a dubious Oscar tradition: the "career" award given for a lousy film. Observers speculated that she must have plied the judges with tea at Pickfair.

But it was too late to reverse the decline of Hollywood's King and Queen of Hearts. While making her next film, *Forever Yours*, Pickford was so aghast watching the rushes that she burned the footage. She made three more talkies, each grossing less than the one before. Her last film, *Secrets*, came out in 1933, the year she and Fairbanks finally separated. Fairbanks made his final picture, *The Private Life of Don Juan*, the following year. Their divorce was finalized in 1936, and three years later Fairbanks died of a heart attack.

Compounding her misfortunes, Pickford's brother, Jack, and her sister, Lottie, both died from causes related to alcoholism. Their father had been a drinker, too, and Mary had managed to avoid the family curse until her own career began to slip. Guests at Pickfair now noticed her retreating to the bathroom and returning with alcohol on her breath. Upstairs, she kept whiskey in a bottle of Listerine. A year after divorcing Fairbanks, she married her *My Best Girl* costar Buddy Rogers, and America's Sweetheart retreated to Pickfair for four decades.

NOT LONG AFTER THE FIRST Academy Awards, Louis B. Mayer summoned actress Anita Page for "special favors." Page, the fair-haired star of *The Broadway Melody*, which in 1930 won the second Academy Award for Outstanding Picture, declined his advances. "I can make you the biggest star in the world in three pictures," Mayer promised. Combining the lure with a threat, he added, "And I can kill Garbo in three pictures."

"But Mr. Mayer," Page said, "I'm already a star."

"I could make you bigger," Mayer pressed. "We could handle things discreetly."

Page turned him down again. Galling Mayer further, she then asked MGM for a raise. "They weren't going to do me any favors anymore," she said later. Within a few years, she was getting loaned out to Columbia and Universal, something MGM did only when it wanted to penalize stars. The Academy Awards were far from the only Hollywood tradition Mayer had helped create; by 1936, Page was out of acting altogether, a victim of what would, many decades later, come to light under the hashtag MeToo.

By late 1929, Mayer had once again beaten back the encroaching unions, but his hold over his kingdom was still under threat—until fate intervened. In July, William Fox was riding through Westbury, Long Island, when his automobile collided with another car. His chauffeur was killed, and Fox lost a pint of blood. He was still recuperating when the stock market crashed in October. Fortunes around the world were wiped out, including Fox's. His shares of Loew's cratered in value, as did those of his own Fox Theatres. With bankers calling in his notes, Fox was forced to cancel his takeover of Loew's/MGM and even lost control of the business that bore his name.

The good times were over, but MGM and Warner Bros., flush with cash from the popularity of talkies, wouldn't feel the effects of the crash for several years. And Mayer, on the verge of losing his kingdom, had held on to his throne, becoming perhaps the only man in Hollywood who directly benefited from the onset of the Great Depression.

He had played his cards—all aces.

TWO

Rebels

1933–39

How Frank Capra joined the establishment only
to turn against it, Bette Davis fought for a role that
matched her fire, and the rise of the guilds nearly
killed off the Academy.

Peg Entwistle grasped the ladder and lifted herself upward. Her shoes
were scuffed. Her coat, made of suede and black leather, was affixed
with a jeweled pin. Earlier that evening, a September night in 1932, she
had told her aunt and uncle in Beachwood Canyon that she was going
to the drugstore and then to see friends. But here she was, climbing rung
by rung, up the back of a fifty-foot capital letter H.

Hollywood had not been kind. Months earlier, Peg had opened in
a play called *The Mad Hopes*, at Los Angeles's Belasco theater, opposite
Humphrey Bogart. The twenty-four-year-old blonde was "a charming
picture of youth," one reviewer wrote. She was set to follow the play to
Broadway, but word of her performance reached David O. Selznick at
RKO, and she was offered a one-picture deal. She broke her contract
with *The Mad Hopes* and reported to RKO, where she was put through a

whirlwind of screen tests and fittings. She was cast in *Thirteen Women*, about a group of former sorority sisters lured to ruin by an ostracized ex-classmate. Entwistle played Hazel, who stabs her husband with a knife.

But her sixteen minutes of screen time were chopped down to four after the Hays Office determined that her scenes with another actress had unacceptable lesbian undertones. By September, the studio had dropped her. Entwistle had alienated the producers of *The Mad Hopes*. At her apartment in Manhattan, her possessions were being held against the back rent she owed. Her ex-husband had a new wife and a revived career—all after *she* had used her own money to cover his alimony from a previous marriage she didn't know about on their wedding day. Her mistakes were all compounding one another. She could go back to New York and grovel for a role or stay in Hollywood and grovel for another screen test.

Entwistle reached the midpoint of the fifty-foot H. The sign, erected in 1923, had been a real estate ploy, with automated lights that flashed to the canyon below: "HOLLY . . . WOOD . . . LAND." Entwistle looked out on a vista that, on a clear day, stretched as far as Santa Monica and out to the Pacific—and leaped into the void.

Two days later, a woman who had been hiking nearby called the police department. She had found a pair of shoes, a coat, and a purse, and down the mountain, she had spotted a woman's crumpled corpse. "GIRL ENDS LIFE IN HOLLYWOOD MOUNTAIN LEAP," read the *Los Angeles Examiner*'s headline. Entwistle's purse had been empty, save for a note, signed "P.E.": "I am afraid I'm a coward. I am sorry for everything. If I had done this a long time ago it would have saved a lot of pain."

THE DEPRESSION WAS SLOW TO reach Hollywood. Talkies gave the industry a well-timed boom. Entire genres—gangster movies, musicals—sprang to life. Movies were an opiate in hard times: Americans who struggled to feed their families pinched their pennies so that they could spend two hours a week in a darkened theater to escape their troubles. More than 65 percent of the population went to the movies in 1930; it was a necessity, like bread or milk.

In Hollywood, aspiring starlets from small towns flocked to the studios' gates, a gold rush that left a trail of broken dreams. The studios did need talent, particularly from the stage—actors who could speak, playwrights who could tell them what to say—but there was never enough work to go around. In the first year of the decade, 17,500 extras registered with the Central Casting Bureau, with only 833 of them averaging a day's work per week. After her death, the press cast Peg Entwistle as an emblem of dashed ambition, another Hollywood hopeful the studios had discarded.

Men like Louis B. Mayer and Adolph Zukor and the brothers Warner didn't flaunt the fact that their profits never seemed to trickle down to the rank and file. They ran their studios as well-ordered fiefdoms, suspending star players when they got out of line and blackballing recalcitrant writers. For most creative professions, Hollywood remained a nonunion town, though the influx of stage talent from the East was bringing in more and more people who were accustomed to labor representation. The coming years would be a time for rebels—not just Hollywood's restive workers but a tempestuous star named Bette Davis and, perhaps most unlikely, the man who more than anyone wanted to affix himself to the establishment: Frank Capra.

By 1933, the Hollywood boom was finally starting to slow. A quarter of Americans were unemployed, and movie house attendance tapered. In January, the mighty Paramount was put into receivership, soon to file for bankruptcy, and MGM was the only major studio operating (just barely) in the black. Then, that March, a match was struck.

Two days into his presidency, Franklin Delano Roosevelt announced a bank holiday to halt a run on the banks. The movie industry went into a tailspin. Fox told its employees that nobody would be paid until the banks reopened; Universal invoked its "national emergency" clause to suspend all its contracts. Unless drastic measures were taken, Hollywood faced a production shutdown. The studio heads huddled. Most of them believed that their top stars were overpaid anyway, and the new urgency gave them cover to institute a pay cut. That's when the Academy, as the industry's de facto parliament, entered the fray, convening an Emergency Committee to broker 50 percent pay cuts across the board.

On March 8, a drained-looking Mayer walked into MGM's largest projection room to address his kingdom. "Don't worry, L.B.," Lionel Barrymore yelled. "We all know why you're here. We're with you."

Mayer gravely informed his subjects that the studios were on the verge of shutting down, leaving thousands out of work and the world without movies—that is, unless the assembled talent and department heads agreed to a temporary pay cut. Barrymore immediately voiced his approval, "for the good of MGM, of Hollywood, and of the country." Only screenwriter Ernest Vajda objected—after all, hadn't MGM been churning out hits?

"Sir," Barrymore intoned, "you are acting like a man on his way to the guillotine who wants to stop for a manicure." After a round of applause, he elaborated: "The tumbrels are rolling; the guillotine is waiting outside and we're haggling over pennies!"

"At least it postpones the execution," Vajda shot back.

The mogul took a pledge: "I, Louis B. Mayer, will work to see that you get back every penny when this terrible emergency is over." Walking back to his office, he asked his talent liaison, "How did I do?"

Vajda's discontent was prescient, and much of the coming strife was about to fall on the six-year-old Academy. The organization had enjoyed a relatively peaceful few years since 1930, when it oversaw a five-year pact between actors and producers that included a "no-strike" provision. Then it moved on to less sensitive matters, like a prospectus to build itself a gleaming, white art deco tower that would stand as a "magnificent temple to the motion picture." Its idealistic president, Conrad Nagel, went on a three-month national tour to counteract "false conceptions of Hollywood." And then there were the Awards of Merit, which had grown in scope and prestige, with radio networks broadcasting the results. As columnist Louella Parsons noted, "You'd be surprised how the greatest of stars who have won the coveted little bronze statues have them sitting in places of prominence in their homes."

Amid widespread grumbling over the 50 percent cut, the Academy's Emergency Committee planned a meeting with studio representatives to hammer out a new plan. About an hour before, one member of the committee was getting his hair cut at the Hollywood Athletic Club. The thirty-five-year-old Frank Capra was preparing to direct his new

Columbia picture, *Lady for a Day*. As he sat at the barber's, he felt the earth begin to shake. He ran outside and watched the building sway, his heart in his throat, then went back in for a steam bath to calm his nerves. He found John Ford reading the paper. Capra introduced himself. "You've heard about the big pay-cut meeting the Academy's holding with the—"

"That's all a lot of horseshit," Ford harrumphed.

Capra finished his steam bath and joined the rest of the Emergency Committee on the top floor of the Roosevelt Hotel. As the group argued, aftershocks rattled the room. "Angry, shaking fingers froze in mid-air during each tremor," Capra recalled. Finally, someone said, "Look, you guys. I'm no hero. Let's get the hell off this top floor." They relocated to the lobby, until another jolt shook a chandelier over their heads. They resumed the squabbling in the parking lot of Grauman's Chinese. "We were just revving up to some good name-calling," Capra recalled, "when police cars trundled by with loud speakers blaring: 'ALL AMERICAN LEGION MEN TO LONG BEACH! EMERGENCY!'"

There could hardly be a more fitting first act to the seismic drama enveloping Hollywood—and, with it, the Academy. With the International Alliance of Theatrical Stage Employees (IATSE) threatening to strike rather than accept the pay cut, Harry Warner persuaded the other studio heads to call the union's bluff and shut down production for a single day. On March 13, soundstages stood empty. When production resumed the next day, the town was rife with recriminations—or, as *Variety* put it, "SQUAWKS GALORE." The Academy emerged with a fourteen-point plan to keep the studios open, with the pay cut lasting no longer than eight weeks. Those making under fifty dollars a week were exempted. To the vexation of the studio heads, the Academy hired the accounting firm Price, Waterhouse and Company to audit their books; if the studios were deemed solvent, they would have to immediately restore salaries.

"All hell broke loose," Capra wrote. "'Traitors!' the company heads called us (the Academy officers), for not making the pay cuts permanent. 'Stooges!' cried the wrathful actors, writers, and directors." Many believed the whole thing was a scheme to cut salaries permanently. By mid-April, though, Columbia and RKO had returned to full pay, quickly followed by MGM and Fox. In its *Emergency Bulletin*, the Academy solemnly promised that "a horizontal industry salary cut will never again be attempted."

But the fallout kept falling. At Warner Bros., Harry and Jack Warner had refused to take pay cuts themselves, while their head of production, Darryl Zanuck, found his own salary unceremoniously sliced in half. Zanuck defied his bosses with a rogue statement announcing that the studio was restoring its salaries. When Jack Warner retaliated with his own statement rescinding Zanuck's order, Zanuck handed in his resignation and (temporarily) withdrew from the Academy. Soon after, he cofounded his own studio, Twentieth Century Films, which became 20th Century–Fox.

As Academy president, Nagel tried to intervene by asking Will Hays to keep the recalcitrant Warner Bros. in line—or to give it a pass. The rogue move enraged the Academy's board, and after a stormy meeting, Nagel offered his resignation. The most utopian of the Academy's original four founders was so beaten up that he fled Hollywood. His replacement, soundman J. T. Reed, promised a new Academy that would be "the kind of an organization that you want it to be." But it was too late. As the face of the pay cuts, the Academy had made enemies on every side. It had always been suspected of being a tool of the producers, but now Hollywood's creative professions, convinced the Academy no longer represented their best interests, were finally pushed to do what they had never managed to: organize.

In April 1933, the Screen Writers Guild, which had existed informally since 1920, was resuscitated. By summer, all but 7 of the 124 writers in the Academy had joined the guild, which commanded its members to resign from the Academy en masse. At the same time, a group of mid-tier actors began meeting secretly at a house in the Hollywood Hills. Unlike the invitation-only Academy, their group would be open to all. In July, seventeen founding members formally became the Screen Actors Guild. They were soon joined by *Frankenstein* star Boris Karloff, who was sympathetic to the actors' cause, having worked backbreaking sixteen-hour days in full monster makeup.

At first, few took the nascent actors' union seriously, and top-level stars were still squeamish about risking their cushy careers. But that fall, the guild saw a chance to prove its mettle. President Roosevelt's National Recovery Administration, or NRA, had invited the Academy to Washington to help codify Hollywood's labor practices, and the Academy was eager to reestablish its authority. When the proposed code was released, with terms favorable to the producers, SAG seized on the discord as a recruiting issue. In early October, the guild arranged a meeting at the home of SAG president Ralph Morgan's brother Frank (who later played the title role in The Wizard of Oz), where some two dozen big-name actors joined the cause. The group—including Groucho Marx, Robert Montgomery, Gary Cooper, and Spencer Tracy—elected a starry new leadership, headed by song-and-dance man Eddie "Banjo Eyes" Cantor. Those among them who were members of the Academy wired in their resignations.

Days later, the newly robust SAG held a mass meeting at the El Capitan Theatre, where Cantor addressed more than eight hundred actors. "Some Academy members say we are going screwy forming a Guild organization," he told them. "We just want to be 100% represented in an organization not subsidized by anyone." The guild issued a strongly worded telegram to Roosevelt opposing the NRA code. Roosevelt responded by inviting Cantor to meet him at his personal retreat in Warm Springs, Georgia, and suspended the objectionable provisions. (The Supreme Court later found the entire NRA unconstitutional.)

The Academy had proven not only ineffectual but disposable. And maybe it was. By December, it had lost 177 people, nearly a fifth of its membership. Its reserve funds were exhausted. The week before Christmas, the Academy confirmed that there would be no Awards of Merit held that year. It ended 1933 with a bank balance of $301, against monthly expenses of $1,700. "The Academy of M. P. Arts and Sciences," Variety eulogized on the last day of the year, "is about to fold up completely and fall into the ash-can of oblivion."

AND YET, THE ACADEMY REFUSED to die. As 1934 dawned, the "skeletonized organization," as Variety put it, was plotting its resurrection. Producers saw the Academy as their best chance to blunt the alarming rise of talent guilds. A revival meeting was held at Irving Thalberg's bungalow at MGM. By the end of January, the weakened Academy set a date in March for its awards banquet.

Though it was now fashionable for writers and actors to send in their Academy resignations, people still wanted Academy Awards. "I wrote and threw away dozens of acceptance speeches; practiced shy humility before the mirror; rehearsed emotional breaks in my voice at just the right spots," one of that year's aspirants for Best Directing recalled. "I ordered my first tuxedo—from a tailor, yet; rented a plush home in Beverly Hills—to be 'seen,' sway votes in bistros. I drove everyone nuts."

This aspirant was Frank Capra, nominated for *Lady for a Day*. In his later films *Mr. Deeds Goes to Town* and *Mr. Smith Goes to Washington*, Capra would heroize the clean-hearted, small-town common man who crashed the halls of wealth and power. In the Academy, he saw a chance to crash the Hollywood establishment: the ultimate happy ending for a grubby, impoverished, immigrant underdog like him.

Like Hollywood's Jewish moguls, Capra was an outsider enamored with the American Dream. He had spent his first five years in Sicily, where his peasant family lived in an "old cracked house of stone and mortar, clinging by its toenails to the rocks," he recalled. He turned six in the steerage hold of the SS *Germania*, "crammed with retching, praying, terrorized immigrants." By 1921, he was in San Francisco, living on pocket change and avoiding the lure of the racketeering life. He spotted an ad for a new movie studio that had set up in a Golden Gate Park gymnasium. The "studio" turned out to be a pomaded eccentric named Walter Montague, who had played Shakespeare in vaudeville. Capra bluffed that he was "from Hollywood," and Montague hired him to direct a one-reel film of a Rudyard Kipling poem, which opened to unexpected raves. "The nutty little Montague affair—a smart aleck scrounging for a quick buck—had backfired into a cockeyed success," Capra recalled in his autobiography, in which he rewrote his life as a snappy Capra comedy.

In Hollywood, he was hired by the comedy king Mack Sennett, known for his bumbling slapstick crew the Keystone Cops. In Sennett's gag room, Capra learned the fundamentals of comedy, including "the topper," that final flourish that caps off a running gag with some outrageous twist—or, as Capra wrote, "the unexpected wow that knocked them in the aisles." But Capra didn't want to be a gag writer; he wanted to be a director. He got a break shooting vehicles for vaudeville star Harry Langdon and directed a First National flop called *For the Love of Mike*. By thirty, he was divorced from his first wife and unemployed, his "dreamy love affair" with the movies on the rocks. Then he got a meeting with Harry Cohn, president of Columbia Pictures. The studio was then a bottom-barrel outfit on "Poverty Row," the area near Gower and Sunset that, Capra recalled, was "infested by shacks and dinky stages where ferret-eyed producers made 'fillums' that cost, and sold for, peanuts."

Cohn was notoriously lewd. He judged the merit of his pictures by the restlessness of his buttocks ("If my fanny squirms, it's bad. If my fanny doesn't squirm, it's good"). He lined his office shelves with perfume and stockings, which he used as bribes, and his sexual coercion of actresses was well known. When Rita Hayworth refused him, he bugged her dressing rooms. Capra nicknamed him "His Crudeness." Cohn gave him a six-by-eight cubicle that looked out onto a dry fountain full of cigarette butts. "Hey, Dago. What've you been doin'? Where the hell's the story?" Cohn would bark. Capra churned out films on a penny-pinching six-week cycle, answering Cohn's coarseness with the only thing the producer respected: cockiness.

But Capra knew that Hollywood looked down on comedy hacks like him. "My goal, as a youth, was to leap across the tracks—to rise above the muck and meanness of peasant poverty," he recalled. "I wanted freedom from established caste systems; and from where I took life's jolts on the chin, freedom could only be won by success." In 1929, Capra released the comedy whodunit *The Donovan Affair*. The film was not only his first all-talking picture, but it marked what he called "the beginning of a secret ambition that would soon aggravate into a manic obsession: win the Academy Award for best film director."

He had an uphill climb. "In 1929," he wrote, "the Academy membership consisted mainly of important Brahmins under contract to major studios. They all had the votes. Winning an Oscar in Poverty Row would be as easy as telling the sex of a fly. Nevertheless, I would have an Oscar on *my* mantelpiece, or bust."

The next year, Capra directed *Ladies of Leisure*, a breakthrough success for its star, Barbara Stanwyck. (Capra had an affair with Stanwyck, whose eventual rejection sent him into the arms of his second wife, Lucille.) Nevertheless, Capra was galled that neither Stanwyck nor the film was considered for the Academy Award. "The major studios had the votes," he reasoned. "I had my freedom, but the 'honors' went to those who worked for the Establishment. I wanted awards as well as independence."

His alley cat instincts kicked in, and he hatched a plan. "First: wangle an invitation to join the Academy by attacking as a howling minority; second: call it 'unfair' to independent producers; third: steam up Harry Cohn into raising a 'stink' with the majors about 'inadequate representation' on the Academy's board of directors." It worked like a charm. In May 1931, Capra received an invitation from Fred Niblo to become an Academy member. By September, he had grabbed a spot on the board. At his first meeting, he asked for clarification on the voting procedures for awards. The disillusioning answer: "The voting was 'kosher'—if you belonged." The trick, Capra realized, "was to get *nominated* by the clique of major studio directors who had achieved membership—and these Brahmins were not about to doff their caps to the 'untouchables' of Poverty Row."

Making good films wasn't enough. To win his "Golden Fleece," Capra created a two-pronged approach. He would get loaned out to a fancier studio and infiltrate the Brahmins. And he would rise up the ranks within the Academy, where he could "become an officer—perhaps President— and preside over the world's most glamorous event, an Academy Award Banquet."

The first tactic backfired. Knowing that Cohn would do anything to win approval from Louis B. Mayer, Capra got himself loaned out to MGM. But, after he dared to revamp a gag that producer Harry Rapf had asked him to stage, he was fired. Back at Columbia, he turned out *American Madness*, starring Walter Huston as an idealistic bank president. Capra was sure this would merit a nomination. "The film was timely, controversial, realistic: the run on the bank was so real many viewers went straight to their banks to withdraw their money," he recalled. "But no! Critics said it was not Academy Award material." Cohn told him, "Forget it. You ain't got a Chinaman's chance. They only vote for that arty junk."

But Capra was single-minded. "I dreamed about Oscars," he recalled. "I *had* to get one." If the Academy wanted arty junk, he'd make "the artiest film they ever saw—about miscegenation!" The film was *The Bitter Tea of General Yen*, about a romance between a Chinese warlord and an American missionary, played by Stanwyck. For General Yen, Capra, unable to find a "real Chinese" of his liking, cast Swedish actor Nils Asther. In January 1933, *The Bitter Tea of General Yen* became the first film attraction at the newly opened Radio City Music Hall. But it failed at the box office—even with two white actors, the interracial romance made ticket buyers wary—and got no nominations. "Damn those Academy voters!" Capra steamed. "Couldn't they recognize a work of art when they saw one?"

His arty films hadn't impressed the Academy. Neither had his hours on the board, serving on the unglamorous Constitutional Amendment Committee. "There was a mystique about Academy voting that confounded trends, predictions and logic," he wrote. "Some years the awards were paradoxical. But those that grabbed off little statuettes didn't give a hang *how* they got one. They just knew an Oscar tripled their salaries and zoomed them to world fame. Salary increases didn't work up my appetite. But world fame—wow! I salivated morning, noon, and night."

If arty didn't cut it, he would try crowd-pleasing. He bought the rights to the Damon Runyon story "Madame La Gimp," in which a haggard apple seller, with the help of her gangster cohort, poses as an aristocrat to impress her daughter's high-born European fiancé. Capra's version, retitled *Lady for a Day*, captured not only Runyon's gangster patois (later immortalized in *Guys and Dolls*) but also the class-hopping fantasy that would please his Depression audiences throughout the decade. When Cohn saw it, he gushed, "You little son-of-a-bitch, you can make shit taste like pineapple!"

When the 1933 pay cut fracas sent the Academy into a death spiral, pitting the fledgling institution against workers, Capra made a choice. "I stayed with the Academy," he recalled, arguing, "We can't let this wonderful thing, the Academy prize, die from lack of interest. Let's keep it alive until we know what to do." He admitted that "stooging for the producers" earned him plenty of detractors: "I was called more names—'scab' and all that shit. The petty guys!" But his belief in the Academy happened to coincide with his ultimate goal of winning one of its prizes.

In February 1934, the back-from-the-dead Academy nominated *Lady for a Day* for four awards, including Best Directing and the top prize, now called "Outstanding Production." Capra, who was busy shooting his next film—about an heiress and a reporter who meet on a Greyhound bus—sprang into action. Even his wife's pregnancy didn't slow his charm offensive at the bistros of Beverly Hills. "Day by day I kept persuading myself that I would win *four* awards for *Lady for a Day*," he recalled. "I looked up the records. No picture had ever won *four* major Oscars. It would set a *record*. Hot damn!"

The Sixth Academy Awards were held on March 16, 1934, at the Fiesta Room of the Ambassador Hotel, with Duke Ellington's band providing music for dancing. Capra's old friend Will Rogers hosted. Watching nervously, Capra recalled, "I applauded like an idiot as each winner squeezed through celebrity-crowded tables to the small dance floor, where a spotlight picked him up, escorted him in glory to the dais where he clutched his coveted Oscar—and grinned like another idiot."

Rogers made a show of opening each envelope, a flourish that became a time-honored tradition. As he read off the directing nominations, Capra took one last glance at the acceptance speech he had hidden under the tablecloth. "Well, well, well, what do you know!" Rogers said, beaming. "I've watched this young man for a long time—saw him come up from the bottom, and I *mean* the bottom. It couldn't happen to a nicer guy. *Come up and get it, Frank!*"

Capra's table cheered as the director snaked his way around applauding Brahmins. On the dance floor, he waved to the searching spotlight and yelled, "Over here!" But the spotlight swung to the other side of the floor, landing on the director of *Cavalcade*, Frank Lloyd. Capra stood stunned in the dark, until he heard someone yell at him, "Down in front!"

The humiliated Capra skulked back to his seat, as spectators scolded him, "Sit down!" It was, he recalled, "the longest, saddest, most shattering walk of my life. I wished I could have crawled under the rug like a miserable worm. When I slumped in my chair I felt like one. All my friends at the table were crying."

Lady for a Day lost all four awards. As Capra slinked out of the ceremony, his shame turned to rage. *Those crummy Academy voters,* he thought. *To hell with their lousy awards!* If he ever won one, he vowed not to accept it. He returned to his pregnant wife and to his new film, *It Happened One Night.*

EACH MORNING WHEN JACK WARNER got into work, the same woman came into his office, pleading. She usually arrived at the same time as the shoeshine boy, bright and early, begging and cajoling, staring with her crazily large eyes. For six months this went on. She haunted him.

What Bette Davis wanted was a part—but not just any part. She wanted "Mildred," the depraved, vindictive, sickly, manipulative waitress who nearly destroys the life of a sensitive painter in W. Somerset Maugham's novel *Of Human Bondage.* John Cromwell was turning it into a film over at RKO, and he wanted Davis. And Davis wanted to play Mildred—not *despite* the fact that the character was as coarse as sandpaper but *because* of it. Only by playing someone so unlikable would she finally prove what she was doing in Hollywood. She just needed Warner, to whom she was under contract, to loan her out.

At twenty-five, Davis wasn't one to back down. "I do not regret the dust I've kicked up," she would later boast. "I always fought people my own size and more often than not they were bigger." Her tempestuous nature was her birthright. The story went that she was born during a raging storm, between a clap of thunder and a bolt of lightning that incinerated the tree outside her parents' house, in Lowell, Massachusetts. Her mother, Ruthie, thought the gods were going mad. To Bette, the story made perfect sense. "Created in a fury," she wrote, "I'm at home in a tempest."

Unlike Capra, Davis came from Episcopalian New England stock, descended from seventeenth-century Puritans. In early 1926, her mother brought her to Boston to see Ibsen's *The Wild Duck.* When the curtain came up, Davis saw a girl of seventeen, like her, playing Hedvig. The actress was Peg Entwistle. "It was my first serious theatre and a whole, new world opened up to me," Davis recalled. Entwistle made her rethink her entire purpose. "I was watching myself," she reflected. "Miss Entwistle had lost herself in Hedvig. Now I did too. There wasn't an emotion I didn't anticipate and share with her."

When Hedvig shot herself in the breast, Davis felt that she had died, too. She turned to Ruthie and declared, "Mother! Someday I will play Hedvig."

"Let her become a secretary!" her absentee father sniffed.

But proving people wrong—particularly him—was one of her specialties. She enrolled at a dramatic academy in Manhattan, where she studied dance under Martha Graham. ("I worshiped her. She was all tension—lightning!") By 1929, Davis was playing Hedvig in a touring repertory company. On opening night, the theater "shook with applause and bravos," she remembered. "People actually stood on their seats and cheered—for *me*." Universal's Carl Laemmle offered a three-hundred-dollar-a-week contract, on the condition that her legs proved satisfactory. "My legs—What had they to do with being an actress?" she recalled thinking. "My Puritan blood curdled as I followed instructions for the silent strip of film of my legs."

She arrived in Los Angeles late in 1930, after a five-day train trip with her mother. After the studio car failed to pick them up, Bette called Universal from the Hollywood Plaza hotel. Apparently, the studio representative hadn't seen anyone who looked like an actress. Dubbed the "little brown wren," Davis was put through a dubious "test," which was more like an assault. "I was simply asked to lie on a couch. Vague doubts assailed me as one male after another bent over me whispering, 'You gorgeous, divine darling. I adore you. I worship you. I must possess you.'" She was disgusted: "I wasn't even a woman. I was a mattress in a bawdyhouse."

She was cast as the second lead in *Bad Sister*, thrilled to be in the presence of its star, Conrad Nagel. But when she watched herself on-screen, all she saw was her embarrassment and her crooked smile. One of the secretaries advised, "When Jean Harlow is a mile away, the men sit up and take notice. You've got to do something about yourself. You've got to look sexy." Davis sighed—was there just one type of "sexy"? When would they just let her *act*? After six pictures (three for Universal, three loans), the studio dropped her option.

Davis was stunned when she read about Peg Entwistle's suicide, but she adopted Peg's legend as part of her own. She would be the great star Entwistle never got to be. Within a year, she made eight pictures with Warner Bros., which had picked up her option. In November 1933, she joined the new Screen Actors Guild, alongside Charlie Chaplin and Clark Gable. When she became pregnant, her husband Harmon "Ham" Nelson told her she'd be a fool to jeopardize her career. Her mother agreed. She did as they asked and got an abortion.

But, for what? In film after film, she was stuck in the role of the "sweet, drab sister." Only Michael Curtiz's *The Cabin in the Cotton* gave her the chance to play her "first downright, forthright bitch." She was dismayed when, in *Fashions of 1934*, she was given fake eyelashes and a platinum wig, like an imitation Greta Garbo. "Spice in pictures has its place," she told *Variety*. "Be sweet and demure all you like—and see how far you get. Just another blonde indistinguishable from all the rest."

So, when Mildred in *Of Human Bondage* came along, Davis knew it wasn't just another role: it was a chance to show everyone (including herself) that she had a place in Hollywood—not as a beauty but as a beast. Lucky for her, Mildred was "such a disagreeable character no well-established actress would play her," Davis recalled. She sat outside Jack Warner's office day after day, imploring him to lend her to RKO.

Mr. Warner was learning how exhausting—and how futile—it was to argue with a thunderstorm. In February 1934, Bette Davis was announced as the "femme" lead in RKO's *Of Human Bondage*.

WHILE DAVIS CLINCHED THE ROLE of the woman you love to hate, the Academy was simply hated, particularly by the newborn guilds. "THE MENACE OF THE ACADEMY," blared the headline in SAG's official magazine. "Hidden behind the mask of an arbiter of taste, and obscured under the cloak of research," it went on, "what the Academy is really trying to do is to destroy the possibility of an honest actor organization—of, by, and for actors." The Academy's recent resurrection was proof that "large appropriations and much propaganda are now being injected into the corpse by Dr. Producer." The editorial quoted Cato the Elder—"Carthage must be destroyed"—and concluded, "So we say of the Actors' Branch of the Academy."

SAG president Eddie Cantor echoed the sentiment at a meeting at El Capitan. "The Academy's one purpose is an attempt to create an apparent division in the ranks of the actors to prevent anything being accomplished for actors," he told the crowd. The guild was now 3,372 strong, with another 3,000 in the "junior" guild, for extras. Now hemorrhaging members, the Academy announced a special new section for musicians— but was rebuffed when twenty-six songwriters enrolled with the Screen Writers Guild instead.

In September, Frank Lloyd—of "Come up and get it, Frank!"—was elected Academy president. Shortly after, rumors floated that some studio heads were willing to withdraw from the Academy altogether, as an olive branch to the guilds. Lloyd officially denied the plan, and the idea of the Academy dumping its "boss section" withered. So did a ploy to replace the Academy with an employee-controlled body called the Motion Picture Institute—which the guilds quickly dismissed as the Academy by another name.

As the Academy planned its awards banquet for 1935, the writers' guild undermined it by announcing its *own* awards, to be voted on by its 750 members and presented at a Christmas dinner dance at the Trocadero. "There will be no personal bias; no corporate influence; no payroll-phobia; no ulterior purpose," the guild promised. Instead, these honors "will be, *for the first time*, an expert and honest award based on one thing only—merit!"

STILL SMARTING FROM HIS HUMILIATION at the Academy Awards, Frank Capra skulked back to Poverty Row. His lofty hopes were on hold; his new picture, It Happened One Night, had received a polite but hardly ecstatic welcome from critics, and it was gone from Radio City Music Hall after a week.

But the enthusiasm for it was building, as audiences spread word of the snappy new comedy, bringing friends for second viewings and selling out theaters. "The quietness," Capra recalled, "burst into the proverbial prairie fire."

Capra was astonished that he had gotten the film made at all. He had discovered Samuel Hopkins Adams's short story "Night Bus" by accident, while sifting through a magazine at a Palm Springs barbershop during a break from writing *Lady for a Day* with screenwriter Robert Riskin. The story, of a runaway heiress who meets a middle-class man on a bus, had romance, humor, and just a pinch of class resentment. Capra bought the rights for "buttons"—five thousand dollars. "Forget bus pictures," Harry Cohn told him. "People don't want 'em. MGM and Universal just made two bus operas and they both stink."

In 1932, Capra had reluctantly returned to MGM, as part of a deal Cohn made with Irving Thalberg: in exchange for Capra making a movie for MGM, Thalberg would give Columbia a fifty-thousand-dollar bonus and loan out one of MGM's stars. Capra hated the studio, which he compared to a "Janus with two hostile heads," Mayer and Thalberg. Once Mayer's "boy wonder" protégé, Thalberg wielded so much influence that Mayer now regarded him as a rival. Thalberg handed a dozen scripts to Capra, who picked out a melodrama called *Soviet*. But, when the frail-of-health producer suffered a heart attack and was sent to Europe to convalesce, Mayer installed his son-in-law, David O. Selznick, as a replacement producer, gleefully spiked Thalberg's projects, and sent Capra back to Columbia. But MGM still owed Columbia a star.

In the fall of 1934, Capra and Riskin returned to Palm Springs to punch out the script for "Night Bus," with a single directive from Cohn: "Get that word 'bus' outta the title. It's poison." They returned with *It Happened One Night*. To play the working-class hero, a cocky newspaper reporter, their first choice was MGM's Robert Montgomery. Mayer turned them down, but added, "I got an actor here who's being a bad boy. Wants more money. And I'd like to spank him. You can have Clark Gable."

And so, the thirty-three-year-old heartthrob stumbled from MGM down to Poverty Row, having evidently "stopped at every bar" along the way—or so Capra surmised, as Gable dragged himself into the director's dingy office and groaned, "That son-of-a-bitch Mayer. I always *wanted* to see Siberia, but damn me—I never thought it would *smell* like this!"

For the restless heiress, Capra and Riskin approached Myrna Loy at MGM, who turned them down. So did Margaret Sullavan and Miriam Hopkins. Flummoxed, Capra asked Bette Davis, who was interested—but Warner Bros. had just lent her to RKO for *Of Human Bondage* and was keeping her on a tight leash. Instead, Capra went to Claudette Colbert, who had starred in his 1927 flop, *For the Love of Mike*. When he arrived at her house, the star's French poodle bit Capra in the pants. Nose in the air, she told him she was leaving for vacation in Sun Valley in four weeks, so if he could get it done by then, she would accept the role for twice her normal salary.

Capra had a meager $325,000 budget and a tight deadline. But the shoot turned out to be a delight. When Colbert was tart, Capra channeled it back into her fussy character. And he watched Gable ease into himself as a "fun-loving, boyish, attractive, he-man rogue." Their saucy interplay contained the seeds of a new genre: the screwball comedy. Colbert made it on schedule to Sun Valley, where, word got back to Capra, she declared, "I've just finished the worst picture in the world."

On February 23, 1934, *It Happened One Night* débuted at Radio City. Its popularity, though gradual, was resounding. In the tale of a working man conquering the heart of a "spoiled brat," audiences saw a retort to the economic stasis of the Depression. After Gable removed his shirt to reveal a bare chest, sales of undershirts were said to have dropped 75 percent.

Bette Davis, meanwhile, was scowling through *Of Human Bondage*. "My understanding of Mildred's vileness—not compassion but empathy— gave me pause," she recalled. "I barely knew the half-world existed. I was still an innocent. And yet Mildred's machinations I miraculously understood when it came to playing her." That vileness explodes late in the film, as Mildred unleashes a torrent of bile at her artist lover, Philip Carey: "You dirty swine! I never cared for you, not once. I was always making a fool of you. You bored me *stiff!*"

Davis punctuated this tirade by shattering a plate on the floor and slamming the door behind her. She believed that her identification with the role—her strongest since Hedvig in *The Wild Duck*—had to do with the way her studio bosses saw her: headstrong, abrasive, insufferable. Davis studied Maugham's prose and hired a Cockney woman to work at her home, without letting on that she was studying the woman's accent. For her final scene, as the consumptive Mildred wastes away, Davis applied her own ghastly makeup. "We pulled no punches," she boasted, "and

Mildred emerged as a reality—as immediate as a newsreel and as starkly real as a pestilence."

When *Of Human Bondage* opened at Radio City in June 1934, the reaction to Davis was visceral. At the first showing, the *New York Times* noted, "the audience was so wrought up over the conduct of this vixen that when Carey finally expressed his contempt for Mildred's behavior applause was heard from all sides." According to Davis, the reaction at her home studio, Warner Bros., was, "Well! RKO knew what type of girl she really was." But Davis was euphoric.

When the Academy Award nominations were announced in February 1935, *It Happened One Night* appeared in all five major categories, with nominations for Colbert, Gable, Capra, Riskin's screenplay, and Outstanding Production. But, in the Best Actress category, there was a startling omission: Bette Davis.

THE REST OF HOLLYWOOD WAS breathing a sigh of relief. With the five-year Academy agreement between freelance actors and producers set to expire on March 1, the guilds had staged a weeks-long standoff that had the industry bracing for a strike. But SAG—which was adding members by the day, including Fred Astaire and Helen Hayes—landed a decisive win, with the studios conceding to new terms that included a twelve-hour rest period between work calls.

The same day that the labor crisis subsided, *Variety* predicted that Columbia's *One Night of Love* was "a cinch to get the best picture palm" at the Academy Awards, though there was "also much pondering of what happened to Bette Davis." It was the first major snub in the Academy's history, and it led to the first backlash of its kind. Actor Francis Lederer wrote a protesting telegram. Joan Blondell and Dick Powell joined the outcry, which grew into what one paper called "a wild burst of indignation." *Movie Classic* published an indignant reader's letter asking if the judges were "near-sighted."

Columnists began questioning the Academy's authority on matters of awards—the only authority on which it hadn't been relentlessly attacked. The cynicism spread to other overlooked performances: why wasn't Myrna Loy nominated for *The Thin Man*, or Mae West for *Belle of the Nineties*?

One SAG official decried the awards as a producer-controlled charade that "was never a sincere expression on the part of the players who voted." There was talk that the upcoming awards might be the Academy's last. "I suppose there was no chance for any part of the process to be fair, because everybody had quit the Academy," Blondell remarked later. "But when they left Bette out, we all began taking a closer look and decided, 'Hey, something's rotten in Beverly Hills.'"

At the Warner Bros. lot, there was an organized effort to send in protest ballots for Davis, inspiring a similar movement at MGM for Myrna Loy. Faced with a growing revolt, the awards committee—which included such interested parties as Frank Capra, Jack Warner, Harry Cohn, and *Of Human Bondage* director John Cromwell—hastily convened and announced that it would, for the first time in its short history, accept write-in ballots. This opened the door for Davis, but every category was now a free-for-all. Unprecedented anger turned into unprecedented interest in the Academy horse race, which now had an infinite number of potential results. There was also a fair degree of cynicism, now that studio employees were sending write-in votes in bulk. "It now appears that the more fortunate candidates must have a Tammanylike organization behind them," observed the *New York Times*. Davis, who kept publicly silent during the affair, could taste victory. "It seemed inevitable that I would receive the coveted award," she recalled. "The press, the public and the members of the Academy who did the voting were sure I would win! Surer than I!"

The awards were held at the Biltmore hotel on February 27, 1935. Capra, surrounded by the same circle of friends who had consoled him the previous year, watched as the emcee, humorist Irvin S. Cobb, presented a special pint-size statuette to six-year-old Shirley Temple. As the envelopes were opened, Capra heard the same sweet phrase over and over: *It Happened One Night*. Riskin won for his screenplay; Gable was named Best Actor.

Claudette Colbert, eager to catch a train east, had been cajoled to the ceremony by studio executives ("just in case") and sat at a far-back table in a tan suit, a taxi waiting outside. Her nomination had been diluted by the surge of write-ins for Davis and others, but, in the end,

Colbert's name was called, and the crowd cleared an aisle for her to rush up, snatch the prize, kiss Cobb on the cheek, and rush out. Halfway to the exit, she spun around, returned to the microphones, and blurted out, "I owe Frank Capra for this."

Davis, after all the fuss, had come in fourth. "I cannot say I wasn't crushed once I had been that close to the prize," she wrote later. "Syndicated columnists spread the word 'foul' and the public stood behind me like an army." Her loss to Colbert was easily explainable as part of the *It Happened One Night* bonanza. But, despite the studio write-in campaign, Davis blamed Warner Bros. for not supporting her, given that *Of Human Bondage* was an RKO film. Karma would breeze her way a decade and a half later, when an injury forced Colbert to relinquish the part of Margo Channing in *All About Eve*.

Capra, at long last, clutched his holy grail: the Best Directing award. By the end of the night, there was no question which of the twelve nominated films would win the grand prize. "You guessed it," Cobb announced over the loudspeaker. "It is something that . . ." The entire audience shouted back, ". . . *happened one night!*"

The film had swept the five top awards—a feat that would not be repeated for four decades. Columbia, which also won several awards for *One Night of Love*, had dominated as no other studio ever had, leaping from scrappy Poverty Row into the big leagues overnight.

Capra returned home, where he and his friends spent a drunken evening toe-dancing and bellyflopping into the fishpond, as his wife flashed a "Mona Lisa smile." "Dizzy night," the director recorded in his memoirs. He passed out on the lawn clutching the statuette in his fist.

THE GUILDS HELD BACK NO chance to knock the Academy, including Columbia's unprecedented sweep. "A little bird tells us that the Academy banquet left a trail of sorely wounded hearts behind it," sneered *The Screen Guilds' Magazine*. "Instead of a spectacle of largesse being bestowed nicely in a friendly way in all directions according to the established rules of Hoyle, the expectant producers at the banquet suddenly found the gifts virtually all going to one spot." The write-up mockingly continued: "Gentlemen, gentlemen! How can you expect to run a big industry like this one when you can't even keep a little Academy on an even keel?"

Bette Davis returned to work. "I was made to trudge through the professional swamp at Warners brimming over with frustration and rage," she remembered. Her brush with artistry in *Of Human Bondage* gave way to more studio fluff. Shooting *Bordertown*, she dabbed her face with cream and mussed her hair for a scene in which her character was just out of bed, and the director objected that she should look pretty. "They still didn't know that I had no desire to be just a glamour girl," Davis lamented.

When her bosses weren't completely baffled by her, they treated her like an "intractable child." At parties, Jack Warner would shake his finger and tell her, "Remember, Bette. You have to be at the studio at six o'clock. Get to sleep soon." At home, Ham, threatened by his wife's breadwinning, tuned out her complaints—so Davis would hop in her car and drive a hundred miles, pondering whether to return. She longed to play Alice in Wonderland, believing that the character had never been played properly—not as a demure little lady but as a spitfire. Instead, the studio handed her *Dangerous*, about a boozy, has-been stage actress convinced that she is a "jinx" who destroys everyone who crosses her path. Davis found the script "maudlin and mawkish with a pretense at quality which in scripts, as in home furnishings, is often worse than junk." Nevertheless, she signed on.

Despite her disdain, Davis's role in *Dangerous*, written especially for her, sharpened her screen persona: she was nervier, brassier, more *Bette Davis*. Her stormy reputation seeped into her lines, as when her character, Joyce Heath, snipes to her architect love interest, "Why *should* I find contentment? I don't want it!" The press immediately began hyping Davis's awards chances. One interviewer claimed that "she thinks she has found it, the role that will compensate for her omission from the list of nominees last year."

Frank Capra, meanwhile, celebrated his Academy coronation by imploding. "I had scaled the Mount Everest of Filmlandia," he wrote. But the only way off a mountain was down. "I had licked poverty and ridicule; I had yet to lick a bigger enemy: myself." He was plagued by fear. What if his next picture failed? Back at Columbia, the director began a "secret malingering campaign," feigning exhaustion and illness. His doctor teased him—"What's the matter, genius, those Academy Awards getting too heavy to carry around?"—and advised him to take his temperature. Capra was amazed when the mercury inched past 100 degrees. Somehow, he had directed his own temperature to do his bidding. "My malingering had maligned on me," he recalled. "I had talked myself into a disease that baffled the experts." (In fact, he was hospitalized for chronic appendicitis.) He would sweat through the night, his fever at 104. When he stood up, the room would swim around him. He lost thirty-four pounds. In his haze, he consoled himself with the romance of dying at the height of his glory, like Rudolph Valentino or Alexander the Great. Maybe this was his fate: win a bunch of Academy Awards and expire.

He confessed his morbid imaginings to his friend Max Winslow, a Christian Scientist. In his autobiography, Capra says that Winslow came back with a "faceless" little man with a bald head and thick glasses. This mysterious visitor sat across from the ailing director and said, "Mr. Capra, you're a coward." He gestured to the radio, from which the voice of Adolf Hitler emanated. "You hear that man in there?" the visitor continued. "That evil man is desperately trying to poison the world with hate. How many can he talk to? Fifteen million—twenty million? And for how long—twenty minutes? You, sir, you can talk to *hundreds* of millions, for two hours—and in the dark."

This "little man" was possibly an invention, a forebear of the angel who coaxes George Bailey from oblivion in *It's a Wonderful Life*. As Capra told the story, he pulled on his trousers and drove to Palm Springs, where he started gaining a pound a day. He was now making a hundred thousand dollars a picture, plus a quarter of the profits, but his approach to filmmaking was forever changed. He no longer saw himself as a gag man chasing success but as an artist with something to say. But what? And how could he say it without boring people with a "message"?

Capra retreated to the St. Lawrence River, between upper New York and Ontario, for a monthlong bass-fishing trip, where he pored over *Anna Karenina* and *Crime and Punishment*. Another novel that caught his eye was *Opera Hat*, about a country bumpkin who inherits twenty million dollars and an opera house, only to get mixed up in the hoity-toity city crowd. Capra found the opera setting "too-too," but he knew that the inheritance plot would strike a nerve with Depression audiences. He changed the title to *Mr. Deeds Goes to Town*.

Longfellow Deeds would be more than a goofy comic hero, Capra vowed; he would be "the living symbol of the deep rebellion in every human heart." It would be the first of a string of social-minded comedies that would burnish Capra's success—even as his detractors dismissed his all-American parables as "gee-whiz" or "Capra-corn." In the title role of the tuba-playing innocent, he cast Gary Cooper, whose star had risen since his breakout role in *Wings*. As Cooper's love interest, Capra picked Jean Arthur, a relatively unknown contract player with a voice that reminded him of "a thousand tinkling bells."

At the end of 1935, while still preparing for *Mr. Deeds*, Capra was elected president of the Academy. It was, he admitted, a dubious honor, because "it would be presiding at a deathwatch," he wrote. "The Academy had become the favorite whipping boy of Hollywood; its membership down from six hundred to forty; its officers dedicated but discouraged." He estimated its chances of folding at ten to one in favor—which would give his hard-won statuette "the patina of a collector's item."

Capra was ambivalent about his new role, which he claimed he was begged to take on by the desperate Academy officers. "Six months before, I would have told them to go fly a kite," he recalled. "I had gotten my armful of Oscars. Let the others sweat. Before meeting 'the little man,' the theme 'get mine, get mine' had been an article of faith in my credo." Now he had been "shocked into realizing that serving self is small potatoes compared with the value of serving man," and he accepted the Academy post out of some combination of vanity and altruism.

His appointment came at a charged moment. That spring, SAG had launched a campaign against the Academy's arbitration system, which resolved disputes between actors and producers. And after the Academy appointed a new committee to revise the standard writer-producer contract, the Screen Writers Guild went on a "warpath against the Academy," *Variety* wrote, warning its members that anyone willing to join the Academy was "committing an act of disloyalty." In a bid clearly designed to undermine the Academy Awards, both guilds bestowed monthly honors, chosen by their members and culminating in an annual best-of-the-best awards gala. (The modern SAG Awards wouldn't be established until 1995.)

But what about the directors? Two days before Christmas 1935, King Vidor hosted a dozen directors at his house in Beverly Hills and made the first moves toward organizing. Vidor had been contemplating the need for a directors' organization since the 1933 pay cut. The Screen Directors Guild received its charter in January 1936. Two days later, at a meeting at the Hollywood Athletic Club, its members elected Vidor as their first president and John Ford as treasurer. Among their grievances were studio practices such as handing directors scripts two or three days before shooting and denying them a seat in the editing room. Those present sent in their Academy resignations. By the end of January, the new guild had seventy-five members. But their ranks had a glaring absence: Frank Capra, Hollywood's golden boy and the face of the Academy.

Hollywood's creative labor force was now a three-headed hydra, though the directors' guild was not, at first, as aggressive as its actor and writer counterparts. Screenwriter Philip Dunne described it as "a company of gentlemen adventuring in unionism." After the conservative Cecil B. DeMille railed against the "Bolshevik" American Federation of Labor at the first general meeting, the guild declined to affiliate with the AFL, as SAG had; it needed to keep big names like DeMille to get traction. But its white whale was Capra. Despite the populist messaging of his films, Capra voted against Roosevelt and distrusted the labor movement—and his stratospheric success gave him little reason to antagonize the producers. But any pretense that the Academy could whistle through the upheaval was about to end. The guilds were coming for the Academy Awards.

APPROACHING THE EIGHTH ANNUAL AWARDS, MGM had the dubious distinction of placing the first-ever Academy Award campaign ads, an eight-page spread in *The Hollywood Reporter* on behalf of *Ah, Wilderness!*, featuring a cartoon Leo the Lion in a tux and a hand offering a gold statuette. Louis B. Mayer's strategy failed. When the nominations came out, the words *Ah* and *Wilderness* did not appear, but *Bette* and *Davis* did.

She was nominated for *Dangerous*, in a category that had doubled from three to six contenders from the previous year.

Without an eligible film, Capra would preside over the March 5 awards as president and host—and he faced an immediate crisis. There was chatter that the actors' and writers' guilds would boycott the banquet and refuse to accept the statuettes. To ensure the integrity of the voting after the Bette Davis uproar, Capra retained Price Waterhouse to perform an impartial tally of the ballots, but this didn't quell the storm. Three days before the awards, the guilds instructed all their members to boycott the Academy Awards. James Cagney, Paul Muni, and Gary Cooper exhorted their fellow actors to stay home.

Having reached the summit of the Academy, Capra now faced the threat of an empty hall—and the potential death of the Academy Awards altogether. He hired Norman Manning, a publicity man from 20th Century–Fox, for "exploitation and entertainment." Behind the scenes, he urged the studio heads to send out telegrams commanding their stars to attend, but this only inflamed the boycott. What Capra needed was a grand gesture that would make Hollywood's elite *want* to show up at the Biltmore. And so, he decided to present an honorary award to the industry's exiled grandfather, D. W. Griffith. The only problem was that no one knew where he was.

More than two decades had passed since Griffith's white-supremacist epic *The Birth of a Nation* had given Hollywood its first blockbuster, and those years hadn't been kind. His 1931 film *The Struggle*, a grim study of alcoholism, was a commercial and critical fiasco. Unable to get financing for more films, Griffith retreated to his home in Manhattan, where he spent his days taking long, rambling walks and scribbling poems and plays. In an effort to extract himself from his estranged first wife, who had been withholding consent to a divorce, the sixty-one-year-old moved to his native Kentucky, hoping to take a new, twenty-six-year-old bride, Evelyn.

Griffith was at a hotel in Louisville when his lawyer sent over the divorce decree. The same day, he received the Academy's miraculous invitation. According to his biographer Richard Schickel, the news put Griffith into an "uncharacteristic dither." He ordered dinner for fifty from the hotel caterer, then changed it to ten, and finally, after a few drinks in the downstairs bar, was dragged to the mezzanine to make Evelyn his wife. The newlyweds were so hasty in rushing to catch a train to Los Angeles that their baggage was sent to the wrong station.

Griffith had no idea that he was a pawn in the war between the Academy and the guilds. "We used him," Capra confessed. "But we had to have a hell of a drawing card to keep the Academy alive, to keep the lights burning." After luring Griffith, Capra would claim that the boycotts "fizzled." This was only half true. The Biltmore Bowl was filled to 1,200-seat capacity, but *Variety* noted that many top-ranking stars were absent, and tickets were "liberally distributed to secretaries."

Bette Davis showed up, accompanied by her mother and her discontented husband, Ham. Davis was convinced that Katharine Hepburn would win Best Actress, for what even Davis considered the finest performance of the year, in *Alice Adams,* so she wore a simple checked dinner dress with white piqué lapels. During the ceremony, she recalled, she went to the ladies' room, where she was accosted by a fan magazine editor. Her back against the tiled pink wall, Davis felt like "a traitor before a firing squad" as she struggled to make out the woman's tirade. "How could you? A print!" the lady screamed. "Your photograph is going round the *world.* Don't you realize? Aren't you aware? You don't look like a Hollywood star!"

"One would have thought that I had defiled the Academy and eaten her young," Davis recalled. The idea that anyone would tell her what a Hollywood star should look like only fed her fire. The more stinging criticism came from Joan Crawford, who looked Davis up and down and pronounced, with a smile of ice, "Dear Bette! What a *lovely* frock."

From her table, Davis watched as Harry Cohn presented Thalberg with the Outstanding Production prize, for *Mutiny on the Bounty.* She watched as Griffith, fighting back tears, was fêted for his "invaluable initiative and lasting contributions to the progress of the motion picture arts"—a mere five years after his banishment. At the end of the night, Capra announced that there was no one better to present the final awards, for Best Actor and Best Actress, than D. W. Griffith himself.

Griffith named *The Informer's* Victor McLaglen as Best Actor. And then, in the final award, he opened the Best Actress envelope: the winner was Bette Davis. Her table mates screamed and flooded her with kisses. Onstage, she recalled, "I stared down at the little gold-plated man in the palm of my hand. He was a Hollywood male and, of course, epicene."

But she couldn't help thinking it was a consolation prize for *Of Human Bondage*. "This nagged at me," she recalled. "It was true that even if the honor had been earned, it had been earned *last* year. There was no doubt that Hepburn's performance deserved the award. These mistakes compound each other like the original lie that breeds like a bunny. Now she should get it next year when someone else may deserve it."

Davis had won, but she felt the pang of an empty victory.

THE PRESS AGREED. IN HIS writeup, gossip columnist Sidney Skolsky called Davis's award the "Hangover Prize." As if to lend the evening a little more dignity, Davis invented a bit of Hollywood lore, claiming that, as she beheld her prize, she noticed that the statuette's "backview was the spit of my husband's. Since the O. in Harmon O. Nelson stood for Oscar, Oscar it has been ever since."

This mythic moment, alas, is false. Two years earlier, Skolsky himself had made one of the first references to "Oscar" in print, noting in his column, "To the profession these statues are called Oscars." Skolsky, like Davis, would take credit for decades, but the more likely story belongs to Margaret Herrick (then Gledhill), the Academy's librarian and later its executive director. Herrick had followed her husband Donald Gledhill to Hollywood in 1931, when he became the assistant to the Academy's executive secretary, and volunteered to build up its reference collection. On her first day, the story went, she was asked what she thought of the gold statuette, and she exclaimed, "Why, it looks like my Uncle Oscar!" (After her origin tale became famous, she confessed that "while I had an Uncle Oscar, I'd never even seen him; he lived in Texas.") Another theory has it that an early Academy staffer named Eleanore Lilleberg, whose mother was Norwegian, christened the award after King Oscar II of Sweden and Norway because it reminded her of a man she knew in Chicago who had been in the Norwegian army and had a stiff, upright bearing.

However the nickname was born, it seems to have been used irreverently. Frances Marion credited Walt Disney for imbuing it with special meaning when he won for *The Three Little Pigs* in 1934—two years be-fore Davis supposedly named the statuette after her husband's backside. "When Walt referred to the 'Oscar,'" Marion wrote, "that name took on a different meaning, now that we had heard it spoken with sincere appreciation."

But the name would be meaningless unless the Academy found a way to survive. Not only were the guilds nipping at its heels, but the write-in policy put in place for Davis the year before had blown up in the Academy's face when Hal Mohr, the cinematographer of Warner Bros.' *A Midsummer Night's Dream*, won over three nominated candidates. The technical branch was furious that its choices had been overridden, and *Variety* reported "storm clouds likely to precipitate wholesale resignations from the Academy groups." Since this was the last thing the Academy needed, the policy was rescinded, making Mohr the sole write-in winner in the Academy's history.

Then there was Dudley Nichols, the screenwriting winner for *The Informer*, who refused his Oscar in an open letter to the Academy: "To accept it would be to turn my back on nearly a thousand members of the Writers' Guild." He had given up his Academy membership three years prior, "convinced that the Academy was at root political," and declared, "My only regret now is that I did not withdraw my name from nomina-tion and thus avoid this more embarrassing situation." Capra insisted that Nichols's victory stood whether he wanted it or not. The prize remained unclaimed, until Nichols finally accepted it in 1949.

In April, the same week *Mr. Deeds Goes to Town* opened to acclaim at Radio City Music Hall, two dozen new members of the new direc-tors' guild—including Howard Hawks, William Wellman, and John Cromwell—sent in their Academy resignations (eight of which were discarded, as their senders weren't Academy members in the first place). When Capra visited the guild's headquarters, at the Crossroads of the World building on Sunset Boulevard, his friend King Vidor pleaded, "Frank, what the hell are you breaking your ass about the Academy for? Why don't you want to do anything for the directors?"

By then, Capra was well into the hundred-day shoot for his next film, *Lost Horizon*, set in a Tibetan utopia called Shangri-La, high in the Himalayas. Capra saw the story as a poetic saga full of mystery and wisdom. He immersed himself in the "strangeness" of Tibetan religion, tracking down rare antique horns from sacred temples. He built the exterior for the lamasery—a monastery of lamas—on Columbia's ranch in Burbank and created blizzards with snow machines inside a cold-storage warehouse.

By the time *Lost Horizon* wrapped, it was thirty-four days over schedule and the most expensive film Columbia had ever made. Capra and Cohn had wrestled bitterly throughout postproduction, with Cohn demanding that the unusual epic be shaped into something leaner and more commercial. Capra would later blame "the Jewish producers" for attempting to sabotage his masterpiece. The feud turned acrid in February 1937, when Columbia withheld the director's semiannual payment of $100,000. But when Harry Cohn watched the three-hour cut, he declared, "I didn't wiggle my ass once." Then he recut it to less than two hours behind Capra's back.

At the Academy, Capra's leadership was more akin to Louis XIV's *L'État, c'est moi.* "It was a one-man show," he claimed later, ignoring the work of Donald and Margaret Gledhill, who handled most of the day-to-day tasks. "It sounds so ridiculous, too me-meish to tell you," Capra recalled. "There's also a point at which people get tired of hearing this— 'Jesus, did he do everything?' The truth is that I *did* everything." His most pressing mission was to save the next year's Oscar ceremony from the drama that had nearly smothered the previous one. Shortly after his reelection in October 1936, he appointed a committee to inoculate the awards from charges of political favoritism. Some of the ideas floated included selecting a jury of critics or even having the public vote in thirty-six major cities.

Instead, Capra formed a fifty-person body to make the nominations, which would then be voted on by the entire membership. In an intriguing twist, there would be two new categories: for Best Supporting Actor and Actress. Janet Gaynor, the Academy's inaugural Best Actress, took credit for having made the suggestion, but the new awards doubled as a sop to recalcitrant actors. Ultimately, the Academy sidestepped another boycott by promising to stand back in labor disputes. SAG, now led by Robert

Montgomery, temporarily held its fire, while warning in a statement that it reserved the right to "change its attitude in future years."

The temporary peace was a victory for Capra, but the Oscars were still roiling with tension and ill will. Most of the drama at the 1937 Oscar ceremony centered on the death of Irving Thalberg, whose health problems had finally ended his life the previous September; he was thirty-seven. The question was now whether his widow, Norma Shearer, would get the sympathy vote for Best Actress for *Romeo and Juliet*. But Mayer, showing little sympathy for his former protégé's wife, successfully pushed for Luise Rainer, star of MGM's *The Great Ziegfeld*.

None of this eased the impression that, as the *New York Times* put it, the Oscars were plagued by "the lurking suspicion of log rolling and political dealing." At the ceremony, Sidney Skolsky reported, the feuding Capra and Cohn had "tables next to each other but they didn't speak." Capra announced the creation of the Irving G. Thalberg Memorial Award, and the Academy put on a show of prosperity by giving each of its guests a small bottle of champagne. But the cynicism spilled over when Capra won his second consecutive Oscar, for *Mr. Deeds Goes to Town*. Called up by the emcee, George Jessel, to help present the award, he put on a show of humility, saying, "I don't see how anybody could look over these nominees for the director of the best picture and pick one out."

Jessel shot back, "Well, they all may be presidents of the Academy some day and then they can select whom they please."

Of all the guests at the ceremony, the *Times* speculated, "Bette Davis of Warners' was probably the unhappiest." As the previous winner, Davis had been summoned to present the Best Actress award. But when the time came to bring her up from the audience, Jessel forgot her completely.

IT WAS THE FINAL RUB in a tumultuous year. After her win for *Dangerous*, Davis hoped that Warner Bros. might reward her with a good script. "My hopes were soon shattered," she recalled. Her roles included the femme fatale in *Satan Met a Lady*, which Bosley Crowther of the *Times* called a "waste of this gifted lady's talents." (John Huston remade the film five years later, with better luck, as *The Maltese Falcon*.) A furious Davis "marched up to Mr. Warner's office and demanded that I be given work commensurate with my proven ability." Instead, she was assigned the idiotic part of a lumberjack in *God's Country and the Woman*.

Davis felt like an "assembly-line actress," a prisoner in a studio system that gave her security without self-determination. "The studio had gained prestige through the Academy's accolade," she recalled. "My popularity had grown immensely. I was now directing the public into Warners' Theatres. To be submissive at this point seemed stupid." She refused the part.

Jack Warner treated her like an unruly child having a tantrum, telling her, "Just be a good girl and everything will work out." If she played the lumberjack, he promised to reward her with a part from a novel he had just optioned, *Gone with the Wind*. Davis, fatefully, waved him away. She was tired of being patronized. When production of *God's Country and the Woman* began in Washington State, she sequestered herself in Laguna Beach.

Her "one-woman strike" earned her a three-month suspension without pay; under the current system, those three months would be added to the end of her contract, which still had five years to go. "In other words, unlike all other forms of employment, the right to strike was not ours," Davis rightfully complained. The press made hay of the standoff, enraging Davis by printing that she was holding out for more money. She held firm, knowing that she wasn't alone. James Cagney was suing Warner Bros. for breach of contract. "Stars were learning that their drawing power entitled them to some consultation about their careers and some greater share of the companies' profits," Davis wrote. "In an attempt to protect themselves from this rising class, Warners now cast me in the role of a spoiled brat."

Undaunted, Davis agreed to star in two pictures for European producer Ludovico Toeplitz, figuring that no one could stop her from working abroad. Her escape was something out of a movie: knowing that injunctions were not served on Sundays, she and Ham flew to Vancouver late on a Saturday night, took a train to Montreal, and sailed to England on the *Duchess of Bedford*. In Britain, she ignored the inevitable injunction, certain that "England and her Magna Charta would see to it that my slavery was ended," and readied herself for what she called "Bette against Goliath." Jack Warner, settling in at William Randolph Hearst's house near London, hit Davis with an ex parte injunction in the English courts. For Davis, there was no way but forward. "Once and for all," she declared, "I had to consolidate my position as an actress and not a painted puppet subject to my masters' whims."

At the trial, she was awed by the wood-paneled English courtroom and the "divine detachment" of the judge, whom she stared at day after day, wide-eyed, in an attempt to hypnotize him to her side. But she was enraged when Warner's barrister, Sir Patrick Hastings, began his argument, "I think, m'lord, this is the action of a very naughty young lady." When Warner himself took the stand, he was so nervous-looking that Davis almost felt pity for him, especially when he was forced to admit under interrogation that he could make her eat oatmeal if the studio wanted it. Davis's lawyer declined to put her on the stand, worried (surely with cause) that she might lose her temper under questioning. As Davis recalled, Sir Patrick "was so furious not to be able to tear me apart, that he took off his wig and threw it across the courtroom."

She was walking along a beach when she learned that she'd lost the case; the Warner Bros. side had argued successfully that movie stars were so well compensated that their subordination was justified. Davis peered at the gray English sky and contemplated the awful fact that her "inhuman bondage" would now last until 1942. She had lost, but her rebellion would open the door for Olivia de Havilland's case against Warner Bros., which in 1944 would end the practice of indefinite contracts.

Upon Davis's return to Hollywood, she was surprised that her standing at the studio had held. Warner Bros. covered her legal fees and offered her acceptable scripts, including *Marked Woman* and *Kid Galahad*, both opposite Humphrey Bogart. And she was pleased to act with de Havilland, whose talent she admired, in *It's Love I'm After*. "In a way, my defeat was a victory," she reasoned. "At last we were seeing eye to eye on my career. I was aching to work and they were eager to encourage me." The only hitch was having lost the role of Scarlett O'Hara in *Gone with the Wind*. Warner Bros. had dropped its option during Davis's protest in London, and when producer David O. Selznick asked to borrow Davis and Errol Flynn as a package, she refused—the idea of Flynn as Rhett

Butler "appalled" her. She was now forced to watch an internationally publicized search for a fresh face to play the role she knew in her bones should have belonged to her.

It was now Frank Capra's turn to rebel. His clash with Harry Cohn over *Lost Horizon* had become a full-blown power struggle. "The trouble was that *I* was becoming Columbia Pictures, not Cohn," Capra said. "I knew that I was getting too big. I could see it coming, and I didn't know what the hell to do about it." In May 1937, Capra was in London when he discovered that Columbia was selling an undistinguished screwball comedy called *If You Could Only Cook* abroad as a "Frank Capra Production." The problem: Capra had had nothing to do with it. Back home, he marched into Cohn's office, but His Crudeness laughed it off. "Oh, *that*, for crissake. Some brain in the New York office got a wild hair about making a few more bucks in England. Does it kill ya, for crissake, to see Columbia make a few more bucks in England? Maybe we can cut you *in* for a slice—"

"Harry," Capra snapped, "If you will cancel my contract, give me freedom—I won't sue you for *If You Could Only Cook*." Cohn didn't, so Capra did: he sued over the unlawful use of his name and demanded a hundred thousand dollars in damages. In the meantime, he sat on his hands at home in Malibu, waiting day after day for a rival studio to snatch him up. But no one called—Cohn had placed him on a blacklist. Without his megaphone, Capra turned into a "twitching, worrisome thing," he recalled. Columbia tied up the suit in the court for months, as Capra's "essential buoyancy, enthusiasm and sunny idealism gave way to hard-bitten, cynical thoughts" about the "Hollywood rat race."

He busied himself with Academy matters, which had only become more fraught. In April, the Supreme Court upheld the Wagner Act, which protected the right to unionize, and the fortified Screen Actors Guild threatened a walkout. At a mass gathering at L.A.'s Legion Stadium—a boxing venue, appropriately—Robert Montgomery announced to a crowd of four thousand guild members that the producers had agreed to the guild's demands, including "closed" union shops at the major studios and the recognition of SAG as the actors' sole bargaining agency. After a four-year battle, the actors were victorious. Joan Crawford, Franchot

Tone, and Ralph Morgan led a resounding standing ovation, and the strike was called off.

This left the Academy officially sidelined from its role as contract arbiter. But hadn't that been the reason for its unpopularity all along? For years, Capra had revered the Academy, plotting and planning to win its prizes and become its face. But now that he was in charge, it was clear that the original function of the Academy was dragging it into an early grave. Capra realized that the only way for the Academy to survive was to relinquish its power. In June, the Academy announced that it would cease to play any role in labor relations in Hollywood. "All contractual relations are now out of the Academy's hands, and the organization will devote itself henceforth to research, the Oscar awards, and inter-branch work of a non-economic character," *Variety* reported, under the headline "In Other Words, the Academy's Just Bowing Out." A decade after its conception as Hollywood's League of Nations, the Academy was now, thanks to Capra, little more than the body that gave out statuettes.

Capra's struggle with Cohn may have tipped him, finally, toward solidarity with the directors' guild. He joined in August—a major victory for the scrappy new group, which had not been formally recognized by the studios. "Our Guild's in trouble, Frank," King Vidor pleaded. "Why don't you come in and help out your fellow directors instead of spending all your life promoting the Academy?" "What the hell," Capra recalled thinking, "my heart's more here than it is any other place." "Any other place" included his beloved Academy. "The Academy job was a figure-head, a pat-on-the-back kind of thing," said his secretary Chet Sticht. "There wasn't a hell of a lot to it except for presiding over the Academy Awards ceremony and a few meetings. The guild had a fight on its hands." That fall, Capra was elected to the guild's board.

When it came to the Academy, Capra's philosophy appeared to be surrender. In November, he announced that SAG would formally oversee the balloting for the Oscars, with the voting pool swelling from the roughly thousand-person membership to some fifteen thousand guild members. The Academy's iron gates had been thrown open to the enemy. As the 1938 ceremony approached, the Academy, facing a doubled increase in ticket demand, was panicking over how to squeeze in the

"Oscar Mob," as *Variety* called it. In a memo, the Academy's Donald Gledhill worried about the cost of printing and mailing the extra ballots, as "the Academy has absolutely no treasury (difficulty in paying rent, in fact)." He added, bitterly, "The various companies and winning individuals spend more in advertising just to boast about the Awards than the Awards themselves cost altogether." And Capra was still dealing with intransigence from wary guild members, this time MGM screenwriter John Lee Mahin, who demanded that his nomination for *Captains Courageous* be withdrawn. Capra told Mahin that if he won the statuette (which he didn't), he could either "accept it or throw it away or deposit it in that well-known place where everything is consigned in Hollywood."

The Tenth Academy Awards were scheduled for March 3, 1938. Days before the ceremony, rainstorms pummeled Southern California with a year's worth of water. Downed trees and deserted cars floated down the flooded boulevards. More than a hundred people were killed. Others were marooned. The Oscars were postponed a week. When the deluge subsided, the shell-shocked denizens of Hollywood reached for their gowns and tuxedos and filled the Biltmore to capacity. The flood was an apt metaphor for the onslaught that the Academy had barely survived. It was a bittersweet year for Capra, who was not even nominated for his mangled masterpiece *Lost Horizon*. But his self-interested craving for Oscars had been supplanted by a hunger for revolt—which was another form of self-interest.

In May, Capra was elected president of the Screen Directors Guild, an anointing that placed him, remarkably, on both sides of the war that had occupied the Academy for the better part of a decade. But his peers figured that anyone who had revitalized the Academy could do the same for the guild; besides, Capra was a changed man. In his standoff with Cohn, he had become more skeptical toward Hollywood's producer-dominated hierarchy and more eager for creative control. "I accepted the challenge with pleasure," he recalled. "I was itching to roll in the dirt with the movie moguls that had ganged up to keep me out of work for a year."

A "TOPPER," CAPRA HAD LEARNED in Sennett's gag room, required a predictable formula to be broken with an unpredictable flourish. In *It Happened One Night*, Clark Gable's character tries hitchhiking on the side of the road, but a car passes him by. He waves his hat, and more cars pass. Then Claudette Colbert's heiress flashes her leg, and—topper!—the next car comes screeching to a halt. For Capra, the pattern went: win the approval of the establishment by sweeping the Academy Awards; *become* the establishment by taking over the Academy; save the Academy from certain doom; then—topper!—join the war against the Academy.

His first step was to get his career back. Capra's standoff with Cohn over *If You Could Only Cook* finally ended when, in Capra's telling, Cohn showed up in the director's living room and told him, "Well, you little dago bastard—gotta hand it to you. You finally put me and Columbia behind the eight ball." After a California court threw out Capra's case because Columbia was officially headquartered in New York, Capra sued him in New York, where the case was thrown out again, this time because the offense had allegedly occurred overseas. It took a lawsuit in England to put Cohn in a vise—but Columbia still had Capra under contract for two more pictures. They could either destroy each other or get back to work. Capra got back to work.

Cohn agreed to buy the rights to the hit Broadway play *You Can't Take It with You*, about a family of free-spirited eccentrics. Capra saw it as "a golden opportunity to dramatize Love Thy Neighbor in living drama." Along the way, he would give Depression audiences the gee-whiz fantasy of a heartless plutocrat learning the simple joys of life while playing "Polly Wolly Doodle" on a harmonica. It would be his first film for which the posters and marquees placed his name above the title—a rare show of directorial might in an era ruled by producers. To trumpet the film's arrival, Capra appeared smoking a pipe on the cover of *Time*, which described him as "Columbia's Gem."

Cohn pulled out all the stops for the movie at an international press preview in August 1938, bedecking Columbia's backlot with flowers and banners, and plying hundreds of journalists with lunch and booze. On his way in from Malibu, Capra and his wife Lu stopped at the Children's Hospital on Sunset Boulevard, so their three-year-old son, Johnny, who was deaf, could get his tonsils removed. After the operation, Capra left Johnny with Lu and the doctors to recover and went to the screening. During the second reel, he got an urgent message to come back to the hospital right away. When he returned, Lu threw her arms around him and cried, "He's dead, Frank. Little Johnny's dead." The cause was inflammation of the brain.

They drove home dumbstruck with grief. "We drove past Columbia Studio," Capra recalled. "The crowds, police, and banners were still here. Somehow they didn't mean much now." The film was a smash hit.

Bette Davis was also back to work, on *Jezebel*, in which she played a nineteenth-century New Orleans vixen. The publication of Margaret Mitchell's *Gone with the Wind* had fueled interest in the antebellum South, and *Jezebel* gave Davis her own version of Scarlett O'Hara—another consolation prize, but a good one. "Julie Marsden, the Jezebel in question, was a blood sister of Scarlett's," Davis observed. "Willful, perverse and proud, she was every inch the Southern belle." As with *Of Human Bondage* and *Dangerous*, her character was also a mirror of Davis. In the most famous scene, Julie scandalizes the Olympus Ball, where maidens traditionally wear white, by showing up in red. That was Hurricane Bette: the rebel who had thundered past the glamour girls and left a trail of stunned executives in her wake.

Jezebel's director was William Wyler, in whom Davis found a creative soul mate. "It was *he* who helped me realize my full potential as an actress," Davis recalled. Wyler treated actors as collaborators, not clay to be molded. "How different," Davis said, "from a Frank Capra who conversely preferred to direct personalities." (She and Capra would collaborate on only one film, 1961's *Pocketful of Miracles*, a remake of *Lady for a Day*. Davis said of the experience, "I didn't always agree with him, but I always respected him.")

The exhilarating shoot of *Jezebel* irked her only because her costar Henry Fonda was expecting a child, and his scenes had to be shuffled so that he could get back to New York. Davis never forgot the trouble that Jane Fonda put her through from the womb. More troubling was her realization that she was no longer in love with her husband: "The fact that I didn't care anymore that I was finding other men attractive was heartbreaking to me." One of those men was Wyler, with whom she began a passionate affair. When Wyler ran behind schedule and Warner Bros. threatened to take him off the film, Davis threatened to "burn the place down." At the end of the year, Ham filed divorce papers. He testified that Davis had read books "to an unnecessary degree" and thought her work was more important than their marriage. Davis had no choice but to concur.

Having lost the Oscar for the right movie and won for the wrong one, Davis was well positioned for the upcoming Best Actress race—provided that the Oscars proceeded at all. By mid-1938, the Academy was formally extracting itself from "responsibility in economic and controversial subjects." But the guilds weren't buying it. On September 14, Capra sent a confidential letter to the Academy board saying that it had been "tough sledding" selling the Academy's new mission. "In fact, we have met with downright opposition. Always the same cry—mistrust of the presence of the Producers." But Capra had come up with a grand gesture that would finally fix the problem for good: the immediate resignation of all producers from the Academy. "I can see no other way out," he wrote. If they objected, he would resign himself.

The next day, Darryl Zanuck sent back a furious response on 20th Century–Fox letterhead. "I sincerely mean it when I say that I was never more astonished in my life," Zanuck wrote of the proposal. "The request for resignation is so basically unfair and the tone of the letter itself is so unreasonable that I cannot help but come to the conclusion that the actual desire for harmony and peace in our industry is nothing but a fantasy." He reminded Capra that he had been at the very first Academy meeting and had even put up his own money during its period of financial emergency. If Capra wanted to resign, have at it. "The Academy is known throughout the world far better than any individual producing company or any individual in our industry or any other Guild or body of workers," Zanuck argued. "It must not collapse now." Rumors of wholesale resignations flamed across the trade papers, and *Variety* ran the headline "ACAD MAY DROP OSCARS: CREATIVE GROUPS THREATEN BOLT."

Capra was deep into preparation for his final film for Columbia, *Mr. Smith Goes to Washington*, with Jimmy Stewart's character waging a lone campaign against Washington corruption on the Senate floor. Capra now took the mantle of righteousness himself. His influence lay with the Academy, but his allegiance was with the directors' guild, which was still fighting for official recognition from the studios. But how would he wage both sides of a war?

It was then, he recalled, that "a clash of events—and egos—shot me into the front lines of a labor-management war which climaxed in my hurling a directors' strike ultimatum at the crowned heads of the Motion Picture Producers Association, and in my plotting the disruption of the Academy which I had labored so long to preserve."

After years of avoiding the unions, Capra had turned noble warrior. To lead the negotiations in his guild's fight for recognition, he hired Mabel Walker Willebrandt, who had overseen Prohibition enforcement under the Harding administration. Meanwhile, he flexed his own influence publicly and in back rooms. In early 1939, to build solidarity with SAG, he directed Bette Davis in a radio play for CBS's *Screen Guild Theater*. He haggled with the producers, even as they exhausted him with meet-and-stall tactics. After Joe Schenck, head of the producers' official trade organization, stood him up for a meeting, Capra chased him down at the Santa Anita racetrack, where he found Schenck in his private box. "Well, well, look who's here," the producer said coolly, and offered to give Capra tips on the next race.

"No, thank you, Mr. Schenck," Capra said. "I just drove out to give *you* a tip. The next time you ask me for an appointment, I'll be there. And so will *you*—with your hat in your hand."

Meeting with the guild's board, Capra proposed a plan to squeeze management into submission. The directors would boycott the Academy Awards, which were eight days away, completely sold out, and expected to be glitzier than ever. "I know," Capra explained, "because as master of ceremonies I've made all the arrangements." He would resign as Academy president and withdraw as emcee, citing the producers' contemptuous attitude. "This accusation will make the world's front pages," Capra explained.

The Oscars, in other words, were being held ransom by the very man who had believed in them the most. "I had to sacrifice the Academy I'd saved," he said.

On February 16, some 250 directors' guild members met in an

emergency session at the Hollywood Athletic Club. When word got out that their leader had been forced to chase Schenck down at the racetrack, the crowd flew into an uproar; Capra had to quell calls for an immediate strike. They unanimously approved Capra's plan to resign from the Academy and lead a boycott of the awards unless Schenck responded to their demands within twenty-four hours.

That night, Capra barely slept. "A boycott of the Academy would be unpopular enough," he recalled. "But a strike would be a declaration of war. It would be asking dedicated filmmakers to be more loyal to their union than to their films. Would I walk out on *Mr. Smith Goes to Washington?* God knows."

The next morning, a frantic Schenck called Capra from a sandstorm in Palm Springs, asking for more time. The answer was no. That afternoon, Capra marched alone, Mr. Smith–style, into 20th Century–Fox's executive room, where he faced a dozen of "Hollywood's high-and-mighties," among them Harry Cohn, Louis B. Mayer, and Darryl Zanuck. Capra repeated his ultimatum: sign an agreement recognizing the directors' guild, or the Oscar banquet gets it. Two hours later, Schenck emerged from the office and handed Capra a letter agreeing to many of the guild's demands, including its official recognition. "Is it okay, Mr. President of the Directors Guild?"

"It's very okay," Capra said. "There'll be no Academy boycott, and no strike, and you're looking at a very happy man, Mr. Schenck."

And so, on February 23, 1939, Capra stood on the dais at the Biltmore, atop an organization that had weathered (and often provoked) six relentless years of attacks, infighting, boycotts, and attempts to be used as a pawn by all sides. "I never felt prouder—or more grateful—for being the head of this beloved Academy which, only days ago, I had conspired to disrupt," he reflected.

Capra had indeed staged a blowout Oscar night, the pièce de résistance being Shirley Temple's presentation to Walt Disney of a special honor for *Snow White and the Seven Dwarfs:* one regular-size statuette, along with seven "dwarf" Oscars. But what happened that night surprised even Capra: he won his third directing award, for *You Can't Take It with You,* becoming the first person ever to have received three Academy

Awards. When the film won Outstanding Production, he said, "my poor numbed brain tail-spinned into total amnesia."

Bette Davis arrived in a sumptuous brown dress with white egret feathers festooning the neckline. The editor who had berated her in the ladies' room "must have been delighted," she imagined, "because I was dressed to the nines." When she heard her name called for Best Actress for *Jezebel*, she took hold of her second Oscar and smiled. Finally, she had won the right award for the right movie. "I was never surer of myself professionally," she recalled, "than at this moment." The rebels had won.

WITH TWO OSCARS AND A box-office smash to her name, Davis arranged a meeting with Jack Warner to discuss the terms of her employment. Her groveling days were over. People were now calling her the "fourth Warner Brother."

"I was now a sovereign state demanding my own tithe—a member of the commonwealth," she recalled. "I had never been able to keep my mouth shut, but now mine was a voice that couldn't be ignored." Davis had won respect; now she wanted money. Her old "battle-worn" contract was torn up and replaced with a new one.

At the end of 1939, Capra stepped down as Academy president after four exhausting years. Having left Columbia to start his own production company, he needed to shed extra responsibilities. Besides, the war he had overseen was over: Hollywood was officially a union town, and the Academy, no longer an industry piñata, was synonymous with the Oscars. One of Capra's final functions was to open the awards to foreign entries—or what *Variety* called "alien films." In January 1940, Walter Wanger took over the presidency. "After chairing five Awards dinners from the rostrum," Capra reflected, "I would again be sitting with my wife and friends in the audience—sweating it out with all the other nominees." (The director of *Mr. Smith Goes to Washington* didn't stand a chance; it was *Gone with the Wind*'s year.)

But a new war was coming—a real one. In December 1941, Capra's production of *Arsenic and Old Lace* was interrupted by the attack on Pearl Harbor. Hollywood, like the rest of the country, was in a state of whiplash. Two days later, a pair of U.S. Army officials came from Washington to discuss a new plan to recruit top Hollywood talent into the Signal Corps, to make training films that would show American soldiers what they were fighting for. Capra agreed. Weeks later, he received a telegram addressed to "Major Frank Capra," ordering him to report for duty in Washington.

His wife drove him to the train station. "Don't go trying to *direct the Army!*" she told him. "Promise?"

THREE

War!

1942

How *Citizen Kane* got blitzed at the Oscars, two sisters battled it out for Best Actress, and the Academy, under General Bette Davis, marched into wartime.

Late on December 6, 1941, a young naval officer named Paul Perrault attended a shipboard screening of the latest Bette Davis picture, *The Little Foxes*. His vessel, the USS *Phoenix*, was anchored at Pearl Harbor, in the U.S. Territory of Hawaii. Afterward, he drifted to bed, hoping to sleep in. Just before eight the next morning, he heard a boom. He peered out the porthole and saw a fireball engulfing a battleship. *Man your battle stations* came over the loudspeaker. *This is no drill.* Perrault raced to the gunnery and looked up at the Pacific sky: it was swarmed by Japanese warplanes.

Some 2,500 miles east, Hollywood awoke to a spate of humdrum headlines. Gossip maven Hedda Hopper filled her inches with a profile of Abbott and Costello. In William Randolph Hearst's papers, Hopper's rival, Louella Parsons, reported that thirteen-year-old Shirley Temple was now reading grown-up novels like *Mrs. Miniver*. It wasn't until late morning that the radio broadcasts brought news of a surprise attack in Hawaii.

Los Angeles readied for a possible air raid. Three thousand sheriff's reserves prepared for emergency service; twenty thousand American Legionnaires stood ready to mobilize. At the harbor, active vessels were ordered to anchor away from oil tanks and warehouses. The mayor told citizens to stay home, drive only when necessary, and avoid jamming the phone lines. The populace, the *Los Angeles Times* reported, was "stiff-jawed" and steeled for revenge. "They've asked for it," a twenty-three-year-old candy store clerk said of the Empire of Japan. "I feel certain we can whip the pants off them. And it shouldn't take very long."

Director John Ford was in Alexandria, Virginia, three months into his service as a lieutenant commander in the U.S. Navy. He had requested the transfer to active duty in September, three weeks after finishing his latest film, *How Green Was My Valley*. He and his wife were luncheon guests of Rear Admiral Andrew Pickens when a maid came in with a telephone and said, "It's the War Department, animal," stumbling over the word *admiral*. Pickens took the call and then gravely informed his guests, "We are now at war."

"It's no use getting excited," said the admiral's wife. She pointed to a hole in a wall made by a musket ball during the Revolutionary War. "This is the seventh war that's been announced in this dining room."

That evening, Orson Welles sat behind a CBS microphone to narrate a radio play called *Between Americans*, a first-person meditation on national ideals, patriotism, and freedom of the press. "Today, particularly, people are thinking about their country pretty hard, some of them for the first time in their lives," Welles began in his resonant baritone. "People are wondering where we're headed. Men are being called on to get ready to defend America. A lot of them are thinking in terms of: What is there to defend?"

At twenty-six, Welles was already an old hand at radio and a Hollywood phenom, having just released his first studio film, *Citizen Kane*. Three years earlier, he'd become a national sensation when his radio broadcast of *The War of the Worlds* convinced some listeners that a real Martian invasion was under way. The breaking Pearl Harbor news had interrupted his morning broadcast. "A few days later, I was talking with the President," he would recall. "Mr. Roosevelt said to me, 'You see, you did that Martian broadcast, and when we brought the news about Pearl Harbor nobody believed it!' They thought it was a rather bad-taste joke on my part."

In L.A.'s Little Tokyo, the streets were closed to traffic, and the FBI was taking Japanese "aliens" into custody on Terminal Island. Some days later, Joan Fontaine heard a knock on her door in Beverly Hills and found FBI agents on her doorstep with instructions to search the houses of Japanese-born Angelenos for guns and shortwave radios. Fontaine, star of the new Hitchcock film *Suspicion*, had been born in Tokyo to English patent lawyer Walter de Havilland. But this was the first time her origins had made her suspect in her own country.

Fontaine's sister, Olivia de Havilland—also Tokyo-born—was relieved to have gotten her naturalization papers on November 28. "Nine days later, I would have been classified as an enemy alien," she said. "I might have been sent to a camp." Unlikely. At the time, she was shooting the Warner Bros. melodrama *In This Our Life*, whose theme was familiar to Joan and Olivia: sibling rivalry. De Havilland played the virtuous sister to Bette Davis, in her usual hellcat mode. Davis abhorred the material, and her unhappiness was inflamed by the open secret that de Havilland was having an affair with their married director, John Huston. "When I saw the first rushes," Jack Warner recalled, "I said to myself: 'Oh-oh, Bette has the lines, but Livvy is getting the best camera shots.'"

The studio had given the rugged, voracious Huston *In This Our Life* as a reward for his smash directorial début, *The Maltese Falcon*. But the shoot was plagued with discord. Both leading ladies were continually walking off the set or falling ill. De Havilland, in particular, was exhausted from overwork. After a row with Davis, Huston abandoned the film, leaving Raoul Walsh to handle reshoots. Like Ford, Huston would soon join the war effort. The day after Pearl Harbor, the rudderless cast and crew assembled on set. With the studio pressuring them to finish, there was no time for reflection.

Davis, meanwhile, had other responsibilities. In November, she had been elected the first female president of the Academy, succeeding Walter

Wanger. But her short reign would be marked by tumult, beginning with a feat of spectacularly bad timing: the Academy had chosen December 7 to announce the date of the upcoming Academy Awards. With all the papers carrying "WAR!" on their front pages, the *Los Angeles Times* buried the Oscar news on page 9.

The Fourteenth Annual Academy Awards would be the first held in wartime, just as Hollywood was repositioning itself as a propaganda arm of the U.S. government. The ceremony—and the clashes over its presentation, down to the dress code—would capture an industry still adjusting to the new American mood. Like the world map, the evening was marked with battle lines, including one between the warring sisters nominated for Best Actress. Ultimately, though, the Oscars of February 26, 1942, would be remembered as the year the Academy made one of its most notorious blunders: a near-total defeat for *Citizen Kane*.

ORSON WELLES HAD ARRIVED IN Hollywood in 1939 on a wave of hype, a "boy genius" who had already achieved more than most people twice his age. "The word 'genius' was whispered into my ear at an early age, the first thing I ever heard while I was still mewling in my crib," Welles noted wryly. By nineteen, he was acting on Broadway, where producer John Houseman discovered him. Welles and Houseman mounted an all-Black staging of *Macbeth*, and in 1937 they formed their own repertory company, the Mercury Theatre. Welles directed a string of boldly envisioned hits, including a *Julius Caesar* in Fascist-tinged military dress, in which Welles played Brutus, establishing himself as a theatrical wunderkind.

The week he turned twenty-three, *Time* gave him the moniker "Marvelous Boy" and put him on its cover, in old-man makeup for his production of Shaw's *Heartbreak House*. Months later, the Mercury's radio program broadcast its adaptation of H. G. Wells's *The War of the Worlds*. Welles wanted to "take the mickey" out of the authoritative voice of radio by mimicking a news broadcast, but a segment of listeners who tuned in without hearing the disclaimers thought that they were learning of an actual Martian invasion. The next day—Halloween—the press whipped the story into front-page news of mass hysteria. Welles claimed shock and remorse that people had taken such an outlandish tale as truth.

Now a national celebrity, he had already rebuffed interest from Hollywood. Warner Bros. offered him a role in *The Adventures of Robin Hood*, costarring Olivia de Havilland as Maid Marian. David O. Selznick, while developing *Gone with the Wind*, dangled a producing job. But Welles wanted to be a director, producer, *and* actor, and Broadway, not Hollywood, gave him that freedom. It was RKO that finally won him over, after an extended courtship. While the studio had weathered the Depression with Fred Astaire and Ginger Rogers musicals, the company was in financial straits by 1938, when George Schaefer became its new president. His strategy was "Quality Pictures at a Premium Price." In 1939, Welles, now in debt after a few Broadway flops, began negotiating. "In my case I didn't want money, I wanted authority," he recalled. "So I asked for the impossible hoping to be left alone, and at the end of a year of negotiations, I got what I wanted." The contract gave him unheard-of creative freedom, including final cut.

RKO's board was alarmed by the latitude Schaefer had given Welles—under the terms of his employ, the studio could approve his budgets but not what he put on the screen. The rest of the industry was skeptical at best. "A genius is a crackpot on a tightrope," *Variety* warned. "Hollywood is watching Orson Welles, wondering if his foot will slip." The trades called him "Little Orson Annie." Even his facial hair, left over from a Broadway role, was ripe for ridicule. (Errol Flynn gave Welles a bearded ham for Christmas.) Everything about the twenty-four-year-old "boy genius" flew in the face of the established order—an order codified by the Academy—in which men like Louis B. Mayer, not parvenu theater directors, were supposed to hold the autonomy. Welles later admitted, "I would have hated myself, too." For both him and Schaefer, who had staked RKO's reputation on a princeling, the price of failure was ruin.

FOR THE REST OF HOLLYWOOD, risk aversion was a way of life. The industry had survived the Depression by keeping America entertained, which meant keeping the escalating events in Germany off the screen. In 1933, the year Hitler took power, an MGM screenwriter named Herman J. Mankiewicz took a leave to write a script called *The Mad Dog of Europe*, about the political rise of an anti-Semitic Transylvanian house painter named Adolf Mitler. No studio would touch it. As Mayer told an agent who was shopping the project around, "We have terrific income in Germany and, as far as I am concerned, this picture will never be made." It wasn't.

The Jewish studio heads were all too aware of their tenuous place in the American power structure—and of the paper-thin acceptance that kept public perception on their side. To take a stand against Hitler would bring attention to their own otherness. Joseph Breen, the Production Code Administration's censor in chief—and a virulent anti-Semite— snipped out any attempts at on-screen criticism of the Nazi regime. In a memo about *The Mad Dog of Europe*, Breen warned that "the charge is certain to be made that the Jews, as a class, are behind an anti-Hitler picture and using the entertainment screen for their own personal propaganda purposes." By this tortured logic, timidity kept the studios Nazi-neutral.

Until, gradually, it didn't. At first, the Warner brothers, especially the vigilant Harry, stood virtually alone. In 1934, after its Berlin representative was beaten by Nazi thugs, the studio shut down its German operations. Four years later—three weeks after the Anschluss—it pulled out of Austria, even as MGM, Paramount, and 20th Century–Fox remained in Germany. Nonetheless, Warner Bros. was oblique about criticizing Hitler on-screen. In 1937, the studio released *The Life of Emile Zola*, starring Paul Muni (born Meshilem Meier Weisenfreund), a chest-beating indictment of injustice and mob violence. But it managed to depict Zola's defense of a Jewish officer in the Dreyfus affair without anyone uttering the word *Jew* aloud. The Academy named it Best Picture.

In January 1938, John Ford spoke to a crowd of nearly seven thousand people at a rally of the Hollywood Anti-Nazi League. At forty-three, Ford was two decades into his studio career. Pugnacious, and prone to weeklong alcoholic benders, he was a walking, bellowing contradiction, subjecting underlings to on-set tirades while publicly crusading on behalf of the little guy. In 1935, he had made *The Informer*, a drama about the Irish War of Independence. Darryl Zanuck had declined to produce the politically charged script at Fox, so Ford brought it to RKO—and won his first Oscar for directing. Even then, his efforts to persuade Zanuck to take on socially conscious material fizzled. Ford groused, "If you're thinking of a general run of social pictures, or even just plain honest ones, it's almost hopeless."

At the Shrine Auditorium, Ford joined a bill with Dorothy Parker, who referred to Hitler simply as "that certain man." The nature of that certain man became harder to ignore that November, when Nazis vandalized Jewish businesses and torched synagogues in the pogrom that came to be called Kristallnacht, or "the Night of Broken Glass." Americans learned about the atrocities abroad in newsreels that played in movie houses—so how could the movies that followed them stay silent? In 1939, Warner Bros. released *Confessions of a Nazi Spy*, the first openly anti-Nazi film produced by a major studio, with the slogan "The Picture that Calls a Swastika a Swastika!" The film ends with a U.S. attorney vowing that "when our basic liberties become threatened, we wake up." A member of Breen's staff called it a "portentous departure."

The movie was not a box-office success, nor was it represented at the Oscar ceremony of 1940, which was all swept up with *Gone with the Wind*. Ford was nominated for *Stagecoach*, his lauded return to Westerns. It was the first ceremony since Hitler's invasion of Poland, and Hollywood, with less to lose now that the European markets were drying up, was allowing more global politics to trickle onto the screen. That summer, MGM released *The Mortal Storm*, starring James Stewart as a German who attempts to flee with the daughter of a "non-Aryan." It was followed by Alfred Hitchcock's spy thriller *Foreign Correspondent*. Hitchcock had reshot the ending after the bombing of Britain began, with a radio correspondent imploring Americans, "Hang on to your lights! They're the only lights left in the world!" That year, Hitler's Germany banned American films from all territories under its control.

In early 1940, Ford came out with *The Grapes of Wrath*, one of the few Hollywood productions to capture the progressive labor politics of the Depression. Ford was no Communist, but the film's sympathetic depiction of organizing farmworkers was enough to raise the hackles of the Red-baiting press. Nevertheless, critics hailed *The Grapes of Wrath* as a masterpiece. After finishing it, Ford set off on the *Araner*, the wood-hulled auxiliary ketch he'd purchased in 1934, to fulfill his fantasies of adventuring at sea. With John Wayne and other friends, he sailed from San Pedro to the Mexican port of Guaymas, where he filed reports to the U.S. Navy on Japanese trawlers he had found suspicious.

Ford's volunteerism was mostly boyish indulgence, but that spring, he wrote a proposal to form a "Naval Photographic Organization" that would use Hollywood talent to counter Nazi propaganda by capturing on film "the Navy's weight, prowess, power, high morale, and striking force." Ford's ragtag group of volunteers, nicknamed "John Ford's Navy," began meeting on the Fox lot on Tuesday nights, training with prop swords in uniforms borrowed from the Western Costume Company. ("I was always afraid that he was going to kill someone the way he waved his sword around," one of his recruits recalled.)

At the same time, Ford was preparing his next film, *The Long Voyage Home*, adapted from four short World War I plays by Eugene O'Neill. Ford updated the action to the present, as the crew of the SS *Glencairn* delivers a cargo of explosives. Once they get to England, a newsboy is seen in a sandwich board with the headline "NAZIS INVADE NORWAY"—an event that had happened eight days before shooting began. *The Long Journey Home*, released in the fall of 1940, joined a spate of films that took the encroaching storm head-on—and failed to ignite the box office. The exception was *The Great Dictator*, in which Charlie Chaplin played both a Jewish barber and the mustachioed tyrant Adenoid Hynkel. But the overall impression was summed up by a *New York Times* column concluding that films "devoted to arousing America against Germany" had proved to be "a costly mistake."

Even so, the conflict in Europe loomed over the 1941 Academy Awards, held ten months before Pearl Harbor. The evening began with a radio address from President Roosevelt commending Hollywood for its "splendid cooperation with all who are directing the expansion of our defense forces." Many of the ceremony's attendees couldn't hear Roosevelt over the voice of the Academy official giving them directions on how to look attentive for the newsreel cameras. It was the first year that the winners' names were kept strictly secret in sealed envelopes, after the *Los Angeles Times* revealed the results prematurely the year before, and the new protocol gave the evening a jolt of suspense. Conspicuously missing was Ford, who had sent word that he and Henry Fonda would be fishing off the coast of Mexico "for as long as the fish are biting." Nevertheless, he won his second directing award, for *The Grapes of Wrath*. The prize was collected by Darryl Zanuck—now Lieutenant Colonel Darryl Zanuck, after he had joined the Signal Corps reserves. When screenwriter Dudley Nichols sent Ford a congratulatory note, Ford wired back, with typical bluster, "Awards are a trivial thing to be concerned with at times like these."

When it came to Best Picture, timeliness proved not to be an advantage: the war-minded *Foreign Correspondent*, *The Great Dictator*, and *The Long Voyage Home* all lost to Hitchcock's *Rebecca*, the film that had made Joan Fontaine a star like her sister.

JOAN FONTAINE AND OLIVIA DE Havilland both had theories about why they never got along. "From birth we were not encouraged by our parents or nurses to be anything but rivals, and our careers only emphasized the situation," Joan recalled. On-screen, both were ladylike ingénues with elegant, heart-shaped faces and impeccable Mid-Atlantic accents. Offscreen, they were oil and water: Olivia was regal, while Joan was flip, sometimes catty. Joan kept their rivalry in the press, while Olivia, when deigning to acknowledge her sister's barbs, was circumspect. "She seems to need what I have," Olivia said.

Olivia was born first, in 1916, to English parents living in Tokyo. Her father, Walter de Havilland, had left Britain in 1893 to teach at Japanese universities. Her mother, Lilian, was a thwarted actress. Joan arrived fifteen months later, a sickly child who needed constant care. That, she surmised, is where the trouble began. "Perhaps my being a puny child had a great deal to do with her resentment," Joan wrote of her sister, "as I am sure I was a fretful infant, and in the nursery she was no longer preeminent with the servants or her parents." Olivia thought that Lilian encouraged her sister's flair for melodrama: "If she got chickenpox, it was a drama of state. When I had it, I went to bed and was told to keep still and not scratch."

After Lilian surmised that her husband had taken their maid Yoki-san as a mistress, she resettled with the girls in California. In San Jose, she married George Fontaine, a department store manager and ruth-less disciplinarian. During the year Lilian was in Japan for divorce pro-ceedings, the girls were left alone with Fontaine, who subjected them to military exercises and rigorous cleaning inspections. Worse, when he bathed them, his washcloth "would tarry too long in intimate places," Joan recalled. "Olivia and I, never given to confidences, did agree that something was odd."

Instead of uniting against their abuser, the sisters turned on each other. One summer, they were invited to a neighbor's pool, and Olivia broke Joan's collarbone on the flagstone edge. Olivia said that Joan had tried to pull her in ("She had never been rambunctious like that before, so it took me completely unaware"); Joan said that Olivia had thrown her down and tackled her. Neither ever forgot the incident. "I regret that I remember not one act of kindness from her all through my childhood," Joan wrote in her memoir, No Bed of Roses, which her second husband liked to call "No Shred of Truth."

Olivia got to Hollywood first, when Jack Warner caught the eighteen-year-old in a touring production of A Midsummer Night's Dream and thought she had "a fresh young beauty that would soon stir a lot of tired old muscles around the film town." He bumped Bette Davis from the film version of Midsummer and signed de Havilland to a seven-year contract. The studio paired her with Errol Flynn in Captain Blood, the first of eight adventure films they would make together over six years. Olivia figured that the worldly Joan would join high society. To her puzzlement, Joan took up acting as well, landing her screen début in MGM's No More Ladies. Threatened, Olivia pushed Joan to relinquish the family name. "Two de Havillands on the marquee would be too many," Joan griped, "so I had to leave Olivia's distinguished name for her and I took my step-father's name." She told the press that a fortune-teller had advised her to take a stage name with eight letters, starting with F.

As both sisters rose through the studio ranks, they continued find-ing ways to undermine each other. When Joan danced in A Damsel in Distress with Fred Astaire, Olivia mocked her flat-footedness, lamenting to a reporter that ever since her sister joined the business, "the sweet closeness of our relationship has slipped away." Both tried to downplay their connection in the press, but the studios knew a juicy story when they saw one. "Rumors of the 'feuding sisters' being circulated by the Warner Brothers' publicity department were not without foundation, yet hardly for print," Joan recalled. "Both of us led such circumspect lives that our studios were at a loss to make the two sisters exciting."

The two also fought over men. In 1939, both sisters attended a party at the home of British actor Brian Aherne, who had briefly been Olivia's beau. A guest claiming psychic powers told Joan that she would marry the host; Aherne proposed not long afterward. Before the wedding, Olivia took Joan to a surprise party at the Trocadero, where Howard Hughes, who was seeing Olivia, declared his love for Joan and wrote down his private number on a slip of paper. Joan showed Olivia the phone number— ostensibly, to warn her of Hughes's disloyalty, but Olivia took out her anger on Joan. "Sparks flew," Joan wrote. "Hell hath no fury like a woman scorned . . . especially in favor of her sister."

By then, de Havilland had filmed what would be her defining role, the earnest, beleaguered Melanie in *Gone with the Wind*. Fontaine claimed that she was the first to receive a call from George Cukor, the film's original director, to discuss the role of Melanie. In her telling, she made the "grave error" of wearing a gray faille coat dress and silver fox furs to their meeting. "Too chic, too chic!" Cukor cried. "Melanie must be a plain simple southern girl." Joan suggested, "What about my sister?" Cukor supposedly replied, "Who's she?" But Cukor would hardly have needed to be told who Olivia de Havilland was. Joan's version not only takes credit for her sister's casting but includes the backhanded suggestion that Olivia got the part of Melanie for being the less glamorous sibling.

At the 1940 Academy Awards, Olivia was nominated for Best Supporting Actress against her *Gone with the Wind* costar Hattie McDaniel, who became the first African American to win an Oscar. Olivia failed to rejoice in the historic achievement. She allowed a single tear to escape before rushing to the hotel kitchen and bursting into tears. "All I could do," she said later, "was think to myself, There is no God." Making matters worse, her sister had found a plum part of her own, in Hitchcock's adaptation of Daphne du Maurier's novel *Rebecca*. Originally, David O. Selznick, who was preparing *Rebecca* while producing *Gone with the Wind*, had wanted Olivia to star opposite Laurence Olivier in the film. But Jack Warner refused to loan her to Selznick a second time. According to de Havilland, Selznick asked her, "Would you mind if I take your sister? She's perfect." Olivia knew she was losing a great role, but admitted, "She was really better for it than I was. She was a blonde; Larry was brunet."

Needless to say, Olivia didn't figure in Joan's version of events. According to Fontaine, she had gone to a dinner at Charlie Chaplin's house and been seated next to a "heavyset, bespectacled gentleman" who turned out to be Selznick. Joan had just read du Maurier's novel and told the man next to her that it would make a good movie. "I just bought the novel today," Selznick exclaimed, and invited her to test for the lead role. In the book, the nameless heroine marries a wealthy English widower and is whisked to his estate, where she's seized with insecurity, afraid she'll never live up to the memory of his beloved first wife, Rebecca. During shooting, Hitchcock told Joan that Olivier had wanted his fian-cée, Vivien Leigh, to star, and that Olivier thought Joan was awful. The insinuation played on Fontaine's overshadowed-younger-sister complex, which only fed into her character's paranoia—perhaps Hitchcock's plan all along. Her self-doubt wasn't alleviated when her mother told Louella Parsons at the film's premiere, "Joan has always seemed rather phony to me in real life, but she's quite believable on the screen."

A year after Olivia's Best Supporting Actress loss for *Gone with the Wind*, she had the displeasure of seeing her sister nominated for Best Actress for *Rebecca*. It was bad enough that Joan was the first to get married—would she win the Oscar first, too? As Olivia said later, "Can you imagine what it's like to be an elder sister and have your younger one do everything first?" *Rebecca* won Best Picture, but Fontaine lost to Ginger Rogers, for *Kitty Foyle*. She claimed to have been relieved. "For me to have won it with my first good role would have been precipitous," Fontaine reasoned. "The voters might well have thought Hitch was my Svengali, that after so many undistinguished performances in the past, surely it was Hitchcock who had mesmerized me into the performance I was nominated for."

On the Academy scoreboard, the sisters were tied at zero. But it would be only a year before Joan—and Olivia—got another chance.

ANYONE WHO SAW ORSON WELLES'S RKO contract as a disaster in the making soon found proof. Welles was living large in a five-bedroom Brentwood estate, preparing an ambitious adaptation of Joseph Conrad's *Heart of Darkness*. To teach himself the cinematic language, he held nightly screenings of Ford's *Stagecoach*, which he called "my movie textbook." He was weeks into planning *Heart of Darkness* when Germany invaded Poland. RKO, already on parlous financial ground, became skittish about the effect that war would have on its foreign markets and put the movie on hold, so that Welles could take on something cheaper first. The Boy Wonder proposed an adaptation of the espionage novel *The Smiler with the Knife*, but that idea imploded when he couldn't find a leading lady.

The vultures descended. "They are laying bets over on the RKO lot that the Orson Welles deal will end up without Orson ever doing a picture there," *The Hollywood Reporter* snarked. Welles started to crack; at a meeting at Chasen's with his Mercury Theatre cohort, he threw a dish at his mentor, John Houseman. He needed to produce something, anything, and the person to help him do it was a sozzled has-been named Herman J. Mankiewicz.

At forty-two, Mank, as friends called him, was as notorious for his acid wit as for his flair for being virtually unemployable. He had begun his career in New York, as *The New Yorker*'s first drama critic and one of the wisecracking intellectuals of the Algonquin Round Table. In 1926, he accepted a lucrative offer from Hollywood, even though he considered moviemaking suitable only for those "in pursuit of a lump sum." Soon after his arrival, he sent a telegram to the reporter Ben Hecht, enticing him to take a job at Paramount: MILLIONS ARE TO BE GRABBED OUT HERE AND YOUR ONLY COMPETITION IS IDIOTS.

Talkies allowed Mankiewicz to inject movies with the Algonquin set's rat-a-tat smartness. He was one of the first ten screenwriters assigned to *The Wizard of Oz*; it was his suggestion that the Kansas scenes be filmed in black and white and the Oz scenes in color. But he was just as talented at self-destruction, prone to drunken invective, racking up gambling debts, and enraging every studio head in town. He was an in-demand dinner guest, notably at the mountaintop estate of newspaper magnate William Randolph Hearst in San Simeon, where he befriended Hearst's mistress, actress Marion Davies—until his excessive drinking got him banished. By late 1939, he was hanging on to week-to-week employment at MGM, where his younger brother, Joseph, was toiling as a writer and producer. Herman pleaded with Louis B. Mayer to give him an advance against his salary, and Mayer agreed—on the condition that he give up gambling. The next day, Mankiewicz was midway through a poker game in the studio commissary when he looked up and saw Mayer glaring back. He packed up his office and was officially fired the next day.

Hoping for a fresh start, Mank borrowed money from his brother and took a ride through the desert with a screenwriter friend. Somewhere near Albuquerque, the car flipped over, leaving Mank with a triple fracture in his left leg. He spent a month in a Los Angeles hospital, "somewhat in the posture of a lower-class Klondike whore," and returned home in a navel-to-toe cast. He crabbily received guests, including his young friend Orson Welles, whom he had met in New York. "Nobody was more miserable, more bitter, and funnier than Mank—a perfect monument to self-destruction," Welles observed. "But when the bitterness wasn't focused straight at you—he was the best company in the world."

Welles took pity on the bedridden writer, paying him two hundred dollars a week to write for Welles's radio program. With Welles scrambling for a feasible film project, the two talked—and talked. "The actual writing came only after lots of talk," Welles said. "Just the two of us, yelling at each other—not too angrily." All that talking led them to the germ that became *Citizen Kane*. But whose idea was it, actually? Welles later said that he had wanted to tell the same story from different perspectives. But, according to Houseman, it was Mankiewicz who had the idea of revealing a man's true character after his death, according to the people who knew him. The main character would be like "a whirling pagoda," radically different depending on the angle from which you viewed him.

But who was this man? They pictured "some big American figure," Welles recalled. "But it couldn't be a politician, because you'd have to pinpoint him. Howard Hughes was the first idea. But we got around pretty quickly to the press lords." Mankiewicz's version: "We were going to do *The Life of Dumas*, and then I told him about how I would be interested in doing a picture based on Hearst and Marion Davies." Hearst loomed larger than myth. At his height, he controlled twenty-six daily newspapers, plus magazines, radio stations, and news services. His empire was a distinctly modern kind, built not on land but influence, which he used to further his personal aims—including movie roles for Davies. Once, when Douglas Fairbanks asked Hearst why he had not pursued a fortune in movies, he replied, "You can crush a man with journalism, but you can't with motion pictures."

Welles offered Mankiewicz a thousand dollars a week to write the screenplay, but his work would be the sole property of Mercury Productions. Also, he would have to lay off the booze, which meant getting away from city temptations. Two weeks after Mankiewicz was put on the payroll, he and Houseman, tasked with keeping the writer on track, left for a desert ranch east of Los Angeles. Houseman allowed the writer one drink per day. Pinned to his bed and dictating to an English secretary, Mank spent six weeks drafting a script initially titled *American*. Among his innovations was the character's cryptic dying word—*Rosebud*—which would set off the hunt for Kane's hidden core. (As one deathless rumor had it, "Rosebud" was Hearst's nickname for Davies's genitalia.) But the script had as much to do with Welles as Hearst. As Houseman recalled, they were "creating a vehicle suited to the personality and creative energy of a man who, at twenty-four, was himself only slightly less fabulous than the mythical hero he would be portraying. And the deeper we penetrated beyond the public events into the heart of Charles Foster Kane, the closer we seemed to come to the identity of Orson Welles."

In April 1940, Mankiewicz delivered the 267-page script to Welles, followed by another 44 pages. Welles slashed down and polished the screenplay, now titled *John Citizen, USA*. Both men were stubborn collaborators. "Herman would rather talk for three days than change two innocuous lines of dialogue," one producer recalled. "Before you knew it, Plato, Kant, and Mencken were involved in whether the leading lady should open or shut the door."

Shortly after the film went into production that summer, the subject of credit became contentious. Louella Parsons was treated to an extravagant on-set luncheon with Welles, who laid on the charm as he told her, between mouthfuls of chicken, calf brains, artichoke hearts, and roast beef, that *Citizen Kane* was about "a dead man." Surely this was a ploy to throw Parsons off its real subject, her boss—and it worked. In print, Parsons cooed over the "brilliant youth." She also quoted Welles as saying, "I wrote 'Citizen Kane.'"

Soon, Mercury publicist Herb Drake was warning Welles that Mankiewicz was threatening to come down on the "juvenile delinquent credit stealer." From his years of studio service, Mankiewicz was used to waiving credit on his work. But, even before *Citizen Kane* was screened, adjectives like "important" and "distinguished" began to stick to it, and Mankiewicz decided that, if he had written a masterpiece, he wanted it known.

Balking, Welles offered Mankiewicz ten thousand dollars to give up his credit. The screenwriter asked his friend Ben Hecht what to do. Hecht advised, "Take the money and screw the bastard." But Mankiewicz refused. In fact, he wanted *sole* credit. This created an additional problem for Welles, whose contract with RKO required him to write his own projects. And there was no question that Welles had made significant contributions to the script. As he saw it, the two men had differing visions, and the film's electricity came from merging them into one. "The script is most like me when the central figure on the screen is Kane," Welles said later. "And it is most like Mankiewicz when he's being talked about."

Mank did not see it this way. He wrote to his friend Alexander Woollcott:

I feel it my modest duty to tell you that the conception of the story, the plot, the characters, the manner of telling the story and about 99 percent of the words are the exclusive creations of

Yours,
Mank

He petitioned the Screen Writers Guild for arbitration, but then withdrew his appeal, suddenly worried that Hearst would retaliate. Finally, Welles, in what he considered an act of goodwill, agreed to share writing credit. Although Mankiewicz maintained that "there isn't one single line in the picture that wasn't in writing—writing from and by me—before ever a camera turned," he gave in. The joint billing would become one of the most scrutinized in Hollywood history. In a line for which Mankiewicz had no trouble getting attribution, he would watch the "boy genius" walk by on set and seethe, "There but for the grace of God goes God."

THE CONVENTIONAL WISDOM THAT WAR pictures didn't sell was about to get upended—by a fifty-two-year-old military veteran. As Hitler plotted his takeover of Scandinavia, producer Jesse Lasky flew to Nashville to try to get a deal from Sergeant Alvin York. In the Great War, York had joined the armed forces despite religious objections and became a one-man fighting force, capturing 132 Germans and killing two dozen. Hollywood came calling immediately, but York was obstinate: "Uncle Sam's uniform," he declared, "it ain't for sale."

By 1940, York was living the hayseed life in Tennessee. Now that another world war was encroaching, Lasky trekked through the mountains to woo the aging war hero, who had taken to calling Lasky a "fat little Jew." Unfazed, the producer reminded York that the profits could help him finish construction of his Bible school. The two struck a deal, and Lasky set up the film at Warner Bros. John Huston, who had cowritten *Jezebel*, was eager to direct his first film, *The Maltese Falcon*, but Jack Warner asked him to first help rewrite *Sergeant York* as the "story of a hell-raising mountaineer who is a conscientious objector but goes to war anyhow and becomes a hero."

Sergeant York opens on the young York as a drunken backwoods ne'er-do-well. After being struck by lightning, York stumbles into a church service during a rendition of "Old-Time Religion" and rededicates himself to God. When war breaks out, he reasons, "I ain't a-goin' to war. War is killin', and the book's agin' killin'. So war is agin' the book." A superior gives a speech about the "struggle for freedom" and sends York off with the Bible and a volume of American history. In a scene that quakes with American folk religion, York brings both books into the mountains, his trusty dog at his side, and the wind blows the holy book open to the words "Render unto Caesar the things which are Caesar's and unto God the things that are God's," giving York an epiphany that allows him to reconcile religion and militarism. He ships overseas and becomes a one-man killing machine, knocking out Germans "like a flock of turkeys."

The real York insisted on being played by Gary Cooper, whose casting made the film's homespun propaganda even more potent; around the Warner lot, people nicknamed *Sergeant York* "Mr. Deeds Goes to War." But getting Cooper required some Hollywood horse trading: Samuel Goldwyn loaned out Cooper to Jack Warner in exchange for Warner allowing Bette Davis to star in an adaptation of the Lillian Hellman drama *The Little Foxes*. Goldwyn also threw in William Wyler to direct *Sergeant York*, but the sensitive Wyler wasn't suited to such a bombastic project, so it went to Howard Hawks. Goldwyn reloaned Wyler to Fox, where Darryl Zanuck put him on *How Green Was My Valley*, an adaptation of Richard Llewellyn's wistful novel about life in a Welsh coal-mining town. All these films went into production in the months before Pearl Harbor, setting the stage for the Oscars of 1942.

At first, Zanuck and Wyler envisioned *How Green Was My Valley* as a four-hour Technicolor extravaganza to rival *Gone with the Wind*, with a star-studded cast including Katharine Hepburn and Laurence Olivier. But the project ran into trouble. Zanuck objected to a version of the script that played up a miners' strike and demanded that it be trimmed and depoliticized, especially once Hitler's attacks on Britain made the idea of vilifying the English industrialists untenable; he insisted that the story be told through the eyes of the little boy Huw Morgan. With Zanuck and Wyler at loggerheads, the director was told that the picture had been canceled, only to discover that it had been reassigned to John Ford.

This left Wyler to focus on *The Little Foxes*, starring his former flame Bette Davis. Their affair had ended sometime after *Jezebel*, though Davis always regretted not marrying him when she could. Both had moved on to other spouses—for Davis, husband number two, the innkeeper Arthur Farnsworth—but she still considered Wyler the only director who had understood how to use her talents. Their mutual affection crumbled during *The Little Foxes*, in which Davis played a conniving southern aristocrat who blackmails her brothers for controlling interest in a cotton mill. Davis had seen Tallulah Bankhead perform the role onstage and couldn't get it out of her head. "It was Willie's intention that I give a different interpretation of the part," she recalled. "I insisted that Tallulah had played it the only way it could be played." In a fit of rage and fraying nerves, Davis walked off the set for three weeks, leaving Wyler to shoot around her. When she returned, a visiting reporter noticed the barely contained discord: "Miss Davis was icy in deferring to [Wyler's] wishes, and each was monstrously patient with the other." She came out believing she had given one of the worst performances of her life.

After *The Little Foxes*, Wyler moved on to MGM's *Mrs. Miniver*, about an English housewife whose life is upended by Germany's bombing campaign. Wyler, who had been born to a Jewish family in Alsace–Lorraine and was receiving increasingly desperate letters from relatives in Europe, saw *Mrs. Miniver* as "an opportunity to, in a small way, make a small contribution to the war effort." The Blitz had shaken Hollywood's sizable British population and even threatened production of *How Green Was My Valley*. "Inopportune to make this film now," one Fox producer warned Zanuck. "Shouldn't throw stone at England. Postpone until after hostilities are over." Nevertheless, Ford shot the film over the summer of 1941, re-creating rural Wales on an eighty-acre set in the Santa Monica Mountains. As the product of a large Irish family, Ford gave the film a personal sense of nostalgia and loss. He was on the Union Pacific to Washington, DC, to be inducted into active duty with the navy, when Zanuck cabled to gush, "If this is not one of the best pictures ever made, then I will eat a film can."

For Joan Fontaine, married to the British Brian Aherne, the war's spread was particularly distressing. "That autumn morning when Britain declared war on Adolf Hitler's Germany, and France speedily followed, the Ahernes' tranquility was abruptly shattered," she recalled. "So it was with all the British in manicured Beverly Hills." Aherne became a flight instructor, and Fontaine joined a women's sewing group that made mufflers and mittens to send overseas. The marriage had begun breaking down as soon as it began, with Aherne criticizing his wife's posture and Fontaine carping at Aherne for leaving his pipe smoking in the ashtray.

She spent long days at the studio, driving herself into a jealous frenzy as she imagined another woman stealing her unattended husband.

All this was good preparation for RKO's *Suspicion*, her reunion with Hitchcock. The story once again cast Fontaine as a wife driven to paranoia, this time an Englishwoman swept off her feet by Cary Grant. No sooner have they eloped than she realizes that her husband is a con artist in chronic debt—and she starts to suspect that he's plotting to murder her for her life insurance. Fontaine herself was consumed with doubts, believing that Hitchcock had stopped paying attention to her. Perhaps he trusted her to do the part without the mind games he had played during *Rebecca*. Her uneasiness on set was echoed at home, where she would find perfumed notepaper or a handkerchief she didn't recognize, which Aherne would dismiss by calling her a "little goose."

Her sister, meanwhile, was dismayed to find that her success in *Gone with the Wind* hadn't translated into better roles at Warner Bros. Something decent finally came from Paramount, the romantic drama *Hold Back the Dawn*. Written by the new team of Billy Wilder and Charles Brackett—who would later be responsible for *Sunset Boulevard*—it was set in the transient world of European émigrés trying to enter the United States from a Mexican border town. One of them, a Romanian gigolo, cajoles a winsome American schoolteacher into marrying him so that he can get his papers, and inevitably, they fall in love. It was yet another film that danced around world events—it's never mentioned exactly *why* these migrants have been driven out of Europe—even though Wilder, an Austrian Jew, was himself a refugee. The role required little of de Havilland except to be winningly naïve, but she wanted it enough to ask Jack Warner for permission, and he begrudgingly agreed.

Joan and Olivia's relationship was as tense as ever. For Olivia's twenty-fifth birthday, in July 1941, Joan prepared a dinner catered to her sister's tastes. But the guest of honor arrived two hours late, with her current beau, James Stewart. When Joan told her that dinner had gone cold, Olivia replied, "It's my birthday. I can arrive whenever I like!" De Havilland, for her part, told columnist Sidney Skolsky about a recurring dream: She's standing on a cliff, watching Joan below on the sand, when she sees a lethal tidal wave coming. "She never knows whether to save herself or go to Joan," Skolsky reported, "and she always wakes up before she decides."

Orson Welles wrapped a cloud of obscurity around RKO Production #281, otherwise known as *Citizen Kane*. Call sheets were labeled "No visitors, please"—except for invited guests like John Ford, who clued in Welles to the fact that his assistant director was an RKO spy. ("How's old snake-in-the-grass Eddie?") When studio executives dropped in, Welles halted shooting and had the cast and crew play baseball until they left. Journalists who were allowed on set were treated to such anodyne scenes that the *New York Times* surmised only that the plot "covers the last 60 years of the American scene." And yet, even before production wrapped, word was spreading that the protagonist of *Citizen Kane* bore a remarkable resemblance to Citizen Hearst.

The culprit for the leak was possibly none other than Herman Mankiewicz, who made the foolhardy decision to show the script to writer Charles Lederer, the nephew of Hearst's mistress, Marion Davies. Mankiewicz was worried, belatedly, that the depiction of Kane's second wife, the boozy, talentless singer Susan Alexander, might upset Davies. It's possible that Lederer showed the script to his aunt, who passed it along to Hearst (though Lederer denied this). However word got out, the issue blew up thanks to the interference of Louella Parsons and Hedda Hopper, the archrival gossip columnists who acted as the industry's public gatekeepers. Both women used their power to uphold the studio system, whether that meant throwing a misbehaving starlet under the bus or squelching rumors in exchange for industry-approved tidbits. Often, one columnist would demand a star's loyalty, with the implicit threat of bad press if the other got favorable treatment. "I walked a narrow tightrope with both ladies," Joan Fontaine recalled, "inviting Louella to one party and Hedda to the next."

At first, both lavished praise on Welles, who knew how to charm the two gossip mavens at once, sometimes sending floral arrangements in thanks for good press. But when whispers began that Charles Foster Kane was based on Hearst, whom Parsons considered not only "the Chief" but her closest friend, she called Welles and asked him directly. "Take my word for it, it isn't," Parsons claimed Welles told her. "It's about a completely fictional publisher." Credulous, she reported back to the Hearst editors that they had no reason to worry.

Parsons considered what happened next "one of the classic double crosses of Hollywood": Welles had not only lied to her, but he showed the movie to Hopper first, at a small press screening in January 1941. Hopper had invited herself, after hearing about the screening and making a fuss. "Come tonight if you must," Welles warned her, "but it still stinks. Many shots are missing or only tests are cut in and we need music like Britain needs planes. Love, Orson."

When Hopper saw the film that night, she had no doubt that Kane—a ruthless propagandist with a massive ego, a Gothic-style lair, and an alcoholic lover—was Hearst. "I was appalled," she wrote, calling the film an "impudent, murderous trick, even for the boy genius, to perpetrate on a newspaper giant." According to Hopper, Welles called her the next day to ask what she thought, and she told him, "You won't get away with it."

"Oh, yes I will," he replied.

Incensed, Hopper took what she knew to Hearst, even though he was the owner of her rival paper. This may have been a matter of principle. More likely, it was a way to embarrass Parsons, who got word that Hopper had called Hearst, feigning horror and saying, "Mr. Hearst, I don't know why Louella hasn't told you this picture is about you." Parsons was further humiliated when, soon after, *Friday* magazine carried a story directly linking *Citizen Kane* to Hearst and including a dubious quote from Welles mocking Parsons: "Wait until the woman finds out that the picture's about her boss."

Welles tried to convince Parsons that the *Friday* story was a "vicious lie," but the infuriated columnist leaped into action. Parsons arranged to see the film with two of Hearst's lawyers. Gasping at the screen, she concluded that *Citizen Kane* was nothing more than "a cruel, dishonest caricature." She walked out without acknowledging Welles and never spoke to him again.

With her own reputation on the line, Parsons dialed "everybody but St. Peter," as publicist Herb Drake put it, starting with the office of RKO's George Schaefer, to whose secretary she promised "one of the most beautiful lawsuits in history." Then she called Will Hays, Louis B. Mayer, Darryl Zanuck, David O. Selznick, Jack Warner, the Rockefellers (who were stockholders in RKO), and the managing director of Radio City Music Hall, where *Kane* was set to premiere on Valentine's Day. For years, Parsons had traded on salacious gossip, using the stories she *didn't* print as leverage. If *Citizen Kane* went ahead, who was to stop her from letting the dirt fly, true or not?

According to Parsons, Hearst himself took a more magnanimous view, telling her, "I don't believe in lawsuits. Besides, I have no desire to give the picture any more publicity." In fact, Hearst executives had already declined an ad for the film in *Cosmopolitan*. Now, Hearst's editors scrubbed every reference to *Kane* or any RKO picture from his papers. Parsons reported back to the Hearst brass that the major theater chains had agreed not to show the film.

The stunned Welles told *Newsweek*, "It looks like my throat has been cut."

The threats were getting louder and stranger. At one point, Welles received a call from journalist Adela Rogers St. Johns, saying that she was working on a story about his "romantic adventures in Hollywood." There were whispers that Welles was a Communist, according to *Variety*, "because of his apparent lack of interest in money." All this took a toll. "Mr. Welles' appearance resembles that of his frightened New Jersey listeners on the night of his Martian broadcast," the *New York Times* observed. "If the trouble becomes more acute, his film career may be ended." Bets against the film seeing the light of day were two to one.

With an infantry surrounding him, RKO president George Schaefer insisted that there was "no serious consideration" to withholding the film. But the studio's board was split. Schaefer argued that the repercussions of scotching the film would be worse than those of releasing it; Welles himself was exploring his legal options against the studio. But it wasn't just RKO being threatened with ruin. *Variety* reported that the Hearst papers were planning "continuous shellfire against the entire industry." This was war.

Louis B. Mayer had seen decades' worth of existential threats to

Hollywood, and he wasn't about to let one lousy RKO picture bring it down. So, he came up with a plan to wipe the problem away: the studios would pool their resources, buy all the negatives and prints of *Citizen Kane* from RKO, and incinerate them.

Mayer was prepared to pay $800,000. A hairsbreadth of cowardice, and Schaefer might have agreed, consigning *Citizen Kane* to oblivion. Instead, he found it in himself to send the vaguest possible reply: "Such an extraordinary suggestion coming from a man in your position must be carefully considered." Schaefer quickly arranged a screening in Radio City's projection room for a group of industry heads, with Welles giving a personal appeal. They agreed not to conspire against the film, as long as RKO made some (relatively painless) trims. Welles agreed.

But *Citizen Kane* was far from liberated. Valentine's Day came and went, with no premiere at Radio City. RKO held a steady stream of screenings to build support, and by March, much of Hollywood's top brass had seen the film. There was little denying that Welles had made a masterpiece. In New York, Welles showed the film to Hearst's competitor Henry Luce, whose magazines proceeded to hype Welles's achievement. As if to needle Parsons, Hedda Hopper announced that she would be doing a six-part biographical series on Welles on her radio show.

The attacks on Welles turned treacherous. Hearst reporters snooped through his draft records, and the insinuations that Welles was a Communist—an omen of the witch hunt awaiting Hollywood on the other end of the war—prompted J. Edgar Hoover to open a file on him. One night, while he was on a lecture tour, a local detective warned Welles, "Don't go back to your hotel. They've got a fourteen-year-old girl in the closet and two photographers waiting for you to come in." Welles was oddly forgiving of Hearst. "Why not fight? I expected that," he later told Peter Bogdanovich. "I didn't expect that everyone would run as scared as they did."

Hearst's campaign may have been a travesty of journalistic ethics, but it was a vain and shortsighted one. His manipulation of his press to squash a rival only confirmed the worst of what the movie had to say about him. Even Hedda Hopper wrote, "If Mr. Hearst had taken his lawyer's advice to ignore *Citizen Kane*, the picture might have died quietly.

Instead it had months of build-up after word spread that W.R. had put thumbs down on it and threatened to sue any theaters which ran it. That tactic was duck soup to every enemy Mr. Hearst ever had." The press baron's vendetta inextricably linked him to Charles Foster Kane, and *Citizen Kane* became the deathless, merciless last word on William Randolph Hearst.

On March 11, after the cancellation of a press preview, Welles summoned reporters to a press conference at his suite at the Ambassador Hotel in New York and issued an ultimatum: if RKO didn't release *Citizen Kane* within three months, he would sue for breach of contract. "I believe the public is entitled to see *Citizen Kane*," he said, warning, "Any attempts at suppression would involve a serious interference with freedom of speech and with the integrity of the moving-picture industry."

Popular sentiment had swung in the film's favor: the more people who saw *Citizen Kane*, the more its release became a noble cause. Even so, Hearst had so cowed theater operators that few were willing to show it, if it was ever released. Finally, RKO announced that the premiere would take place at New York City's Palace Theatre on May 1, 1941, five days short of Welles's twenty-sixth birthday. It would scale back the wide release to just seven cities. Welles was unfazed. "Show it in tents," he urged Schaefer. "It will make millions—'the film your local theater won't let you see.'"

The reviews were rapturous. In the *New York Times*, Bosley Crowther wrote that "it can be safely stated that suppression of this film would have been a crime" and called *Citizen Kane* "far and away the most surprising and cinematically exciting motion picture to be seen here in many a moon." The Hearst papers, of course, had nothing to say. But Hopper, never one to ignore an egged face, gushed that "the boy who was spat upon, jeered, and ridiculed, has made the town swallow its words."

The *Film Daily* confidently predicted, "Welles can prepare his mantel for a couple of Oscars."

THE JULY 2, 1941, PREMIERE of *Sergeant York*, at New York City's Astor Theatre, had the pomp of a military parade. A four-story-tall image of Gary Cooper towered over the theater, lit up with fifteen thousand red, white, and blue lights. Eleanor Roosevelt and Wendell Willkie joined a crowd of World War I veterans, including a Tennessee delegation headed by York's former commander in the Eighty-Second Division. Mayor Fiorello La Guardia gave a hero's welcome to York, who expressed his hope that the film would contribute to "national unity in this hour of danger."

For young men who felt stirred to follow in his footsteps, army officials were on hand with recruitment materials. The critics, though charmed by the film, were hardly blind to its agenda. "The suggestion of deliberate propaganda is readily detected here," Bosley Crowther wrote. *Time* called the film "Hollywood's first solid contribution to national defense." The blurring between movie and military went even farther when, at Jack Warner's behest, the Veterans of Foreign Wars gave Cooper a "Distinguished Citizenship Medal" just for *playing* Sergeant York. Even before it was released nationwide, *York* became the country's highest-grossing film of the year, revving up an American public that had been skeptical about entering the "war in Europe" and proving that anti-German drum beating wasn't a noble cause but a profitable one.

It was certainly better business than baiting the press lords, as proven by *Citizen Kane*'s lumbering box office. When the film expanded in the fall, the Hearst papers were still refusing to advertise it, and some local theaters were so frightened of legal retaliation that they declined to play it. Those that did found that small-town audiences weren't showing up; Welles's Gothic cynicism didn't sell like the folksy Americana of *Sergeant York*. "It may be a classic," a theater manager in North Dakota reported, "but it's plumb nuts to your show-going public."

Even *How Green Was My Valley*, which had nothing to do with the war, garlanded its late-autumn premiere with military embellishment. The gala opening night, at New York's Rivoli Theatre, was presented under the auspices of the Navy Relief Society of the Third Naval District, preceded by a dinner at which the film's star Walter Pidgeon mixed with Rear Admiral Adolphus Andrews. The story of a disintegrating idyll had added resonance as the world fell into chaos, and Bosley Crowther praised Ford for capturing "the beauty which shines in the souls of simple, honest folk." For the director, the premiere was a last gasp of showbiz glitz before returning to his war duties; the next night, he was at the White House, dining with Franklin and Eleanor Roosevelt.

Hollywood's pivot toward interventionism had the immediate side effect of provoking Washington's isolationist faction, already frustrated by its failure to win over the press. North Dakota senator Gerald P. Nye, an isolationist firebrand, singled out *Sergeant York* and *The Great Dictator* among the movies "designed to drug the reason of the American people" and "rouse them to a war hysteria." Perhaps more to the point, Nye blamed the "foreigners" with "non-Nordic" names who ran the industry, and warned, "Go to Hollywood. It is a raging volcano of war fever. The place swarms with refugees." Nye and Missouri senator Bennett Clark introduced a resolution on the Senate floor to investigate Hollywood, claiming that the industry was a monopoly controlled by "groups interested in involving the United States in war."

To defend itself, the Motion Picture Producers and Distributors of America hired Wendell Willkie. Since losing the previous year's landslide election to Roosevelt, Willkie had become the Republican Party's preeminent interventionist, and he charged into the hearings with unapologetic fervor. "Frankly," he opened, "the motion-picture industry would be ashamed if it were not doing voluntarily what it is now doing in this patriotic cause." When Nye rattled off a list of films meriting investigation, including *Sergeant York*, Willkie interjected to ask if the senator had actually seen them. Nye confessed that he hadn't seen "all of them," and Willkie triumphantly offered to arrange screenings for the committee.

Nye's cause slipped farther downhill when Charles Lindbergh, the country's most outspoken isolationist, upstaged the hearings with a speech at an America First rally in Des Moines, in which he warned that the "greatest danger" that the Jews pose to America "lies in their large ownership and influence in our motion pictures, our press, our radio, and our government." The backlash came from all over, including from Alvin York himself, who, despite his own anti-Semitism, declared, "I'm anti-Nazi and proud of it, and I'll be glad to tell that to the Senate committee investigating what they call 'war propaganda' in Hollywood."

The industry now had the upper hand in Washington, where Harry Warner and Darryl Zanuck gave heart-tugging testimony that cast

Hollywood as a beacon of courage, liberty, and the American way. "In truth," Warner said, "the only sin of which Warner Bros. is guilty is that of accurately recording on the screen the world as it is or as it has been." In October, the defeated senators adjourned the hearings until January 1942. Instead, the inquiry evaporated the day after Pearl Harbor.

IN HOLLYWOOD, THE DAYS AFTER the attack were mired in uncertainty. Gala premieres were canceled. Studios improvised air raid shelters. Nightly blackouts along the Pacific coast eliminated night shoots, and workers went home at five. It was desperately unclear if anyone wanted to go to the movies. The day after the attack, *The Hollywood Reporter* ran the headline "War Wallops Boxoffice." Hedda Hopper urged her readers, "Let's continue to play golf, go to the movies, go on with our music." It would take until Christmastime for attendance to bounce back. But would the public want escapism or grit?

"Much speed will be shown by all studios in contriving productions dealing with the war in the Pacific," the *Los Angeles Times* predicted before the attack was three days old. "The scope and possibilities afforded are, of course, terrific." RKO rushed *Bombardier* into production and moved the release date of *Call Out the Marines* from March to as soon as possible. Paramount scrapped *Absent Without Leave*, a military desertion story. And Fox announced *Secret Agent of Japan*, jump-starting a shameful trend of movies that portrayed the Japanese as bucktoothed, subhuman caricatures.

As the Nye Committee hearings faded into oblivion and the United States barreled into the war, a new relationship emerged between Hollywood and Washington. President Roosevelt tasked Lowell Mellett, his liaison with the studios, with helping Hollywood stay on track in its patriotic messaging. Lieutenant Colonel Darryl Zanuck made monthly trips to Washington to coordinate with the War Department. The Academy had already joined the war effort, in part thanks to its former president Frank Capra, who had arranged a meeting between its "Research Council" and the president's son James Roosevelt. They agreed that the Academy would oversee production of military training films for the Signal Corps, a project that Capra's successor, Walter Wanger, called "a source of pride to the organization." The films instructed the swelling ranks of military personnel on everything from horsemanship to cryptographic security. As chair of the Research Council, Zanuck assigned John Ford the direction of *Sex Hygiene*, a half-hour tutorial on the perils of venereal disease. Before Pearl Harbor, the council delivered eighty-eight reels of training film to the government. Afterward, production ramped up.

By then, the Academy had a brand-new president: Bette Davis, who was elected in November 1941. "Being a Jeffersonian democrat, it was only logical that the Queen be constitutionally chosen," she quipped. One paper unironically predicted, "It's Miss Davis' talents as a diplomat that will come in handiest at board meetings." As the Academy's first female president and the biggest star in the role since Douglas Fairbanks, Davis dove into her responsibilities, poring over the bylaws and the rights of her new office.

Within weeks, Pearl Harbor gave Davis her first major crisis: What to do about the Academy Awards, a mere two and a half months away. With a wartime spirit of austerity at hand, it would be unseemly to hold a glitzy, self-congratulating banquet. Just before Christmas, the Academy announced that "in view of existing war conditions," the prizes would be handed out in a "quiet" fashion to be determined—or, as *Variety* put it, "[T]he Golden Boy of Hollywood . . . has covered his gilded epidermis with a coat of camouflage." The Oscars were effectively canceled.

Until they weren't.

Days later, the astonishing news broke that Davis had quit her post after less than two months. Her predecessor, Walter Wanger, would reassume the presidency. Various reasons were given: studio demands, poor health. But Parsons had a different story. "Bette would be the last to want me to print this, but I feel it is so important it should be told," the gossip columnist wrote, disclosing that Davis had objected to the cancellation of the Academy Awards, which would have been a "wonderful opportunity for morale." The actress had offered a counterproposal: Move the ceremony from a ballroom to a theater and donate the ticket proceeds to war relief. They could even hand out wooden statuettes in place of metal ones.

This was the version that Davis told, with relish (and perhaps a dash of invention), in her memoir *The Lonely Life*. When she presented her plan to the Board of Governors, the members were "horrified," thinking that such an evening would "rob the Academy of all dignity." Then she stepped on a more personal minefield when she suggested that Rosalind Russell, the only other woman on the board, run the Oscars planning committee—a job that had previously gone to Mervyn LeRoy.

Furthermore, she proposed revoking the voting privileges of the six thousand extras in the Screen Actors Guild, as many of them "didn't speak English, let alone know anything about excellence of performance." The inclusion of the extras had been part of the tenuous détente between the Academy and the guilds, and at this suggestion, according to Davis, a "pall fell on the room." An aghast Wanger asked Davis what she had against the Academy. It was clear to her that she was expected to be little more than a figurehead. "I was not supposed to preside intelligently," she wrote. "Rather like an heiress at her deceased father's board of directors' meeting, I felt quite capable of holding the gavel." Days later, she submitted her resignation. Zanuck, who had sponsored her candidacy, threatened that she would never work in Hollywood again.

"I took a chance," Davis said, "and resigned anyway."

With Davis out, the board waited out the first months of 1942. The press had not taken well to the cancellation. Hedda Hopper was up in arms, clucking, "The more I think of our Academy award dinner being called off, the madder I get about it." Military officials, now in bed with Hollywood, signaled that they had no problem with the Oscars being held. On February 1, Wanger announced that the banquet would indeed take place—but, *Variety* reported, "sans orchidaceous glitter." As decreed by the planning committee, headed by Rosalind Russell after all, there would be no dancing, and the dress code, excepting military uniforms, would be casual—black tie was "strictly tabu."

The Oscars were back on. Nominations were out in eight days.

RKO HAD ENDED 1941 ON a high note. On December 30, the members of the New York Film Critics Circle went into a room and emerged two hours later—the shortest deliberation in seven years—with a winner for

Best Picture: *Citizen Kane*. John Ford won his third consecutive directing prize, for *How Green Was My Valley*, and Gary Cooper won a nearly uncontested race for Best Actor, for *Sergeant York*. Joan Fontaine was named Best Actress for *Suspicion*, after what the *New York Times* described as "a closely waged contest with her sister, Olivia de Havilland," for her role in *Hold Back the Dawn*.

Suspicion was not scheduled to play in Los Angeles until late January, but RKO, sensing an opportunity, booked the Pantages for the last day of eligibility for the Academy Awards. The film was a triumph for Fontaine, of whom Bosley Crowther wrote, "This young lady has unquestionably become one of the finest actresses on the screen, and one of the most beautiful, too." But the move put her in direct competition with de Havilland, who began the New Year with the news that she had lost the starring role in Warner Bros.' *The Constant Nymph* to her sister. Fontaine was not only horning in on de Havilland's home studio, but was becoming the more popular employee, thanks to de Havilland's continuous absences. After the retakes of *In This Our Life*, combined with her contentious affair with Huston, Olivia was exhausted. Within an hour of finishing the shoot, she received orders to report to another Warner film. When she declined, she was given another assignment, *Saratoga Trunk*, and sent producer Hal Wallis a telegram, pleading, IN SPITE OF AN OPERATION AND ILLNESS I HAVE DONE FIVE PICTURES IN A YEAR AND NOW NEED FOUR WEEKS REST. She was given a four-week suspension without pay.

Darryl Zanuck also scheduled the Los Angeles premiere of *How Green Was My Valley* for the last possible moment, hoping to keep it at the top of Academy voters' minds. He had an opening, but a narrow one. *Citizen Kane* was the critical darling. *Sergeant York*, the popular favorite, was the biggest hit of the year, and Cooper the most lucrative star.

When the Oscar nominations came out on February 9, 1942, *Sergeant York* led with eleven nominations, proof that it was not only wildly popular but a serious awards threat. *How Green Was My Valley* had ten nominations, and *Citizen Kane* and *The Little Foxes* tied with nine. All four were included in a stacked ten-way race for Best Picture, along with Huston's *The Maltese Falcon*, *Suspicion*, and *Hold Back the Dawn*. The stars of those last two, Fontaine and de Havilland, were up against each other for Best Actress, along with Bette Davis for *The Little Foxes*.

The good showing for *Citizen Kane* represented a last chance to turn around its box-office numbers. Even sweeter: the list of Oscar nominations marked the first time that the Hearst papers were forced to print the title *Citizen Kane*.

Welles was personally nominated for directing, acting, and writing (though he shared the last distinction, uncomfortably, with Mankiewicz). The *Los Angeles Times* named Welles "menace No. 1 to much-longer-established stars, directors, producers and others of cinema," so much so that "he might almost be entitled to a special award." *Variety* predicted that Welles was "Doped to Win a Flock of Oscars." *Kane* was a "walkaway" for cinematography, an "easy win" for editing, a shoo-in for screenplay. The Best Picture contest was thought to be a three-way race among *Kane*, *How Green Was My Valley*, and *Sergeant York*, and Best Directing was between Welles and Ford. "If he gets a substantial block of extra votes, he may make a clean sweep of the field," *Variety*'s prognosticator said, while warning of the "considerable jealousy over acclaim his picture has received throughout country."

Hedda Hopper, for her part, used her column to boost *Sergeant York*, whose producer, Jesse Lasky, had "worked long, hard and faithfully." Louella Parsons continued her vendetta against *Kane* behind the scenes—there were rumors that she was enlisting her lackeys to boo if it won anything—but she devoted her column to the Battle of the Sisters, each of whom gave Parsons gracious quotes about the other. As for their supposed feud, de Havilland said, "Of course we fight. What two sisters don't battle?"

Fontaine had learned of her nomination on the set of *The Constant Nymph*. She claimed that she didn't expect to win, as *Suspicion* was not the "classic" *Rebecca* was. On the day of the ceremony, the Academy called her at the studio in Burbank to ask if she planned to attend. She said no—she had an eight-o'clock call the next morning. Immediately, she got another call, this time from Olivia, who told her that she *must* attend the banquet, because her absence would "look odd."

"But I haven't anything to wear!" Joan said.

Within an hour, Olivia swanned into the dressing room with a saleslady from I. Magnin, bearing striped boxes of every size-six dress from the store. "Between takes," Fontaine recalled, "I tried on the dresses, finally selecting a ballet-length black number with a lace skirt and mantilla, which was hastily basted to fit me." The sisters' job that night was clear: to put on a good face, both to the watchful crowd and to each other. In short, to act their hearts out.

The Hollywood that arrived at the Biltmore on February 26, 1942, had even more cause than usual for dread. Weeks earlier, the beloved star Carole Lombard was flying back from a war bond rally, along with her mother and fifteen servicemen, when their plane crashed in the mountains near Las Vegas; a beacon had been turned off out of fear that Japanese warplanes were poised to attack. Lombard's death left Clark Gable a widower and gave Hollywood an omen of the costs of war to come.

Then, two nights before the Oscars, military radar picked up what seemed to be enemy aircraft some 120 miles off the coast of Los Angeles. Air raid sirens blared, the city was put under a blackout order, and searchlights swept the sky, as if for a movie premiere. Just after 3 a.m., artillery batteries blasted more than 1,400 rounds of anti-aircraft ammunition, lighting up the sky with what the Los Angeles Times called "beautiful, if sinister, orange bursts of shrapnel." But when the smoke cleared, there were no warplanes; it was all a false alarm, possibly caused by a weather balloon. The "Battle of Los Angeles" was, in true Hollywood fashion, an illusion.

Less than forty-eight hours later, sixteen hundred of Hollywood's elite arrived at the Biltmore—a record-high turnout, requiring the hotel staff to cram in extra tables behind the orchestra. The ballroom was festooned with Allied flags in lieu of flowers. The military makeover extended to James Stewart, the previous year's Best Actor, who showed up in uniform on a one-day furlough from Moffett Field. Others had defied the Academy's edict against formal dress, with Hedda Hopper leading the charge. "Would it break down anyone's morale to see our girls beautifully dressed?" she had written, complaining that the toned-down affair would be "no dressier than a missionary's sewing bee."

De Havilland was the first sister to arrive, along with her date, Burgess Meredith, who was to be inducted the next day as a buck private. Fontaine came on her husband's arm, and the sisters were seated at David O. Selznick's table, face-to-face. They barely touched their plates as they sensed a roomful of stares. As one columnist observed, "the two girls faced each other, chatting and smiling with forced gaiety and nonchalance. Meanwhile 1,600 sets of eyes shifted curiously from the entertainment above to the sisterly drama below." De Havilland couldn't hide how she felt about seeing John Huston, who was nominated for two writing awards, for *The Maltese Falcon* and (with three cowriters) *Sergeant York*. Though he was there with his wife, he and de Havilland blew kisses across the dance floor, a display that William Wyler's wife described as "uncomfortably obvious."

At least none of them had to deal with Bette Davis—the sisters' competitor, Wyler's ex-lover, and Huston's ex-tormenter from *In This Our Life*. She had stayed home in New Hampshire, rather than make a scene after her Academy abdication. Also absent was John Ford, who was in Hawaii working on *December 7th*, a documentary for the U.S. Navy recounting the attack on Pearl Harbor. Orson Welles, expected to be the man of the hour, was in Rio de Janeiro filming *It's All True*, an ill-fated documentary he had been compelled to make by RKO and the Office of the Coordinator of Inter-American Affairs, Nelson Rockefeller's agency promoting "hemispheric solidarity" to counter the Axis powers.

The after-dinner presentation began at ten thirty, with an address by the guest of honor, Wendell Willkie, after his winning defense of the industry on the Senate floor. Willkie's speech was a blast of militarism. "We will not win this war on the defensive," he thundered. "Let's begin to strike. Let's begin to win." He couldn't help but point out the irony that, six months earlier, he had been defending Hollywood for producing propaganda against the very forces with which the United States was now at war.

The ceremony's host, Bob Hope, came out in a "Willkie for President" button and joked, "I haven't given up yet, and there's one for Hoover under it." With that out of the way, it was on to the awards, including two special prizes for Walt Disney's *Fantasia*. The Academy inaugurated a prize for documentaries, to recognize the glut of wartime reels such as *Soldiers of the Sky*, *Christmas Under Fire*, and the winner, *Churchill's Island*, chronicling the Battle of Britain.

And then another sort of blitz: the near-total annihilation of *Citizen Kane*. The black-and-white cinematography award—instead of going to Gregg Toland for his groundbreaking use of deep focus—went to Arthur Charles Miller for *How Green Was My Valley*. There was an unusually loud burst of applause—from Louella Parsons' minions. The same group turned to booing when Welles and Mankiewicz won Best Original Screenplay. Mixed with the jeering were shouts of "Mank! Mank! Where's Mank!"

Mankiewicz had stayed home. "He thought he'd get mad and do something drastic when he didn't win," his wife explained. In his bedroom wearing a bathrobe and slippers, he'd been feigning lack of interest in the radio broadcast of the ceremony. When he heard his name, he leaped up and waltzed around the room with his wife, despite having rebroken his leg in a drunken tumble.

That, as it turned out, was the only bright spot for *Kane*. The strange mixture of contrived boos and dumbfounded applause continued through the night, as it lost for scoring, sound recording, art direction, and editing. Cecil B. DeMille came out to present the Best Directing award not to Welles but to "Major Ford," flubbing John Ford's actual rank, which was commander. Ford's boss, Lieutenant Colonel Darryl Zanuck, accepted the prize, then returned to the dais when *How Green Was My Valley* won Best Picture.

The acting prizes came last. Welles's last chance for a comeback was dashed when James Stewart presented Best Actor to Gary Cooper, who said, "It was Sergeant Alvin York who won this award," and then forgot to take his statuette.

The Academy had saved the Battle of the Sisters for last. Fontaine was so down on her chances that she bet Wendell Willkie ten dollars to his twenty-five that she would lose. Now both sisters watched Ginger Rogers read off the Best Actress nominees. Rogers later said that she was hoping neither sister would win, which may explain why she haplessly held the card upside down. She turned it around: the winner was Joan Fontaine.

As the room erupted in cheers, Fontaine froze. From across the table, she heard a dominating whisper. It was de Havilland, ordering her, "Get up there!" The younger sister had won the Oscar first. "Now what had I done!" Fontaine recalled thinking, as their enmity came roaring to the surface. "All the animus we'd felt toward each other as children, the hair-pullings, the savage wrestling matches, the time Olivia fractured my collarbone, all came rushing back in kaleidoscopic imagery. My paralysis was total. I felt Olivia would spring across the table and grab me by the hair. I felt age four, being confronted by my older sister. Damn it, I'd incurred her wrath again!"

Fontaine gave her speech in a daze and then returned to their table, where she grasped de Havilland's hand, "appalled that I'd won over my sister." Hedda Hopper, reviewing Fontaine's attempt at graciousness, sniped that the younger sister "could have learned naturalness and sincerity from her sister Olivia, who sat across the table from her. It was the worst performance of Ophelia I've ever seen—and I've seen some bad performances in my time." Olivia smiled faintly. Later, a *Life* reporter overheard her whispering to friends, "If *Suspicion* had been delayed just a little, it wouldn't have gotten under the wire for this year's Award and I might have won . . ."

Fontaine returned to the set of *The Constant Nymph* the next day, cradling her statuette like a doll. "That Oscar can be a jinx," she reflected years later. "Winning an Academy Award is undoubtedly a great accolade, supreme praise from one's peers, a recognition to be accepted gratefully and graciously. It can also damage irreparably one's relations with family, friends, co-workers, the press. In those days, winners of the Oscar seemed like minor members of royalty suddenly elevated to the throne. All eyes watched to see the slightest sign of arrogance, inflated ego, disdain . . . It was a fishbowl existence until the next year's awards, when a new winner would occupy the throne. Naturally, there was many a doubter, many a detractor, many an ill-wisher. It's an uneasy head that wears the crown."

WRITING IN 1971, NEW YORKER critic Pauline Kael cast the drubbing of *Citizen Kane* not just as an embarrassment for the Academy but as a moral failure. "The Academy members had made their token gesture to 'Citizen Kane' with the screenplay award," she wrote. "They failed what they believed in; they gave in to the scandal and to the business pressures. They couldn't yet know how much guilt they *should* feel: guilt that by their failure to support 'Citizen Kane' at this crucial time—the last chance to make 'Kane' a financial success—they had started the downward spiral of Orson Welles, who was to become perhaps the greatest loser in Hollywood history." This wasn't just a problem for Welles, Kael believed, but one with epochal consequences. If the Academy voters "had backed the nation's press and their own honest judgment," she speculated, "the picture might have got into the big theatrical showcases despite the pressures against it. If they had, 'Kane' might have made money, and things might have gone differently for Welles—and for American movies."

So, why *did* the Academy get it so wrong? The finger-pointing started the very next day, when Welles's near washout was, according to *Variety*, "the chief topic of conversation around the gin rummy tables." The trade paper blamed the unwashed masses, writing, "That most of the 6,000 extras who voted scuttled his chances is foregone. The mob prefers a regular guy to a genius." Under this theory, *Citizen Kane* might have won had Bette Davis been allowed to disenfranchise the extras during her presidency. But the extras voted only for Best Picture, Best Original Song, and the four acting awards, so they couldn't be blamed for Welles's directing loss. And it certainly didn't explain editing and cinematography, which were chosen by small committees of experts. *Citizen Kane* had been rejected by commoners *and* the elite.

Another theory was that Welles was an outsider. "The fact that every mention of Welles or the picture at the Academy dinner drew scattered boos and catcalls suggests that the voters resented him as an inexcusably brilliant newcomer," the *New York Times* observed; his treatment had revealed the "clannishness of the town." Kael echoed the idea: "The members of the Academy destroyed Orson Welles that night, but they probably felt good because their hearts had gone out to crazy, reckless Mank, their own resident loser-genius." In that version, it was only because Mankiewicz had insisted on screen credit that *Citizen Kane* won anything at all.

But there were other factors. After Pearl Harbor, *Kane*'s tragic ruth-lessness, its skepticism toward mass media, was even more out of step with the zeitgeist than when it premiered. And the Hearst papers had spent months campaigning against or ignoring *Kane*, which blunted it at the box office. The Hearst saga had put the entire industry through a painful months-long ringer, and for what? A critical hit that couldn't turn a profit?

Compare Welles to John Ford, a master craftsman whose movies also made money. *How Green Was My Valley*, unlike *Kane*, had a sentimental heart and not an ounce of cynicism. Fox had mounted a major campaign for the film, late enough in the season that it was fresh in voters' minds. Also, Ford had won for *The Grapes of Wrath* the year before, but it hadn't won Best Picture. The *Times* further theorized that the Best Picture win was a way to make amends to Fox, which had never won the top prize under Zanuck, including for *The Grapes of Wrath*.

But there may have been a deeper disconnect between the Academy and *Citizen Kane*. Ever since Welles's arrival in Hollywood, his excep-tionality had threatened the way of doing business, one that favored the assembly line over a single artist's vision. Welles modeled a version of auteurism that wouldn't catch on in Hollywood until the sixties—not incidentally, the era in which Welles and *Citizen Kane* would be embraced by European critics and young countercultural directors like Peter Bogdanovich. But unlike Ford or Capra, he wasn't a hitmaker, just a troublemaker. In 1942, Welles wasn't merely an *enfant terrible* in need of a spanking; he was a weapon pointed at the entire business model.

Unsurprisingly, Hollywood gatekeepers were pleased with the results. "Everybody was happy about the way the voting went," Hedda Hopper wrote, though she was dismayed to see "most of our girls wearing street clothes, which robbed Hollywood of its glamour." Louella Parsons ignored the Welles shutout completely, beaming, "Good to see Darryl so happy and to feel the awards were so well deserved."

ULTIMATELY, IT'S LESS SHOCKING THAT *Citizen Kane* lost than that *Sergeant York*, the film that introduced Hollywood's flag-waving next chapter, didn't win. The Bureau of Motion Pictures, which President Roosevelt formed in 1942, now worked arm in arm with the studios to make sure the movies carried patriotic messaging with clear heroes and villains. The government vetted scripts, scotched objectionable plotlines, and provided manuals on how to aid the war effort. (Question No. 1: "Will this picture help win the war?") Hollywood eagerly played along, churning out spy thrillers, tropical romances, and morale-boosting musicals like *Star Spangled Rhythm*. Laurel and Hardy became air raid wardens. Bugs Bunny battled "slant-eye" Japanese soldiers. The public ate it up, rewarding Hollywood with record-breaking profits. By the end of 1943, 264 of the 545 films in production or development were related to the war. Once a taboo, the war was now the driving force in American movies.

In October 1942, Bette Davis found a new role that gave her the sense of largesse the Academy presidency could not—as the cofounder of the Hollywood Canteen, a nightclub on Cahuenga Boulevard where servicemen headed for the war front could mix with Hollywood personalities for one last hurrah. Betty Grable danced with soldiers. Rita Hayworth served pie. "I found the work exhilarating and rewarding," Davis recalled. The Canteen was so successful—not only for its patrons but for Hollywood's image—that in 1944, Warner Bros. turned it into a star-studded movie, in which Davis played herself. Olivia de Havilland gamely served coffee at the Canteen, while Joan Fontaine trained to be a nurse's aide and worked shifts at local hospitals. Down the street, Orson Welles (who, for medical reasons, had been deemed unfit for the military) staged *The Mercury Wonder Show*, a variety-and-magic spectacle in which "Orson the Magnificent" entertained the troops by sawing starlets in half.

John Ford learned about his Oscar victory for *How Green Was My Valley* while in Hawaii shooting *December 7th*. "The Navy is very proud of me," he wrote his wife. "It's made a tremendous impression. Admirals, generals, etc. have called to congratulate me. Strange!" That June, he was dispatched to film the Battle of Midway, pointing his 16-millimeter handheld camera at the oncoming Japanese planes. The four-day clash ended with a decisive win against the Imperial Japanese Navy, but in his documentary, Ford tempered the triumphalism with the elegiac tone he had brought to *How Green Was My Valley*. When President Roosevelt watched *The Battle of Midway*, he turned to his chief of staff and said, "I want every mother in America to see this film."

The Battle of Midway gave the public an indelible view of the war in the Pacific. It was also Ford's chance at another Oscar. Though the director professed to disdain awards, he made sure to screen the film for Academy president Walter Wanger and persuaded him to open up the new documentary category to multiple winners. Of the astounding twenty-five nominees in 1943, more than half were produced by the government or the military. *The Battle of Midway* was among the four cowinners.

The Oscars in 1943 were even more bathed in regalia than the year before. Jeanette MacDonald sang multiple verses of the national anthem, and Wanger read a letter from Roosevelt praising the industry for "turning the tremendous power of the motion picture into an effective war instrument." Due to the metal shortage, the Academy announced that the statuettes that year would be made of plaster, to be redeemed for gold-plated ones after the war. The winners received them in front of a giant banner reading "27,677," the number of motion picture workers in uniform. The Best Picture winner was Wyler's *Mrs. Miniver*, a film that had stirred such fervent emotion that Winston Churchill had (supposedly) told Louis B. Mayer that it was "propaganda worth a hundred battleships." Colonel Frank Capra presented the directing prize to Mrs. Wyler, who let the crowd know that her husband was filming a bombing raid in Germany.

By 1944, the Academy had its wartime act down pat. Three months before D-day, the ceremony played out in front of ten rows of soldiers and sailors, who sat onstage as honorary guests. *Casablanca* took the top prize, over other wartime pictures, like *In Which We Serve* and the Bette Davis vehicle *Watch on the Rhine*. Ford's *December 7th* won the Best Documentary, Short Subject award on behalf of the U.S. Navy and the Field Photo Unit. And the Oscars were no longer a banquet: the Academy had moved them for the first time to a theater, Grauman's Chinese, and invited members of the public. Just two years after asking Davis what she had against the Academy, Walter Wanger had done exactly what she had suggested.

HOLLYWOOD MAY HAVE BEEN THREATENED by Welles, but it missed the danger lurking closer to home: Olivia de Havilland. After she lost the Oscar to Joan, Warner Bros. placed her in the middling comedy *Princess O'Rourke*, another romance with a wartime hook. De Havilland was miserable, ill, and—now that Huston was off at war—lonely. Her temperament and her health worsened when she was put into a hackneyed period piece called *Devotion*, playing Charlotte Brontë. Fed up by years of inferior roles, she walked out on her contract. Over her eleven years at Warner Bros., she'd been suspended six times, with each suspension tacked to the end of her contract, leaving her in a state of perpetual indentured servitude. So, she took the studio to court, attempting to win where Bette Davis had failed in 1936. In late 1944, California's Second District Court of Appeal decided in de Havilland's favor, a landmark ruling that limited studio contracts to seven calendar years. The "De Havilland Law," as it became known, was a major blow to the exploitative treatment of Hollywood actors and contributed to the unwinding of the studio system over the next two and a half decades.

Even Fontaine was impressed. "Every contract player owed Olivia a great debt of gratitude," she conceded. That same year, Fontaine was nominated for Best Actress again, for *The Constant Nymph*, but lost to Jennifer Jones. Fontaine's Oscar for *Suspicion* seemed to have changed the balance between the sisters. The press marveled that Joan, once a "frail, sickly child," had now become "a picture of radiant vitaminity." She must have taken special satisfaction when de Havilland called her up and said, "Well, it's happened."

"What's happened?"

"*It.*" Olivia read aloud from a newspaper clipping: "'Olivia de Havilland, who is Joan Fontaine's sister . . .'"

Liberated from Warner Bros., de Havilland could finally pursue better roles, despite Jack Warner's attempts to blacklist her. In 1947, she was nominated for Best Actress for Paramount's *To Each His Own*. Joan, now married to her second husband, William Dozier, was presenting the Best Actor prize. By then, the sisters' relationship had become strained even farther. De Havilland was newly married to author Marcus Goodrich, about whom Fontaine had cracked, "All I know about him is that he has had four wives and written one book. Too bad it's not the other way around." When the remark got back to Olivia, she was furious.

The incident was still fresh at the 1947 awards. De Havilland had told her publicist, "If you don't see us together there is a reason—if I happen to win, I won't acknowledge any gesture on her part in public unless she comes to me privately first." De Havilland finally did win her first Oscar, but when Fontaine rushed over to congratulate her, Olivia turned her back and walked away. A *Photoplay* photographer captured the icy moment on camera. The snapshot—smiling Joan, stony Olivia—gave the public proof that the feud wasn't just a press invention.

The sisters didn't speak for several years, during which de Havilland won a second Oscar, for *The Heiress*, and divorced Goodrich. By then, de Havilland said, "it seemed ridiculous to demand this apology after I'd separated from the man about whom the issue arose." The sisters resumed "diplomatic relations" but led separate lives. De Havilland moved to Paris and married French writer Pierre Galante, occasionally returning to Hollywood for movie roles or appearances at the Academy Awards. On the rare instance when the sisters got together, it didn't go well. At a birthday party for Joan's daughter Deborah, they started squabbling while posing for a family portrait. "It was like two little girls," Deborah recalls. "'Look at what she's doing!' 'Well, she knows what *she's* doing!' Joan had a way of getting under her skin, and [Olivia] thought it was deliberate. It might have been. It was amazing how childish they became. I thought they were going to slap each other."

In 1975, Fontaine was doing dinner theater in Rhode Island when she got word that their eighty-eight-year-old mother had terminal cancer. Unable to leave her tour, she cabled de Havilland in Paris. Two weeks later, she got a call from Santa Barbara: it was her sister, who, according to Fontaine, wasn't convinced their mother had cancer at all and who proposed an exploratory operation. Joan was aghast; Olivia had taken control again. After Lilian died, Fontaine found out that her mother had been cremated without her consultation and that Olivia had planned a memorial while Joan was still on the road. Joan threatened to go to the press unless the service was postponed. At the memorial, the sisters kept their distance from each other. "As for Olivia," Fontaine wrote, "I had no words at all."

The sisters refused to speak to each other—for the rest of their lives.

The legend of Hollywood's most long-standing sibling rivalry only grew. In 1978, both were invited to the Oscars' fiftieth ceremony, to appear in a lineup of living winners. They stayed on opposite sides of the stage. A decade later, they were brought back for another anniversary broadcast. When Fontaine found out the two were staying in adjacent hotel rooms, she asked to switch rooms and vowed never to attend the Oscars again. "I got married first, got an Academy Award first, had a child first," she said. "If I die, she'll be furious, because again I'll have got there first!"

Fontaine did die first, in 2013, at ninety-six. Her daughter Deborah Dozier Potter called her aunt Olivia with the news. Deborah recalls, "She said, 'Oh, how are you this morning?' I said, 'Your sister died.' 'Oh, and what are your plans for this Sunday?' 'Your sister died.' 'And how is your wonderful husband?' 'Your sister died.' And she said, 'What are we going to say when the press calls?' She just went right there. And we decided to say we were 'shocked and saddened.'"

De Havilland died seven years later, at 104. The feud followed them to their obituaries. "Imagine," Fontaine once said, "what we could have done if we had gotten together. We could have selected the right scripts, the right directors, the right producers—we could have built our own empire. But it was not to be."

AFTER THE *CITIZEN KANE* BLOODBATH, Orson Welles good-humoredly wrote his cowinner. "Dear Mankie: Here's what I wanted to wire you after the Academy Dinner: 'You can kiss my half.'" Mankiewicz quipped back that his acceptance speech would have gone, "I am very happy to accept this award in Mr. Welles' absence because the script was written in Mr. Welles' absence."

Welles wouldn't have resented his cinematic master, John Ford, for winning the directing award, but the Oscar might have saved his Hollywood career from hitting a wall. That spring, RKO pulled *Citizen Kane* from circulation, at a loss of over $150,000. George Schaefer was forced to resign as the studio's president, and the new management pulled funding from Welles's South American documentary, which was never completed. While he was in Brazil, RKO took control of his latest film, *The Magnificent Ambersons*, and tacked on a happy ending over his objections. The movie was unceremoniously released on a double bill with the Lupe Vélez comedy *Mexican Spitfire Sees a Ghost*. The new regime terminated Welles from RKO and announced a new studio motto that disowned even the idea of him: "Showmanship in Place of Genius."

Citizen Kane was the beginning and end of Welles's artistic autonomy in Hollywood. He spent the rest of his career fighting with studios, scrounging for funds, and taking acting roles and commercials to pay for his passion projects. In 1943, he agreed to play Mr. Rochester in Fox's *Jane Eyre*, opposite Joan Fontaine. Fontaine, who cracked that "everything about him was oversized, including his ego," could sense Welles bucking against his restraints. On the first day, he arrived three hours late and announced to everyone (including the director), "Now we'll begin on page four." Although his oeuvre would include lauded works like *Touch of Evil*, Welles never regained the golden chance he'd been given for *Citizen Kane*. He lamented, "I had luck as no one had; afterwards, I had the worst luck in the history of cinema."

Citizen Kane, meanwhile, was largely forgotten in America. It wasn't until French cineastes such as André Bazin championed it in the fifties that it began its road back to the pantheon. In 1962, a once-a-decade survey in the British film magazine *Sight and Sound* ranked it as the best movie ever made, and it kept the top spot for five decades. In 1971, with the New Hollywood anointing a new generation of star directors, the Academy gave Welles an honorary Oscar, presented by his friend John Huston. The prize was an apology for its rejection of *Citizen Kane*. But Welles didn't show up, and sent a videotaped acceptance instead. Huston explained that he was "filming abroad." In fact, he was watching from a house in Laurel Canyon.

Perhaps he had been too burned by the Hollywood establishment. Or perhaps he was still reeling from a two-part takedown by Pauline Kael that had appeared weeks earlier in *The New Yorker*. In the same piece in which she derided the Academy for snubbing *Citizen Kane*, she passionately undercut the idea that Welles deserved sole credit for its brilliance, which she thought belonged to Herman Mankiewicz, who had been dead for eighteen years. Kael's fifty-thousand-word broadside deeply hurt Welles and drew vigorous pushback from his defenders, including Peter Bogdanovich, who wrote a ten-thousand-word rebuttal in *Esquire*. Even John Houseman, who had been one of Kael's sources, said, "Orson brings these things on himself by trying to take credit for everything. Pauline Kael got all her facts right but just carried her conclusions too far."

Nevertheless, the debate over *Citizen Kane*'s authorship continued year after year, eclipsing even the Hearst saga in the public perception of the film. The movie's sole Oscar, awarded to both men, was like a "Rosebud" pointing back to some unsolvable riddle: Who wrote *Citizen Kane?* The legend of Mankiewicz's underappreciation reached its apotheosis with David Fincher's *Mank*, in which Gary Oldman played Mankiewicz as a slurring, acid-tongued genius and Welles barely appeared at all. In 2021, *Mank* was nominated for ten Academy Awards, the most of any film that year. In true *Citizen Kane* fashion, it lost all but two.

FOUR

The Greatest Star

1951

How the women of *Sunset Boulevard, All About Eve,*
and *Born Yesterday* navigated Hollywood's double
standard—and a Best Actress race for the ages.

B illy Wilder knew that his next film had the explosive potential of
dynamite. That's why he made sure word didn't get out: not to the
trade press, not to industry people, and certainly not to the president
of Paramount, Barney Balaban, who might well cancel the project if he
knew what they were up to. Every night when he and his writing partner,
Charles Brackett, left their office on the lot, Wilder's secretary locked
their papers in an iron drawer. On Thursdays, Brackett would have to
report their progress to the higher-ups, so Wilder made up notes on a
fictitious project called *A Can of Beans*—a film as innocuous-sounding
as it was phony and which had nothing to do with the movie they were
actually making, *Sunset Boulevard.*

The real title finally appeared on the sixty-one pages they submitted
on December 21, 1948, marked "For Limited Distribution." "This is the
first act of *Sunset Boulevard,*" the first page read. "Due to the peculiar

nature of the project, we ask all our co-workers to regard it as top secret."
Wilder and Brackett had the clout to pull off such shenanigans thanks
to the success of *The Lost Weekend*, their 1945 film, which had won four
Oscars, including Best Picture and Best Directing. They followed it with
The Emperor Waltz and *A Foreign Affair*, both in 1948, and were now
Paramount's princes of smartly cynical entertainments.

A *Foreign Affair*, with its irreverent view of American officialdom,
was denounced on the floor of the U.S. Congress. But *Sunset Boulevard*
would do something bolder: it held a disenchanted mirror up to their own
industry, one that chewed people up and left them desperate, wasted,
and mad. Wilder and Brackett had been toying with the idea for five
years before they sat down, in the summer of 1948 (along with a third
writer, D. M. Marshman Jr.), and started hashing out the story of a down-
on-his-luck young screenwriter entangled with a washed-up silent movie
"queen" who declares, in her delusion, "I'm the greatest star of them all!"
Her bouts of madness had elements of silent stars Clara Bow and Mae
Murray, and her name, "Norma Desmond," recalled scandal-struck ghosts
like Mabel Normand and William Desmond Taylor.

But who could play this glamorous monster? "We needed a passé star
who has gone down the tubes," Wilder explained later. "And the reason
we needed a *real* passé star to play her was because it's very difficult to
find a woman in her sixties, let us say, who is undiscovered—where was
she until sixty? It would be hard to believe she was ever a big star. So we
went after one who had been big."

Hollywood's first generation of stars had now reached middle age,
holed up in mansions like fossils no one had bothered to excavate, their
films disintegrating in studio vaults. For women, valued for their youth
and beauty—while it lasted—the calculus was particularly cruel. To be a
star was to have the most visible power a woman could get in Hollywood,
but it was power in a vise. You had to be pretty, thin, and, with rare
exceptions, white. You had to endure the attentions of influential men
who treated sex as a form of droit de seigneur, the "right" of feudal lords
to bed women on their wedding nights. If you strayed from a narrow
moral path—like Ingrid Bergman, who became pregnant during an affair
with Roberto Rossellini—you were banished. You were pitted against

one another, if not by yourselves (as with Joan Fontaine and Olivia de Havilland), then by the gossip columns, the studios, and the Oscars, where the Best Actress race served as a contrived catfight. And if you did nothing wrong at all, you would commit the crime of aging. Hence a plethora of potential Norma Desmonds.

Wilder called first on Hollywood's most famous absentee, Greta Garbo, seven years into her self-imposed exile. Her very name conjured stardust. In 1939, Wilder and Brackett, along with Walter Reisch, had written her role in *Ninotchka*. As they contemplated *Sunset Boulevard*, Wilder invited Garbo to his house on North Beverly Drive for a drink and peppered her with story ideas. But the only role she wished to play—which, of course, she never did—was of a woman posing as a male clown. Wilder suspected that she wanted to "hide behind greasepaint," he said. "She could play the clown in white makeup so no one would be able to see her face."

A more radical road not taken was Mae West. When Wilder and Brackett pitched her *Sunset Boulevard*, it was a comedy about an aging burlesque star. West, who hadn't done a film since 1943, enjoyed the thought of being around handsome young fellas. But she didn't consider herself someone who'd need a gigolo to flatter her—more like the other way around. "The idea of Mae West was idiotic," Wilder said. Next on the list was Mary Pickford, living in extravagant seclusion. "Mr. Brackett and I went to see her at Pickfair," Wilder claimed, "but she was too drunk—she was not interested."

Yet another rejection came from Pola Negri, the imperious Polish-born star. In her Jazz Age heyday, she was a tempestuous glamour puss, carrying on high-profile romances with Chaplin and Valentino, demanding fresh orchid petals on the floors of her dressing rooms, and walking a pet leopard down Sunset Boulevard. With those credentials, she might have been a grand Norma Desmond. But she supposedly told Wilder, "I'm too young to play a fifty-five-year-old woman!" (Negri was somewhere around her early fifties at the time, but her birth date was a moving target.) Before her death in 1987, she clarified, "I had pneumonia at the time."

Perhaps it's not surprising that Wilder had trouble casting the part of an aging has-been, even if Norma Desmond herself would have leaped at the opportunity. But, by the time they turned in their "top secret" draft, Wilder and Brackett had a strong idea of who they wanted to play the main roles. Under "The Actors We Hope to Get," they listed Gloria Swanson. "We knew no time would be wasted getting into the story as soon as Swanson appeared on the screen," Brackett said. "Youngsters who never saw her would immediately accept her as an old-time movie queen. Older fans would identify her with the characterization and get a bigger emotional wallop from the story."

Whether Swanson, who had not appeared in a feature since 1941, would feel differently from Mae West, Mary Pickford, or Pola Negri was another matter.

"THAT TERRIBLE GIRL" IS HOW Elisabeth Bergner described the real-life woman who would come to be known as Eve Harrington. This was the summer of 1944, or thereabouts, and Bergner was in the kitchen of a Vermont farmhouse showing a young acquaintance how to make Wiener schnitzel and rambling about the understudy who had taken over her life.

Born in the Austro-Hungarian Empire in 1897, Bergner fled Hitler. In 1936, she lost the Best Actress Oscar to Bette Davis, for *Dangerous*. Now in her forties, Bergner had just starred in the Broadway play *The Two Mrs. Carrolls*. The director was Reginald Denham, and the young acquaintance Bergner was instructing was Denham's soon-to-be-wife, Mary Orr, an actress and playwright. En route to Maine, the couple had stopped in Vermont to see Bergner and her husband. As the two men talked, Bergner invited Orr to the kitchen, where she started confiding to her about "that terrible girl," also known as "that awful creature" or "that little bitch."

Every night after the performance of *The Two Mrs. Carrolls*, "that terrible girl" had stood outside the stage door in a little red coat. She claimed to have seen every performance. Curious and touched, Bergner invited the young woman to her dressing room one night, where she recounted, speaking with an English accent, how she had also fled Europe in the thirties. A few days later, Bergner arranged for the girl in the red coat to be her husband's secretary. When a replacement was needed for Bergner's castmate Irene Worth, the girl volunteered to read Bergner's role at the auditions. But then the girl had insinuated herself into the older actress's life, even gone after her husband. She wasn't even British—she'd picked up her accent from the movies. "It certainly became an obsession with Elisabeth about that girl," Orr recalled.

The next morning, Orr asked her hotel for a typewriter and stationery and didn't stop writing for three days. Written from the perspective of a playwright's wife, "The Wisdom of Eve" was a short story about an actress named Margola Cranston and her manipulative protégée, Eve Harrington. The first line: "A young girl is on her way to Hollywood with a contract for one thousand dollars a week from a major film company in her pocketbook." The last: "She's going to marry my husband, Lloyd Richards." *Cosmopolitan* paid Orr eight hundred dollars and published "The Wisdom of Eve" in its May 1946 issue. (Decades later, author Sam Staggs tracked down the real "Eve," Martina Lawrence, who said, "I read the story and was flattered and fascinated, but shocked by its slant, by its erroneous point of view.")

Three years after the story was published, Orr, who was scrambling for money after her husband had busted both legs during a bird-watching trip, turned "The Wisdom of Eve" into a radio play. It aired on NBC's *Radio Guild Playhouse* in January 1949, with Orr in the role of the playwright's wife, Karen Richards. Within days, 20th Century–Fox offered to option "The Wisdom of Eve" for five thousand dollars.

Orr never met Joseph L. Mankiewicz, but both saw something in this tale of a fan gone rogue: the lure of the phony, the way that show business dreams curdle into treachery. Eve Harringtons were everywhere in the theater—and in Hollywood, where Mankiewicz had followed his older brother, Herman, and labored as a screenwriter for Paramount and then a writer and producer at MGM. Herman's Oscar for *Citizen Kane* only spurred Joseph's ambitions. With his reputation for blade-sharp, literate dialogue, Joseph was now well into his career as a director at 20th Century–Fox. Like Billy Wilder, he was coasting off an Oscar-laureled success, having won Best Directing and Best Screenplay for *A Letter to Three Wives*.

The Oscar campaign had brought Mankiewicz face-to-face with the ugliness of show business. Fox's Darryl Zanuck had told him that the studio wouldn't campaign for *A Letter to Three Wives* and would instead put its efforts into *Twelve O'Clock High*, which Zanuck had produced himself. The shoddy treatment made Mankiewicz's double win extra sweet, but it also made him wonder about the "cockamaimy immortality" of the award, along with "the conniving and soliciting and maneuvering that goes on for the acquisition of it—and, in the end, the strangely unenduring gratification it provides," he recalled. "Award-winning can often be followed, almost reactively, by a period of depression—not unlike suddenly going off amphetamines. Anyway, I found myself pondering these and other ramifications of 'The Award' syndrome; it would make an excellent frame, I thought, for a film . . ." The Academy Award, born as an afterthought, was now inspiring movies itself.

Mankiewicz had read "The Wisdom of Eve" nearly a year before winning his Oscars, and he urged Zanuck to act on Fox's option. In a memo dated April 29, 1949, he proposed combining the story with an "original idea" of his, and added, "Superb starring role for Susan Hayward." Later that year, Mankiewicz retreated to a ranch near Santa Barbara and wrote a treatment in longhand, titled *Best Performance*. Zanuck read through it with a pencil in hand. On one page, the acerbic drama critic Addison DeWitt says in a voiceover, "Eve . . . but more of Eve, later. All about Eve, in fact." Zanuck underlined the words "All about Eve."

Hayward had starred in Mankiewicz's latest film, *House of Strangers*. But, at thirty-two, she was too young to play Margo Channing—as Margola Cranston had been renamed. Zanuck's first choice was Marlene Dietrich, but Mankiewicz "simply could not visualize—or 'hear'—her as a possible Margo." Fox drew up a list of potential cast members. For Eve: Elizabeth Taylor, Olivia de Havilland, Donna Reed. For Margo: Katharine Hepburn, Ginger Rogers, Joan Crawford, Gloria Swanson, Rosalind Russell, Barbara Stanwyck, Bette Davis.

Soon the pieces fell into place. In February 1950, Fox announced that it had signed the forty-six-year-old Claudette Colbert to play Margo. For Eve, Zanuck had thought of Jeanne Crain, fresh off an Oscar-nominated role in *Pinky*, but Mankiewicz didn't think she had the "bitch virtuosity" for the role. He suggested Anne Baxter, who was under contract with

Fox. Born in Indiana in 1923, Baxter was a granddaughter of architect Frank Lloyd Wright. She'd made her Broadway début at thirteen, showing flashes of Eve when she told the *New York Evening Journal*, "There is no stopping ambition. I always like to dramatize things in my life."

Now twenty-six, Baxter had won the Best Supporting Actress prize in 1947 for *The Razor's Edge*. Zanuck thought she was a "cold potato," but she had an overriding asset: a resemblance to Claudette Colbert, which would establish Eve as a mini-Margo who morphs into her idol. It wasn't to be. Colbert was shooting a scene in the war drama *Three Came Home* in which her character fends off a would-be rapist. After a particularly vigorous take, she suffered several fractured vertebrae and a ruptured disc.

Mankiewicz, bereft that his Margo had been waylaid, sent Colbert flowers tied to a pogo stick. Fox tried to postpone production of *All About Eve*, but the studio had rented San Francisco's Curran Theatre for location scenes, and production had to begin on April 3, 1950. Mankiewicz tried Gertrude Lawrence, who had just filmed the role of Amanda Wingfield in *The Glass Menagerie*. As Mankiewicz recalled, Lawrence's lawyer replied with two conditions: that the drunk scenes be eliminated and that the pianist in the party scene not play "Liebesträum" but, instead, "accompany Miss Lawrence as she sang a torch song."

So much for that. Now it was up to Zanuck to do something he surely did not want to do: call Bette Davis and offer her the role of Margo Channing. The last time Zanuck had spoken to her was in 1941, when she resigned as Academy president and he bellowed, "You'll never work in Hollywood again!" And here he was, about to offer her a job.

When Gloria Swanson got the call about *Sunset Boulevard*, she was in a hospital in New York. Shortly before Christmas, she had been shooting a holiday decorating segment for her new lifestyle TV series, *The Gloria Swanson Hour*, when she found herself bent over the banister in pain. The doctors told her she needed an appendectomy. She disagreed. After the surgery, she was still in agony. As she recuperated, she turned on a television set that had been sent to her by one of the networks. She had been so busy appearing on this new contraption called television that she hadn't bothered to watch any of it. "That's awful," she said as she watched one "cheap and thrown-together" program after the next, then dictated a letter to her secretary resigning from WPIX.

Half an hour later, the phone rang. A casting director from Paramount was asking her to come back to Hollywood for a screen test.

"I've made two dozen pictures for Paramount," she replied. "Why would they need to test me?" Besides, she said, she'd have to ask the doctor.

"Doctor!" the man said. "What's wrong?"

"Look, you called me, I didn't call you. This is a hospital number you've reached. I'm recovering from surgery."

Swanson had given up on the idea of "comebacks." Her last attempt had been in 1941, with *Father Takes a Wife*. It hadn't gone well, and she was content to return to "cinematic obscurity." She was more interested in her engineering company, Multiprises, which was exploring how to make buttons out of plastic. She had founded it in 1938, to satisfy her flair for inventions, and had helped rescue four Jewish scientists from Europe to work there. Meanwhile, her fifth marriage, to a rich man she barely knew, had ended after little more than a month.

Unlike Norma Desmond, Swanson preferred to look forward, not back. But in her mind's eye, she could still see lavish bungalows, jewels, her name on marquees. At her height, in the silent era, she had led every box-office poll and averaged ten thousand fan letters a week. She had helped define movie stardom as a form of American royalty—the movie magazines named her "Queen of the Screen." Central to her reign was her penchant for fabulous clothes: peacock feather headdresses, gowns of satin and gold, the finest Belgian lace. As one writer put it, "Is there anyone who can flaunt a superb wardrobe with more dash than Gloria Swanson?"

Inevitably, her career lurched to a halt. By the thirties, new stars were on the rise; in 1937, Warner Bros. had remade Swanson's film *The Trespasser* as *That Certain Woman*, starring Bette Davis. "On the one hand, I was a lucky American girl, picked at random out of millions, who had succeeded admirably and could therefore take it easy for a while," she recalled. "On the other, I was a legend—a sacred monster, in Jean Cocteau's phrase—a fading star the public had worshiped long enough, who was in search of a new type of role to fit." After a row with Harry Cohn, Swanson canceled her contract with Columbia and moved to New York, having concluded, approaching age forty, that her time as a star was up.

So, she could be forgiven for not jumping for joy when Paramount called, a decade later, about a screen test for what she assumed would be a bit part. Back at her apartment, another call came—this time from Charles Brackett, promising her that this was a major role in a major film to be directed by Billy Wilder.

"I know Mr. Wilder," Swanson said. "That is, he was a writer on one of my films, *Music in the Air*."

"I know," Brackett said. "Now, can you come out for the test? We're very anxious to talk to you." He said they would put her up at the Beverly Hills Hotel. If all went well with the test, the pay would be $50,000.

Swanson had been making $350 a week at WPIX. She turned to her mother, who sat nearby, and said, "Mother, we've had a dreadful Christmas. How would you like to make up for it and go to Beverly Hills with me for a few weeks?"

BETTE DAVIS WAS ON THE set of her latest film, *The Story of a Divorce*, when she received a call from someone claiming to be Darryl Zanuck. Of course, that was ludicrous—why would Zanuck deign to telephone her? Surely this was a prank. She decided to play along.

The man asked if he could send her a script. "Right away, right away, Darryl dear," Davis replied, keeping up the charade. At forty-one, she was used to battles of will. "In these years I made many enemies," she wrote later. "I was a legendary terror." Her roles only fed her "Hurricane Bette" reputation. In *The Story of a Divorce*, which would be retitled, to her dismay, *Payment on Demand*, she played what Bosley Crowther called one of "those woman-you-love-to-hate roles" that Davis had become famous for, the kind that required her to smoke, slap, and bristle as she delivered lines like "You tell me what it's worth to me to be civilized—or I'll show you how *uncivilized* I can be!"

The Story of a Divorce was a story Davis knew well. She was now on husband number three, who was about to become ex-husband number three. William Grant Sherry was a painter and physiotherapist whom Hedda Hopper would describe as a "handsome Greek God" with "mahogany tanned skin." Sherry had decided the moment they met that he would marry Bette Davis, and his determination was a turn-on. *What drive the man has!*, Davis told herself.

After their wedding, they left for Mexico on their honeymoon. On the drive down, Sherry threw his new bride out of the car, for reasons she later claimed to have forgotten. The bickering continued the first night in their hotel, when Sherry threw a steamer trunk across the room. Davis had to admit she was stimulated by his irascibility, which matched her own. But she was already in a tempestuous marriage—to the movies. "I was possessed with my career," she said. "Sherry was possessed with me."

She went back to work, in a remake of an Elisabeth Bergner film, *A Stolen Life*, around when Bergner was fending off "that terrible girl." At thirty-nine, Davis gave birth to a baby girl, Barbara Davis, called B.D. Being a mother shifted something in Davis: she had no desire to give up her career, but she was increasingly aware of the conflict between two Bettes, the actress and the "woman." The end of World War II had pushed working women back into the home, and, years before *The Feminine Mystique* and *Ms.* magazine, there was no road map for a woman like Davis. She could see her desire for a career and a family only as a battle, and she wasn't sure who would win. But, as with all Bette Davis battles, it would be a knockout fight.

After a year away from the screen, Davis's box-office draw had slipped. Her big return, *Winter Meeting*, was the rare Bette Davis film to lose money. Even she found it "dreary." She hated to be away from B.D. and was growing weary of marching into Mr. Warner's office to argue. She begged him not to saddle her with King Vidor's melodrama *Beyond the Forest*, but she succumbed. It was an embarrassment for Davis, who is remembered in the film only for her line "What a dump!" During dubbing, she delivered her last line for Warner Bros.—"I can't stand it here anymore"—and walked out after nineteen years.

By the time she started filming RKO's *The Story of a Divorce*, things with Sherry had worsened. Davis was terrified of her daughter becoming a target of his violent eruptions. He wanted dominion over his wife, but submission was not among her talents. It became clear that Sherry's attraction had been not only to Davis but to her earning potential, now on the wane. In April 1950, the cast and crew of *Payment on Demand* threw her a forty-second birthday party. Sherry wasn't invited, but when he showed up anyway, he found Davis sharing a drink with her costar Barry Sullivan and slugged him. The next day, Davis filed for divorce.

Amid all the turmoil—a career slump, a crumbling marriage—Davis could hardly believe that another adversary was calling her in the form of Darryl Zanuck. It soon became clear, however, that this wasn't an impersonator, but the real thing. He told her he was sending a script along; if she agreed to it, she'd have to start in ten days. *Why worry?*, she thought. *It's probably a lousy script, anyway.* But when *All About Eve* arrived, Davis was elated. In Margo Channing, she saw a woman much like her: an actress on the wrong side of forty, full of fight, torn between being a star and being a woman, whatever that meant. She would later tell Mankiewicz that he had "resurrected me from the dead."

WHEN GLORIA SWANSON'S CAR PULLED up to Paramount, it was a return twenty-three years in the making. California was celebrating the centennial of the California gold rush, and Paramount was playing along by flaunting its wealth of stars. Gazing up at the studio gates, Swanson saw a sign in the shape of a comet. From the tail to the head were photographs of Paramount players past and present, presumably in order of importance. Swanson looked for herself at the tail end: nothing. Out of curiosity, she glanced at the head of the comet and was shocked to see her once-famous profile. Her name still meant something here after all.

"Baby, am I glad to see you," she heard someone say. It was the chief casting director. "You took me off a helluva spot. If I'd put Crosby's picture on the front end of that comet, Hope would've blown his top, and Crosby would've had a fit if Hope was up there. Stanwyck or Hutton would've scratched my eyes out if one got top billing over the other. You turned out to be a real lifesaver."

So, that's what this was about: massaging egos. "That's how I knew I was home," Swanson would recall. "Right back in the jungle, up to my ears in the old rat race."

She had arrived by train with Mother, without so much as a clue to what the film was about. She still wasn't sure about the screen test, but her friend George Cukor assured her that Wilder and Brackett were "the brightest things in Hollywood" and advised, "If they ask you to do ten screen tests, do them, or I'll personally shoot you."

She found Wilder to be elfin and witty and "a bit overactive." He and Brackett assured her the test was a formality, mainly to try out the young actor they had in mind for the male lead. Swanson had never heard of Montgomery Clift, but she agreed. Wilder and Brackett admitted they hadn't finished the script, but they had the basic story: former movie queen returns, seduces a young writer, and somewhere along the way there's a murder.

"Who murders whom?" Swanson asked.

"We honestly aren't sure yet," said Wilder.

Over the next few days, Swanson took care of the screen test, the contract, and finding a temporary place to live. She reported to Paramount for publicity shots, where Brackett broke a delicate piece of news: Montgomery Clift had pulled out of the film, apparently because he didn't want to play love scenes with an older woman. Would she submit to a second screen test, this time with one William Holden?

"Joe Gillis, the writer in the script, is supposed to be twenty-five and you're supposed to play fifty," Brackett explained. "But Bill Holden is thirty-one and nervous that you'll look too young. We may have to age you with make-up. Not too much. Just a little."

Swanson, who was in fact fifty, shot back, "But women of fifty who take care of themselves today don't look old. That's the point. Can't you use make-up on Mr. Holden instead, to make him look more youthful?"

The few script pages she had been given included a description of Norma Desmond: "There is a curious style, a great sense of high voltage about her." As Wilder and Brackett finished the script, they melded Swanson's vanished world with Norma Desmond's. With some reluctance, Swanson agreed to supply stills in old frames, turning the Desmond mansion into a Swanson museum. Norma's "curious style" would be a decadent mix of turbans, furs, and (perhaps in a nod to Pola Negri) leopard prints. Working with Edith Head on her costumes, Swanson designed a peacock feather headdress like the one she wore in 1919 in *Male and Female*, in which she had played a scene with a live lion.

Her first day on set, Swanson was mobbed by old-timers: extras and technicians angling for a look of recognition, some of them having come over from adjacent sets to see if *the* Gloria Swanson was really there in the flesh. Swanson took her rightful place in front of the lights, and a hush descended across the studio. It was a scene that would recur in the film almost exactly, when Norma visits Paramount and an old studio hand bathes her in light, shouting, "Let's get a good look at you!"

Nancy Olson, the twenty-year-old ingénue hired to play winsome script reader Betty Schaefer, had never heard of Swanson, but she knew about Hollywood. "As inexperienced as I was, I sensed part of what was going on in *Sunset Boulevard*," Olson said decades later. "Even I realized they might not get away with it, because they were telling the story of how Hollywood makes promises it doesn't keep."

Swanson would go home each night with pages to memorize, then come in the next morning to find a fresh batch in her dressing room. She handled the changes like a pro, but they made it difficult for her to find her character. Frustrated, she told Brackett, "But I've got to know more about her—is she really nuts? Is her arrogance genuine, or is she faking it?" The truth is that Wilder and Brackett didn't know, either. But their open-endedness allowed them to tailor *Sunset Boulevard* to their star like a bejeweled gown.

In his effort to merge reality and fiction, Wilder cast the living ghosts of Swanson's era. Vienna-born Erich von Stroheim, who had directed Swanson in his 1932 film *Queen Kelly*, was playing Max, Norma's devoted butler; when the characters watched one of Norma's old films, they would be watching *Queen Kelly*. Buster Keaton had agreed to play himself. So had Cecil B. DeMille. Swanson had starred in six DeMille pictures between 1919 and 1921, and the scene showing Norma's big return to Paramount would be shot on the actual set of his latest film, *Samson and Delilah*. (Somehow, though he was in his sixties, DeMille's career hadn't ebbed like Swanson's.) "We're really going to mix up Hollywood then and now, real and imaginary," Brackett said. "What do you think?"

"I don't know," Swanson said. She meant it. When she heard that

DeMille was nervous about appearing on camera, she assured him, "Mr. DeMille, if you're just yourself, you'll be wonderful." With that, she recalled, "I grasped with fearful apprehension, for the first time, that the same certainly applied to me to a great extent, that I would have to use all my past experience for props, and that this picture should be a very revealing one to make, something akin to analysis."

During the two days they shot the final scene—Norma Desmond's deranged descent down the staircase—the set rustled with nervous excitement, as if something historic were about to happen. It was. Wilder had written Norma a breathtaking final aria, in which her delusions of fame come nightmarishly true just at the moment she descends into madness. The entire cast gathered to watch—even William Holden, whose character was by now floating dead in a swimming pool. Hedda Hopper, herself a former silent film actress, was playing herself. Naturally, she wrote up the proceedings in her column, snarking that Swanson "spent the first day sitting on a bed."

Descending the staircase, Swanson maintained her concentration, her eyes crazy-wide and her hands writhing like snakes. The staircase was curvy and narrow, and her feet were tiny, but she didn't want to break character by looking down. "On high heels I would have tripped for sure, so I played the scene barefoot," she recalled. "I imagined a steel ramrod in me from head to toe holding me together and descended as if in a trance." As Norma drifted toward the camera, ready for her close-up, Wilder let the camera lose its focus, as if Norma were cross-fading into her movie fantasies. Wilder yelled, "Print it!" Swanson burst into tears. The cast and crew handed her a gift with the inscription:

TO PROCLAIM THAT
GLORIA SWANSON
IS
THE GREATEST STAR OF THEM ALL

BETTE DAVIS ARRIVED IN SAN FRANCISCO in a panic: she had woken up that morning with her voice reduced to a croak. She found Mankiewicz, who blanched—they were due to start filming *All About Eve* in two days.

He found her a doctor, who advised her to go on vocal rest. But when she showed up at the Curran for the first day of principal photography, she still sounded hoarse. "Oh, what am I going to do about it?" she asked Mankiewicz.

The wily director smiled. "Honey, we're going to keep it," he said. "It's the whiskey-throated voice that Margo should have," perfect for rasping lines like "You can always put that award where your heart ought to be." He added, "If your throat improves, make sure you keep your voice deep throughout the picture."

Bette joked that she sounded like Tallulah Bankhead, but she and Mankiewicz kept that little secret to themselves. Mankiewicz would maintain that Margo was modeled on the eighteenth-century Irish actress Peg Woffington. But Edith Head, who was designing Davis's wardrobe, asked her researchers to bring her stills of Bankhead. When reporters asked about the resemblance, Davis would play coy. "We never mentioned her name on the set," she told Hedda Hopper. "Basically 'Eve' is the story of any woman in the profession. Personally I have a great admiration for Tallulah. We've had strange careers." And that shoulder-length bob? "Coincidental."

As for Margo's raspy voice, Davis insisted it was the result of a burst blood vessel from shooting *Payment on Demand*. But the real explanation was darker. The night before she left for San Francisco, Sherry had shown up at her Beverly Hills home. She met him on the front lawn, still in her nightgown, where their confrontation turned into a screaming match. Davis knew exactly how to hurt him—by undermining his manhood—so she taunted him with the idea that she was having an affair with Mankiewicz. "He's a *real* man," she said. "He's a genius! He makes a living *all his own*."

"Shut up!"

The next day, her voice was gone, and she left by train for San Francisco with B.D., her nurse, and a bodyguard.

Gary Merrill, who would be playing her lover, Bill Sampson, made the trip north in Zanuck's seaplane, along with Hugh Marlowe and Celeste Holm, cast as playwright Lloyd Richards and his wife, Karen. Merrill, a man's man with thick eyebrows, had met Davis at her makeup test and was appalled to find the makeup people "twirling her around, rather callously examining her facial lines," instead of treating her like royalty. Over the din of the plane's engine, Holm shouted, "I wonder what it's going to be like working with the Queen Bee!"

"I know one thing," Merrill said. "It'll all be over in eight weeks."

But Merrill, despite being married, couldn't stop thinking about Davis. Their first night in San Francisco, he joined the cast for drinks. "Everybody was showing off," Holm recalled. "Bette had taken one look at Gary and Gary had taken one look at Bette, and something had happened." Rehearsing one scene, Davis, in character, took a cigarette out of a case, waiting for Merrill to light it. To her surprise, he told her, "I don't think Bill Sampson would light Margo's cigarettes."

Davis studied him, wondering if this was a character decision or if Merrill was trying to prove who was boss. "You're quite right, Mr. Merrill," she said. "Of course he wouldn't."

Anne Baxter, meanwhile, was getting to know Eve. In her early scenes, Eve was as meek as a lost lamb, with flashes of the manipulator to come. Even Davis admitted that Baxter had the more difficult part, always playing two things at once: the "sweet bitch," as Davis called her. Baxter thought back to her stage début, at age thirteen, and to her first understudy, a girl who was "nice to everybody but me and would always be in the wings watching me like a hawk." As Eve, she would follow Margo with her eyes, for the same effect.

Given that *All About Eve* revolves around backstage rivalry, it was inevitable that rumors would circulate of bad blood between Davis and Baxter. George Sanders, who played critic Addison DeWitt, would stir the pot even more when he recalled, "Bette upstaged Anne Baxter at every turn, and drove Anne to distraction. Playing a woman of forty who was jealous of a much younger woman, Bette played it as if it were happening to her personally. Anne caught the underlying tensions and viciousness. It is to her credit that it spurred her to act even better than she would have with a gracious co-star."

But Baxter dismissed this narrative as a too-easy invention. "The studio tried to play that up all during the filming," she said of the supposed feud. "But I liked Bette very much. She'd come on the set and go 'S-s-s-s-s' at me, but it was just a joke between us." Davis said that the real "bitch" in the equation was George Sanders.

If there was a feud, it was between Davis and Celeste Holm. Holm, a Broadway actress, had won a Best Supporting Actress Oscar in 1948, for *Gentleman's Agreement*, but she had little regard for movie acting. "Hollywood," she said, "is a good place to learn to eat a salad without smearing your lipstick." She had even less regard for her costar. "Bette Davis was so rude, so constantly rude," she claimed. "I think it had to do with sex."

Holm could tell that something was going on between Davis and Merrill the first week of filming. "And from then on," she complained, "she didn't care whether the rest of us lived or died." On one of their first days, Holm greeted Davis with a cheery "Good morning." Davis replied, in her Tallulah Bankhead rasp, "Oh, shit, good manners."

"I never spoke to her again," Holm claimed. "Ever."

As far as Davis and Merrill were concerned, Holm was absolutely right. Merrill was infatuated. Davis began confiding to him about her turbulent divorce from Sherry. "My first feeling of compassion for this misunderstood, talented woman was quickly replaced by a robust attraction," Merrill would recall. "Before long we were walking about holding hands, going to the movies, and doing other things together. From simple compassion, my feelings shifted to an almost uncontrollable lust. I walked around with an erection for three days."

Word of the flirtation reached Sherry, who responded with a telegram pleading with his estranged wife not to go through with the divorce. Davis was pitiless as she read the message aloud for the entire cast, howling with laughter. "It was a beautiful, tender, sweet letter," one observer recalled. "The only one who didn't go along with ridiculing it was Anne Baxter. She was offended by the whole thing. As was I." The observer was Marion Richards, B.D.'s young governess, who had her own Eve Harrington tendencies: in August 1950, after both *All About Eve* and Davis's marriage were in the can, Richards became the next Mrs. William Grant Sherry.

When shooting was done in San Francisco, Merrill spent a weekend with Davis in L.A. Not long after, Merrill and his wife went to a dinner party, where he had a few too many drinks for a man with a secret. He recalled, "In my alcoholic haze, while talking to the other guests about Davis, I stated that I'd marry Bette if she'd have me—not exactly the sort of thing to say in front of one's own wife. When we returned to the beach house, the dishes began to fly."

The heat between Merrill and Davis only inflamed the brush fire they were creating on-screen, particularly during the film's greatest set piece—Margo's booze-soaked party for Bill. The party spanned more than thirty pages of the script and took almost a week to film. A shot of the guests' coats piled up on the bed required extra precautions: Fox hired security guards to watch the five hundred thousand dollars' worth of furs. As Davis and Merrill filmed their quarrel, Mankiewicz watched closely. When he hired Davis, Edmund Goulding, who had directed her in *Dark Victory*, warned him, "Dear boy, have you gone mad? This woman will destroy you, she will grind you down into a fine powder and blow you away." But Mankiewicz wasn't destroyed. Between camera setups, he told Davis, "I expected you to be Lady Macbeth—and instead you're Portia." She saved her Macbeth-ishness for the scene in which she gulps a martini, dumps her olive in the empty glass, and announces, "Fasten your seat belts. It's going to be a bumpy night."

Amid the poison of the party scene, one actress managed to make an impression with honey. Marilyn Monroe had won the small role of Miss Caswell, an aspiring actress from the "Copa Cabana School of Dramatic Arts," for five hundred dollars a week, over studio ideas ranging from Angela Lansbury to Zsa-Zsa Gabor. Gabor might have gotten the part, too, if not for her third of nine husbands—George Sanders. When the former Miss Hungary got ahold of the script, she imagined herself playing Phoebe, the teenage Eve Harrington fan who appears in the final scene—no matter that she was hovering around thirty. She begged her husband to put in a good word with Zanuck, but Sanders shot back, "Don't be silly. Acting isn't for you."

Gabor was now relegated to the sidelines as her husband acted the party scene with Monroe. At twenty-four, Monroe was struggling to turn her stint as a pinup model into a full-fledged acting career. Hollywood had given Norma Jean Mortenson a new hair color, a new name, and a slew of screen tests. Zanuck had signed her for a six-month contract in 1946, before she was unceremoniously dropped. "Mr. Zanuck feels that you may turn into an actress sometime," a studio official told her, "but that your type of looks is definitely against you." Disappointed, she found an advocate, and a lover, in Johnny Hyde, a senior agent at William Morris, who managed to get her real parts in good films—including *All About Eve*. Mankiewicz would later say, "There was a breathlessness and sort of glued-on innocence about her that I found appealing."

Everyone connected to *All About Eve* would have something to say about Monroe. Holm called her a "poor little thing," when not dismissing her as "quite sweet and terribly dumb." Baxter found her "eminently braless." Sanders, her scene partner, recalled, "She was very beautiful and very inquiring and very unsure—she was somebody in a play not yet written, uncertain of her part in the over-all plot." Lunching in the Fox commissary, Sanders noted, "She showed an interest in intellectual subjects which was, to say the least, disconcerting. In her presence it was hard to concentrate." (Their lunches did not sit well with Gabor.)

Then there was Davis. Monroe was terrified of her costar, telling Joan Collins in 1955, "That woman hates every female who can walk. She made me feel *so* nervous. She didn't talk to me at all, just sort of swept around the set, nose and cigarette in the air. She's a mean old broad." Sanders, who enjoyed fanning the gossip about actress-on-actress cruelty, reported that, after they shot one scene, Davis stage-whispered, "That little blonde slut can't act her way out of a paper bag!"

Davis was more focused on Merrill, whom she saw as a test she was determined to pass. For all her similarities with Margo, the one that cut the deepest was Margo's inner tug-of-war between her career and her womanhood, which she saw as incompatible. As Margo says to Karen, "It's one career all females have in common, whether we like it or not: being a woman. Sooner or later, we've got to work at it, no matter how many other careers we've had or wanted." Delivering the speech in her mink and her white gloves, Davis held back tears. "Margo Channing was a woman I understood thoroughly," she wrote. She knew how much she needed love, and how bad she was at receiving it. "I sensed in Gary my last chance at love and marriage," she wrote. "I wanted these as desperately as ever. I had been an actress first and a woman second. I had proved what I wanted to prove about the actress part."

On July 4, 1950, a quickie Mexican divorce finally ended Davis's marriage to Sherry. At the Los Angeles airport, she told reporters, "No one is very happy, really, about a divorce." Sherry was less contrite, announcing, "I shall set off a great big firecracker in honor of my own independence." By July 28, Merrill was free of his own wife, who would claim in their divorce proceedings that "Anne Baxter had been Gary's first choice for an affair in San Francisco." Davis and Merrill married in Juárez, Mexico. The ceremony was performed in Spanish, with Merrill in a gabardine suit and Davis in a navy-blue dress and white gloves.

"An hour after I married him," Davis would say, "I knew I had made a terrible mistake."

Merrill would soon discover Davis's "stubborn insistence on perfection. She would empty the ashtray before the cigarette was out, and she had the bed made before my feet hit the ground." Davis's zeal to be a successful wife alienated her new husband. "I loved making a home for him, but he did not at all like that domestic side of me," she said. "He wanted me to be Margo Channing."

As much as Margo Channing was other people—Bette Davis, Elisabeth Bergner, Tallulah Bankhead—she was also none of them, a screen invention with a life of her own. The same went for Norma Desmond, who was and wasn't Gloria Swanson. Both *All About Eve* and *Sunset Boulevard* traded in show business archetypes—the high-strung diva, the scheming understudy—making them hyperreal. On one level, *All About Eve* told the oldest tale in Hollywood: the overnight success. Most of the time, it was fantasy. But, every so often, a star really is born in an instant. It had happened to Judy Holliday, who was about to give Davis, Baxter, and Swanson all a run for their money.

JUDITH TUVIM NEVER DREAMED OF being a movie star, and she never quite reconciled herself to the fact that she became one. It had all been a crazy fluke. Even after she became Judy Holliday, and after Judy Holliday became a bona fide celebrity, she wondered whether acting was a "proper career for a serious-minded person."

Holliday was a bundle of contradictions. She was serious-minded, but her livelihood was comedy. She was painfully self-conscious about her weight and her looks, but she'd thrust herself into the role of a Hollywood beauty. She was ambivalent yet driven, shy yet theatrical, incandescent yet prone to depression. She was bookish and witty, yet her defining role—the one she could never quite escape—was as the ultimate dumb blonde.

Born in 1921, she was the only child of Abe and Helen Tuvim, New York Jews of Russian descent. (Helen's father had made epaulets for the czar in St. Petersburg.) When she was ten, the story went, Judy took an IQ test and placed in the genius range. Big-boned and awkward, she preferred reading *The Brothers Karamazov* to talking with boys. The Tuvims became habitués of Café Royale on Second Avenue, a fashionable spot for Yiddish theater actors and Jewish intellectuals. Judy's uncle Joe was active in the Socialist Party, and she was encouraged to participate in social causes. At twelve, she wrote a prize-winning essay called "How to Keep the Streets, Parks and Playgrounds of Our City Clean and Wholesome." By the end of high school, she had decided to enter the theater, not as an actress but as a writer and director. She took a job as a switchboard operator for Orson Welles's Mercury Theatre, but no opportunities arose. "I just sat at the switchboard from nine to five and cried," she recalled.

At a camp in the Catskills, she met a young songwriter named Adolph Green and his friend Betty Comden, and they formed a comedy troupe they eventually called the Revuers. They performed blackout sketches and songs at the Village Vanguard, a bohemian spot in Greenwich Village. Adrift at first, Holliday became a deft comedienne. Comden said, "It was truly phenomenal; in a matter of a few weeks she picked up what the rest of us had learned over a period of years." They started entertaining at benefits—some of which, it would later be claimed, were arranged by Communist-front organizations. Though the troupe members were all left-leaning, their material was hardly subversive. One sketch imagined a meeting of the Joan Crawford Fan Club.

After they got glowing notices at the Trocadero, offers came in from Hollywood—not for the Revuers, but for Judy alone. Her gazelle-like brown eyes and crack comedic timing had made her the group's standout star, but she didn't want to betray her friends. She reached a compromise with Fox: she would make her first screen appearance as part of the Revuers, and if that went well, the whole troupe would get signed. They filmed a pair of their nightclub sketches for a Fox musical called *Greenwich Village*, but both were cut from the final print. Unsurprisingly, the studio dismissed all the Revuers but Judy, who was distraught. Comden and Green returned to New York, where they wrote the musical *On the Town*.

Meanwhile, Fox gave Judith Tuvim the star treatment, which meant finding her a less Jewish-sounding name. "Holliday" was a play on her original surname, *yom tovim* meaning "holiday" in Hebrew. One day, the newly minted Judy Holliday was informed that Darryl Zanuck wanted to meet her. Holliday, self-conscious about her physical imperfections—she thought her ankles were too big, her face too wide—stuffed her bra.

She was escorted past four secretaries to Zanuck's office, where she found him in an electric wheelchair, staring at her over his unkempt salt-and-pepper mustache. Instead of a meeting, she got an assault. He rolled toward her, swinging a polo mallet, and the startled Holliday fell onto a couch. "I must have you!" Zanuck said, launching onto her lap.

"But, Mr. Zanuck," she pleaded, "you can have any beautiful girl in the studio. Why pick me?"

He pawed at her and explained, "You belong to me. You belong to me."

Horrified, Holliday leaped to her feet, reached into her dress, and threw the falsies in his face. "These belong to you, Mr. Zanuck, but I don't," she said, and stormed out.

She knew she was risking her career. For the next six months as a contract player, Holliday collected her four hundred dollars a week and hoped the studio would make good use of her. It didn't. She had all but decided to quit when Fox saved her the trouble by dropping its option. Maybe she had sabotaged her chances by rejecting Zanuck's advances. Or maybe she was too heavy to be a movie star. Or too Jewish. Or both.

Back in New York, she landed a zingy supporting role in the Broadway play *Kiss Them for Me*. She would join her theater friends at the steakhouse across the street from where *On the Town* was playing to ecstatic crowds. Comden would catch her watching everyone eat while she sipped on a coffee and then discreetly ask the waiter to wrap up the leftovers for her dog. The truth was that she was broke, living in her mother's apartment, and spending her days doing crossword puzzles and putting on weight.

Then she got the break of a lifetime. One day in 1946, her agent called. There was a play out of town called *Born Yesterday*, and there were problems with its leading lady. The show, by Garson Kanin, was a newfangled Pygmalion comedy about a junk dealer named Harry Brock who brings his moll, Billie Dawn, to Washington in a scheme to buy off a congressman. A showbiz floozy with a tart mouth and a Brooklyn drawl, Billie lacks the polish for Washington etiquette, so Harry hires a newspaper journalist to educate her. It turns out that Billie has more brains than anyone knew, including her, and her awakened intellect allows her to expose Harry's skullduggery—all while she falls in love with the newsman.

The problem was Jean Arthur, Frank Capra's former leading lady, who was fighting the role more than playing it. She rewrote her lines, trying to assuage her unease. The show opened in New Haven in December 1945, to mixed reviews. Patrons were demanding their money back. After the Boston opening, Arthur called in sick. She would have to sit out the play until it opened in Philadelphia the following Tuesday. Back in New York, as rumors swirled of Arthur's troubles, the producers sought possible replacements and heard about Holliday, who had just made a splash in *Kiss Them for Me*. The script described Billie as "stunningly beautiful and stunningly stupid." Holliday saw herself as neither, but her knack for the character was uncanny. When news came that Arthur was leaving the show for good, Holliday was told to pack her bags for Philadelphia. "When do we open?" she asked.

"Whenever you're ready," Kanin told her.

The producer corrected him: "Saturday night." Saturday was in three days.

Holliday rehearsed for hours, fueling herself with Dexedrine and chop suey. There was no time for her usual self-doubt to distract her. "In that space of time," Kanin recalled, "she changed from a bright young girl to an exhausted old woman of sixty." At the final run-through, she wept uncontrollably every time she left the stage, knowing that if she screwed up in Philadelphia, the producers would have to replace her before New York.

Playing Paul, the newspaper man, was none other than Gary Merrill, who had not yet become ensnared by Bette Davis. "Judy was a big girl, a contrast to Jean Arthur," he would ungenerously recall. "In her own way, she was as talented as Jean. Hers was a much tougher, harder quality." But what Holliday brought to the role wasn't toughness so much as innocence, a naïve curiosity that radiated through Billie's brassy exterior, her voice a disarming, high-pitched squeal. Merrill wrote, "Judy could get a laugh with her squeaky voice and her blank expression more easily than anyone I knew."

In February 1946, the play opened on Broadway to raves. Holliday, now the toast of the town, settled in for a long run. By 1949, her name was above the title, and she had married David Oppenheim, a clarinetist with the New York Symphony Orchestra. But there was still one prize just out of reach: the chance to play Billie Dawn in the movie version of *Born Yesterday*.

Harry Cohn had paid a million dollars for the film rights for Columbia, imagining it as a vehicle for Rita Hayworth. When it came to Holliday, His Crudeness expressed nothing but disgust. "On the stage you can get away with a broad [who] looks like that, because the audience sits far enough away," he told Kanin, "but with the camera movin' in she'd drive people out." What Cohn didn't realize was that *Born Yesterday* was Kanin's way of sticking it to him; the playwright had used Cohn as a prototype for the sleazy galoot Harry Brock, and Cohn's prickly relationship with Jean Arthur had been baked into that of Brock and Billie Dawn. The play may have purported to satirize Washington, but under the surface, it contained nearly as jaundiced a view of Hollywood as *Sunset Boulevard*.

As Columbia's resident bombshell, Hayworth could have snapped up *Born Yesterday* if she wanted it. Instead, she broke her contract to marry Prince Aly Khan, the playboy son of the Aga Khan. More than thirty-five actresses were considered for Billie Dawn, among them Lucille Ball, Gloria Grahame, Celeste Holm—and Marilyn Monroe, then briefly under contract at Columbia. As the casting call entered its second year, people began comparing it to the search for Scarlett O'Hara. It seemed like everyone in America was up for the role except the woman who had made it famous. When Holliday read that Hayworth was attached to the project, she said, "I was inconsolable. But you can only carry a torch for so long."

Salvation came in the form of Katharine Hepburn. Kanin and his wife Ruth Gordon had written the screenplay for *Adam's Rib*, in which Hepburn and Spencer Tracy played married lawyers opposing each other in court. Hepburn had seen Holliday onstage in *Born Yesterday* and insisted on her for the part of the loudmouthed defendant. In June 1949, Holliday shot her scenes for director George Cukor. She had put on weight, inspiring Kanin to sing, "Judy's Busting Out All Over." Despite the mockery, she turned in a winning performance, with Hepburn making sure the camera angles in their scenes favored Holliday. If some columnists noted that Holliday had stolen the picture, it did not come as a slight to Hepburn—she had planted the rumor herself. On New Year's Eve, *Born Yesterday* closed on Broadway after 1,642 performances. Less than two weeks later, Columbia finally announced the results of its search for Billie Dawn: the role would be played by Judy Holliday.

Holliday put herself on a regimen of vegetable broth, poached eggs, cottage cheese, and liver, but that didn't stop Cohn from looking her up and down and declaring, "Well, I've worked with fat asses before." In lieu of the natural blond curls she had worn on Broadway, the studio refashioned Billie as a platinum bombshell in the mold of Jean Harlow. Holliday starved herself to fit into her gowns, with only her mother reminding her to "eat, darling." In June 1950, she arrived in Washington, DC, for six days of location work, shooting a handful of scenes in which her newsman love interest wises her up to the glories of American democracy. (The role formerly played by Gary Merrill now belonged to William Holden, who was also playing Joe Gillis in *Sunset Boulevard*.)

Columbia had gotten clearance to film Billie's Washington education at real landmarks like the Jefferson Memorial and the Capitol Rotunda, where she wonders, "How could anybody paint upside down like that?" Dressed in a flowered hat and a polka-dotted jacket, Holliday peered at the 159-year-old Bill of Rights. Holden delivered his line: "This whole country is practically founded on these three pieces of paper."

"*This* whole country?" she squealed back in delight. Billie recites part of the Second Amendment—but it was the First Amendment that Holliday would need in the coming years.

ONE EVENING, THE PARAMOUNT SCREENING room opened its doors to some three hundred industry people. The big question: How would *Sunset Boulevard* play in the town it mirrored so unsparingly? Swanson arrived directly from a twenty-person dinner party thrown by Louis B. Mayer. "Gloria made a grand entrance wearing a floor-length silver lamé dress," Edith Head recalled. But the guest of honor was tentative. "These affairs are known for being morbidly restrained, devoid of the slightest overt reaction, but that night the whole audience stood up and cheered," Swanson recalled. "People clustered around me, and I had trouble moving up the aisle. Barbara Stanwyck fell on her knees and kissed the hem of my skirt. I could read in all their eyes a single message of elation: If she can do it, why should we be terrified?"

She looked around for Mary Pickford. "Where's Mary?" she asked.

"She can't show herself, Gloria," someone told her. "She's overcome. We all are."

Head recalled a more conflicted reaction: "As everyone watched the film, the screening room was silent. The credits rolled, the screen went black, and still there was silence. Then there was thunderous applause. A few people walked out, murmuring that the film would be the ruination of Hollywood, but the rest swarmed around Swanson and Wilder."

Among the scandalized was Mayer himself. Now sixty-six, he had helped create the very dream factory mythology that *Sunset Boulevard* wickedly punctured. Outside the theater, he barked at Wilder, "You bastard! You have disgraced the industry that made and fed you! You should be tarred and feathered and run out of Hollywood!" Wilder's response was something along the lines of: "Go shit in your hat."

Luckily, Mayer did not get the last word on *Sunset Boulevard*. By the time it premiered, on August 10, 1950, in front of seven thousand spectators at Radio City Music Hall, it was one of the most-talked-about films of the year. The *Post* called it "a major work of Hollywood art." The *Journal-American* raved, "It elevates Gloria Swanson, a fine actress, to heights she never before has attained." (A rare dissent came from *The New Yorker*, which called it "a pretentious slice of Roquefort.") Swanson's return was heralded with gushing headlines like "Gloria Swanson's Magnificent Comeback—'20s Siren Still Glamour Queen."

Bette Davis was en route to Maine for her honeymoon with Merrill when she spotted *Sunset Boulevard* advertised in a small-town theater, and they stopped for the night just to see it. "I was interested in it because, you know and I know, it's a true story," she told Hedda Hopper. "It was a relief to find one actress portrayed on the screen who wasn't starving. Gloria Swanson was loaded with money. Incidentally, I think she gave a heavenly performance."

"Didn't you find the film a trifle brutal?" Hopper asked of the picture in which she played herself.

Hopper's column, "Life Begins Anew at 40 for Bette Davis," was subtitled "Back from Retirement, Brilliant Actress Is Contender for Third 'Oscar.'" Davis may have been surprised to learn she had ever entered retirement, but life had indeed begun anew. *All About Eve* premiered at New York's 6,200-seat Roxy on October 13, two months after *Sunset Boulevard*. In November, Davis kneeled outside Grauman's Chinese Theatre and stuck her hands in wet cement. Staring into the flashbulbs, she quipped, "Too bad there's no way to imprint my poached-egg eyes down there." The West Coast premiere followed three days later, drawing stars like Lana Turner, Ava Gardner, and Gregory Peck. Marilyn Monroe came on the arm of her agent, Johnny Hyde, who would drop dead less than six weeks later. Across the street, the Roosevelt Hotel blacked out all the letters on its big electric sign except for "EVE."

The picture opened to raves, with the *Times* critic Bosley Crowther calling it "a withering satire—witty, mature and worldly wise." He added, "Although the title character—the self-seeking, ruthless Eve, who would make a black-widow spider look like a lady bug—is the motivating figure in the story and is played by Anne Baxter with icy calm, the focal figure and most intriguing character is the actress whom Bette Davis plays. This lady, an aging, acid creature with a cankerous ego and a stinging tongue, is the end-all of Broadway disenchantment, and Miss Davis plays her to a fare-thee-well." Crowther concluded, thunderously, that Davis's performance "merits an Academy award."

Still five months away, the Best Actress competition had already appeared to narrow to a two-way race. Both Davis and Swanson were stars who had passed their glamorous heydays and were playing actresses who had passed their glamorous heydays. And yet, both had been resurrected from professional "death" in pictures that wittily tore show business apart. Margo and Norma were cautionary tales—women who had passed forty or fifty without learning to survive away from the spotlight. In real life, Davis and Swanson had proven the opposite: that actresses north of forty didn't have to pass gently into oblivion.

Charles Brackett, who had been elected Academy president in 1949, foresaw the coming showdown. He and Wilder had ended their collaboration after writing *Sunset Boulevard*, when Wilder turned to him and abruptly announced, "You know, Charlie, after this, I don't think we should work together anymore." Now Brackett had moved from Paramount to 20th Century–Fox, placing himself officially on Team Eve. "*Sunset Boulevard* and *All About Eve* being squared off against each other for 1950 honors, I feel a little as though I were slipping out this letter from the stronghold of the enemy," he wrote Swanson in late 1950. "And I'm going to add to the treachery by whispering that I think *Sunset* a much better performance than Miss D's."

Before *Sunset Boulevard* even opened, Swanson toured the country drumming up publicity, traveling by train from Boston to Philadelphia to Memphis to Salt Lake City. She worked herself ragged bantering with radio hosts and signing autographs. At one point, she wrote to Paramount's New York office saying she was having symptoms of a nervous breakdown, pleading, "I know I cannot take this grind much longer."

Publicly, she put on a game face, acting as goodwill ambassador for the industry to which she had at long last returned, "as if from the dead." The studios were desperate to distract from twin scandals that had broken months earlier. The first was the birth of Ingrid Bergman's baby with Rossellini. "Americans everywhere went purple at the thought that the good girl, the saint, the nun of pictures, should flaunt her adultery in their faces, and the studios were once again spending millions to prove that all Hollywood wasn't bad," Swanson recalled. "The second source of fearful scandal was Senator Joseph McCarthy, who announced in Washington that he had lists of Communists all over America bent on the overthrow of our government. Hollywood was trembling."

It all seemed familiar to Swanson, who had weathered the Hollywood scandals of the twenties and suffered the intrusions of morality clauses and a gossip-hungry press. As for this McCarthy business, she "doubted that there were Communists hiding behind every corporation desk and director's chair." Or, for that matter, hiding in plain sight on the screen.

THE SAME MONTH THAT JUDY Holliday was in Washington shooting *Born Yesterday*, a 213-page pamphlet began circulating in offices on both coasts. Executives at every television and radio station got a copy. It arrived without fanfare, though the cover image was alarming: a radio microphone threatened by a menacing red hand. The title, framed by zigzagging radio waves, was *Red Channels: The Report of Communist Influence in Radio and Television*.

This strange volume was the product of *Counterattack*, a "Newsletter of Facts to Combat Communism" published by an organization calling itself American Business Consultants. It brought urgent news that the Communist Information Bureau was seeking "domination of American broadcasting and telecasting." One of the bureau's tactics was to enlist "glamorous personalities" to appear at front meetings and rallies. What followed was a list of 151 of those personalities, among them Lena Horne, Leonard Bernstein, Gypsy Rose Lee, Arthur Miller, Zero Mostel, Dorothy Parker, Edward G. Robinson, and Orson Welles. Garson Kanin, writer of *Born Yesterday*, was also named, having apparently signed a "Statement Defending Communist Party" in the *Daily Worker* on April 16, 1947. So was José Ferrer, the Puerto Rican star of *Cyrano de Bergerac*. And on page 78 appeared the name "Judy Holliday."

The Red Scare had been rumbling since 1947, when the House Un-American Activities Committee, or HUAC, began investigating Hollywood figures with possible Communist ties. A group of "unfriendly" witnesses, among them screenwriter Dalton Trumbo, refused to answer

HUAC's questions and denounced the inquisition as an attack on their constitutional rights. The Hollywood Ten, as the group became known, were cited for contempt and sentenced to jail time, while the industry washed its hands of them. But the air of paranoia remained. By the time Mankiewicz was writing *All About Eve*, self-policing had become second nature. When Zanuck read the treatment, he slashed out one of Margo Channing's would-be zingers, directed to the watchful Eve: "You're not on one of those congressional committees, are you?"

With the Hearst papers fanning the theory that Hollywood was a hotbed of leftist propaganda, other entities stepped in to do the work that the studio brass wouldn't—entities like *Counterattack*. Published by three former FBI agents and bankrolled by Alfred Kohlberg, a textile importer and central member of the anticommunist China lobby, the newsletter culled names from petitions, membership lists, and programs from questionable rallies and fund-raisers. By 1949, Ed Sullivan was consulting it to avoid booking "pinkos" on his program.

Red Channels was the climax of that culling: a handy guide to show-biz subversives, many of whom happened to be Black or Jewish. The evidence against Judy Holliday spanned two pages. In May 1947, she'd been listed on the board of sponsors for People's Songs, an organization founded by Pete Seeger, whose productions, according to *Red Channels*, "follow the Communist Party line as assiduously as do the people behind the organization." In December 1948, she had signed an ad in *Variety* in support of the Hollywood Ten. And as recently as March 25, 1950, she had entertained at a carnival for the New York Council of the Arts, Sciences and Professions, a suspected Communist front.

By late summer, the release of *Red Channels* produced its first shock wave when actress Jean Muir was dropped from NBC's *The Aldrich Family* after protesters complained to its sponsor, the General Foods Corporation. The Muir affair rattled the industry, with Jack Gould, in the *Times*, worrying, "There is now under way in both radio and TV a 'Red purge' which could lead anywhere." Holliday was now an immediate target, and her background—she was a descendent of Russian socialist Jews—made her even more vulnerable. The trade paper *Hollywood Life* warned, "Judy only acts dumb. She's a smart cookie . . .

the Commies got her a long time ago." If Holliday was panicked, she didn't show it. "Of all those who were harassed in the ugly days of *Red Channels* and blacklisting, no one was more steadfast or less craven than Judy," Garson Kanin would recall. "Her behavior under pressure was a poem of grace."

As the release of *Born Yesterday* approached, Hollywood was divided. The Screen Directors Guild proposed a bylaw requiring its members to take an anticommunist oath, an initiative led by enthusiastic Red hunter Cecil B. DeMille. The board overwhelmingly voted for the measure, all while the guild's president, Joseph L. Mankiewicz, was sailing from France with his wife on vacation after the completion of *All About Eve*. Upon his return, he was shocked to discover that DeMille had gone ahead with the vote behind his back. "It seems to me that kind of thing only happens in Moscow," he said, to which DeMille replied, "Well, maybe we need a little of that here." On October 12, DeMille's pro-oath faction hatched a secret plan to recall Mankiewicz for opposing the board and making the "incendiary" claim that they were instituting a blacklist. Motorcycle messengers hand-delivered the ballots late into the night.

The next evening—as *All About Eve* was premiering at the Roxy—Mankiewicz gathered at Chasen's with his own faction of supporters, including John Huston, William Wyler, and Billy Wilder, and they worked through the night to get twenty-five signatures on a petition to hold a full membership meeting on the matter. On Sunday, October 22, in what Mankiewicz called "the most dramatic evening of my life," the entire guild packed the Crystal Ballroom of the Beverly Hills Hotel, for an acrimonious meeting that lasted until 2:20 a.m. DeMille, over boos and hisses, produced dossiers on the twenty-five Mankiewicz supporters, including a list of "Red front" organizations to which they supposedly belonged. Rouben Mamoulian, who was born in the Russian Empire, said that for the first time in America, he was afraid to have an accent. After five hours of impassioned speeches, John Ford, who had been sitting quietly with a pipe, rose and said, "I don't think we should . . . put ourselves in a position of putting out derogatory information about a director, whether he is a Communist, beats his mother-in-law, or beats dogs."

Defeated, DeMille withdrew from the stage and left the hall.

Mankiewicz had seized back control of the guild. But even then, the pressures of the blacklist proved too great, and in a confounding about-face, he kept the oath in place.

Three weeks before its Christmastime premiere, Born Yesterday itself came under attack. William H. Mooring, a reviewer for the Catholic newspaper the Tidings, called it "the most diabolically clever political satire I have encountered in almost thirty years of steady film review-ing." This was not a compliment. The MPAA fired back in a telegram to twenty-three Catholic newspapers, insisting that THE PICTURE GIVES WARMTH AND POSITIVE SUPPORT TO THE DEMOCRATIC IDEALS, PRINCIPLES AND INSTITUTIONS OF AMERICA. A more influential defense may have come from Louella Parsons, who wrote in Hearst's anti-Red papers that "if there are any pink ideas infiltered into 'Born Yesterday' they are way over my head." Soon, Mooring's pearl-clutching review became a laugh-ingstock, with Variety's Frank Scully surmising that he was suffering from "mass hysteria emphasized by an acute personal hallucination."

To see Communist propaganda in Born Yesterday, with its wide-eyed tour of Washington landmarks, one would have to read Marxist senti-ment into the very idea of government corruption, or into Billie's win-some protest that "some people are always giving and some taking—and it's not fair!" By the time the public saw Born Yesterday, the controversy had ebbed. The film and its star had been saved, for the moment, by the fact that its critics had overstepped.

"TWO FILMS ABOUT AGING ACTRESSES—'ALL About Eve' and 'Sunset Boulevard'—won the most nominations tonight to compete for Academy Awards," the Associated Press reported on February 12, 1951. Eve led the pack with fourteen nominations, beating Gone with the Wind's rec-ord by one. Sunset Boulevard followed, with eleven nominations. Both would compete for Best Picture with Born Yesterday, which was up for five awards.

The Best Actress category was a glut. Swanson earned her first nom-ination since 1930 and Davis her eighth (not counting the write-in vote for Of Human Bondage). Judy Holliday was nominated for the first time. And then, a curveball: Anne Baxter was also nominated for Best Actress.

Baxter, who had already won in the supporting category, for her role in *The Razor's Edge*, had perhaps sensed her chance to win as a lead. Because the studios designated eligibility, she had taken her campaign to Zanuck and convinced him that Eve Harrington was a leading role. "The film, after all, was about how different people saw Eve," Baxter argued. Besides, if she had been in the supporting category again, she would have had to compete against two of her costars, Celeste Holm and Thelma Ritter. By competing against Davis, though, Baxter appeared to be pulling an Eve Harrington herself. Years later, she would say, "I've decided recently that I was wrong. I *should* have accepted another supporting Oscar." Davis's response: "Yeah, she should have."

The fifth Best Actress slot went to Eleanor Parker, the twenty-eight-year-old star of the prison drama *Caged*. Dubbed the "Woman of a Thousand Faces," Parker had signed with Warner Bros. on her nineteenth birthday and made a modest impression in war pictures like *Pride of the Marines*. But she had trouble finding her footing as a star. In 1946, she played the Cockney shrew in an *Of Human Bondage* remake. The reviews inevitably compared her to Davis, even accusing her of imitating the elder actress's walk. In 1947, Parker finally got a break, in *The Voice of the Turtle*, opposite Ronald Reagan. (Her defining role was still ahead: Baroness Elsa von Schraeder in *The Sound of Music*.)

In *Caged*, Parker had the chance to play fragility and grit, as a fretful teenager who is sent to a women's prison for abetting her husband's armed robbery. Warner Bros. had envisioned *Caged* as a spicy vehicle for Bette Davis and Joan Crawford, until Davis supposedly declined to appear in a "dyke movie." Like Baxter, Parker had the challenge of completely transforming over the course of the film, from doe-eyed innocent to hardened schemer.

In another year, Parker might have had a chance, but not with Davis, Swanson, and Holliday duking it out in what Oscar watchers considered a three-way race. Swanson was now back in New York, starring in a Broadway revival of *Twentieth Century*, costarring and directed by José Ferrer. She'd been savoring her comeback, showing off her hundred pairs of shoes to *The Saturday Evening Post* and receiving a fashion award from Neiman Marcus. In one scene in *Twentieth Century*, Swanson's character, a Hollywood star, brandishes her Academy Award. "Best Actress," Ferrer's character reads off the plaque, then scolds, "Good God! It's pathetic. Don't fall for this sort of thing." After the real nominations came out, Broadway audiences would whistle and cheer, Swanson recalled, "as if they wanted Norma Desmond, my character in *Sunset Boulevard*, to step out of Lily Garland, my character in *Twentieth Century*, and take a bow or do a turn."

Ferrer, who was up for Best Actor for *Cyrano de Bergerac*, found his own standing in question on March 6, when it was revealed that he had been subpoenaed by HUAC to testify on possible Communist ties. Ferrer swore to his patriotism, but word spread that, if he won the Oscar, Hedda Hopper would unfurl an American flag and storm out of the theater. When Hopper heard the rumor, she said it wasn't true—but that she wished she *had* thought of it. Holliday, meanwhile, was avoiding any hint of political controversy, but she was not out of the woods; days before the awards, the New York Anti-Communist Committee of the Catholic War Veterans announced that it would protest a Times Square screening of *Born Yesterday*.

To boost her dumb-blonde persona, Holliday became a semi-regular guest on *The Big Show*, an NBC Radio program hosted by "the glamorous, unpredictable Tallulah Bankhead," who addressed her "dahlings" with the raspy hauteur of Margo Channing. Holliday's skits cast her as a version of Billie Dawn, a bubble-voiced foil to the imperious hostess. Bankhead had turned the widespread perception that she was Davis's model into a one-woman comic vendetta, growling with mock indignation, "Dahling, just wait till I get my hands on *that woman*. I'll pull out every hair in her mustache."

As the ceremony approached, columnist Bob Thomas declared "a wide-open race, particularly among the fillies." Swanson had the "sentimental vote," but Davis had the "sheer artistry." It was possible she would split the vote with Anne Baxter, handing the win to Swanson. Then again, Davis could split the living legend vote with Swanson and clear the way for Holliday to "upset the dopesters and walk home with the statuette." On a plane bound for Los Angeles two days before the Oscars, the stewardesses handed out ballots to all the passengers, who, at 18,000 feet, predicted that *All About Eve* would win Best Picture, but that Gloria Swanson would be named Best Actress.

SWANSON BEGAN THE MORNING OF the Academy Awards interviewing Tennessee Williams at her apartment in New York. As part of her publicity blitz, she was hosting her own half-hour radio program, in addition to becoming the face of Jergens All-Purpose Cream. ("Will you look as young as Gloria Swanson on your 52nd Birthday?" the ads asked.) She and Williams talked about his new play, *The Rose Tattoo*, and he wished her luck at the Oscars.

Then she and her secretary sorted through her correspondence, including a letter from actor Clifton Webb: "I want to see you get your satiny little hand on that nude little Oscar." But Swanson felt in her bones that she wouldn't win, and she refused to miss a night on Broadway to attend the ceremony. The studio had pestered her for a written acceptance speech. Even Billy Wilder sent a telegram: DEAR GLORIA: I UNDERSTAND YOU WILL BE UNABLE TO ATTEND ACADEMY AWARDS. THE STUDIO INFORMS ME THAT I AM TO ACCEPT YOUR AWARD IF YOU SHOULD WIN. PLEASE LET ME KNOW WHAT YOU WANT ME TO SAY BUT MAKE IT SHORT AS MY DELIVERY IS SINCERE BUT DECIDEDLY AMATEURISH.

Swanson had skipped the first Oscar ceremony, for which she was nominated for Best Actress. Twenty-two years later, she professed the same lack of interest. She would spend the evening performing in *Twentieth Century*, then listen to the ceremony by radio at a little party thrown in honor of her fifty-second birthday, which was two days earlier. José Ferrer planned to host the post-show get-together for the cast of *Twentieth Century* and their spouses at La Zambra, a Spanish restaurant five minutes from the theater. But the little get-together turned big. ABC Radio, which had an exclusive on the Oscar broadcast, got wind of the bash and asked if other nominees in New York could be invited, too. The initial list of 45 turned into 110 invited guests, which word of mouth inflated to 280, including 6 nominees (Judy Holliday, Celeste Holm, and *Born Yesterday* director George Cukor among them) and reporters from *Time*, *Newsweek*, and *Variety*, which called it "one of the most exciting parties New York has seen in a long time."

After the curtain call, Swanson changed into a sleeveless black dress, a feathered hat, and a white fur jacket. "Good luck," her maid, Carrie, told her. Swanson had bet Carrie fifty dollars that she wouldn't win, and responded, "I'll see you tomorrow—have your money ready."

Bette Davis was even farther from the action—in the Yorkshire moors, on the set of the British film *Another Man's Poison*, in which she and Merrill were costarring. In the wee hours, the couple convened a small gathering to listen to the awards by radio.

In California, meanwhile, guests arrived at the Pantages Theatre: Gene Kelly, Debbie Reynolds, Marlene Dietrich. Charles Brackett, as Academy president, kicked off the evening in front of a giant Oscar flanked by Greek columns, saying, "Did Americans ever watch the passing of a year with such a sense of relief?" As he gravely ticked off geopolitical calamities—the "Russian land grab" of Czechoslovakia, "young American blood" spilled in Korea—it was easy to hear a hint of strategic patriotism. To make sure no one missed the message, Brackett argued for the importance of motion pictures to affirm "our faith in the importance of individual man and his God-given rights," before bringing on the host, Fred Astaire.

Backstage, Marilyn Monroe, dressed in a low-cut gown with black tulle encircling her neck, waited to present the award for Best Sound Mixing. After the sudden death of her agent, Johnny Hyde, she was unmoored. Moments before she had to go on, she saw that her sequined skirt had ripped. As a seamstress quickly repaired it, actresses Jane Greer, Debra Paget, and Gloria DeHaven attempted to calm her nerves. When she heard Astaire call her name, Monroe went out and breathily announced the winner: *All About Eve*.

In the pressrooms downstairs, director-producer Stanley Kramer noticed a throng of photographers surrounding Monroe. "Her beauty was so arresting I couldn't just walk casually by this wild scene," he recalled. As he watched Monroe beguile the press corps, Marlene Dietrich, having just presented Best Foreign Language Film, swept in majestically. "When the press spotted her, I felt sorry for Marilyn Monroe," Kramer wrote. "The entire crowd of photographers ran after Dietrich into the next room. Marilyn was left virtually alone. She looked around, bewildered at first, then realized what had happened. She shrugged and smiled sheepishly, as if to say, 'Well, what could I expect? That was Marlene Dietrich.'"

It was Monroe's first and only time attending the Oscars.

Just after eleven o'clock East Coast time, Swanson arrived at La Zambra. In the smoke-filled room, she saw packs of reporters with microphones and notepads, but no one she knew. A waiter led her to her table with Ferrer, where she asked, "Is it all over?"

"No," someone told her. "They're still awarding songs and special effects and short subjects—all that stuff."

A columnist sidled up and asked, "Are you nervous?"

"Not in the least," she said. "I've been through all this before, and I don't expect to win."

Swanson strained to follow the broadcast over the restaurant's clamor, but the occasional calls for quiet went unheeded. The press persuaded the nominees to move to a table in the center of the room, where their every facial expression could be documented by photographers. There, Swanson saw Holliday, wearing a maroon taffeta dress and matching velvet choker. They shook hands and laughed, then sat on either side of Ferrer, along with Celeste Holm, George Cukor, and *The Asphalt Jungle*'s Sam Jaffe, in front of a row of ABC Radio microphones.

Over the sound system, Holm learned that she had not won Best Supporting Actress. Neither had her *All About Eve* costar Thelma Ritter, *Sunset Boulevard*'s Nancy Olson, nor Hope Emerson, the prison matron from *Caged*. The winner was Josephine Hull, for *Harvey*. There was another jolt of excitement as Jaffe and *Sunset Boulevard*'s Erich von Stroheim lost Best Supporting Actor to *All About Eve*'s George Sanders. Holm leaned over to Jaffe, her fellow loser, and deadpanned, "Shall we dance?" At the Pantages, Sanders ascended to the stage and wordlessly bowed his head, then burst into tears in the wings, stammering, "I can't help it. This has unnerved me." (In his excitement, he left Zsa Zsa Gabor in the audience and completely forgot about her.) Recounting the evening years later, Sanders adopted Addison DeWitt's insouciance, writing that "everyone wants an Oscar, and the handing out of these coveted trophies takes place at a highly emotional ceremony which makes strong men weak and turns egocentric actresses into weeping and blushing maidens.

The correct procedure for winners is to disclaim all credit for their victory and to look stunned and transported with ecstatic disbelief and surprise. This is the moment when one draws to the limit one's reservoir of histrionic skill." In 1972, Sanders checked into a hotel near Barcelona and swallowed five bottles of Nembutal, writing in his suicide note, "Dear World, I am leaving because I am bored."

The nominees' table at La Zambra was now down to four. "What a sleazy affair," Cukor told Swanson over the din. "You can't hear yourself think. Are you going to make a speech if you get it?"

"Heavens, no," Swanson replied. She noticed Cukor smiling past her at Holliday, who flashed an anxious grin. A hush descended as the sound system piped in Helen Hayes reading the list of Best Actor nominees. Swanson felt a tug of allegiance as she heard the names "William Holden"—her costar in *Sunset Boulevard* and Holliday's in *Born Yesterday*—and "José Ferrer," now her Broadway costar and the man seated to her right. *Neither one of them could have played the other's part*, she thought. *That was what was so stupid about awards and contests.* The winner was Ferrer, who had overcome the black mark of the HUAC subpoena.

The prop Oscar from *Twentieth Century* somehow wound up on the table, and photographers urged Swanson and Holliday to pretend-fight over it, or to kiss Ferrer on either cheek. "It was a tasteless exercise, even for the press," Swanson recalled, "and Judy and I were both acutely embarrassed to go along with the galumphing horseplay, which, thank heaven, couldn't go on for long because the next fraught moment had come."

The tension in the room ratcheted up again as Broderick Crawford (the goon from *Born Yesterday*) walked out to present Best Actress. Swanson leaned toward Holliday and said, "One of us is about to be very happy." In England, where it was nearly dawn, Davis stood up in expectation—as if, somehow, she might step onto a stage an ocean away.

"The winner," Crawford announced, "is Judy Holliday."

Holliday stood up, unable to speak. "Judy, darling," Swanson said, attempting to reach for her. According to Swanson, Holliday looked "lost, as if she didn't recognize anyone. She was laughing and crying at the same time, and everyone was applauding her." A man brought her a microphone to give a speech to the Pantages. She opened her mouth to speak, but an ABC sound engineer had accidentally turned off the switch. No one heard what she had to say at the Pantages, where Ethel Barrymore was already accepting the award on her behalf. As Holliday griped to a friend the next day, "I don't even get a chance to say thanks before the ax falls."

In England, Bette Davis announced, surely dry as a martini, "Good. A newcomer got it. I couldn't be more pleased." With that, she returned to her hotel, with strict instructions to the front desk that she not be disturbed for the rest of the night.

Mankiewicz, who would end the evening with his second consecutive director-screenwriter double win, must have regretted that one of cinema's best showcases for actresses, *about* actresses, did not receive a single Oscar for its female cast. Years later, the director remarked, "Bette lost *because* Annie was nominated. Annie lost *because* Bette Davis ditto. Celeste Holm lost because Thelma Ritter was nominated, and *she* lost *because* Celeste ditto."

In the hubbub at La Zambra, Swanson waved Holliday back over and said, "Why couldn't you have waited till next year?" It wasn't clear if she was kidding or not. "I hadn't thought I would be greatly affected one way or another, and I wasn't," Swanson wrote later. "I had been through this all before, at times when winning might have been considered crucial to any other person. Both times I had shrugged and moved on. The simple truth of the matter was, I just happened to be the sort of person who couldn't be motivated by competition or prizes."

She surveyed the chaos at La Zambra. There was Holliday, looking at her as if "pleading for forgiveness." There was Ferrer, giving her a consolation hug. And there was the press, peppering her with questions: "Would you care to make a statement, Miss Swanson?" She gamely quipped, "Now there's nothing else but for the old warhorse to go back to work."

But she was becoming increasingly disgusted. "It slowly dawned on me that they were unconsciously asking for a bigger-than-life scene, or better still, a mad scene," she recalled. "More accurately, they were trying to flush out Norma Desmond. In the final analysis, from the moment Judy Holliday was announced, they had been waiting, and rather hoping, to see the *Hindenburg* go up in flames." Unwilling to play along, Swanson waved goodbye to Ferrer and signaled to her mother and daughter that it was time to go. In the car, they were silent as stones, which only bothered Swanson more. Didn't they see that it was all a farce?

As she readied herself for bed, she took stock: five failed marriages, a seesawing career. "But tonight I had seen for the first time with perfect clarity that I had a huge specter in the spotlight with me," she reflected. "She was just about ten feet tall, and her name was Norma Desmond." Swanson had played the role all too well: "I may not have got an Academy Award for it, but I had somehow convinced the world once again of that corniest of all theatrical clichés—that on very rare occasions the actor actually becomes the part."

MINUTES AFTER THE BEST ACTRESS winner was announced, Charles Brackett returned to the Oscar stage to present an honorary award to Louis B. Mayer. The white-haired mogul looked out over the organization he had concocted, clutching the prize he had all but invented, and professed his "great sense of responsibility to the future years to come."

Those future years were in doubt. MGM had been plunged into a civil war between Mayer and his protégé turned rival Dore Schary. Raging with paranoia, Mayer would pace his office and mutter, "I don't know what it is, the picture business. Everyone wants to see *this*," then grab his crotch. Weeks after the Oscars, Mayer delivered an ultimatum to Nicholas Schenck, president of MGM's parent company: it was either him or Schary. The choice wasn't hard. Schary had cut costs and boosted the bottom line, and he had his best years ahead of him. By May, Mayer was out. As *Sunset Boulevard* had shown, Hollywood was no place for has-beens. He lived another six years.

In the end, the night belonged to *All About Eve*, which walked away with six Oscars, including Best Picture. Like *Sunset Boulevard*, it told a story about the life-span of actresses: how youth was destined to wither, ambition to detonate or disappoint. As if to prove the point, a bulletin from the Allied Theatre Owners of the Gulf States reveled in Holliday's triumph a week later. "The nationwide cry of theatre owners for new faces and talent takes on infinitely more significance when fresh talent walks away with the year's Oscars," it read. "Suffice to say, who knows but what infinite gains could result from a bit of purging of our washed-up and washed-out galaxy of so-called stars."

Swanson realized she was in a bind: if she insisted that she didn't care about losing, people would cry sour grapes. If she said that, as an Aries, she wasn't prone to melancholia, they would assume she was as batty as Norma Desmond. Even Charles Brackett felt the need to cheer Swanson up. In April, the Academy president wrote her about how much he had wanted her to win. "Never forget that a great many of our members had seen *Sunset* not in early 1950 but in late '49," he reasoned. "All sense of timeliness was gone."

That couldn't have been much comfort to Swanson: her big comeback after nine years, and already the bloom was off the rose. As scripts came in, she realized that Norma Desmond would be her legacy. All of them were "awful imitations of *Sunset Boulevard*," she wrote, "all featuring a deranged superstar crashing toward tragedy." In her later years, she would be called to play a Norma Desmond-ified version of herself. In a 1966 episode of *The Beverly Hillbillies*, she descends a grand staircase in a pink turban to meet the Clampetts, who try to engineer her comeback in a silent movie. In *Airport 1975*, she boards a 747 in white gloves and a cape, recalling, "In 1917 I was flying in something wilder than this. Do you know who the pilot was? Cecil B. DeMille." In her 1980 autobiography, published three years before her death, she lamented that many of her silent films had disappeared, the celluloid disintegrated.

One of those awful *Sunset Boulevard* imitations might have been *The Star*, which became a vehicle for Bette Davis in 1952. Still in her Margo Channing high-dudgeon mode, Davis played a faded movie queen desperate to revive her career. In one sequence, she grabs her Academy Award, cries, "Come on, Oscar, let's you and me get drunk," and takes the statue on a boozy tour of Hollywood mansions. (Davis was nominated for Best Actress for the role.) *All About Eve* may have brought her back from the dead, but it also set her on the path toward *What Ever Happened to Baby Jane?*, the 1962 film in which she played a deluded has-been actress. The film, which pitted her against her rival Joan Crawford, kicked off a short-lived genre called "hagsploitation," which turned its aging stars into decrepit, campy monsters.

By then, Davis was in her fifties, only slightly older than Swanson had been in *Sunset Boulevard*. She realized that it was probably her last chance at a third Oscar, but she lost to Anne Bancroft, for her role in *The Miracle Worker*. Crawford, who was not nominated, had conspired to accept on Bancroft's behalf. The offscreen feud between Crawford and Davis became legendary—a grotesque funhouse mirror of the catfighting in *All About Eve*.

By the time *Baby Jane* came out, Davis and Gary Merrill were divorced. Like Margo Channing, Davis wrestled with whether the star and the wife could coexist. Margo had chosen Bill. Davis chose herself. "I am sure I have been uncompromising, peppery, untractable [*sic*], monomaniacal, tactless, volatile, and ofttimes disagreeable," she wrote in her 1962 memoir, *The Lonely Life*. "I stand accused of it all. But at forty I allowed the female to take over. It was too late. I admit that Gary broke my heart. He killed the dream forever. The little woman no longer exists." Davis never married again.

Judy Holliday also found herself trapped in her signature role: the dumb blonde. Months after the Oscars, she played the sophisticated heroine in a New York stage production of the comedy *Dream Girl*. Several critics warned that audiences would not hear her squeaky Billie Dawn voice, and Holliday pushed back, saying, "I couldn't use the same voice even if I wanted to." But Harry Cohn wasn't getting the message, and he tried securing the rights to the play *Gentlemen Prefer Blondes* for Holliday's next film. He was outbid by Fox, and the part of the gold-digging Lorelei Lee went to Marilyn Monroe.

Instead, Holliday reunited with George Cukor in *The Marrying Kind*. But she never took to Hollywood, or to the award it had given her. "She didn't trust an award or the world of the award," says her son, Jonathan Oppenheim. At their apartment at the Dakota, in Manhattan, the Oscar was not displayed prominently. "I think it was probably in my grandmother's room," Oppenheim guesses. His mother "wanted to be rooted, and I think that the Oscar and its trappings were a rootless entity for her."

Near the end of 1951, Holliday was called to testify before a Senate subcommittee. Though Cohn still thought of her as "that fat Jewish broad," he was determined not to lose his Oscar-garlanded star to the blacklist. He enlisted the Columbia legal team and even hired an investigator—a former FBI agent who had done research for *Counterattack* before switching sides—to monitor evidence that might be used against her. On March 26, 1952, Holliday entered a Washington chamber in a black dress, white gloves, and a veiled hat. She had a tricky line to walk: professing her innocence without seeming defiant, appearing cooperative without being compelled to name names. Sitting before the stone-faced senators, she found a brilliant solution only she could have pulled off: playing dumb.

When the committee's counsel pressed her on her acquaintances, she professed winsome ignorance of their political views. The counsel, who may have read one of the many movie magazine profiles boasting of Holliday's genius IQ level, asked if she knew about Thomas Mann's or Albert Einstein's affiliations with Communist fronts.

"I am sure that Mann and Einstein got into it the way I did, because I am sure none of them are Communists," she said, with Billie Dawn reasoning. "I mean, if you are a Communist, why go to a Communist front? Why not be a Communist? Whatever you are, be it!"

By the end of the hearing, her "Who, me?" act had worked like a charm. "Well, I guess you've learned to watch it now, haven't you?" Arthur Watkins, Republican senator from Utah, told her.

"Ho, ho!" she said. "Have I ever!" As for lending her name to causes, she added, "Now I don't say yes to anything except cancer, polio, and cerebral palsy." The line, which could have come straight out of *Born Yesterday*, sent Holliday out on a cloud of goodwill. She had outsmarted them all. But she had also foretold her own fate: in 1965, she died of breast cancer two weeks short of her forty-fourth birthday.

The 1951 Best Actress race pitted Hollywood's past against its present, with one up-and-coming starlet stealing the crown from two seasoned comeback queens. In the end, none could escape the shadows of Billie, Norma, and Margo. Holliday, Swanson, and Davis had wedged themselves into the spotlight despite the strictures of Hollywood's standards: they were too old or too difficult or too fat or too Jewish. What they couldn't have predicted was that the "dumb blonde" archetype of *Born Yesterday* would morph into the blond bombshell, or that female stardom in the fifties would be defined by Marilyn Monroe. Like Eve Harrington, she was the bit player who would upstage them all.

FIVE

Who Is Robert Rich?

1947–60

How the screenwriters of *Roman Holiday*, *High Noon*, and *The Bridge on the River Kwai* fought the Hollywood blacklist—and turned the Academy Awards into a farce.

On March 27, 1957, Deborah Kerr walked onstage at the Pantages to present the Academy Award for Best Motion Picture Story. The nominees that year (the last of the category's existence) included French philosopher Jean-Paul Sartre, for *The Proud and the Beautiful*. But when Kerr opened the envelope, the winner was an unknown: Robert Rich, for RKO's *The Brave One*. The film told the treacly tale of a Mexican boy trying to save his pet bull from slaughter in the matador's ring. Jesse Lasky Jr., as vice president of the screenwriters' branch of the Writers Guild of America, accepted the prize on behalf of Rich, who was not present.

In the days that followed, the winner's identity became a mystery that enveloped Hollywood. Before the ceremony, a Robert Rich had called the Academy requesting two tickets, then called back to cancel because his wife was sick. It emerged that the film's producers, the B-movie impresarios the King Brothers, had a nephew named Robert Rich who had once worked as their bookkeeper. The nephew, now employed at a casting company, admitted that he had asked for the tickets, but, amazingly, was not the same Robert Rich who had written the movie treatment. He was terribly sorry for the deception and told the *New York Times* that he wished to "clear this thing up before I lose my job."

The King Brothers compounded this preposterous story with another one. According to Frank King, Robert Rich was an American ex-GI he had met in a hotel in Munich in 1952. He had bought the movie pitch for a modest sum, but Rich was now "somewhere in Europe," or maybe Australia—King had sent five cables and was "trying to locate him." *Life* magazine, reporting on the Hollywood "Whowonit," ran an illustration of the phantom Oscar winner based on King's recollections: brown hair parted on the left, aquiline nose, small goatee, thirty-one years of age, 175 pounds. "I'd recognize him anywhere," King said. He dismissed the "ridiculous" speculation that "Robert Rich" was a front for a blacklisted screenwriter.

The plot thickened when Paul Rader, a television and radio producer in Cambridge, claimed that *he* must be Robert Rich, given that he had sold a similar story, called *Ring Around Saturn*, to Nassour Studios in 1951. Another version had it that a writer named Willis O'Brien had sold a tale called *Emilio and the Bull* to Jesse Lasky Sr., who then gave it to his son; the Nassour brothers later acquired it and hired Rader to do a rewrite. Director Fred Zinnemann said that Robert Flaherty, the documentarian known for *Nanook of the North*, had come up with the story back in 1931. Flaherty had died in 1951, but his widow confirmed, "My husband wrote a story idea about a boy who loves a fighting bull. But now I would not think of protesting the award." Orson Welles backed up the Flaherty claim, saying that *he* had bought the idea in 1941 and shot some of it, as part of his doomed post–*Citizen Kane* project in Latin America. "But if they used our stuff and it worked," Welles said, "hurrah for them."

Frank King countered that the story was a popular legend, and if you gave it to ten thousand writers, "they all must come to the same conclusion: you can't kill the bull and you can't kill the boy." Nevertheless, less than two weeks after the Oscars, the King Brothers and RKO settled a $750,000 lawsuit brought against them by Nassour Studios, apparently because Robert Rich was unavailable to testify—meaning that the enigma would not be solved in the courts. Meanwhile, Academy officials held a three-and-a-half-hour meeting and emerged with a statement: "To date no clear proof of authorship has been established. Until such time as the writer presents and identifies himself as the true author of the story and is qualified to receive the award, the 'Oscar' will remain with the academy."

But no one came forward, and the question remained: Who is Robert Rich?

A DECADE EARLIER, ON A sweltering afternoon in September 1947, two small children were cooling themselves on the terrace of their ranch house in Kern County, a few hours north of Los Angeles. Gazing toward the sagebrush-covered valley, they saw a glint of sunlight off a car winding through the country road. The ranch was so secluded that days could pass without any sign of the outside world; more unusual was that the car was headed toward the house. A stranger in shirtsleeves stepped out and said, "Hey, kids, your folks around?"

The children led the man through the kitchen door to their father. "Mr. Trumbo?" the stranger said.

"That's right."

"Mr. Dalton Trumbo?"

He nodded. The man, a deputy U.S. marshal, handed him an envelope. Inside was a folded pink paper instructing him to appear before the House Un-American Activities Committee in Washington, DC, on October 23, 1947, at 10:30 a.m. Trumbo looked up and said, "Would you like some water before you leave?" Then he handed the man a glass of fresh mountain water that the family had pumped from a creek.

Trumbo and his wife, Cleo, explained to the children that he was being investigated by the government. "It has subpoenaed me because of my political beliefs," he said. "We are Communists, and I have to go to Washington to answer questions about my communism." When the children asked what communism was, they said, "It's a system of government that provides to each person according to his need and that gives according to each person's ability. Capitalism, on the other hand, is based on making profits." Then Trumbo told them that he might go to jail.

The subpoena, though alarming, was not a surprise. At forty-one, Trumbo was one of Hollywood's highest-paid screenwriters and one of its most outspoken leftists. The Committee was widely known to be investigating Communist infiltration in Hollywood, and the family had moved to the ranch from Beverly Hills to save money in case they were caught up in the dragnet. Days before receiving the HUAC subpoena, Trumbo had warned a meeting of concerned Hollywood leftists that the Committee was waging "intellectual terror" that echoed the "poisonous features of Fascism itself."

A sly fox with an instinct for arguing, Trumbo had an acid wit, a bushy mustache, a drinking habit, and an epistolary flair. (His screenplays were second to his eviscerating letters.) He often wrote in the bathtub, a cigarette holder dangling between his lips and a typewriter perched on a board laid across the tub. Words were his ammunition. "My father could be so dominant, irascible, and tenacious," his daughter Mitzi would recall. "He enjoyed confrontation; he never hesitated to jump into a dispute full throttle, and he rarely let anyone else win."

Dalton Trumbo had come to political radicalism relatively late in life. Born in 1905, he spent most of his childhood in Grand Junction, Colorado. His father moved with the family to Los Angeles in 1925, to work at a Harley-Davidson dealership, and Trumbo joined them after his first year of college. He found a job as a nighttime bread wrapper at a bakery, where he worked for eight years while churning out short stories, novels, and essays. The bakery job was grueling, but it did not turn him toward class warfare. "I never considered the working class anything other than something to get out of," he cracked.

Despite considering the movie studios "consanguineous societies chartered to fry the fat out of the stockholder," Trumbo was hired as a script reader at Warner Bros. in 1934. He had ambition and a knack for showmanship. After publishing a short story in The Saturday Evening Post—a satire of government corruption called "Darling Bill"—he managed to pose for the Los Angeles Examiner with Bette Davis holding up a copy. He joined the Screen Writers Guild as it was battling the studio chiefs. Union work suited Trumbo's belligerence, but he wasn't alone. The labor movement spurred by the Depression was politicizing many Hollywood workers, particularly screenwriters. The Spanish Civil War and the rise of Hitler and Mussolini further galvanized the town's growing left wing. In 1936, the same year that Columbia signed Trumbo to a $250-a-week writing contract, the Communist Party of the United States of America made its first major inroads in Hollywood. Though it kept its member rolls secret, the party gave left-leaning citizens an outlet for political activism on issues like antifascism, labor rights, racial equality, and the Spanish Republic. By the middle of World War II, more than half of the party's Hollywood membership consisted of screenwriters.

Trumbo established himself as both a lightning-fast scenarist and a gadfly with a colorful tongue. He edited the guild's magazine, *Screen Writer*, which became a hotbed of progressive argument. In 1939, the FBI, which was slowly collecting information on what it considered a Soviet plot to take over the American cinema, opened a dossier on Trumbo. Leftist screenwriters were often conflicted about their inability to reconcile their political views with their participation in a capitalist studio system that—contrary to the FBI's paranoia—squelched any attempt to put radicalism on-screen. But during World War II, with the U.S. government, the Soviets, and Hollywood all aligned against a common enemy, the studios welcomed antifascist messaging. Trumbo wrote a string of patriotic hits, including *Tender Comrade*. He was on a roll, especially after his screenplay for the Ginger Rogers vehicle *Kitty Foyle* received an Oscar nomination in 1941.

Although his FBI file labeled him a "Communist fellow traveler" in 1942, Trumbo did not join the party until the following year. Cleo recalled a night on which Trumbo came home "full of energy and a little drunk. Not terribly drunk, but a little drunk. It's kind of like he blew in and announced that he had just joined the Communist Party and I was also a member, and then blew out again." The decision stemmed largely from his friendships with other left-wing writers (and fellow drinkers) like Ian McLellan Hunter, Ring Lardner Jr., and his frequent correspondent Michael Wilson. "Joining the Communist Party had no more importance for him than joining the Catholic Church," Trumbo's son, Christopher, recalled. He quit five years later, finding the party meetings "dull beyond description." (He usually showed up tipsy.)

The war's denouement brought a drastic change in the political winds. With the Soviet Union now standing as the only threat to American hegemony, the right-wing critics of the New Deal, who had been muted during the war, brought anticommunist rhetoric to a roar. Proximity to communism, which in the thirties had been a fact of political life, was recast as "anti-American," and those who had been early to criticize foreign authoritarianism were now suspected of "premature antifascism." Sam Wood, who had directed *Kitty Foyle*, was among the new crop of Hollywood conservatives whose hatred of communism turned into witch-hunting frenzy. His daughter Jeane remembered that the subject "transformed Dad into a snarling, unreasoning brute," though she traced his obsessive Red-baiting to bitterness over losing the directing Oscar for *Goodbye, Mr. Chips*.

Wood became the founding president of the Motion Picture Alliance for the Preservation of American Ideals (or MPA), an organization formed, according to screenwriter John Lee Mahin, to "turn off the faucets which dripped red water into film scripts." In 1944, its members—who included John Wayne and Walt Disney—wrote to Senator Robert R. Reynolds, a conservative Democrat from North Carolina, warning of the "flagrant manner in which the motion picture industrialists of Hollywood have been coddling Communists." The letter, signed "A Group of Your Friends in Hollywood," was all but an invitation to a witch hunt, and Reynolds read it into the *Congressional Record*. HUAC, created in 1938, had threatened to probe Hollywood before, but after the midterm elections of 1946, in which Republicans took both chambers of Congress, Trumbo began hearing "ominous word from Washington" about what it had in store.

Now the highest-paid screenwriter at MGM, Trumbo attacked the MPA with withering disdain, writing of his former collaborator Sam Wood, "There seems to be no way of confirming a report that he proposes to spend his twilight years engraving the Lord's Prayer on the head of a Communist." (Wood hit back at "Comrade Trumbo" in a full-page ad in *The Hollywood Reporter.*) But Trumbo's enemies were bigger than one angry director. In May 1947, HUAC sent a three-person subcommittee to Los Angeles to question "friendly" witnesses about the Communist influence in Hollywood. On September 21, it issued more than forty subpoenas to members of the film industry, including nineteen deemed "unfriendly" witnesses. One of them was Trumbo.

At first, much of the industry rallied around "the Unfriendly Nineteen." "Nobody can tell me how to run my studio," Louis B. Mayer squawked. A liberal cadre, including William Wyler and John Huston, founded the Committee for the First Amendment, which produced a radio broadcast called "Hollywood Fights Back" and flew a chartered plane of stars, among them Humphrey Bogart, Lauren Bacall, and Katharine Hepburn, to voice their support in Washington. The Nineteen and their lawyers, meanwhile, hashed out a strategy. If they invoked the Fifth Amendment to avoid self-incrimination, they'd be admitting that membership in the Communist Party was incriminating. If they proudly declared their political affiliation, they would be asked to name names of other members. Trumbo and Lardner argued that they should use their testimony to turn the tables and question HUAC's legitimacy, hanging their right to political privacy on the First Amendment. If they were cited for contempt, they believed they would be on firm footing to win through the courts, thus destroying the Committee. This became the plan.

The hearings began on October 20, at the beaux-arts Caucus Room of the Old House Office Building. They opened with "friendly" witnesses, including Sam Wood, who, when asked if he knew any Communists, replied, "Well, I don't think there's any question about Dalton Trumbo." Ginger Rogers's archconservative mother, Lela, testified, having told investigators that her daughter was forced to say Trumbo's line in *Tender Comrade* "Share and share alike—that's democracy." Jack Warner, breaking the studio heads' intended stonewall, withered under the spotlight, perhaps nervous that his own studio had produced the pro-Soviet *Mission to Moscow.* Without being asked, he named twelve Communists he professed to have "spotted" and fired, including Trumbo. (Warner later admitted that he hadn't fired any of them.)

The Committee then moved on to the Unfriendly Nineteen. When

Trumbo's turn came, he sat behind two radio microphones, surrounded by lawyers and popping flashbulbs, poised for a battle of wits. But the chairman forbade him to read his opening statement. "I would like to know," Trumbo asked, "what it is in my statement that this committee fears to be read to the American people?" When the chairman gaveled over his attempts to answer questions with speeches and demanded responses of "yes" or "no," Trumbo retorted, "Very many questions can be answered 'Yes' or 'No' only by a moron or a slave."

Then came the big question: "Are you now, or have you ever been, a member of the Communist Party?"

Trumbo tried to circumvent an answer, saying, "I believe I have the right to be confronted with any evidence which supports this question. I should like to see what you have."

"Well, you will, pretty soon," he was told. "The witness is excused. Impossible."

Trumbo tried to get the last word, warning, as he left the stand, "This is the beginning of an American concentration camp." But Committee chairman J. Parnell Thomas shot back, "Typical Communist tactics." He cited Trumbo for contempt of Congress.

The hearings went on for two more days, churning through ten "unfriendly" witnesses, all of whom refused to answer the Committee's questions. (An eleventh, German playwright Bertolt Brecht, denied being a Communist and promptly returned to Europe.) Then the hearings, having grown repetitive, were adjourned indefinitely, with Chairman Thomas warning the movie industry to "clear its own house."

The so-called Hollywood Ten returned to Los Angeles feeling victorious. Trumbo resumed work at MGM. But the triumph disintegrated like a film dissolve. The witnesses' truculence struck many observers as evidence that they had something to hide. The liberal allies of the Committee for the First Amendment, under pressure from the studios, backed off; Bogart later published a piece in *Photoplay* titled "I'm No Communist." Wyler recalled, "People got scared . . . All our heads were going to be on a chopping block." The right-wing press, including Hedda Hopper and William Randolph Hearst, kept the heat on. In November, a large group of industry leaders, among them Louis B. Mayer, Harry Cohn, and Samuel Goldwyn, met at New York's Waldorf-Astoria and released a decree: in addition to discharging the Ten, the studios would "not knowingly employ a Communist or a member of any party or group which advocates the overthrow of the government of the United States by force or by any illegal or unconstitutional methods." The Waldorf Statement, as it became known, was the opening bell for one of Hollywood's darkest chapters. The blacklist had begun.

MGM suspended Trumbo indefinitely. In Washington, the House approved his contempt citation by a vote of 240–16. Plummeting from the top of his profession, Trumbo immediately felt the financial strain. By December, he agreed to write an uncredited screenplay called *Gun Crazy*, for King Brothers Productions, for a dramatically reduced fee. This was the beginning of the black market, an alternative economy that operated through pseudonyms, verbal contracts, and shady middlemen. If a producer failed to pay him, he had little recourse but to "take the loss in silence," Trumbo wrote. In May 1948, a jury found him guilty of contempt of Congress, and he was sentenced to twelve months and a one-thousand-dollar fine. "As far as I was concerned, it was a completely just verdict," he said later. "I had contempt for that Congress and have had contempt for several since."

As Trumbo waited for his appeals to go through, he wrote a pamphlet called *The Time of the Toad: A Study of Inquisition in America*, decrying the moral bankruptcy of the era, while scrounging for money on the black market. "It simply requires that I work three times as fast for about one-fifth my former price," he wrote to his aunt and uncle. *Gun Crazy*, based on a *Saturday Evening Post* story by MacKinlay Kantor, was released in late 1949, under the title *Deadly Is the Female*. The screenplay was credited to Kantor and Millard Kaufman, a writer who was acting as a front.

In April 1950, the Supreme Court declined to hear Trumbo's appeal, delivering a final blow to his freedom. That June, Prisoner No. 7551 entered the Federal Correctional Institution in Ashland, Kentucky. Before leaving for prison, he had written an original screenplay that was as fanciful as his reality was bleak but that mirrored it in exactly one respect: it was about going incognito. The story was about a princess who poses as a commoner and falls in love with a reporter. It was *Roman Holiday*.

By the time Trumbo emerged from prison, in the spring of 1951, it was clear that the contagion could not be limited to the Hollywood Ten. Four years after the original hearings, the newly aggressive HUAC widened its net with a second round. Hundreds in Hollywood now waited with dread for men with crew cuts to arrive with pink subpoena papers—as helpless, as one journalist put it, as "a group of marooned sailors on a flat desert island watching the approach of a tidal wave."

The options were grim: take the Fifth and get blackballed from the industry, name names and get branded a snitch, or somehow clear your name without doing either, as Judy Holliday did. Even without a subpoena, you could wind up on the "graylist," an unofficial roster of the unemployable. Alleged subversives were now asked to sign loyalty oaths, and a cottage industry emerged to "clear" those presumed guilty. "It was like a pall that fell over," recalled screenwriter Howard Koch. "People began to be suspicious of each other. Should you go and see a Russian movie, or would they take your license plate and send it in to the FBI? Suddenly, fear enveloped the atmosphere of Hollywood."

Carl Foreman received his subpoena on June 13 from a friendly man in a gray suit who apologized for being the bearer of bad news. At thirty-six, the stocky, bespectacled screenwriter was a man's man of the Frank Sinatra school: he drank dry martinis, played poker and gin rummy, bet on football games. He wrote with two cigarettes going at once, one on either side of his typewriter. Foreman had boxed in his youth and still had the toughness and street smarts of a scrappy Chicago kid. When his temper went hot, which it did easily, he would swell his barrel chest and bellow—a skill he'd learned as a carnival barker.

Foreman had just been nominated for two Oscars in a row: for *Champion*, in which Kirk Douglas played a boxer, and *The Men*, starring Marlon Brando, in his film début, as a war veteran in a wheelchair. Both were collaborations with director-producer Stanley Kramer, Foreman's business partner, who ran the biggest independent film company in town. When he got the subpoena, Foreman was finishing the script for their next picture, *High Noon*.

He left work early and went home to Brentwood to his wife Estelle and their four-year-old daughter. A former member of the Communist

Party, he knew that someone had named him. "Who do you suppose the son of a bitch was who did this to us?" he fumed.

Snitching was something Foreman could not abide. Back in the Chicago of his youth, no one would ever have ratted out a friend to the cops. Foreman was born to Russian-Jewish immigrants, in 1914, and was steeped in the working-class left. For a time, he wanted to be a lawyer like Clarence Darrow, but then fell in love with the movies, which he considered "the people's art." He made his first attempt to get to Hollywood at nineteen, at the invitation of his aunt, who was married to a well-connected furniture dealer. The trip was a bust: somewhere in Missouri, his car hit a cow and knocked over a lettuce truck. He took a bus the rest of the way, only to find that his aunt had divorced the furniture guy. There, Foreman worked as a janitor, subsisted on peanuts, and slept in public parks. After a year, he slumped back to Chicago and joined a traveling carnival. In 1938, he returned to Los Angeles on a circus train packed with elephants.

To learn screenwriting, Foreman took night classes at the League of American Writers, an organization founded by the Communist Party. He saw the party as the only political organization truly agitating for causes such as labor rights and antifascism. He and Estelle became members a few years after getting married, and the party became the center of their social world. "If you left the party," he said, "you were leaving the friends you had." After Pearl Harbor, he joined the Signal Corps, specifically the unit overseen by Frank Capra, and spent nine months working on a documentary called *Know Your Enemy: Japan*. While working out of a studio in Astoria, he met Stanley Kramer, then a young lieutenant and film editor with what Foreman called a "brooding aura of fighting injustice about him." Both were passionate about what was wrong with Hollywood and their desire to change it.

After the war, Kramer founded his own company, with the intention of making movies that had something to say; in the late forties, there was an opening for socially conscious dramas like *The Best Years of Our Lives* and *Gentleman's Agreement*. Kramer hired Foreman as a writer, and they set up shop in a warehouse. Their first picture, *So This Is New York*, was a flop, but they bounced back with *Champion*, which used the rise of a brutish boxer as a metaphor for capitalism and corruption. ("Aw, it's like any other business," the boxer says. "Only here, the blood shows.") Kirk Douglas, still a relative unknown, won the part when he ripped off his shirt in Kramer's office and flexed his muscles. After screening *Champion* at the paraplegic ward of a veterans' hospital, Kramer devised *The Men*, another socially minded drama, highlighting the plight of wounded veterans. Foreman's screenplay lost the Oscar to *Sunset Boulevard*'s, but he used his gathering clout to push Kramer on an idea he'd been working on for years: a Western about a small-town lawman facing down a band of outlaws.

Foreman had originally conceived *High Noon* as a parable of postwar global interdependence, inspired by the United Nations. But as the Red Scare took hold, his mood darkened, and so did the script. Foreman had followed the 1947 HUAC hearings with horror—and relief that he was too small potatoes to be targeted. By then, he and Estelle had left the Communist Party, mostly because of the pressures of Carl's work schedule and caring for their daughter, Kate. By 1951, the crackdown had reduced the party to fewer than a hundred members in Los Angeles, but Foreman's successes made him vulnerable to the Committee's attentions. He was disgusted by the kangaroo court hearings and by Hollywood's cravenness. "It was these events," he said, "that made me think of a story about Hollywood under the political gun."

High Noon became a story about cowardice, about facing down evil alone when no one has the guts to stand with you. The hero, Marshal Will Kane, of Hadleyville (the name scans like "Hollywood"), learns on his wedding day that a dangerous man he once sent to prison has been released and is headed into town with his goons on the noon train to take revenge. The marshal looks for help, but, one by one, the townspeople— his new bride, his deputy, the judge, the churchgoers—turn him away. When the clock strikes twelve, Kane walks down the abandoned main street alone to face his destiny.

Foreman conceived the story as unfolding in real time, to heighten the suspense of the coming train. After he finished a treatment, someone told him that a story with a similar premise had run in *Collier's* magazine, under the title "The Tin Star," so Foreman bought the rights and called

his screenplay an adaptation. He hoped to direct, but Kramer was closing in on a huge deal to bring the Stanley Kramer Company under the
umbrella of Columbia Pictures and needed Foreman to focus on scripts.
Instead, Kramer hired the director of *The Men*, Fred Zinnemann, who
saw *High Noon* as "a picture of conscience as against compromise."

As Foreman fine-tuned the screenplay, the war between conscience
and compromise was raging in Washington. In April, lapsed Communist
Richard J. Collins gave HUAC twenty-three names, among them a
little-known screenwriter named Martin Berkeley. When an investigator came to his home, Berkeley turned out to be a geyser, spouting an
astounding 150 names. One of them was "Carl Foreman." When he got
the subpoena, Foreman called Kramer, who assured him that everything
would work out. But others in the company worried that Foreman's situation would disrupt their deal with Columbia and sided against him, just
as Foreman had seen supposed allies do to others. "It was now happening
to me rather than to friends of mine," Foreman said, "and it was all falling into line." As he finished *High Noon*, he borrowed the townsfolk's
cowardly dialogue directly from life. "You could walk down the street
and see friends of yours recognize you, turn, and walk the other way,"
he recalled.

Surprisingly, one person who didn't turn his back was the movie's
star, Gary Cooper. Cooper had been a friendly HUAC witness in 1947
and was a charter member of the Red-baiting Motion Picture Alliance;
at one of its first meetings, he warned against "the lukewarm Americans
who dally with sedition in the guise of being liberals." Foreman told him,
"If you want to leave the picture, now's the time to do it." But Cooper
flashed his twinkling eyes, called Foreman an honest man, and said that
he wasn't going anywhere.

Foreman was willing to go to jail rather than name names, but his
lawyer had a tactic he called the "qualified Fifth," in which Foreman
would state that he was not a member of the Communist Party currently, then invoke the Fifth when asked if he had ever been a member
in the past. It was a risky path, but so was Marshal Kane's in *High Noon*.
Foreman and Zinnemann were still debating the ending: Should Kane
defeat his persecutors or, as Foreman put it, "go down bravely but dead"?

He urged the director, "Freddy, if we let him go, if he dies, what we'll be saying is you can't win, you just can't win, so just give in."

Kane would survive. But would Foreman?

During the second week of filming, the Stanley Kramer Company asked Foreman to resign from the company and cease work on *High Noon*, for which he was also an associate producer. Foreman pleaded with Kramer in a two-hour private meeting. "I tried to explain, but Stanley wouldn't listen," Foreman recalled. "Don't tell me about the qualified Fifth," Kramer told him. "They'll say, 'Do you know Stanley Kramer?' and you'll take the Fifth and then *I'll* be in trouble." Kramer claimed that Foreman had not been forthcoming about his political past and that he had even threatened to use Kramer's liberal reputation against him, "depending on how the negotiations turned out." "We had a couple of meetings in which I locked the door and looked him right in the eye," Kramer lamented, "and I just felt he didn't look me back in the right way, and we parted." The two men never spoke again.

The next day, Foreman visited the set of *High Noon*, on the Columbia Ranch. Martin Berkeley had just spelled out his name in a hearing on television, and he wanted to warn the cast and crew. As he turned toward the parking lot, Gary Cooper threw his arm around him and said, "Do what you have to do. But kid, don't let them put you in jail."

On September 24, Foreman arrived at the Federal Building in Los Angeles. He had been fantasizing about showing up dressed as Abraham Lincoln and giving a speech so rousing that he would end the witch hunt forever. Instead, he wore a "very sincere tie" and tiptoed through the legal minefield. Had he renounced his membership in the Communist Party? "I have never admitted that I was a member of the Communist Party." Could he say so now? "I decline to answer." He asserted, "I am an American. I was born here and I love this country. I love it as much as any man on this committee."

None of it stirred the hearts of the officials. The hearing was over after an hour.

Although he and Kramer had agreed to wait sixty days to decide on his employment, the producer immediately released a statement through Columbia Pictures citing a "total disagreement between Carl Foreman and myself." Foreman, now living out his own screenplay, recalled, "They quit right then and there and threw me to the wolves." His legal strategy had saved him from prosecution but not from the blacklist. By October, his lawyer finalized a severance agreement stripping Foreman of his associate producer credit. Foreman announced that he was founding his own production company, with backing from Gary Cooper. But after John Wayne pressured the star and Hedda Hopper scoffed in print, Cooper reluctantly backed out, like the last ally to abandon Marshal Kane in *High Noon*.

After meeting personally with Wayne, who made it clear that Foreman would never work in Hollywood unless he gave friendlier testimony, the screenwriter realized that he was truly alone. "My partners, you know, saw their own futures and careers trembling in the balance, because of their guilt by association with me, and they behaved as a great many other people did," he said. He got a passport and, in May 1952, boarded the ocean liner the SS *Liberté* on a one-way trip to England. When he arrived in Southampton six days later, he felt "completely liberated." He settled in London, where his family soon joined him in exile. The problem was that he couldn't write. "When I sat down at the typewriter," he recalled, "instead of writing 'Fade in' or 'Scene One,' I would find myself writing, in effect, a letter to the editor, any editor! *'Dear sir. Do you know what they're doing to me?'* You see, I was full of rage and self-pity."

Back in Hollywood, *High Noon* was nominated for seven Academy Awards. *Variety* predicted, "'HIGH NOON' LOOKS TO SWEEP OSCARS." Few recognized the film as a blacklist allegory, but Foreman's screenplay nomination opened it up to attack nonetheless. After Foreman won the Screen Writers Guild award, *The Hollywood Reporter*'s Billy Wilkerson called the honor "an affront to the upholders of our democracy." Paramount executive Luigi Luraschi, who was on the Academy board, told a CIA contact that he'd been working to kneecap its Best Picture chances. Before the ceremony, *The Hollywood Reporter* revealed that "none of the Kramer boys wanted to accept the screenplay award if Carl Foreman won it for *High Noon*."

On March 19, 1953, at the first Oscar ceremony to be televised, *High Noon* won four awards, for its editing, score, theme song, and star, Gary

Cooper (his second Best Actor win, after *Sergeant York*). But it lost Best Picture to Paramount's circus spectacular *The Greatest Show on Earth*, directed by staunch conservative Cecil B. DeMille, which became notorious as one of the worst Best Picture winners in Oscar history. "I still believe *High Noon* was the best picture of 1952," Stanley Kramer wrote later. "But the political climate of the nation and the right-wing campaigns against *High Noon* had enough effect to relegate it to an also-ran status." Foreman lost the Best Screenplay award, but he wasn't the only blacklisted writer in the category. It was a distinction he shared with Michael Wilson.

MORE THAN TRUMBO OR FOREMAN, Michael Wilson was a committed Marxist. Handsome and clean-shaven, with penetrating blue eyes, he was serious, taciturn. But beneath his shell was a deep ethical center, a quiet fervor that made him almost priestlike, especially when it came to the downtrodden, for whom he had a passionate, bleeding heart. Wilson abhorred small talk, but when discussion turned political, he became fervid, even cutting. An alcoholic who could hold his whiskey so well that few noticed, Wilson was a deliberate writer—he would pace the room as he hashed out scenes, twirling a lock of his hair—and could never understand how his friend Trumbo churned out scripts so fast. "I grew up hungry, you didn't," Trumbo would say.

Wilson was born in 1914 in Oklahoma and raised as a religious Catholic who lived in "mortal terror of salvation." As a teenager, he rebelled against his successful yet uneducated salesman father, whose "world I wanted to shun," Wilson recalled. "But I had no idea what to replace it with." In 1932, he enrolled at the University of California, Berkeley, where he studied philosophy and dreamed of becoming the next Hemingway. He stayed for graduate school and became radicalized. He read Marx and Engels and thought of writing novels about the "struggles of modern man." During a year in Europe, he tried joining the Abraham Lincoln Battalion in the Spanish Civil War, but no recruits were needed, and he was consumed with guilt over not being able to fight. "I was still a very immature, hopelessly romantic young man," he said. When he returned to Berkeley, he joined the Communist Party.

In a short time, he became the chairman of the campus branch. He tried writing a novella about Mexican laborers and taught classes on Marxism. "He was a positively gorgeous-looking guy, and all these wonderful ideas were coming out of him," recalled his future wife, Zelma. In need of money, he joined an Alaskan salmon expedition and instructed the Chicano fishermen on class struggle. In 1940, Zelma's brother-in-law, leftist screenwriter Paul Jarrico, persuaded him to come to Hollywood. Wilson believed that movies were "a secondary art form," but he figured it could pay the bills while he wrote fiction.

He and Zelma moved into a one-room shack behind the Hollywood Roosevelt, and he got his first credit revising a regrettable script called *The Men in Her Life*, which had already passed through sixteen writers. Like many left-wing screenwriters, Wilson felt a looming gap between his beliefs and his craft. In one of several Hopalong Cassidy Westerns he wrote, a group of ranchers organize to fight a monopoly over water rights. He used the Marxist idea of the dialectic to infuse scenes with human tension. He quickly befriended Dalton Trumbo, who later joked, "We saw a lot of each other in those days, spending many evenings together planning ways of bringing down Warner Brothers by force and violence, injecting the noodles in MGM's chicken soup with a red dye."

After Pearl Harbor, Wilson enlisted in the Marine Corps and served in the Pacific, rising to first lieutenant. Zelma saw his desire to join "the most aggressive, dangerous aspect of the war" as overcompensation for his failure to fight in Spain. After three years, he returned to Hollywood and was hired by Liberty Films, a new company formed by Frank Capra, George Stevens, and William Wyler. His first assignment was to retool a script that Capra planned to direct, about a man who considers suicide on Christmas Eve but is redeemed by a guardian angel. Zelma recalled, "I remember him coming home groaning about having to write dialogue with an angel." In the end, he did not receive a credit on *It's a Wonderful Life*.

In 1946, Capra assigned him an adaptation of *The Friendly Persuasion*, a book of vignettes by Jessamyn West based on her Quaker ancestors in Indiana. Wilson managed to locate dialectical conflict in one of the stories, in which a Confederate raid spurs the family's teenage son into battle, despite the Quakers' pacifist principles. As a peace lover who had fought in a just war, Wilson recognized this conflict, and he wanted his script to show "how the serenity of Quaker life is disturbed by the alien values of the outside world." Capra, however, worried that the project might be "construed as being antiwar." After Wilson finished his second draft, Liberty Films was sold to Paramount, and *The Friendly Persuasion* was shelved.

Wilson followed the company to Paramount, where he was assigned an adaptation of the novel *An American Tragedy*, to be directed by George Stevens. Released as *A Place in the Sun*, it told the dark tale of a working-class striver (Montgomery Clift) who fantasizes about murdering the factory girl he has impregnated (Shelley Winters) when he falls in love with a glamorous socialite (Elizabeth Taylor). Though the taut, Hitchcockian screenplay was light on politics, Wilson said that he and Stevens "came into conflict on ideological points" when the director worried that he was being "too stubbornly Marxist."

A Place in the Sun was released in August 1951. Wilson had moved to Fox, where Darryl Zanuck assigned him *5 Fingers*, Joseph L. Mankiewicz's adaptation of a memoir by a former Nazi attaché in wartime Turkey. Wilson was finishing his script when, on June 13, 1951, he received his pink invitation to testify before HUAC.

Zanuck fired him three days later. "I have been 'laid off,' which is the studios' temporary euphemism for blacklisting me," Wilson wrote to a friend. "There was a time when studios waited until a man was in contempt of Congress before blacklisting him; but today the mere announcement that I have a subpoena and that I oppose this committee's aims costs me my job." Wilson's own parents urged him to cooperate, but, five days before his testimony, he wrote them, "Surely, whatever your beliefs, you cannot see this as an alternative for a decent human being—to turn Judas, to sell my birthright and worship the Almighty Dollar for the sake of expediency, for the sake of my career, or for the sake of your shame as to what people will think. It is not my career that is really at stake at all—it is my survival as a free writer."

On September 20, four days before Carl Foreman, Wilson appeared at the hearing room in Los Angeles. The Committee did not allow him to read his opening statement, in which he had written, "The consequence of these hearings will be appalling pictures, more pictures glorifying racism, war and brutality, perversion and violence. I do not think any honest pictures will be written by frightened writers; and I know they will not be written by informers." When asked what knowledge he had of Communist activity in Hollywood, Wilson took the Fifth and added, "I think subversion is being committed against the Bill of Rights here today." Capra, who watched on live television, later wrote to the Committee, "I was bowled over by Michael Wilson's connection with the party. He wouldn't have lasted two minutes with Liberty Films had I the slightest inkling he was a Red."

Five months later, Wilson's screenplay for *A Place in the Sun* won the Oscar, beating *The African Queen* and *A Streetcar Named Desire*. Zelma was eager to attend the ceremony, and friends urged Wilson to seize the chance to speak out against the blacklist. But he refused; he had nothing but contempt for Hollywood's hypocrisy and cowardice. Instead, his cowinner, Harry Brown, who had done revisions on the script, accepted the prize alone, apologizing that Wilson "couldn't be here to appreciate the thrill." The win showed that there was still room for Academy voters to embrace a worthy screenplay by a blacklisted writer, perhaps as a form of silent protest. By the next year, when Wilson was nominated for *5 Fingers*, and Foreman for *High Noon*, that window had evidently closed.

Banished from Hollywood, Wilson and twenty-two others filed a lawsuit alleging that the studios had conspired to refuse them employment. The Supreme Court would dismiss the case five years later. In the meantime, Wilson and other blacklistees made their own movie outside Hollywood, one that would express their political views free of studio interference. The film was *Salt of the Earth*, inspired by the Empire Zinc Company strike in New Mexico. Wilson's screenplay, radically unlike anything in Hollywood of the era, foregrounded Chicano workers and had a distinctly feminist thrust, as the strikers' wives prove their mettle on the picket line. Unsurprisingly, the movie came under attack even as it was being filmed. Planes roared overhead to ruin shots, and there was an arson attempt on the local union hall. Right-wing groups pressured projectionists not to show the film, and it was barely seen upon release in 1954.

Wilson was relegated to working on the black market for cheap. He recalled one humiliating job for a producer who refused to meet him: "He was so frightened of being associated with me he would bring cash to the corner druggist, a pharmacist. The degradation came when the man didn't like what I had done and I couldn't even get a hearing to prove to the man I was working for—whom I never met—that the way I wanted to do it was right."

In 1956, Wilson quit the Communist Party, along with many other disillusioned members, after Nikita Khrushchev's speech detailing Stalin's abuses of power. But as his daughter Becca says, he maintained the "heart of a socialist." That year, Wilson moved his family to Paris, where he could work far from the hysteria and fear of Hollywood; they would stay in France for eight years. He and Zelma joined a cohort of expatriates living in exile, for whom they held open houses every Sunday. Wilson kept his Oscar for A *Place in the Sun* with a black hood over its head, a symbol of his disdain for the craven Hollywood establishment.

William Wyler, meanwhile, had purchased Wilson's old screenplay for *The Friendly Persuasion*, about Quakers during the Civil War, and brought it to Allied Artists. He summoned Jessamyn West, who had written the book, to revise it, along with his brother, Robert Wyler. It was released in 1956 as *Friendly Persuasion*, with Gary Cooper as the Quaker patriarch and a young Anthony Perkins as his conflicted son, who defies his faith to fight against the Confederates. ("Thee did what thee had to do," his father tells him.) But Wyler had a problem: its original writer had been blacklisted—or, as Wilson put it, "I had been a naughty boy." Allied Artists invoked the "credits escape clause"—which the Screen Writers Guild had shamefully approved in 1953, relieving producers of the obligation to credit politically unclean writers—and the studio submitted Jessamyn West and Robert Wyler as cowriters. The director, who wanted his brother to win an Oscar, claimed that denying Wilson credit was "a decision I regretted but had no control over." But Wilson was furious. He appealed to the Writers Guild of America West (as the Screen Writers Guild was now called). To Allied Artists' horror, the arbiters found that the sole author of *Friendly Persuasion* was Michael Wilson.

Unwilling to credit Wilson and unable to credit Jessamyn West and

Robert Wyler, Allied Artists made the remarkable move of releasing the movie with no screenwriter credit at all. It was simply "Based on the Book by Jessamyn West." In France, where Wilson watched in disbelief, the press called the resulting outrage *L'affaire Wilson*. The same day that *Friendly Persuasion* opened in Los Angeles, Wilson filed a lawsuit in Los Angeles Superior Court. (It was later settled.) "The illogic of the blacklist," Wilson said in a statement, "has been reduced to an absurdity."

That illogic was suddenly of urgent concern to the Academy, which faced the real and awkward prospect of a screenplay with no official author getting nominated. On February 6, 1957, the Board of Governors voted for their own shameful rule: according to a new clause in Article VIII, Section 1 of its bylaws, any member of the Communist Party or former member who refused to publicly renounce it, or who defied a federal investigation, "shall be ineligible for any Academy Award so long as he persists in such refusal." The Oscars had officially joined the blacklist. Twelve days later, Wilson's screenplay for *Friendly Persuasion* was nominated—and disqualified.

This Orwellian turn made the Academy a laughingstock. *Variety* called it the "biggest boo-boo in Academy nomination history." The WGA gave Wilson its award for Best Written Drama in defiance, despite the fact that the guild's "credits escape clause" had started the whole mess. At the WGA dinner, Groucho Marx quipped that the producers of *The Ten Commandments* were "forced to keep Moses' name off the writing credits because they found out he had once crossed the Red Sea."

On Oscar night, only four nominees for Best Adapted Screenplay were named, and the prize went to *Around the World in 80 Days*. But if the Academy hoped that this would end the farce, it was to be disappointed, because this was the same night that Robert Rich won for *The Brave One*.

IT HAD BEEN A ROUGH few years for Dalton Trumbo. After getting out of prison, he returned to the ranch, which had been flooded with hate mail. His finances were a wreck. He kept working on the black market, but the new HUAC hearings made things harder. "Since I have been released from jail," he wrote in one letter, "I find that most of the friends who accommodated me have either left town or are themselves blacklisted or are under some kind of cloud—the variety of clouds in Hollywood is enormous." Mostly, he worked for the chintzy King Brothers, who hired him and Michael Wilson to write a picture about a woman who joins a carnival. (It was released in 1954 as *Carnival Story*, starring Anne Baxter.) Desperate to live cheaply, the Trumbos put the ranch on the market, packed up their lives, and drove to Mexico in late 1951.

In Mexico City, they settled into a pink house in a nice neighborhood and hired a chauffeur. Trumbo developed a passion for collecting pre-Columbian artifacts. For a time, they were joined by friends—Hugo Butler, Ian McLellan Hunter, Ring Lardner Jr.—and their families. The men would spend their evenings drunk on cheap liquor; the kids would play baseball. But expat life wore thin. "I dreamed of living in luxurious exile in Mexico City," Trumbo recalled. "Well it was luxurious for the first year but absolutely hellish during the second year." The FBI was still tracking them. He took whatever work he could get but was "heroically broke."

Trumbo was in Mexico in September 1953, when *Roman Holiday*, directed by William Wyler, opened to raves. The idea had come from Ian McLellan Hunter, after reading about Princess Margaret's tour of Rome. Hunter, before he himself was blacklisted, agreed to be Trumbo's front man, and after delivering the script, he was hired, along with several others, to do rewrites. When Paramount released the film, Hunter got sole story credit, and he shared screenwriting credit with English writer John Dighton. The following spring, *Roman Holiday* won three Academy Awards: Best Actress (Audrey Hepburn), Best Black-and-White Costume Design (Edith Head), and Best Motion Picture Story, awarded to Hunter, who did not show up to accept the prize from Kirk Douglas. Lardner wrote to Trumbo, "Never has a man been so appalled by the success of work credited to him." As if haunted by a telltale heart, Hunter kept the statuette in the bottom drawer of his filing cabinet—but he wasn't haunted enough to hand it over to Trumbo.

One day in Mexico, the Butlers invited the Trumbos to a bullfight, where they watched a particularly gruesome slaughtering. Jean Butler recalled, "The Trumbos, who had kept a cow and several horses on their ranch that they'd been quite fond of, were pro-bull from the outset and came away from the plaza white-faced and outraged." On a trip to Los Angeles to attend to the sale of the ranch and other financial matters, Trumbo outlined an idea for the King Brothers about an extraordinary bull who receives an *indulto*, a rare pardon granted by the spectators. Months later, he sent the producers a 133-page draft of a script called *The Boy and the Bull*, which became *The Brave One*.

"Robert Rich" was Dalton Trumbo.

As Maury King explained later, "I needed a name for the script, so I picked my nephew's. He knew as much about writing as I know about fixing cars."

After two years abroad, Trumbo, as he wrote to Michael Wilson, was "living out an old truism: 'The first time you see Mexico City you are struck by the horrible poverty; within a year you discover it's infectious.'" He informed his family, "If you want to suck, you better get close to the tit," and moved them back to Los Angeles. Trumbo found a modest home in Highland Park, where he set up shop in a converted shed and wrote from six in the morning until late at night, fueling himself with cigarettes and Scotch. He opened multiple bank accounts under different names and used upward of thirteen pseudonyms, including "Theodore Flexman," "Peter Flint," and "Sam Jackson." In one sense, screenwriters were lucky: unlike blacklisted actors or directors, they could work undercover. But the black market was demoralizing, and producers were only too happy to pay bargain rates to top-shelf writers. Trumbo longed to "totally revolt against the sense of martyrdom that lay so heavily over all of us." From behind his typewriter, he fixated on one goal: demolishing the blacklist.

But how? After the Senate censured Joseph McCarthy in 1954, the Red Scare seemed to be ebbing. But the courts had swatted away every legal challenge to the blacklist, and the studios had grown accustomed to the cheap labor of the black market. Even if they did have some incentive to end the blacklist, there was no clear way out. Although the studio heads had adopted the Waldorf Statement banning the hiring of Communists and uncooperative witnesses, they never formally acknowledged keeping a list, black or gray. If they announced that they were ending what they had never officially admitted to instating in the first place, it could open them up to a fusillade of lawsuits for having violated contracts or run a hiring conspiracy. Everyone was stuck in place. Hollywood ran on fear and publicity—and would budge only if it were too embarrassing to stand still.

Trumbo hit on a master plan: win by talent. If blacklisted writers could convince the world that they were writing the most lauded films in Hollywood, they could, in the words of historian Larry Ceplair, "defeat the blacklist by outwriting the white market."

Step one was to broaden the black market. From his shed, Trumbo became a kind of central command. Blacklisted writers collaborated and helped one another get jobs; before Michael Wilson decamped to Paris, he and Trumbo wrote a string of Westerns, mailing drafts back and forth through what they called the "pony express." Step two was to unmask the studios' hypocrisy for hiring the very people they had made untouchable. When the Academy passed its no-Oscars-for-Communists rule for *Friendly Persuasion*, Trumbo sensed a golden opportunity: if one of them won an Academy Award, they could expose the black market for the sham it was.

The Brave One opened in October 1956 and was an unexpected hit, turning the King Brothers into prestige producers—though Trumbo still had to haggle over every one of the ten thousand dollars he was owed for it. "The horse you refuse to feed can no longer haul your wagon," he wrote them in a huff. Trumbo, who considered *The Brave One* a "very simple and simply made family film," was as surprised as anyone when it was nominated for Best Motion Picture Story. He delighted in dropping hints that he was Robert Rich. "It has kept me happily absorbed in tossing dead cats and false leads into the steamy cesspool that now lies exposed for all to see," he wrote one correspondent, sneering at the "solemn asses at the Academy."

He was even more amused when "Robert Rich" actually won. "That it should have been voted the best original story that year is a comment on the Academy's idea of originality," he later scoffed. His daughter Mitzi, who was eleven, recalls, "The weird part, all during my childhood, was that my father was a writer, but I couldn't say what he wrote." On Oscar night, she says, "we watched on TV, and I do remember saying, 'Daddy, this is great! Let's go get it!' And he said, 'We can't. This is still a secret.'

Going to school the next day was so sad, not being able to say. But we were kind of used to that."

Nevertheless, the flurry of speculation provided an opening. "You see," Trumbo said later, "all the press came to me, and I dealt with them in such a way that they knew bloody well that I had written it. But I would suggest that maybe it was Mike Wilson, and they would call Mike and ask him, and he would say no, it wasn't him. And they would come back to me, and I'd suggest they try somebody else—another blacklisted writer like myself who was working on the black market." Amid the teasing, Trumbo realized "that all the journalists—or most of them—were sympathetic to me, and how eager they were to have the blacklist exploded. There had been a certain change in atmosphere, and then it became possible."

The heart of Trumbo's plan was to keep people guessing, to make it a game. If he outed himself, it might provoke HUAC. But if he turned "Robert Rich" into anybody, he could make the black market seem ubiquitous. When *Life* inquired, Trumbo would neither confirm nor deny that he was Robert Rich, adding, "In that way I am able to steal a part of the credit for practically every good picture ever made." Then he sent in a little poem:

> *Come back, Robert Rich, whoever you are,*
> *Return so the ghost can be shriven.*
> *Do you live on the moon, do you live on a star?*
> *Is that where your legends are scriven?*

Trumbo reveled in having—or appearing to have—the upper hand. After the Academy confessed not to know whom it had awarded, he gloated in *The Nation*, "The Academy, giddy by now with patriotism, flushed with its victory over Wilson, anxious to proclaim itself Cerberus of the blacklist, and sensing that a second barbarian"—meaning Robert Rich— "might have breached the defenses and profaned the sanctuary, rushed into print with the most disastrous publicity release of its twenty-nine-year history." He facetiously suggested that the Academy "turn the Oscar over to the next highest man in the vote, or maybe shoot craps for its custody."

But as the weeks, then months, went by, Trumbo realized that drollery alone wouldn't work. At a speech to the Citizens Committee to Preserve American Freedoms, he turned lofty: "I choose to think of Robert Rich as a symbol of disgrace; as the personification of a nation-wide blacklist . . . As such, he has as many faces as the blacklist itself." In another speech, at Carnegie Hall, he went farther: "Robert Rich is the Unknown Artist—the man who has been suppressed so mercilessly by his own government that he has forsaken not only his own name but all the honors which may accrue to his work."

Meanwhile, he plotted his next move. Perhaps "Robert Rich" could write a second King Brothers movie—Trumbo imagined ads drawn by Saul Bass showing an Oscar statuette covering its eyes with golden hands. The fanfare would culminate with the Kings identifying Trumbo as Rich. "Thereupon," Trumbo wrote his lawyer, "I would claim the Oscar from the Academy, and if they didn't come through with it, bring suit against them. The whole idea being to stir up as much stench as possible, and to laugh this fucking blacklist out of existence." When that idea fell through, he wrote to Academy president George Seaton threatening that if the board did not resolve the matter, the identity of Robert Rich would be revealed "in the most public way possible."

But the endgame was unclear, and the blacklist, though punctured, was still alive. Then, a full year into the Robert Rich circus, the Academy handed Trumbo and company another gift: a screenwriting nomination for *The Bridge on the River Kwai*.

CARL FOREMAN WAS MISERABLE IN London: exiled from home, plagued by writer's block. When his wife Estelle joined him, "Carl was kind of a different man," she recalled. "He was not the husband who had left. He was angry now, all the time." Homesick, he would ask friends visiting from the United States to come bearing hard salami from Chicago. He drank too much, lost money in high-stakes gin rummy games. "I felt it was important," he said, "to project the image of a normal, red-blooded American who liked to play cards and who could stand the smell of cigar smoke."

Even abroad, he was unemployable, despite the acclaim for *High Noon*.

A deal with the Rank Organisation, a British entertainment conglomerate, was canceled after its American partners at United Artists objected. When Kirk Douglas passed through town, Foreman said, "Well, Kirk, if you don't want to have lunch with me I'll understand." *Jesus*, Douglas thought, *this is what happens to a guy who thinks all his friends have turned on him.* On the Fourth of July 1953, Carl and Estelle were summoned to the U.S. embassy and told that their passports were no longer valid; they were essentially trapped. "That was when I really began to feel very sorry for myself," Foreman said. Estelle recalled, "I think he felt at that time that nothing was any use anymore, including loyalty to one's spouse. So he began leading a completely different life."

He started working on the black market, under pseudonyms like "Derek Frye." "A writer without a credit on a script he has written," Foreman said, "is professionally emasculated." In 1954, he discovered a translation of a French novel called *Le pont de la rivière Kwai*, by Pierre Boulle. Set in the Burmese jungle during World War II, it follows a group of British POWs who help their Japanese captors build a railway bridge connecting Bangkok and Rangoon—and who become so diligent in their efforts that they lose sight of friend and foe. Foreman, an outsider in Britain, enjoyed "the Frenchman's cold, detached, sardonic view of the English and the Japanese," in which the two colonels, English and Japanese, were "both somewhat ridiculous, and both potentially dangerous in their obsessions." He bought the rights for three hundred British pounds.

Foreman brought the novel to producer Sam Spiegel, of *The African Queen* and *On the Waterfront*, who commissioned Foreman to adapt it for British director David Lean. The film was being distributed by Columbia, so, naturally, Foreman would not get credit. In early 1956, Foreman won a years-long legal battle to regain his passport and went to New York to work on the script with Spiegel. In Boulle's novel, Allied commandos fail to destroy the bridge; Foreman and Spiegel knew that the movie had to end with the bridge's spectacular destruction. Spiegel promised Lean a "magnificent screenplay," but when the director—a notorious perfectionist who did things his own way, often to the exasperation of his collaborators—finally read Foreman's script, he was underwhelmed.

Boulle's novel, Lean wrote to Spiegel, had set the stage for a "tremendous clash of wills," but the screenplay "has discarded practically all of this." The Japanese colonel behaved "like a stock B-picture villain." All in all, Lean concluded, "Mr. Foreman hasn't got the first glimmer and he is offensive. Monsieur Boulle, on the other hand, knows what he's talking about."

Foreman chalked up Lean's disapproval to "the somewhat built-in antipathy to Americans that you find in some Britons." Spiegel convened a script conference at the Hotel George V in Paris, hoping to spark some healthy creative friction. But the dislike between Lean and Foreman was palpable. Foreman took Lean's edits and sailed for Ceylon, revising from port to port. By the third or fourth draft, "it was getting a little wearing, because the changes were very minor," he said. "We began to have friendly arguments about whether a character would scratch his face or not." Finally, in June 1956, the exasperated Lean told him, "Either you go, Carl, or I go." Spiegel chose Lean.

Foreman was off the project he had originated. But he urged Spiegel to replace him with another blacklisted writer: Michael Wilson.

Wilson signed a contract that September. As an ex-marine who thought deeply about war and peace, he was well matched to the material. The movie, he thought, would show how "the military mentality, if it's allowed to take power, becomes completely irrational." (The last line: "Madness!") As he rewrote *The Bridge on the River Kwai*, he signed his communications with the name "John Michael." He fine-tuned the new American protagonist, played by William Holden, and transformed the Japanese colonel from a "psychotic barbarian" into a "man of stature." Lean found Wilson to be "a very civilized, good chap, and he wrote the American part and sort of polished up and tightened up all that I had done. It was really Mike's and my script." Wilson was paid ten thousand dollars for five months of work, including six weeks on location in Ceylon. Then he returned to Paris.

Foreman, meanwhile, had a chance to get off the blacklist. A Columbia executive told him that the studio was eager to hire him as a UK-based writer-producer, if he could "clear" himself. That meant naming names, which Foreman refused to do. But he *was* willing to criticize the Communist Party. He asked his lawyer, Sidney Cohn, to talk to the Committee, hoping that he might "deal with the devil with a long pole." Cohn approached the new HUAC chairman, Pennsylvania Democrat Francis E. Walter. The congressman was incensed that his daughter, a student at Sarah Lawrence, was being "punished among her peers" because of his position, while the children of the blacklisted received sympathy. Cohn promised that Foreman's testimony would let those Sarah Lawrence kids know all about the evils of communism—but he wouldn't name names. Walter agreed. Estelle Foreman recalled, "I was opposed to the whole thing. I said, 'Fuck them all. Who needs them? You're earning a living and why reappear before the Committee?'" But Foreman hoped that if he could get away with this, it might open the gates for everyone else.

On August 8, 1956, Foreman and his lawyer walked into the Old House Office Building in Washington. Only Congressman Walter and a staff director named Richard Arens represented the Committee. Foreman admitted his former affiliation with the Communist Party, saying that he had been "a very unimportant little fellow who came to meetings and listened." When he declined Arens's request to name names, Walter interjected, "I do not think that is important." Foreman denounced communism, but he also criticized HUAC, telling his inquisitors that, as an expatriate, "I find myself in the position of apologizing for and explaining America overseas."

With this uneasy ritual, Foreman was "cleared"—without naming names. In March 1957, Columbia announced that it had signed him to a four-picture deal.

The other blacklistees were wary. Some suspected that Columbia had paid off Chairman Walter, or that Foreman had secretly named names. It wasn't clear whether he had set a precedent or gotten a one-off deal. (In fact, the blowback from conservative watchdogs embarrassed the Committee into closing the loophole for anyone else.) Foreman agreed to meet with two dozen skeptical colleagues at an all-night meeting in Los Angeles. He assured them that there had been no under-the-table dealing. Not everyone was willing to absolve him, but one of the attendees who did was Dalton Trumbo. "Obviously there was corruption somewhere," Trumbo reasoned, "but so long as a man didn't inform, if he had been fucked by a corrupt system and could take advantage of that corruption without harming anyone else, possibly without harming himself (except to the degree he did something that he preferred not to do), I see no harm in it. It seems a mild sin, a venial one, and with a few exceptions forgiveness can be granted."

The Bridge on the River Kwai premiered in London in October 1957, a CinemaScope spectacular. David Lean had told Sam Spiegel, "If anyone's going to get a credit for the script—and particularly if Carl Foreman's going to get a credit—I want a credit, because I certainly did much more than he did." But the director was stunned when he went to a screening and saw the script credited not to him, not to Carl Foreman, not to Michael Wilson, but to the original novelist, Pierre Boulle—a patent absurdity, given that Boulle barely spoke English. Foreman, for his part, felt "very badly about seeing Boulle's name on the credits." Wilson brought his daughters to see the film at a cinema on the Champs-Élysées. "My memory," Becca Wilson recalls, "is that he was crying when we watched those credits go by."

The movie was an international smash. In early 1958, it was nominated for eight Academy Awards, including for its screenplay, supposedly adapted by Boulle from his novel.

Once again, the Oscars shone an uneasy light on the black market. Spiegel panicked that Wilson's "wicked name" would leak and "ruin our chances, baby." Lean assured Wilson, "By now, whether you like it or not, everyone knows you did it. They all know, Mike—I must say I am very glad. You are in fact the top screen writer this minute—but it's acknowledged in whispers! A real farce." Publicly, Lean and Spiegel furiously denied that Foreman had had anything to do with the final script, even though he had sold them the rights to the novel. But the truth was impossible to contain. Days before the Oscars, *Newsweek* asked, "Who wrote the screenplay for 'The Bridge on the River Kwai?'" and pointed to both Foreman and Wilson. Even Boulle admitted, in tortured English, "I did not actually pen the screenplay, but I had numerous talks with both Lean and Spiegel during which we created its main carcass."

On March 26, 1958, *Kwai* swept through seven categories, including the sham screenplay award for Boulle, who, as Foreman said later, "had the good taste not to return in person to accept the Academy Award." Kim Novak, representing Columbia Pictures, accepted on his behalf. After the ceremony, Spiegel and Lean were led to the press area, toting their Oscars for Best Picture and Best Directing. A reporter stuck a microphone in the director's face and asked, "Mr. Lean, who wrote the script of *The Bridge on the River Kwai?*"

Lean was conflicted. "In the wildness of my distress," he said later, "I could have pulled down the whole edifice and exposed its rottenness." Instead, he blurted out, "You're asking the $64,000 question, and as you have not got $64,000 I'm not prepared to tell you."

Spiegel was irate, knowing that the quip would inflame the issue in the press. Outside the Pantages, he shook his Best Picture statuette at Lean in a rage. Lean shook his Best Directing Oscar right back. "It was," Lean recalled, "a ridiculous scene." The next day, Foreman, who was at work on *The Key*, the first film to bear his name since *High Noon*, gladly told the press that he had written *Kwai*, with "some contributions by David Lean." He was now off the blacklist and had nothing to hide. The proof of his authorship, he said, was that every one of his original screenplays wove in the surnames of three friends of his—"Weaver," "Grogan," and "Baker"—like a secret code. He did not mention Michael Wilson.

Dalton Trumbo was elated. "All in all," he wrote Wilson four days after the ceremony, "the writing Awards were gloriously screwed for the second time running, and a great glow of health runs through the community." In the space of thirteen months, the Academy had tripped over screenplays credited to nobody, to an imaginary person, and to a Frenchman who barely spoke English. All this showed how unworkable, how *ridiculous*, the blacklist was. Trumbo readied his next move.

ANOTHER PART OF TRUMBO WAS less giddy than he let on. "After eleven years of investigation, blacklist, jail, pamphleteering, platform rhetoric, TV debates and interviews, I lift my shaggy old head above the horizon, and I behold—nothing," he confessed to Wilson. "Only a bunch of blacklisted artists doing work they shouldn't do because they're prevented or forbidden from doing work they should." Subsumed with black-market gigs that barely covered his expenses, he worked so hard that he suffered a mild heart attack—but continued to get up as early as 3 a.m. to write, taking Dexedrine to stay awake and Seconal to get to sleep.

If he derived any pleasure, it was from the press circus around the blacklist and the Oscars, which he told Wilson he had been "quietly active in stimulating." He continued to go on talk shows, to pen scathing articles, and to release waggish statements that tiptoed around which blacklisted writer had written what movie. He knew that martyrdom wouldn't work; the key was making the black market seem so insidious that its unmasking was inevitable. Not all his compatriots agreed. Some thought that Trumbo was a showboat. Some wanted to win through the courts. But Trumbo was convinced that legal action was pointless. They had to succeed with cleverness.

He had one ace to play: the identity of Robert Rich. But how? When? If HUAC subpoenaed the King Brothers, Trumbo realized, it could "totally destroy the subterranean market for blacklisted work it had taken almost a decade to develop." He had to implicate the entire Hollywood establishment, which meant the Academy. In September 1958, he saw another opportunity: the release of *The Defiant Ones*, about two escaped convicts handcuffed to each other, one white (Tony Curtis), the other Black (Sidney Poitier). The screenwriters were Harold Jacob Smith and Nedrick Young, who were handcuffed to each other in their own way. Smith wrote under his own name, while Young was blacklisted and used the pseudonym "Nathan E. Douglas." The film's producer and director was Stanley Kramer, seven years after he had cut off Carl Foreman during the making of *High Noon*. Kramer was willing to hire Young, he said, because, unlike Foreman, "the guy was warm and truthful" and "I was willing to take a stand with him." *The Defiant Ones* was now an awards contender, which meant that the Academy would again be in a bind: How could it honor one cowriter and not the other?

Just before Christmas, Smith and Young were approached at a luncheon by two Academy officials, including George Seaton, who had just ended his term as Academy president. Wary of yet another awards season scandal, they were hoping to convince the rest of the board to overturn the Academy's bylaw banning blacklistees from winning Oscars, and they proposed that the two *Defiant Ones* screenwriters give a "friendly" interview to the *New York Times* exposing Young's identity. This seemed like the opening Trumbo had been waiting for—but he told the two writers to hold off. "I felt it was the Academy's problem, not theirs," he explained, "and that they should save all their fire for a fight if one developed, rather than wasting a single inch of newspaper space when they did not need it." If Trumbo couldn't control the plan, he didn't trust it.

Then, on New Year's Eve, the duo won the New York Film Critics Circle Award, and the *Times* threatened to expose Young with or without cooperation, in a story to run on New Year's morning. Trumbo leaped into action and got Los Angeles TV broadcaster Bill Stout to interview them that evening, so they could scoop the *Times* "in a most dignified and advantageous way." Calls poured in to the station—all but one in *support* of Young. "For 3 days," Trumbo wrote to Michael Wilson and Hollywood Ten member Albert Maltz, "the industry greeted this with a silence which convinced me (and still does) that we have the best chance of our lives."

With Seaton planning to bring up the Academy rule at the next board meeting, Trumbo made plans for Stout to reveal "Robert Rich" live on television the following Wednesday. The tone, he hoped, would be "history hurt everybody, all made mistakes, and la-de-da-da-do." This was critical, he reasoned, because "there can never be an *official* end to the blacklist—this is as close as we shall presently come. Therefore we must *pretend* this is the end (which it damned near is), and pose not as angry martyrs, as the persecuted, but as good *winners*."

If the Academy failed to rescind the rule, however, Trumbo resolved to go on TV anyway and "blast the hell out of them."

The Board of Governors met on the evening of January 12, 1959. Seaton, who had a liberal faction behind him, introduced a motion to repeal the blacklist rule. After much deliberation, his motion passed 18 to 1, and the Academy announced that the ban had proved "unworkable and impractical." After just two years, a pillar of the blacklist had fallen.

Trumbo's carefully stage-managed interview aired over two nights. As proof that he had written *The Brave One*, Trumbo held up a draft. "Through grotesque chance," he said impishly, "Robert Rich is probably the best-known screenwriter in the history of motion pictures. I should like to be associated with him, because I should like to be as well known myself." When Stout asked if he planned to claim his Oscar from the Academy, Trumbo said, "I imagine if they consider me qualified, they, in their time and in their way, will make arrangements to confer it." Then he turned emotional. He had been blacklisted, he said, since his youngest daughter, Mitzi, was three. "I think I will give this Oscar, if I get it, to that girl. I think I will tell her, 'Well, here is one secret you no longer need to be burdened with.' I'll tell her, we have our names back."

The interview was immediately followed by another one, with producer Frank King, who confirmed that Trumbo had indeed written *The Brave One*. Asked if he had questioned Trumbo's Communist affiliation before hiring him, King said, "Of course not. I'm not interested in his politics or his religion or his color. I was interested in his work." *The Brave One*, after all, was "the story of a little Catholic boy and his pet. Is there anything Communistic in that?"

The delicate situation now swung back to the Academy. The new president, George Stevens, sent a statement to the *Los Angeles Times* blasting Trumbo's "deception," but his predecessor, George Seaton, persuaded him to retract it before the morning edition. Trumbo tried to maintain the peace. "It seems to me it will be rather difficult for the Academy to withhold the award and still maintain its dignity," he wrote to Seaton. "If, however, they do decide to withhold it, I shall cooperate with them so that the least harm possible be done to everyone concerned." A war of words would benefit no one, Trumbo argued: "For when the Academy attacks an individual, the object of its anger instantly becomes a brave little underdog—and the whole press corps takes out happily after the big-bully institution which has precipitated so unfair a fight."

The Academy did not hand over the Oscar to "Robert Rich," but, no matter. On April 6, Elizabeth Taylor announced the winners of the 1959 original screenplay award: Harold Jacob Smith and "Nathan Douglas," for *The Defiant Ones*. Both writers were present. Working from Trumbo's playbook, the blacklisted Nedrick Young didn't make a soaring political speech. He simply held his statuette and said, "Thank you very much," as if it were the most normal thing in the world.

The plan was working. As Trumbo wrote Michael Wilson, "Revocation of the Academy rule was the nearest thing to an official rescission of the blacklist that could or will occur." But the blacklist wasn't over—not as long as they were still writing, and receiving awards, under pseudonyms. What came next, Trumbo told Wilson, was "guerrilla warfare, the almost unscrupulous use of our only weapon (which is our excellence)." As it happened, rising up against an oppressive system was the plot of Trumbo's latest screenplay, about a Roman slave named Spartacus.

THE RED SCARE AND SPARTACUS were intertwined long before Trumbo got ahold of the latter. In 1950, Howard Fast, a onetime Communist Party member, served a three-month prison sentence for defying HUAC. While incarcerated, he had an idea for a novel about the slave uprising against the Roman Republic in 71 BCE, which would serve as an allegory for McCarthyism. After seven publishers rejected it, Fast self-published the book. It became a surprise hit.

In late 1957, Kirk Douglas, who was looking for projects for his own company, Bryna Productions, got wind of Spartacus and thought that the title character would give him a plum leading role. The catch: Fast wanted to write the screenplay himself. Months later, he delivered a 102-page outline that Douglas hated. Yul Brynner was developing his own Spartacus project for United Artists, called The Gladiators, which was also being written by a blacklisted writer, Abe Polonsky. Racing to get his own version made for Universal, Douglas needed "the quickest and most skillful writer in the business." That was Dalton Trumbo.

Trumbo was already working on another script for Bryna, The Brave Cowboy, under the name "Sam Jackson." He drove to Douglas's palatial home in Beverly Hills. "It's a pleasure to finally meet you, Sam," Douglas said.

"So this is how the other half lives," Trumbo said, looking around.

Within days, Trumbo delivered a long outline that diagnosed the problem with Fast's Spartacus: the protagonist was a blank. "The gladiator's revolt," Trumbo wrote, "must mark, in the personal story of Spartacus, his rise from animal to leader." Douglas was thrilled. Fast blew up when he learned of the outline, but his blessing was essential to getting the movie made, so Douglas had both men work on different drafts simultaneously.

Douglas and Trumbo, who shared a birthday, became close; the star bought Trumbo a gray parrot, which would perch on his shoulder as he typed away in the bathtub. When Douglas was invited to meet Vice President Richard Nixon, who had been a member of HUAC in 1947, Trumbo sent him to Washington with talking points about the ills of the blacklist—including the disastrous press surrounding the Oscars. "Academy night is probably the most widely publicized cultural event in the world," Trumbo wrote. "It is also uniquely American. A situation that brings it into disrepute year after year is greatly damaging to American prestige." (Nixon declined to publicly denounce the blacklist.)

When both writers turned in their screenplays, Trumbo's was clearly superior. Douglas used it to lure British stars Laurence Olivier, Peter Ustinov, and Charles Laughton to play the Romans, which was enough to get *Spartacus* green-lit at Universal and win the race with *The Gladiators*. Trumbo finished his revised "final" draft in January 1959. Days into the massive shoot in Death Valley, Douglas fired director Anthony Mann and replaced him with the thirty-year-old Stanley Kubrick, who had directed Douglas in *Paths of Glory*. Mann began spreading rumors that *Spartacus* was written by Trumbo, which leaked into the gossip columns. The panicked Douglas told his wife, "If I rock the boat, we might lose everything—the picture, the company, my career, *everything*."

Trumbo became more invested in *Spartacus* than any screenplay he'd ever written, even as Kubrick wrested it away. As Trumbo wrote to Pablo Picasso, "The theme of the film, for which I take full responsibility, is simple and, I feel, curiously appropriate to our times: in waging a life-and-death struggle to keep Spartacus and his followers enslaved, the senate and the people of Republican Rome inevitably produced the conditions for their own enslavement under a dictatorship of the right." Although Spartacus is ultimately crucified, Trumbo wanted the audience to see him as "not a tragic figure, because he wins," just as he had positioned the blacklisted screenwriters not as martyrs but as victors. To that end, he wrote a new scene in which the Roman general Crassus, played by Olivier, asks the captive slave army to identify their leader, and one of them answers, "We're all Spartacus." Douglas expanded the idea: what if *all* the slaves, one by one, came forward as Spartacus? The famous "I am Spartacus" scene was the opposite of Carl Foreman's bleak ending of *High Noon*: instead of an abandoned hero facing down evil alone, Spartacus is saved by an act of collective bravery. The scene was about the power of the pseudonym; if everyone is Spartacus, then no one is. In that sense, Spartacus was Robert Rich, the Unknown Artist who, in Trumbo's words, had "as many faces as the blacklist itself."

Four months into production, Trumbo learned that Peter Ustinov was rewriting his scenes with Laughton. "Sam Jackson" sent a fiery telegram quitting the picture, signed, "With a good deal of affection, but with far more resentment and disgust."

Kirk Douglas drove to Trumbo's house in a panic. "I got a telegram from your 'friend' Sam Jackson. Is he here?"

"No," Trumbo deadpanned, "I killed him. We just buried him in the backyard. It was a lovely ceremony. Too bad you missed it."

Douglas apologized for not sending flowers. "What will it take to bring him back to life?"

"It's too late," Trumbo told him. "Easter was last month. Besides, you're a Jew. You don't believe in resurrection."

Then, in his telling, Douglas realized what he had to do. He took a breath and said, "I *don't* want Sam Jackson back. Let's leave him dead and buried. I want Dalton Trumbo." Once the picture was in the can, the actor promised, he would insist that Universal credit Trumbo by name. He extended his hand, and Trumbo shook it. (Trumbo's biographer Larry Ceplair suspects that the reverse was more likely: that Trumbo knew that he had leverage and offered to resume work only if he got credit.)

In late 1959, Douglas met with Kubrick and producer Eddie Lewis to discuss the screenplay credit. When Kubrick offered to take it himself, the star was so appalled that he invited Trumbo to the Universal commissary for lunch: a simple, impulsive gesture that, in Douglas's eyes, "broke" the blacklist. In the tale of the blacklist's endgame, the star was quick to cast himself as the hero, downplaying the role of another man: Otto Preminger. While Trumbo labored over *Spartacus*, the Austro-Hungarian director had hired him to adapt *Exodus*, Leon Uris's mammoth Zionist novel. Despite Preminger's autocratic reputation, Trumbo "had more pleasure working with Otto than with anyone in my life." Preminger stayed at the Trumbo household over Christmas, allowing the writer an hour off to give his children their presents.

In January 1960, as Douglas was carefully negotiating studio politics over the *Spartacus* credit, Preminger gave a bombshell interview with the *New York Times* in which he announced that Dalton Trumbo was writing *Exodus* and "naturally will get the credit on the screen that he amply deserves." The article, which also mentioned Trumbo's work on *Roman Holiday* and *Spartacus*, called this the "first open defiance by a producer-director of Hollywood's 'blacklist.'" *Exodus* was being distributed by United Artists, which didn't produce its own pictures and had not signed the 1947 Waldorf Statement. Because Preminger had complete autonomy, there was nothing its executives could do but shrug.

Kirk Douglas later claimed that Preminger had decided to hire Trumbo only after hearing about his own defiant lunch with the screenwriter on the Universal lot. But the fact was that Preminger had blown up Douglas's best-laid plans. "You've got to hand it to Otto," Douglas said to his wife. "He saw that the train had already left the station with *Spartacus* breaking the blacklist. Not only did he run to catch up with it, he jumped into the front car and claimed to be the engineer!"

With the American Legion warning of a "renewed invasion of American filmdom," Universal stalled. The question was whether it would continue the charade or acknowledge what everyone already knew: that Dalton Trumbo had written *Spartacus*. Months went by, with the studio refusing to say anything definitive. Then Howard Fast, the original *Spartacus* novelist, heard that "Sam Jackson" might receive sole credit and panicked. He asked the Writers Guild for an arbitration and received the unwelcome verdict that the credit should read "Written by Dalton Trumbo, based on the novel by Howard Fast." Five days later, on August 7, 1960, Universal announced that it would do just that, becoming, after thirteen years, the first major studio to break the Waldorf pledge.

Spartacus opened in October 1960; *Exodus* followed in December. "If these films are economically damaged by my name," Trumbo wrote to Michael Wilson, "the ban against everyone will be absolute." Instead, *Spartacus* became the highest-grossing film of the year, and *Exodus* the third-highest. Some audiences applauded when they saw Trumbo's name on the screen. The American Legion could only muster thirty-six protesters at *Spartacus*'s Los Angeles premiere, a rounding error next to the fifteen hundred attendees. Hedda Hopper, in a predictable tizzy, warned, "If Dalton Trumbo gets an Oscar for either *Exodus* or *Spartacus*, the roof may blow off the Santa Monica Auditorium from boos and hisses." He wasn't nominated for either, but in February 1961, the newly inaugurated President Kennedy slipped into a showing of *Spartacus* in Washington, on his brother Bobby's recommendation. Seeing Trumbo's name, Kennedy elbowed a friend and said, "Do you think he's Irish? I hope so." Afterward, he told reporters, "It was fine." Trumbo's credit, at long last, was a political nonevent.

THE BLACKLIST DID NOT EVAPORATE overnight. Like a wounded grizzly bear, it lumbered around, dying a slow death. Trumbo had triumphed, but his fellow blacklistees wondered whether the breakthrough was for everyone or just for him. Many had fallen out of the industry altogether and couldn't find their way back after years away from the game. Trumbo himself predicted that only a few writers had the talent to follow his path. But even the top tier found that the door had creaked open only so wide. There was, for instance, Michael Wilson, who was working on another David Lean epic, *Lawrence of Arabia*.

After *The Bridge on the River Kwai*, Lean had turned his mind to T. E. Lawrence, the British officer who joined the Arab Revolt against the Ottoman Turks during World War I. Michael Wilson's terms included "screen credit for the rightful author"; producer Sam Spiegel agreed to a credit in the Eastern Hemisphere and, if Wilson signed an affidavit saying he was not a Communist, possibly the Western Hemisphere, too. Wilson, who had no interest in signing such a thing, began work anyway. In September 1959, he delivered a ninety-two-page outline and thematic treatise. Wilson saw Lawrence as an antihero, someone caught between two cultures, and who betrayed both. "The contrast between

the legendary figure and the actual man is the meat of drama," Wilson
wrote. Lean used the treatment to secure the rights to Lawrence's memoir, *Seven Pillars of Wisdom*, and cabled Wilson from Bombay to praise
his "masterly job."

The accord was short-lived. Wilson worked through the summer
at the Palace Hotel in Bürgenstock, Switzerland, and finished his first
draft in August 1960. True to his lifelong interest in the follies of war,
Wilson depicted Lawrence as opportunistic, self-deluded, and only passingly devoted to the Arabs he professed to love. The script's disillusioned
tone was a mismatch for Lean, who was location-scouting in Jordan and
swooning over the romantic desert vistas. As he revamped the script,
Wilson told his agent that he would stay on only if Lean wanted a mere
polish going forward. "On the other hand, if Lean behaves like Lean,
and remains fraught with insecurity and later demands a new departure
to the material (and that is quite possible), then I'm afraid they'll have to
find themselves another boy."

Wilson flew to Jordan to meet the director, who made plain his unhappiness with the second draft. Wilson, who had replaced Carl Foreman
on *Kwai*, now found himself in the Foreman slot. When Lean asked
him to spend six months in the desert reworking the screenplay, he declined. He turned in a third revision in early 1961, to fulfill his hundred-
thousand-dollar contract, and exited the project.

As Lean prepared for the shoot from Amman, frantic that Wilson
had "walked off the picture in circumstances partially beyond my com-
prehension," Spiegel hired English playwright Robert Bolt, of *A Man for
All Seasons*, to take over the *Lawrence* screenplay. Weeks before the film's
December 1962 premiere, Wilson learned that Bolt was to get sole credit
and demanded a copy of the final script. In a letter to Spiegel, he conceded that Bolt had rewritten most of the dialogue, but the underlying
architecture was his own. Spiegel denied Wilson's request for joint credit,
with the stipulation requiring an anticommunist statement providing a
convenient pretext.

Desperate, Wilson wrote directly to Bolt. "For the past eleven years,"
he pleaded, "I have been one of the blacklisted American writers. I have
just begun to emerge from that shadowy realm." He went on: "If I were

'clean,' my name would already be alongside yours as co-author of this picture. I implore you to believe this is not a paranoid assertion. I am not a man for all seasons; but while martyrdom ill suits me, there are aspects of the blacklist that do fill me with mirth. If I could tell you (and if you're interested someday I shall) the enormous pressures the top brass of this production put on me to 'clear myself,' you would see that this is the heart of the matter."

Bolt replied that Wilson's letter had come as a "bombshell" and denied having used his script at all. Two years after Trumbo's credit appeared on *Spartacus* and *Exodus*, *Lawrence of Arabia* opened without Wilson's name, even as he pursued (and won) an arbitration through the British writers' guild. In 1963, the film was nominated for ten Academy Awards and won seven, including Best Picture. Bolt was nominated for the screenplay; the award, presented by Bette Davis, went to Horton Foote, for *To Kill a Mockingbird*. Wilson's contributions to the classic were all but erased.

Wilson did not receive his first post-blacklist credit until 1965, the year after his family ended its eight-year French exile and settled in Ojai, California. The movie, unfortunately, was *The Sandpiper*, a trite Elizabeth Taylor–Richard Burton vehicle and an unhappy collaboration between Wilson and Dalton Trumbo. Wilson wrote a seventy-three-page treatment and handed it off to Trumbo in Rome, where the two old friends ate at the same restaurant each night. Whoever arrived first would arrange for the musicians to play either the *Lawrence of Arabia* or the *Exodus* theme for the other. When Trumbo was done writing, though, he abruptly tried to block Wilson's credit. Trumbo, Wilson chided him, had once been determined to "get my name up there on the screen alongside your own," but was now acting "without grace or candor." Many letters and an arbitration later, they reconciled and shared credit on what Trumbo considered "one of the most frightful cinematic abortions of recent history."

Three years later, Wilson's name finally appeared on a movie worthy of his talents. *The Twilight Zone* creator Rod Serling had adapted the French novel *La Planète des singes*, by the same Pierre Boulle who had written *The Bridge on the River Kwai*. Fox hired Wilson to do a rewrite, and he and Serling shared credit on *Planet of the Apes*. Wilson kept

Serling's inspired ending, in which Charlton Heston's astronaut comes upon the destroyed Statue of Liberty and realizes he's been on Earth the whole time. Wilson saw the story as political satire. In one scene, the captive Heston and his chimpanzee allies are brought before a tribunal of orangutans, where he is found to have "no rights under ape law." It was Wilson's send-up of the now moribund HUAC, reenacted by simians like the travesty it always was.

THE BLACKLIST LEFT BEHIND BROKEN careers, broken lives, and unfinished business—including Academy Awards.

In the spring of 1975, Dalton Trumbo was sixty-nine and in declining health. The King Brothers, realizing time was short, sent an affidavit to the Academy certifying what everyone had known for years: that Trumbo had written *The Brave One*. The Board of Governors voted to give him the Oscar originally awarded to Robert Rich. On May 15, Academy president Walter Mirisch drove to Trumbo's house at St. Ives Drive. Trumbo, his mustache a bushy white, sat for a photographer, eyeing the Oscar ambiguously as Mirisch flashed an effortless smile. "He was very ill by that time, but he managed to get downstairs, pose for that picture," recalls his daughter Mitzi. "I wasn't too thrilled. It just seemed . . . a little late."

The award prompted Trumbo to think not just about his own legacy but others'. Michael Wilson was also in poor health, after suffering a stroke in 1970. After *Planet of the Apes*, he had received just one other screen credit, for a Che Guevara biopic so mangled that Wilson tried to get his name *off* it. In early 1976, Trumbo wrote to the Writers Guild recommending Wilson for its prestigious Laurel Award. Trumbo was too ill to attend the ceremony, so Carl Foreman presented the award. Since getting off the blacklist, Foreman had bounced back. In 1962, he was nominated for two Oscars, for writing and producing the Gregory Peck wartime adventure *The Guns of Navarone*. Winston Churchill was so taken with the film that he asked Foreman to adapt his memoir *My Early Life*. When Foreman disclosed that he had been blacklisted, Churchill said, "Oh, I know all about you. But we don't like political blacklists in England." *Young Winston*, released in 1972, earned Foreman his fifth screenplay nomination under his own name. But his only winning script had been *The Bridge on the River Kwai*, credited to Pierre Boulle.

He returned to Hollywood in 1975, after two and a half decades in England. He had divorced Estelle and married a young production assistant, Eve, with whom he had two children. Despite his change in fortune, the blacklist was "a shadow that was always there," says his son Jonathan. "The wrongs that were done, they stay wrong." Presenting the Laurel Award to Wilson, Foreman sardonically proposed that they send a letter to Pierre Boulle: "Dear Pierre: Hello there, how are you? We are fine, and hope you are the same. Say, by the way, do you think you might send us our Oscar . . ."

When Wilson collected his Laurel Award, he recalled the absurdity surrounding *Friendly Persuasion*, perhaps the "only time a Hollywood picture was released that wasn't written by anyone." To the spectators who were too young to remember "the Great Witch Hunt," he warned, "I fear that unless you remember this dark epoch and understand it, you may be doomed to replay it."

Months later, on September 10, 1976, Dalton Trumbo died of congestive heart failure. He had told Wilson that he was writing his own eulogy, because "his estimate of himself was neither as awesome as that of his enemies nor as aweless as that of his friends." Wilson died of a heart attack two years later.

In 1984, Carl Foreman was dying, too, of a brain tumor. One day, while he and his old friend John Weaver were walking down a street in Beverly Hills, Weaver asked him if there was anything he could do, and Foreman said there was: help get him that Oscar for *The Bridge on the River Kwai*. Foreman's draft had supposedly been lost, but Weaver found a copy in Wilson's archives at UCLA, complete with Foreman's secret code—references to his friends' surnames "Weaver," "Baker," and "Grogan" sprinkled into the screenplay. "A cold chill ran up my spine," Weaver recalled. "I brought it to Carl and he clutched it with tears in his eyes." That June, the Writers Guild awarded credit to Foreman and Wilson. Weaver went to Foreman's sickbed and told him that he would get his Oscar after all. At ten o'clock the next morning, Foreman died.

That December, the Academy Board of Governors unanimously

voted to give Foreman and Wilson posthumous Oscars for *Kwai*. The ceremony was held in March 1985, at the Academy's in-house theater. Their widows accepted. Eve Foreman reflected, "During the time he was very ill, lots of his films were on television, and it hurt to see somebody else's name on the screenplay for *Bridge on the River Kwai*." It was an ambivalent occasion: a wrong was being righted, but too late for either man to see it—or, as Jonathan Foreman puts it, "It's amazingly shitty that it took them that long." Zelma Wilson told her daughters that it was a "cop-out" that the Academy wasn't including the honor in that year's Oscar telecast. "It wasn't announced with fanfare," Becca Wilson says. "I felt, and I think our mother felt, that the Academy just went through the motions."

Seven years later, the Academy board voted to reassign the Best Motion Picture Story Oscar for *Roman Holiday* to Dalton Trumbo. Ian McLellan Hunter, who had received the award in 1954, had recently died, and the *Los Angeles Times* published a posthumous interview in which Hunter said that "it was certainly Trumbo's story." A ceremony was held at the Academy theater in May 1993, attended by Trumbo's family and the aging blacklist community. Presenting the statuette to Cleo Trumbo, Academy president Robert Rehme expressed his hope that "one more dark chapter in American history can be closed." Then Cleo, in a white blazer and pearls, fought back tears and said, "I don't want to leave you with the impression that living under the blacklist was a steady procession of motion picture assignments and secret honors. It was not. Earning a living was a precarious business." She added, "It was a time of fear, and no one was exempt."

But even the story credit was a ruse; Trumbo, according to Cleo, had written the *screenplay*, something that Hunter, perhaps out of guilt, had never admitted. After years of stalemate between the Hunters and the Trumbos, Dalton Trumbo's screenwriting credit was finally given in 2011. In the meantime, the Academy voted in 1995 to reinstate Michael Wilson's nomination for *Lawrence of Arabia*, alongside Robert Bolt's. In 2002, it reinstated his nomination for *Friendly Persuasion*. The longer the time line got, the more tragic and absurd.

When Cleo Trumbo died in 2009, she left her husband's Oscars to their granddaughters. The *Roman Holiday* statuette, its head scratched up by Cleo's cat, went to Mitzi's daughter Samantha. The *Brave One* award went to her other daughter, Molly. As of 2022, it was at Mitzi's house, in Los Altos, for safekeeping. "I guess I don't feel the reverence I'm supposed to for these Oscars, simply because they were awarded twenty and forty years too late," Mitzi says. "He didn't get to go onstage in a fancy suit at a fancy event and make a speech. He would have loved to have done that." She keeps the *Brave One* award—once the source of the saddest, most complicated prank in Oscar history—on a bar. In a tutu.

SIX

X

1970

How Midnight Cowboy *and* Easy Rider *brought
the counterculture to the Oscars, Candice Bergen
reached across the generation gap, and Gregory Peck
led the Academy into a groovy new world.*

On April 14, 1969, a tuxedoed Gregory Peck strode across the empty lobby of the Dorothy Chandler Pavilion like a weary cowboy crossing an abandoned prairie. Peck had become Academy president two years earlier, and his job was to introduce the Forty-First Academy Awards. On camera, Peck descended a mirrored stairwell, looked around with his thick eyebrows furrowed, and pronounced in his deep, godlike voice, "It's kind of lonesome out here. The audience is already on the inside."

The cameras cut to the stage, where Frank Sinatra crooned the title song from *Star!*, a new Julie Andrews vehicle from 20th Century–Fox. The most nominated films that year were the splashy studio musicals *Oliver!* and *Funny Girl*, whose star, Barbra Streisand, showed up to the ceremony in a see-through pantsuit. Streisand was a new kind of old star—"ethnic," but with showbiz chops. In an effort to make the Oscar broadcast less lugubrious, Peck had hired stage director Gower Champion. In place of Bob Hope, hosting duties were shared by "Oscar's best friends," among them Ingrid Bergman, Sidney Poitier, Burt Lancaster, and, for the youth vote, Jane Fonda, her short hair marcelled for *They Shoot Horses, Don't They?*

When Bergman opened the Best Actress envelope, she found a shocker: Streisand had tied with Katharine Hepburn, for *The Lion in Winter*. Because Hepburn was absent, Streisand, who was ten days away from twenty-seven, had no chance of being upstaged. She cooed to her statuette, "Hello, gorgeous." *Oliver!* won five awards, including Best Picture. Only six months earlier, the MPAA had instituted a new ratings system, replacing the old Production Code after three and a half decades. *Oliver!* was rated G, designating it as the kind of wholesome studio entertainment that could be enjoyed by "general audiences," whoever that was.

But a closer look revealed another Hollywood—and a more unconventional kind of movie—clawing at the gates. *Rosemary's Baby* was nominated only for Roman Polanski's screenplay and for Ruth Gordon, who won Best Supporting Actress. Stanley Kubrick's *2001: A Space Odyssey* had managed four nominations, Best Picture not among them, and won for special effects—the only Oscar that Kubrick would ever receive. And sitting next to Streisand (but cut out of the frame) was her estranged husband, the little-known Elliott Gould, wearing the droopy mustache he had grown for Robert Altman's *M*A*S*H*.

After the awards, congratulations on a smashing show poured into Peck's Academy mailbox. "At a time when the morals within movies are being pushed to the outer edges of chaos," Vincent Canby wrote in the *New York Times*, awards for the likes of *Oliver!* "reassure everyone in the industry that all is well, that Hollywood really isn't some giant bordello that's about to be raided."

He spoke too soon. Just a year later, Gould would be nominated for a movie about spouse swapping, Fonda would hold up a fist on the red carpet, hippie frocks would turn the Oscar stage psychedelic, and the winning picture would be rated X.

BENEATH THE GILDED SCHMALTZ, HOLLYWOOD was falling apart. Movie attendance, which had peaked at 78.2 million a week in 1946, was on a downward slide that would bottom out at 15.8 million by 1971. The old studios, desperate to distinguish themselves from television, had spent the decade filling screens with musical extravaganzas and *Spartacus*-like swords-and-sandals epics that displayed the industry's bloat, but they had little idea how to speak to anyone younger than Streisand. *Star!* would lose $15 million and all seven of its nominations, hammering another nail into the coffin of Hollywood's business model since 1965: re-create the success of *The Sound of Music*. Popular music didn't sound like *Oliver!* anymore. Vietnam had marred the innocence of *Doctor Dolittle*. The sixties were almost over, and Hollywood *still* hadn't caught up.

Despite a wave of corporate takeovers, the last of the golden age moguls held the studios in an arthritic fist. In 1966, Jack Warner, at seventy-four, had sold his controlling interest in Warner Bros. to Seven Arts Productions—but he ran the studio until late 1969. Darryl Zanuck, in his late sixties, remained on the throne of 20th Century–Fox, having installed his son, Dick Zanuck, as head of production in 1962. At Paramount, newly acquired by Gulf and Western, Adolph Zukor, in his nineties, and Barney Balaban, in his eighties, sat on the board, which Zukor would chair until his death in 1976 at the age of 103.

Viewed from another angle, though, the corporate decay presented an opportunity. In 1966, Robert Evans, a braggadocious thirty-six-year-old producer, had been appointed Paramount's head of production. "The strongest period in Hollywood history was in the thirties, when most of the creative people were young," Evans proclaimed the next year. "The trouble is that most of them are still around making movies." One of his first projects was *Rosemary's Baby*. As his consigliere, Evans hired Peter Bart, a journalist who had written about him in the *Times*. When Bart arrived in Hollywood, he found an industry in free fall. "At that point it was too disarrayed to *be* an industry," he recalls. "It was a community that couldn't quite figure out how to communicate to its audience. So there was a certain degree of alarm. The reason I decided to take this job offer is that I felt it could be a great adventure, because everyone was hoping by dint of necessity. Everyone was open to new ideas." At Paramount, Bart welcomed poets and rock stars to pitch projects, while the old stars seemed conspicuously glamorized and adrift: "Sometimes

a big star would come in and say, 'I don't know where the fuck I am.'"
The town was primed for an Oedipal showdown: parents versus children,
square versus hip.

Outside the studio lots, Los Angeles was enveloped in the din of the
Hells Angels and the scent of marijuana. "It was like the ground was in
flames and tulips were coming up at the same time," Peter Gruber, who
was then a young Columbia executive, would recall. While the Byrds and
Joni Mitchell played the Troubadour, Evans found himself saddled with
grandfathered projects like *Paint Your Wagon*. The "don't trust anyone
over thirty" side of the generation gap looked at Hollywood and saw a
tone-deaf establishment. "Nobody had ever seen themselves portrayed in
a movie," recalled one of the town's rowdiest rebels, Dennis Hopper. "At
every love-in across the country people were smoking grass and dropping
LSD, while audiences were still watching Doris Day and Rock Hudson!"

Not that the kids were uninterested in movies; they were ravenous for
them. But the exciting movies weren't coming out of Los Angeles. They
were the European avant-garde of Truffaut's *Jules and Jim* and Antonioni's
Blow-Up, which married fluid narrative style with risqué sexuality and
drew titillated crowds into art house cinemas. They were embraced by
intellectuals such as Susan Sontag and argued over by celebrity critics
like Pauline Kael and Andrew Sarris. A new generation of American
directors, reared on Fellini and Godard, was itching to rewrite the rules:
Francis Ford Coppola, Martin Scorsese, Peter Bogdanovich. A 1968 study
sponsored by the Motion Picture Association of America brought the
unnerving news that sixteen-to-twenty-four-year-olds had accounted for
48 percent of box-office sales the year before and that "being young and
single is the overriding demographic pre-condition for being a frequent
and enthusiastic moviegoer."

In 1967, two raucous hits blasted through Hollywood, hinting at a return to relevance. Warren Beatty, as lore has it, had kissed Jack Warner's
feet to get him to finance *Bonnie and Clyde*. The movie was about
Depression-era gangsters, but its freewheeling insolence drew from the
French New Wave; the bad guys were good, the good guys were squares,
and it all ended in a shocking geyser of blood. *The Graduate* had sex—
the taboo kind, with your girlfriend's mom—and an unconventional

new star. Charles Webb's novel described its young hero as athletic and
Waspy—a role for Robert Redford, perhaps—but Mike Nichols gave the
part to Dustin Hoffman, a twenty-nine-year-old Jewish stage actor. The
press touted Hoffman as a new kind of star: "a swarthy Pinocchio," as *Life*
not so delicately put it, proclaiming, "Dusty is one of the few new leading
men in Hollywood who look like people rather than profiles in celluloid."

The new batch of talent was leery of the studio system. Dyan Cannon,
a young actress in the midst of ending her three-year marriage to Cary
Grant, was offered a five-picture deal with Universal, the first of which
would be a Don Knotts vehicle called *The Love God?* "A bird in the
hand," her agent told her. But Cannon had also received a script for an
unusual comedy about free love. "It was new. It was not safe. It was edgy,"
she recalls. "I had a feeling that something was changing, and I wanted
to be a part of the change." She turned down the Universal contract just
for the chance to audition for *Bob and Carol and Ted and Alice*.

In 1968, Jack Valenti, the president of MPAA, introduced the new
ratings system, which replaced the sclerotic Production Code with letters: G (for General Audiences), M (Mature), R (Restricted), and X (no
minors allowed). After scuffles over exposed breasts in Sidney Lumet's
The Pawnbroker and the "screws" and "goddamns" in Nichols's *Who's
Afraid of Virginia Woolf?*, the change was a long time coming. In early
1969, the Swedish erotic film *I Am Curious (Yellow)* caused a sensation
when it was released in the United States, only to be seized by customs.
As its obscenity was debated by the courts, audiences flocked. Suddenly,
Paramount's Peter Bart recalls, "all the nice Jewish boys in New York
dreamed of dating a Swedish girl."

If Hollywood had arrived late to the sixties, the Academy arrived
even later. *The Graduate* and *Bonnie and Clyde* made the Best Picture
cut in 1968, but both lost to the Sidney Poitier drama *In the Heat of the
Night*, one of Hollywood's belated acknowledgments of the civil rights
movement. The next year, the thirty-six-year-old Peter Bart watched
Rosemary's Baby lose the adapted screenplay award to *The Lion in Winter*.
"I was by far the youngest person in the audience," he says. On the eve
of the forty-first awards, the *Times* mocked the Academy for its byzan-
tine membership procedure, "a trying ritual that rivals finding a cheap

apartment in Manhattan," noting that its three-thousand-odd voting body was "heavily weighted with older people, many of whom are no longer very active in the film business." The nominations only proved the point. As *Variety* observed, "Over-50 demographic age characteristics of Academy members was brought sharply home with lack of a best picture nomination for *2001*, this year's youth fave."

If anyone could lead the Academy out of obsolescence, reincarnating it like *2001*'s star child, it would have to be someone who understood what the sex-drugs-and-rock-'n'-roll kids were looking for. And yet, the job had fallen to a square-jawed fifty-three-year-old whom most of America thought of as Dad: Gregory Peck.

IN FEBRUARY 1969, *TIME* PUT Dustin Hoffman and Mia Farrow, the break-out stars of *The Graduate* and *Rosemary's Baby*, on its cover. "Many of the young stars are, in fact, anti-stars," the story announced. Anti-stars chose Manhattan apartments over Beverly Hills swimming pools, political activism over Paramount: "The once-desirable studio contract now looks like slavery." Summing up the past two years of upheavals, the article continued, "As comedy grew steadily blacker and as audiences grew steadily younger, hipper and more draftable, the old concepts began to erode. The invulnerables like Peck and Holden and Wayne seemed lost in a country full of people whose destinies were not in their own hands."

Peck would not have been pleased to appear on this list of "invulnerables." How could his resonant baritone compete with Hoffman's adenoidal whine? Peck was inarguably a product of the star system now being compared to slavery. Born in 1916, Eldred Gregory Peck had arrived in Hollywood in 1943, a former varsity rower with the clean-cut handsomeness to match. He could be stalwart to the point of being stiff, but with the war depleting Hollywood's roster of leading men, Peck's robustness had appeal. Louella Parsons wrote in her column, "You couldn't go to a party without hearing the buzz about this wonder man's rugged handsomeness, his thin height, his magical speaking voice." In 1946, Peck was nominated for Best Actor for his second picture, *The Keys of the Kingdom*, in the role of a Roman Catholic priest.

He was nominated again the next year for MGM's *The Yearling*, playing the father-knows-best role. In 1948, he received a third consecutive nomination, for Elia Kazan's *Gentleman's Agreement*, which won Best Picture. Peck played a journalist who poses as Jewish to expose anti-Semitism, a role that chimed with his offscreen liberalism; he collected books on Lincoln by the hundreds, and in response to HUAC, he joined the liberal protest group the Committee for the First Amendment. In 1950, he was nominated a fourth time, for the war drama *Twelve O'Clock High*. On-screen and off, he exemplified valor, the reasonable man who takes a principled stand. But it wasn't until he was forty-six, well past his matinee idol *Roman Holiday* period, that he found the role that burnished his legend: Atticus Finch, in *To Kill a Mockingbird*. From behind his round spectacles, Peck embodied the citizen hero, the gentle father, the fair-minded dissenter. "In that film," Harper Lee said, "the man and the part met."

Lee gave Peck a gold watch and chain that had belonged to her late father, the model for Atticus, and he carried it with him to the Academy Awards on April 8, 1963, where he finally won Best Actor, beating *Lawrence of Arabia's* Peter O'Toole. The moral glow of Atticus propelled Peck to a new role as civic figurehead. The next year, he was elected to the Academy's Board of Governors. He campaigned for California's Democratic governor, Pat Brown, in his failed reelection bid against Ronald Reagan. Unlike Reagan, Peck declined to run for office, instead becoming Hollywood's unofficial mayor, Reagan's liberal shadow. In June 1967, he was elected Academy president.

His first crisis in office came the following April, when Martin Luther King Jr. was assassinated four days before the Fortieth Academy Awards were to be held. After four Black stars who were slated to participate— Sidney Poitier, Sammy Davis Jr., Louis Armstrong, and Diahann Carroll—withdrew in mourning, Peck postponed the ceremony two days, the first time the Oscars had been delayed since the flood of 1938. He opened the April 10 broadcast with a speech worthy of Atticus Finch, the archetypal white liberal. "Society has always been reflected in its art, and one measure of Dr. King's influence on the society we live in is that of the five films nominated for Best Picture of the year, two dealt with the subject of understanding between the races," he said, referring to *In the*

Heat of the Night and *Guess Who's Coming to Dinner*, nominated against *The Graduate*, *Bonnie and Clyde*, and (improbably) *Doctor Dolittle*. Peck returned later in the evening to receive the Jean Hersholt Humanitarian Award.

Peck's role as Hollywood's liberal ambassador came at a cost to his acting career. In the first month of 1969, Lyndon Johnson awarded Peck the Presidential Medal of Freedom, calling him a "humanitarian to whom Americans are deeply indebted." Three days later, Vincent Canby panned Peck's new film, *The Stalking Moon*, writing, "Peck is so grave and earnest it seems he must be thinking about his duties on the board of the American Film Institute, rather than on survival." Children who were eleven in 1962, when they first saw Peck as Atticus Finch, were now dropping acid and burning their draft cards. They didn't want a dignified father figure; they wanted rebellion, and that made Peck's gentle authority a liability.

Peck wasn't blind to the sea change. "Film turns young people on like nothing else," he said in 1968, predicting an "American New Wave" brought on by directors like Nichols and Coppola. It was an open question, though, where Peck belonged in that future. He certainly didn't live like an "anti-star," splitting his time between his Brentwood mansion and his house in the South of France and socializing with the likes of Fred Astaire and Ava Gardner. He preferred Trollope to *Portnoy's Complaint*, and his taste in films, he told one paper, fell "somewhere in between the esoteric tastes of the young and the more conventional tastes of the Academy."

Peck entered 1969 with his mind pulled in different directions. His son Stephen had received his draft card and joined the Marine Corps. "He was very patriotic, my dad, even though he was against the war," Stephen recalls. "He stoically said, 'Well, you gotta do what you gotta do.' And off I went." In the spring of 1969, Stephen shipped out to Da Nang, where his father sent him boxes of Dickens and Brontë.

At the Academy, Peck was putting out various fires. Robert Evans wrote from Paramount to lodge an "emphatic appeal" against the rejection of Peter Bart for Academy membership, on the grounds that Bart had not yet been a film executive for three years. "I take it that the three year rule is seldom waived," Peck wrote to Evans. But everyone knew that the rules could be bent: Streisand had been made an Academy member before her film début in *Funny Girl*. After her tie with Hepburn, there was renewed speculation that the Oscar voting was rigged for maximal drama. As observers pointed out, Streisand, having skipped the line on membership, presumably cast the tie-making vote for herself. In addition, the Academy had received "some bruising comments [about the Oscar telecast], especially about Barbra Streisand's derriere," Peck wrote to a friend. "For whatever a few dozen letters are worth, the indication is that professional people liked it, but the common folk thought it was too far out." The efforts to jazz up the broadcast had failed to halt a rating slump. The indefatigable Margaret Herrick, who still handled the Academy's day-to-day administration, sent Peck a cache of press clippings about the falling viewership, saying, "This is not only surprising to me but very alarming, as I am sure it will be to you."

Peck had to do something bold to bring the Academy up to date. He had already kicked off a study of the membership rolls, with the idea of demoting administrators and public relations people to nonvoting status. In a letter to Peck, Herrick predicted that "the worst that can happen is that we have some bruised egos to deal with." Then he got a nudge from an unlikely source: twenty-two-year-old starlet Candice Bergen.

IN 1967, BERGEN HAD RETURNED to Los Angeles after nearly two years of jet-setting, making films in France and Greece, shooting pheasant, and liaising with an Austrian count. Bergen had the statuesque beauty of a Nordic deity, with silken blond hair and a long nose that ended in elegantly flared nostrils. Her wardrobe was stocked with Dior and Hermès, and her style fell somewhere between Holly Golightly and Princess Grace.

But the world she came back to was unrecognizable. "Men in page-boy haircuts preened, ruffled and jeweled, lurching in high-heeled buckled boots, fashionably foppish," she recalled, "while women's heads were shorn: they were more eyelashes than hair, peering out from under the spiky black thatch shading each eye and trying to look like Twiggy, their patron saint." In New York, Bergen had attended Truman Capote's Black and White Ball at the Plaza, with a mink bunny mask loaned to her by

Halston. As she swanned among the glittering crowd, a *Women's Wear Daily* reporter inquired: Wasn't it inappropriate to be hobnobbing at a ball while war was raging in Vietnam?

"Oh, honestly," Bergen sniffed in her bunny ears.

Back home in Los Angeles, Bergen prepared for her twenty-first birthday, sending out invitations to "mourn the passing of my youth" to guests who included Rosalind Russell and Cary Grant. This was the world she knew: the world of her father, ventriloquist Edgar Bergen, whose fame had come courtesy of his top-hatted wooden alter ego, Charlie McCarthy. When Candice was born, in 1946, the press called her "Charlie's sister." Young Candy's life was surreal. Christmas parties featured David Niven as Santa. Her friends included Liza Minnelli, whose sixth birthday party was held at Ira Gershwin's house in Beverly Hills. At six, Candy made her début on Edgar's radio show, bantering with her wooden "brother." In her father's office, she would gaze at his special Oscar, awarded in 1938—made of wood, with a movable mouth.

Candice's first date, at thirteen, was with Gloria Swanson's grandson. The next year, she was sent to finishing school in the Swiss Alps, where, to her parents' horror, she learned to flip open a Zippo lighter and order "*un* Bloody Mary." She enrolled at the University of Pennsylvania but lost interest in school as her modeling career took off, when she became the face of Revlon's campaign for Tawny cosmetics. In 1966, she made her film début, in Sidney Lumet's *The Group*, as a lesbian graduate of a women's college. She explained to her scandalized parents, "This is an *art film*, not a Ross Hunter production," referring to the producer of *Pillow Talk*. But she was only passingly interested in her craft, and Pauline Kael, observing the shoot for *Life*, called Bergen a "golden lioness of a girl" who "hasn't yet discovered what acting is all about." After *The Group* came Bergen's extended European jaunt, during which she made films for Claude Lelouch and Michael Cacoyannis, while polishing her refinement to a sheen.

By the time she returned to L.A., her fame eclipsed Edgar's—the "father of Charlie McCarthy" was now the "father of Candice Bergen." The sixties had rendered him prehistoric—Charlie McCarthy's impish humor was in saying the unsayable, and now everything was sayable—and he was reduced to performing at county fairs. Not that Candy was up with the times. "Evidently the Sweet Bird of Youth had passed me by like a Boeing," she recalled, "and I found myself, at twenty-one, peering at the generation gap like a tourist—from the far side." Her arrival at a "hippie party" in Beverly Hills confused her more: the guests included Sammy Davis Jr. and Frank Sinatra, and a maid passed out brass ankhs. One middle-aged producer chided a colleague, "Take that goddamned flower off your ear."

Ah, Bergen realized, this wasn't a real "hippie party," just Hollywood playacting. The next night, she got a dose of the real thing when she went to a party in Benedict Canyon in her Dior lounging pajamas. Inside the candlelit house, she smelled burning sandalwood. Janis Joplin's voice blasted from the sound system. The women wore moccasins; the guys were shaggy-haired and festooned in beads and bells. "People were sitting and passing a joint and listening to the music," she recalls, "and I'm there with my crocodile bag and my little kitten heels. It was just, like, where *am* I?"

Bewildered, Bergen found the host, Terry Melcher. Melcher, Doris Day's son, had been Bergen's first love when she was sixteen and he was a college dropout in Italian loafers. Five years later, Melcher wore jeans and an Indian shirt, his sandy hair down to his shoulders. His job at Columbia Records had placed him at the center of the California rock scene: he produced the Byrds' *Mr. Tambourine Man* and played on the Beach Boys' *Pet Sounds*. "You seem so old," Melcher told the sophisticated Bergen. "Don't you ever miss being a kid?"

Melcher's honesty pierced Bergen's armor of archness. They took motorcycle rides through the mountains, and she tried to fit in among his hippie circle, including Brian Wilson and the Mamas and the Papas' John and Michelle Phillips. "I was *beyond* straight," she recalled. "No number of robes and beads, no amount of dope was going to change that, though God knows I tried." She moved into Terry's house in Benedict Canyon, where the party had been: 10050 Cielo Drive.

The house, built in the forties in ersatz Normandy style, had stone fireplaces and rose-covered fences. "You waited to find Bambi drinking from the pool," Bergen recalled. They hired a butler to cook them romantic dinners and ate by candelabra under the cherry blossoms, a

Hollywood fantasy on a not-insignificant budget. Among their dinner guests was shaman Rolling Thunder, who asked Bergen if she had any fresh meat for a sacrifice; she gave him chicken legs and ground sirloin from the freezer, and he took them up the mountain and burned them.

Bergen had finally found her side of the generation gap. By 1968, she was covering the Oregon primaries for *Cosmopolitan* and expounding to the *Los Angeles Times* on the Maharishi and "cosmic consciousness." Her Republican father disapproved of Melcher, whose radical politics were rubbing off on his Candy, with her lectures on materialism and vegetarianism. "One week it's ducks, the next it's Indians!" her exasperated father would exclaim.

Candice's relationship with Melcher became strained, too. His casual cool left her restless; staring into space stoned bored her. "Your problem is you have no soul," he told her.

"I do, too!" she protested. But part of her believed him.

One day, Melcher and one of the Beach Boys came home talking about a commune they'd visited at an old movie ranch, where sunlit young women doted on their Christ-like leader, singing in the nude. "Why can't they sing *dressed*?" Bergen cracked, eyes rolling. Melcher halfheartedly asked if she wanted to join them, but she had no interest in Charlie Manson.

One Monday in January 1969, Melcher abruptly announced that they were moving to his mother's beach house in Malibu. Manson had been dogging Melcher for a record contract, and the producer asked friends not to tell Manson his new address. "He was suddenly very threatened by Manson," Bergen says, "and I didn't know that was why he wanted to move." Soon after they left the Cielo Drive house, Roman Polanski and Sharon Tate moved in.

Terry's stepfather, Martin Melcher, had died nine months earlier, leaving an unpleasant parting gift: he had embezzled millions from Doris Day, and now Terry was saddled with mountains of financial briefs. He leaned on sleeping pills and liquor. Bergen saw the life drain out of him. Left alone to walk her Saint Bernard on the beach, she felt adrift. In April, she watched the Academy Awards and saw that something was missing: people her age. "The Academy needed new blood," she says. "It seemed to need *blood*, period. It skewed way too old, and I don't think until then it was as obvious."

She was uniquely qualified to act as a bridge—bred by the Old Hollywood but versed in the New. She had crossed paths with Gregory Peck growing up but didn't know him well, only that he was a gentleman. Nine days after *Oliver!* won Best Picture, Bergen sat down with her stationery pad and wrote in blue cursive:

Dear Mr. Peck,

Not being an Academy member, I am most certainly out of place in writing you. I *am* a film lover and you seem to be the most receptive and constructive of all Academy Presidents.

Among the rising questions provoked by antiquated Academy rules is that of membership. Many or most members are anachronisms clogging the works of an incredibly facile mechanism called motion pictures.

I would be very grateful if I could help in any way to recruit newer, younger members. Perhaps one way is compiling a list of those whose creativity and energy the Academy never before solicited. And by mailing memberships to those people voted upon jointly by the Academy or its Board of Directors. Application procedures are somewhat lengthy & discouraging.

In this way the Academy might be more of a vital, social organism improving higher, more honest standards and encouraging new talent.

I know you are concerned with these very same things. I don't mean to be rude, I am simply offering my help and interest if it is needed. (Attested by the fact that I used 3 pieces of good stationery . . .)

Congratulations to you and Mr. Champion on such an exciting show. You do us proud.

Sincerely,
Candice Bergen

Two days later came a reply on Academy letterhead, along with the closely guarded membership list. "Why don't you go over it, and then make out a list of young people who should be in the Academy," Peck suggested. "I agree with you that the Academy must break down resistance to new ideas, and indifference to the kinds of films which have meaning today to younger audiences. Since we can't put older members, who in their time made important contributions, out on the icebergs to die, we must do our best to balance things by encouraging all of the qualified younger people to join and exert their influence."

Peck assured her that "the process of application and approval isn't as cumbersome as you think. For actor members, we require as a rule, three credits in major films. Exceptions are made if the talent is special. Dustin Hoffman, although he hasn't applied, would probably be accepted at once. The practical purpose behind the selectivity is the protection of the Academy. We want voting members who will still be in films ten or fifteen years from now, and not in the laundry business in Glendale."

Empowered by her latest crusade, Bergen got to work. Among her recruits was Dennis Hopper, who was about to release a film that would tilt Hollywood on its axis: *Easy Rider.*

IN 1955, A BLUE-EYED NINETEEN-YEAR-OLD was shown into Harry Cohn's offices at Columbia. Dennis Hopper was new to Hollywood but had made an impression, beating out thirty-two actors for a part as an epileptic on *Medic* by faking a seizure in the casting director's office. Hopper wandered awestruck into Cohn's office, where the mogul sat with a cigar next to his second-in-command, Abe Schneider, framed, Hopper recalled, by "a rainbow of Academy Awards."

"We're going to make a big star out of you," Cohn said to the perspiring young man. "What have you been doing, kid?"

"Well, I've been doing Shakespeare in San Diego," Hopper offered—he had been an apprentice at the La Jolla Playhouse, the theater cofounded by Gregory Peck.

"Shakespeare?" Cohn barked. "Oh, God, not Shakespeare! Shakespeare ruins movie actors!" He turned to his casting director: "Max, get him some numbers and send him to school."

Hopper exploded. "What the fuck are you talking about? You're tell-ing me I have to go to fucking school to learn how to be a movie actor?" He told Cohn to go fuck himself and was escorted out the door.

Hopper's loathing of authority ran deep. When he got to Hollywood, he would tell people at parties, "I come from Kansas, which is nowhere. And I hate my parents, who are no one." Born in Dodge City during the Dust Bowl, he spent much of his childhood on his grandparents' farm, wearing a gas mask to school during dust storms. After his father went off to fight in World War II, his mother informed Dennis that he had been killed in an explosion during basic training. Not long after, nine-year-old Dennis was stunned when his father returned home from Peking; his death had been a cover story for his work with the Office of Strategic Services in Asia. "Now," Hopper recalled, "wouldn't that make you a paranoiac?"

Suspicious of everything, Hopper got mixed up with juvenile gangs. He spent his first months in Hollywood stealing milk from porches. But his main rebellion was acting; his parents thought that creative people were bums who ended up behind bars. Hopper had landed a contract with Warner Bros. and was cast as Goon in *Rebel Without a Cause*, part of the teen gang that pesters James Dean's character. Hopper worshiped Dean: his spontaneity, his iconoclasm. The two took peyote and smoked marijuana together. They were both cast in *Giant*, where Dean upstaged Elizabeth Taylor by peeing on the set. When Dean died in a car crash, Hopper felt "cheated," he said. "I had dreams tied up in him, and suddenly that was shattered."

Hopper resolved to take on the mantle of Dean's unlived life: his drugging, his reckless driving, his intransigence. He racked up so many parking tickets that he lost his driver's license. When Warner Bros. sent him a letter chiding him for lateness, he framed it. Jack Nicholson, with whom he shared an agent, would marvel, "Man, this is suicide! What the fuck's he doing?" In 1958, Hopper was cast in *From Hell to Texas*, directed by the old-school Henry Hathaway. After Hopper called him "a fucking idiot," Hathaway told the actor, through cigar smoke, "Kid, there's one thing I can promise you: you'll never work in this town again." Warner Bros. canceled Hopper's contract.

Hopper decamped to New York and found a hip new circle, including Allen Ginsberg and Miles Davis. While acting in a Broadway play, he met Brooke Hayward, the daughter of agent and producer Leland Hayward and actress Margaret Sullavan. The morning of their wedding, Leland told his daughter, "Brooke, it's not too late to call it off." She married him anyway. At the reception, thrown by Brooke's friend Jane Fonda, Hopper met Jane's brother, Peter, who thought, *This guy is looney tunes, but he sure is interesting.*

The Hoppers moved back to L.A. "We'd go to these parties where you'd have the crème de la crème of Hollywood, and [Dennis would] tell them that when he ran things, heads were going to roll, they'd be in chains," Hayward recalled. "Someday he'd make a movie, and the old dinosaurs would be slain." Friends were dazzled by the couple's home, festooned with art by Duchamp and Lichtenstein. One writer called it "the Prado of Pop." "There was some sort of circus poster in the front hall," remembers Candice Bergen, who knew Hayward from childhood—they were both second-generation Hollywood. In Hopper, Bergen saw the wild thing she could never be. "He was sort of a brilliant lunatic," she says. "Totally unedited and uncensored, just this force of nature, without any impulse control."

One day at Peter Fonda's house, Hopper jumped up on the sofa and exclaimed, "Everyone talks about making an independent film, but nobody's willing to go through with it!" In 1966, the two men went to New York to try to find funding for a comedic screenplay they'd devised called *The Yin and the Yang*, but Hopper's attitude warded off anyone with money. He thought of turning their failed expedition into a movie itself, called *Second Chance*, which would begin with him telling Fonda, "We've gotta save the movie industry, man. We gotta save it, or it's all over for the movies!" He had a treatment titled *The Last Movie, or Boo Hoo in Tinseltown*, which he thought would be his masterwork, but when plans to finance it fell through, Hopper spiraled. "I was into peyote and drinking, and I'd fly into uncontrollable rages," he recalled.

He went up to Haight-Ashbury in San Francisco for a be-in and came back transformed. "He had a three-day growth of beard," Brooke Hayward recalled, "he was filthy, his hair was crazy—he'd started growing a ponytail—he had one of those horrible mandalas around his neck, and his eyes were blood-red. Dennis was altered forever." Convinced the FBI was tracking him, he took karate for self-defense. He believed he would die at thirty-three, like Jesus Christ. One afternoon, after Hayward criticized one of his photographs, he broke her nose. Terrified, she fought the abuse with withering criticism. The day that Hopper began working on a new project—temporarily called *The Loners*—she told him, "You are going after fool's gold." The movie was *Easy Rider*.

The origins of *Easy Rider* are as hazy as a pot cloud, but it emerged from the wave of scuzzy, cheap biker flicks that proliferated after Roger Corman's 1966 *The Wild Angels*, starring Peter Fonda and Bruce Dern. The next year, Hopper starred in *The Glory Stompers* and played a drug dealer in Corman's *The Trip*, which costarred Dern and Fonda and was written by Jack Nicholson, who also starred in *Hells Angels on Wheels* that year. These B-movies existed in an alternative Hollywood, rawer and more defiant than the established one that won Oscars. In Fonda's telling, he was at an exhibitors' convention in Toronto to promote *The Trip*, winding down with some beer and grass in his hotel room at four thirty in the morning, when he looked at some *Wild Angels* publicity stills showing him and Dern on motorcycles. "Suddenly I thought, that's it," Fonda recalled, "that's the modern Western; two cats just riding across the country, two loners, not a motorcycle gang, no Hell's Angels, nothing like that, just those two guys."

Hopper was the only person he knew who was crazy enough to dig his late-night brainstorm, so Fonda called him in L.A. and pitched the idea: "I figure you direct it, I produce it, we'll both write it, and both star in it, save some money."

Hopper was speechless. "You'd let me direct it, man?"

Fonda and Hopper named their stoner characters Wyatt and Billy, invoking the icons of the Wild West. In Rome, where Fonda visited his sister on the set of *Barbarella*, he picked up Terry Southern, one of its gaggle of screenwriters, to help write the script. Fonda owed a movie to American International Pictures, but when the company threatened to seize the film if it went three days over schedule, he refused. It was then that the pair wound up at Raybert, an ultrahip production outfit run by Bob Rafelson and Bert Schneider, producers in their mid-thirties. Both were scions of show business. Rafelson was the nephew of Samson Raphaelson, who wrote *The Jazz Singer*. Schneider, a voracious pot smoker with seductive eyes and a nimbus of blond curls, was the son of Columbia president Abe Schneider, who had been sitting beside Harry Cohn during his fateful meeting with Hopper. In 1965, Rafelson and Schneider had sold an idea to Columbia's TV arm to create a television answer to the Beatles' *A Hard Day's Night*, starring an ersatz band called the Monkees.

Now riding high (in more than one sense) on the Monkees' success, the young producers were eager to bottle the counterculture—and they had the grass to prove it. By the time Fonda and Hopper arrived at the Raybert offices, Rafelson was directing the Monkees film *Head*, which he had written with Jack Nicholson. Fonda pitched a short film he wanted to make, featuring LBJ feasting on live lobsters as he planned the Kennedy assassination. Rafelson asked, "Peter, how's that motorcycle movie coming?" By the end of the meeting, Schneider was handing Hopper and Fonda a forty-thousand-dollar check to go film Mardi Gras, telling Hopper, "This is your test."

Driving Hopper to the airport in February 1968, Brooke Hayward told her husband, "You're making a big mistake. This is never going to work. Peter can't act. I've known him since I was a child. You're just going to make a fool out of yourself."

"You've never wanted me to succeed," Hopper said. "You should be encouraging me, instead of telling me I'm going to fail. I want a divorce."

"Fine."

Mardi Gras was, indeed, a disaster. Hopper began the first morning haranguing the crew: "This is *my* fucking movie, and nobody is going to take *my* fucking movie away from me." He would carry a loaded gun, raving about how the government was monitoring them. People started quitting. At their hotel, a paranoid Hopper demanded film stock from one of the cameramen, and they got into a brawl involving a thrown TV set. The night before they came home, Fonda called Hayward and warned her, "I think you ought to take the children and get out of the house. Dennis has gone berserk."

Back in L.A., Hopper was arrested on the Strip for possession of marijuana. (He insisted that they had stopped him only because of his long hair.) Bert Schneider bailed him out and sent him off to scout locations in Texas. Hayward filed for divorce and got a restraining order. Her father told her, "Congratulations on the first smart move you've made in six years."

Rip Torn was set to play George Hanson, the ACLU lawyer whom the two drifter heroes pick up in Louisiana. But after Hopper pulled a steak knife and pointed it between Torn's eyes, Torn either quit or was fired, depending on whose version you believe, and was replaced with Jack Nicholson. At thirty-one, Nicholson was virtually unknown to "straight" Hollywood; after starting out as an office boy in the MGM cartoon department, he'd spent a decade in Roger Corman's B-movie shanty town. Schneider had asked him to be his eyes and ears on *Easy Rider*.

The shoot somehow continued, a seven-week ramble through California and the South. According to Hopper, Fonda hired bodyguards to protect him from his drugged-out director. Terry Southern had exited the tumultuous project after supplying the script, the movie's new title (a slang term for a prostitute's boyfriend), and the ending, in which the two heroes are shot down by rednecks. Southern saw it as "an indictment of blue-collar America, the people I thought were responsible for the Vietnam War."

Hopper's first cut of *Easy Rider* was four and a half hours long. Fonda was too scared to confront him—he worried that Hopper would jump him with a pistol. To distract him, Schneider coaxed Hopper into taking a small part as a dirtbag horse thief in *True Grit*, a John Wayne Western directed by Henry Hathaway, who had fired Hopper years before. "C'mon, man, go and work for the old man," Schneider said. "I won't touch the movie while you're gone."

Wayne and Hopper were an odd couple: Hollywood's archconservative and its upstart hippie. On set, Wayne would arrive by helicopter from the minesweeper he kept in Newport Beach, a .45 strapped to his side. Hopper recalled, "This one day he arrived, and he wanted to know where 'that Pinko Hopper was hiding.' I was actually in Glen Campbell's trailer, hiding from him. He was screaming, 'My daughter was out at UCLA last night and heard Eldridge Cleaver cussing, and I know he must be a friend of that Pinko Hopper! Where is he?'"

Afterward, Schneider convinced Hopper to take a holiday in Taos, while *Easy Rider* got pared down to ninety-six minutes. "You've ruined my film," Hopper said as he watched the results. "You made a TV movie out of it." The film was finished with a groundbreaking rock score featuring Steppenwolf and the Byrds. Like Hopper, *Easy Rider* was rebellious and self-aggrandizing—and an Oedipal rebuke to the Old Hollywood of Abe Schneider and Henry Fonda. When Bert Schneider and Bob Rafelson screened it for the Columbia brass, most of the executives walked out halfway through. One lamented, "What's Bert doin' to his father?" As the bewildered Columbia planned the film's release, United Artists was readying another racy property, also about two men living on the edges of society, called *Midnight Cowboy*.

IN 1965, AN ARTIST FRIEND sent British director John Schlesinger a new novel about a Texas stud named Joe Buck who goes to Manhattan to be a gigolo for Park Avenue society ladies but winds up servicing men, with help from a consumptive con man known as Ratso Rizzo. Schlesinger, an Oxford-educated, Jewish son of a London doctor, was on a hot streak thanks to *Darling*, starring Julie Christie. The film won three Oscars, including Best Actress, but had the misfortune of competing with *The Sound of Music*.

Schlesinger was intrigued. A flamboyant, bawdy wit who kept a male lover in the attic of his home on Peel Street, he was still putting on the pretense of heterosexuality. When he brought the novel to his regular producer, the response was "This is faggot stuff. This will destroy your career." But an American producer Schlesinger knew, Jerome Hellman, thought they could do something with it—something that would be nearly impossible to finance, in the days when *Who's Afraid of Virginia Woolf?* was still straining against the old Production Code.

Hellman took the novel to United Artists, whose president warned him, "My partners here, the older men in the company, aren't going to understand it." But the studio offered to fund it for no more than a million dollars. They hired playwright Jack Gelber to write the screenplay but weren't happy with his drafts. While they were looking for a replacement, an agent who represented formerly blacklisted writers walked into Hellman's office and plunked down some forty pages of an unproduced screenplay called *The Artful Dodger, or, If You Can't Join 'Em, Lick 'Em,* by Waldo Salt.

A gentle, jug-eared, otherworldly man, Salt had been in the show business wilderness for decades. He was one of the original Unfriendly Nineteen called before HUAC in 1947, and in exile he sold scripts under his wife's name. By the early sixties, he was free to write under his own name again—but all he could turn out was junk like *Wild and Wonderful,* about an alcoholic French poodle. Convinced that he no longer knew how to write, he left his wife and children and holed up in a dilapidated hotel room in New York, where he drank too much and labored over a screenplay about Don Quixote. But Schlesinger thought that Salt's *Artful Dodger* script had the fragmented quality he wanted for *Midnight Cowboy,* and they agreed that what propelled the story was, in Salt's words, the cowboy's "infantile need for touch."

One night, Hellman went to the Off-Broadway play *Eh?* Watching the young actor playing the factory caretaker, the producer thought, *Oh, shit, this guy was born to play Ratso Rizzo.* Plus, they could get him cheap. It was Dustin Hoffman. Then, as Salt and Schlesinger worked on *Midnight Cowboy* at a beach house in Malibu, something unexpected happened: *The Graduate* turned Hoffman into an overnight sensation. He was now getting offered every script in Hollywood—and turning most everything down. But he still wanted to do *Midnight Cowboy.* Mike Nichols was flabbergasted, telling him, "I made you a star, and you're going to throw it all away?"

But the success of *The Graduate,* paradoxically, made Schlesinger less sure about Hoffman. He wasn't interested in big names and couldn't picture the preppy Benjamin Braddock as a limping street rat. Hoffman begged the director to meet him at a seedy Times Square automat at 1 a.m., and he showed up in a dirty raincoat, his hair slicked back, with days-long stubble. Schlesinger agreed to keep him, if he stayed out of the sun.

The search for Joe Buck was more fraught. Michael Childers, a young photographer who became Schlesinger's assistant and lover, would recall that Elvis Presley's rep showed interest, saying, "If you'd clean up this script, get rid of some of the smut, it could be a vee-hicle for Elvis!" Fortunately, no one was interested in that solution, least of all Marion Dougherty, the New York casting director who had an eye for the kind of offbeat talent that would define the New Hollywood. Her idea for the midnight cowboy was Jon Voight, an unknown Off-Broadway actor with a Little Dutch Boy handsomeness. Voight was ravenous for the part. It came down to him and Canadian actor Michael Sarrazin. Schlesinger asked Hoffman to watch both screen tests; Voight had understood Joe Buck's innocent phoniness—that the cowboy thing was all an act. Hoffman said later, "When I was watching these tests with [me playing against] Michael, I was looking at myself. When I was watching the test with Jon Voight, I was looking at Jon Voight." They released Sarrazin, who instead took a role opposite Jane Fonda in *They Shoot Horses, Don't They?*

Voight, who came from Yonkers, spent a week roaming around Texas with a tape recorder, studying accents, while Hoffman surveyed the denizens of the Bowery. During preproduction, Hoffman practiced his consumptive cough with such gusto that he threw up on his costar's cowboy boots. Voight, who was separated from his wife, began dating the screenwriter's daughter, Jennifer Salt, cast as his girlfriend in flashbacks. While filming their scenes, they watched the 1968 Democratic convention in their motel room. Voight was very much on the "counterculture bandwagon," Salt says. "His politics were 'take care of the underdog' to the tenth power"—a far cry from his turn toward Trumpism decades later.

Voight seemed to have no qualms about his sex scenes, including his movie theater rendezvous with a young male client played by Bob Balaban, the nephew of former Paramount president Barney Balaban. "We sat there up in the balcony, with me pretending to go down on Jon Voight, for a day, while this outer space adventure was playing," Balaban recalls. "There were millions of shots, and all I remember is my knees were red from rubbing against the stiff, tough carpet." Even more involved was Voight's bedroom scene with Brenda Vaccaro. "My first film of any consequence," Vaccaro recalls, "and I said, 'My mother's going to see my tits before my face?'" The costume designer, Ann Roth, gave Vaccaro a fur coat to cover herself, and when Schlesinger saw it, he exclaimed, "How divine! Fucked in fox!"

The year before Stonewall, Schlesinger's sexuality was an open secret. "We had a lot of problems with the crew," Childers recalls. "All those Irish and Italian union workers, who just were so antigay. So we had that wall of prejudice against us." The homoeroticism between Ratso and Joe Buck was a delicate matter. As Hoffman recalled, he and Voight were looking around the set of the tenement apartment the two men share when "it hit us: 'Hey, these guys are queer.'" But Schlesinger waved off the idea, saying, "Oh, God! Please! It was hard enough to get the financing. Now all we have to do is tell them that we're making a homosexual film."

In one sequence, Joe Buck and Ratso visit a psychedelic party featuring Warhol Factory "superstars" like Viva and Ultra Violet. Warhol would hang around the set, observing; Brenda Vaccaro recalls Schlesinger complaining, "Fucking Andy Warhol is always behind the camera, driving me fucking crazy. Get him out of here!" The artist was meant to appear in the party scene, which re-created the Factory in a studio in Harlem. But, a few weeks before the shoot, Viva was in the makeup room doing tests. She was taking a call from Warhol when she heard a *bang* on the other end of the line—Warhol had been shot by radical feminist Valerie Solanas.

The party scene was "like a six-day bacchanal," Hellman recalled. Vaccaro says, "Every crazy person in New York showed up. There was a girl with green hair and a green monkey sitting on her shoulder, but it was a stuffed monkey. And she had green nails, and she said, 'Hi, I'm a monkey in a tree.' I walked into my dressing room, and two people were on my bed making love. I said to Jerry Hellman, 'What's going on? This place has turned into a rat's nest!' And half of them were on acid."

Schlesinger filmed it all through the eyes of his marginalized protagonists. Where *Easy Rider* reveled in the counterculture, trying to bottle its defiant cool, *Midnight Cowboy* observed it from a bemused distance. Both films follow a pair of male friends chasing a mirage-like dream across America, and both subvert the traditional Western: *Easy Rider* with its motorcycles subbing for horses, *Midnight Cowboy* with its poseur Texas stud adrift in sexual ambiguity. *Easy Rider* is a time capsule, but *Midnight*

Cowboy is a portrait of two lost souls, and its gritty New York City milieu anticipated the New Hollywood tone of the seventies.

On the last day of shooting, Voight found Schlesinger alone by a camper, looking like he was having a stroke. "What will they say about this?" he told Voight in a panic. "A dishwasher goes to New York to screw older women? What will they think of us? What have we *done?*"

Voight, who could fake confidence as well as his character, grabbed the director by the shoulder and told him, "John, we'll live the rest of our artistic lives in the shadow of this great masterpiece."

DENNIS HOPPER AND PETER FONDA strode into the Cannes premiere of *Easy Rider* in May 1969 in Union Cavalry garb: a loophole to the *comme il faut* rules (uniforms, technically, counted as evening wear) and their signal that the United States was on the verge of another civil war. There was no question which side *Easy Rider* was on. "It's America today," Fonda told the press. "A simple picture, but heavy, as they say on the street."

The film opened at Manhattan's Beekman theater on July 14 as the world-rocking summer of '69 was under way, and made back its budget in one week. Teens lined up barefoot and smoked so much pot in the theater bathrooms that the staff had to remove the stall doors. Like *The Graduate, Easy Rider* was a youth phenomenon; *Life* credited Hopper with creating "a style of a New Hollywood in which producers wear love beads instead of diamond stickpins." In the *New York Times*, Vincent Canby called the film "a ballad of joy and sorrow, something felt as poetry, not intellectualized as prose." But he reserved special praise for Jack Nicholson, who stood out as "a real-life character set into a cartoon." Even Henry Fonda praised the raffish thirty-two-year-old, declaring, "If there's any justice, he'll get a nomination."

Audiences studied *Easy Rider* like a road map for a new America, one epitomized not by Atticus Finch but by Abbie Hoffman. "We were living in a society that was amoral," Hopper said later, "because we could no longer believe in the mores of the society and that we were all breaking the laws of society. Because of smoking marijuana, and the kinds of things we were doing in the '60s, it seemed like everyone was outside of the law at that time."

For its young producers, Bert Schneider and Bob Rafelson, the success of *Easy Rider* brought their pot-scented operation new clout. With the addition of a third partner, Steve Blauner, they had changed their company name to BBS, using their first initials, and set up in a four-story building on La Brea. The offices had a pool table and secretaries who delivered bowls of grass on silver trays. It was the indie hothouse of the New Hollywood, with a pipeline including *Five Easy Pieces*, directed by Rafelson and starring Nicholson, and Peter Bogdanovich's *The Last Picture Show*. The older studio executives, meanwhile, questioned whether their decades of experience were an asset or a liability. Peter Fonda recalled, "Bert's father, Abe Schneider, resigned as chairman of the board of Columbia, stating that if *Easy Rider* was the way the industry was going to go, he did not understand it and did not want to be a part of it."

At Paramount, executives Bob Evans and Peter Bart were still working through the archaic projects they'd inherited from the old regime while fast-tracking youth-oriented pictures like *Medium Cool* and *Love Story*. When Bart was invited to an industry screening of *Midnight Cowboy*, he took Evans. At the end, Bart recalls, "he looked at me in total bewilderment, and he said, 'We just saw dailies on *Paint Your Wagon*. This picture—it's a different industry. It's a different *epoch*.' The eras were changing so rapidly that you'd be caught in the backdraft." Bob Balaban visited his uncle Barney's office and saw a pile of reels on his desk labeled *Midnight Cowboy*. Perhaps flummoxed by his nephew's oral sex scene, the former Paramount president didn't say a word.

Under the new ratings system, United Artists chairman Arthur Krim was certain that *Midnight Cowboy* would be the first studio movie to be branded with a scarlet X. When the ratings board gave it an R, he should have been thrilled: more papers could advertise it, and more audiences could buy tickets. Instead, he rejected the rating and pushed for the X. He was worried about the movie's influence on children—could it turn them gay? Besides, he realized, the X would give *Midnight Cowboy* cachet with the hippie crowd. "The quality was there, no question—I was sure Hoffman and Voight would be Academy Award nominees," UA executive Gabe Sumner recalled. "The question was how to make the movie more potentially exciting to the general public. I felt the controversy over the X rating would give it an extra dimension. The movie needed to get out of the art house and into the public square."

Midnight Cowboy was a smash hit when it opened at New York City's Coronet in May. John Schlesinger hid out in Bloomingdale's to gawk at the crowds, which stretched from Third Avenue to the Fifty-Ninth Street Bridge. It made $44.8 million on a budget of around $3 million—another score for pictures that were cheap and risqué. The critics did not unanimously swoon. "It's not a movie for the ages," Vincent Canby incorrectly judged, "but, having seen it, you won't ever again feel detached as you walk down West 42d Street, avoiding the eyes of the drifters, stepping around the little islands of hustlers and closing your nostrils to the smell of rancid griddles."

Schlesinger heralded the film's success as a sign of the times. "As the old moguls and old systems are dying off and young people are coming in, the studios are beginning to take risks," he told the *Los Angeles Times* in June, the same week the Stonewall riots erupted in downtown Manhattan. He warned, though, "Change is very tough. Hollywood is a very big Establishment factory." Driving the point home, the July 11 issue of *Life* split its cover in half: Dustin Hoffman in a winter coat on top, John Wayne in a cowboy hat on the bottom, with the headline "Dusty and the Duke: A Choice of Heroes." Which would Hollywood choose?

NINE DAYS LATER, IN A victory for clean-cut, laconic heroes, the world stopped still to watch Neil Armstrong walk on the moon. Candice Bergen was in Eugene, Oregon, shooting her latest film, Columbia's *Getting Straight*, a comedy about a campus protest starring Elliott Gould as a sardonic teaching assistant, Bergen as his coed girlfriend, and twenty-seven-year-old Harrison Ford as a long-haired undergrad. It was the sort of studio concoction that tried too hard to chase the youth vote, up to its ludicrous last shot of Gould and Bergen getting it on mid-riot.

Watching the moon landing with the cast in a hotel room reeking of pot smoke, Bergen rolled her eyes. "Candice said, 'While you were all downstairs watching the moon landing, I was upstairs watching *The Prisoner of Zenda*,'" Gould recalls. At thirty, the rangy, eccentric Gould had already shot Paul Mazursky's *Bob and Carol and Ted and Alice* and

Robert Altman's M*A*S*H, the movies that would soon turn him into the New Hollywood's next groovy Jewish hero, but neither had been released. To the world, he was still Mr. Barbra Streisand, although their marriage was effectively over.

After *Getting Straight*, Bergen returned to Malibu and to Terry Melcher, who was still mired in his mother's wrecked finances and hooked on Placidyl. Their two-year romance was on its last legs. And weird things were happening. One morning, they woke up to find that the telescope on the beach veranda had gone missing. Days later, a friend passed on the message that Charlie Manson was looking for Melcher—and if he happened to be missing a telescope, that's because Manson had borrowed it. A week later, Hollywood awoke to absolute horror: Sharon Tate and four others had been murdered in Terry and Candy's old house on Cielo Drive. Bergen was panicked. "It could have been *me!*" she wailed to Melcher. "I could have been *killed!*"

"*We* could have been killed," he corrected her. But it was too late. Bergen moved out soon after.

She wasn't the only freaked-out celebrity. Rumors swirled that the unidentified killers had a movie star hit list. Los Angeles was upended with fear and speculation. Was it the Black Panthers? A celebrity stalker? Who was next? All the wildness and paranoia of the sixties seemed to break through to the surface; the center, as Joan Didion observed, no longer held. Throughout Hollywood, people armored their mansions with automatic gates and guard dogs. To protect his home in Brentwood, Gregory Peck hired a night guard, who would leave a slip of paper wedged in the back door to prove he had been there.

Peck was spending the summer at his home in the South of France, conducting Academy business from afar while he tried in vain to evict a French groundskeeper whom he suspected of spying and grift. The most pressing Academy matter was Peck's plan to move noncreative members to "associate" status, without Oscar-voting privileges. "I am most anxious to get on with the branch and membership reforms," he wrote to Margaret Herrick. "We must assign people who are wrongly placed and shift people from all branches who are deadwood."

Part of his mind was on his son Stephen, in Vietnam. "He spent a year in almost terror of the Western Union," recalls his younger son Carey, who, at the time, was starting at Georgetown's School of Foreign Service. During his first semester, he was arrested twice for civil disobedience. His father's agent, using Old Hollywood logic, chided Carey for exposing Peck to potential scandal. But his father saw shades of Atticus Finch, telling his son, "These days, if you don't have an arrest record, you're not young and alive and standing on the right side of things."

Bergen was in Mexico making a new film, *Soldier Blue*, when she called Terry Melcher and heard that Charles Manson had been arrested in the Tate killings. (Manson later invited Dennis Hopper to see him in prison, hoping that he would play him in a movie.) She received a subpoena but arranged to testify in private. She sat in the back of the courtroom when Tex Watson was brought out. She was asked if she recognized him, but she didn't. Hippies all looked alike to her.

Bergen had bought her own place, the Aviary, on the old John Barrymore estate. Having once housed exotic birds and, later, Katharine Hepburn, it was an impractical but romantic dwelling: a Mediterranean tower nestled amid cypress trees, with stained-glass windows and moldy murals that reminded Bergen of *Arabian Nights*. Life was dreamy: she had a horse named Herschel and spent her days practicing photography and contemplating ecological causes. But after the Manson murders, everything seemed darker. "I remember John Phillips came over to visit once, with Quincy Jones, and left me a gun," she recalls. "I said, 'Why are you giving this to me?'"

Bergen had kept up her offer to Peck, cajoling Dennis Hopper and other friends to join the Academy. Her father and Peck had cosponsored her membership, and she sponsored her flock in turn. In the fall of 1969, she handwrote a letter to the Academy president:

Dear Mr. Peck—

Thank you so much for the application forms and the opportunity of suggesting new members. I have filled out forms for nine people. All of them are people who are a vital and creative part of our industry (perhaps the *only* vital and creative part of the industry).

The thing of it is—that I am stuck for a co-sponsor. So, I was
wondering . . . if perhaps you wouldn't mind doing the honors of
being a sponsor—if you agree on the people I've suggested.

I will be in Mexico now till January—so I hope my friends make
the grade.

Thank you again,

Best,
Candy Bergen

By then, Peck was in Tennessee shooting *I Walk the Line*, in which
he was miscast as a married small-town sheriff who has an affair with
a mysterious young hillbilly. Peck was uneasy performing midlife crisis
abandon, much less raw sensuality. From the Holiday Inn in Cookeville,
he kept up on Academy affairs by post. ABC was "adamant" that they
invite back Bob Hope to host the Oscars, but Peck was keen to draw in
the New Hollywood set. "We have checked all of the sponsorship cards
which you sent in," Margaret Herrick wrote him. "Warren Beatty and
Katharine Ross have been members since 1968; Julie Christie was invited
in 1967 and never responded; Dustin Hoffman was invited in 1968 and
never responded, but Jack Nicholson, [Elliott] Gould, Peter Fonda, Dennis
Hopper and Robert [Forster, the star of *Medium Cool*,] should definitely
be invited before the end of this year as they are certainly more than
eligible."

The indifference of young talents like Christie and Hoffman was
bad news. Peck sent out personal appeals, writing, "I urge you to accept
membership in the Academy when it is offered to you, as it will be in
December. It is not your dues we are interested in. We do want your point
of view reflected in the annual voting for awards." He assured them that
even a single vote could change the outcome: "Witness last year's tie vote
between Katharine Hepburn & Barbra Streisand."

Peck happily joined Bergen in cosponsoring Dennis Hopper's application. The drawbridge was lowering, and fast. Peter Bart, whose membership Peck had earlier rejected, recalls one day at Paramount when the

previous head of production, Howard W. Koch, came into his office and said, "You are now a member of the Academy."

"Wait a minute," Bart stammered. "They're a bunch of old guys!"

"Look," Koch told him, "the average Oscar voter is someone in their mid-seventies. We've got to change the demo. You are hereby conscripted." He then plunked down an application card, which informed Bart that Billy Wilder had sponsored him. Bart didn't know Billy Wilder. "They were just so desperate to change the voters," he recalls.

But Peck had something bolder in mind. Over the winter, the Board of Governors finalized a radical new plan: anyone who had not been active in the movie industry for seven years would be made an "associate" member, without an Oscar vote—in other words, put "out on the icebergs to die." But it had to be done carefully. Secret lists were drawn up; lawyers were consulted. As the minutes of February 19, 1970, recorded, Peck "stressed the importance of keeping this information from becoming known prematurely." The board agreed that the purge would be kept under wraps until after the Forty-Second Academy Awards.

THE NEW DECADE DAWNED IN Hollywood with uncertainty and a little hope. MGM, Fox, and Paramount had lost well more than fifty million dollars in 1969. "I used to be able to tell how much money a picture would make just by looking at it," one executive lamented. "Nowadays, there are times when I haven't the faintest idea." And yet the industry, despite everything, had a future. "The movies entered the 60s as [a] mass family entertainment medium in trouble," Charles Champlin wrote in the *Los Angeles Times*, "and they leave them as a mass but minority art-form, important and newly influential, wildly divergent and addressed to many and divergent audiences." He singled out *Midnight Cowboy*, "one of the prime candidates for an Academy Award as Best Picture" that "could not and would not have been made a decade ago and could not have been exhibited."

When the nominations came out, though, they seemed to flash a gigantic arrow pointing backward. The highest number of nominations, ten, went to *Anne of the Thousand Days*, a costume drama starring Richard Burton as Henry VIII, in the vein of *A Man for All Seasons* and

The Lion in Winter. Also in the Best Picture race was *Hello, Dolly!*, which was struggling to earn back its $25 million budget. Barbra Streisand—at twenty-seven, playing a widow—was considered the miscasting feat of the year, and she was conspicuously not nominated. It was Elliott Gould who was now a sensation, thanks to the release of *M*A*S*H* and *Bob and Carol and Ted and Alice*, for which he was nominated for Best Supporting Actor.

The former Mr. Streisand was not impressed. "The Oscars are some sort of masturbatory fantasy," he told the press. "People think, an Academy Award—now if I get a parking ticket I don't have to pay it. I don't put the award down, but at my sanest, I would rather have a good three-man basketball game than sit there in my monkey suit." Gould shared the category with Jack Nicholson, who was now so in demand that he doubted whether he'd have the night off to attend the ceremony. But he didn't play humble, telling Rex Reed, "If I get an Oscar, I won't feel like I've stolen anything."

Nicholson's nomination was one of only two for *Easy Rider*, along with the original screenplay award, for the uneasy trio of Hopper, Southern, and Peter Fonda. Jane Fonda was nominated for Best Actress, for *They Shoot Horses, Don't They?*, and her novel campaigning methods included smoking joints in interviews ("You don't mind if I turn on, do you?") and expounding on the military-industrial complex. Henry Fonda, who had been nominated twice, captured the air of patricide when he griped, "How in the hell would you like to have been in this business as long as I and then have one of your kids win an Oscar before you did?"

The top-grossing movie of 1969 was *Butch Cassidy and the Sundance Kid*, a gun-toting adventure featuring comely young stars Robert Redford and Katharine Ross, William Goldman's zippy dialogue, and Burt Bacharach and Hal David's catchy "Raindrops Keep Fallin' on My Head." The charm offensive had worked on the public and on the Academy, which nominated the movie for seven Oscars. It was the rare film that appealed to both sides of the generation gap. Like *Bonnie and Clyde*, it ended with its heroes gunned down in a blaze of glory. And like *Midnight Cowboy*, *Easy Rider*, and *M*A*S*H*, it centered on an exalted male friendship unencumbered by the presence of women, who had little place, so far, in the New Hollywood revolution. The frame had been widened, but only so much: the new movie heroes were young, free, and defiant, but they were predominantly white and male.

Midnight Cowboy tied Butch Cassidy and Hello, Dolly! with seven Oscar nominations, including Best Picture. Hoffman and Voight would compete with each other for Best Actor, though the category was seen as a shoo-in for John Wayne, for True Grit. Before the awards, Midnight Cowboy producer Jerry Hellman ran into George Roy Hill, director of Butch Cassidy, who told him, "Midnight Cowboy is a terrific movie. You should be very proud. And don't be too disappointed, but the studio's told me that we've got a lock on it." The poor showing for Easy Rider, meanwhile, seemed "somehow an inadequate reflection of the impact the movie has had on the industry," Champlin argued. "It is in the nature of Academies to celebrate the doing well of what has been well done before: How else to explain the dimensions of the honors to 'Dolly!' and 'Anne of the Thousand Days'?"

The studio machinery, though creaky, had scarcely ground to a halt. Before the nominations, three men in suits took Midnight Cowboy's Brenda Vaccaro to lunch at the Beverly Hills Hotel. "They said, 'Give us three thousand dollars and we'll get you the nomination,'" she recalls. "I said, 'What? I have to pay you?' Stupidly, I turned away from it. I should have just given them the three grand." Universal held thirty-five special screenings of Anne of the Thousand Days, preceded by cocktails with beef Stroganoff and assorted French pastries and followed by midnight champagne suppers. Fox hosted lavish buffets for Hello, Dolly!, with an open bar and prime rib au jus, rerunning its campaign for Doctor Dolittle. One industry insider predicted a sweep for Hello, Dolly! out of a "save-the-town sentiment."

Five weeks before the Oscars, dyspeptic critic John Simon published a broadside in the New York Times, titled "Oscars: They Shun the Best, Don't They?" He tore into the nominees: Anne of the Thousand Days ("sluggish dullard of a film"), Butch Cassidy ("a mere exercise in smart-alecky device-mongering"), Hello, Dolly! ("a vacuous, unwieldy, over-produced musical"), Midnight Cowboy ("your typical social-significance film"). But his sharpest words were for the Academy: "The main trouble with the Oscars is, of course, that an award of artistic significance cannot be adjudged by a large, unwieldy, semi-anonymous body of *any kind*—any more than a court case can be tried by a panel of several hundred or thousand judges."

Under fire, Peck deputized board member Michael Blankfort to write a response to the *Times*, which ran the Sunday before the awards and called Simon a "hungry Cassius" with "the hauteur of an 18th-century French aristocrat." The year had been rocky for Peck. In January, Vincent Canby wrote that the end of the decade had brought "no less than four Gregory Peck performances that can only be described as 'ambassado-rial'"; in his roles as a retired army scout (*The Stalking Moon*), a sher-iff (*Mackenna's Gold*), a scientist (*The Chairman*), and a NASA official (*Marooned*), Peck looked "as if he were on some high-level mission on behalf of clean, resonant speech."

No matter. With the Oscars days away, Peck was on a high-stakes mission: to lure Cary Grant to the ceremony. At sixty-six, Grant had shunned the Oscars for twelve years after getting passed over one too many times. His bucking of the studio system had made him anathema to the Academy's elders, but Peck spent months making top-secret preparations to give Grant an honorary award, even hiring Mike Nichols to prepare a highlight reel. In March, Grant promised Peck that he would end his Oscar boycott and receive the honor in person. Two days later, a former call girl named Cynthia Bouron filed a paternity suit against Grant. As the scandal rippled through the trade papers, Grant fled to the Bahamas and hid out in Howard Hughes's private villa. At a press conference, Bouron threatened to show up at the Oscars and reveal her baby's name on the red carpet. If Grant showed up, she'd have him slapped with a subpoena.

Peck scrambled to get Grant back, despite speculation that the Academy brass had planted the scandal to keep him from showing his face. Princess Grace was scheduled to present him the award, but Grant urged her to cancel for her own sake, and Peck subbed in Frank Sinatra. On April 1, Grant flew to Las Vegas to get advice from Hughes, who told him that the best way to squelch the story was to show up and receive his Academy Award as if nothing were wrong. Grant called Peck the next day and agreed to come.

Grant went to stay with his ex-wife Dyan Cannon, who had been nominated for Best Supporting Actress for *Bob and Carol and Ted and Alice*. "Cary was very nervous to be out in public, and he told me he didn't know what he was going to say," Cannon recalls. "I just thought he should let all his fans see him. 'The world loves you. Go shine your light.'"

DENNIS HOPPER FORGOT ALL ABOUT the Academy Awards, until someone reminded him to show up. On April 7, 1970, he arrived in a velvet tux, cowboy boots, and a Stetson, along with his new girlfriend, the Mamas and the Papas singer Michelle Phillips, newly divorced from John Phillips. Jane Fonda, wearing her *Klute* shag, held up a fist to the roaring fans and yelled, "Right on!" Her political opposite, John Wayne, also received a swell of cheers, though one picketer held up a sign reading "JOHN WAYNE IS A RACIST." Other protesters objected to the fact that there were only three Black musicians in the orchestra, and down the street, some fifty Mexican Americans demonstrated against Hollywood's stereotypical depiction of Latinos in movies like *Butch Cassidy*, chanting "Power to the Chicanos!"

As if to underline how much things had changed in the past year, viewers at home were given a disclaimer that all film clips had been edited "regardless of the ratings of the motion pictures referred to tonight." When the curtains opened, Gregory Peck walked onto an empty stage and struck a philosophical tone: "Most of us these days are asking ourselves and each other these questions: What is the meaning of the new freedom of the screen? Is it something to be feared? Should the screen be censored?"

Bob Hope, who had been invited for his usual yuks, said a hammier version of the same. "It's such a novelty seeing actors and actresses with their clothes on," he joked, after coming onstage wearing a *True Grit* eye patch. He went on: "This will go down in history as the cinema season which proved that crime doesn't pay, but there's a fortune in adultery, incest, and homosexuality." Summing up the new epoch of sex, drugs, and violence, Hope said, "This is not an Academy Awards. It's a freak-out, ladies and gentlemen."

So it was. The audience was the generation gap made visible:

Vincente Minnelli, Frank Sinatra, and Mickey Rooney on one side, Jane Fonda, Jack Nicholson, and Dennis Hopper on the other. "These X-rated movies are really something," Hope continued. "One theater manager told me he's been popping corn for six months and still hasn't plugged the machine in." The audience laughed, with some groans. "You could feel there was a kind of buzz when Bob Hope would host anything, because he was the conservative," Candice Bergen recalls. "And so it was very much us against them."

Bergen, one of the recurring presenters ("Oscar's best friends") wore a sequined purple poncho with gold fringe, loaned from her friend Arnold Scaasi. She and Gould came out for the first award, Best Sound, won by *Hello, Dolly!* Gould was surprised to find himself seated next to John Wayne and his wife. When Wayne was called onstage, he turned to Gould and said, "When I go up there, you look after her." It was unclear whether he knew that he was talking to the guy from the spouse-swapping movie.

Presenting Best Cinematography to *Butch Cassidy*, Wayne marked his turf in the culture war, grumbling, "I'm John Wayne, an American movie actor. I work with my clothes on." Like Hope, Wayne was despised by the hipper members of the audience. "We all were politically opposed to his position about the war and therefore not big fans," recalls Jennifer Salt, who sat with her boyfriend, Jon Voight, and her father, Waldo. It was Voight, along with Katharine Ross, who presented the adapted screenplay award to Salt. "I want to thank all the beautiful people who helped to make *Midnight Cowboy*," Salt said from behind his sunglasses. It was a short speech but redolent of meaning: nearly two decades after his HUAC hearing, Salt had been welcomed back to the Hollywood fold. To the hippies, the blacklisted screenwriters weren't traitors but heroes.

Each award was a shot across the battle line between the two Hollywoods, Old and New. At the Oscar rehearsal, Gould had run into Jack Nicholson, his competition for Best Supporting Actor. "I'm winning this," Nicholson told him with a smirk. But both lost to the fifty-six-year-old Gig Young, for *They Shoot Horses, Don't They?* The writers of *Easy Rider* and *Bob and Carol and Ted and Alice* lost the original screenplay award to William Goldman, for *Butch Cassidy.* Streisand, in a pink pillbox hat, came out to present Best Actor. Both *Midnight Cowboy* actors lost, inevitably, to John Wayne.

When Cary Grant came out to accept his honorary award, looking grayer but no less twinkling than his public remembered him, he struck a note of comity. "I've been privileged to be a part of Hollywood's most glorious era," he said, before praising "the astonishing young talents that are coming up in our midst. I think there's an even more glorious era right around the corner." In the audience, Dyan Cannon, in a Sant'Angelo's Indian princess midi, sat next to Elizabeth Taylor. "At the moment he came out," Cannon recalls, "Elizabeth put her hand on my knee and turned and looked at me and gave me a look I'll never forget. The look said, 'I understand. You were married to him. You gave him his only child. You're divorced from him. Are you okay with this moment?' That's what that look said. I just smiled and said, 'It's okay.'"

Midway through, Hope came out with Fred Astaire. "You've never danced in the Academy show, huh?" Hope said, cuing the conductor. The orchestra played a funky riff, and Astaire, who was born in 1899, took center stage, moving his seventy-year-old frame to an unmistakably seventies sound. He swayed, he jerked, he twirled, an old man matching his rhythm to an unfamiliar beat. Then a big-band tune played, and Astaire broke into an exuberant tap routine, dancing away the decades, lighter than air. It was a dance to ward off mortality, to reawaken the schmaltzy Hollywood that was falling into the sea. Later in the night, Jon Voight was crossing backstage when he saw Astaire coming toward him. "We reached each other in the middle of this thing, me six foot two or three and Fred, slight of figure, shorter," Voight recalled later. "And he looked up and said, 'Oh, Jon! Hi. Let me stand aside.' I said, 'No, no, please—let me stand aside for you.' 'Great work,' he said. 'Well, thank you, thank you.' Then I stepped aside. He went on, and I looked back, and it was Fred Astaire! That was the meeting of the two generations in the appropriate way, with tremendous regard for each other."

John Schlesinger, nominated for directing *Midnight Cowboy*, was in London shooting his next film, *Sunday Bloody Sunday*. His boyfriend, Michael Childers, recalls, "John refused to shut down his movie to go to Hollywood [for the Oscars], even though the studio was willing to pay for the shutdown and was begging John to fly. 'You're the dark horse,' they kept saying." The couple followed the proceedings on TV from London at four in the morning. Schlesinger's ex-secretary, who was working as the production manager for the Oscar broadcast, had them on the phone from backstage when Schlesinger won Best Directing. "She started screaming hysterically," Childers recalls. "We were in our pajamas in the house jumping up and down."

Finally, Elizabeth Taylor came out to present Best Picture. The winner was *Midnight Cowboy.*

For the first time, the counterculture had won. "It was an earthquake, a tsunami for the Oscars," Childers says. Peter Bart recalls, "*Midnight Cowboy* was a total 'fuck you' to every way that the town was doing business. An X picture was acceptable by the Academy. Would that mean that we all should get into the porn business? It was a serious discussion inside closed doors."

At the end of the night, Bob Hope delivered a farewell that was more like an elegy, or perhaps a white flag of surrender:

Never again will Hollywood be accused of showing a lollipop world. Perhaps by showing the nitty-gritty, by giving the world a glimpse of the element of violence and its destructive effect, it will help cool it. Whatever violence the screen has shown is not an example to follow but to see in its full destructive power. The troubled, kooky characters that people the screens are not examples to emulate but to learn from and try to understand and hopefully, perhaps, contrive help for. More and more films have explored the broad spectrum of human experience. They have fearlessly, and for the most part with excellent taste, examined behavior long considered taboo.

"The evening," Charles Champlin wrote, "was a reminder of how much and how swiftly the world has turned."

At the Beverly Hills Hotel, Elizabeth Taylor and Richard Burton hosted a losers' afterparty. Dyan Cannon, who had lost to Goldie Hawn for *Cactus Flower,* danced with Burton. Taylor wore a Cartier necklace displaying the pear-shaped diamond that Burton had bought her at an auction. At the party, she gave it to Gould and Rupert Crosse—the first Black actor nominated for Best Supporting Actor, for *The Reivers*—and let them toss it around like a softball. "It was the size of the Statue of Liberty," Gould recalls, "and she gave it to us." If there was a baton to be passed, this was it.

Hollywood's warring generations scraped uneasily into the night. John Wayne, Oscar in hand, caught up on his drinking at the Polo Lounge. When his *True Grit* costar Dennis Hopper approached, Hopper recalled, "he took one look at me and called me a Communist. Then he asked me to come out on his yacht—it's actually a minesweeper— and he'd explain to me why he's worth a million per picture." At the Governors Ball, Frances Bergen expressed her and Edgar's disapproval of their daughter Candy's psychedelic smock. "She didn't have to agree to be a presenter," Mrs. Bergen huffed. "But once she did, she should have conformed and worn something elegant."

FOUR DAYS AFTER THE OSCARS, the Academy announced that it had "revised and democratized" its rolls by reclassifying 335 of its members as nonvoting "associates," effective immediately. Peck called it "a just determination concerning the voting privileges of members who have been professionally inactive in motion pictures for a number of years." As one headline put it, "Stodgy Old Oscar Gets a Facelift." Ironically, many in the same voting body that had just awarded *Midnight Cowboy* Best Picture were being told they were obsolete.

Peck set up a committee to review grievances, which poured in. Gossip columnist Sidney Skolsky, who still claimed that it was he who had given Oscar its name, objected that he was "actively engaged" in producing, even though his last outing was in 1953. There was the "distressed" former MGM producer who understood the need to embrace new talent but did "not understand what is to be gained by tossing others to the crocodiles." (His case was reviewed, and he was reinstated.) There was the producer of *Bud Abbott and Lou Costello in Hollywood*, who blasted the Academy's "prejudice and favoritism." (His appeal was denied.) A Spanish director turned newspaperman admitted that he had retired from pictures, but wrote, "I believe that YOUTH should be given a voice in the Academy, but NOT at the expense of those who, like myself, have served it well over the years. I feel that we are just as qualified to vote at Oscar time as any newcomer such [as,] for example, Barbra Streisand."

One newly deemed "associate" was Jack Warner Jr., son of the mogul, who had produced films like *The Hasty Heart* (1949) before his father dismissed him from the company that bore their name, in 1958. The bitterness of the family feud was evident in Warner's letter to Peck, in which he wrote of the industry, "The way we act towards our own shows that we think little of the feelings of our own people." He added, "I sincerely hope someday the Academy will grow a conscience—and that it will happen during your administration."

Peck wrote gracious but firm replies, took phone calls, went out to lunches. In the end, the Academy reversed only thirteen decisions. In *To Kill a Mockingbird*, Atticus Finch exemplified the idea of courage as taking an unpopular stand. The Peck purge of 1970 may or may not have been courageous, but it was certainly an unpopular stand, and a self-sacrificial one. By putting the golden age out to pasture, Peck was hastening the demise of the Hollywood that had created him, the only one in which he made sense.

THE TRIUMPH OF *MIDNIGHT COWBOY* embarrassed the new rating system. What was X if it applied to a Best Picture winner? Some thought that instead of relegating dirty movies to the garbage dump, the rating would only give cachet to pornography and would kneecap boundary-pushing art films. Not long after the Oscars, United Artists, which had lobbied for the X rating for *Midnight Cowboy* in the first place, went back to the ratings board and asked for the film to be reclassified as an R. The request was granted without a single frame having been changed.

Hollywood was still adjusting its eyes to the altered landscape. It was perhaps the biggest talent turnover since the talkies, and Old Hollywood wasn't going quietly. "To be an idol, there must be worshipers at the shrine," Joan Crawford told the *San Francisco Examiner*. "All the dream-hungry kids who used to buy fan magazines by the dozens and live vicariously in the worlds of their movie gods are now living it up and loving it up in their various Woodstocks. Personally, I'm glad I belonged to that other era."

MCA mogul Lew Wasserman, who had taken over Universal, was scrambling to catch up with the world of *Easy Rider*. A fiftyish man of middlebrow tastes, he created a division for youth-oriented films, which would produce George Lucas's *American Graffiti*. Its first project was *The Last Movie*, Dennis Hopper's metafictional epic about a Peruvian village that takes up filmmaking after a B-movie crew leaves town. Hopper starred as a stuntman, a character he saw as "blindly American, a guy with preconceived ideas about everything"—he had offered the role to John Wayne. Universal gave him final cut.

By then, Hopper was on the outs with every member of the Fonda clan. Just before Christmas, Jane had visited his ex-wife Brooke Hayward and learned that his present for his daughter was a Polaroid camera box filled with his dirty hair. "So I don't know what kind of scene he's into now," Jane said. In June, Hopper sued Peter Fonda, claiming that he was owed a third of the *Easy Rider* profits. Henry Fonda, meanwhile, made no secret of his feelings. "If you want to know what I think of Dennis Hopper, the man is an *idiot!*" he told the *New York Times*, adding, "He's a total freak-out, stoned out of his mind all the time. Any man who insists on wearing his *cowboy* hat to the Academy Award ceremonies and keeps it on at the dinner table afterward ought to be spanked." "Henry Fonda said I was an idiot?" Hopper retorted. "Wow! I guess it just goes to show you what the establishment view of me is. Of course, I *did* make his son a star in *Easy Rider*."

Production of *The Last Movie* began in Peru, where Hopper immediately made himself a pariah by offering a reporter his unfiltered thoughts on marijuana and homosexuality. (He'd lived with a lesbian and said it was "groovy.") Things went downhill from there. The first day of shooting, a local woman attacked the crew, yelling in Quechuan, "Go away! This is sacred Inca land!" In Chinchero, high in the Andes, Hopper had seven sheep tied up for an ersatz native sacrifice, with hundreds of locals as extras. He paid them less than a dollar apiece, plus whatever sheep remains they could grab. There were hailstorms, mud slides. Hopper fantasized about living in an adobe hut for six months, even as he imported

Argentinian beef for his stoner set, who stayed in a European-style hotel. "Man, the movies are coming out of a dark age," he opined on set,
claiming that his was the most creative generation of the past nineteen
centuries. "And we're going to make groovy movies, man."

As much as Hopper styled himself as an alternative to the old studio
system, he somehow magnified its abuses. Kris Kristofferson recalled later,
"He got a priest defrocked because he got him involved in some kind
of weird mass for James Dean. He antagonized the military and all the
politicians. It was crazy." At one point, Hopper slammed a local actor's
head through a coffee table. The seven-week shoot was "one long sex-
and-drugs orgy," Hopper said. "Wherever you looked, there were naked
people out of their fucking minds on one thing or another." The junta
finally told him to get out of the country.

He returned to the States with some forty hours of footage and retreated to the twenty-two-room adobe compound in Taos he'd bought
with *Easy Rider* money. On Halloween 1970, in front of two hundred
guests, he married Michelle Phillips, who said she was drawn to him
by a "Florence Nightingale instinct." The marriage lasted eight days.
Phillips claimed Hopper had shackled her in handcuffs, believing she
was a witch. (Hopper denied handcuffing her and later explained that
he abused women only "after *days* of abuse by them.")

After more than a year of editing, interrupted by LSD-soaked bacchanals and telephone fights with the studio, Hopper screened *The Last
Movie* at Universal's Black Tower. In the silence that followed the final
frame, the projectionist said, "They sure named this movie right, because
this is gonna be the last movie this guy ever makes." *The Last Movie*
was a fiasco. "That sound you hear is of checkbooks closing all over
Hollywood," *Time*'s critic wrote. "I had final cut," Hopper said, "and cut
my own throat."

His Academy membership lapsed in 1972, owing to nonpayment
of dues.

A MONTH AFTER HOPPER'S PERUVIAN misadventures were catalogued in
a damning cover story for *Life*, Candice Bergen covered another issue of
the magazine, alongside the phrase "Activist Actress." Like Jane Fonda,

Bergen was fully politicized: speaking at rallies for L.A.'s teachers' union, joining peace demonstrations. She would pick up her eight-year-old brother at school so she could "de-condition" him. But she knew there were limits to actor activism. "To *really* help the Indians, for example, I should be on a reservation giving penicillin, not talking on the *Dick Cavett Show*," she admitted.

Bergen had finally found a role that excited her, in Mike Nichols's *Carnal Knowledge*, opposite Jack Nicholson, whose fame was unstoppable after *Easy Rider*. From her bedroom at the Aviary, she could spy with her telescope on the pool across the canyon, where girls sunbathed topless. Bert Schneider had just moved in. The producer of *Easy Rider* intrigued her, as did his pedigree: a child of Old Hollywood who had helped forge the New, just like her. They had met in passing, first at a premiere and then at the Columbia dining room, where Bergen saw Schneider, Hopper, and Peter Fonda looking like a shaggy commune amid the aging executives. "He was very tall. He kind of slumped," Bergen recalls. "He had a very full head of ash-blond curly hair. But he had piercing blue eyes—sort of Paul Newman blue eyes. He was deeply handsome and very rangy and slim. And very successful, because he got *Easy Rider* made and made movies that changed movies."

Schneider was becoming less interested in making movies and more interested in revolutionary politics. In one heady weekend, he introduced Bergen to Joan Baez, guru Baba Ram Dass, and Huey Newton, the Black Panthers' "minister of defense." Her parents were even more appalled by her new boyfriend than they had been by Terry Melcher. Edgar would only call him "that producer fellow." When Schneider implored Mrs. Bergen to "go with the flow," she snapped, "No."

Schneider pressed Bergen to renounce her old friends. "The difference between you and me, Bergen," he scoffed, "is that if it were the Russian Revolution you would be inside dancing with the nobility and I'd be outside with the peasants, with my face pressed against the window." (*True*, she thought, *but then he'd drive away in a Porsche.*) The couple would house Abbie Hoffman when he was on the run, or host the zonked-out Dennis Hopper when he was in from Taos. In Washington, DC, they joined an antiwar demonstration, lying down in the Senate chamber and getting arrested. By 1972, Bergen was crossing the country with Huey Newton campaigning for George McGovern while her father stumped for Nixon, baffled that she would throw away her inheritance on some socialist tax rate.

That same year, Schneider arranged for Charlie Chaplin to come to America with his wife Oona to receive an honorary Oscar—his first time in the country since he was effectively exiled during the Red Scare two decades earlier. Schneider arranged for Bergen to have exclusive rights to shoot Chaplin for the cover of *Life*, and the couple accompanied the Chaplins to the ceremony, where Bergen watched Chaplin bound offstage after a twelve-minute ovation, beaming like a schoolboy, so emotional that he misplaced his statuette.

Three years later, Schneider made his own controversial splash on the Oscar stage when his antiwar film *Hearts and Minds* won Best Documentary Feature. "It is ironic that we are here at a time just before Vietnam is about to be liberated," he said in his speech, then read a telegram from the Vietcong expressing "greetings of friendship to all the American people." Backstage, the appalled Bob Hope scrawled a statement on behalf of the Academy and handed it to Frank Sinatra to read onstage, disowning "any political references made on the program."

But the days of the apolitical Oscars were over. And so, by then, were Bert and Candy. Schneider, now past forty, had made it clear that he considered monogamy a "bourgeois concept." He informed her that "the only realistic base for any love relationship is sexual non-exclusivity."

"What do you mean by that exactly?"

"Where two people feel secure enough and free enough to explore sexually with other people."

"What do you mean, 'other people'? What does that mean, 'explore sexually'?"

After two years, Bergen realized that Schneider was just another ventriloquist like her father, and she his dummy. "It was just too fraught," she says. "And I did move out and gradually take charge of my own life—and met a lot of interesting people on my own steam. I didn't need the credentials of a man any longer to be a middleman for me."

In June 1970, Gregory Peck declined to run for another term as Academy president. His tenure had been transformative, even if his entreaties to the New Hollywood didn't always stick. "The Academy is only two or three years behind the critics," he said backstage at the 1971 ceremony, adding ruefully, "I tried to get the young people involved in the Academy, but it's impossible to reach them. People like Dennis Hopper and Peter Fonda belong to the Academy, but they wouldn't get involved."

Peck's next film was *Shoot Out*, a Western that turned out to be the latest in a string of disappointments, serving, as Charles Champlin put it, "mostly as a glum reminder of the inadequate use the movies have lately made of one of their principal personalities, Gregory Peck." Peck reflected, "It was humiliating to work in mediocre films—not that I ever felt a lowering of self-esteem, but it was embarrassing to know that people who had liked my earlier work weren't enjoying my latest movies." It would take five more years for the New Hollywood to find a role for him, in *The Omen*.

His son Stephen returned from Vietnam the spring that *Midnight Cowboy* won. "I was pretty shut down," he recalls. "I was a sensitive kid, and everything that I saw and did over there was a real shock to my system." His father tried, in vain, to draw him out, asking, "Was there a time when you nearly got killed?"

"Some artillery landed, you know, ten feet from me and killed two guys," Stephen muttered. Then he'd clam up, and Peck wouldn't press further. His war movies had always carried a message of peace, but his experience with Stephen "helped solidify that he saw the futility and the uselessness of war," his son Carey says. But where in the antiwar movement did Peck fit? He felt, he admitted, "a bit overage for carrying placards, marching in the streets, and lying down in front of the Justice Department."

Not long after Stephen came home, Peck saw a play called *The Trial of the Catonsville Nine*, about a group of activists who burned 378 draft files in the parking lot of a Maryland draft board office and were sentenced to prison terms of two to six years. Peck bought the rights to the play, drawn from the trial transcripts, and raised $250,000 to film it. It was his first time producing something that he wasn't acting in, and the studios were uninterested. Paramount president Frank Yablans, now flush with New Hollywood profits, told Peck, "This film must be distributed, but not with my *Godfather* money."

The film was praised at Cannes but did little business back home. Peck joked, "All things considered, it may have shortened the war by about fifteen minutes." The movie didn't win him an Oscar, but he received a different sort of honor: when Nixon's enemies list was made public, in 1973, the name "Gregory Peck" was on it. America's dad had finally joined the revolution.

SEVEN

Running the Asylum

1976

How *One Flew Over the Cuckoo's Nest*, *Nashville*, *Barry Lyndon*, and *Dog Day Afternoon* raced to the heights of the New Hollywood, while *Jaws* bit off a piece for itself.

The night that Richard Nixon announced his resignation, on August 8, 1974, five movies were in the anguished process of getting made. One, shooting in Martha's Vineyard, involved a corrupt mayor who covers up a deadly shark attack. Another, shooting in Brooklyn, was about a bank robber who seemed, even in folly, more heroic than the lawmen sent to bring him down. Yet another, limping to the end of a three-hundred-day shoot in Ireland and England, was about an opportunist who claws his way to high society only to come toppling down. In a fourth, about to shoot in an Oregon mental institution, a nurse abuses her authority by lobotomizing her charismatic challenger. And a fifth, filming in Nashville, revealed a town overrun by climbers and sleazy politicos, ending with an assassination without a clear motive or message—except that America, approaching its bicentennial, was deeply, comically sick.

It would be too easy to take these five movies as a collective diagnosis of the country's ills, despite the editorials deconstructing what *Nashville* said about America, or the political cartoons recasting the shark from *Jaws* as inflation. But each bore the cynical aftertaste of the sixties, the psychedelic revolution having soured into seventies vinegar. Between 1964 and 1974, Americans' trust in government plummeted from 64 to 36 percent. In *One Flew Over the Cuckoo's Nest*, you could see a nation at war with itself, each side staring down the other across a group therapy circle. Jack Nicholson's Randle McMurphy was a scoundrel, a madman, a martyr—a symbol of the wild human spirit itching to break free. Louise Fletcher's Nurse Ratched was orderly, rule-bound, the banality of evil in a crisp white cap. Their escalating fight to the finish was the same one that had split America into two incompatible halves: the establishment versus the counterculture. Who would win?

Even the Oscars were in the grip of irreverent hijinks, with the ceremony upended by one sideshow after another. In 1971, George C. Scott refused his nomination for *Patton*, calling the Oscars a "two-hour meat parade." Two years later, in protest of Native American stereotypes in Hollywood and the siege at Wounded Knee, Marlon Brando sent Apache activist Sacheen Littlefeather to decline his award for *The Godfather*. Though ridiculed, the stunt was a triumph of guerrilla activism, and it opened the door to decades of political Oscar speeches, including Bert Schneider's missive from the Vietnamese. Then, in 1974, as David Niven was introducing Elizabeth Taylor, a man named Robert Opel streaked across the stage in the nude; he later announced his campaign for the presidency with the slogan "Not just another crooked Dick."

Respect for authority may have been at a low point, but the movies, not coincidentally, were ascendant. Five years after *Easy Rider* and *Midnight Cowboy*, directors bent the ailing studios to their will, working far outside Hollywood and taking bold artistic risks. The New Hollywood had brought a cast of renegades to the forefront, auteurist McMurphys thumbing their noses at the studio Nurse Ratcheds. The lunatics now running the asylum included Robert Altman, Sidney Lumet, Stanley Kubrick, and Miloš Forman, each of whom rode a wave of nonconformity to the Best Picture race of 1976. But lurking in that wave was a young "movie brat" named Steven Spielberg, who gave Hollywood's moneymen an inkling of a comeback. Of the five Best Picture nominees, one would gobble up all the others—and it wasn't the one that won every major Oscar of the night.

EVERY TUESDAY MORNING AT EIGHT o'clock, Ken Kesey would show up at Menlo Park veterans' hospital, where a doctor would hand him pills and a shot of juice and keep him under observation in a tiny room with a chicken-wired window. It was 1960, and Kesey, a student of creative writing at Stanford, was a guinea pig in a CIA-funded study of the effects of psychoactive drugs. "Patients straggled by in the hall outside, their faces all ghastly confessions," he wrote. On occasion, a nurse would check in, her face full of "painful business," he recalled. "This was not a person you could allow yourself to be naked in front of."

Kesey kept detailed accounts of his acid trips, the beginning of a life-long fascination with hallucinogenic drugs. Six months later, as a nurse's aide, he observed the patients from the other side of the chicken wire and drew their haunted faces. One night at the hospital, a very high Kesey had an epiphany. As his wife, Faye, said later, "He began to wonder, you know, what's the difference between the orderlies and the nurse and the patients? And he began to see that they were all damaged in some way or another."

The novel that resulted was Kesey's indictment of postwar American conformity. Its narrator was Chief Bromden, a Native American patient who pretends to be deaf and mute and believes that the world is run by the "Combine," a kind of authoritarian conspiracy that keeps humanity in line. The Combine is personified by the Big Nurse, described as a giant-breasted harridan with a frozen smile, "big as a damn barn and tough as knife metal." The men of the ward, meanwhile, are "victims of a matriarchy"—that is, until a charismatic new inmate, McMurphy, riles them to disobedience.

Published in 1962, One Flew Over the Cuckoo's Nest tapped into a rambunctious energy burbling beneath the surface of American life—so much so that it was frequently banned by school libraries. The book made Kesey an instant literary celebrity, joining a wave of subversive fiction that included *Catch-22* and *A Clockwork Orange*. Among its fans was Kirk Douglas, fresh off *Spartacus*. Douglas, determined to play McMurphy, bought the rights. "It was a great character for him," recalls his son Michael, then a college student. "You don't get that many great parts in your career." The subject matter was iffy for Hollywood, so the elder Douglas decided to establish it as a theatrical property first. In 1963, he played McMurphy in a Broadway adaptation. It closed after just two months.

The play's failure left *Cuckoo's Nest* in limbo, but Douglas held out hope. On a trip to Prague as a goodwill ambassador for the U.S. State Department, he met Miloš Forman, a leading light of the Czechoslovak New Wave—young, voluble, with a cigar perched perpetually between his lips. Douglas told him he had a novel he wanted him to read; Forman said to send it along. Douglas put a copy in the mail, but it never arrived, apparently confiscated at customs.

Each man thought the other had dropped the ball. Nothing happened for ten years.

IN MARCH 1969, A NINETEEN-YEAR-OLD Californian with flowing hair arrived in New York City with eighty dollars and an electric guitar. Keith Carradine knocked on the stage door of the Biltmore Theatre, home of the musical *Hair*. "I was off on life's great adventure," he recalls. The first face he saw belonged to a fine-boned woman named Shelley Plimpton, who was playing a lovesick flower child. "We saw each other," Carradine says, "and there was an instantaneous moment of . . . whatever that is."

Carradine was cast in the musical's tribe of hippies. Plimpton was married to a castmate, but the relationship was rocky, and Carradine saw an opening. Idling in his brother David Carradine's hotel room with his Gibson, he picked out a song that might win Shelley's heart. Breezy and yearning, it made love seem like a no-brainer. Carradine called it "I'm Easy."

The song did its job. "It was a very short liaison," Carradine says. But it had two enduring outcomes. One was a child, Martha Plimpton. The other was the song.

After *Hair*, Carradine went back to Los Angeles, where he heard that Robert Altman was directing a Western for Warner Bros. Carradine had no idea who Altman was, until it was explained to him that he was the director of M*A*S*H. Carradine was sent to Lion's Gate Films, the production company that Altman had created so that he could make whatever the hell kind of movies he wanted.

Puckish and fun-loving, with flashes of cruelty, Altman was a "bombastic-rebel, bomb-thrower son of a bitch," as his agent George Litto put it. Lion's Gate was his kingdom on Westwood Boulevard, a Tudor-style courtyard duplex outfitted with pinball machines, a bar stocked with Cutty Sark, and a pool table. "A 'through these portals . . .' sign above the front door would not have been inappropriate," his protégé Alan Rudolph recalls. "No one else in America was doing what went on there."

Carradine was pointed to Altman's quarters and found the director at the foot of the bed in a bathrobe and a T-shirt, unwrapping a package from Colombia. Carradine guessed it was a kilo of cocaine, but Altman said, "Oh, I was at the Cartagena Film Festival and I bought some pre-Columbian art." The part of the young cowboy in McCabe and Mrs. Miller was supposed to play the banjo, and Carradine had been practicing his finger-picking. Instead of asking him to play, Altman simply said, "Well, you want to do it?"

Carradine was now part of Altman's ensemble of oddballs, including Shelley Duvall, whom Altman had discovered in Texas while shooting Brewster McCloud. Three years later, Altman cast Carradine and Duvall as a pair of Depression-era outlaws in Thieves Like Us. One Sunday, Altman gave a party for the cast and crew at the hilltop house where he was staying with his wife. ("Bob's three favorite things were being on the set, having parties, and editing," Carradine says.) Carradine took out his guitar and played some of his songs for the guests, including "I'm Easy" and a folksy number called "It Don't Worry Me."

Altman was delighted. "When I heard them," he said later, "I knew I wanted to base a whole movie around them, a movie that would simply give me an excuse to put them in." The movie was Nashville.

IN THE SUMMER OF 1968, as moviegoers tripped out over 2001: A Space Odyssey, MGM and Stanley Kubrick announced their next project: an epic film about Napoléon Bonaparte. "He fascinates me," Kubrick explained. His *Napoleon* would be not a "dusty historical pageant" but a drama about "the responsibilities and abuses of power." He saw Napoléon's romance with Empress Joséphine as "one of the great obsessional passions of all time."

Obsessional passion wasn't just fodder for Kubrick: it was his way of life. Headquartered at his home at Abbots Mead, north of London, the Manhattan-born director ransacked hundreds of books, extracting details on everything from Napoléon's appetites to the weather during particular battles. Production would begin in winter 1969, and Kubrick envisioned gargantuan battle scenes that would have the poetry of "two golden eagles soaring through the sky from a distance." He determined that they would need two hundred thousand gallons of Technicolor blood. He summoned a Thomas Gainsborough expert and dispatched an assistant to Versailles, to view Napoléon's personal lavatory. He wanted verisimilitude, from the epic to the quotidian. "Most people don't realize, for example, that Napoléon spent most of his time on the eve of battle immersed in paperwork," Kubrick said.

Surely Kubrick knew, on some level, that he was describing himself: a man immersed in paperwork, gearing up for battle, possibly doomed. His identification with his subject took bizarre forms. Actor Malcolm McDowell once remarked on the director's peculiar dining habits: scooping up a mouthful of dessert, then a forkful of steak, then back to dessert again. "This is how Napoléon used to eat," Kubrick explained. Borrowing Napoléon's management style, Kubrick rotated his acolytes in and out of favor at random, just to keep them on their toes. Eventually, some of his subordinates revolted. One designer quit after an argument over whether rhododendrons had migrated to England from India by Napoléon's time. Adrienne Corri, the Gainsborough expert, groused that the director was "a vampire on people's brains."

Ten days after seeing *Easy Rider*, Kubrick wrote to its breakout star, Jack Nicholson, whom he saw as the perfect Napoléon. Nicholson was drawn into Kubrick's obsessive spell, saying that the director "Napoleonized" him. But the obstacles were piling up. Two rival Napoléon films came out and lost money. MGM announced that it would downscale film production to focus on television. By that time, Kubrick had turned his attentions to *A Clockwork Orange*, which premiered in late 1971.

"I plan to do *Napoleon* next," Kubrick announced. "It will be a big film but certainly not on the scale that big films had grown to just before the lights went out in Hollywood."

By 1973, the project had become his directorial Waterloo. But Kubrick had found a new outlet for his obsessional passion—and his mass of eighteenth-century research. He sent a 243-page draft script to Warner Bros., under the title *New Stanley Kubrick Film Project*, about an Irishman who climbs his way to position, wealth, and romance, and then, like Napoléon, loses it all. Paranoid that someone might steal the idea, he changed the names, dates, and locations. Only a literary scholar would have recognized the plot of William Makepeace Thackeray's 1844 picaresque, *The Luck of Barry Lyndon*.

SHORTLY BEFORE 3 P.M. ON August 22, 1972, three young men entered the Chase Manhattan bank on the corner of Avenue P and East Third Street, in Brooklyn. One of them, a boyish eighteen-year-old named Sal Naturile, sat at the bank manager's desk and quietly introduced himself. "Freeze," Naturile said. "This is a holdup. I'm not alone."

Nearby, a teller was at her adding machine and spotted a man in a white V-neck shirt. John Wojtowicz was twenty-seven, a Vietnam vet with mussed hair, a bulging nose, and a New York bark. Their third accomplice had chickened out moments earlier, saying, "I can't do it." "What the fuck do you mean you can't do it?" Wojtowicz squawked. *Fuck it*, he thought. He crossed himself, pulled out a shotgun, and said, "Okay, nobody move!" He assured the staff, "Everybody does what I tell them and everything will be alright—and we'll be out of here in five minutes."

As Wojtowicz filled his attaché case with cash and traveler's checks—not as much as he'd hoped, but they might as well finish what they started—bank manager Robert Barrett, with a gun to his head, got a call from Chase headquarters about a personnel transfer. "You're talking funny, Bob," the guy at headquarters said. "Is something wrong down there?"

"Yep!" Barrett said cheerily. Minutes later, Wojtowicz looked out the glass storefront and saw police and FBI men staring at the bank from the fire escapes. As word whipped through the city, they were joined by a scrum of onlookers and TV crews. Wojtowicz negotiated an escape in exchange for the hostages while answering calls from reporters and charming their pants off.

"What are your terms?" one journalist asked him.

"Well," Wojtowicz said, "I want them to deliver my wife here from Kings County Hospital. His name is Ernest Aron. It's a guy. I'm gay."

The news channels soon broadcast an incredible tale: Wojtowicz was an "admitted homosexual" whose crime of passion was hatched to fund his lover's sex-change surgery. To the general public, loud and proud gay men—to say nothing of transgender women—were a novelty, and Wojtowicz played his role to the hilt. At one point, in a kind of perverse street theater, he ordered a pizza and chucked a thousand dollars in singles onto the sidewalk, as some two thousand spectators hooted and cheered.

Aron arrived under police escort, her hair like an explosion of mattress springs. Too terrified to talk in person, she called Wojtowicz from a barbershop. "But Ernie," Wojtowicz pleaded, "I did this for you, so you could have your operation. Why are you afraid of me?"

The hostages, meanwhile, were starting to like their captors. "If they had been my houseguests on a Saturday night, it would have been hilarious," a teller said later. They passed the hours listening to the Mets–Astros game, and Wojtowicz would peer at the snipers outside and say, "What d'ya think of that sonofabitch! He really wants me—he wants me in the worst way." Barrett, the bank manager, said, "I'm supposed to hate you guys, but I've had more laughs tonight than I've had in weeks."

By 2 a.m., Wojtowicz was still negotiating his escape, demanding a car to Kennedy Airport and a plane to take them wherever they wanted to go. By 4:45, a car carrying the robbers and the hostages led a convoy down Rockaway Boulevard. The limo, driven by an FBI agent named Murphy, arrived at the runway. As Wojtowicz and Naturile joked about stopping inside the terminal for hamburgers, Murphy swiped a .38 from under the floor mat and shot Naturile in the chest. Wojtowicz was quickly disarmed. The hostages were freed.

Life ran the story under the headline "The Boys in the Bank," a nod to the gay drama *The Boys in the Band*, and noted Wojtowicz's "broken-faced good looks." When Martin Bregman, producer of Sidney Lumet's *Serpico*, saw the story, he noticed something even stranger: the bank robber bore an uncanny resemblance to Al Pacino.

By 1973, MILOŠ FORMAN WAS living at the Chelsea Hotel, mid-nervous breakdown. He had come to the United States six years earlier, after his subversive comedy *The Firemen's Ball* was banned in Czechoslovakia. After the 1968 Soviet invasion, he'd managed to get his wife Věra and their twin sons to Paris. Then Věra decided to take the children back to Prague, and Forman returned to New York. His first American film was *Taking Off*, a failure that left him flat broke. He applied for a green card when he realized he couldn't afford a ticket home.

In his eighth-floor room, he subsisted on a dollar a day, plotting his way back to a filmmaking career. One day, he received a package from California, from producers Saul Zaentz and Michael Douglas, containing Ken Kesey's *One Flew Over the Cuckoo's Nest*. Kirk Douglas was still unable to get the project off the ground and had handed off the rights to his twenty-nine-year-old son.

Forman, who had lost both parents to Nazi concentration camps and then lived under the Communist regime, was captivated by the novel, which "vividly dramatized the never-ending conflict between the individual and the institution." He flew to Los Angeles to meet with Douglas and Zaentz over Chinese food. When he ran into Kirk Douglas at a party, the actor barked, "Mr. Forman, aren't you a real son of a bitch?" A hush fell. "When I sent you the book, you didn't even have the decency to write 'Kiss off' back to me. But now that you live here, you're all gung-ho to direct it!" It was only then that both men realized that the project had gotten lost in the mail. Now that he had taken over the reins, Forman thought Kirk Douglas was too old to play McMurphy. It fell to Michael Douglas to fire his own father. "It *killed* him not to get to play that part," Michael recalls.

A first version of the script was too slavishly faithful to the novel, so the producers hired screenwriter Bo Goldman. Each morning, Goldman and Forman met by the pool of the Sunset Marquis, bottles of Czech beer at the director's feet. Dreamlike psychedelia was passé, so they went for documentary-style objectivity, which meant dropping the Chief's narration and the idea of the Combine. When it came to Nurse Ratched, though, Goldman didn't stray from Kesey's misogynistic depiction. "I thought about her like my wife's mother," Goldman says. "'Control' is the operative word. You don't ever think of them romantically or sexually. They use their femininity to control people."

Marlon Brando and Gene Hackman both passed on the part of McMurphy. Forman was briefly intrigued by the "cheap charisma" of Burt Reynolds, but he soon set his sights on Jack Nicholson. "He was always very friendly to me," Forman recalled, "but he spoke such vivid slang that my English simply couldn't keep up." Nicholson was in. "Hell, Miloš," he said, "I tried to get the rights to the fucking book, if you know what I mean, but old boy Douglas beat me to the punch."

To cast the patients, Forman held bicoastal "group therapy" sessions and assembled a team of eccentric-looking character actors: Christopher Lloyd, Vincent Schiavelli, Danny DeVito. But two roles were difficult to cast. One was Chief Bromden, for which the filmmakers needed someone as big as a tree. After a continent-wide search, a used-car salesman whom Douglas had met on a plane reported that he'd spotted "the biggest son of a bitch" he'd ever seen. It was Will Sampson, a forest ranger from Yakima, Washington, who stood at a commanding six foot seven.

Then there was Nurse Ratched. "In the book," Forman recalled, "she is portrayed as an order-mad, killjoy harpy. At one point, Kesey even describes her as having wires coming out of her head, so I searched for a castrating monster." Forman cycled through stars—Anne Bancroft, Geraldine Page, Angela Lansbury—but they turned him down. "Women, in terms of the women's movement and what was happening at that time, were uncomfortable being the villains," Michael Douglas says.

It was only after a year of searching that an actress who'd been begging for the role persuaded Forman to take a chance on her. The director thought that Louise Fletcher's "prim, angelic" manner didn't seem evil at all. But that, of course, was the genius of it.

ROBERT ALTMAN WAS UNDERWHELMED WHEN United Artists sent him a script called *The Great Southern Amusement Company*, which it saw as a possible vehicle for Tom Jones. Altman took one look and balked: "It was a movie script!"

Altman didn't do movie scripts. Still, he was intrigued by its milieu. The country-western industry was on the ascent, thanks to breakout acts like Tammy Wynette and Loretta Lynn. Keith Carradine's crooning on the set of *Thieves Like Us* planted the idea of using all original songs, rather than country standards. Altman asked Joan Tewkesbury, who had cowritten *Thieves Like Us*, "Do you know anything about country-western music?"

"Not really," she said.

"Would you like to learn?" He sent her to Nashville.

"The first time I went, it was really the antiseptic tour," Tewkesbury recalls. She was paired with a public relations chaperone and spent three days being shepherded around the *Grand Ole Opry*'s Ryman Auditorium and a country-western museum, where she was shown Patsy Cline's hairpins. When she tried to ask about *real* life in Nashville, the conversations somehow wound back up at the hairpins. She returned to Altman and said, "I've got to go by myself and do this differently, because nobody's giving me a straight answer here."

In the spring of 1973, Tewkesbury made her second trip, unattended. Nearly everything she saw wound up in *Nashville*, starting with the moment she landed at the airport and witnessed a chaotic scene of country stars, gawkers, bewildered residents, and hippies. "Their hair was long. They were wearing these weird clothes," Tewkesbury says. "And it was just wrong. So that made it absolutely right as far as I was concerned."

Armed with a yellow notepad, she watched recording sessions with Loretta Lynn and Conway Twitty. When she asked the recording engineers where to see live music, they sent her to a hole in the wall called the Exit/In, where she sat in a banquette and listened to a group called

Barefoot Jerry singing, "The words to this song don't mean anything at all." She surveyed the crowd: industry executives, a girl who seemed to be overdosing at the table in front of her. A man sat next to Tewkesbury and shoved a joint up her sleeve, explaining that he'd just gotten out of jail for premeditated murder. "I thought, *This is it. This is the construct for this movie*," Tewkesbury says. "Everything was happening simultaneously."

Tewkesbury returned to Los Angeles and mounted a huge graph, with the time of day on one axis and character names on the other, methodically planning where they would intersect over a five-day period. The ex-con who had given her the joint became Wade. Her driver, who had a habit of getting lost and vomiting, became Norman.

For Altman, the city had a familiar dynamic. "Nashville to me is like Hollywood was forty years ago," he said. "It's not even just a place—it's a state of mind, just in the way Hollywood was. It's the place where the kids get off the buses and hope to make their fortunes." Glued to television coverage of the Watergate hearings, he concluded that *Nashville* needed politics and created a fictitious presidential candidate, Hal Phillip Walker of the Replacement Party. With Walker came a slew of new characters; the total was now twenty-four. The second thing Altman added was a killing. "Assassination has become acceptable in this society," he said later, "and it's going to spread, the way hijacking did." To shake the audience out of complacency, Altman decided that the gunman would assassinate the wrong person—not the candidate but Barbara Jean, the Loretta Lynn–like country star to be played by Ronee Blakley.

But before he could worry about casting, Altman had to save the movie. United Artists' David Picker thought the script was a downer. The two men faced off at Chasen's. "Fuck you," Picker said. "Fuck you, too," Altman replied. At a party for John Denver, Altman met touring producer Jerry Weintraub, who brought *Nashville* to the newly installed head of ABC Pictures, Martin Starger. Altman's renegade reputation was a mixed blessing—as much as studios wanted to harness the creativity of New Hollywood auteurs, they knew they were signing up for an unpredictable ride. At his house in Malibu, Altman played Starger and Weintraub a tape of Carradine singing "I'm Easy" and "It Don't Worry Me." Once again, the songs worked their magic. Altman would have $2.2

million and his cast of twenty-four, but any overages would come out of his salary. Still, whatever excesses Starger imagined would be nothing compared to the ones that would plague *Jaws*.

"CECIL B. DESPIELBERG" WAS HIS mother's nickname for him, and Steven Spielberg did not resist the comparison. "I want to be the Cecil B. DeMille of science fiction," he told the ragtag crew of his first full-length film, *Firelight*. The movie, made for under six hundred dollars, was about a group of aliens abducting the inhabitants of an Arizona town to create a human zoo on their home planet. It played one night at a local cinema and turned a profit of one dollar. The director was a high school junior.

The oldest child of an Orthodox Jewish family, Spielberg was a self-described "wimp in a world of jocks." He made his first movie in the fifth grade, a nine-minute, 8-millimeter Western, for which he earned his Boy Scout photography badge. By the time *Firelight* premiered, in March 1964, Spielberg had already made contact with a family friend at Universal Studios, where he hoped to turn his spit-and-Scotch-tape production into a big-budget sci-fi epic. Soon after, the family moved from Arizona to Silicon Valley, where Steven finished high school as his parents ended their twenty-one-year marriage. He vowed to make his first major film before the age of twenty-one; to ensure his wunderkind status, he shaved a few years off his age. At Universal, he parlayed a one-day studio pass into an office and some clerical work. "Every day for three months in a row," he boasted, "I walked through the gates dressed in a sincere black suit and carrying a briefcase."

Unlike his circle of "movie brats"—Coppola, Scorsese—Spielberg wasn't interested in subverting the studio system. Like DeMille, he wanted to exploit every trick of the trade. Two decades younger than Kubrick and Altman, he had grown up on television and still acted like a kid into his twenties, gorging on Twinkies and Oreos. The counterculture seemed to pass him by completely: he was clueless about sex, wary of drugs, and enamored of the Hollywood machine just as it was falling apart. In 1967, he said, "I don't want to make films like Antonioni or Fellini. I don't want just the elite. I want everybody to enjoy my films." Soon after, he made *Amblin'*, a short film about free spirits hitchhiking across the California desert. "It was very mature work," said Universal's Sidney Sheinberg. "It was all the more impressive since the guy that did it was twenty years old and was very anxious to do a film by the time he was twenty-one. I thought he deserved a shot." He signed Spielberg to a seven-year-contract.

Spielberg directed *Duel*, a made-for-TV thriller about an oil tanker truck stalking a Plymouth Valiant, and then his first feature, *The Sugarland Express*, starring Goldie Hawn as a beautician ensnarled in a police chase. The latter thrilled *The New Yorker's* Pauline Kael, who called it "one of the most phenomenal film débuts in the history of movies." Spielberg cast around for his next project. One idea—about the toilet impresario Thomas Crapper—thankfully died in infancy. He still dreamed of remaking *Firelight*, his alien flick from high school. Columbia agreed to finance the film, now called *Watch the Skies*. Paul Schrader was hired to write the screenplay, but the pugnacious writer of *Taxi Driver* was Spielberg's aesthetic opposite. After reading his draft, all about a military cover-up, Spielberg said, "I want these people to be people from the suburbs, just like people I grew up with, who want to get on the spaceship at the end."

Schrader spat back, "If somebody's going to represent me and the human race to get on a spaceship, I don't want my representative to be a guy who eats all his meals at McDonald's."

With the UFO idea in limbo, Spielberg reassessed. The producers of *The Sugarland Express*, David Brown and Richard Zanuck, had formed their own production outfit in 1972, two years after Zanuck was fired as the president of 20th Century–Fox by his own father, Darryl, and they were now coming out with Universal's *The Sting*. A synopsis by a studio reader alerted them to a soon-to-be-published novel called *Jaws*. Peter Benchley, a former *Newsweek* editor, had been contemplating the story since 1964, when he read a *Daily News* item about a Long Island fisherman who had harpooned a 4,500-pound shark. The paperback sold for a whopping $575,000, setting off a sharklike feeding frenzy for the movie rights.

Spielberg was in postproduction for *The Sugarland Express* when he spotted the unpublished galley of *Jaws* in Zanuck's office. "I can make something of this—it'll be fun," he said. The producers realized that a seasoned studio hand was the wrong way to go; they would offer the shark project to "the kid." Spielberg saw it as the kind of commercial movie that could make him, at last, Cecil B. DeSpielberg. He told the producer of his UFO film, "I've got an offer to do a movie about a shark. It will take me six months. Then I'll get back and finish *Watch the Skies.*"

But as soon as Spielberg landed the job—which Universal's Sheinberg saw as *Duel* with a shark instead of a truck—he fretted: "Who wants to be known as a shark-and-truck director?" Only later did he realize that a deeper force than ambition was driving him: fear. "I wanted to do *Jaws* for hostile reasons," Spielberg said. "I read it and felt that I had been attacked. It terrified me, and I wanted to strike back."

ON THE MISSISSIPPI SET OF *Thieves Like Us*, Robert Altman and Joan Tewkesbury were busy creating the topsy-turvy world of *Nashville.* The two stars of *Thieves*, Shelley Duvall and Keith Carradine, would both have roles, Duvall as a groupie and Carradine as a folk-singing lothario.

And then there was Louise Fletcher, who in *Thieves* was playing the sister-in-law of one of the outlaws. Fletcher grew up in Birmingham, Alabama, the child of deaf parents. Having deaf parents, Fletcher said, is "like having immigrant parents. You feel a special responsibility, and you're a translator. You try to explain the world and how it works to them." Her mother was a movie lover, and every weekend at the cinema, Fletcher would interpret the plots in sign language. "People used to tease me and say that's how I got started, redoing old Bette Davis movies."

When Fletcher's parents visited the *Thieves Like Us* set, Altman and Tewkesbury watched her translate their sign language to her husband. It gave them an idea for a character: Linnea Reese, a gospel singer with deaf children who cheats on her husband with Carradine. Fletcher filled in Tewkesbury on "what it's like to have to translate everything." She assumed she would play the character they were developing, but months later in Los Angeles, she was on the phone with Altman's wife Kathryn, who mentioned that Lily Tomlin had joined the cast.

"Who's she going to play?" Fletcher asked.

Kathryn blanched. "Oh, my God, Louise, I shouldn't have said anything."

That's how Fletcher found out she wasn't going to star in *Nashville.*

She was furious. Perhaps to make amends, Altman showed footage from *Thieves Like Us* to Michael Douglas and Miloš Forman, who were still scrambling to find their Nurse Ratched. Every few weeks, Forman and Fletcher met at the Sunset Marquis to discuss the character, though she was unaware of the big-name actresses turning him down. Fletcher knew that Kesey's version of the character was unplayable, because "she's got smoke coming out of her ears." But she had a solution.

Fletcher had spent 1974 consumed with the unfolding Watergate scandal, even writing letters to senators, and she saw elements of Nixon in the Big Nurse's perversion of power. She thought back to her childhood in segregated Alabama and to the "paternalistic way that people treat other people there." Moving to California had opened her eyes to how warped things were back home. "White people actually felt that the life they were creating was *good* for Black people," she said—a dynamic she recognized in that of Nurse Ratched and her charges. "They're in this ward, she's looking out for them, and they have to act like they're *happy* to get this medication or listen to this music. And make her feel good about the way *she* is."

Like Fletcher, Forman had lived under an oppressive system, in Communist Czechoslovakia. "I slowly started to realize that it will be much more powerful if it's not this visible evil," he said later. "That she's only an *instrument* of evil. She doesn't know that she's evil. She, as a matter of fact, believes that she's *helping* people." Late in 1974, Fletcher got a call from her agent. She was due in Salem, Oregon, in one week.

In 1848, Thackeray subtitled his book *Vanity Fair* "A Novel Without a Hero." *Barry Lyndon* has a hero without heroism. Its protagonist, a low-born Irishman with aspirations of nobility, bumbles and connives his way in to high society by seducing his cousin, dueling her suitor, fighting in the Seven Years' War, deserting the army in another man's uniform, spying for the Prussians, gambling, and, finally, marrying into wealth via the widowed Countess of Lyndon. Then comes the fall, swift and pitiless, leaving him with a lost leg, a dead son, and a mass of debt.

Lyndon was perfectly matched to Kubrick's curdled view of humanity and to the cynical culture emerging under Nixon. The director, according to actor Leon Vitali, was interested in "man's folly." Once again, Kubrick threw himself into the period, researching the eighteenth century down to condoms, toothbrushes, and wig lice. He scrutinized—and, in some cases, directly borrowed the composition of—paintings by Watteau and Gainsborough, which would give *Barry Lyndon* the look of a museum brought to life.

To re-create the atmospheric glow of historic castles, Kubrick decided to use only candlelight, an idea he'd considered for *Napoleon*. But no matter how many candles you used, contemporary film stocks weren't fast enough to capture their low light. After a three-month search, Kubrick discovered that a German manufacturer had created a super-fast 50-millimeter lens with an unusually wide aperture for use in satellite photography in outer space. Kubrick bought three. He personally went to Battersea, London, to visit a dripping factory that supplied beeswax candles to the Roman Catholic Church and acquired enough to illuminate a hundred ballrooms.

As they prepared to shoot in Ireland, his overworked production managers squabbled over logistics, begging the director to answer simple questions. Finally, Kubrick agreed to address their concerns—but only if they got him a bell to ring when he felt like moving things along. But what kind of bell should it be? Someone suggested a servant's bell. Too snobby, Kubrick said. A buzzer? Too annoying. "Have the art department go out and get an example of every available bell, and I'll choose one," he instructed. Realizing that he had coerced them into another wild goose chase, his exasperated staff dropped the subject.

In spring 1973, Kubrick, his wife Christiane, and a cast and crew of 170 descended on Dublin. In the title role was Ryan O'Neal, who had submitted to months of fencing lessons and fittings. (His fifteen wigs were crafted from the hair of Italian women entering religious life.) With his actors, Kubrick could be exacting, cryptic, warm, funny, or aggravating— sometimes all at once. "He was like a very strict headmaster," recalls Gay Hamilton, who played Barry's cousin. Vitali, who played his stepson, Lord

Bullingdon, had a scene in which Barry gives him six lashes on the behind for misbehavior. "I can't tell you how many times we went through
the scene," he said. "My ass was absolutely black and blue."

Barry Lyndon arrived in Ireland at a perilous moment. Sectarian violence had escalated since Bloody Sunday, the previous January, and
the papers reported a stream of bombings, abductions, and intimidation
campaigns on the part of the Provisional Irish Republican Army. Strange
things started happening. As Jan Harlan, Kubrick's producer and brother-
in-law recalls, "Two men arrived at the rented house west of Dublin; neither Stanley nor Christiane or the children were at home. The resident
Irish staff was told to tell their master 'to get his ass out of the country
and fast, or else.' Stanley and Christiane heard this hours later from their
lovely, weeping, and almost hysterical staff, who said that these lunatics
had to be taken seriously." Kubrick, who was used to death threats after
A Clockwork Orange, told Christiane, "We might as well go." The next
morning, they fled back to England by ferry.

Production resumed in England at the start of 1974, with the crew
moving from one estate to another, "like an Emerson, Lake and Palmer
road tour," Vitali said. The candles, besides making the corseted actors
unbearably hot, melted quickly and had to be constantly replenished for
continuity—which only inflated the sizable candle budget. By the time
Barry Lyndon wrapped, it had been shooting for three hundred days over
the course of two years. Warner Bros. hadn't seen a frame.

IN LATE 1973, SPIELBERG CALLED a meeting to figure out just how on God's
green earth he could make a movie starring a shark. Production designer
Joe Alves, an ex-race car driver, had consulted ichthyologists, who said
that the biggest great white sharks were, at most, nineteen feet long, and
untrainable. But the shark in Peter Benchley's (still-unpublished) novel
was a whopping twenty-five feet—which would require a lifelike mechanical monster that could swim and thrash in the open ocean. Nothing like
that had ever been done.

The production team searched for a special effects expert who could
help them do the unprecedented. The one person they needed had retired: Bob Mattey, who had been responsible for the giant squid in *20,000*

Leagues Under the Sea. Pulled back into service like a movie sheriff, Mattey planned to mount his mechanical shark on a twelve-ton submersible platform with a track, requiring a location with a sandy ocean floor, small tides, and an unbroken horizon. In the dead of winter, Alves traveled to Long Island, where Benchley's novel was set. Nothing looked right. On a whim, he took a ferry to Martha's Vineyard, which, besides meeting the nautical requirements, had a quaint little village. Perfect.

Benchley's novel was released in February 1974 and stayed on the best-seller list for forty-four weeks. Universal, which had been preoccupied with disaster pictures like *Airport 1975*, now realized it had momentum to ride, which meant filming *Jaws* as soon as possible—say, April? Instead of a year and a half, the shark designers now had a matter of months. Oh, and could they get the picture done before a potential actors' strike in late June? A panicked Spielberg pushed them off a month. On May 2, the *Jaws* circus descended on Martha's Vineyard, with a budget of $3.5 million to cover fifty-five days of filming.

By then, Spielberg at least had a screenplay. Benchley's initial script had been reworked by playwright Howard Sackler. Unsatisfied, Spielberg sent it to Carl Gottlieb, a writer on *The Odd Couple*, with the note "Eviscerate it." Gottlieb sent back a long memo, saying, "If we do our jobs right, people will feel about going in the ocean the way they felt about taking a shower after *Psycho*." Spielberg asked Gottlieb to find himself a role to play, and he chose the corrupt publisher of the local newspaper, a part he himself later cut to near oblivion (and "my heart bled with every cut"). Instead, the town cover-up would be orchestrated by the mayor, who, Gottlieb noted at the time, "bears a passing resemblance to Richard Nixon."

Charlton Heston had shown interest in the role of the police chief, but Spielberg didn't want big names. The star was the shark. He cast Roy Scheider, best known for his sidekick role in *The French Connection*. To play Quint, the Ahab-like shark hunter, producer David Brown suggested Robert Shaw, the burly Englishman from *The Sting*. As for Hooper, the marine biologist, Spielberg had tried unsuccessfully to get Jon Voight. With days to go before shooting, Gottlieb tracked down his old friend "Ricky."

At twenty-six, Richard Dreyfuss was a newfangled star after George Lucas's *American Graffiti*. He heard about *Jaws* and told Spielberg, "I'd rather just watch it than shoot it." Then, after seeing himself in *The Apprenticeship of Duddy Kravitz*, Dreyfuss had a crisis of confidence and reassessed. He met Spielberg and Gottlieb in Boston. Over "drinks and dinner and consciousness-raising," as Gottlieb delicately put it, they promised to deepen the role. The cast was complete with three days to spare.

The Hollywood crew, in Gottlieb's words, tumbled into the quaint New England town like "a boisterous three-hundred-pound child." Alves and his team had built three sharks that could be filmed from different angles, which Spielberg collectively named "Bruce," after his lawyer. At the hangar in San Fernando Valley where Bruce was built, the designers had gotten the two-thousand-pound machines to swim, snarl, gnash, flip their tales, and dive—in a freshwater tank. They hadn't counted on saltwater corroding the sharks' insides. On the Vineyard, Zanuck, Brown, and Sheinberg came to watch a test run. "We had all the executives there," Alves recalls, "and the thing flipped over. It was embarrassing. It didn't work." Spielberg's friend Brian De Palma, who was visiting as everyone watched the first horrendous rushes, said it was "like a wake."

"What happened in May and June was just one disaster after another," production executive Bill Gilmore would recall. "Every single day the shark was put in the water, something went wrong: A hose burst, there would be geysers that would go a hundred feet in the air. The sea-sled shark ran aground." Stalling, Spielberg shot everything not involving the shark, and they began writing it out of scenes. Gottlieb says, "The decision was: if we don't absolutely have to see the shark, why make trouble for ourselves?"

For Spielberg, it was an epiphany. "I just went back to Alfred Hitchcock," he would explain. "What would Alfred Hitchcock do in a situation like this? So, imagining a Hitchcock movie instead of a Godzilla movie, I suddenly got the idea that we can make a lot of hay out of the horizon line and not being able to see your feet, not being able to see anything below the waistline when you're treading water. What is down there? It's what we *don't* see which is really truly frightening."

ON FOURTH OF JULY WEEKEND, Altman threw a welcome barbecue for the cast of *Nashville* at the stone ranch house he and Kathryn had rented on the edge of town. As steaks sizzled and ice cubes cracked in Scotch, the director said, "More than anything I want you to have a good time this summer. You've all read the script. Now I want you to put it down and forget about it."

"At the time, I thought, *What the fuck are you talking about?*" recalls Tewkesbury, who had taken care with her screenplay. "Bob was perverse, and what he basically meant by that was: Don't be married to what's on the page. Don't be afraid to do some exploration on your own. In other words, he gave everybody permission."

That's not to say the actors weren't prepared. Jeff Goldblum, cast as the daredevil Tricycle Man, had taken magic lessons. Tomlin, making her film début after breaking out on *Rowan and Martin's Laugh-In*, took three months of sign language lessons. Duvall raided thrift shops for halter tops and platform shoes. Gwen Welles, who played the tone-deaf Sueleen Gay, spent three days working at the soda fountain in the Nashville airport.

According to Michael Murphy, who played a political advance man, Altman told the actors, "All right, I put all my money into film stock. Take these characters as far as you want to take them. But if you bore me, I'll just cut to somebody else." Most of the actors thrilled at the chance to supply their own material. Barbara Baxley, who played local matriarch Lady Pearl, brought in a long monologue about her love of the Kennedys, drawn from her own experience working for Robert Kennedy's campaign; Altman let her ramble for two reels of film. "I would try anything," he said. "I had no linear obligations, necessarily." To make the overlapping dialogue decipherable, Altman hired sound designer Jim Webb to create a sophisticated eight-track system by which he could body-mic multiple actors at once and then feed their chatter into individual tracks, which Altman could then mix and match in the editing room.

Altman saw his loose style in contrast to the perfectionism of his fellow auteurs. "I admire Kubrick, but I can't say I like him," he said later. "I mean, I don't know him personally. What he does is terrific and the opposite of what I do. He supervises every little detail of his films down to the last inch. But I leave a gap so wide that anything between A and X may be acceptable. With Kubrick, it's between A and A 1."

Peppered over the madness were moments of heart-stopping seriousness. One of the film's most poignant scenes was filmed at the Exit/In, where Tomlin's character watches Carradine's Tom sing "I'm Easy." Back when he was wooing Shelley Plimpton, the song was a guileless declaration of love. But Altman gave it a manipulative undertone: we see Tom dedicate the song to "someone kinda special who just might be here tonight," and the camera cuts to four women who think he's singing for her.

As Linnea, wrestling with possible infidelity at Tom's invitation, Tomlin sat in the back, her mouth slightly agape, eyes in shadow, full of lust and hesitation. Tewkesbury, who was in the midst of a divorce, had written her own restlessness into the character. Linnea "hadn't had passion in her life in how many thousands of years," she says. "Someone is encouraging to her, and she takes the bait." Tomlin, who was only partly out of the closet as a lesbian, recalled saying to Altman, "I don't think Linnea can go to bed with this guy. He has no character." He told her, "Well, when the time comes, if she can't do it, she just can't do it."

Tomlin watched Carradine, her left hand brushing against her collar. "I knew this was an important scene for me," she recalled. "I was working for a place for myself internally. I thought I was putting out so much. This kind of conflicted yearning. I was counting on my eyes being so expressive." The next night, she went to a screening room at the Jack Spence Motor Hotel, where everyone gathered nightly with Budweiser, pot, and Cheez Doodles. Tomlin was aghast. On-screen, her eyes were barely visible. "I left the screening early, because I was just in tears," she recalled. But her understated, wordless performance would help clinch her Oscar nomination.

The night that Nixon announced his resignation, "we were all in a celebratory mood," says Carradine. Their Tennessean hosts were less mirthful. Altman had taken over the *Grand Ole Opry* and gathered 4,400 locals. After Tomlin warmed up the crowd with her *Laugh-In* characters Ernestine and Edith Ann, the crowd got a welcome from Roy Acuff, a former singer and fiddler for the Smoky Mountain Boys who had become a Nashville power broker. When the Nixon news hit, he was devastated. "Look at what you've done to our President!" he bawled at a group of actors milling around backstage, then slammed the door to his dressing room. The cast soon heard mournful fiddle wafting from inside.

JAWS HAD BECOME A WAR zone, with the exhausted crew calling it *Flaws*. The schedule had long been tossed out. The "panic scenes" on the beach, which required hundreds of splashing locals, were pushed back once it became clear that no one dared go into the cold Nantucket Sound until after the Fourth of July. *Jaws* author Peter Benchley showed up to play a small role as a television reporter. The week before, *Newsweek* had quoted Spielberg saying Benchley's characters were so unlikable that "you were rooting for the shark to eat the people—in alphabetical order!" Upon his arrival, Benchley stopped for lunch with a reporter, who told him, "Spielberg says your book is a piece of shit."

Benchley snapped back, "He knows, flatly, zero. He is a twenty-six-year-old who grew up with movies. He has no knowledge of reality but the movies." With relish, the author added, "Wait and see. Spielberg will one day be known as the greatest second-unit director in America."

The director had been dreading the day when the scenes on land were done and it was time to shoot on open water. The third act would take two and a half months to shoot, double the budget, and drive everyone to a breaking point. Bruce was still as temperamental a star as Bette Davis. The shark would drag through the water, looking, as Spielberg put it, "like a 26-foot turd." On good days, they would snatch something usable. On bad days, they got nothing at all. The crew, working out of an overstuffed barge christened the SS *Garage Sale*, was given a No Beer order, followed by No Card Playing.

Cabin fever ensued. "It was almost mutiny," Alves says. Things got even worse when the local boat jockeys who had been hired to shuttle equipment went on strike. They resorted to acts of sabotage, like filling the gas tanks of Quint's fishing vessel, the *Orca*, with water. The actors started to crack. "Dreyfuss would say, 'What am I doing on this island? Why am I here? I should be signing autographs in Sardi's,'" Scheider recalled. Shaw, who thought Dreyfuss was a "young punk," goaded him, "Look at you, Dreyfuss. You eat and you drink and you're fat and you're sloppy. At your age, it's criminal. Why, you couldn't even do ten good pushups!" Pouring himself a drink one day, Shaw remarked, "I would give anything to be able to just stop drinking." "Okay," Dreyfuss said—and hurled his glass through a porthole.

When Universal's Sid Sheinberg visited, he was appalled to see the haphazard attempts to shoot at sea and asked Spielberg if he would consider moving production to a studio tank. "Well, I wanted to shoot this in the ocean for reality," the young director replied.

"Reality is costing us a lot of money," Sheinberg said. "If you want to quit now, we will find a way to make our money back. If you want to stay and finish the movie, you can do that."

"I want to stay and finish the movie," Spielberg said.

Inwardly, he was panicking. "I thought my career as a filmmaker was over," Spielberg later admitted. "I heard rumors from back in Hollywood that I would never work again because no one had ever taken a film a hundred days over schedule—let alone a director whose first picture had failed at the box office." Crew members, Gottlieb reported, would catch Spielberg "sitting morose and alone on the bowsprit of the *Orca*."

Out at sea one day, the crew set up a harrowing shot in which the shark rams into the *Orca*. When Spielberg called "Action," underwater cables yanked the vessel sideways, causing an eyebolt on its hull to rip out a three-foot-long plank. The *Orca* was sinking. "She's going over!" someone bellowed. Radios blared. Frogmen leaped into the ocean to rescue stray equipment, while everyone yelled to save the actors.

"Fuck the actors!" a sound engineer screamed. "Save the sound department!"

On their last night, in September 1974, the delirious filmmakers got into a food fight after Scheider poured a fruit cocktail over the director's head. The shoot had lasted 159 agonizing days. "I feel like an old man who has been doing this for twenty years," a weary Spielberg complained. He had heard rumors that the mutinous crew was planning to throw him overboard after the last shot, so he showed up the next morning in leather and suede, hoping it would dissuade them. He checked the final shot through the lens, slipped onto a waiting speedboat, and hightailed it toward land, yelling triumphantly, "I shall *not return!*"

That night in Boston, he woke up before dawn, palms sweaty and breath short. He caught a morning plane home to Los Angeles. For the next three months, he had nightmares that he was still surrounded by ocean, waiting for the damn shark to work.

WHEN JOHN WOJTOWICZ'S LAWYER VISITED him in jail with news that some producers wanted to make his story into a movie, he snarled, "Hell, no. I don't want no movie." Then he got a visit from his transgender wife, who was on her way to becoming Elizabeth Eden. "You make the movie, you get the money—I get the sex change," she reasoned. He signed the papers.

Under the advisement of her psychiatrists, Liz then informed Wojtowicz that it was time to start her new life as a woman and leave him behind. Heartbroken, he slit his wrists and forearms, but survived. He was brought before a federal judge in bandages. "Love is a very strange thing," he told the court. He was sentenced to twenty years in Lewisburg Federal Penitentiary, in Pennsylvania.

Every so often, screenwriter Frank Pierson came to the prison hoping to interview him for the project that would become *Dog Day Afternoon.* Wojtowicz refused to see him. A Hollywood veteran whose credits included *Cool Hand Luke*, Pierson couldn't figure out the main character, renamed "Sonny." Finally, Pierson said, he realized that this was a story of "a guy who imagines that he's a magician that can make everybody happy and whole—but who lashes out in rage when he inevitably fails."

This was the pitch he gave Sidney Lumet. The son of Yiddish theater actors, the forty-nine-year-old director had been nominated for the Best Directing Oscar in 1958, for *12 Angry Men*, but lost to David Lean for *The Bridge on the River Kwai*. Unpretentious, with thick glasses and a bushy mustache, Lumet worked steadily without ever living in Hollywood. "A utopian city where artists have to create I find ridiculous," he said. "One needs to rub oneself against something real in order to create."

There was no better place to rub up against reality than New York

City, a decaying Babylon hurtling toward bankruptcy. It was the city's desuetude that had set the stage for Wojtowicz's hapless robbery and the ensuing media circus, but its funky, dangerous energy had also inspired a filmmaking renaissance that included, post–*Midnight Cowboy*, movies like *The French Connection*, *Mean Streets*, and Lumet's own *Serpico*, starring Al Pacino.

A Lumet-Pacino reunion seemed ideal for *Dog Day Afternoon*, but the actor was burned out. "I had just done *Godfather II* and I was tired of films," he said later. After an initial commitment, he reneged. Lumet grudgingly sent the script to Dustin Hoffman. Whether it was the thought of a rival or the producers begging him to reconsider, Pacino changed his mind.

Despite Hoffman's turn in *Midnight Cowboy* five years earlier, it was still risky for a star of Pacino's stature to play a gay man with a transgender lover. But Lumet saw the story as a window into a subculture—only, instead of gawking, as the TV news crews had done, *Dog Day Afternoon* would look for humanity. Lumet boiled down the theme: "Freaks are not the freaks we think they are. We are much more connected to the most outrageous behavior than we know or admit."

From the start, Lumet knew that the test lay in a single moment. Late in the script, Sonny, under siege by law enforcement, dictates his will to the captive bank tellers, saying, "To my darling wife, Leon, whom I love more than any man has loved another man in all eternity, I leave $2,700 from my $10,000 life insurance policy, to be used for your sex change operation." Lumet thought back to his working-class Brooklyn childhood and to the crowd at the Loew's Pitkin that would heckle from the balcony at the effete Leslie Howard in *The Scarlet Pimpernel*. He knew if the audience laughed at Sonny's final gift to Leon, the picture would be finished.

To play Leon, Lumet auditioned the young theater actor Chris Sarandon, who was living on the Upper West Side with his wife Susan. Most of the other auditioners were in drag; Sarandon wore jeans and a men's jacket. After reading with Pacino, Lumet gave him a note: "A little less Blanche DuBois and a little more Queens housewife."

"I knew exactly what he was talking about," says Sarandon, who immediately nailed the blabby accent and won the role. Despite warnings from friends—"God, do you *really* want to play this part?"—Sarandon was committed. He plucked his eyebrows, grew his fingernails out, clomped around the apartment in heels. He set up a spaghetti dinner downtown with two drag queens and two transgender women on hormone therapy, asking questions like "When was the first time you knew that you were a woman trapped in a man's body?"

As the summer of 1974 limped into the dog days of September, Lumet's crew took over a block of Brooklyn's Windsor Terrace. To play the gaping mob, Lumet brought in more than five hundred extras per day, a mix of professionals and locals. From the top of a ladder, he gave detailed character descriptions. There were four truck drivers, sixteen kids playing hooky, sixteen gay-liberation protesters, and sixteen yentas, whom Lumet broke down even farther: "You two know each other, you four hate those two because they're too good at mah-jongg."

"My part of the crowd was the pizza shop," recalls Lionel Pina, who got a bit part as the Pizza Boy. "If there was something going on, I'd come out of the pizza shop and see." Just as Sonny was playing to the raucous bystanders, Pacino was playing to his fans. "Al was a star, but also *Sonny* was a star," says Carol Kane, who played a hostage. When it came time for Pina to film his big pizza-delivery scene, Lumet pointed to Pacino and told the teen actor, "You can explode. He's the guy you were *just* watching on TV." Just like Wojtowicz, Pacino tossed a spray of cash to the rabid crowd. After delivering the pizza, Pina spun around to the cameras and declared, to wild cheers, "I'm a fucking star!" To Pacino, it was the film's defining moment.

Like McMurphy, Pacino's Sonny joyously upends the system—but, in the end, the authorities reassert their control. The system wins, the outlaws lose, just as they had in *Bonnie and Clyde* and *Easy Rider*. The New Hollywood directors saw themselves the same way. Marcia Jean Kurtz, who played one of the hostages, recalls, "Sidney would tell us stories about filmmaking and his ideas about films. Once, he said that this was the end of the small movie, because what's coming is the *big*."

IN MARCH 1975, A SNEAK preview of *Jaws* was held in Dallas, far from the jaded eyes of executives and industry people. Spielberg worried the film would be a laughingstock, along with his career. What if the shark looked fake (which it was) and clumsy (which it was)? What if people guffawed when they were supposed to jump out of their seats?

His fears melted away with the first big scream. "The first show was dynamite, boffo, exciting," Carl Gottlieb recalled. Producers Zanuck and Brown clutched each other, stunned. "It was that moment that we knew we had a giant hit," Zanuck said later. "They bought it! They bought that dummy shark!" During one harrowing scene, Spielberg was dismayed to see a guy fleeing the theater—but then he watched gleefully as the man ran for the bathroom and vomited.

Spielberg and the producers celebrated until 4 a.m. with champagne in the Registry Hotel penthouse. With them was composer John Williams, who had added the score—Spielberg had at first found it "too primitive," but its sinister simplicity had done more than anything to heighten the suspense. Word got back to Wall Street about the film's good reception, and the next morning, MCA/Universal's stock was up several points.

Two days later, another preview was held, in Long Beach, where Spielberg, partly soothed by a Valium, stood in back biting his nails. The response was so dead-on—screams when there were supposed to be screams, laughs when there were supposed to be laughs—that Spielberg thought there had to be paid plants in the audience. One comment card read, "This is a great film. Now don't fuck it up by trying to make it better."

But Spielberg wanted to make it better. "I have a four-scream movie," he concluded. "I think I can get it up to a five-scream." The extra scream was found in the scene in which Dreyfuss's marine biologist is searching underwater wreckage—and out pops a fisherman's disembodied head. With better timing, it could give the audience a jolt. Spielberg shot a new version in editor Verna Fields's swimming pool, using a gallon of milk to muck up the water.

After the Long Beach screening, the Universal brass met in the men's room of the theater. "We realized it could be a monster picture,"

Sheinberg recalled. MCA chairman Lew Wasserman asked his head of marketing how many movie theaters they had *Jaws* booked in for its June release. The answer was nine hundred—an unprecedented number, based on the surge of interest after Dallas. Typically, releases that wide were reserved for duds, so they could Hoover up money before audiences caught on. *Jaws* would create a new template: a massive promotional campaign, climaxing in a massive release. For now, Wasserman decided to *drop* a few hundred screens, to create just enough demand that, say, people in Palm Springs would have to drive to Hollywood to see it.

He told his staff, "I want this picture to play all summer long."

DR. DEAN BROOKS HAD READ Ken Kesey's *One Flew Over the Cuckoo's Nest* in 1962 and hated it. He thought it totally misrepresented Oregon State Hospital, where he happened to be superintendent. But by the time Michael Douglas came scouting for locations, Brooks had begun to realize that the story was an allegory about "the use and misuse of power." Forman gave him a part in the movie.

Like Lumet, Altman, and Kubrick, what the director wanted was realism; his mantra was "Is it natural?" Before a single frame was shot, the cast spent two weeks in the ward, observing patients and sitting in on group therapy. Each actor got a private cell with a cubby, where he could keep a toothbrush and some personal effects. "I would go up to the maximum-security level on the third floor," recalls Christopher Lloyd, "and there was a guy—a young guy, a wonderful cartoonist, really talented. He was up there because he killed his girlfriend or something like that."

"It was rather striking how normal everybody appeared, particularly in maximum security," says Brad Dourif, who played the stuttering Billy Bibbit. At one group therapy session, mixed in among real patients, he noticed something about the head nurse. "I had the feeling that she felt everybody should be more like her, that she was the 'normal' one. I remember saying that to Louise as we walked away, asking if she got the same impression. And she said, 'You're really onto something there.'"

Before she left for Oregon, in early 1975, Fletcher had met with celebrity hairdresser Carrie White, who came up with Nurse Ratched's signature pageboy. Fletcher wanted a hairstyle that looked "stuck in time," as if her character hadn't bothered to change it since World War II. Since Ratched is never seen outside work, it was up to Fletcher to fill out her life beyond the hospital grounds. She concocted a detailed backstory: "She hasn't married, hadn't done this, hadn't done that, and was self-sufficient on her own, leading this life, because she dedicated her life, her earlier life, to other people who needed her." Also, she decided, Nurse Ratched was a forty-year-old virgin who was "very turned on by this McMurphy guy."

As the shoot began, friction surfaced between Forman and Haskell Wexler, the Oscar-winning cinematographer of *Who's Afraid of Virginia Woolf?* Forman, preferring a raw, documentary look, thought that Wexler was taking too long to light each hospital scene perfectly. As with Nurse Ratched and McMurphy, the power struggle was winner-take-all. "The most difficult thing I ever had to do," Michael Douglas says, "was to fire Academy Award–winning Haskell Wexler." He was replaced by Bill Butler, who months earlier had shot *Jaws*. There, Butler had developed a waterproof camera box that allowed him to film from a shark's-eye view, and he persuaded Spielberg to let him shoot at sea with a handheld camera, so that he could cancel out the wobbling by shifting his knees. *Cuckoo's Nest* required more psychological than technological ingenuity. "The director had something in mind, and he wasn't getting it," Butler recalls. "I had to find out who he was. I had only overnight to do that." Studying Forman's footage of the 1972 Munich Olympics, Butler noticed the director's interest in the faces of the crowd—and translated that into reactive close-ups of the patients during group therapy.

Reality and fiction started to blur. "You began to perceive that the line between being sane and being crazy is thinner than you think," Dourif says. Sydney Lassick, who played the childlike Cheswick, would tap-dance in the hallways. Danny DeVito started talking to an imaginary friend. Fletcher found herself gently instructing her castmates at lunch, "Come on, now. Eat up." There were real patients assisting with set decoration and props. "We had somebody working in the art department who was an arsonist," recalls Douglas. Nicholson's girlfriend, Anjelica Huston, passed through town to visit. "At one point, some grip was opening a window that had a grille behind it, in order to put through some cable," she recalls, "and one of the patients who had a very low-level clearance jumped out the window."

The actors had a game room where they could play billiards and *Pong*. At night, they'd go out drinking in Salem. Fletcher instinctually knew that she had to distance herself from the camaraderie. "I thought, I can't do this," she said. "I can't be in this motel and be with these guys. It's too much fun!" She made up a story that she was receiving threatening phone calls and had the producers move her to her own apartment. She had a like-minded costar in Nicholson, who found canny ways to keep her on her toes. Early on, he asked Fletcher what Nurse Ratched's first name was. "Mildred," she told him. Weeks later, he surprised her mid-scene with the line "I'm proud to join the group, *Mildred*." Fletcher blushed so hard that it was visible on camera.

Still, something inside Fletcher was itching to be let loose; she wanted to show the guys she wasn't the virginal killjoy she was playing. One day, she shocked herself—and everyone else—by stripping off her nurse's uniform to reveal a slip and a bra underneath: "It was like, 'Here I am. I'm a woman.'" As a wrap gift, she gave them all a photo of herself topless and peeking over her naked back, Betty Grable style, in her nurse's cap.

AMONG THE FIRST PEOPLE TO see *Nashville* was Barbra Streisand, who was invited to a special screening at the Lion's Gate offices, along with Martin Scorsese, Harvey Keitel, and Streisand's boyfriend, producer Jon Peters. The couple was preparing to shoot a rock-'n'-roll remake of *A Star Is Born*, to be directed by *Dog Day Afternoon* screenwriter Frank Pierson.

Altman had finished the latest cut with mere minutes to go before the eight-o'clock screening. According to the director, Streisand approached him afterward and didn't say "diddly-squat" about the film; she was instead looking for pointers on how to shoot the concert sequences for *A Star Is Born*. "This is my picture," he chided her, "and we're here to sit here and wallow in it. Just take your unappreciative ass and walk out the door!"

As the picture was screened, raves poured in, including from Sidney Lumet, who told Altman, "I can take things when they are good—but *brilliant?* Then I get sick." *Casablanca* screenwriter Howard Koch declared it "the *Citizen Kane* of this generation of moviemakers." Not all of Hollywood's old guard agreed; Tewkesbury recalls Altman reading an infuriated letter from Billy Wilder, who wrote something along the lines of "It simply isn't a movie!" At sixty-eight, Wilder had apparently become the establishment pooh-pooher that Louis B. Mayer had been toward *Sunset Boulevard.*

"It was a time when the hierarchy had definitely shifted," Tewkesbury says. "And it made for great filmmaking, but it made the hierarchy uncomfortable, because they were losing whatever had been established as what a good film had to be." Not that the reaction broke down along strictly generational lines. Barry Diller, the thirty-three-year-old recently handpicked to run Paramount Pictures, was baffled. As the film's editor, Dennis Hill, later recalled, Diller approached him after a screening in New York and said, "Mind if I ask you a few questions? Because everybody loves this picture and, between you and me, I can't fuckin' figure it out."

Paramount, which was distributing the film, had not set a release date when Pauline Kael stepped into the Magno Screening Room in New York City in January 1975, along with Kurt Vonnegut and Paul Newman. Kael viewed her position as more than a referee. A decade earlier, over dinner at Lumet's apartment, she and Broadway caricaturist Al Hirschfeld had gotten to debating the role of a film critic. Pointing to Lumet, Kael declared, "My job is to show *him* which way to go." Lumet said later, "I thought, This is a very dangerous person." Altman, however, was one of Kael's princes, and she sensed that Paramount was skittish. Tewkesbury recalls, "Lights barely went up, and she was out of her seat and back to Bob in an instant," heady with praise. Kael later said, "After I saw it, it occurred to me that he might want it reviewed to keep the studio from hacking away at it." Her review appeared in the March 3 issue of *The New Yorker*—months before the film's release. "I've never before seen a movie I loved in quite this way," Kael gushed. "I sat there smiling at the screen, in complete happiness."

Kael's fellow critics balked at her preemptive love letter. In the *Times*, Vincent Canby took an entire column, headlined "On Reviewing Films Before They're Finished," to condemn the practice. "If one can review a film on the basis of an approximately three-hour rough cut," he wrote, "why not review it on the basis of a five-hour rough cut? A ten-hour one? On the basis of the screenplay? The original material if first printed as a book? On the basis of a press release? Gossip items?" Nevertheless, Kael's rave set the tone for a media frenzy, in which *Nashville* was greeted as not only a party but a statement. *Newsweek* put Ronee Blakley on its cover, with an accompanying story that invoked Walt Whitman and declared *Nashville* "that rarest thing in contemporary movies—a work of art that promises to be hugely popular."

On August 8, *Nashville* played Nashville. The splashy homecoming came with a parade of antique autos and a tricolor Peterbilt truck pulling a forty-foot stage, where a country band played under an American flag alongside the Rutherford County Square Dancers. Altman skipped the hoopla, but Carradine was there to receive a gold-plated key to the city jail.

Dozens of Music City personalities were in the audience. As they walked out, it became clear that they had just glimpsed themselves in a funhouse mirror—and they didn't like what they saw. "I don't think it said the truth about Nashville," Betty Blanton, the Tennessee governor's wife, complained. At a reception at the Exit/In, *Opry* singer Jeanne Pruett remarked, "I thought it was hokey from start to finish. I can see how they might like it in New York. They think we're a bunch of hayseeds to begin with. The only thing Mr. Altman and I agree on is how to spell the title." Notably absent was Loretta Lynn, who sent word that "I'd rather see *Bambi*."

JAWS OPENED NINE DAYS AFTER *Nashville*, on June 20, 1975, and from then on, the summer belonged to it alone. Universal had spent a massive $1.8 million on advertising, the most in the studio's history. More than half went to radio and television ads, which saturated the country in the two weeks before the film's release, while Spielberg, Benchley, Zanuck, and Brown toured eleven cities. The hype campaign culminated in a *Time* cover story predicting that *Jaws* would "hit right in the old collective unconscious."

The dismissal of the critics hardly mattered. Nor did the fact that Jacques Cousteau had blasted Benchley's novel for shark-related inaccuracies and warned, "I'm afraid the movie will compound all the errors in the novel." By its fourteenth day, *Jaws* had recouped its once-unthinkable budget. As Spielberg would observe, it was less a movie than a phenomenon on par with the hula hoop. Naïve about merchandising, the director had suggested that the studio sell chocolate sharks that would spurt red cherry juice; the studio vetoed that one and instead flooded America with branded T-shirts, beach towels, and toys. Sales of shark teeth surged. A *Jaws* discotheque opened in the Hamptons. Ice-cream stands renamed their flavors "sharklate" and "jawberry." Lifeguards were flooded with false shark sightings from terrified swimmers. In Seattle, the National Association of Skin Diving Schools groused that the film had caused a sudden drop in diving instructors' courses. By August, the *Christian Science Monitor* was bemoaning that *Jaws* had become "the compulsory topic at parties, the desperate comedian's fail-safe joke, and the political cartoonist's all-purpose symbol." As critic Molly Haskell recalled, it was "open season for Freudian sleuths." Was the shark a symbol of liberated womanhood, devouring the impotent modern male? Was the town cover-up, as Fidel Castro postulated, an indictment of capitalism? Or did the film offer a post-Watergate thrill in the expulsion of a monster?

Robert Altman had called *Nashville* "my metaphor for America," but it was *Jaws* that now seemed to match the description. Despite the paeans, *Nashville* disappointed at the box office. The reason, Altman lamented, was that "we didn't have King Kong or a shark." On September 5, *Jaws* surpassed *The Godfather* as the highest-grossing movie ever made.

SIDNEY LUMET KNEW SOMETHING WAS wrong with *Dog Day Afternoon*. He and editor Dede Allen had shaved off nearly five minutes from the first half, re-creating the rapid-fire thrill of the bank heist. After they watched the cut at a Broadway screening room, Lumet was still worried about the dictation of Sonny's will and about the potential hecklers who would take any excuse to laugh. After the ramped-up pace of the first half, the will scene now seemed jarringly slow, and Lumet realized he had to even out the pace. "We talked for about a half hour," he recalled, "standing there on the street as cabs, hustlers, porno customers, and passersby moved past us. The next day, I went back to the cutting room and restored two and a half minutes of the four and a half we had cut."

When the film came out, on September 21, Vincent Canby hailed it as a "gaudy street-carnival of a movie." In the *Washington Post*, Gary Arnold described it as "the picture to beat for the next set of Oscars." Even Kael, setting aside her dislike of Lumet, described it as "one of the most satisfying of all the movies starring New York City," singling out the scene that had so bedeviled Lumet: "In the sequence in which Sonny dictates his will, we can see that inside this ludicrous bungling robber there's a complicatedly unhappy man."

Perhaps the most conflicted review came from John Wojtowicz. He had been shown the film privately at the Lewisburg Federal Penitentiary. When the warden refused a screening for the rest of the inmates, Wojtowicz threatened, "If you don't show this in the prison I'll go to the press and I'll hang you by your fucking cannolis! I'll start the biggest prison riot you ever saw!"

The warden relented. But Wojtowicz had mixed feelings about what he saw. In a long and self-contradicting letter he submitted to the *New York Times*—part review, part screed, part attempt to clear up the "truth"—he claimed that the "Movie People" had reneged on a verbal agreement to pay him 2 percent of the gross and estimated that the movie was "30% true." Like a film critic hedging his bets, Wojtowicz then U-turned into praise for Lumet's "fantastic" direction. Ultimately, he concluded, "I felt the movie was in essence a piece of garbage," though he conceded that Pacino's acting was "out of sight": "I feel he deserves an Academy Award for Best Male Actor for his unbelievable performance."

In an observation that would have pleased the director, Wojtowicz added, "I was very touched and cried in the most moving scene in the entire movie, the one in which he dictates my last will and testament. During this memorable scene over 1,300 men in here were completely silent, and you could hear a pin drop."

THE FIRST TIME THAT LOUISE Fletcher saw *One Flew Over the Cuckoo's Nest* was in Oakland. On the way home, her agent told her, "Well, it's not going to hurt you." Soon after, at a screening in Chicago, she realized the movie had hit a nerve. During the climactic scene in which McMurphy strangles Nurse Ratched, audience members stood up and yelled, "Kill her!" It was a sign, perhaps, of the movie's unsettling gender dynamics, but Fletcher was thrilled. When spectators swarmed her afterward, it was "the first time in my life that I had experienced what fame is."

Her instinct was right. After being passed on by every studio but United Artists, *Cuckoo's Nest* opened on November 19, 1975, and sailed past the $100 million mark, second only to *Jaws* at the year's box office. It was perfectly suited to an era in which heroism meant being an outsider—who wouldn't want to see himself as a renegade McMurphy, waging a fun-filled war against the system? Kael called it "a powerful, smashingly effective movie—not a great movie but one that will probably stir audiences' emotions and join the ranks of such pop-mythology films as 'The Wild One,' 'Rebel Without a Cause,' and 'Easy Rider.'"

One notable critic was Ken Kesey, who was living on a blueberry farm in Oregon. Kesey had long since fallen out with the producers, whom he was now suing for 5 percent of the grosses plus $800,000 in punitive damages for "breaking our verbal agreement and ruining the book." "Ken Kesey was kind of an enemy of the movie," says screenwriter Bo Goldman. According to Michael Douglas, "He didn't believe in lawyers and this and that, so there seemed to be a miscommunication of what the deal was. And then it all kind of blew up." Among Kesey's complaints: the film had dropped the all-important idea of "the Combine," stripping its critique of "the conspiracy that is America." Kesey was now part of an unlikely fraternity that included Loretta Lynn, John Wojtowicz, and Jacques Cousteau. The directors of *One Flew Over the Cuckoo's Nest, Nashville, Dog Day Afternoon,* and *Jaws* had gone to extreme lengths to ensure authenticity—braving open waters and psych wards—and yet all now faced detractors. Stanley Kubrick was starting to look like a real genius, as William Makepeace Thackeray had been dead for two hundred years and couldn't complain.

When Warner Bros. executives flew to London to see *Barry Lyndon,* Kubrick declined, assuring them that, once the movie won its Oscars, it would "go through the roof." The studio backed off. "It would make no sense to tell Kubrick, 'O.K., fella, you've got one more week to finish the thing,'" production chief John Calley said. "What you would get then is a mediocre film that cost say, $8 million, instead of a masterpiece that cost $11 million." Kubrick extended his Napoléonic control to every advertisement and publicity still. From his manor house in England, he labored for up to eighteen hours a day, living, as one friend put it, "like a medieval artist living above his workshop."

The Hollywood brass was finally allowed to see *Barry Lyndon* three weeks before its release. The executives "were polite but worried," producer Jan Harlan recalls. "The lyrical ending, edited to the slow movement of the Schubert Piano Trio, did not meet their expectation." But at that point, what were they going to do about it?

Barry Lyndon opened on December 18, heralded by a *Time* cover story that called it "Kubrick's Grandest Gamble." Critical reaction ran from mixed to hostile, especially in America, where Kael called it "a coffee-table movie." Jerry Oster, in the New York *Sunday News*, called it "an egocentric film, made by a man who has lost touch with his peers, his critics and his audiences." *The Harvard Lampoon* named it Worst Movie of the Year.

"I fucking knew it," Kubrick said of the criticism. Christiane recalls, "He was prepared, thinking that it wasn't going to go over very big in America. It went best in Japan, funnily enough. And Europe also, people liked it. They didn't like it in America at all. They found it really boring." Its defenders—including Vincent Canby, who found its pacing "luxurious, like sinking into a fine long book"—saw *Barry Lyndon* as a different kind of moviegoing experience, if you could sit back and let it wash over you like rain. Still, when Canby wrote that *Barry Lyndon* was "about foolish, gallant overreaching," it seemed like a dig at Kubrick and, by extension, the New Hollywood model that turned directors into emperors.

For all Kubrick's obsession over period details, the movie didn't pass Joan Tewkesbury's smell test. "The first movie done by candlelight, yada yada yada," she says. "All I remember about *Barry Lyndon* was that Ryan O'Neal's feet were beautifully manicured, and nobody living in that time would ever have had feet that beautiful."

SPIELBERG FELT BULLISH ON THE morning of February 17, 1976. "*Jaws* is about to be nominated in eleven categories," he told a documentary crew he had invited to film him watching the Oscar nominations. "You're about to see us sweep the nominations."

He had reason to be confident. In July, Sid Sheinberg had gloated, "I want to be the first to predict that Steve will win the best-director Oscar this year." The *Los Angeles Times* had included *Jaws* in its "short odds" for Best Picture nominees, alongside *One Flew Over the Cuckoo's Nest*, *Nashville*, *Dog Day Afternoon*, and the Neil Simon comedy *The Sunshine Boys*. "The odds lengthen" on *Shampoo*, the paper said, and "a bit further" on *Barry Lyndon*.

Spielberg, in a red sweater and big glasses, called out from his desk, "Carol? Can everybody in this room have coffee, with the exception of myself who would like a cup of tea?" He hunched over on an office chair, fists planted in his cheeks and a camera in his face, and watched the nominations announced for Best Directing: Robert Altman, Miloš Forman, Stanley Kubrick, Sidney Lumet, and . . . Federico Fellini, for *Amarcord*.

"Oh, I didn't get it! I didn't get it!" Spielberg moaned. He turned to his friends, all shaking their heads, and said with disbelief, "I got beaten out by Fellini." Best Actress was up next, and the director quickly papered over his disappointment with shtick: "Wait a second. The shark was an actress." As his pals pronounced it "a dark day in Hollywood," Spielberg turned comedian: "Cancel my day! Cancel my week! I'm going to Palm Springs!"

For Carl Gottlieb, whose screenplay was also passed over, the forced levity was "a very honest look at Steven. That's how he looks when he's upset." Spielberg went on to rationalize for the cameras, whose presence he must have instantly regretted: "This is called commercial backlash . . . Everybody loves a winner, but nobody loves a *winner*." "It didn't fit his master plan at all," Gottlieb says. "He was going to be acclaimed as an auteur director. It was like Hitler getting to the English Channel and not being able to cross it."

The rest of Hollywood was stunned. "It's the biggest disappointment for me of the whole Oscars," said Michael Douglas, who was at Jack Nicholson's ski house in Aspen with Miloš Forman. Czech director Ivan

Passer, riding in a car with Forman, reasoned, "At least he has something to look forward to. Imagine, to get everything when you are twenty-eight. It's good for him he didn't get it."

"I don't think it's good for him," Forman countered.

Neither Douglas nor Forman had reason to complain. *One Flew Over the Cuckoo's Nest* led the pack with nine nominations, followed closely by *Barry Lyndon* (seven) and *Dog Day Afternoon* (six), which would compete for Best Picture with *Nashville* and *Jaws*—the only contender without a nominated director and the only one with a happy ending.

Nashville had already won what Altman called the "New York primary," tying with *Barry Lyndon* for Best Picture and Best Director at the National Board of Review Awards and winning Best Film, Best Director, and Best Supporting Actress (for Lily Tomlin) at the New York Film Critics Circle Awards. *Cuckoo's Nest* had won the "foreign primary," cleaning up at the Golden Globes and the BAFTAs. Perhaps the only *Cuckoo's Nest* nominee to be dismayed was Bill Butler, who was nominated with Haskell Wexler for his pinch-hitting cinematography but overlooked for his much more innovative work on *Jaws*. "I don't think *ironic* is the word," he says. "Irritating maybe closer."

Joan Tewkesbury, whose screenplay for *Nashville* was left out, could not understand how Frank Pierson's script for *Dog Day Afternoon* was considered "original," given that it was based on a magazine article. "Frank was such a good friend," she recalls, "and I said, 'You cheated! It's not fair!' He said, 'Tough shit.'" Altman was also steaming. *Nashville* had earned five nominations, including for Lily Tomlin and Ronee Blakley (Best Supporting Actress) and "I'm Easy" (Best Original Song), but the Academy hadn't recognized its inventive sound design or its score—a technicality, due to its multiple songwriters. Altman wrote a scathing mailgram to Academy president Walter Mirisch, decrying "the destructive effect of the discriminatory and arbitrary action of the executive committee of the music branch."

Lily Tomlin had no such indignation. At a costume store in Studio City, she tried on a purple sequined dress and a white stole worthy of Princess Grace. She cooed at herself in the mirror. "How fabulous!" she said, twirling like a tongue-in-cheek Miss America. "Oh, this is good for *accepting.*" Accessories followed: earrings, bracelets, gloves. "The real quandary I have is whether or not to go in this dress and a fox or a mink cape and full clown makeup," she deadpanned.

Forman, sensing his Oscar fortunes rising with *Cuckoo's Nest's* run-away box office, had written to the Czech government for permission to bring over his two sons, Petr and Matěj, whom he had not seen in six years. "The old rule that nothing impressed the Communists as much as success among the imperialists kicked in," he recalled, "and my boys were allowed to come." In late March, he picked them up at the Los Angeles airport in the biggest limo he could find, nervous to see the twelve-year-olds they had become. In the car to the Beverly Hills Hotel, they seemed unimpressed by the pools and the Porsches—until one of them exclaimed, "Dad, they got women driving cars here?"

Forman asked if they wanted to see his film, which they pronounced "Couscous Next." The boys replied, "We'd rather see *Jaws.*"

OF THE NOMINATED DIRECTORS, PERHAPS Altman could have best captured the schmaltzy absurdities, missed connections, and muted disappointments of the Forty-Eighth Academy Awards, held on March 29, 1976, at the Dorothy Chandler Pavilion. His camera would have cast a droll eye on the screaming fans in the bleachers, hoping to glimpse Jack Nicholson or Goldie Hawn. Or on Lily Tomlin, waving to her royal subjects with a silver glove. Or on Robert Shaw, grabbing a reporter's microphone to give the fans a sexy "Hello, girls." Or on Louise Fletcher—dressed in a decidedly non-Ratched chiffon gown, with a cuckoo bird pattern—asking her limo driver, "Who's screaming? This is like the Alabama State Fair!"

Altman surely would have caught the tension between the now-separated Chris and Susan Sarandon (by then the star of *The Rocky Horror Picture Show*), who had declined the studio limousine for a chauffeured Nash Rambler. Or the wide-eyed Americana of the TV announcer welcoming O. J. Simpson, "actor and athlete nonpareil." He would have cut from the European glamour of Audrey Hepburn, swathed in a black shawl, to the California hucksterism of the Polaroid pitchman showing off the latest Pronto! model, available for only sixty-six dollars.

And Altman would have relished the unbridled kitsch of the opening number, sung by the seventy-two-year-old Ray Bolger, the Scarecrow of *The Wizard of Oz*, winking at the chasm between his top-hat-and-tails Hollywood glitz and the shaggy defiance of the nominated films, all shot far from Los Angeles, by directors who considered themselves rambunctious outsiders—save for Spielberg, who had proven himself a rambunctious insider.

That was exactly why Altman didn't have much hope for *Nashville*. "It is not a Hollywood movie," he had said weeks earlier, when asked about his Oscar chances. "It was made outside the establishment and, after all, it is the establishment doing the voting." Now he watched *Nashville* immediately lose two awards in one blow, as *Shampoo*'s Lee Grant beat both Tomlin and Blakley for Best Supporting Actress.

Kubrick, who dreaded flying, was watching from his bedroom in England. He hated parties, according to his wife. "He just stood there like an idiot." Plus, Christiane says, "He knew the tidal wave was against him." Nevertheless, *Barry Lyndon* racked up four early awards, for its costumes, score, cinematography, and art direction, as if the film were a museum with a string quartet playing inside. *Jaws* picked up three awards, for sound, film editing, and John Williams's score. Accepting her award, editor Verna Fields thanked "our wonderful, fabulous, talented director, Steven Spielberg," who was nowhere in sight.

Keith Carradine sat with his father and girlfriend, until it was time to sing "I'm Easy." The Academy had asked him to appear alone with a single guitar, as he did in the film. "I remember feeling really naked, sitting in front of that audience," Carradine recalls. "I threw in one extra bar out of nerves, but no one knew that but me." He was convinced that Best Original Song would go to the "Theme from Mahogany," performed in a live satellite broadcast from Amsterdam by Diana Ross. But "I'm Easy" won, giving *Nashville* its sole Oscar, seven years after Carradine first played it for Shelley Plimpton. "True love inspired it," he told the pressroom.

Dog Day Afternoon's screenwriter, Frank Pierson, was on the set of *A Star Is Born*, shooting a night scene in a parking lot. When the Best Original Screenplay award came up, everyone crowded into a bar and cheered when Pierson's name was called, then watched presenter Gore Vidal accept on his behalf. "We went back to the set and shot until midnight," Pierson said. "That was my Oscar night." It was the only award for *Dog Day Afternoon*.

Midway through, Gene Kelly introduced an honorary Oscar for Mary Pickford, now nearing eighty-four. Pickford was too frail to receive the statuette in person, so there had been a prerecorded handoff at Pickfair. The Academy cameras had invaded the estate, which appeared as ghostly and frozen in time as Norma Desmond's mansion. An oil painting of Little Mary, in her curls, hung between golden candelabra. Pickford, tiny and elegant, sat in a silk robe in the Regency dining room where she had once entertained the King and Queen of Siam. Walter Mirisch held out the Oscar statuette and said, "He hasn't changed very much in all this time, has he?"

"Well, I hope not," America's onetime sweetheart replied, with honey and a hint of drollery in her voice. Dwarfed in her armchair, she stroked its gold head and promised, "I shall treasure it always." She died three years later.

Michael Douglas had to persuade Jack Nicholson to come to the ceremony. The actor had lost four Oscars since 1970, most recently for *Chinatown*. "I don't want to do this anymore. I can't stand it," he told Douglas, who argued, "Jack, we have nine nominations. *Nine*." So Nicholson came, with Anjelica Huston on his arm and sunglasses affixed to his face. But *Cuckoo's Nest* immediately started losing awards—to *Jaws* for editing and score, to *Barry Lyndon* for cinematography. Nicholson turned to Douglas and said, "I told you, Mikey, it's not going to happen."

They were all aware that *Chinatown* had gotten eleven nominations the year before and lost all except one. Now, Miloš Forman recalled, "I could feel the nerves of the *Cuckoo's Nest* family stretching. We sat in the same section of the orchestra, so I could see Saul, Michael, and Jack, who all wore very serious, very composed expressions. I knew they were thinking what I was thinking: *Chinatown*."

Cuckoo's Nest's Brad Dourif and *Dog Day Afternoon*'s Chris Sarandon were both certain they would lose Best Supporting Actor to George Burns, for *The Sunshine Boys*—and they were right. When Burns won,

Forman's sons clapped and jumped in their chairs. "It's nice of you to applaud, guys, but we didn't win," Forman whispered. As the night wore on and "Couscous Next" kept losing, he looked down and saw that Petr and Matěj were fast asleep.

But then, excitedly, he woke them up. *Cuckoo's Nest* had won the adapted screenplay award. Then it never stopped winning.

Louise Fletcher, nominated for Best Actress, had been spared the angst of competing against Lily Tomlin, who was in the supporting category. She expected to lose to Glenda Jackson, for *Hedda*. When she heard her name, Fletcher bounded onstage in a whirl of chiffon. "All I can say is I've loved being hated by you," she told the Academy, and thanked the cast for making "being in a mental institution like being in a mental institution." Tearing up, she spoke in sign language to her parents in Alabama: "I want to say thank you for teaching me to have a dream. You are seeing my dream come true."

When Jack Nicholson won Best Actor, he kissed Anjelica Huston and finally removed his shades. "I guess this proves there are as many nuts in the Academy as anywhere else," he purred from the stage. Then he thanked Mary Pickford, for being "the first actor to get a percentage of her pictures." Al Pacino was not present to see Nicholson beat him. He later said that Nicholson deserved the prize because he'd "been out there a while," but that he would have turned down the role of McMurphy. "I thought *Cuckoo's Nest* was a kind of trap," Pacino said. "It's one of those built parts: I don't think it has much depth. Commercially it's very good, but as far as being a really terrific role, I don't think it is."

To present Best Directing, William Wyler joined Diane Keaton, who was dressed in a white suit, striped shirt, and black tie. When Miloš Forman heard his name called, he was "numb." He thanked the Academy for putting him in the "company" of his fellow nominees, Altman and Lumet (who were watching from the audience) and Kubrick and Fellini (who weren't). As he rattled off names, Forman recalled, the world was "a goulash of impressions and feelings":

> I had reached the top of my profession, I was in Hollywood, I was in America, and I was happy and overwhelmed. I didn't know

what to think about first, the money, the smiles of the world's most glamorous women, the doors that had been closed to me suddenly opening. In the glare of lights, I could just make out my two boys in tuxedos clapping away and beaming. They were my blood, which was the blood of people who had died behind barbed wire . . . There was a strangeness between us, the strangeness that's between all the people, the concertina wire separating me from the cheering crowd, the deep strangeness of it all, the barbed-wire heart.

Audrey Hepburn came out to present Best Picture. It was a *One Flew Over the Cuckoo's Nest* sweep—the first film to win the "Big Five" since *It Happened One Night* in 1935. (The sweep would not be repeated again until 1992, with *The Silence of the Lambs*.) Like Capra, who had tapped into a yearning for class mobility, Forman had captured something elemental about the country. The wild yell of *Easy Rider* had crescendoed into McMurphy's mad fury—and, in both films, Nicholson's character had been snuffed out by an uncomprehending world. Producers Michael Douglas and Saul Zaentz ascended the stage with arms around each other and thanked everyone from Kirk Douglas, who had stayed with the project for fourteen years, to the state of Oregon.

One name that went conspicuously unmentioned: "Ken Kesey." The author was watching with a rowdy crew of friends at his blueberry farm. The group applauded every time *Cuckoo's Nest* won, jeered whenever the winner failed to mention Kesey. (Only Forman did, while Kesey was doing chores in the milkshed.) When it won Best Picture, he switched off his ratty TV and announced, "Any one of them could have thanked me for writing the book and won all the arguments. But they blew their big chance to be in the big times, the big league." As congratulatory calls poured in, he groused, "I'm sure it's a good movie in the sense that Nixon's '72 campaign was a good campaign because he won."

Moments after *Cuckoo's Nest*'s triumph, Elizabeth Taylor emerged in a red dress and invited everyone to celebrate the United States bicentennial with a rendition of "America the Beautiful." The audience awkwardly rose to its feet, and out marched a line of uniformed sousaphone players—Altman couldn't have staged it better. Fletcher went back up with her Oscar. As she looked out, she saw Altman staring at her from his seat, twiddling his hands in mock sign language. "I was shocked," she said. "I just was shocked."

The next morning, Forman read his pile of congratulatory telegrams, including one from the seventy-eight-year-old Frank Capra. Four decades after *It Happened One Night*'s sweep, he wrote: WELCOME TO THE CLUB.

SEVERAL MONTHS LATER, ALTMAN WAS asked about the single Oscar for *Nashville*. "Well, the Academy is a private club, so its members can do whatever they want with it," he groused. Awards campaigning had put him off. "I don't know what United Artists spent promoting *Cuckoo's Nest*, but I'll guarantee you it was over $80,000. That's the trouble, the whole thing becomes like a national election."

Four years later, when John Lennon was assassinated, a *Washington Post* reporter called Altman and asked if he felt responsible. "What do you mean, 'responsible'?"

"Well, you're the one that predicted that there would be an assassination of a star."

"Don't *you* feel responsible," the director replied, "for not heeding my warning?"

Louise Fletcher, meanwhile, was still fuming at Altman. "I have nothing against Lily Tomlin, and I understand she was wonderful in the part," she said in 1976. "I have not been able to see the movie myself." Before *Cuckoo's Nest*, she had been rejected by fifteen agencies, but now the offers were rolling in. For whatever reason, she turned down the part of the mother in *Carrie*, which became a star-making role for Piper Laurie. Soon, other parts—Norma Rae among them—slipped out of her grasp. In 1987, playing the evil grandmother in *Flowers in the Attic*, Fletcher realized just how good she'd had it with *Cuckoo's Nest*, when her new director instructed her, "Scare me to death." "The director didn't understand about villains," she said. "What's so familiar can be the most frightening thing."

John Wojtowicz was released from prison in 1978, after the parole board recommended a reduced sentence. For a while, he cleaned toilets on Park Avenue, but he quickly embraced his newfound notoriety from *Dog Day Afternoon*. He would stand outside the Chase Bank on Avenue P and East Third Street, signing autographs in a T-shirt that read, "I Robbed This Bank." When a television reporter chided him for "expecting to make money out of committing a crime," he shot back, "What about Hollywood? Hollywood can make a movie—namely Warner Bros.—make fifty million dollars off of it, get six Academy Award nominations, and win an Oscar for it. They can make money off of a crime."

After Stanley Kubrick finished *Barry Lyndon*, he stored the costumes in a warehouse in England, on the off chance that he could use them again for *Napoleon*. The movie was never made. But he did finally get his chance to work with Jack Nicholson, whom he cast in the lead role of his next project, *The Shining*. He hired Shelley Duvall after seeing her in Altman's *3 Women*. Miloš Forman's next move was the film version of *Hair*, a decade after the show brought Keith Carradine to New York City. Sidney Lumet followed up *Dog Day Afternoon* with another defining film of seventies malaise, *Network*, which would join a 1977 Best Picture race full of more discontentment, more post-Watergate cynicism and dread, including Martin Scorsese's *Taxi Driver* and Alan J. Pakula's *All the President's Men*. But all would lose to *Rocky*, signaling a shift toward triumphalism that would carry into the eighties.

Asked by *Playboy* in 1976 which of the young "movie brats" would endure, Altman said, "I think Steven Spielberg will endure, though it's tough when a picture like *Jaws* brings you a lot of success and money overnight that may not strictly be related to the merit of your work. I am not knocking *Jaws*, which was a magnificent accomplishment for a kid that age. But will he now be able to go off and make a small personal film?"

Despite his gift for prophecy, Altman was misreading the moment. Spielberg did not want to make a small, personal film. He wanted, finally, to make the big-budget version of his juvenile alien flick *Firelight*, which he retitled *Close Encounters of the Third Kind*. *Jaws* had given him "a free ticket for half a dozen rides," Spielberg said. He marched into Columbia and asked for a $12 million budget. The executives agreed, of course. Every studio wanted the next *Jaws*.

Jaws remained the highest-grossing movie of all time only until 1977, when it was beaten by *Star Wars*. Spielberg would beat *that* record five years later, with *E.T. the Extra-Terrestrial*. Universal would follow *Jaws* with *Jaws 2, Jaws 3-D*, and *Jaws: The Revenge*. If the Oscar triumph of *One Flew Over the Cuckoo's Nest* was the high-water mark of the New Hollywood, there was nowhere to go but down. After all, McMurphy loses. Nurse Ratched survives. The lunatics can run the asylum for only so long.

EIGHT

Fiasco

1989

How a caftan-wearing bon vivant introduced Rob
Lowe to Snow White and saw his Hollywood dream
turn into a career-ending nightmare. But were the
"Worst Oscars Ever" really that bad?

Pee-wee Herman dangled from the rafters of the Shrine Auditorium. Onstage, a killer droid clomped toward him, raised its machine-gun arms, and demanded an Academy Award.

"*He-e-elp!*" Pee-wee shrieked.

From the back of the hall, RoboCop marched down the aisle and shot cartoon-green laser beams at the droid, landing a direct hit. "Yeah!" Pee-wee yelled.

The audience—among them, Jack Nicholson, Glenn Close, Paul Newman—clapped tentatively. "All right, Pee-wee," RoboCop said in robot monotone, "it's safe to continue giving the award now."

"Thanks, RoboCop," Pee-wee said. He floated down to the stage, loafers wriggling, and presented the award for Best Live Action Short Film to *Ray's Male Heterosexual Dance Hall*.

If the Oscars of 1988 had a credo, it was "more is more." The hair was big. The movie budgets were big. Understated elegance was not the fashion. Tom Selleck presented an award with Mickey Mouse. Cher, the Best Actress winner for *Moonstruck*, wore one of her outrageous Bob Mackie gowns. Michael Douglas won Best Actor for playing Gordon Gekko, the era-defining corporate raider from *Wall Street*, and the character's "greed is good" ethos could have doubled for Hollywood's; the previous year's top domestic grosser was *Beverly Hills Cop II*. This was the world created by *Jaws*.

The show had kicked off with a musical number featuring chorines on a honeycomb-shaped set. Midway through, lasers flashed, and fourteen Oscar statues came to life on pedestals and danced in gold spandex suits. Lavish opening numbers were now an Oscar tradition. The previous year, Telly Savalas, Pat Morita, and Dom DeLuise had crooned "Fugue for Tinhorns," from *Guys and Dolls*. The year before that, Teri Garr had piloted an airplane onstage, in a re-creation of the aerial song-and-dance extravaganza from the 1933 film *Flying Down to Rio*. These numbers had a schmaltzy, vaudevillian excess that was brazenly out of step with the times, as variety television gave way to MTV.

The ratings had been in decline since 1984, and the 1988 broadcast, which ended in an underwhelming win for *The Last Emperor*, managed to stem the bleeding. But the critics gave the ceremony a drubbing. The *Los Angeles Times* said that the "parched, drab and leaden" show had "curiously lacked oomph." Janet Maslin, in the *New York Times*, diagnosed the Academy Awards with "a serious identity crisis," with its "snail-paced" presentations and "exceptionally irrelevant" opening number. The presence of emissaries from Hollywood's past—including Gregory Peck and Audrey Hepburn, who looked "like visiting royalty"—only emphasized the tacky commercialism of its present.

The show's producer that year was Samuel Goldwyn Jr., the son of the golden age impresario. For years, the Academy had tried to inject the ceremony with Hollywood magic by hiring producers with filmmaking pedigree, among them Jack Haley Jr., Norman Jewison, Stanley Donen, and, most strangely, *Exorcist* director William Friedkin. It wasn't working. The Oscars were a big, embarrassing yawn. After two years running, Goldwyn bowed out, telling the papers, "I wish the next guy luck."

To revamp its big night, the Academy needed someone who could bridge what was left of classic Hollywood with a young audience more interested in the Brat Pack than in Bette Davis. It needed someone who knew that the Oscars were sacred—but not *boring* sacred. It needed a showman. In October, the incoming Academy president, publicist Richard Kahn, announced the producer of the 1989 awards. The papers called him "Glittermeister." He called himself Allan Carr.

EVERYONE IN TOWN KNEW THE name "Allan Carr." Allan Carr had made sure of that. He was the man who had produced *Grease*, but that hardly covered his self-perpetuating legend. At five foot seven, Carr lived as if his name were perpetually spelled out in lights, festooning his rotund frame with looping Elsa Peretti diamonds, glasses patterned with pink and blue clouds, and an array of shimmering designer caftans.

If Carr had a genius, it was for throwing fabulous parties, whether Babylonian movie premieres or house parties at his Benedict Canyon home, a brick mansion with the genteel name "Hilhaven Lodge." He had bought the place in his first flush of success, and it fulfilled his life-long fantasy: to inhabit the myth of Old Hollywood. As Carr knew well, David O. Selznick had bought Hilhaven for Ingrid Bergman, to entice her into staying in Hollywood instead of returning to Sweden with her husband, and it was there that she and Roberto Rossellini began their world-scandalizing affair. By the time Carr bought Hilhaven, in 1973, for $200,000, *Godfather* star James Caan was renting the house, sleeping on a mattress on the floor. But Carr saw its potential. As his friend Bruce Vilanch recalls, "He reveled in the lore of the place."

Carr transformed Hilhaven into a kitschy fantasia. In the living room were a granite fireplace, bay windows looking out on to a pool, and a clear Lucite grand piano under a crystal chandelier. Upstairs was the Olivia Newton-John honorary bedroom, after the star of his greatest hit, decked out in girlish gingham. And in the basement, the pièce de résistance: his own Egyptian-themed disco. "It used to be the laundry room," recalls Don Blanton, who for a time was Carr's personal deejay. "He wanted to lie on the couch like Cleopatra. He had all the couches done in gold lamé and named each after a famous person." The bar was named for the Polish film star Bella Darvi, a kind of in-joke for anyone who fed on Old Hollywood arcana. "Most everybody was chemically altered, so it was a great place to sit and trip," recalls Vilanch. Outside the front door, Carr placed a six-foot-tall Oscar statue.

Sooner or later, every boldface name wound up at Hilhaven. "I want to bring glamour back to Hollywood," Carr would say. "Everybody, let's dress up!" At his bacchanals, where even the security guards wore tuxedos, Carr mixed Old Hollywood royalty with the pretty young things he collected like baubles. "The takeaway was whatever you wanted to take away," Vilanch says. "If you wanted to take the pool boy, well, that was available. But if you just wanted to take away the glamour and the overflowing hospitality, that was also great."

At the center of the action was the host, who cycled through as many as ten caftans a night before retiring. "The caftans allowed him to look kind of great without having to show the figure of his body," says Don Blanton; Carr struggled with his weight, even after having his stomach stapled. To the world, he projected a front of glitzy excess, cajoling caterers into working his house parties for free in exchange for the publicity. One night, his friend Gary Pudney recalls, "I went into the kitchen, where he had all these people working, and they were pouring cheap champagne into Dom Pérignon bottles that were empty. Gives you a little clue."

The press invariably described Carr as "flamboyant"—a code word for what he really was, which was loudly, unapologetically gay. "Everybody knew, but I don't think he ever said anything publicly about it," Vilanch says. "He never declared himself like baggage." His parties, particularly the raunchier ones, gave closeted celebrities a place to flaunt their open secret. "You would see the Velvet Mafia—all the high-powered gay guys—who were not afraid to be there," Vilanch says: David Geffen, Barry Manilow, Rock Hudson, Liberace. Even ultraconservative lawyer Roy Cohn made appearances. ("He would pretend he wasn't there," Vilanch jokes, "and if you claimed he was, you would be murdered.") There was his notorious "Mattress Party" for Rudolf Nureyev, a male-only affair where each guest brought a mattress for admittance and Hilhaven overflowed with caviar, Stolichnaya vodka, and rent boys. Carr populated his parties with a bottomless list of handsome young "twinkies," but he rarely took part in the orgiastic fun himself; his preferred sexual mode was to watch two young hunks engage in a late-night wrestling match.

Carr loved to titillate his A-list guests. Days after Robert Opel streaked the Academy Awards in 1974, Carr threw a party honoring Marvin Hamlisch's triple win, for *The Sting* and *The Way We Were*; a visit from Nureyev; and the birthday of Grace Robbins, wife of the author Harold Robbins. The guests—Jack Nicholson, Anjelica Huston, Bianca Jagger, Diana Ross—found a giant Oscar replica, named "The Marvin," and a cake in the shape of the Robbinses' yacht. Opel, the streaker, wore black tie and a silver codpiece, and at Carr's cue—"Everyone should take their clothes off and be counted!"—Opel stripped to his collar and tie.

Carr pushed the envelope, but he was careful not to lose his grip on classic Hollywood. Alice Cooper later recalled, "We'd go to Allan's and it would not be surprising to find Mae West sitting next to Rod Stewart or Salvador Dalí or Jack Benny." In 1979, Carr threw a wedding party for Stewart and his bride, Alana. "There was everyone from Rod's band to Gregory Peck and Fred Astaire," Alana recalls, rattling off the incongruous guest list: Contessa Marina Cicogna, Irving "Swifty" Lazar, Hugh Hefner. Peck and his wife Veronique lived next door to the Stewarts, and they were unlikely habitués at Hilhaven. "This scene, it's hilarious," the bemused Peck would tut, taking in the pandemonium.

Carr traced his yearning for Tinseltown glamour back to 1956, when, as a teenager living in the Illinois suburb Highland Park, he saw producer Mike Todd come to Chicago to roll out his epic Oscar winner, *Around the World in 80 Days*, with the help of his bride-to-be, Elizabeth Taylor. "He named a theater after himself and one after her and gave a party that lasted three days," Carr would recall. "I went to that party and I knew what I wanted to do with my life."

Carr was an only child; his father ran a furniture store, and his mother had a fur and leather boutique. As an overweight gay boy, Carr found an alternative reality in show business, and the Academy Awards were its pinnacle. He could recall being seven years old, listening in the dark to the Twenty-Second Academy Awards on his bedroom radio. "Many stars took part in that show in 1950," he said decades later, as if he could still picture it. "When 'Baby, It's Cold Outside' was nominated for best song, the producer had Red Skelton, Betty Garrett, Ricardo Montalban and Arlene Dahl to sing it—but I was upset that he hadn't gotten Esther Williams, too, because she, not Arlene Dahl, sang it in 'Neptune's Daughter.'" By eleven, he was telling classmates that he wanted to be a Hollywood producer. Back then, he was "Alan Solomon," a name he changed in his teens because he was angry at his parents for getting a divorce and because "Allan Carr" ("rhymes with star") would look better on a marquee.

His flamboyance hid a deep unease. "At home I was secure," he said, "but at school I felt I was not physically attractive and this exaggerated my desire for approval, to be amusing, to be liked. That's why I came on so strong." Showbiz was where he made sense, and his parents were happy to indulge him. Still a teenager, he persuaded them to invest in a touring Tallulah Bankhead revue. At Lake Forest College, he wrote an anonymous gossip column, "Through the Keyhole," and advised the girls of Gamma Phi Beta on how to dress. By the end of college, he weighed over two hundred pounds, but by making himself so over the top, so audacious, he insulated himself from ridicule. The only way to survive was to be the center of attention.

After college, he used more of his parents' money to reopen Chicago's Civic Theatre. For his first season, in 1958, he landed Bette Davis and Gary Merrill, who were touring the country with their stage show, *The World of Carl Sandburg.* Carr went to see it in a tiny town in Wisconsin, then barged into the dressing room, saying, "I don't want to be rude, but why are you playing this auditorium?"

"Good question," Davis rasped.

When the Civic's season failed to turn a profit, Carr found another opportunity. Hugh Hefner was spinning his magazine into a TV show, *Playboy's Penthouse,* and he hired Carr to be the talent coordinator. In Los Angeles, he launched a management firm, Allan Carr Enterprises. His prize client was Ann-Margret, the Swedish-born sex kitten whose career was on a downslide. With her husband, Roger Smith, Carr booked her a

Las Vegas act and a TV special. "I was like a career doctor," he recalled. In 1972, Ann-Margret was nominated for an Oscar for *Carnal Knowledge*, and Carr attended the Academy Awards for the first time. He and Smith had gone into business as Rogallan Productions, turning out a biker flick called *C.C. and Company*. Carr had an eye for a quick buck. On a trip to Mexico, he saw moviegoers lining up to see *Supervivientes de los Andes*, an exploitation thriller about a 1972 Uruguayan plane crash in the Andes that had left the survivors resorting to cannibalism. John Schlesinger, on a roll after *Midnight Cowboy*, had made the mistake of telling Carr he planned to adapt a best-selling book about the disaster. Working fast and dirty, Carr bought the rights to the Mexican film and reopened it in the United States under the title *Survive!* It made him a millionaire.

"I hit California at just the right time," Carr said. "Right after *The Graduate* changed everybody's life. Before that movie, they thought everybody old was brilliant. Afterward, anyone who was young was smart. I rode in on the youth movement." But Carr had little in common with the Dennis Hoppers and Bert Schneiders. "His whole life was based on the studio system model that had gone away and that he was trying to bring back," Vilanch says. "He wanted to be Mike Todd or David Selznick or names that meant something only in Hollywood. There was nobody like that around anymore, and for good reason—because the business had changed. The barracudas had taken over."

Carr's career as a marketing wizard was born while he was persuading music manager Robert Stigwood to cast Ann-Margret in his movie adaptation of the Who's *Tommy* and said, "Columbia doesn't have a clue how to advertise this movie." Carr came up with a plan to rival Mike Todd's *Around the World in 80 Days* bash. On March 18, 1975, he threw an opening night party for six hundred people inside a new subway station at Sixth Avenue and Fifty-Seventh Street. The guests, including Elton John and Tina Turner, wore "black tie or glitter funk" and ate from an underground buffet that included fifty pounds of Bahamian octopus. Months later, Carr topped himself by throwing a party for Truman Capote in the defunct Lincoln Heights Jail in Los Angeles. Guests, including Diana Ross and Lucille Ball, received their invitations by "summons," from actors dressed as policemen. After cruising up to the jailhouse by limo, they were sent to "booking," on the second floor, where a lobster spread awaited.

Thanks to Carr's party-throwing prowess, in 1977 he was put in charge of the Governors Ball after the Academy Awards. He staged an elegant black-and-white affair with a revolving dance floor and Petrossian caviar. The next year, the Academy hired him as "executive consultant" for the fiftieth annual ceremony, a role he happily inflated in the press. "I have more enthusiasm for the Academy Awards than anybody my age," Carr told the *Times*—he placed his age in the nebulous late thirties—detailing his adventures in celebrity wrangling: "Lana Turner wouldn't answer my phone calls. Claudette Colbert was having thirty people for Easter in Barbados. I sent Esther Williams little gifts and roses. She said she was retired, and nothing could coax her back. Kim Novak wanted the Academy to fly designer Jean Louis to her home in northern California twice to fit her dress, and the Academy simply won't do that. Gloria Swanson said since she had never won an Oscar she didn't belong on the show."

Even more indiscreet was Carr's criticism of the previous year's broadcast ("a disaster"), produced by Friedkin. A few days after the ceremony, Carr was getting a massage when he had a revelation: the stars of the Oscar broadcast should be the *presenters*, not the nominees. But even after he was brought back the next year to oversee the afterparty, no one asked him to produce the show. He was, he admitted later, "frankly a little disappointed."

In 1978, Carr pitched himself to Universal's Sid Sheinberg to run the marketing campaign for *The Deer Hunter*. Universal saw the Vietnam War drama as a hard sell, but Carr insisted it could be a box-office hit *and* an Oscar winner. He urged the studio to open the film in New York and Los Angeles at the end of the year, then expand after the nominations. Oscar consulting was still an embryonic profession, but Carr's tactics anticipated what was to come—and they worked. *The Deer Hunter* won five Oscars, including Best Picture. Best Supporting Actor winner Christopher Walken told Carr, of his statuette, "I want you to keep this six months out of the year, because if it weren't for you I wouldn't have it." *The Deer Hunter*, Vilanch recalls, "was considered a turd in the pool, and he turned it around and made it the Academy Award–winning movie of the year, because it satisfied his bent to be involved in something serious—which he could never really make happen, because he wasn't a serious person."

By then, Carr had made his name as a producer, thanks to his adaptation of the Broadway hit *Grease*. He saw in *Grease* a version of his own suburban high school years—only, this time, he could rewrite it to suit his movieland fantasies, with bit parts for aging icons like Eve Arden and Joan Blondell. Splashy movie musicals were hardly in vogue in 1978, but Carr sold *Grease* as an antidote to the New Hollywood. "If you can explain to me *Apocalypse Now* in the last half hour, good luck," he said from a talk show chair. "Let's see movies like we used to see." The film's world-conquering success made Carr feel "like I was the president of my class," he said. He relished his newfound place in the establishment, bragging, "I'm thrilled when Gregory Peck and his wife come to my house for dinner."

The mass-market kitsch of the eighties should have suited Carr, but his own tackiness kept getting in the way. In 1980, he produced *Can't Stop the Music*, an MGM-style spectacular chronicling the rise of the Village People. (The original title, *Discoland*, had to be thrown out after disco was declared dead.) Carr heralded the film's arrival with a circus-themed party at Lincoln Center Plaza, complete with trapeze artists, clowns on stilts, and live elephants. The limo bill alone was $118,000. But the film was a high-camp disaster—so bad that publicist John J. B. Wilson, after seeing it on a double feature with *Xanadu*, invented the Golden Raspberry Awards, and Carr's film won the first-ever "Razzie" for Worst Picture. He continued his losing streak with *Grease 2*, a misbegotten sequel that gave Michelle Pfeiffer her first major film role but had the misfortune of opening on the same weekend as *E.T.*

Carr drowned his disappointment in booze and coke. In 1983, he struck gold again with the Broadway musical *La Cage aux Folles*. To herald his comeback, he threw a "tasteful minor extravaganza" at Pan Am headquarters—the airline was one of the show's sponsors—giving the lobby an around-the-world theme, with an entrance tricked out like Saint-Tropez. *La Cage* was a Tony Award–winning hit, though its box

office suffered as the public learned more about the AIDS crisis, which
sparked a homophobic backlash. The ribald gay culture of the seventies
was over. Carr's attempt to get his footing back in movies, a 1984 remake
of *Where the Boys Are*, came and went. His parties were smaller now—
dinners with old friends like Bea Arthur—and his substance abuse was
worsening. "He was just really horrible with the drinking, and I arranged
an intervention," his assistant Tony Lutz recalls. Carr agreed to go to
rehab, but on his way back, he had his limo pull over for wine and was
drunk by the time he got home.

By 1988, Carr was in his fifties and past his prime. He had snapped
up the rights to a tell-all memoir by Lana Turner's daughter, and he hoped
to turn opera star Plácido Domingo into a crossover sensation with a
bio-musical about Francisco Goya, which Carr told people would be "my
Gandhi." He tried to drum up interest by staging a star-studded concert at the Hollywood Bowl, but the investors didn't come. And he was
having trouble climbing stairs. He scheduled hip-replacement surgery for
mid-October. Then, two days before the operation, he got a call from
Academy president Richard Kahn, asking to talk in person. "Allan was
a showman," recalls Kahn, whose wife still raved about Carr's swanky
Governors Balls. "He had demonstrated in a number of different venues,
not just *La Cage aux Folles* and *Grease*, that he was an imaginative and
creative producer." Poolside at Hilhaven, Kahn asked the question Carr
had been waiting to hear his entire life, or at least since "Baby, It's Cold
Outside": Would he consider producing the Academy Awards?

Carr accepted, telling the Academy president, "I want to bring glamour back to the awards." Inside, he felt like he'd scaled Mount Olympus.
"It was the biggest thing he'd ever done," Alana Stewart says. "He grew
up watching the Oscars and dreaming of coming to Hollywood and being
someone. He was so enthusiastic." His Hollywood dream come true had
arrived at the exact moment he needed it. What could possibly go wrong?

MINUTES BEFORE THE ABC SUITS arrived at Hilhaven, Carr placed Cristal
bottles on ice. "But they're coming here to talk business," Bruce Vilanch
pointed out. "I don't think anyone will want to drink champagne in the
middle of the day."

"It doesn't matter," Carr insisted. "Just make sure the label shows. I want those bastards to know I have class!"

Vilanch had known Carr since he was a journalist at the *Chicago Tribune* and Carr came to town promoting *C.C. and Company* with Ann-Margret. Vilanch began writing for Ann-Margret's Vegas act, and "Allan and I just became really friendly—as friendly as you could become with Allan." A born jokester with shaggy hair, a bulbous nose, and a gay sensibility that matched Carr's in wattage, Vilanch had a knack for writing celebrity patter, a career he'd fallen into during an interview with Bette Midler. "She said, 'You're a very funny writer.' I said, 'Well, you should talk more onstage.' And she said, 'You got any lines?'" Vilanch could make Lily Tomlin sound more like Lily Tomlin, Joan Rivers sound more like Joan Rivers—and he was the perfect match for Carr's star-studded Oscar plans.

When the network brass arrived at Hilhaven, the clash was obvious. On one side of the white poolside tent were executives in business casual. On the other were Carr in a caftan and Vilanch in a T-shirt and jeans. A houseboy came out and, in a move Carr had filched from Joel Schumacher, asked, "What kind of water would you like? Perrier? Pellegrino? Crystal Geyser? Poland Spring?"

Vilanch looked on skeptically as Carr trumpeted his Oscar fanaticism. "I watched every year," he told the executives. "I remember Jo Van Fleet coming down the aisle in a gorgeous dress to get her Oscar."

One of the men said, "What was a guy named Joe doing in a dress?"

Carr's planning had begun the moment he got the gig. "This will be a nice thing to do in my recovery period, when I can't climb the stairs that lead from my house," he told himself. He went into Cedars-Sinai for his hip surgery with a notepad, jotting ideas in his painkiller haze: Would Lana Turner appear alongside Ava Gardner? After two weeks of bed rest, he got to work. He hired Marvin Hamlisch, a client from his managing days, as music director, and Vilanch as head writer. Jeff Margolis, who'd been brought on to direct the broadcast, came to meet Carr at Hilhaven. "Allan told me that this was a dream come true for him," Margolis recalls. "He was going to change the face of the Academy Awards. And he wanted to do something that was very young and hip and Hollywood. He wanted to mix the old and the new." In a move that would prove fateful, Carr also hired a personal publicist, Linda Dozoretz, to make sure the world knew that these were "the Allan Carr Oscars."

Carr also wanted to ramp up the fashion, reasoning, "Women watch the Oscar show to see what the women are wearing." He went straight to Fred Hayman, "the father of Rodeo Drive," where Hayman had opened his boutique, Giorgio Beverly Hills, in 1961. Carr knew it well—he liked to try on the women's caftans—and asked Hayman to be the Oscars' first "fashion consultant." Edith Head had helped out in the old days, but Carr envisioned something grander. "The fashions have gotten boring," he said. (Or, as Hayman put it, "Edith is dead, and it shows.") Red-carpet coverage had consisted of two-minute clips, but Carr thought it could be at least five or ten minutes, so that viewers had more time to salivate over the gowns. "The designers weren't eager to loan," Hayman said later. "This was before all the top designers fought to get an actress to wear their fashions at the Oscars. There's been a whole evolution, and it began with Allan Carr."

Not everyone was bullish about Carr's plans. In December, *Los Angeles Magazine* reported that Carr "has some of the Academy's conservatives edgy about what the flamboyant producer may come up with." There was that word again, and its obvious subtext. Claiming an "Oscar rash," Carr escaped to Fiji for Christmas, where he puzzled over his list of potential presenters like Fermat's Last Theorem.

At his meeting with the ABC executives, Carr spelled out his master plan for pairing the presenters, which he called the "four Cs": compadres, costars, couples, and companions. His dream roster included Warren Beatty with Shirley MacLaine, Robert Mitchum with Deborah Kerr, Debbie Reynolds with Carrie Fisher, and Mia Farrow with Robert Redford. The show would coast on chemistry. Plus, he told them, "We don't need a host." Instead, he laid out his "baton theory," in which each couple would introduce the next. His production designer, Ray Klausen, had mentioned that the phrase "And the winner is . . ." made everyone else feel like a loser, so Carr decided to change it to "And the Oscar goes to . . . ," which would help soften the blow while acting as subliminal branding.

Carr also wanted to do away with the Best Original Song performances. There were only three nominated that year, but Carr thought
they were all "turds," with the exception of Carly Simon's "Let the River
Run," from *Working Girl*—and Simon wouldn't sing it herself. Instead,
he told the executives, he would have two production numbers. One
would be a showcase of Hollywood's up-and-coming stars—the Brat Pack
types—which would help appeal to the eighteen-to-thirty-four demographic. The other would be the opening number, for which he had big,
big plans.

Carr was a longtime fan of *Beach Blanket Babylon*, a zany San
Francisco musical revue that had been in existence since 1974, when
director Steve Silver staged it as an outdoor happening that spoofed
old Annette Funicello beach movies, with costumes from Rent-a-Freak.
The show moved into a club and became a local institution, beloved
for its Hollywood send-ups and its homespun sight gags—especially
the sky-high headdresses in the shape of Buckingham Palace or the
San Francisco cityscape (with working trolleys). By 1988, the revue had
expanded to Las Vegas, with custom headgear displaying a miniature
Caesars Palace.

Naturally, the show's camp extravagance tickled Carr, who was
partial to an edition called *Beach Blanket Babylon Goes to the Stars*,
featuring Snow White searching for her Prince Charming. Beneath
its wackiness was a reverence for Hollywood lore—what better match
for the Oscars? Carr envisioned a new version for his opening number,
with re-creations of Hollywood landmarks like the Cocoanut Grove
and Grauman's Chinese Theatre. "It exploded full-born from his head
like Zeus," Vilanch says. "The headdresses struck me as being in perfect
Oscars bad taste. I didn't try to talk him out of it. I just sort of said,
'That's a signature San Francisco thing.' And he said, 'Oh, but it's so
different and new and hip!'"

When Carr contacted Silver, the director was so excited that he
turned down an offer to perform at one of George H. W. Bush's inaugural
balls. But when it came time to pitch the idea to the ABC brass, they
were dumbfounded.

"We listened to it, and it was very complicated and quite long," recalls

John Hamlin, the vice president for special programs. He was more worried about the show finishing on time. "At the end, I said, 'Please don't go over three hours and twenty minutes.'"

The chatter at the salon L'Ermitage died down the moment Carr swept in—usually, you could hear him before you saw him, from the clattering of his post-surgery cane. It was a Monday night in Beverly Hills, and fifteen or so people had gathered to prepare for a Wednesday-night fashion show for the press.

"The first thing people will see is Cyd with me," Carr announced, referring to veteran MGM dancer Cyd Charisse. He added, "I'll bring my good gold cane, my Susan Hayward cane."

The dapper Fred Hayman doled out fashion wisdom to a reporter. "The eye tells you immediately if a star is secure enough to dress herself properly," he said. "People like Geena Davis and Anne Spielberg know what to wear. But sometimes insecurity masks itself as security." Whether this rule applied to the man with a hundred caftans and a gold cane he did not say. Carr wandered past some models and looked at the faux Modiglianis hanging nearby. "Do these come off the wall?" he asked. "Or are they screwed on the wall? It would be nice if we could replace them with Academy-winning posters."

"It's called Only in Hollywood," one of the models snarked to another. "Posters are more important than art."

Two days later, Carr returned to the salon, announced by his gold cane. "You took care of Angie today, so she's happy?" he asked his assistant Tony Lutz, who'd been assigned to escort Angie Dickinson to the technical awards when Carr decided that he was "sick."

"Should we use your Cadillac to pick up Angie or Cyd Charisse?" Lutz inquired.

"Use the Cadillac for Angie."

As the ladies primped, production designer Ray Klausen fed the press tidbits about the big night, which would feature a forty-six-piece orchestra and a thirty-foot-high curtain: "I've designed it with more than fifty thousand beads and sequins, to be hand-applied. There are the million tulips from Holland, six million stems altogether."

"Don't tell too much," Carr intervened. "Let's say there will be eleven sets and 106 stagehands."

"It's like an obsession," Klausen added. "Everything is overstated and very glamorous." The street outside the Shrine would be covered in red carpet, and, according to one Academy press release, the draperies alone would be enough to cover one side of the Empire State Building. As Klausen went on about the sparkling drapes, one of the models dead-panned, "It sounds like planning an invasion."

It was. Most days, Carr worked the phones from his bedroom at Hilhaven, massaging egos and coaxing stars. Loretta Young sent word that she would only present solo, because "I stand on my own two feet." Susan Sarandon was too pregnant to fly from New York, so Carr slotted in Michelle Pfeiffer. Doris Day required a ride from Carmel and some-one to take care of her dog. ("Then get her a fucking dog sitter!" Carr barked.) Brigitte Bardot would appear only if she could talk about animal rights. ("We're on her side," Carr said. "And I promise there are no furs on the show. But also no speeches.") Warren Beatty couldn't present with his sister, Shirley MacLaine, because he was shooting *Dick Tracy*. Ava Gardner wanted the public to remember her as she was. Ditto Lana Turner. And so on.

Carr knew how to play this game. "I was afraid I'd either be desperate for stars, or driven crazy by them," he said. "But, nope. People want to be in the business again." When a name came in—or didn't, or almost did—he would alert the press, creating a drip, drip, drip of anticipation. Both *Variety* and *The Hollywood Reporter* began relaying each morsel un-der the new banner "Oscar Watch." When Lana Turner wouldn't budge, Carr took to the gossip pages, saying, "For some reason, Lana doesn't want to take part in the program. I don't know what her problem is, but I'm working on it." Mostly, he puffed himself up, telling one reporter, "I'm going to shock people with glamour and humor."

The relentless buildup was more than the Academy could keep up with. "Generally, there would be a release from the Academy and the net-work announcing so-and-so was going to be on the show," says Vilanch. "But Allan would tell Liz Smith that somebody was going to be on, and she would break it exclusively, and the Academy hated that, because it got them in bad trouble with other columnists. This was Allan playing one against the other and giving everybody an exclusive. The Academy didn't know how to play that game. They had done it their way all of these years."

The results—besides Carr's name constantly in the press—were bruised egos. He had wanted to pair Gregory Peck with Sophia Loren, but Loren couldn't be lured from Florida, so Peck's invitation never went out. Word of Peck's annoyance got back to Carr, who brushed it off. The American Film Institute's tribute to Peck had just aired, he reasoned, and Peck was overexposed. Same with Elizabeth Taylor, a perennial Oscar presenter, who was the subject of an ABC tribute the week before the ceremony. When Carr's own *Grease* star John Travolta hedged on presenting a musical montage, Carr nabbed Patrick Swayze. "Ungrateful!" he would gripe of any intractable star, showing his snappish side. "If you disagreed with him, you were betraying him," Vilanch says. "He had to push you away."

The ceremony would once again be at the Shrine, the Moorish Revival behemoth that had opened in 1926 and seen better days. When Carr surveyed it, he was appalled. "I'm not doing the show here unless they redo all the bathrooms," he announced. "I want the bathrooms redone, and I want all the hallways and the lobby painted." Vilanch worked out of a dingy office building on La Cienega Boulevard, next to a hotel. "You could hear people having sex, and there was a homeless encampment behind the hotel," he recalls. Carr would limp through at least once a day with news of which stars were in or out of the lineup, leaving Vilanch with his own set of negotiations. "I had to deal with everybody: their publicists, their agents, their holistic pet psychiatrists. *Everybody.* One person's trainer would come in: 'Oh, I saw the script, and I don't think she's going to say this.'"

Down the hall, Marvin Hamlisch worked on the "young Hollywood" number, a ditty called "I Want to Be an Oscar Winner," which he wrote with Broadway lyricist Fred Ebb. Carr corralled nineteen "stars of tomorrow," among them teen tap phenom Savion Glover, matinee idol Patrick Dempsey, and brassy *Hairspray* star Ricki Lake. "When he ran out of people who were talented enough and famous enough," Vilanch recalls, "he began casting people who were just known because they were young Hollywood, *literally*," including Carrie Hamilton (daughter of Carol Burnett), Patrick O'Neal (son of Ryan), and Tyrone Power Jr. As the *Los Angeles Herald-Examiner* put it, "Hooray for Nepotism!"

Carr hired *Dirty Dancing* choreographer Kenny Ortega, who asked each of the participants to show off some special skill. Corey Feldman had a Michael Jackson impression. Christian Slater wanted to swing in on a rope. Patrick Dempsey could swashbuckle. Ricki Lake could belt. Chad Lowe, younger brother of Rob, couldn't sing or dance, so he played a pretentious thespian. ("I am a serious actor! I was on *Dynasty!*") "Instinctively, it just felt like something I shouldn't be doing," Lowe says. But he convinced himself it was a good idea. "I mean, you had Allan Carr and Kenny Ortega and the Academy. How do you say no to that?"

They rehearsed for weeks. "It was very loose and somewhat haphazard," Lowe recalls. They improvised dialogue, spending their breaks schmoozing. "We immediately would form little cliques," says Keith Coogan, a teen actor who just happened to be the grandson of silent film star Jackie Coogan. The prom king was Dempsey, who revealed himself to have golden feet. "He was like Fred Astaire," Ricki Lake recalls. "I was completely in love with him." Blair Underwood, who'd been roped into the number by his friend Holly Robinson, says, "I was very new to the business and to this town, and to be in that room and considered an up-and-coming talent was really overwhelming."

Every so often, Coogan recalls, "Allan Carr would breeze in, say hi to everybody, like he was on his way to go meet with somebody else." Carr expounded in the press, "This generation sees Oscar in a different way. They have this burning desire for it, but it's unspoken." It was a misreading of Generation X, whose reputation was for jaded cool. Instead of tap-dancing for Oscar glory, the number should have had them rolling their eyes and smoking cigarettes. Carr was the one with the burning desire, which he practically shouted from the rooftops.

A WEEK BEFORE THE CEREMONY, ninety-three of the 1989 Oscar contenders gathered at the Conrad International Ballroom for the nominees' luncheon. There was Kevin Kline, from *A Fish Called Wanda*; Sigourney

Weaver, double-nominated for *Working Girl* and *Gorillas in the Mist*. River Phoenix, the eighteen-year-old star of *Running on Empty*, was unsmiling as he cleared his long hair from his eyes and fielded inane questions from reporters.

The most nominated film was *Rain Man*, starring Dustin Hoffman as an autistic savant and Tom Cruise as his slick brother. Barry Levinson's film may have resembled the small, relationship-driven dramas of the New Hollywood, but it in fact represented something different: the rise of the superagent. The movie had come to Creative Artists Agency in 1986 and landed on the desk of its Wizard of Oz–like founder, Michael Ovitz. By the eighties, superagents had edged in on the power once held by studio heads like Mayer and Warner, and Ovitz was a make-them-fear-you bogeyman who brokered megadeals and minted stars. (Steven Seagal had been his martial arts instructor.) He also bolstered the rise of packaging, in which an agency lassoes several of its clients into a single project. "CAA's goal," as Ovitz put it, "was to have all the clients, and therefore all the conflicts; we used to say, 'No conflict, no interest.'"

Ovitz was the driving force behind *Rain Man*. "The script had no sex, no car chases, and no third act," he reasoned, "but I was convinced that if we could keep the budget to $25 million, we could earn back $50 million from date-nighters and grown-ups." In a packaging meeting, two of his agents suggested Cruise, who had just been in *The Color of Money* and was bankable, even though, at twenty-four, he was half Hoffman's age. Word around town, Ovitz admitted, "was that the project was CAA packaging run amok." *Rain Man* made more than $350 million internationally, with lucrative back-end profits for director Barry Levinson and the two stars. The Cruise character, with his Armani suits and imported Lamborghinis, epitomized the ascendant Hollywood yuppie—not to mention the new brand of wheeler-dealers like Ovitz. The impish New Hollywood of *One Flew Over the Cuckoo's Nest* was long gone; instead of subverting the psychiatric ward like Jack Nicholson's McMurphy, Hoffman's character counts cards in Vegas and helps his brother win $86,000. The brothers' tense yet symbiotic relationship was not unlike the dynamic between Hollywood power brokers and directors: as long as the artistic "crazies" kept the money train moving, they tolerated one another.

It was a corporate milieu in which a gaudy throwback like Allan Carr had diminished stature. At the nominees' luncheon, he was still hyping the ceremony: "It will be shorter than *Lawrence of Arabia* but longer than *Who Framed Roger Rabbit*." Some of his friends worried about his press blitz. Talk show host Nikki Haskell remembers getting calls from Warren Cowan, of the PR firm Rogers and Cowan, "asking me to please see what I could do to calm Allan down. The papers were beginning to turn against him because he was making it too much about himself." Vilanch worried about Carr's badmouthing of his predecessors. "He was giving these interviews saying, 'Sam Goldwyn Jr. didn't know what he was doing.' I said, 'You have to stop saying that, because they're going to come gunning for you if it isn't perfect.'"

Some of Carr's press tactics bordered on cruel. When *People's Court* judge Joseph Wapner, who had a cameo in *Rain Man*, asked for Oscar tickets, Carr planted a story with the *Los Angeles Times* claiming that Wapner had tried to get himself a spot as a presenter. "I don't think he's a member of the Screen Actors Guild," Carr snickered. "He called on my car phone to plant the story," recalls Carr's assistant Robert Newman. "Allan made stuff up."

Carr seemed to be aware of his inflating ego. "For three weeks you are the most powerful person in the town," he said of his spot in the producer's chair. "But don't worry. I'm not turning into Little Caesar." Two days before the ceremony, he told the press, "Right now I think the show is a triple. But with a little luck, by the time it goes on it'll be a home run." Carr had leaked a heady roster of celebrities. But one was still top secret, and he promised that she was the biggest star of them all.

THE MORNING OF HER AUDITION, Eileen Bowman drove up from San Diego with her fiancé. Bowman was twenty-two, a good girl who didn't drink or swear. She had never worked outside San Diego and had, as her sister put it, "no more sense of business or money than a gerbil." With her fair skin and dark brown hair, Bowman had, as far back as St. Martin's Catholic grade school, been called "Snow White."

She hated the nickname and then grew to love it. As a teenager, she collected Snow White memorabilia and played the character at the San

Diego Junior Theatre. She was performing show tunes at a restaurant in San Diego and singing with a Youth for Christ choir when the opportunity came to audition for Snow White in the Vegas rendition of *Beach Blanket Babylon*. Or, at least, that's what she *thought* it was for.

Bowman was told to be at the Beverly Hills Hotel by 8 a.m. While her fiancé waited by the bar, she was led into the ballroom and handed fifteen pages of sheet music. She quickly learned the score—songs like "The Way We Were" and "Proud Mary," with jokey new lyrics—then was brought up to a room with a hair-and-makeup artist and two identical Snow White costumes on the bed. "We want to see if you fit into the dress," Steve Silver, the *Beach Blanket Babylon* director, told her.

"At that point, I just stopped asking questions," Bowman says. "I thought, *These are big people. I need to be grateful for whatever this is*." They asked her to get in a Mercedes and close her eyes. On her way out, she passed her fiancé. "I don't know what's going on!" she said.

"Well, I'm not going to let you get in a car with someone you don't know."

"I think I'm okay," she reassured him. "If I'm not back by four, call the police. Just look for Snow White!" Was she kidding? Sort of. But she was anxious—she had to get back to San Diego for her sister's wedding the next day, and who knew how long this was going to take?

She got in the Mercedes with another girl dressed as Snow White. Silver didn't say much. "It was 'This is all top-secret. Close your eyes, because you're going to someone's house, and you can't know how to get there.'" She and the other girl shared a "What the hell is happening?" look—but obeyed.

When she opened her eyes, they were at Hilhaven Lodge. Each Snow White went in one at a time. Bowman looked in awe at the giant Oscar by the front door and the pink water in the swimming pool. "It was beautiful, but I thought, *Oh, boy, we're in Hollywood*," she said. She was taken inside, where she stared at the Lucite piano. Then Allan Carr came in the room. "He was wearing a kimono robe," Bowman says, "and it was uncomfortable, because he wasn't crossing his legs. I thought, *Where do I look? Over here? Over there?*"

The audition was quick. Bowman heard Carr make a flippant

comment about her that she didn't think she should have heard and would not repeat. Back in the car, Silver said, "Okay, one more stop." They drove to Marvin Hamlisch's office, and the Snow Whites walked through a building "like those tin soldiers with the little round cheeks. We looked like demented Snow Whites—like the sisters in *The Shining*." Even weirder was the fact that Silver insisted that they walk everywhere hand in hand. "*Insisted*," Bowman says. "He got the biggest thrill out of all this. And so we went and sang for Marvin Hamlisch, again, one by one, and then we got back in the car, and he said, 'Okay.' I'm like, *Oh, now what, we're going to go see Charo?*"

Silver told them, "I want you guys just to walk down Rodeo Drive hand in hand."

"Now, *wait a minute*," Bowman objected. It was now early evening. "I need to know what's going on here. I need to get home."

"Listen," Silver quieted her. "This is going to change your life if you get this. I can't tell you what it is, but I would probably stop asking questions." Back at the hotel, Silver split the Snow Whites into separate elevators and went with Bowman. "You should be very grateful, and we are thinking about using you," he said as they rode up.

"Yes, thank you," the baffled actress said.

Then he asked, "How are you with famous people?"

"Well, they're just like anybody else."

That was the right answer. After a thirteen-hour day, she was told she got the job. "Do you know what this is for?" Silver asked.

"*Beach Blanket Babylon?*"

"No, honey. This is for the Oscars."

Bowman assumed she was going to be escorting the winners offstage in a gown. In fact, she had been hired as the star of the opening number. The more she learned, the less sense it made. The broadcast would start with *Variety*'s Army Archerd showing Snow White into the Shrine. Then Merv Griffin would sing "I've Got a Lovely Bunch of Coconuts" at a replica of the Cocoanut Grove, which would be full of the aging legends who used to go there. Then she'd sing "Proud Mary" with Prince Charming, and that would lead into a kick line with the dancers playing the ushers from Grauman's Chinese. At the end, the theater would turn into a hat, and a movie star—maybe Bette Midler?—would jump out. "It was a lot to put on an unknown girl who just fell off of a turnip truck," Bowman says. It was her first AFTRA job, and she'd get $350 a week.

Rehearsals, on the Fox lot, lasted a week and a half. "They were closed, meaning *nobody* could get in," Bowman says. "Allan Carr watched that door like a mother hen. He was like, 'Out! No!' Because it was all top secret. They wanted it to be a big surprise, the whole number." The production team scrambled to keep up. "I mean, the phone calls go all night and all day," costume designer Pete Menefee complained to a camera crew. "'The gorillas are in, the gorillas are out.' I'd never even *heard* about the gorillas when they were in."

Every other day, Carr would call for attention and tell the dancers that they were canceling the number—"Thank you so much for your work"—as a prank. Bowman says, "It was the cat playing with the mouse: 'Let's see how much we can play with these toys.' 'Toys' meaning people and their feelings." Sometimes Carr would come through with celebrity offspring like Lucie Arnaz or Judy Garland's daughter Lorna Luft, warning Bowman that they had wanted her part. "With the publicity and career you're going to have after this, you should be paying *us*," he told her.

In fact, Luft, who had starred in Carr's *Grease 2* and *Where the Boys Are '84*, had been summoned to Hilhaven over the winter, for what she hoped was another movie role. Instead, Carr told her, "As you probably know, I'm producing the Oscar telecast. It's a dream come true for me. And I'd like you to be a part of it." But when he explained that she would be dressed as Snow White, Luft was baffled. The next day, Carr called her for an answer, and she told him, "I'm sorry, Allan, I can't do that." Carr turned from Jekyll to Hyde, screaming, "I made you!" and hurling swears, until Luft hung up the phone in tears.

Of course, Bowman knew none of this. On the second day of rehearsal, Carr told her, "I wanted Tom Cruise, but he shaved his head for some movie he's doing"—*Born on the Fourth of July*—"and I don't like it, so we're getting you another prince." Instead, he got Rob Lowe. The twenty-five-year-old heartthrob was a member of what the media had pejoratively labeled the "Brat Pack," along with his *St. Elmo's Fire* costars Emilio Estevez, Demi Moore, and Andrew McCarthy. He was coming off a string of box-office duds when the Oscars called. "Without hesitation, I said yes," Lowe recalled later. "Mistakenly, I take this as an honor, if not a duty. After all, I'm from Ohio; if someone asks you nicely, you do it. Particularly if it's the Academy of Motion Picture Arts and Sciences!"

Bowman didn't know who her Prince Charming was until the day Lowe strolled onto the lot with an entourage. She was starstruck—but a little concerned when Lowe warbled his song. "I don't know what he's telling you to do," she told Lowe, nodding at his vocal coach, "but that's not singing." Lowe had no musical experience, and he was petrified. "How do you guys *do* this?" he asked the ensemble.

As the number came together, everything seemed to get bigger—including the Chinese Theatre headdress, which got so huge and unwieldy that it could no longer be balanced on Snow White's head. It was an apt metaphor for the whole number, which had ballooned to the length of a sitcom episode. Marvin Hamlisch was unsure about the tone, warning Carr, "We need to let the audience know that this is a spoof. Otherwise, I'm not sure how they'll react." Even Steve Silver, the *Beach Blanket* creator, was worried. "At one point, which was very, very painful, Steve said to Allan, 'This number is too long. It will not work,'" his widow, Jo Schuman Silver, recalls. "And Allan said, 'Maybe you better not come to rehearsals anymore.'"

Heading into what Carr called "White Knuckle Week," opinion was split. "People were saying, 'If this works, it's going to be the most incredible number that's ever been on television. And if it doesn't work, boy, are we fucked,'" director Jeff Margolis recalls. They cut a tap interlude pairing the veteran vaudeville act the Nicholas Brothers and thirteen-year-old *Beaches* star Mayim Bialik, who had shown up day after day in her tap shoes. "I was devastated," Bialik says, "because I was mercilessly teased in junior high for being a weirdo, and I was very proud that I actually was doing something legitimate in my acting career." The Nicholas Brothers had been the only Black entertainers in the number, and, despite looking frail, they could still do their splits and jumps. "That would have brought the house down," Vilanch laments. "I told Allan I thought [cutting them] was a mistake. I said, 'The audience will go wild.' He didn't see it that way."

At rehearsal, it became clear that the "dinosaurs" featured in the Cocoanut Grove segment weren't all in great shape. Some couldn't walk unassisted, so Carr and company dropped the idea of a grand procession and instead placed them at tables from which they could simply wave. Thirties starlet Alice Faye griped that she had been reduced to "a dress extra." Others dropped out, including Doris Day, who sent word that she had tripped over a sprinkler in Carmel and had a swollen ankle.

Bette Midler hadn't come through, either, so Lily Tomlin was tapped to emerge from the headdress and give a quick "Welcome, we'll be right back." Watching the dress rehearsal, Tomlin turned to Vilanch and said they'd need something self-deprecating to undercut the excess. They decided that she'd lose a shoe on the staircase and crack, "Well, I told them I'd be thrilled to do the Oscars if they could just come up with an entrance." At the final dress rehearsal, Bowman wore her street clothes, and Snow White was given a code name in the script. Margolis recalls, "Nobody knew who it was going to be except us guys, who had to sign a nondisclosure agreement."

Hours before showtime, Bowman recalls, Rob Lowe paid an unexpected visit to her dressing room. "Hey," he said, "my manager loves the chemistry that we have together, and he's going to come up to you and want to sign you." Bowman looked hopeful, until Lowe added, "Don't do it, because I'm leaving him."

He leaned in. "If I were you, I would get out of this town tonight," he warned. "Because there's blood in the water, and the sharks are circling. There are people who are going to take advantage of you, and I don't want to see that happen."

Bowman was astonished. They both knew that they were in for something bizarre. "Never trust a man in a caftan," Lowe told her.

ON MARCH 29, 1989, THE scent of a million Dutch tulips was enough to cover up the stench of rush-hour exhaust fumes enveloping the Shrine. Traffic had been a notorious problem on Oscar night, but Carr had thought of everything, meeting with limo drivers with a map of the desired routes. The plan worked so well that the first celebrity to hit the street-long red carpet, Sylvester Stallone, got there a half hour early.

Soon, Carr's roster of celebrity couples appeared: Bruce Willis and Demi Moore, Kevin Kline and Phoebe Cates, Don Johnson and Melanie Griffith. River Phoenix and his date, Martha Plimpton, the eighteen-year-old product of Keith Carradine and Shelley Plimpton's "I'm Easy" romance, looked like jaded Gen X royalty. Cybill Shepherd flexed her biceps for the cameras, while Cher arrived in a marginally toned-down Bob Mackie strapless mini. Among the carpet walkers was Donna Rice, best known for her scandalous appearance in 1987 with presidential candidate Gary Hart on a yacht called *Monkey Business*. Carr had instituted a dress code even for the press, and one photographer was banned until he found a bow tie. On Jefferson Boulevard, a group of San Francisco drag queens, calling themselves the Sisters of Perpetual Indignity, stood in Mae West wigs and gowns, saying that they had come "to show our support for Allan Carr" for producing the first "gay Oscars."

Carr wore a black sequined dinner jacket, taking in the hoopla he had summoned like a sultan. Outside the Shrine, he turned to Academy president Richard Kahn and told him with heartfelt sincerity, "Thank you for making my dream come true."

As the Shrine's 6,300 seats filled up, an announcer promised over the speaker system, "The star of all time will be here soon." Some wondered whether Garbo herself had been coaxed into service.

Bowman, in her Snow White dress, hid in a broom closet with a guard keeping watch, like a fairy-tale princess trapped in a tower. Her helmet-like wig was topped by a twinkling red bow. Her costume, which she hadn't ever rehearsed in, was the weight of a small child. "You know, I'm really scared right now," she said to the guard. "I could just go right out this door and run down Jefferson Boulevard!"

"You could," the man said kindly. "But you're not going to."

"Yes, sir. I'm going to sit right here."

At showtime, she was led to the theater entrance, where Army Archerd stood with a microphone and announced, "And now, ladies and gentlemen, here's one of the great legends of Hollywood. She's back with us tonight: Miss Snow White!" Bowman greeted him in a voice that squeaked like a rubber duckie: "Can you tell me how to get into the theater?"

"Just follow the Hollywood stars!"

Snow White cooed as chorines in gold star outfits breezed by, leading her inside. Bowman sauntered up the aisle, giggling and shaking hands with unsuspecting audience members. In rehearsal, she had practiced with placards of spectators' faces. Now that they were real, the job was trickier. She tried going for Melanie Griffith, but found a seat filler in her place. "I was told by the director, 'Do not go to Robin Williams, because he'll start to get involved,'" she recalls. "So, I thought, *Okay, no Robin Williams, no Robin Williams, no Robin Williams.* I was supposed to go to Kevin Kline, but the back of their heads kind of looked the same, and it was dark, so what do I do? Go to Robin Williams. I went in my head: *Abort! Abort! Abort!*" Martin Landau later recalled Bowman's look of panic: "I empathized with her. Poor Snow White. She didn't have the dwarves to support her."

The spectators were just as unnerved as the rogue princess descended on them in the dark. "The minute that it started, everybody sucked in their breath and felt something awful was going to take place," recalls Peter Bart, then the editor in chief of *Variety.* Tom Hanks looked baffled as Snow White grabbed his hand while singing a corny Oscar rewrite of "I Only Have Eyes for You." Sigourney Weaver buried her hand in her lap, so Bowman passed her over for Dustin Hoffman, who flashed a get-the-hell-away-from-me grin. Michelle Pfeiffer was "so embarrassed, she couldn't even give me her hand," Bowman said afterward. "Then she started to laugh and giggle, and that made me feel better." Jeff Margolis, directing the cameras from a remote truck, recalls, "It was like shooting a football game, because I kind of didn't know who Snow White was going to go to in the audience. I heard the network people go, 'Holy shit, she got Meryl Streep!'"

Bruce Davis, who would soon become the Academy's executive director, had another concern: intellectual property. "I actually got bumped by the actress dressed as Snow White," he recalls. "And I'm thinking, *Oh, Christ, have we cleared Snow White?*"

Finally, Bowman reached the stage, where the curtain of fifty thousand beads parted to reveal the Cocoanut Grove set. Performers in coconut cocktail headdresses flounced behind Merv Griffin, who introduced the living legends from their seats, including Roy Rogers and Dale Evans in fringed cowboy garb. But the effect was less than glamorous. "It looked like a condo party in Boca Raton," Vilanch says. Things got worse when Griffin told Snow White, "Meet your blind date, Rob Lowe!" Lowe looked into Bowman's eyes and saw what he called "that thousand-yard stare common to all performers who are going into the tank." He tried to steady her nerves as they sang "Proud Mary," which veered into the surreal when the cocktail tables behind them stood up and boogied.

Lowe recalled losing all hope when he spied Barry Levinson in the audience. "His mouth is agape. He almost looks ashen. He turns to his date, his face a mask of shock and disgust. Even in the middle of singing a duet I can very clearly read his lips as he says, 'What the fuck is *this?*'" Even *Beach Blanket Babylon* creator Steve Silver was appalled. In the audience, his wife leaned over and whispered, "Oh, my God! Steve, you have a big hit!" Silver responded, "It's a piece of shit." When it was all over, the number had lasted eleven interminable minutes.

Carr spent the ceremony watching from different angles: from the audience, from the wings, from the greenroom he had spruced up and christened "Club Oscar," a glam version of his basement disco. He had gotten Waverly fabrics to sponsor the room, so the Academy wouldn't have to foot the bill, and became so obsessed over the furniture that some staffers wondered if he was more focused on the greenroom than the show. As Carr watched the ceremony move along, the stink bomb of the opening number hung in the air. "It just wasn't classy enough," Marvin Hamlisch recalled. "And the rest of the evening was putting a Band-Aid on something that was hemorrhaging." But Carr thought it was all marvelous. "He'd come over to me wherever I was, saying, 'That worked, that was fine, they liked that,'" Vilanch recalls.

The ceremony did have its moments, particularly the celebrity pairings that Carr had curated. Jacqueline Bisset and Candice Bergen—now forty-two and coming off her first season as Murphy Brown—delivered the foreign-language award in French, with Bergen reminding her husband Louis Malle, "Don't forget to walk the dog." Carrie Fisher and Martin Short came out in identical dresses and heels. (Short: "All right, I'll change. But the shoes stay!") Demi Moore and Bruce Willis showed home movies of their baby daughter, Rumer; when Willis slipped up and said, "And the winner is . . . ," Moore corrected him with the Carr-mandated "And the Oscar goes to . . ." And Billy Crystal killed with his Edward G. Robinson and Yul Brynner impressions. But the undercurrent of the evening may have been summed up by Jeff Goldblum, wading through scripted banter with his wife Geena Davis, as they presented the documentary awards: "Have we lost our sense of dignity?"

Carr watched the "young Hollywood" number from the back of the house. At nine minutes, it was also bloated, but most of the kids considered themselves lucky. "We flew under the radar because of my brother's performance that night," Chad Lowe says. The number was introduced by Bob Hope and Lucille Ball, in Ball's last major appearance before her death. (People later joked that Allan Carr killed her off.) Backstage at "Club Oscar," Ricki Lake got to meet Tom Cruise, while Ball held court in the corner. "Young, man," she said to Rob Lowe, "I had no idea you were such a good singer. Please come sit with me." Then she sent him for some aspirin, rasping, "My goddamned head is killing me, sweetheart."

It was, more than anything happening onstage, an Allan Carr party for the ages, with the golden age mingling with the new guard. As far as the producer was concerned, everything was going great. When his publicist, Linda Dozoretz, walked him to the pressroom, he assumed more adulation awaited. Instead, *USA Today*'s Jeannie Williams asked skeptically, "Don't you think the Snow White opening was a bit . . . over the top?"

"Are you kidding?" Carr beamed, digging his fingers into Dozoretz's arm. "Did you hear the ovations out there? It was magical."

Williams pressed, "But Allan, why Snow White? What's the connection between her and, well, the whole Cocoanut Grove theme of the show?"

"It's called theatrical!" Carr retorted, his smile increasingly forced. It was his first indication that the opening number had been received less than glowingly.

"So, Allan, tell us," Williams continued. "Would you do it all again?"

"Ask me tomorrow," he joked. Then he muttered to Dozoretz, "Get me out of here."

Sweat was pouring through his jacket, but the extent of the fiasco hadn't dawned on him. After Cher presented Best Picture to *Rain Man*, Carr zipped to the Governors Ball. The Shrine's cavernous Expo Hall was festooned with red and white chiffon, with three jumbo Oscars towering over a twenty-piece orchestra on a revolving pedestal. Richard Kahn accepted compliments on a great show. The Academy president had been in the men's room during the opening number, taking a final piss before his speech. In what he should have seen as an omen, he saw a penny on the floor in a puddle of toilet water, kicked it into a dry spot, and picked it up for good luck. By the time he got to the ball, the opening number was three hours in the past, and most attendees had forgotten about it. Margolis, who arrived just in time to be toasted along with his collaborators, says, "I remember being up on the stage with Allan and Dick Kahn, and Allan was just six inches off the ground in all his glory. Everybody was buzzing. 'Oh, my God, *finally* they did something different.'"

After the ball, Carr and Vilanch rode to Swifty Lazar's party at Spago, where more royalty awaited: Jack and Anjelica, Jane Fonda, Plácido Domingo. Carr, on his third bottle of champagne, seemed aware that his weeks of maneuvering had poked at some Hollywood egos. Looking out the car window during a momentary quiet, he told Vilanch, "I burned a lot of bridges on this one."

EARLY THE NEXT MORNING, JEFF Margolis got a call from Carr. He sounded shaken. "Oh, my God, have you gotten any phone calls? Have you heard anything yet?"

"No," Margolis said. "What's the matter?"

The matter, for one thing, was the reviews. The *Sacramento Bee* called the show a "flatulent gas bag." The Associated Press: "a flaming wreck." Perhaps the harshest pan came from the *New York Times's* Janet Maslin, who wrote that the opening number "deserves a permanent place in the annals of Oscar embarrassments" and advised Lowe to "confine all future musical activities to the shower." Like other critics, she singled out the man who had put his stamp all over the ceremony: "The contributions of Allan Carr, who produced the show for the first time, involved camping up the musical numbers and cleansing the format of most of its fun." The young Hollywood number "inspired no confidence in Hollywood's future." The celebrity pairs "were made to sound like near-strangers as they traded cozy remarks." But she did have a word of praise for Billy Crystal, who "left the distinct impression that he should have been the evening's host."

Carr had expected to spend the morning basking in congratulatory telegrams by the pool, maybe even to get a call from the Academy asking him to return the next year. But no one called. "His balloon had been deflated," Margolis says. Carr took to his bedroom and stayed there.

At around 9:15 a.m., Richard Kahn was delighting in the numbers: the ceremony had been watched in 26.9 million American homes, the Oscars' biggest ratings in five years. But any pride was punctured by a call from Frank Wells, the president of Disney, who told him, "Dick, we got a problem."

The problem was the use of Snow White, which apparently had not been cleared with the studio. Had the number been universally praised, that would have been one thing. Instead, Disney's most famous princess had been dragged into a campy train wreck. Kahn had barely hung up the phone when a messenger arrived with an aggrieved telegram from Gregory Peck. Wells called him. "The show reminded me of those Photoplay Awards!" Peck grumbled, recalling the chintzy medallions delivered by the erstwhile fan magazine. At seventy-two, Peck still saw himself as the Academy's moral center, and the broadcast had threatened the institutional dignity he felt duty-bound to protect.

Rousing himself, Carr decided to keep his lunch plans at Morton's, where he might soak in some reassuring praise. "He walked into Morton's for lunch expecting a standing ovation, and instead people wouldn't even talk to him," says his friend Gary Pudney, who tried to cheer him up by touting the telecast's good ratings. The rest of the diners treated him like the bubonic plague. "Allan was having lunch right up at the front," recalled Hollywood historian Robert Osborne. "You had to go by to pay your bill and get out of the restaurant. And I remember people climbing over chairs so they could get out of the restaurant without going by his table." The banishment of Allan Carr had begun.

EILEEN BOWMAN HAD FLED THE Oscars soon after the opening number. Coming offstage, she thought, *I will never be this scared again in my entire life*. In the dressing room, she saw Olivia Newton-John borrowing her blush; the singer turned to her and said, "Oh, my God, I don't know how you did that! I could never have done that."

An Academy staffer asked Bowman to go to the Governors Ball on Rob Lowe's arm, dressed as Snow White. But she had been pushed too far. "No," she said. "I've had enough." Then she left: "I was out of that side door quicker than you could say 'Allan Carr's caftan.' I mean, I was *out*." All she kept were her eyelashes. Before driving back from L.A., she stopped to see her sister, who had been watching on TV and said, "Wait, I just saw you get offstage an hour ago. What are you doing?"

"I'm going home," Bowman said. "I've had it with L.A."

She thought that was the end of it. But the next morning, she woke up in San Diego and turned on the news to see a story about how Disney was angry at the Academy. Then the doorbell rang. She opened it to find a lawyer in a suit with a thick packet of papers. "Is this normal after you do something on TV?" she asked, flipping through the documents in a panic.

"They left me out there as the little lamb to be slaughtered," she says. "Of course I signed it, because I was scared." The documents forbade her from speaking about the Oscars for thirteen years.

ALL DISNEY WANTED WAS AN apology. "For its own reasons, however, the academy unfortunately did not accede to our request," Disney president Frank Wells told the papers. By the end of Thursday's business, the studio filed a trademark infringement lawsuit in U.S. District Court.

The parties met on Friday to try to resolve the dispute, without success. Disney maintained that the use of Snow White had been unauthorized and unflattering; a spokeswoman said, "We thought it was extremely unrepresentative of our creative work and of the quality of our creative work." The Academy was baffled: how had this slipped through the cracks? "Obtaining rights is one of the things we do routinely," the Academy's Bruce Davis told the press. "Yes, it is very puzzling. We are exploring the reasons for that."

Carr gave no comment. Jeff Margolis had advised him to keep his distance: "Why don't you just let the attorneys handle that?"

But Carr couldn't escape his own emotional devastation. When Steve Silver and his wife, Jo, visited Hilhaven to check on him, they found Carr in his basement disco, drunk and alone at the Bella Darvi bar. "Allan was very despondent," Jo recalls. "He felt horrible. We went over to try and cheer him up, because he didn't deserve all of the bad press he got." The couple handed him a gift from Tiffany engraved with the words "You Are a Star!" He burst into sobs.

Once he collected himself, Carr drew on one skill he could always count on: spin. He called Army Archerd at *Variety* claiming that Ronald Reagan himself had called to compliment him and had reminisced about how he used to go to the Cocoanut Grove. Carr told *The Hollywood Reporter* that he'd hired an extra secretary to respond to all the kudos. He invited over Charles Champlin, the *Los Angeles Times*'s affable arts editor, who arrived that afternoon to find what he called "vast and artful, top-of-the-budget floral arrangements and towering sprays of spring blossoms" in the living room. Carr claimed that he had run out of room and had already sent some of the flowers to hospital children's wards. In fact, Carr had asked his staff to order them from Harry Finley's floral shop.

In bare feet, Carr sipped a vodka and grapefruit juice and showed Champlin what he claimed was a pile of congratulatory messages. Jennifer Jones: "You delivered." Michael Ovitz: "You brought show business back to the movie business." Candice Bergen had supposedly called him to express her wrath at the critics. "What have we done?" Carr asked rhetorically. "We've touched the heart of America and won the town."

The town insisted otherwise. Letters poured into Champlin's paper in response to his piece, including one calling the show "an overstuffed turkey with a ghastly opening number." By the next Thursday, the Disney feud had begun to subside when the Academy issued a formal apology for "unintentionally creating the impression that Disney had participated in or sanctioned the opening number on the Academy Awards telecast." The agreement forbade the Academy from ever reusing the Snow White material, meaning that Carr's extravaganza was now officially banned. Kahn tried to shield Carr from blame, saying, "If there was a fault, it rests with me and the Academy." But any pretense that he had "won the town" was smashed when the next bomb dropped: the letter.

Seventeen Hollywood luminaries, including Gregory Peck, delivered a letter to Kahn calling the ceremony "an embarrassment both to the academy and the entire motion picture industry" and proclaiming, "It is neither fitting nor acceptable that the best work in motion pictures be acknowledged in such a demeaning fashion." The signers included two of Carr's Oscar-producer predecessors, Stanley Donen and William Friedkin, as well as Paul Newman, Julie Andrews, Blake Edwards, Billy Wilder, Joseph L. Mankiewicz, Alan J. Pakula, and Sidney Lumet. Kahn later claimed, "I collared the people one by one, and most of them expressed no recollection of putting their names on that letter." But word was that Peck and Edwards had spearheaded it, and plenty of others were vocal in their condemnation. "What we're responding to," said one of the signers, *Jaws* producer David Brown, "is a free-floating sense of dissatisfaction about the overly glitzy nature of the show."

The letter cemented the Hollywood establishment's rejection of the ceremony and, by extension, its producer. "It crushed his spirit," Alana Stewart recalls. "I don't think he ever got over it. I think it was really cruel." He had spent his career trying to find a place alongside these golden age icons, and he had considered Peck a friend. Now he was an Icarus who had flown too close to the Oscar sun. "This was his dream," Vilanch says. "He wanted to be one of them. He *was* one of them for a while. And then . . . he stepped on his cock."

"They just froze him out," Carr's friend Jeanne Wolf says. "And it took a while for him to figure that out, but once he did, he was devastated. He was *devastated*. He talked about being a nerd when he was in school, and he talked about always being the fat kid, the guy who looked like he wanted to be different but wanted to be part of the crowd. If you're wearing a caftan and if you're on a constant diet your whole life, you want to be accepted, you want to be one of the A-listers. And he could feel this ultimate rejection."

Rob Lowe felt that the fatal flaw had been the opening number's silliness. "Don't ever try to take the piss out of the Oscars," he wrote later. "The ceremony is not merely escapist fare for the average American; it is of cancer-curing importance, an evening of the highest seriousness, to be revered at all costs." But whatever career fallout Lowe may have suffered was overshadowed in May, when word got out of a sex tape he had made while campaigning at Michael Dukakis's Democratic National Convention. The mother of a girl in the video filed a lawsuit, which was eventually settled, but the tabloid feeding frenzy only prolonged the Academy's nightmare. Vilanch says, "Every time [the story of the sex tape] was shown, it was 'Rob Lowe, most recently seen dancing with Snow White in the disastrous opening number of the Academy Awards, which resulted in a lawsuit from Walt Disney . . .' So it built, it built, it built."

Carr's greatest gift, his ability to create a hoopla, had become his downfall. If he hadn't been so determined to give the Oscars his neon-bright imprimatur, the blame would have diffused instead of ricocheting back at him. "The show's reputation was 'You're the captain of the *Titanic*, Allan Carr,'" Vilanch says. "'You slammed into the iceberg, because you wanted to get to New York on time. You didn't give a shit, you didn't heed any of the warnings, and it's on *you*.'" But friends saw other forces at work. Jeanne Wolf sensed "somewhat of a gay backlash. Had [the show] been a success, they might have giggled behind his back. But he gave them the ammunition to speak more publicly, even if they didn't totally say what they were rejecting."

Vilanch wasn't "consciously aware" of a homophobic undercurrent, but he did sense personal resentment toward Carr. "There was a lot of schadenfreude going around, because he had dumped on a lot of people. He had been mean to a lot of people over the years, and there were a lot of people who said, 'He got what was coming.' Or others who said, 'It's too bad, because there's a talented guy in there, but there's so much ego and so much insecurity.'"

Days after the Gregory Peck letter, the Academy board convened an Awards Presentation Review Committee to assess the damage and make recommendations for how to rescue the ceremony going forward. It was chaired by Gil Cates, a well-liked TV director-producer who had been president of the Directors Guild, and its members included Carr's immediate predecessor, Samuel Goldwyn Jr., who promised, "For the first time, the board of governors is really going to take a hard look at what the show is going to be."

At the end of 1989, the *Los Angeles Times* looked back on a decade that, it assessed, had been "a black hole for serious film makers." The risk taking of the New Hollywood had given way to *Porky's*, *Police Academy*, and *Can't Stop the Music*. Five of the top-grossing films of the eighties, including *E.T.*, *Gremlins*, and the three Indiana Jones movies, had been produced by Steven Spielberg. And the Oscars had "continued to be criticized for the bloat of its antiquated variety-show format," culminating in the now-famous letter "complaining that the event had been a professional embarrassment. Hey, the *decade* was a professional embarrassment."

CARR BECAME RECLUSIVE. "NOTHING WAS happening afterward that he could focus his attention on, so he could just live in a pity pool for a while," Vilanch says. The disgraced producer carried around a bag overflowing with pills—Percocet, Halcion, anything—popping a dozen per day. Even with the medication, his mood seemed to permanently sour. "If I said something was black, he'd say it was white, and we would have an argument," recalls Carr's assistant Tony Lutz, who quit a few months after the Oscars. "Finally, one day, I said, 'Allan, I can't do this. Have it your way. But I'm not going to fight this fight with you every day.' So, that was just the end."

Carr disappeared to Mexico for a while, then spent a few weeks in Palm Springs, trying to get the Lana-Turner's-daughter project off the ground, but it never got made. "At bottom, a producer has his taste," Vilanch says. "And when your taste is invalidated by so many of your peers, there's nothing you can do but go into a depression. And God knows his taste was invalidated." Vilanch didn't hear from Carr for a while. "He doesn't want to talk to you," Roger Smith told him. "He doesn't want to talk to *anybody* involved with that show."

"I frankly wasn't that eager to talk to him," Vilanch says, "because I knew what was coming. I knew there would be the Night of the Long Knives, where eventually he would say, 'You! You fat queen Jew fag! *You* talked me into that shit with the young kids!' Which isn't true. But there would be a blanket condemnation. Or there would be, 'It was just you and me. We were the only ones who got it. *They* defeated us.' And I didn't particularly want to be *there*, either." The two never spoke face-to-face again.

In December, Carr booked a trip to Fiji, as far from Hollywood as he could get. He arrived at the airport in a beige caftan, carrying a suitcase full of sedatives. As he sank into his seat in coach, lulling himself to sleep with pills and champagne, he babbled to himself, "Those bastards in Hollywood! Those ungrateful SOBs! I gave them everything. I did everything for them. And then those assholes treat me like this." He remained defiant about the opening number. "He didn't understand why people thought it was so bad," Don Blanton says, "because, in his mind, it was fabulous."

Few people saw Carr for the next two years. "He didn't have those parties, because he was persona non grata with the people who he wanted to be in with, and he couldn't really cultivate a younger crowd because he represented a squarer, older thing," Vilanch says. "So he wasn't going to chase after them, and he was miserably unhappy. And so, he began drinking and using, which he always had been doing, but apparently it just got worse and worse."

So did Carr's health, which was never great to begin with. He installed an underwater treadmill in his pool and hired a personal trainer, who became a pseudo-boyfriend. He lost his Central Park South apartment ("Viewhaven") when his landlady, Leona Helmsley, discovered that he was subletting it to Billy Joel and terminated the lease. He spent days in bed glued to CNBC, screaming on the phone at his financial analyst. For the twentieth anniversary of *Grease*, Carr persuaded Paramount to rerelease the film. To mark the occasion, the studio booked the Chinese Theatre, the site of Carr's original world-premiere party, though it now had darker associations thanks to Snow White's hat. Carr hit the red carpet in a branded T-shirt, out of shape but managing without a cane. It was a brief moment back in the sun—a nostalgia trip in honor of a nostalgia trip. But it turned out to be a last hurrah. Carr tried to rustle up a new theater project, a musical version of *The Adventures of Tom Sawyer*. At the first rehearsal, he appeared in a wheelchair, with acupuncture needles coming out of his ears.

Over Christmas 1998, Carr had a kidney transplant. When he was discharged, he threw a party for his new kidney. It seemed like a return to the old Allan, who could find any excuse to celebrate in style. But the guests worried about his orange complexion. Midway through, he retreated to his bedroom and called for an ambulance to take him to Cedars-Sinai. The truth was that he had liver cancer, which was spreading through his body like a deadly glitter bomb. Friends were alarmed when they'd call the house and get brushed off with an "Oh, he's just not feeling up to it today." Some suspected that his handlers were keeping him isolated, but it may have been that Carr, ever the showman, didn't want to be seen in his condition. Ann-Margret simply showed up and treated him to a song and dance.

Carr died on June 29, 1999, at the age of sixty-two. "He had no family at that point," says his oldest friend, Joanne Cimbalo. "His parents were gone, he had no brothers or sisters. So, it was his staff that made the arrangements. It was very sad, very odd." As Carr would have noted, it was all very Norma Desmond. Paramount chair Sherry Lansing held a memorial on the lot. Two weeks later, Ann-Margret spread his ashes off the beach in Hawaii. Not long after, Hilhaven Lodge was sold to producer Brett Ratner, who inherited the Oscar curse: in 2011, he resigned as Academy Awards producer after remarking that "rehearsal is for fags."

Those who knew Carr best knew that he had been dying, cancer or not, ever since the 1989 Oscars. "That was the end of his life," Nikki Haskell says. "What did he do that was so terrible that everybody got so hysterical? He made it too much about himself; that was the problem. He made it so much about Allan that, when it wasn't flawless, they killed him."

THE 1989 CEREMONY LIVES ON in infamy as the Worst Oscars Ever, a symbol of Hollywood excess run amok. But how bad was it? Most of the show, after the opening number, was fine, even charming. And was Snow White's duet with Rob Lowe any tackier than RoboCop's rescue of Pee-wee Herman the year before? Teri Garr's *Flying Down to Rio* number had been "every bit as bad as the Cocoanut Grove," Vilanch observes. "Except that Rio didn't sue."

But Carr had committed multiple Hollywood sins: he'd been too

self-aggrandizing, too tacky, too gay. He'd slipped past the line that sep-
arates schmaltz from schlock. More than anything, he was the victim of
a snowball effect: If the reviews hadn't been so damning, Disney might
not have sued. And if Disney hadn't sued, Hollywood's elder statesmen
might not have felt the need to stage an intervention.

In late 1989, the new Academy president, Karl Malden, announced
that the next year's ceremony would be produced by Gil Cates, the head
of the damage-assessment committee. The panel recommended a single
host, more film clips, and a $150,000 fee for the show's producer, tradi-
tionally an unpaid post. Naturally, eyebrows rose over the fact that Cates,
whose committee had suggested the fee, would be the first person to
receive it. But the "even-tempered, rabbinical" Cates, in Vilanch's words,
was the opposite of Carr, buttoned up and resistant to overhyping. "He
was the Academy doctor, Mr. Fix-It," Margolis says. Cates wound up producing fourteen Oscar telecasts.

If Carr's Oscars were New Coke, Cates's were Coca-Cola Classic. The
1990 ceremony moved the proceedings back to the Dorothy Chandler
Pavilion, and Cates hired Billy Crystal to host, a return to the Bob Hope
and Johnny Carson days. "Carr did a good job," Cates told the *New York
Times* diplomatically. "He wanted to do a show with lots of glitz and glitter. I'd like to do a show that is contemporary and reflects the changes in
the world." The Berlin Wall had fallen, and, to celebrate a hopeful new
decade, Cates hooked up live satellite links to London, Moscow, Tokyo,
Buenos Aires, and Sydney. Instead of an extravagant opening number, the
show began with Crystal strutting out onto a sleek, purplish set. "Thank
you," he said, quieting the applause. "Is that for me, or are you just glad I'm
not Snow White?" It was an Allan Carr exorcism.

And yet, some of Carr's contributions remained, notably the line
"The Oscar goes to . . ." and Vilanch, who became the ceremony's comic
Yoda for two and a half decades. Perhaps most influential was Carr's
attention to Oscar fashion. With his nudging, the red carpet became a
spectacle unto itself, a contest within a contest. By 1995, it had attracted
another transformative figure: Joan Rivers, whose coverage for E! with
her daughter, Melissa, turned the carpet into a catty danger zone, where
stars found themselves swooned over or viciously panned. Measured in

hours and eyeballs, the red carpet came to compete with the ceremony itself, realizing the potential that perhaps only a man in a caftan could have foreseen.

If the 1990 ceremony signaled an end to eighties glitz, the nominated films were still sentimental Hollywood fare, including the Best Picture winner, *Driving Miss Daisy*. But there were signs that the pendulum was swinging once again. The original screenplay award went to the studio tear-jerker *Dead Poets Society*, but the losers included *Do the Right Thing* and *sex, lies and videotape*, two films that barely made a blip in the Oscar race otherwise. As in the late sixties, Hollywood had gotten bloated. It was time for another insurrection. Only, this time, it would be as ruthless as a shiv in the gut.

NINE

The Harveys

1999

How Harvey Weinstein made the Oscars dirty,
Steven Spielberg built his dream factory, and
Shakespeare in Love vs. *Saving Private Ryan* became
the nastiest Best Picture fight ever.

Bruce Feldman was running the Oscar campaign for *Schindler's List*, a job even he knew was a cakewalk. "It's not rocket science," he says. "You just—duh! Don't fuck it up!" Not that the expected triumph wasn't momentous. Since his snub for *Jaws*, Steven Spielberg had become notorious for losing Oscars. He lost for *Close Encounters of the Third Kind*, then *Raiders of the Lost Ark*. The year *E.T.* was nominated, he lost Best Directing and Best Picture to *Gandhi*. The message was clear: Spielberg was a hitmaker, not an artist. In 1985, he made *The Color Purple*, a period drama based on an acclaimed novel. It was nominated for eleven Oscars and lost all of them.

But now he had done it: directed a watershed Holocaust drama that simply could not lose. "Everyone universally agrees that the picture is going to win, end of discussion," recalls Feldman. "So, who goes in and tries to outrun that tidal wave? Harvey."

One morning in December 1993, after *Schindler's List* had won the New York and Los Angeles critics' awards, Feldman opened his stack of newspapers and trades and saw a full-page ad for *The Piano*, the feminist erotic drama by Jane Campion. At the top, in giant letters, were the words "BEST PICTURE." Below, in parentheses and tiny print, was "Runner-Up." Feldman was stunned but not surprised. *The Piano* was a Miramax film, and Miramax meant Harvey Weinstein.

Feldman went to Spielberg's longtime publicist, Marvin Levy, and said, "This is outrageous. Can you believe this?" Instead of confronting Weinstein, they decided to call the critics' groups and have them take care of it. "We won't get our hands dirty," Feldman reasoned. The misleading ads stopped.

A month later, Feldman was at Sundance, sitting with his wife in a crowded restaurant, when he felt someone looming over him. "Hello, Bruce," Weinstein sneered. "Why did you tell the L.A. and New York film critics on me? Why didn't you call me?"

Feldman stammered, "Uh, well . . . it didn't occur to me to do that."

"Well, next time, you do that," Weinstein said, and turned to leave. At the door, he spun his head around and screamed across the room, *"I'll get you, Bruce Feldman. I will!"*

"He just had no shame," Feldman says. "Nothing would stop him. And as the years went on, he got bolder and bolder, particularly as he started to win a lot. It just emboldened him. He doesn't have any humility. He doesn't have any sense of propriety or proportion. None."

This is the story that people always liked to tell about Harvey Weinstein: the brazen, bullying mogul who treated art house cinema like a mob boss and who would stop at nothing to win awards. Whether you loved him, loathed him, feared him, or revered him, there was no denying that he had chutzpah, that he played the game better than anyone else, that he was "passionate about film." (As director James Ivory said of him, "He's passionate about films in the same way a dog is passionate about meat.")

That story wasn't wrong, but it was incomplete, because Weinstein's appetites weren't confined to statuettes. There were two Harveys: the browbeating producer in a tuxedo getting thanked from the Oscar stage alongside God and the serial sexual predator covering his tracks. It took years for the second Harvey to be brought to light, in part because he was protected by the first Harvey: the P. T. Barnum of the indies, the one who boasted in 1994, as he was plastering *Variety* and *The Hollywood Reporter* with up to seven ads per day for *The Piano*, "Look, you have to keep it interesting. No one wants to be told by the media that the whole thing is wrapped up."

Schindler's List won Best Picture, of course, though *The Piano* made it out with three awards. You could scarcely find two movie heavyweights less alike than Spielberg and Weinstein. Spielberg was L.A.; Weinstein was New York. Spielberg was studio; Weinstein was indie. Spielberg was a mensch; Weinstein was an asshole. But the two were on a collision course that would bring them head-to-head five years later, when Weinstein once again challenged a vaunted Spielberg drama about World War II—only, this time, he would be in a position to win. The year of *Saving Private Ryan* versus *Shakespeare in Love* was the year that Oscar campaigning got big and got ugly, the year that both sides still talk about as if it were the Spanish Civil War. But it was also the year that Weinstein burnished his legend as the man with the magic Oscar touch, and that was a story that nobody could resist. Oscar by Oscar, he built himself a golden shield.

In 1963, Max Weinstein called his two small sons, Harvey and Bob, into the living room of their two-bedroom apartment in Queens. Max, a cutter in the Diamond District, asked the boys to sit in the "club chairs" usually reserved for company. They braced for a dressing-down. Instead, Max gave a soaring speech about the Kennedy brothers: how Jack had appointed Bobby as his attorney general, how their loyalty to each other was first and foremost. "And you guys can accomplish as much as them," Max said. "If you stick together, nothing is impossible."

Harvey and Bob were streetwise kids who spent their days bouncing Spaldeens off parked cars in Flushing. Harvey was full of angry bluster, while Bob was quieter but no less full of rage. On Saturdays, while their mother, Miriam, was at the beauty parlor, Max would take them to the movies: Westerns, musicals, war epics. In the late sixties, the teenage Harvey insisted on going to an artsy foreign film. Before Bob could protest, Harvey pulled him aside and explained that the movie was *I Am Curious (Yellow)*, the Swedish sensation that contained full-frontal nudity. Max chaperoned them but fell asleep thirty minutes in. Already, Harvey understood that you could sell sex under the cover of art, or vice versa.

In 1979, the brothers formed a film distribution company, Miramax, a portmanteau of their parents' names. Its first office in Manhattan shared a building with a working madam. The art house scene was small potatoes—with luck, a film could make a few million dollars—but Weinstein had a knack for provocation. At Cannes in 1983, he picked up *Eréndira*, a Brazilian drama based on a Gabriel García Márquez story. When one of his gofers wondered how to sell it, Harvey replied, "Easy! You got a Nobel Prize winner and you got sex. You work both ends." On one end, Harvey made a fuss when García Márquez was denied a visa to attend the American premiere. On the other, he got the film's young star Cláudia Ohana a spot in *Playboy* and gave her extra cleavage on the movie poster. "I had never seen anything so crass," publicist Reid Rosefelt recalled. "Would art filmgoers want to see the film more if they believed that Claudia had slightly bigger breasts?" But Weinstein didn't want "art filmgoers." He wanted to break out of the "art house ghetto" by whatever means necessary.

In 1987, another path opened up when Merchant Ivory's *A Room with a View* scored eight Oscar nominations, including for Best Picture, and grossed more than twenty million dollars for the indie distributor Cinecom. Weinstein took Cinecom's Ira Deutchman out for lunch and asked how he had done it. Deutchman ran him through his Oscar strategy, which included sending the voters VHS tapes, a new technology that was leveling the playing field for small movies; licensing the film to a local L.A. TV station; and mailing out wall calendars with stills from the movie and dates marked for upcoming screenings. Weinstein listened and learned. "Harvey was still not a threat, or he didn't appear to be one," Deutchman says.

The next year at Cannes, Miramax picked up for American distribution the Palme d'Or winner, *Pelle the Conqueror*, a bleak Danish drama featuring Max von Sydow. Miramax ran ads foregrounding the naked back of a peasant woman who barely appeared in the film. At the Academy Awards—the Allan Carr year—von Sydow was nominated for Best Actor, and *Pelle* won Best Foreign Language Film. It was Weinstein's first taste of Oscar.

But another time line was taking shape. By then, Weinstein had allegedly raped a woman named Hope Exiner d'Amore in a hotel, forced a woman named Cynthia Burr to give him oral sex, sexually assaulted a Buffalo waitress in a car, asked an aspiring actress named Tomi-Ann Roberts to show him her breasts while he was in a bathtub, and demanded a back rub from a young Miramax employee named Lisa Rose. "Well, other people do it," he said when Rose refused. When the time came, he would deny it all.

NINETEEN EIGHTY-NINE WAS A WATERSHED year for Miramax. In January, Steven Soderbergh, twenty-six and broke, won the Audience Award at the U.S. Film Festival (the future Sundance) for *sex, lies and videotape*. With its slacker cool factor and psychosexual thrills, it was Gen X's answer to *Bob and Carol and Ted and Alice*. When Weinstein caught wind of it, he flew to L.A. with mock-ups of posters and promised the producers he would outpay the competition. Miramax was a shoestring operation, but the Weinsteins were known as hardball negotiators who would blow up when they didn't get what they wanted. Harvey's rough-edged persona rankled the cerebral indie world. Though he positioned himself as a champion of auteurs, his meddling in the editing room earned him the nickname "Harvey Scissorhands." Worse, he would acquire movies and then bury them if he lost interest.

Deutchman, now a marketing consultant, had the unenviable job of mediating between Weinstein and Soderbergh. "Harvey, if he was left to his own devices, would have called the film *sex, sex and sex*," Deutchman says. "And, of course, Soderbergh was horrified. But then, his alternatives were just as horrifying to Harvey, because they didn't feel that entertaining. They felt very arty and very severe."

Sex, lies was the big bang of the indie movement, grossing $24.7 million domestically and giving Gen X a noncorporate alternative to Hollywood. At the 1990 Oscars, Soderbergh was nominated for his original screenplay. Miramax had also distributed *My Left Foot*, which was nominated for Best Picture and Best Actor for Daniel Day-Lewis, playing an Irishman with cerebral palsy. Weinstein had acquired the rights from a British production company in part by promising to get Day-Lewis an Academy Award.

Oscar nominations served a number of Weinstein's aims at once: they were publicity fodder, box-office fuel, carrots to dangle in front of talent, and a ticket out of the "art house ghetto." Campaigning was largely a gentlemen's game consisting of "For Your Consideration" ads, private screenings at homes in Bel Air, and screener copies festooned in lavish packaging. "In those days the studios had a lock on the Oscars, because none of the indies campaigned aggressively," Weinstein said later. "The only thing that we did to change the rules was, rather than just sitting it out and getting beat because somebody had more money, more power, more influence, we ran a guerrilla campaign." A week before the nominations, he accompanied Day-Lewis to Washington, where the actor urged Congress to pass the Americans with Disabilities Act. Did it help humanity? Sure. Did it raise *My Left Foot*'s profile at just the right time? Sure. "It is not as cold and calculating as it sounds because he helped to get the bill passed," Weinstein said. If you saw it as cynical, what did that say about *you*?

Day-Lewis won Best Actor, and Brenda Fricker, who played his mother, won Best Supporting Actress. That, plus a foreign film prize for *Cinema Paradiso*, brought the Miramax tally to three. Miramax had just moved to new headquarters at Robert De Niro's Tribeca Film Center, giving the company an aura of downtown cool. The offices were a rabbit warren of desks, with Weinstein in a smallish room of his own. "Harvey would keep the blinds closed, and he would chain-smoke cigarettes and drink a thousand Diet Cokes," publicist Teri Kane says. "Then he would put his cigarette down in his one big marble ashtray and he would pour the diet soda over the cigarette. I mean, it was just so disgusting." On a shelf were biographies of the great Hollywood kingpins: Selznick, Thalberg, Mayer. "He just loved the idea of being a mogul with great power and great taste," marketing executive Mark Gill recalls. "That's what got him up in the morning."

After the successes of My Left Foot and sex, lies and videotape, Miramax seemed ascendant, but its next two years were full of misfires and mismanagement. "There was no business plan," one former executive says. "There was never a spine in the company. There was no infrastructure, ever." Aside from Madonna's Truth or Dare, which made fifteen million dollars, the company careened from flop to flop. Even with hits, the accounting was iffy; My Left Foot producer Noel Pearson complained that expecting a dime of profit from Miramax was like "waiting for Godot to come."

By 1992, the company was teetering upon bankruptcy. Weinstein was forced to sell off a package of films to Disney, a deal that first introduced him to Jeffrey Katzenberg, chairman of Walt Disney Studios. In what seemed like another act of desperation, Miramax started a horror division, Dimension, which became Bob Weinstein's domain and put out the likes of Hellraiser III: Hell on Earth. Even as Miramax staff was instructed to save pennies by using both sides of paper in the copy machine, the brothers would treat themselves to first-class flights, limos, and rooms at the Beverly Hills Hotel and London's Savoy, where Harvey spent a curious amount of time. "Everybody knew he cheated on his wife," one employee says. "He stayed at a totally different hotel from the staff. So, we didn't see this stuff, we just knew. We'd always get a call about a girl we'd have to invite to a premiere."

The company's financial savior came in the unlikely package of The Crying Game, an Irish drama about a conflicted IRA volunteer who falls in love with a hair stylist named Dil. The twist: Dil, played by Jaye Davidson, reveals herself to be transgender in a full-frontal nude scene. Weinstein had seen the script during development and given it a "good luck and goodbye," but when the brothers saw the finished product, Bob snatched up the North American rights. One of his competitors was Deutchman, then at Fine Line. "The Crying Game is a source of a lot of grief for me," Deutchman says, "because I could have bought that film, and if I had, maybe we never would have heard of Harvey Weinstein again. The reason I turned it down for distribution is because I really believed that there was no way that, once the word got out about the secret at the end, anybody would want to see the movie."

Weinstein realized that the opposite was true: the secret was the *solution*, because you could dare audiences not to reveal it and create intrigue. After opening the film in New York and L.A., Weinstein would stalk the lobbies incognito and dare patrons to tell him the secret. To his delight, they were keen to play the game. Every audience member was now a willing participant in a Miramax marketing scheme. But the more attention the secret got, the harder it was to keep. Weinstein called one *Time* editor eighteen times in one day in an unsuccessful attempt to keep the magazine from blowing the big reveal.

In February 1993, *The Crying Game* was nominated for six Academy Awards, including Best Picture, with additional nominations for Miramax's *Enchanted April*, *Passion Fish*, and *Close to Eden*. The press hailed the nominations—including nine for Merchant Ivory's *Howards End*—as a triumph for the indies. In the *Los Angeles Times*, Kenneth Turan speculated that "the poohbahs of Hollywood have lost touch with their mandate." Even Katzenberg, one of those poohbahs, castigated the studios, telling the *New York Times*, "Commerce has overwhelmed art, which is why Hollywood movies aren't as good as they used to be."

The only problem was that Jaye Davidson had been nominated for Best Supporting Actor—probably the only Oscar attention Weinstein *didn't* want, because it spoiled the secret. To hide the enigmatic star from the press, Weinstein sent Davidson to Egypt. Ultimately, *The Crying Game* won a single Oscar, for its screenplay, but the nominations boosted its grosses from $20 million to $63 million. And Miramax, having proven itself as "mighty monarch of the indies," in Turan's words, was finally positioned to cash out.

In April, Katzenberg called Disney's CFO, Chris McGurk, and proposed that they buy Miramax. It was, on one level, an outrageous idea: how would the crude, rude purveyors of *sex, lies and videotape* fit into the wholesome Disney empire? But if anyone had credibility, it was Katzenberg, who had followed CEO Michael Eisner from Paramount in 1984 and was largely responsible for revitalizing the moribund studio with Touchstone Pictures comedies like *Three Men and a Baby* and cartoon megahits like *The Little Mermaid*. What Disney didn't have was Oscar-caliber prestige—aside from music prizes and a Best Picture nomination for *Beauty and the Beast*. The Weinsteins, meanwhile, were "tired of being in the minor leagues and being undercapitalized," Harvey said later. The unholy alliance would give each something it needed: for Miramax, financial security; for Disney, an Oscar gold mine. In May, the brothers signed the deal, estimated between sixty and eighty million dollars. At a news conference, Katzenberg promised that Miramax would remain "a stand-alone, independent and autonomously run company." Hollywood waited skeptically.

Amid the negotiations, Weinstein was acquiring *The Piano*, which would vindicate Disney when the film got eight Oscar nominations. Weinstein's estimated $750,000 campaign, one insider said at the time, "cost almost as much as the movie did to make." The race belonged to *Schindler's List*, which won seven Oscars. Three more went to *Jurassic Park*, crowning Spielberg Hollywood's undisputed king of art and commerce. But Spielberg's next move wasn't directing a movie. It was building his own dream factory.

ON THE MORNING OF OCTOBER 12, 1994, three men walked into the Verandah Room of the Peninsula hotel in Beverly Hills. A scrum of reporters awaited, alerted the previous afternoon by a blizzard of cryptic faxes that Jeffrey Katzenberg would be holding a press conference. By nightfall, reporters had sussed out the extraordinary news: Katzenberg, Spielberg, and music magnate David Geffen were founding a brand-new studio.

At the Peninsula, the three men, casually attired in khakis, danced around the open secret. "There's a pretty giant misunderstanding here," Katzenberg began. "The reason that we wanted to have this press conference this morning is to announce that the next Dive! restaurant opening will be in Las Vegas on April 15." The crowd laughed. Dive! was the chain of family eateries that Katzenberg had started with Spielberg.

Katzenberg passed the baton to Spielberg, who read from a statement. "Hollywood studios were at their zenith when they were driven by point of view and personalities. Together with Jeffrey and David, I want to create a place driven by ideas and the people who have them. I regard Jeffrey and David as pioneers. I'd like to be one, too."

One reporter asked how the three titans would divide the work, and Geffen joked, "I'm going to direct *Jurassic Park 2*." That would be fine, Spielberg shot back, if he could be a billionaire. Then Katzenberg, waxing utopian, said, "There's an opportunity for us to have a revolution."

The idea, in truth, had been born of tragedy. Thirteen days after *Schindler's List* won the Oscar, Disney president Frank Wells was returning from a ski trip when he died in a helicopter crash. Wells, who carried a slip of paper in his pocket reading, "Humility is the final achievement," had been a buffer between his boss, Michael Eisner, and Katzenberg, the studio's production chief and the man Eisner called his "golden retriever." Neither was big on humility.

With Wells gone, the two men's animosity came to a head. Katzenberg, on the verge of overseeing the release of *The Lion King*, lobbied hard for the number two spot. But Eisner was wary. At forty-three, Katzenberg was alternately lovable and despotic. In the words of *Lion King* producer Don Hahn, "You never knew if he was gonna hug you or kick you." His entourage of loyalists included whip-smart, acid-tongued publicist Terry Press, with whose help Katzenberg made himself the face of the Disney renaissance. But Eisner wondered whether Katzenberg's self-aggrandizing, cutthroat style would fly with Disney's board of directors, and so, Katzenberg was, astonishingly, passed over. Two months after *The Lion King* premiered, he was forced to resign.

Spielberg was vacationing with his wife at Robert Zemeckis's house in Jamaica when he heard the news and called Katzenberg to check in. Katzenberg needed something to do, preferably something that would put Eisner to shame. Spielberg, filching a line from *Back to the Future*, assured him, "Where you're going, you don't need roads."

"What do you mean *you*," Katzenberg said. "I'm talking *we*."

Geffen had encouraged the ousted executive to pursue a venture with Spielberg, but Spielberg was hesitant: he had everything he could want, including his own production company, Amblin, housed in a eucalyptus-lined bungalow on the Universal lot. But the more Katzenberg gave him the hard sell, the more Spielberg warmed to the idea of overseeing his own studio, especially considering that Lew Wasserman, his longtime corporate godfather at Universal, was in his eighties and diminished in power.

Geffen also resisted Katzenberg's entreaties. Having already launched two music labels, the fifty-one-year-old billionaire didn't need to work another day in his life. Why not spend his days jetting around in his Gulfstream IV and lounging in his $47.5 million Beverly Hills estate, once owned by Jack Warner? But part of him wanted to stay in the game—plus, joining up with Spielberg would be a poke in the eye of his rival Michael Ovitz, the director's agent. In September, the three men attended a White House dinner for Boris Yeltsin. In the late hours, they met at the Hay-Adams hotel and decided to invest $33 million apiece. Katzenberg, significantly less wealthy than his partners, would have to mortgage two homes. But each was getting something he craved: for Spielberg, a chance to chart his own destiny; for Geffen, a new way to pull Hollywood's strings; and for Katzenberg, a job, a comeback, and revenge.

Even before the new enterprise had a name, the press went wild over the "dream team," as if they were a rock-'n'-roll supergroup. So what if the details were vague? This would be the first major Hollywood studio to be launched in sixty years. "This is as if Babe Ruth, Lou Gehrig, and Joe DiMaggio got together," Harvey Weinstein raved when asked for a comment. Within weeks, the company announced its name, with each founder pitching in an initial: "DreamWorks SKG."

The next March, the triumvirate appeared on the cover of *Time*, with the headline "THE PLAYERS: How the men who gave you *Jurassic Park*, *The Lion King* and Nirvana are creating a media colossus overnight." The story hyped DreamWorks as "the prototype plugged-in multimedia company of the new millennium." Where scrappy Miramax had risen from the gutter, DreamWorks had descended from the clouds. Katzenberg would oversee a two-hundred-million-dollar animation unit. Geffen would run a music division. Spielberg might expand into software. Unlike the old studios, they wouldn't churn out crap just to make a buck but would limit their output to maybe ten movies a year. "And if we can't find ten good movies a year," Spielberg promised, "we won't make five good ones and five bad ones. We want quality over volume."

Spielberg dreamed of building a state-of-the-art movie facility, eyeing a development called Playa Vista, a 1,087-acre expanse of marshland north of LAX. Geffen worked mostly from his Beverly Hills Xanadu, while Katzenberg moved into the studio's temporary headquarters at Amblin. Spielberg remained in his office upstairs, with its mantel of hard-won Oscars. To the new DreamWorks employees, many of whom came from the buttoned-up legacy studios, the House of Spielberg was a laid-back fun factory. "It was movie nirvana," one recalls. "Filmmakers and writers and musicians and animators and game makers and every actor on the planet—everyone was coming through the lobby and hanging out and enjoying lunch that was complimentary and was there to talk about the promise of what a next-gen studio could actually be."

Suits were out; business casual was in. "Next time I see you in a tie, you're fired!" Katzenberg would joke. Unlike at the old, bureaucratic studios, no one had official titles. "It was a little Mickey Rooney–ish, 'Hey, kids, let's put on a show!' type of thing," one early joiner says. Another employee was less sanguine: "They gave us some bullshit thing about how everyone's going to have no titles and we're all going to pitch in. It basically meant they didn't have to give us raises every year."

But the perks were plentiful: an on-site masseuse, a video game lounge. Chefs, on call to make free meals, would interrupt meetings with freshly baked cookies. "The snack thing was big," says Mike Gottberg, who joined the skeleton crew marketing team. "You'd go down there, and there'd be Dove Bars. It was like a fully stocked 7-Eleven." At Miramax, employees would talk about the Miramax Twenty, the weight they would either gain or lose from stress. At DreamWorks, you'd put on the DreamWorks Ten, which meant only one thing: happiness.

Everyone was having fun and eating well, but could any DreamWorks film possibly live up to the hype? As Tom Hanks predicted, "I guarantee that, when their first film premieres, everyone will say, 'This is it? This is what these three geniuses have come up with?'"

Miramax knew exactly what kind of movies it put out. There was "literary" foreign fare such as *Like Water for Chocolate*, which became the highest-grossing foreign film in a decade. (To celebrate, the company threw a banquet in TriBeCa for a thousand guests, who were invited before dinner to watch actress Claudette Maillé re-create her nude horseback scene on the West Side Highway.) And there were grungy, provocative American movies like Kevin Smith's *Clerks* and Quentin Tarantino's *Reservoir Dogs*.

A motormouthed, kung fu–obsessed cinephile, Tarantino had quit high school and in 1984 started working at the Video Archives in L.A.'s Manhattan Beach. There he found his cadre of movie geeks and began writing *Reservoir Dogs*, a bloody, postmodern heist film made for $1.3 million. With its B-movie violence, blaring seventies soundtrack, and revenge-of-the-nerd nihilism—all ending in a hailstorm of bullets—it was an unapologetic assault on the refined art house aesthetic. After one Sundance screening, a spectator asked, "So, how do you justify all the violence in this movie?" Tarantino shot back, "I don't know about you, but I love violent movies. What I find offensive is that Merchant Ivory shit."

Reservoir Dogs left Sundance without a distributor, but Miramax's acquisitions team implored Weinstein to take a look. He thought that the gore would alienate women, a thesis that held up when his wife and sister-in-law left the room after the ear-slicing scene. Tarantino objected, "I didn't make it for your wife!" After a standoff, Weinstein blinked. He opened the movie in October 1992, ear-slicing included. It grossed some $2.5 million—hardly *Crying Game* money. Meanwhile, Tarantino, with an option from TriStar on his next project, holed up in a one-room apartment in Amsterdam, hopped up on twelve cups of coffee per day and filling composition notebooks with indecipherable scrawl. After three months, he emerged with *Pulp Fiction*.

The script—nonlinear, ultraviolent, with a leather-clad character called the Gimp—was too weird for TriStar, but Miramax production head Richard Gladstein gave it to Weinstein, who was catching a plane to Martha's Vineyard. Within three hours, he called Gladstein and said, "The first scene is *fucking brilliant*. Does it stay this good?" An hour later, he called again: "Are you guys crazy? You just killed off the main character in the middle of the movie." Keep reading, Gladstein urged him. "Start negotiating," Weinstein said. He called back a third time. "Are you closed yet?" he asked. "Hurry up! We're making this movie."

The film shot in the fall of 1993, with John Travolta and Samuel L. Jackson as hitmen and Uma Thurman as a crime boss's wife. At Cannes, the newly flush Weinstein brothers showed up with the *Pulp* gang. The movie hit Cannes like dynamite. Crowds chanted Tarantino's name. "Quentin brought back that thing that only had existed theretofore in the seventies, the idea of the rock-star director," says his then publicist, Bumble Ward. On Tarantino's way up to accept the Palme d'Or, a woman shouted, "*Pulp Fiction* is shit!" He flipped her off and said, "I don't make movies that bring people together. I make movies that split people apart."

That fall, *Pulp Fiction* went to the New York Film Festival, where spectators included Katzenberg, Demi Moore, and Tom Cruise. During the scene in which Travolta stabs Thurman in the heart with a syringe of adrenaline, a woman screamed, "Is there a doctor in the house?" A diabetic man had fainted. Miramax sent the guy home in a limo, and the film resumed. The incident made headlines, but not everyone was convinced. "It could not have been a bigger—in my opinion—*stunt*," says Fine Line's Liz Manne, who was sitting a few rows behind the fainter. "Either that or Harvey made the most of an opportunity that arose organically. Many people in the industry thought that it was a fake."

Pulp Fiction opened in October 1994 on 1,100 screens, and made back more than its $8.5 million budget on the first weekend. "The hero ain't the hero. The villain ain't the villain. And the outcome of the story might happen an hour before the end. It's defying everything," Weinstein told the press. A true cultural phenomenon, *Pulp Fiction* became the first independent film to blast through the $100 million mark, and Tarantino the rare director famous enough to host *Saturday Night Live*. He was the face not only of the exploding indie movement but also of Miramax. "I'm their Mickey Mouse," he'd say.

Pulp Fiction was nominated for seven Academy Awards, including Best Picture, among twenty-two total nominations for Miramax. "I'm drinking sweet vintage champagne through the faucets of Miramax," Weinstein told the *L.A. Times*. (The press knew he was good copy.) His competition was *Forrest Gump*, a feel-good studio drama that located America's soul in a sweet simpleton played by Tom Hanks. At more than $600 million worldwide, it was the highest-grossing film in Paramount's history. *Gump* vs. *Pulp* reflected the two antipodes of American movies: big-budget Hollywood versus the rude, ascendant indies. "They kept calling it the David-and-Goliath year," says Bumble Ward, "but it really was a sort of litmus test: Are you a *Forrest Gump* person or are you a *Pulp Fiction* person? Are you groovy or not?"

Although Weinstein had about half of *Gump*'s campaigning budget, he used his resources shrewdly. Miramax staff would visit the motion picture retirement home in the Valley, where some elderly Academy voters lived, and, according to Tarantino's agent Mike Simpson, "have lunch with little old ladies and make a personal connection with each one of them, saying, 'Watch the movie and vote for our film.'" The tactic, like others for which Miramax became notorious, wasn't new, but Weinstein was relentless. The studios were now showering voters with so much swag—including Disney's fifty-dollar coffee table books for *The Lion King*—that the Academy had to warn against items that "tread dangerously close to the definition of a bribe." "I'm always going up against the huge Hollywood establishment, and this time it's no different," Weinstein said mid-campaign. "You have Bob Zemeckis and Tom Hanks, who could both be mayor of Beverly Hills."

The *Gump* campaign was overseen by Cheryl Boone Isaacs, Paramount's head of worldwide publicity and one of the few Black executives in Hollywood. A few years earlier, Weinstein had tried to poach her, saying, "You're the kind of person Miramax would love," but she declined. Now she was in direct competition with him. "It was heated," she recalls. "*Pulp Fiction* was the darling of the New York press, which didn't make life easy by any means. I remember saying to the staff, 'Okay, this is the deal: every nomination that is offered, I want it.'" Although *Gump* got thirteen nominations, Boone Isaacs wasn't taking anything for granted. "We had already known he was good at this," she says of Weinstein. "But I didn't think he was any smarter than I was, to be honest."

In March 1995, the Miramax crew touched down at LAX like a band of renegades from a Tarantino movie. Two nights before the Oscars, *Pulp Fiction* swept the Independent Spirit Awards, but Weinstein predicted, "Monday night, we'll be the fucking homeless people." Like *Citizen Kane*, *Pulp Fiction* lost every Oscar but the original screenplay award, which Tarantino shared with his old video store chum Roger Avary. (In another *Citizen Kane* echo, the two had squabbled over Avary's credit.) Onstage, they looked like crashers from a skateboarding contest. Avary, a long-haired art school dropout, announced, "I really have to take a pee right now."

Miramax had taken over Chasen's, the storied West Hollywood eatery that was about to shut its doors. The party was a kind of Irish wake, both for the restaurant and for *Pulp's* Oscar chances. The guests reveled in being the cool-kid losers—even Madonna, who watched the telecast from the party. When *Gump* won Best Picture and one of the producers invoked its values of "respect, tolerance, and unconditional love," she heckled the screen, "What about mediocrity?"

By 12:30 a.m., the party was packed, the atmosphere unhinged. When Courtney Love, in mourning for Kurt Cobain, recognized the woman sitting next to her as Lynn Hirschberg, the journalist who had written a damning *Vanity Fair* profile of her, she said, "You have blood on your hands," grabbed Tarantino's Oscar off the table, and tried to clobber Hirschberg with it, as the director scrambled to intervene. After Love gathered herself and left, Tarantino turned to Hirschberg and quipped, "If she had killed you with an Oscar, it would have been like a scene from one of my movies."

Late into the night, Weinstein told the *New York Observer* that he hadn't given up on those Oscars after all: "At 4 a.m., we're going to Hanks' and Zemeckis' houses. We're taking them back." He smirked. "And if they don't give them up, we're going to get *medieval* on them." He enjoyed playing troublemaker, but he knew what to keep hidden. Among the revelers was Uma Thurman, who later revealed that, amid the *Pulp Fiction* juggernaut, Weinstein had assaulted her at his suite at the Savoy: "He pushed me down. He tried to shove himself on me. He tried to expose himself. He did all kinds of unpleasant things. But he didn't actually put his back into it and force me. You're like an animal wriggling away, like a lizard."

The next day, he had sent her yellow roses and a card that read, "You have great instincts."

DREAMWORKS HAD THREE SUPERMOGULS, $2.7 billion in capital, and no movies to speak of. The mostly absent Geffen played godfather and signed George Michael for DreamWorks Records. Katzenberg, obsessed with his vendetta against Disney, poached animators with mid-six-figure contracts and fashioned an $85 million animation campus in Glendale, with a koi pond and a helipad. There, his hires could work on *The Prince of Egypt*, an epic Exodus musical to rival *The Lion King*, plus an irreverent computer-animated comedy called *Shrek*, which would spoof wholesome Disney fairy tales. But those would take years to complete.

Then there was Spielberg, the boy-man around whom the DreamWorks solar system spun. The studio's logo encapsulated his worldview: a boy sitting on a crescent moon dropping a fishing line from the clouds. He threw himself into plans for an arcade/restaurant chain and the designs for his filmmaking Valhalla at Playa Vista, taking breaks to play video games. But where were the movies? After *Schindler's List*, Spielberg took a hiatus from directing, which he finally broke to make a *Jurassic Park* sequel, *The Lost World*—for Universal. To oversee DreamWorks's live-action division, he installed Walter Parkes and Laurie MacDonald, married producers known for their discriminating taste, who could identify and shepherd potential Oscar winners. But they were so deliberate that, despite Katzenberg's push to get *something* out in theaters, the better part of 1995 flew by without anything greenlit. Even the press was getting impatient running "dream team" stories.

Finally, in late 1995, DreamWorks announced its inaugural feature, *The Peacemaker*, a thriller starring George Clooney and Nicole Kidman. The next summer, the studio announced more upcoming films, but the lineup was a head-scratcher: a slapstick film called *MouseHunt* and a comedy about a talking parrot, called *Paulie*. (Those who saw DreamWorks as Katzenberg's elaborate revenge scheme against Disney couldn't help but notice that one of its first films was about two men trying to kill a mouse.) And Spielberg would not direct his first DreamWorks feature, *Amistad*, about a slave ship uprising in 1839, until he was done with *The Lost World*. When *The Peacemaker* came out, in September 1997, it drew a modest $41 million, hardly a groundbreaker. "Nothing would have lived up to the amount of expectations," a DreamWorks employee recalls. "It was when the reality started to hit. Not everything's going to be *Schindler's List*."

Reality was also hitting Miramax. Almost immediately after the *Pulp Fiction* Oscars, the company was engulfed in controversy over *Priest*, about a Catholic priest grappling with his homosexuality. The Catholic

League seized on the fact that Disney was releasing sacrilege. Uncowed, Weinstein vowed to open the film on Good Friday—until Disney persuaded him otherwise. Without Katzenberg, the Disney-Miramax marriage inevitably soured. Disney would audit Miramax's books; the Weinstein brothers would threaten to join Katzenberg at DreamWorks. After another provocative acquisition, Harmony Korine's *Kids*, got slapped with an NC-17 rating and the Weinsteins had to form a separate company, Shining Excalibur Films, just to distribute it, Weinstein backed away from provocation. "I don't want to cause Disney any problems," he told the *New York Times*. "Why ruin a perfect relationship?"

At Miramax headquarters, though, there was no mellowing. "We worked like crazy," says Amy Hart, who started as a receptionist. "We did not get lunch breaks. We were not allowed to leave the building. Harvey talked one of his assistants off an airplane as she was leaving to go to her honeymoon: 'Come back to the office! You can't go this week!'" Hart recalls an "atmosphere of intense blaming," especially around awards season. "If a film won, everyone patted each other on the back; if a film did not win or get the box-office return they anticipated, there was a lot of finger pointing, and it could get vicious." Donna Gigliotti, who joined as an executive vice president in 1993, shared an office wall with Harvey. One day, she leaped from her desk thinking there was an earthquake. She rushed out, saying, "What *was* that?" "He had thrown this marble ashtray at the wall," Gigliotti recalls. "He was mad at somebody."

Stockholm syndrome set in. "You think, *Well, yeah, he did kick me, but not as hard as he kicked that other person*," says PR executive Teri Kane. "You just started to lose your mind." Now that Miramax was the studio that released *Pulp Fiction*, the staff knew they were replaceable. "It was just ridiculous how many résumés were slamming in that door," Hart recalls. Then there were cases like Amy Israel, whom Weinstein promoted to cohead of acquisitions. In 1994, she went to see him in his hotel room during a film festival and found him barely clothed, asking for a massage. "I reported the incident to someone more senior," she said later. "And I was told that another one of my other colleagues had also been harassed. But no one had ever bothered to warn me. Even after reporting it, nothing was done."

Weinstein was careful to keep employees siloed so that nobody knew everything that was going on. But the bullying, the harassment—it was all of a piece. "He was just a person who never took no for an answer," says one staffer. "I would describe him to my therapist, and she would say, 'He's like a hole that's never filled up. He's constantly needing affirmation.'" One way he filled that hole was with Oscar nominations, which increasingly obsessed him. "*Gluttonous* is just the smallest word you could say for his appetite," Amy Hart says. "He wanted to own every square on the Monopoly board, and if it cost him a million dollars, he really didn't care." With Dimension turning out to be an unlikely cash cow, especially after the release of *Scream*, the breakdown became: Bob makes the money, Harvey wins the Oscars. Kane recalls Weinstein ending one strategy session by saying, "So, who's ready to go to war with me?"

By 1996, Miramax's Oscar game was well honed. Marcy Granata, who had come in to run the publicity department two years earlier, knew how to imbue a campaign with an emotional through line. Cynthia Swartz, who had joined the company in 1989 and oversaw its full-time awards operation, was a nebbishy whiz kid who hated parties but understood Academy math. She instituted a ground game that complemented Granata's messaging skills—it was like a presidential campaign that knew how to give soaring speeches *and* get people to the polls. Both prongs became crucial in the 1996 campaign for *Il Postino*, an Italian-language film about a postman who befriends Pablo Neruda. It was the kind of foreign heart-warmer that increasingly made up Miramax's catalogue. The problem was that it had been released in Italy in 1994 and was ineligible for Best Foreign Language Film—but it *was* eligible for Best Picture, a technicality of which Miramax had to remind voters, using ads, screeners, and even personal calls.

Calling voters was not uncommon at indie companies, and Miramax's operation was intended as a reminder to Academy members—who were expected to review hundreds of hours' worth of screeners—to watch the Miramax contenders, plus as a kind of focus group to gauge where to put campaigning resources. But Weinstein pushed it farther. "We would sit and go through the list of Academy members, and everybody was assigned who they knew," one staffer remembers. "You were supposed to call them and somehow convince them to vote for your movie, and there were also times when Harvey wanted us to get people's ballots and vote for them." That level of soliciting, which Miramax continually denied doing, was against the Academy's intermittently enforced rules.

To fan *Il Postino*'s literary cred, Miramax recorded a CD of celebrities reading Neruda poems, including Madonna, Wesley Snipes, and Julia Roberts, who, Weinstein claimed, was "nearly a Neruda scholar." The album spawned a star-studded poetry reading at the Tribeca Film Center. When Roberts failed to show up, Weinstein himself subbed in and growled through her poem, "Poor Fellows," about two lovers longing for privacy ("Everyone pries under your sheets"). "No one appreciated my reading it," Weinstein admitted. *Il Postino* got five nominations, including Best Picture, but won none—it was *Braveheart*'s year.

The next year, Miramax finally had a front-runner. Michael Ondaatje's novel *The English Patient* had the makings of a David Lean–style epic: a World War II backdrop, sweeping vistas, a doomed romance. But when producer Saul Zaentz and director Anthony Minghella pitched it to studios, including Miramax, they were met with what Minghella called "polite indifference." Zaentz, a cantankerous man with a Santa beard, who had collected Best Picture Oscars for *One Flew Over the Cuckoo's Nest* and *Amadeus*, put in $5 million of his own money. The project finally went to Fox, starring Ralph Fiennes, Kristin Scott Thomas, and Juliette Binoche. But in Zaentz's telling, the studio got cold feet and demanded that Demi Moore replace Thomas. (Fox denied this.) Four weeks before shooting began, Fox pulled the plug. The Weinsteins, playing deep-pocketed indie saviors, scooped up the world rights for some $28 million. "I regarded them as angels," Minghella said, "though given what I'd heard about Harvey and Bob's invasiveness, angels with claws."

The English Patient opened to rapturous reviews in late 1996 and got a whopping twelve Oscar nominations. "This is a terrific vindication for a movie that was five days away from not being made," Weinstein boasted. The press called the Oscar race the "Year of the Indies." Of the five Best Picture nominees, four were independents (*The English Patient*, *Fargo*, *Shine*, and *Secrets and Lies*) and only one was a studio release, Sony's *Jerry Maguire*—a benchmark that showed how far the taste line had moved, in large part because of Miramax's doggedness.

With *The English Patient* making him the biggest fish in the pond, Harvey cranked up his Oscar apparatus. He carpet-bombed the trades with ads, so much so that *Variety* gave the studio a volume discount. Ramping up from the *Il Postino* poetry night, he staged a star-studded event at New York City's Town Hall, where a crowd that included Candice Bergen, Mike Nichols, and Diane Sawyer listened to Bach's *Goldberg Variations* and Ondaatje reading from his novel. "We flew the *English Patient* cast around the world and back again for four months straight promoting the film," recalls Miramax's Amy Hart. "There were huge premieres and high-end parties all over the globe for months on end. They absolutely exhausted those actors."

But the Oscar promises could backfire. Weinstein had acquired Billy Bob Thornton's microbudget drama *Sling Blade* for an absurd ten million dollars and spun Thornton into a Tarantino-style celebrity auteur. When Thornton was nominated for acting and screenplay, Weinstein sprang into action. One day, he picked up his office phone and got Bill Clinton on the line; eager to become a political power player, Weinstein had become a fund-raiser for the Clintons and part of their social circle on Martha's Vineyard. Realizing that both Clinton and Thornton were Arkansas boys, Weinstein picked the president's brain for tips on Thornton's Oscar campaign. "I was so appalled that the president of the United States would spend half an hour with us on the phone," says a Miramax staffer who was there. "I lost all respect for him well before Monica Lewinsky, because I could see how much access the Clintons were giving to Harvey."

Thornton was the kind of charismatic eccentric who could win over Academy voters through nonstop cocktail parties, but his campaign irked Minghella, who was nominated against him for the adapted screenplay prize. "You're doing too good a job on *Sling Blade*," Minghella scolded the Miramax publicity staff. Paul Zaentz, Saul's nephew and producing partner, recalls Cynthia Swartz telling the *English Patient* team, with complete confidence, that Minghella would win Best Directing, because Thornton was going to win the screenplay race: "They were so dialed in to the voters that they knew who to push, who to contact, who had influence over other voters."

But the pushiness rankled some Academy members. John Ericson, a retired actor in Santa Fe, complained to the *New York Times* that he had received multiple calls about *Sling Blade*, first urging him to watch the screener copy he'd been sent and then following up to see what he thought. Miramax even set up a screening at a local movie theater, for the handful of voters in New Mexico. "We would have screenings in Telluride, Vail, anywhere anybody had vacation homes or went over Christmas," a former Miramax staffer recalls. "We started screenings in London and Paris, because maybe if you got three Academy members there, if we had the screening and no one else did, we got them to see our movie."

After the nominations, *The English Patient*'s box office leaped from $42 million to $60 million. "We wanted people to think they couldn't go to a party unless they saw this movie," Mark Gill told the *L.A. Times*. So successful was its takeover of the zeitgeist that, eleven days before the Oscars, *Seinfeld* aired an episode in which Elaine is tortured by the film's ubiquity. Amy Hart says, "The joke around the office was 'Well, we've made it.'"

On Oscar night—which the host, Billy Crystal, dubbed "Sundance by the Sea"—*The English Patient*'s domination started early when Binoche won Best Supporting Actress over Lauren Bacall. Despite speculation that studio employees would go all-in for *Jerry Maguire*, *The English Patient* won nine Oscars, including Best Picture, accepted by Saul Zaentz. He thanked the Weinsteins for saving the film, but got a knowing laugh when he added, "We had final cut, though."

The honeymoon wouldn't last. *The English Patient* went on to gross more than $230 million worldwide, but Zaentz saw none of the profits. He later audited Miramax and compared Weinstein to "a pushcart peddler who puts his thumb on the scale when the old woman is buying meat." Weinstein countered, "Did we want the Academy Award? Yes! Did we overspend? Yes! We did whatever we had to do." Zaentz sued in 2006. The two-decade dispute finally ended with a settlement in 2014, after Zaentz had been dead for six months.

On Oscar night, though, it was all smiles. The Miramax party at the Mondrian was so packed that the fire department had to stop the influx of guests. ("And then, of course, Miramax charged [the producers of] *The English Patient* with the entire cost of the party," Paul Zaentz says.) Among the fifteen hundred guests were Mira Sorvino and Ashley Judd, who would later accuse Weinstein of sexually harassing them and then blacklisting them when they resisted. Not even Steven Soderbergh, a personal guest of Minghella, could get in—a sign that this was no longer the Miramax of *sex, lies and videotape*.

Standing near the banquettes, Weinstein had ditched his bowtie and, in the words of the *Observer*'s Frank DiGiacomo, had "so rumpled his monkey suit that he looked like a Tahoe lounge singer after his third set of the night." Besieged by ring kissers, he asked *Pulp Fiction* producer Lawrence Bender, "Can't they let me just be happy for one night?"

"Nope," Bender replied. "Tonight, you're the Godfather." Now that Miramax had won the top prize, Weinstein had an insatiable hunger for another—only, next time, it wouldn't be Saul Zaentz onstage accepting Best Picture. It would be Harvey Weinstein.

LOST AMID THE *ENGLISH PATIENT* sweep was the fact that DreamWorks took home its first Academy Award, for *Dear Diary*, a failed ABC pilot that the studio had submitted for Best Live Action Short Film. Fine, but hardly the stuff that dreams were made of. That December, *Amistad*— the first Spielberg movie from Spielberg's studio—opened under a cloud. A Black writer named Barbara Chase-Riboud had sued DreamWorks for copyright infringement, claiming that the film bore "shocking similarities" to her novel *Echo of Lions* and asking for ten million dollars in "reparations."

Months later, she withdrew the lawsuit and, in a strange about-face, praised Spielberg for his "splendid piece of work." But that didn't save the film from weak box office and mixed reviews. Even the DreamWorks marketing team called it "the spinach movie." Spielberg, whom one consultant describes as "mad for awards," had his hopes on another Oscar, but he shunned campaigning, believing the movie should speak for itself. "He really didn't get involved at all in the *Amistad* campaign," recalls Mike Gottberg. "He just felt it was distasteful. It was an old-school thing." It fell on Terry Press, the studio's marketing head, to tell him it wasn't looking likely. Press had come to DreamWorks in 1995 from Disney, where she was known as one of "Jeffrey's Girls"; Katzenberg had even hosted her wedding, where he gave her away to Andy Marx, grandson of Groucho. She had what one colleague called "truthful brazenness." Once, when a male executive offered a marketing idea for a Reese Witherspoon film, Press retorted, "When you have a vagina, you can tell me how to market this movie!"

Press could tell powerful men what others would not, an asset at DreamWorks. "She did speak the truth to the partners," one DreamWorks veteran says, "but she also kind of spoke the truth to what each one of them wanted to hear. Terry did an incredible job telling Steven what he needed to hear about Jeffrey, and Jeffrey what he needed to hear about David, and David what he needed to hear about Steven. She could engender goodwill amongst the partners, or she could get one of them complaining about the other one and use soft power to say, 'Oh, I need Steven to do this,' but then riling up the other one to get him to do it."

When it came to *Amistad*, Press was right: neither the picture nor Spielberg was nominated. If 1997 was the "Year of the Indies," 1998 was the year of *Titanic*. Even Miramax looked like small potatoes, with its breakout hit *Good Will Hunting*—though that didn't stop Weinstein from proclaiming, "*Titanic* has great special effects, but in *Good Will Hunting*, the special effects are the words." "Harvey didn't get crazy about winning until we won with *The English Patient*," Swartz says. "And then I remember him being stupidly crazy about *Good Will Hunting* beating *Titanic*, which wasn't going to happen." But *Good Will Hunting* made instant celebrities of its young stars and cowriters, Matt Damon and Ben Affleck, whom Weinstein sent out "whoring for Oscars," in Affleck's words. In the end, they won the original screenplay award. At the afterparty, Weinstein joked, "I offered Sean Connery $1 million for three seconds of work. All he had to do was open the envelope . . . and say that the Best Picture went to *Good Will Hunting*. But the bastard was too ethical."

If *Amistad* had turned out to be another *Color Purple*, Spielberg's next project might be another *Schindler's List*. *Saving Private Ryan* had originated with screenwriter Robert Rodat. In his small New Hampshire town, Rodat would get up at dawn to walk with his crying baby. "We would often walk through the graveyard, which was always shrouded in morning mist, and pass a monument that has the names of the men from the village who had died in combat, from the Revolution up through Vietnam," he recalled. He saw names of brothers, sons, and fathers; one family had lost five members in the Civil War. "And so, with this infant son in my arms and another sleeping in the house, the idea of losing a son to combat was painful beyond description."

Rodat's wife had given him Stephen E. Ambrose's book *D-Day*, published on the invasion's fiftieth anniversary, and there he read about the Niland family of Tonawanda, New York. One day in 1944, Mrs. Niland received telegrams from the War Department informing her of the deaths of three of her four sons. (One turned out to be in a Japanese POW camp and survived.) The fourth son, Fritz, of the 101st Airborne, was plucked from the front lines and returned to safety. Rodat, whose own father had been injured in World War II, saw in this tale a moral conundrum: Is it worth endangering a band of soldiers to save one?

He pitched the idea to producer Mark Gordon. "I said, 'That's the greatest fucking story I've ever heard,'" Gordon recalls. They made a deal with Don Granger, an executive at Paramount who was on the hunt for war pictures, and turned in a script in January 1996, expecting a hero's welcome. They got back alarming news: the studio now had two other World War II films in development, one with interest from Bruce Willis and another attached to Arnold Schwarzenegger. Whichever one came together first would get the green light.

Gordon raced to get a director and star attached. He had given the script to an agent at CAA named Carin Sage. She told her boss, Richard Lovett, that the part of Captain John H. Miller, who leads his men on the mission to save Private Ryan, would be perfect for Tom Hanks. Sage also knew that Spielberg was coming to CAA the next day, where a gaggle of agents would pitch him projects. Spielberg didn't typically take his ideas from agents, but Sage gave a passionate pitch for *Saving Private Ryan*. The director seemed intrigued.

Just as Gordon was about to land director Rob Cohen, who was in postproduction on Paramount's *Dragonheart*, Lovett called and said enigmatically, "Don't make an offer yet." Hours later, he called back with word that Tom Hanks wanted to have lunch. Gordon and his business partner listened to the actor expound on Captain Miller, whom Hanks saw as a conflicted "citizen-soldier." After his back-to-back Oscars for *Philadelphia* and *Forrest Gump*, Hanks had acquired the Decent Soul of America status previously held by Gary Cooper and Jimmy Stewart. "He said, 'How would we feel about giving the script to Steven?'" Gordon recalls. "I was like, 'Yeah, please!'" That Friday, Paramount chair Sherry Lansing was driving home and got a call from Lovett at CAA. "How would you like it if Steven Spielberg and Tom Hanks did *Saving Private Ryan?*" he asked, as if taking her order at a diner.

"Yeah," she said, dumbstruck, "that'd be just fine."

The movie would be a Paramount–DreamWorks joint venture. To determine who would get domestic versus foreign rights, David Geffen and Sumner Redstone, chairman of Paramount's corporate parent, Viacom, flipped a coin. Redstone called heads, Geffen called tails. It was tails; DreamWorks took domestic rights.

Spielberg then got to work taking apart *Saving Private Ryan* and refashioning it in his own image. During the summer of 1996, he beamed in by teleconference from his house in the Hamptons, while Rodat, Gordon, Walter Parkes, and others sat in his home office in Pacific Palisades. When Rodat mentioned that he originally wanted Hanks's character to die—Paramount thought that he should live—Spielberg replied, "You bet he's got to die." Then there was Private Ryan. "We had different iterations of who Ryan could or should be," says producer Gary Levinsohn. "Could he be someone you never saw, perhaps, and all of that risk was taken for someone who you never got to see? Could he be a bully? What if you had gone all this way and found out that the guy that you had done all this for was someone you found reprehensible?" Spielberg settled on an all-American son of the Iowa cornfields and cast the Miramax-anointed star Matt Damon.

The biggest change, though, was to the D-day invasion scene that opened the film. In Rodat's script, it had run just a few pages, but Spielberg saw it as an extended battle sequence that would lay bare the carnage of combat. "I remember him saying, 'When people finish that sequence, they're going to think they were in the war,'" Gordon recalls.

"One of Steven's gifts is to be able to be simultaneously very micro and very macro," says Walter Parkes. "On one hand, the morality of risking six or seven lives to save one is a really interesting 'big idea.' And on the other, I think it was about, 'Boy, I could shoot the heck out of D-day.'"

World War II had a special hold over Spielberg. His father had been in a B-25 bomber squadron in Burma, and Spielberg had been raised on war movies like *Back to Bataan* and *Sands of Iwo Jima.* "So, between my father's stories and John Wayne's presence in these films, as a youngster I got the impression that war was something to be glorified, to be looked at with a kind of awe," he said. But *Ryan*, a kind of companion piece to *Schindler's List*, would strip the romance from the old war movies. "I didn't want to shoot the picture in a way that would seem like a Hollywood production coming to Omaha Beach and making a gung-ho extravaganza," he said.

The pull of *Ryan* went even deeper. Since his parents' divorce in 1966, Spielberg had harbored anger toward his father that turned into a fifteen-year rift. "In my heart, I loved my dad," he said later. "But resentment can build up layers and barriers, and I just felt more comfortable not thinking about it." After his mother told him that the split had been her fault as well, Spielberg realized that he had been putting too much blame on one parent, and he "began to try to figure out how I could earn my father's love back." *Ryan* would be an act of filial piety, a way to honor not just his father but the generation that had saved the free world.

The cast went through a grueling basic training, hiking through the rain and cold and sleeping on the ground. Spielberg didn't arrive on set until three days before the D-day shoot began on a beach in County Wexford, Ireland. "He wanted to be like those young men and put himself directorially in a position where he didn't exactly know what he was going to do," producer Ian Bryce recalls. The Irish Defence Forces lent hundreds of reserves as extras. Spielberg modeled the grainy, handheld cinematography in part on John Ford's Oscar-winning footage from *The Battle of Midway*. They spent nearly three weeks "laboring to get it accurate," Hanks said, "despite how gruesome and despite how painful."

When Terry Press first saw the film, she realized she had a hard sell. The invasion sequence lasted nearly half an hour, and though everyone who saw it was awestruck, it could easily scare moviegoers away. She insisted that the trailer include a shot of the wordless scene of Ryan's mother receiving the news of her sons' deaths. "I thought that the actual idea of the movie would appeal to females: the army will save your remaining son," she says. "That is a mother's message." When Spielberg resisted, the two fought it out. Press won.

Her bigger challenge was getting Spielberg to play pitchman. As with *Amistad*, the director worried about looking crass, given the gravitas of the subject matter. Press knew that no one could match Spielberg's promotional might, and she got Katzenberg, along with Spielberg's publicist Marvin Levy, to press her case. Spielberg agreed to a five-city tour, along with historian Stephen E. Ambrose, whose presence gave the film a legitimacy that had eluded *Amistad*. When *Ryan* was screened for aging veterans and their families, the impact was seismic; many had never found the words to describe to their loved ones what they experienced. "Some of the more overwhelming responses we had were from children and spouses of veterans, who said to us, 'Oh, my God, thank you so much for doing this,'" Levinsohn says.

DreamWorks slated *Ryan* for the summer of 1998, a season that Spielberg had owned since *Jaws*. But would the audiences flocking to *Godzilla* and *Armageddon* show up for a harrowing World War II drama? At the movie's premiere in Westwood, which was attended by Tom Cruise, Sylvester Stallone, and Oliver Stone, Spielberg, seeming particularly boyish and energetic, would tell anyone who would listen about his strict new fruit-and-vegetable diet. Privately, he'd confess his doubts that young audiences would understand the stakes of the fifty-year-old war.

Nevertheless, *Ryan* took in more than $30 million on its opening weekend. It went on to gross $216 million domestically and an astonishing $485 million worldwide. Critics lavished praise on the D-day sequence, which *Time*'s Richard Schickel called "quite possibly the greatest combat sequence ever made." *Ryan* represented more than a movie: it was a commemoration of the aging "Greatest Generation." For DreamWorks, it was also the film that finally made the studio click. "You were like, *This is a Steven Spielberg movie. This is why we joined this company*," one employee says. "*Saving Private Ryan* was a flag flying on top of the building."

Or, as Geffen put it, "We don't have to take any shit for a while."

For Spielberg, tap-dancing for awards was out of the question. "He held—and still holds—the Academy in great esteem and didn't feel like it needed to be debased," publicist Mitch Kreindel recalls. No matter: as summer turned into fall, *Saving Private Ryan* was the undisputed Best Picture front-runner. How could it lose? One day in December, Terry Press filed into an Academy screening room to see the latest release from Miramax. It was light, it was frothy, and it was about love and creativity instead of war and sacrifice. And it was about actors, by far the largest branch of the Academy. It was *Shakespeare in Love*, and the crowd absolutely adored it. Press turned to her husband and said, "Houston, we have a problem."

A DECADE EARLIER, SCREENWRITER MARC Norman was living in Santa Monica, with a master's in English and a few undistinguished credits. "I'd written a bunch of screenplays," he recalls. "The ones I really liked had never gotten made, and the ones that *had* gotten made, I didn't like that much." One day, his college-age son, who was taking an Elizabethan Theater class at Boston University, called him with an idea: the young Shakespeare, just starting out. "That's fucking brilliant!" Norman replied.

But how to approach such a lofty subject? Shakespeare "was like the Death Star," Norman says. "How do you attack the Death Star?" He was researching in the UCLA library when he realized that the Elizabethan theater world felt strangely familiar: there were money-grubbing producers, warring companies, preening stars, contract disputes, lawsuits. It was, in short, Hollywood. If Shakespeare were alive today, he thought, he would be living in Bel Air and driving a Porsche, with a three-picture deal at Warner Bros. The idea of Shakespeare as struggling screenwriter—as a version of Norman—was the germ of *Shakespeare in Love*.

Norman brought the concept to Ed Zwick, cocreator of *thirtysomething*, who lived on his street and had an office in the same building. They sold the idea to Universal; Zwick would direct, and both would produce. But when Norman turned in a draft, the studio was lukewarm. That's when Zwick had the masterstroke of getting British playwright Tom Stoppard, whose dazzling wit and erudition had animated plays like

Rosencrantz and Guildenstern Are Dead, to rewrite it. News of the now-buzzy screenplay got to Julia Roberts, in her post–*Pretty Woman* after-glow. Roberts wanted to play Viola, the stagestruck young noblewoman who disguises herself as a man to infiltrate the theater and becomes Shakespeare's lover, muse, and the star of his new play, *Romeo and the Pirate's Daughter*, which of course becomes *Romeo and Juliet*.

The sets were being built at Pinewood when, in late 1992, Roberts flew to the United Kingdom to audition with would-be Shakespeares. She was determined to land Daniel Day-Lewis, who had already turned the part down, as he was busy with *In the Name of the Father*. Roberts had a history of becoming entangled with her leading men; she had recently ditched her *Flatliners* costar Kiefer Sutherland at the altar. She and Day-Lewis allegedly had a fling, after which he declined the role anyway. (Universal's Tom Pollock reportedly said, "Couldn't she have waited to fuck him until we had his name on a piece of paper?") Spurned, Roberts showed up to test with potential leading men, including the pre-*Schindler* Ralph Fiennes, but seemed disengaged. Six weeks before production, she dropped the movie as she had Sutherland. The sets were destroyed. "All of a sudden, Universal pulls the plug," Zwick recalls, "and the tabloids are all about how Julia Roberts (and probably me) had destroyed the British film industry."

Zwick tried to repackage the movie with Stephen Dillane and Emily Watson, then with Kenneth Branagh and Winona Ryder. But the project, Zwick says, had a "stink on it," plus around eight million dollars in sunk costs. He met with Weinstein, who loved the script and professed to love Zwick, but couldn't or wouldn't meet Universal's asking price. Years passed. In 1996, Zwick was shocked to read in the trades that Miramax was doing *Shakespeare in Love*. Weinstein had acquired it as part of a horse trade: Universal wanted Peter Jackson to direct *King Kong*, but Miramax had an option on him after distributing *Heavenly Creatures*.

Zwick realized he'd been frozen out. "No one tells me a word—this thing that I have *bled* over," he says. "It's not just that [Weinstein] controls the rights to *Shakespeare in Love*, but he decides that he doesn't want me to have anything to do with it. He's stealing my movie." Zwick hired a lawyer to play hardball. He was with his dying father when he got a 2 a.m.

call from Weinstein, screaming, "You little fucker! I'm going to kill your family! I'm going to make sure you never work again!" Zwick, thinking, *You picked on the wrong hippie*, replied, "You can go fuck yourself." Finally, Weinstein called Zwick and his agent to the Peninsula, where he wept crocodile tears and said, "I can't help it. I do bad things." He offered Zwick credit for his production company, Bedford Falls, plus the right to see dailies and acknowledgment in marketing materials. He later reneged on all but the credit, which appeared in the finished film over a shot of horse manure. "That, I have to believe, was just his utter malice," Zwick says.

Weinstein saw *Shakespeare in Love* as a vehicle for Gwyneth Paltrow, whom he was building up to be "the First Lady of Miramax"—like Jack Warner molding a new queen of the lot. Years earlier, Paltrow had reluctantly agreed to play the love interest in Miramax's *The Pallbearer*, only because Weinstein made it a precondition of her starring in *Emma*. "He was obsessed with her," says marketing executive Matthew Cohen. "He loved pretty blond things." Shortly before *Emma* filmed, the twenty-two-year-old actress got a fax from CAA summoning her to meet Weinstein at the Peninsula, where, after some business, he proposed that they move to the bedroom for massages. Petrified, Paltrow, who had thought of him as "Uncle Harvey," refused. She told her boyfriend, Brad Pitt, who warned Weinstein to back off. Weinstein called Paltrow and screamed at her for the disclosure. In the kind of internal compromise that many sexual harassment survivors make, Paltrow told herself she would keep quiet and nudge the relationship back toward professionalism.

The day that *The English Patient* was nominated for twelve Oscars, Paltrow failed to get a nomination for *Emma*, something she was apparently told to expect. Now there was another chance, with *Shakespeare in Love*. Weinstein hired British director John Madden and reportedly wanted Ben Affleck to play Shakespeare, but the actor was tied up with Kevin Smith's *Dogma* and hesitant to costar with Paltrow, whom he was currently dating. Weinstein browbeat Affleck into taking a comic part as a vainglorious actor. Ralph Fiennes was now long in the tooth for the young Shakespeare, but the part went to his bedroom-eyed brother Joseph.

Weinstein took a producer credit, an unusual move for an executive.

But it meant that, if the movie won Best Picture, he would get his own statuette. Was that *the* reason he took the credit? "Zero question about that in my mind," says Miramax marketing executive Mark Gill. But the heavy lifting at Shepperton Studios, where Elizabethan London had been painstakingly reproduced, was split between Donna Gigliotti and English producer David Parfitt. Gigliotti recalls, "Harvey would show up for half a day: 'This set looks really good.' 'Hi, Gwyneth!' 'Oh, hi, Ben!' 'Hi, whoever.' And that was it." Still, Weinstein left an impression. Goofing off during one take, Geoffrey Rush, playing a smalltime impresario, ad-libbed, "Let us have pirates, clowns, and a happy ending, and you'll make Harvey Weinstein a happy man."

Stoppard, picking up on the Elizabethan-London-as-Hollywood analogy, had stuffed the script with jokes about back-end points, above-the-title credits, and L.A. neurosis. (When Shakespeare visits a confessor, complaining of writer's block, he reclines as if on a therapist's couch.) Lording over the action was Judi Dench's Queen Elizabeth, who, in her indelible eight minutes of screen time, swoops in to issue directives, part lovers, and generally throw her weight around, finally ordering Shakespeare to write "something more cheerful next time." In other words, she was Weinstein—the mogul whose opinion is the only one that matters, who gives notes, asks for a happy ending, and leaves. "Except he wouldn't go away," says Mark Gill. "Judi Dench exited stage left. Harvey stuck around."

When *Shakespeare in Love* tested in New York, the numbers were mixed. "We could feel in the first test that people wanted to like the movie, but they were just left cold by the ending," Gigliotti says. In Stoppard's script, the lovers say a hasty goodbye, and, at the Queen's command, Viola leaves with her betrothed, Colin Firth's Lord Wessex, to claim his fortune in the New World. In Shakespeare's imagining, Viola survives a shipwreck and steps on to a beach to become the heroine of his next play, *Twelfth Night*. Stoppard envisioned the camera tilting up to reveal the modern Manhattan skyline. Too postmodern. They shot a version in which Viola approaches two figures on the beach and they enact act 1, scene 2, of *Twelfth Night* ("What country, friends, is this?"). Too obscure. Weinstein argued for a rom-com ending: Viola falls into

Shakespeare's arms, saying, "All the world's a stage," to which he replies, "And all the men and women merely players." Somehow everyone talked him out of that one.

Ultimately, they airbrushed out the figures on the beach, allowing Viola to walk alone into her unwritten future. The producers also realized they needed a more satisfying goodbye scene between Will and Viola. After some arm-twisting, Stoppard rewrote it so that Viola gives him the idea for *Twelfth Night*; she has healed him creatively and sexually, which he repays by immortalizing her in his art. Weinstein, who swore by test scores, agreed to pay for a quickie redo. This time, the test audience cried—bingo! But Weinstein, in Harvey Scissorhands mode, was still driving everyone crazy by insisting they needed to cut individual frames of Firth drowning in the shipwreck. Postproduction dragged.

The barely finished film premiered at Manhattan's Ziegfeld Theatre on December 3, 1998. "It literally was presented wet," says Tony Angellotti, one of the army of consultants Weinstein hired to push the movie. "The crowd went fucking nuts." In a PR coup, the guest of honor was Hillary Clinton, who gave a fifteen-minute speech praising "my friend Harvey," then watched beside him from the front row.

Weinstein was initially uncertain of the movie's Oscar chances. At Sundance, he sat his marketing brain trust in a circle and quizzed them: "Do you believe *Shakespeare in Love* can win?" Some thought so, some didn't. But audiences seemed to delight in the movie, which the *New York Times's* Janet Maslin praised for its "exhilarating cleverness." The only exception seemed to be the Academy screening—Terry Press remembered the crowd reaction as ominously enthusiastic, but Weinstein found it so muted that he hauled Angellotti outside and asked what the hell was going on. The audience, Angellotti explained, was his competition. "What did you expect?" he said. "This is Hollywood. You think they're on your side?"

SAVING PRIVATE RYAN HAD BEEN the front-runner for so long that the arrival of a major competitor gave the industry a jolt. On February 9, 1999, *Ryan* got eleven Oscar nominations; *Shakespeare* got thirteen, garnering "most nominated film of the year" bragging rights. With twenty-three nominations in total, including seven for Roberto Benigni's *Life Is Beautiful*, Miramax led every other distributor. Unlike in the "Year of the Indies," the lineup pitted Miramax directly against a studio block-buster. Over the decade, Weinstein had made the indies big business. But *Shakespeare* vs. *Ryan* was the ultimate test: Could he really beat *Spielberg*?

For the *Shakespeare* campaign, Miramax took everything it had done for *The English Patient* and put "more gas on the fire," says Mark Gill. The company flooded the trades with ads, which Miramax marketing exec-utive David Brooks describes as "very colorful and fun and romantic—a distinct contrast to *Private Ryan*." Radio spots ran on a dozen different L.A. stations, stalking commuters with the *Shakespeare* theme music. Pricey brochure booklets were made, and, according to Gill, "we over-printed an extra hundred thousand and 'accidentally' left them all over every Starbucks in West Los Angeles."

The no-stone-left-unturned philosophy extended to the ground game. At one point, Weinstein asked Donna Gigliotti, "Has Red Buttons seen the movie?" She said that the Borscht Belt comedian was dead, but Weinstein corrected her—Buttons was not only alive and well at eighty, but he was living in Palm Springs, represented by William Morris, and an Academy voter. They arranged a screening. "Harvey made the Academy feel like *Shakespeare in Love* was a classic," publicist Dale Olson said. "He made it so it was almost criminal not to vote for it. He said, 'This is the kind of thing that's never been done before.' It was like *Gone with the Wind*." Weinstein was particularly focused on Paltrow's Best Actress cam-paign. When he heard that the Waspy-looking starlet was half Jewish—in fact, descended from the Paltrowitch rabbinical dynasty—he instructed his office to book her an interview with the *Jewish Chronicle*.

Miramax hired a battalion of freelance consultants to push every conceivable angle, to the point where its own executives didn't know everything that was going on. In February, Bobby Zarem, the "superflack" who had created the "I ♥ New York" campaign, arranged a "Welcome to America" party for *Shakespeare* director John Madden at Elaine's and invited Academy members Sidney Lumet, screenwriter Jay Presson Allen, and composer David Newman. The Academy received a complaint that this violated a 1997 rule against improper receptions, and Zarem got a panicked call from Miramax. "This is thirty-six hours before the supper," Zarem remembered. "I got Betsy and Walter Cronkite, Blaine Trump, Keith Hernandez—there were probably one or two more civilians—so that it was no longer correct to say that it was *just* Academy members."

Miramax was simultaneously pushing *Life Is Beautiful*, which one critic derided as "the first feel-good Holocaust weepie" but which Weinstein had spun into the highest-grossing foreign-language film ever released in the United States. It was nominated for Best Picture and Best Foreign Language Film, and Benigni got the nod for Best Actor and Best Directing. At Weinstein's request, the impish Italian star moved to L.A. for months for a nonstop charm offensive. More Bugs Bunny than human, Benigni added a madcap touch to Oscar season, jabbering in exuberant broken English over Miramax-arranged dinners with Kirk Douglas, Jack Lemmon, and Elizabeth Taylor. At the Directors Guild of America Awards, where Spielberg called him "an Italian Furby," Benigni hopped onstage, exclaiming, "I can't believe I won! I am full like a watermelon!" Actually, Spielberg had won; Benigni was being given a nomination plaque.

When the Vatican included *Life Is Beautiful* on its list of films "suitable for viewing by the faithful," Miramax sent out a press release trumpeting the movie's place in "the Pope's Oscars," implying that the Pope had endorsed its Academy campaign. It was Weinstein's old *My Left Foot* playbook, but at Miramax, where the underdog mentality was ingrained, nothing was overkill. "Everybody had to figure out where they drew the line with him," Mark Gill says, "otherwise he would just ask you to do anything: 'Go kill a baby seal to win the Academy Award!'"

Shakespeare screenwriter Marc Norman noticed a shift. "I'd go to these parties in the months before the Oscars and run into people I knew, and they'd say to me, 'Gee, I really liked your movie, I voted for it, but of course Steven's gonna win.' After the third or fourth person said it to me, I began to think, *Well, who's voting for Steven?*" Little did Norman know that Miramax's lavish campaign spending was cannibalizing his 7.5 net points. Later on, he says, "I had an accountant look over the books. They basically said, 'Miramax spent so much money promoting this movie, there's not going to be any profit for *you*.'"

DreamWorks now looked complacent next to the Weinstein machine, but Spielberg was still resistant to campaigning for *Saving Private
Ryan*. "It really was a full-court press to try to get Steven out in the world
telling people how proud he was of this film," Mike Gottberg recalls. Five
years into DreamWorks's existence, its utopianism had hit multiple rocks.
The company had blown through a billion dollars in start-up capital,
and Spielberg's plans for his Playa Vista studio had stalled amid lawsuits,
red tape, and environmental protests. (It never got built.) When *The
Prince of Egypt* finally came out, it was neither a flop nor the next *Lion
King*. Within months, the company would have to ban first-class travel,
bar employees' families from Christmas parties, and wind down its TV-
animation division. It was looking less like a dream factory than a regular
studio with regular problems, and just about the only thing propping it up
was *Saving Private Ryan*. Even then, there was what one observer calls an
"undercurrent of resentment" building toward Spielberg, whose success
was so out of proportion to that of his peers.

Then the tinderbox exploded. One day, Terry Press was at
DreamWorks, on the phone with Lynn Hirschberg, the journalist who
had nearly suffered death by Oscar at the *Pulp Fiction* party. Hirschberg,
who was covering the awards race for the *New York Times*, gave Press a
heads up: Weinstein had tried to persuade her to write that *Saving Private
Ryan* peaked after the first twenty-five minutes and then became a standard World War II drama.

By casting *Ryan*'s bravura D-day sequence as a liability, Weinstein had
channeled one of Karl Rove's rules of the political dark arts: attack your
opposition's *strength*, not its weakness. Press had tangled with Weinstein
before, when she was at Disney and he was creating a PR nightmare with
Priest. But negative campaigning was against Academy rules, and this was
beyond the pale. Murray Weissman, a consultant working for Weinstein,
gave Press the impression that the line was a coordinated talking point.
"It was shocking to my system," she says, "which shows how completely
naïve I was."

Incensed, she marched into Spielberg's office and told him what she
had heard. The director was crystal clear: "No matter what, I do not want
you to get in the mud with Harvey Weinstein."

"Are you sure?" she asked.

"I don't want any negative campaigning."

If Press was working with one hand tied behind her back, that didn't mean she was backing down. "Very quickly, we were all on red alert," one of her staffers recalls. "We all knew we were at war." DreamWorks pumped an extra million dollars or two into the campaign and rereleased the film in more than a thousand theaters. On a single Sunday, it ran ads in more than sixty major-market papers, reminding everyone that *Ryan* was the best picture of the year. "We started to do special inserts in the trades, which Steven was actually very involved in," says Gottberg. "I would show him layouts. There were a few things we suggested that he killed—like, 'No, I don't want to go that far.' He just didn't like the gauche-ness of it all." Press implored him, "You don't have to campaign, but you really need to get out there."

Katzenberg was aghast that they were spending so luxuriantly, especially for a movie that had already made its box-office money. For Press, though, it was personal. "Terry was always the angriest of the people in the room," one staffer recalls. "She was the most competitive, the savviest at realizing exactly what was happening, how dangerous it was. Jeffrey's no shrinking violet—he's very intense and tough—but Terry *really* is. My memories of that era are of Jeffrey trying to calm Terry down, because she was livid."

Weinstein's response was simple: deny, deny, deny. He insisted that he had loved *Saving Private Ryan*. "I called Steven to congratulate him," he protested. "I told Mrs. Clinton that the movie was a masterpiece and she should see it, and Mrs. Clinton has an aversion to films with violence." He called the accusation "scurrilous and an effort by people to ruin long-standing friendships." But other journalists had heard Weinstein's knock against *Ryan*, too, including *Variety* editor Peter Bart, who got weekly phone calls from Weinstein and Press carping about each other. "She was always pissed off, and rightly so," Bart recalls. "She would say, 'Well, surely you don't believe a word that *he* said.' But, in point of fact, I was taking his phone calls. And why not? He was usually kind of funny. But he also clearly was a pig."

The rivalry soon spilled over into the press. In the *New York Times*,

Bernard Weinraub wrote that *Ryan* had been "virtually anointed" until Miramax began "spinning journalists and spending lavishly." More incendiary was a *New York* magazine piece by Nikki Finke, calling the upcoming Oscars "one of the most contentious ceremonies in the 72-year history of the Academy" due to "what many view as Miramax's over-the-line campaign." Finke laid out every supposed breach: the phone banking, the overspending, the "fleet" of publicists hired to "schmooze prominent Academy colleagues," the Elaine's party, the alleged attacks on *Saving Private Ryan*. One journalist recounted getting a phone call from consultant Tony Angellotti offering "a little guidance when you write your Oscar story," which Angellotti began by "totally trashing *Saving Private Ryan*." (Angellotti called this a "lie.") "Miramax, for some reason, thinks that because they are media darlings, they're above scrutiny," a competitor griped. "We wouldn't get away with this stuff for two minutes."

"The payoff," Finke wrote, "may well be that the Oscar goes to two hours of Elizabethan froth instead of to one of the most gut-wrenching war movies ever made."

Weinstein's staff, working grueling hours to promote *Shakespeare*, felt smeared. "DreamWorks was having a conversation in the media about the process," Miramax's Marcy Granata says. "They didn't use their considerable microphone to go back and emphasize how Steven *made* those twenty-five minutes. You could win Best Picture alone on those twenty-five minutes." And what was wrong with hanging out at Elaine's, when L.A. people habitually gathered in their private screening rooms? The Academy, meanwhile, declined to intervene; all the marketing for the two front-runners would be good for ratings, and, as AMPAS executive administrator Ric Robertson told Finke, "We don't want to be Big Brother."

In March, as recriminations flew, Weinstein and Katzenberg set up a conference call with their respective campaign heads, Marcy Granata and Terry Press. The two men mostly stayed silent as Press lit into Miramax for overspending and overreaching—even running a *Shakespeare* ad during Barbara Walters's interview with Monica Lewinsky. Granata replied that DreamWorks could have done the same if they had thought of it, and that, because *Shakespeare* was still in theaters, Miramax was simply trying to open its movie wide. Granata, who was pregnant and trying to minimize her stress, was speaking from a town car steps from her apartment. "All I wanted to do was get out of the car and get into the house," she recalls. "But I was holding my own, because I didn't understand why someone had to explain doing a hundred percent for their movie."

As for negative campaigning, Press said carefully, "We're not saying it's you, and I don't think it's you. But what if people you hired are doing this despite you?"

Granata insisted that she had grilled the freelance consultants and been assured the rumor wasn't true. Weinstein asked her to vouch for his effusive praise for *Ryan* when it came out. Then Granata went on offense, accusing Katzenberg and Press of shopping around the story about Miramax's tactics. The DreamWorks side dismissed the idea.

The call ended without a resolution. Weinstein had wanted to make the accusations against him go away, but Katzenberg wanted to mitigate the spending, which Weinstein was not going to do. The two men were "admiring frenemies," Mark Gill says: Katzenberg had made Weinstein through the Disney deal, but now Weinstein was a thorn in Katzenberg's side. "There was an audacity in competing with the person who gave you your shot," Granata says.

After hanging up with DreamWorks, Granata stayed on the phone with Weinstein, who was stunned that she'd been so forthright with his former boss. "You get that this is a choice," Granata told him. "They think you are trying too hard to win—not just to make your money, but actually *win*. They believe Best Picture is theirs, and that's what's fundamentally going wrong here. They're upset, because you're trying to take something away from Steven that they feel Steven deserves." Not realizing that her boss had been attacking *Ryan* out of the other side of his mouth, Granata felt that Weinstein was being played for a caricature: the "rough, rude street player who could bully his way into winning Oscars." Years later, she says, "Did I get used? Was I used by a serial, sociopathic liar? Was I just a pawn? Was *everybody* a pawn?"

As the Oscars approached, both parties felt aggrieved. Miramax thought that DreamWorks was playing the victim card as its own form of negative campaigning, particularly when Press made passive-aggressive zingers to reporters: "My legs are hurting from being on the high road," she told the *Times*. "I believe the award is for achievement in motion pictures and is not an award for spin," she told the *Wall Street Journal*. DreamWorks staffers felt that their noble movie was getting assassinated, and Spielberg had forbade them from fighting back. "We were hamstrung," one publicist recalls. "These street fighters have come here from New York, and we're being out-trashed by them. And we have our hands tied behind our backs, and we can't respond. We can't fight dirty like they are."

ON MARCH 21, 1999, DONNA Gigliotti was leaving for the Seventy-First Academy Awards when she got a call at her hotel room. It was Harvey and Bob Weinstein. In the event that *Shakespeare in Love* won Best Picture, Harvey would have to share the stage with four other producers: Gigliotti, David Parfitt, and the pair he considered vestigial at best, Marc Norman and Ed Zwick. Weinstein had offered Norman a hundred thousand dollars to relinquish his producing credit and even his screenwriting credit, but the matter was dropped when Norman threatened to take the matter to the Writers Guild. There was no way, however, that Weinstein was going to let Norman and Zwick talk if they won Best Picture. After Harvey's rambling speech at the Golden Globes, the team had decided that Gigliotti would speak solo. Then, a week before the Oscars, Parfitt privately asked her if she could cue him up for a few words, and Zwick asked the same.

Now Gigliotti heard the voice of Bob Weinstein on the phone, saying in a tone she found threatening, "How are you going to introduce Harvey?" She understood that this was an offer she couldn't refuse. She pondered what to do.

The *Saving Private Ryan* producers had no such angst over who would speak: Spielberg. At the Dorothy Chandler Pavilion, the director had an aisle seat unmissable by the cameras. But the evening kicked off with a nod to *Shakespeare in Love* and *Elizabeth*, when the host, Whoopi Goldberg, entered in Elizabeth I garb and announced, "I am the African queen." She teased the dueling Oscar campaigns: "Those boys fought World War Three over World War Two!"

From then on, the night was like a pickup basketball game: *Shakespeare*'s Judi Dench won Best Supporting Actress, *Ryan* won Sound. *Shakespeare* won Score, *Ryan* won Editing. A memorable detour came when *Life Is Beautiful* won Best Foreign Language Film, and Benigni climbed over the seats—with a helping hand from Spielberg—and babbled, "I want to kiss everybody because you are the image of the joy!" Amid a torrent of Italian names, he thanked *Haar-vay Wayn-steen*.

"The score," Goldberg said after a commercial break, "is Shakespeare, four; World War Two, two; insane Italians, one." Moments later, Benigni beat Tom Hanks for Best Actor and took the stage again, saying, "This is a terrible mistake, because I used up all my English!" Insane Italians: two. Later, when Marc Norman and Tom Stoppard won for their screenplay, Stoppard deadpanned, "I'm behaving like Roberto Benigni *underneath*," then thanked Gigliotti and Parfitt for playing "good cop and very sweet cop to Commissioner Harvey."

The *Shakespeare* vs. *Ryan* feud had not been the Academy's biggest headache that year. Its decision to present an honorary award to Elia Kazan, forty-seven years after he named names to HUAC, had brought weeks of hand-wringing; Michael Wilson's daughter Becca was among those who stood outside the theater protesting. This unwelcome visitation from Hollywood's past ended with an anticlimax when Kazan came out to a standing ovation. A few stars, including Nick Nolte and Ed Harris, refused to applaud. Spielberg split the difference by clapping from his seat. The ghost of Dalton Trumbo presumably started typing an angry letter.

Then it was back to the main event. *Ryan* got an imprimatur when General Colin Powell showed up to salute World War II veterans. Then Best Actress went to a teary Paltrow, a Hollywood princess in her pink Ralph Lauren dress.

The penultimate award, Best Directing, went, unsurprisingly, to Spielberg, who momentarily dropped his above-it-all humanitarianism when he said, "Am I allowed to say I really wanted this?" Then, snapping back to form, he thanked the families who had lost sons in the war and dedicated the award to his father, who raised a fist from the audience.

Spielberg rushed back to his seat for the final award. The score was now *Shakespeare*, six; *Ryan*, five. The *Ryan* team, bracing for a photo finish, sighed in relief when Spielberg's friend Harrison Ford came out to present Best Picture: the Indiana Jones reunion seemed tailor-made for television. "I couldn't imagine not winning," *Ryan* producer Mark Gordon says. "I mean, for God's sakes, we had no competition!"

The *Shakespeare* team had already lost hope. It had been nine years since a Best Directing–Best Picture split. When Ford walked on, Mark Gill recalls thinking, "This is just a coronation. We're the court jesters." Ford opened the envelope and looked glum. Even as he spoke, no one could believe it. "When Harrison said, 'The winner is Ssss'—I stood up and buttoned my tuxedo, or started to," Gordon says. "Then I sat back down. It was horrible."

The winner was *Shakespeare in Love*.

As Weinstein leaped to his feet and gave out bear hugs, the spectators looked as if an anvil had fallen on them. Something had gone deeply wrong: in Hollywood, the bad guy wasn't supposed to win. In the wings, DreamWorks publicist Mitch Kreindel turned to Tony Angellotti and said, "Don't ever talk to me again." Terry Press, standing in the mezzanine, could feel her legs wobble. "I felt," she said later, "like my face was on fire, which was probably blood rushing to my face."

Onstage, Weinstein was unfolding his speech. As Gigliotti and then Parfitt spoke, Ed Zwick waited his turn, his head bobbing toward the microphone. The wrap-it-up sign was flashing. Gigliotti recalls, "I'm thinking, *What do I do?* Because I have this nine-hundred-pound gorilla, who is frankly frightening, breathing down my neck." Just as Zwick was about to speak, Gigliotti pulled Weinstein to the mic, praising him for having "the guts, the courage, the commitment to make this picture." Zwick's head drooped as he watched the man who had stolen his movie filibuster through the play-off music. "I had to make a choice between an act of violence in front of a worldwide viewing audience of several million people, or false modesty," Zwick says. "And I made the wrong choice."

Some forty-five million viewers watched Weinstein go on about how "art and life combining is called magic" and thank Disney, his wife, his mother, and his "two rotten kids." Appearing on the Oscar stage for the first time, Weinstein had completed his ten-year ascent, but to those he had threatened, bullied, cheated, harassed, and screwed over, it looked more like a hostile takeover.

As the audience cleared out, Mitch Kreindel found Spielberg at his seat and said, "I don't expect that you are comfortable going upstairs to do the press?" "No, I'm not," Spielberg replied weakly and walked away. The press corps was so insulted not to have access to the Best Directing winner, as protocol dictated, that Kreindel got booed on his way to the parking lot. The Academy called DreamWorks the next day to complain.

The five *Shakespeare* producers, meanwhile, headed to the pressroom. (Five producers was too many for the Academy, which soon issued a rule limiting the nominees to three per film.) "I don't think I spoke to any press," David Parfitt recalls. "That was Harvey front and center, pulling Gwyneth to the front. We were marginalized. So, that was a very embarrassing forty minutes." In the elevator to the Governors Ball, Weinstein lit a cigarette, and the female elevator operator brought the elevator to an abrupt halt and told him, "Sir, you're going to have to put out that cigarette." With the hand that wasn't holding his Oscar, he took one last defiant drag and put it out on the bottom of his shoe.

Terry Press, still in shock, followed the crowd through a narrow corridor to the Governors Ball. Her disappointment was hardening into raw fury, especially when she saw Weinstein talking to Katzenberg right in front of her. She congratulated her bête noire through gritted teeth. When he was gone, she turned to Katzenberg and said, "This will *never happen again*." She had played by Spielberg's rules, and what had it gotten her? Humiliation and loss. "I will *never* take the high road with these people again," she seethed to Katzenberg. "The next time, you'll find me in the mud."

Eventually, Press made it to the *Ryan* party at Barnaby's, where, the *Washington Post* observed, she had the "pale, haunted look of too-much-stress-not-enough-statues." The mood was funereal. Spielberg sat at a table with Harrison Ford, clutching his Oscar with cold rage. Guests whispered that Katzenberg looked "even shorter this evening." The *L.A. Times* snapped a photo of him and Spielberg not even feigning smiles. "They were the kings, and Harvey was a renegade prince," Mark

Gill says. "And the renegade prince, it turns out, brought a much better army. In many ways, it was a coup."

The Miramax party, at the Beverly Hills Hotel's Polo Lounge, was only marginally happier. They had won—but had gone from underdogs to the town villains. When Michael Eisner saw Marcy Granata, he told her, "What's wrong? You're supposed to smile." But she didn't feel like smiling. "It was this phenomenal moment where we *arrived*, we did it—and we're not being allowed to celebrate," she recalls. She told the *New York Observer*, "Just wait and see what they do to us." An *L.A. Times* reporter approached a group that included Tony Angellotti and said, "I hope you guys are happy, because they're really miserable over there at the DreamWorks party." Angellotti recalls, "It was all we could do not to tell him to fuck off."

At the Governors Ball, Weinstein had gone over to congratulate Spielberg, but the director turned away. "Steven was no longer naïve about what Harvey was capable of," Press said. Never mind. Weinstein made the rounds, statuette in hand, before finally showing up at his own party, where the crowd included Jennifer Lopez, Ben Affleck, and Quentin Tarantino. By 1:30 a.m., it was standing room only, except for a VIP section where Weinstein sat, in the vivid words of the *Observer*, "with tense pleasure, a mat of sweat dampening the close-cut fur of his Ursus major skull." Having beat the industry on its own turf, he was likely the most hated man in Hollywood. When the *Observer* asked for a quote, Weinstein smiled and said, "It's good to be alive."

EARLY THE NEXT MORNING, MIRAMAX's David Brooks woke up to a phone call from Weinstein. "They're saying we bought it," he said. "I need you to go in now and count their ads and our ads." The marketing team, now in defensive mode, spent hours going through piles of trade magazines. In the final tally, Miramax had run 118 pages of print ads. DreamWorks had run 165 pages.

In the heat of campaign season, Katzenberg had made a wager with Warren Beatty that Miramax would run more ads than DreamWorks. The ante was ten thousand dollars, to be donated to a charity of the winner's choice. Now that Beatty was the winner, Katzenberg suspected a miscount. But Weinstein was vindicated. Either his extravagant spending had been overstated or, more likely, DreamWorks's counterspend had blown Miramax out of the water.

It hardly mattered. Everyone believed that Weinstein had corrupted the Oscar race—and wasn't shy about saying so. "It's no longer about the material or the merit. It's about how much money you spend," Fox's Bill Mechanic told the *New York Times* the morning after, singling out Miramax for bad behavior. Mark Urman, of the newly formed Lionsgate, said, "The machinery Harvey puts in place is like a juggernaut. All predictions, all sense of logic and in some instances a sense of fairness is thrown out the window." In an *L.A. Times* story headlined "'Shakespeare' Hit by Snipers," one executive complained, "They're distorting the process. It's just like a political campaign."

Miramax vigorously defended itself, insisting that the campaign had cost much less than the reported fifteen million dollars and that *Shakespeare* was simply better liked. "The movie itself is about putting on a show, what all of us do every day," Marcy Granata argued. The *Observer* tracked down Weinstein, on vacation at Disneyland. "The newspapers report the town from the executive suite, and that can be a very self-serving executive suite," he said, in underdog mode, adding, "The executive suite wants to make money. Miramax wants to make movies."

Days later, Vincent Canby published a scathing column in the *New York Times*, accusing Weinstein's detractors of snobbery and hypocrisy. "There's still nothing quite as exhilarating as the spectacle of some of Hollywood's toughest wheeler-dealers, each of whom has an average income exceeding the G.N.P. of many countries, as they take umbrage at the shabby behavior of an upstart not yet in their club," he wrote, concluding, "This post-Oscar outrage is a joke. Come on, fellows: shut up or invite the Weinsteins to join the club."

The truth was that *Shakespeare in Love* had plenty of advantages. It had come out later. It played better than *Ryan* on VHS screeners. It had showed Hollywood a mirror of itself, in which every anxious screenwriter was a potential Shakespeare. It was about a woman succeeding in a man's world, a resonant idea in Hollywood. Amid the sordidness of the Lewinsky affair, it was a witty, romantic escape. Besides, could Sidney Lumet's vote really be bought by a party at Elaine's? Could a whisper campaign to a handful of journalists really change who won? *Shakespeare in Love* didn't need dirty pool to win, but now that it had won, the narrative solidified into two words: Harvey cheated.

WHAT HAPPENED NEXT WAS AN arms race.

"We would hear from our friends all over Hollywood that everybody decided that the only way to win an Oscar was to leave no stone unturned," Mark Gill recalls. "Harvey's approach had taken over." Executives, agents, and stars now demanded that marketing teams replicate the "Weinstein playbook" for them. "Oscar strategist" became a cottage industry, not just at indie houses but at big studios, too. "You always hired a strategist," a Universal publicist says. "The difference was you didn't hire an army and create a war room, and after that you did."

In September 1999, DreamWorks released *American Beauty*, a dark comedy directed by Sam Mendes and starring Kevin Spacey. Miramax had passed on Alan Ball's script, but Spielberg championed the project over the skepticism of some of his colleagues. Once it emerged as an Oscar contender, Terry Press took no chances. DreamWorks dropped $774,000 of ad spending within four weeks, doubling every other studio's, and hired a trio of consultants—among them Bruce Feldman, who had battled Weinstein on *Schindler's List* vs. *The Piano*. Feldman whisked Ball to the Santa Barbara International Film Festival and had him shake hands. "We figured five, ten or twenty-five votes could make a difference," he reasoned. Spacey poured tea at the motion picture retirement home. The once-aloof DreamWorks "couldn't afford the embarrassment of losing again," a rival executive observed. "They bought an insurance policy."

The 2000 Oscars were the Empire Strikes Back year. "Harvey skunked us last year," Katzenberg said of his "buddy." Miramax put its Oscar chips on *The Cider House Rules*, Lasse Hallström's stately adaptation of a John Irving novel, set at an orphanage in Maine. Far from *Pulp Fiction*, Miramax was now making the kind of mid-budget, middlebrow period piece that used to belong to the studios, while DreamWorks was putting out an edgy, low-budget upstart. It was as if the two companies had switched places: the indies were more studio-ish, the studios more indie-ish. *The Cider House Rules* had provocative themes—abortion, incest—but Miramax downplayed them, prompting Press to crow that she "never hid the darkness or the unsavory elements" of *American Beauty*. Weinstein was off his game. On his Christmas vacation on St. Bart's, he had come down with a mysterious bacterial infection and spent weeks hospitalized in New York, returning to work with a tracheotomy scar, forty pounds lighter, and in a foul temper. Nine days before the Oscars, he called Katzenberg on the DreamWorks jet and said, "Congratulations. You saw the playbook and outplayed us."

Sure enough, *American Beauty* won Best Picture. The producers thanked Spielberg, who stood in the wings, palms pressed as if in prayer, having just handed the directing Oscar to Sam Mendes. The next day, DreamWorks's offices were festooned with vases of five red roses apiece—one for each Oscar won by *American Beauty*.

Meanwhile, a parallel arms race heated up in the press, aided by the burgeoning blogosphere. The explosive coverage of *Shakespeare* vs. *Ryan* had exposed the Oscar machinery to a mass readership and helped create an appetite for gossip and prognostication. In 1999, a film school dropout named Sasha Stone started OscarWatch.com (renamed AwardsDaily.com after the Academy sued). The next year, Tom O'Neil founded GoldDerby.com, which provided year-round predictions. The rise of "Oscarologists" gave the newly busy consultants more receptacles for ads, spin, and swag. "I would be invited to private screenings of Harvey movies, where they try to make you feel special," O'Neil says. One year, Weinstein sent him a gift basket of cheeses and French wines.

GoldDerby.com was in full swing by the 2001 Oscar race. DreamWorks had *Gladiator*, which critics dismissed as a swords-and-sandals throwback. But Press, proving she could win with a big-budget popcorn movie as well as an indie-style dramedy, took out double-truck ads, billboards, and a Super Bowl spot. DreamWorks rented out a theater in Century City, where every night for a week, Russell Crowe and others made appearances. Live Q&As became an awards season staple, condemning actors and directors to a never-ending circuit of explaining themselves. *Gladiator* won Best Picture against Miramax's treacly *Chocolat*. For the first time in a decade, Miramax won none of its ten nominations, despite

Weinstein's procuring *Chocolat* endorsements from Jesse Jackson and the Anti-Defamation League's Abraham Foxman.

Weinstein hoped to rebound in 2002 with Martin Scorsese's *Gangs of New York*, even taking a producer credit. But when the $97 million behemoth got mired in postproduction, he was left with the chamber drama *In the Bedroom*. Universal and DreamWorks were sharing distribution of *A Beautiful Mind*, about schizophrenic mathematician John Nash. After it got six Golden Globe nominations, the online tabloid the Drudge Report posted an "exclusive item" that the movie had scrubbed out "repeated homosexual references" from Sylvia Nasar's biography. After the Oscar ballots went out, Drudge hit again, saying that Academy members were "discovering shocking Jew-bashing passages" in Nasar's book. No matter that Nash had made these comments in the midst of a schizophrenic rant decades earlier—he also expected to be named emperor of Antarctica—or that the film sought to destigmatize mental illness. The whisper campaign was the ugliest Oscar clash since *Shakespeare* vs. *Ryan*—uglier, as the ascendant online media could chew on every turn. Everyone blamed Weinstein, who denied it. Later, someone from the *Lord of the Rings* team apologized to a Universal publicist for their part in the smear campaign; others accused Universal of using the controversy to win sympathy votes. Whatever Weinstein's part, his mere presence pushed the boundaries. "Other competitors had protective cover," someone connected to *A Beautiful Mind* says. "If he was in the race, you could behave badly, knowing that he would be the first one people suspect."

At the 2002 Golden Globes, Weinstein heard that Nikki Finke was about to publish a column blaming him for the *Beautiful Mind* smear campaign. Convinced this was the doing of Terry Press, who lived rent-free in his head, he marched into the CAA afterparty and found Universal's Stacey Snider, all of five foot two. "You're going down for this!" he screamed, jabbing a thick finger in her face. The partygoers watched the tirade in shock. *"You fat fuck,"* Press shrieked. *"Get away from her."*

The next morning, Katzenberg called Weinstein and scolded, "You can't work this way. You are endangering my friendship, and you must apologize to Stacey." Weinstein vowed to take anger management classes. But the industry had seen his brutality in plain sight. Less than two weeks before *A Beautiful Mind* won Best Picture, Miramax laid off seventy-five employees. Others left out of sheer exhaustion. The Weinstein era seemed to be coming to an ignominious end. "This is a town that smells blood," one Disney executive told *The New Yorker*, in a damning profile by Ken Auletta. "When they smell blood, they circle like sharks. In Harvey's case, there is a sense that his streak has waned, that the magic may be gone."

But when Weinstein got cornered, he got angry, and anger was his fuel. In December 2002, Miramax released *Gangs of New York* and *Chicago*, which became Miramax's highest-grossing film. By then, the Oscar ecosystem had become more bloated than ever; that year, by some estimates, "For Your Consideration" ads cost the studios a combined fifty million dollars. The Academy scrambled to tamp down the hijinks with what became known as "Harvey Rules" or "Terry Rules," worn like badges of pride by their instigators. When Miramax took out ads for *Gangs of New York* with a testimonial by Robert Wise, the eighty-eight-year-old director of *The Sound of Music*—it was ghostwritten by a Miramax consultant—the Academy outlawed third-party endorsements from voters. But Weinstein was resurgent. "Three months ago they were saying I was dead," he gloated after *Chicago* won the Golden Globe. "Well, guess what? I've come back to life."

While one Harvey rebounded, the other Harvey had allegedly raped *Scream* star Rose McGowan in a hotel room; pinned actress Liz Kouri to a wall and digitally penetrated her; summoned Lauren Holly to a hotel room and asked for a massage; offered actress Dawn Dunning a contract on the condition of a three-way; and assaulted sixteen-year-old model Kaja Sokola at his apartment.

When the 2003 Oscar list came out, Miramax dominated with forty nominations. Of the five Best Picture contenders, Weinstein had produced two, *Chicago* and *Gangs of New York*, and had a hand in two others, *The Hours* and *The Lord of the Rings: The Two Towers*. In its headline the next morning, the *L.A. Times* nicknamed the awards "The Harveys."

One Harvey had remade the Oscars in his image. The other Harvey had done much worse.

Tokens

1940, 1964, 2002

How Hattie McDaniel, Sidney Poitier, and Halle
Berry broke through the Oscar color barrier—and
discovered how lonely being the first and only can be.

When the Oscar nominations were announced in 1996, *People* noticed something odd, or oddly typical. Its reporters started calling up the nominees, asking, "Are you white?" Of the 166 nominees, only one, short-film director Dianne Houston, was Black. Two weeks before the ceremony, the magazine published its findings in a cover story, with the damning words "HOLLYWOOD BLACKOUT."

The article blasted Hollywood's "shocking level of minority exclusion," from sound departments to executive suites, of which the whiteness of the Oscar nominees was a dispiriting reflection. The issue of the magazine sold poorly, but in a Los Angeles whose racial fault lines had been aggravated by the O. J. Simpson trial, it hit a nerve. Jesse Jackson announced that his Rainbow/PUSH Coalition would protest the ceremony, saying, "It doesn't stand to reason that if you are forced to the back of the bus, you will go to the bus company's annual picnic and act like you're happy."

The Academy, unused to a racial audit, went on the defensive. "The Academy is probably the most liberal organization in the country this side of the N.A.A.C.P.," protested executive director Bruce Davis. He demanded to see "the wonderful performances that have been over-looked," despite the fact that *People* had highlighted several on its cover, including Laurence Fishburne in *Othello* and Angela Bassett in *Waiting to Exhale*. The Academy had planned a ceremony it considered laudably diverse, produced by Quincy Jones and hosted by Whoopi Goldberg. Jones was careful not to undermine the cause—he said the *People* article was "thirty-five years too late"—while maneuvering behind the scenes to mollify Jackson, who vowed to "open up the consciousness of Hollywood." They reached a compromise: instead of picketing the Dorothy Chandler Pavilion, Jackson would move his protest to the ABC lot, and church leaders across the country would instruct their congregants to picket ABC affiliates.

On Oscar night, ushers carried trays of rainbow ribbons—another concession to Jackson—so that Black attendees could show their solidarity. Only Quincy Jones wore one. (Will Smith said it would clash with his tuxedo.) In Goldberg's opening monologue, she could barely contain her irritation, quipping, "Jesse Jackson asked me to wear a ribbon. I got it. But I had something I wanted to say to Jesse right here, but he's not watching, so why bother?" (The line got huge applause.) Some seventy-five people had joined Jackson's protest, plus three hundred in Chicago and a dozen in Washington. The press called the action a "box-office flop."

To present the Best Picture award, Goldberg introduced "the first Black man to win the Best Actor award, something that has yet to be repeated." At sixty-nine, Sidney Poitier was used to being trotted out as a totem of tolerance from a bygone age: "a living repository, and not much more," he later wrote. Before presenting the award to *Braveheart*, Poitier spouted some lofty words about the "mystery called the creative process." He said nothing about the firestorm that had pushed Hollywood, however briefly, to confront its racial imbalance, or the conflicted position into which it had put Jones and Goldberg—a conflict he knew all too well. In 1964, Poitier had expanded the club of Oscar-winning Black actors from one to two; four decades later, the group was just five, including

Goldberg, who had won for *Ghost*. A Black woman would not win Best Actress, astoundingly, until 2002.

These victories occurred years, sometimes decades apart. Each time, the winner was celebrated as a symbol of progress, an exception to the rule that gave the industry a chance to pat itself on the back for "making history." Most often, though, the statuette wasn't just a prize but a trap, in which the walls didn't expand so much as tighten. To "win" in a game ruled by white Hollywood—or, in Jackson's metaphor, to smile at the bus company's annual picnic—was to become a compromise, a paradox, and a target.

And yet, each of these Oscar pioneers laid the groundwork for the next. These are the stories of three of them, across the ages.

HATTIE MCDANIEL KNEW THE TRUTH about the Civil War because it was written on her father's face. Henry McDaniel, like his wife, Susan, was born into slavery. The name "McDaniel" came from his second owner, Tennessee farmer John McDaniel, who purchased Hattie's father and two of his siblings when Henry was about nine years old. (He had no record of his birth.) In December 1864, Henry fought in the Battle of Nashville, a major Union win in which the Black troops, used as decoys to lure the secessionists, lost 64 percent of their forces. Henry survived, but an explosion shattered part of his jaw, leaving an oozing open wound inside his mouth, and his legs were scarred from frostbite. Because he couldn't afford to see a doctor, his injuries festered, even as he was compelled back into physical labor during Reconstruction, when the backlash to the Union victory drained the freed slaves of rights and opportunities. He married Susan in 1875, and they moved to Kansas looking for work. Susan bore thirteen children. Only seven survived, the last of whom, Hattie, was born on June 10, 1893.

Hattie saw firsthand the Civil War's terrible aftereffects, the kind that would be washed away in the film that made her an Oscar winner, *Gone with the Wind*. Her father applied over and over for a disability pension, undergoing medical examinations to prove that his health problems stemmed from his military service, only for the government to reject his claims. After eighteen years, he was finally awarded six dollars a month.

By then, the family had moved to Denver, where Susan worked in white households as a maid and cook—practically the only form of employment for Black women. Hattie would accompany her mother to work, where she learned how to fold laundry and serve meals.

Big-boned, bawdy, and endowed with a devilish sense of humor, Hattie recalled, "I knew that I could sing and dance. I was doing it so much that my mother would give me a nickel sometimes to stop." Her parents, instilling a devoutness that stayed with Hattie all her life, joined an African Methodist Episcopal church, and the choir became her gateway to performance. When she was seventeen, McDaniel married Howard Hickman—the first of four husbands—who had been Denver's first Black pianist to accompany silent films. With her sister Etta, she formed an all-female minstrel troupe, the McDaniel Sisters Company, supplementing her income as a maid. McDaniel wrote the songs and scripts, and they performed to ecstatic audiences at fund-raisers. Minstrelsy had blossomed during the nineteenth century as a way for white performers in blackface to lampoon African Americans for white audiences. Over the decades, minstrel shows gave rise to derogatory stock characters like the lazy, bumbling slave Jim Crow, who became synonymous with southern segregation laws. Another popular "type" was the mammy, the plump, grinning matron who happily raised the children of her white bosses, doting on them as her own.

McDaniel fit the mammy look, but in *her* shows, she poked fun at minstrel stereotypes by exaggerating them for Black audiences: a lampoon of a lampoon. Slathered in burnt cork, she rendered stock characters so ridiculous that the joke was ultimately on the white audiences who gave them credence. In 1914, the *Denver Star* raved over her ludicrous appearance: "cactus hair," skin painted "deeper black than ten midnights without a sun," "awkward feet filled with corns." The next year, McDaniel, now a local comedy sensation, planned a solo show in which she would appear as "different nationalities in their native brogue and dress." She booked an auditorium for what would be her biggest showcase yet. The night before, her husband died of pneumonia. She canceled the show and returned to domestic work.

She eventually eased back onto the stage and found a second career as a blues singer, winning a spot on the Pantages vaudeville circuit and refining her brash, defiantly sexy persona. (She was billed as the "Sepia Sophie Tucker.") With her husky voice and brazen, lustful stage presence, McDaniel was everything the servile, sexless "mammy" archetype was not. By 1929, she was recording saucy original duets for Paramount Records; in one, "Dentist Chair Blues," the male singer plans to "put my drill in your cavity," and McDaniel snarls back, "You make me moan and groan."

Those years, she recalled, were filled with "ups and downs"—but "mostly downs." Despite her successes, she still had to support herself with maid work, and she often went hungry. She got a part in Florenz Ziegfeld's touring production of *Show Boat*. After the stock market crash, the show laid her off in Milwaukee, where she stayed and worked as a bathroom attendant at an inn before making her way into the nightly floor show. Her brother Sam was living in Hollywood, headlining the radio show *The Optimistic Do-Nuts*. In 1931, already thirty-eight, Hattie joined him in South Central Los Angeles, the heart of Black Hollywood.

Black roles in the movies were confined to maids, cooks, and servants, and the performers who broke through embodied hand-me-down minstrel types. They included Stepin Fetchit, the screen persona of Lincoln Perry, who specialized in sleepy-eyed, shiftless nincompoops; and Louise Beavers, who played warm, docile maids in films like *Coquette*, in which she was cast as Mary Pickford's servant. McDaniel picked up jobs as an extra for $7.50 a day, padding her income doing laundry in white homes. Although she appeared in hundreds of films as an extra, her focus was on the stage, where she could flex her subversive comedic muscles for Black audiences. She even appeared on her brother's radio show as her own brassy character, Hi-Hat Hattie.

In 1932, she finally got a plum speaking role in a movie, playing Marlene Dietrich's maid in Paramount's *Blonde Venus*. But she didn't conform to the template of the happy help; McDaniel was beginning to craft her own type, a back-talking, eye-rolling "sassy" servant who called out the foibles of her white employers—behavior that, if an actual maid did it, would likely get her fired. She landed a larger role in *Judge Priest*, a 1934 Will Rogers vehicle directed by John Ford and set in

1890 Kentucky—part of a growing genre that cast a nostalgic gaze on the Old South. As the competent Aunt Dilsey, McDaniel served as a foil to Stepin Fetchit's mumbling layabout. McDaniel, who was asked to wear padding and dark foundation for the role, clashed with Fetchit, but Rogers warmed to her so much that he asked for her role to be enlarged so they could sing a duet together. One wonders what McDaniel, the child of a Union soldier, made of the film's ending, in which Priest wins a case by invoking the "War of the Rebellion" as Fetchit plays "Dixie" from the street, followed by a parade of Confederate veterans.

The film won the attention of Louella Parsons, who noted in her column, "There is a colored woman, Hattie McDaniels"—as her name was misspelled in the movie's opening credits—"who sings Negro spirituals as I have seldom heard them sung." By the end of 1934, McDaniel had brought her brassy style to eight studio features and a background role in *Imitation of Life*, Universal's groundbreaking drama that starred Beavers as a domestic who starts a pancake business with a white widow. The film was nominated for an Academy Award, the year that Capra swept with *It Happened One Night*. "But of course, the Academy could not recognize Miss Beavers," noted the Associated Negro Press. "She is black."

The success of *Imitation of Life* sparked a momentary demand for Black roles, but more parts didn't mean better ones. In *The Little Colonel*, another wistful Old South period piece, McDaniel appeared in her usual headscarf and apron, this time serving six-year-old Shirley Temple, who starred as the plucky granddaughter of a Confederate colonel. McDaniel's mammy character sweetly scolds Temple ("No use you stompin' your foot at me"), but her authority extends only to her pipsqueak boss. McDaniel walked a tricky line, smuggling in bits of comic defiance that winked at Black audiences without threatening white ones. With a quick glare or a cocked head, she could signal disapproval of her characters' white employers, played by Katharine Hepburn (*Alice Adams*) or Jean Harlow (*China Seas*). But she always remained tethered to them.

By mid-1935, one Black columnist predicted that McDaniel would "surpass Louise Beavers in prominence within a year." She played eleven credited film roles in 1936, including Queenie, the spiky dockworker's wife in Universal's *Show Boat*. She picked up a white agent and bought her first home, which she decorated with a baby grand piano. Unlike her aproned mammy characters, she threw lavish house parties and dressed in what the *Baltimore Afro-American* called "smart tailored gowns and jaunty hats."

With prominence came the scrutiny of the Black press. In the *Pittsburgh Courier*, Earl Morris decried her stereotypical "handkerchief head roles." McDaniel tried to duck the criticisms, believing that her mere presence on-screen was a mark of progress. In what became her most quoted justification, she is reported to have said, "I can be a maid for $7 a week, or I can play a maid for $700 a week." She was content to maintain the status quo and do what white Hollywood asked of her—and her personal success was all the proof she needed that she was doing something right.

It was a philosophy that would be tested by the runaway success of *Gone with the Wind*, Margaret Mitchell's sweeping novel about the fall of the antebellum South. A month after it was published, in the summer of 1936, David O. Selznick snapped up the rights for fifty thousand dollars. The Black press was aghast at the prospect of Mitchell's lacy paean to the Confederacy getting to the big screen. But no one knew just how enormous the film version would be. "Unless the propaganda is CUT from the *Wind* opus (and that comprises four-fifths of the story)," the *California Eagle* remarked, "it could just as well be a forgotten foul breeze anyway."

ONE MORNING IN 1944, A young private walked into the office of the head of a veterans' hospital in Northport, Long Island. Not yet eighteen, he had lied about his age to join the army because it was better than sleeping on a bench in Penn Station, where he'd been picked up for vagrancy the year before. "Yes, what can I do for you?" the hospital chief asked from behind his desk. Then the young man picked up a chair and hurled it at the administrator, who ducked just in time for it to crash though a bay window and land two floors down, in a spray of broken glass. With that, Private Sidney Poitier calmly walked out of the office, crossed to the recreation center, and began shooting pool.

Poitier had enlisted nine or ten months before, but he quickly soured on the military. He heard that you could get discharged under Section 8 if you were declared mad, and he had rehearsed his Hamlet act like a role in a movie. It was a risky gambit: if his ploy were discovered, he could get court-martialed and jailed. After attacking the hospital chief, he was taken to a psychiatric ward in Amityville, where he realized that he was on the wrong floor: the *truly* crazy inmates weren't permitted shoelaces or belts, as he was. When the dinner cart came around that evening, he waited until it got close and then toppled it over with his feet.

The next day, the head psychiatrist threatened to give him shock treatments, so Poitier confessed his entire plan. Instead of turning him in, the doctor, perhaps sensing that the young man's instability was less phony than he professed, began seeing him five days a week for psychoanalysis. He noticed that Poitier had a ferocious sense of pride; he kept insisting that *no man* was better than he was. As Poitier later wrote, "He helped me to understand that because I was surrounded by a society that was perpetually hostile to blacks, I assumed a position, a pose, designed to say: I am *not* going to let you dismiss me, hostile world." After five weeks, he was sent to New Jersey for processing and discharged from the military.

Poitier's exposure to American racism came relatively late. The youngest of seven children born to poor tomato farmers, he spent his first ten years on Cat Island, in the Bahamas. At birth, he was so premature that his father bought a shoebox to use as a casket, but a soothsayer told the baby's mother not to worry: "He will walk with kings. He will be rich and famous. Your name will be carried all over the world." Life on the tiny island was simple. There was no electricity or plumbing, and the Poitier children ate with their hands or with spoons made from sea-grape leaves. Sidney was free to wander among the coco plum trees and swim in clear waters. He had little notion of race or class until the family moved to Nassau. There, Sidney first encountered cars and ice-cream cones and movie theaters—he loved Westerns and thought that working in Hollywood meant being a cowboy—but also whites and wealthy Blacks. A congenital risk taker, he was arrested for stealing corn with a band of boys. At fifteen, he was sent to live with his older brother Cyril in Miami, where his real education in difference began.

By then, Poitier, having been raised "free of the crushing negative self-image hammered into black children" in the Jim Crow South, had a fully formed sense of self-worth. At first, the rules simply flummoxed him. Working as a delivery boy, he biked to a fancy house in Miami Beach and rang at the front door. When the white woman there asked him to go around to the back entrance, he said, "But I'm here. Here is the package." Two nights later, his panicked sister-in-law said that white men in hoods had been looking for him. Soon after, an unmarked police car followed him home from the cleaner's, threatening to shoot him if he turned around. "From the moment I got off that fucking boat," he recalled, "I began to experience this new, different, strange, complex, crazy society. And once I became attuned to the strangeness of the racial situation in Miami, that did weird things to my head."

Driven by his "terrible, fierce pride," at sixteen he rode the rails to Georgia and caught a Greyhound to New York, because it was the farthest away from Florida he could get and because he'd heard of a place called Harlem. He worked as a dishwasher and, for a time, slept on the roof of the Brill Building. During a race riot on Lenox Avenue, he got shot in the leg. When winter came, the cold was unfathomable. That was when he joined the army, hoping to be sent somewhere warm.

By the time he got out, in late 1944, he had learned that he had a terrible capacity for anger, the kind that could destroy him if it weren't bottled up under his "enormous effort at being likable and friendly and fair and honest and dependable." He learned that he must never let that anger out, because it frightened him, and coming from a Black man, it certainly frightened others. He returned to New York, to more dishwashing and more cold. He wrote to President Roosevelt asking for a hundred dollars and was dismayed when he didn't write back. That was when he saw a headline in the *Amsterdam News*: "Actors Wanted by Little Theatre Group." At the basement headquarters of the American Negro Theatre, he was handed a script. Poitier could barely read, and his Caribbean accent made him indecipherable. "Just go on and get out of here and get yourself a job as a dishwasher or something," the man there told him.

Poitier quaked with shame, because he *was* a dishwasher. But that wasn't all he was. He bought a thirteen-dollar radio and practiced speaking in an American accent. At the restaurant, a kindly customer helped him improve his reading. After six months, he returned to the American Negro Theatre in a dapper brown suit and recited a passage from *True Confessions* magazine. He was taken into the theater's school on a trial basis, because they were short on men. After three months, he was told he wasn't progressing, so he offered to mop the stage if they let him remain. Finally, he got to understudy for another Caribbean American actor, named Harry Belafonte, with whom he forged a tense, competitive friendship.

Poitier was offered a small role in an all-Black production of *Lysistrata* on Broadway. The show lasted four days, but he got good notices, which led to another job, touring with a hit production of *Anna Lucasta*. In 1949, Joseph L. Mankiewicz, on a hot streak between *A Letter to Three Wives* and *All About Eve*, cast him in *No Way Out*, about a young Black doctor who treats a pair of white outlaw brothers; when one dies during treatment, the other accuses the doctor of murder, vowing, "I'll get you for this, you black rat!" Poitier took the Twentieth Century Limited to Los Angeles, where he was put up in an all-white hotel. "I soon found that living exclusively among white people with no other blacks around was like being a visitor in a foreign culture," he recalled, "on the alert and at the ready twenty-four hours a day." He brought his watchful discomfort to the film, which set the Poitier mold: a bright, clean-cut professional whose skill and equanimity make him "acceptable" in the white world and who is typically bound by circumstance to a racist counterpart. This was a vast improvement over the Stepin Fetchit roles that preceded him—and Poitier had the megawatt charisma to pull it off—but it became another kind of trap. His characters were rarely able to show anger or sexuality, and they were defined by their exceptionalism.

Poitier was exceptional in Hollywood, too, where his only real competition was Belafonte. But the work still wasn't steady enough to pay the bills, especially after Poitier had a child with his first wife, Juanita Hardy. For a time, he and a business partner ran a chain of restaurants in New York, where his political consciousness flowered. Because of his association with left-wing activists, MGM asked him to sign a "loyalty oath" before he acted in the 1955 film *Blackboard Jungle*, and he refused. Fortunately, the director, Richard Brooks, said "Fuck 'em." Somehow it worked. The movie made Poitier a sui generis heartthrob.

Aware of his singular place in Hollywood, Poitier turned down roles he found demeaning, perplexing his white agents. Back in the Bahamas, his parents were selling cigars and breaking down rocks into gravel, but with dignity, and he would never dishonor their name or his race. He stunned Samuel Goldwyn by turning down the lead role in the film adaptation of the Gershwin opera *Porgy and Bess*. Despite the fact that Poitier was tone-deaf, Goldwyn offered him $75,000 to play Porgy, but Poitier resisted. "*Porgy and Bess* is an insult to black people," he told his New York agent, "and I ain't gonna play it and that's all there is to it."

Goldwyn invited Poitier to a meeting at Harry Cohn's house and told him, "I understand how you feel, Mr. Poitier, but I disagree with you—this is one of the greatest things that has ever happened for the black race." Poitier promised to think about it. In the meantime, he took a meeting with Stanley Kramer, who was planning his film *The Defiant Ones*, about a pair of convicts, one Black and one white, who escape a chain gang handcuffed to each other. This was the movie Poitier wanted to make—one that he thought would open up new possibilities for Black roles—but his agents made it clear that Goldwyn could blackball him from *The Defiant Ones* if he said no to *Porgy and Bess*. Poitier realized he'd been outplayed: "As smart as I thought I was, that time the white folks were smarter."

He agreed to do both, gritting his teeth through *Porgy and Bess*, in which his singing was dubbed. He was cast opposite Dorothy Dandridge, who in 1955 had become the first Black woman to be nominated for Best Actress, for *Carmen Jones*. But the film's real significance for Poitier was meeting Diahann Carroll, with whom he began a tempestuous nine-year affair. *The Defiant Ones*, meanwhile, brought Poitier acclaim, with Bosley Crowther praising his "deep and powerful strain of underlying compassion." And yet, the movie's conciliatory message wasn't necessarily what Black audiences wanted to hear. Writing in 1968, James Baldwin recalled, "When Sidney jumps off the train at the end because he doesn't want to leave his buddy, the white liberal people downtown were much relieved and joyful. But when black people saw him jump off the train, they yelled, 'Get back on the train, you fool!'"

In February 1959, Poitier became the first Black man to be nominated for Best Actor. His costar Tony Curtis, who was nominated in the same category, had no illusions about either man's chances, writing in his autobiography that "they weren't going to give an Oscar to a black man or a Jew." He was right. Although *The Defiant Ones* was an Oscar breakthrough for blacklisted screenwriter Nedrick Young, both actors lost to David Niven, for *Separate Tables*. Like his character, Poitier was handcuffed, but to a white industry, and neither was able to move forward without the other. He didn't attend the ceremony; he was back in New York, starring in the Broadway play *A Raisin in the Sun*. Hailed as the Jackie Robinson of the movies, he felt the heavy burden of representation. "As I see myself, I'm an average Joe Blow Negro," he told the *New York Times*. "But, as the cats say in my area, I'm out there wailing for us all."

WHEN HALLE BERRY WAS AT the mostly white Bedford High School, in suburban Cleveland, she ran for prom queen and barely edged out a blond, blue-eyed competitor. An overachiever who craved approval, Berry was already president of the class of 1985, editor of the school newspaper, an honor roll student, and a cheerleader. But prom queen was a step too far. Her classmates spread a rumor that she had stuffed the ballot box, and the two girls flipped a coin to determine the winner. Berry won again, but the victory was compromised. "I had worked so hard to be accepted, but when it came to being a standard of beauty for the school, they didn't want me," she said later. "That taught me. No more being a dancing bear."

When she became famous, some version of this story was repeated in nearly every article about her. It was Berry's existence in a nutshell: no matter how talented, accomplished, or beautiful she was, she would always have to surmount some double standard that left asterisks on her achievements. And she *was* gorgeous, in a way that didn't stray far from white beauty standards; those same articles swooned over her "flawless cafe au lait skin," "exquisite cheekbones," and eyes like "huge dark caramels." But beauty, she discovered, was just another trap.

Berry was born in Ohio in 1966, to a white mother who worked as a psychiatric nurse and a Black father who was a hospital orderly and a violent alcoholic. He left the family when Halle was four, leaving her mother to raise her and her older sister alone. The couple got back together temporarily when Berry was ten, in what she called the worst year of her life. Her father would kick her mother down the stairs or smack her head with a wine bottle. One time, he threw their dog against the wall. "I felt a lot of guilt," Berry recalled. "When my sister saw him hitting my mother, she would jump in and get hit, but I would run and hide."

Once he was finally out of the picture, her mother was left to raise two biracial daughters. She taught Halle that when she left the house, the world would consider her Black, so she should embrace it: "She said if I fight it, I will have a battle with them and a battle inside myself." Being biracial, she learned, was like being in a "secret society" that allowed her to shape-shift depending on who was in the room. But it was a hard-won lesson. In elementary school, kids left Oreos in her locker and called her a zebra. In high school, she tried to prove herself with accomplishments, to "show who I was without being angry or violent." But the prom queen incident taught her that it didn't always work out that way.

Berry had few Black role models, including the ones in the movies—glamorous women like Dorothy Dandridge and Diahann Carroll. "My mother tried hard," she said. "But there was no substitute for having a black woman I could identify with, who could teach me about being black." In search of money and confidence, Berry entered the beauty pageant circuit, winning Miss Teen All-American and then Miss Ohio USA, which fed into the 1986 Miss USA competition. Berry got first-runner up, which sent her to London for the Miss World contest, the first Black contestant to represent the United States. She caused controversy when she wore a revealing star-spangled bikini, meant to show "America's advancement in space." "It makes me very proud to be the first," she said, already an anomaly and a lightning rod, though she clarified that she wasn't on a "crusade for black people."

She lost to Miss Trinidad and Tobago, but by then she was pageanted out. She dropped out of community college and moved to Chicago to be a model. In 1989, she signed with a manager named Vincent Cirrincione, who was looking for a Black pageant queen for a role on a soap opera. The part didn't pan out, but he got Berry a commercial for the NYNEX phone company. When she showed up with her hair cropped short, Cirrincione said, "Well, there goes your commercial career." "That's not why I'm here," she told him. Within two months, she landed a role on the sitcom *Living Dolls*, a *Who's the Boss?* spinoff about a group of models. She collapsed on set and was diagnosed with diabetes. The show lasted twelve episodes.

At the time, Spike Lee's *Do the Right Thing* was leading a boom in Black filmmaking that took an unflinching approach to race, romance, and inner-city life. These movies, notably John Singleton's *Boyz n the Hood*, were a launchpad for Black talent, including Cuba Gooding Jr., Angela Bassett, and Samuel L. Jackson. Berry auditioned for Lee's film *Jungle Fever*, about a Black architect (Wesley Snipes) who has an affair with a white temp (Annabella Sciorra). She was cast as Samuel L. Jackson's junkie girlfriend, a part that would strip down her beauty queen image and prove that she could do "street." Around the same time, a boyfriend—someone "well known in Hollywood"—hit her so hard that she lost 80 percent of her hearing in one ear. "I left so fast," she recalled, "there were skid marks."

Berry kept getting parts written for Black women—Eddie Murphy's girlfriend in *Boomerang*, Alex Haley's grandmother in the miniseries *Queen*—but she yearned to cross over into "anything" roles. The live-action film of *The Flintstones* featured a bombshell secretary role originally conceived for Sharon Stone, but Cirrincione got Berry a meeting with the director. "I convinced him that in this day and age, Bedrock should be integrated," she said. Berry viewed her own sex appeal as a litmus test for what white audiences would accept: "It was important to me that a black woman be seen as the object of desire."

The Flintstones creaked the door open, but only so much. Working the phones, Cirrincione heard all kinds of racist rationalization. "Some executive explained it to me by talking about milk," he recalled. "They said milk is milk until you add a little Hershey. It doesn't matter if you add a little Hershey or a lot." She wanted the part of a park ranger in John Woo's *Broken Arrow*, but the studio didn't think a park ranger would be Black. Conversely, she had nearly lost her role in the Black comedy *Strictly Business* because the producers thought she was too light-skinned. "I identify with being a black woman, even though I'm half-white, because that's how the world identifies me," Berry said. "But still, I often don't get called for black-women parts because I don't seem right to the producers. I'm in that gray area."

Throughout the nineties, Berry found her place in that gray area, often with lucrative results. In 1996, she was paid a million dollars to play a flight attendant in the action flick *Executive Decision*, opposite Kurt Russell, and Warren Beatty picked her as his love interest in *Bulworth*. She did Revlon ads alongside Cindy Crawford. But her personal life was rocky; after marrying Atlanta Braves outfielder David Justice, in early 1993, they moved to a woodsy house in Atlanta. Justice said that Berry would have jealous fits; Berry got a temporary restraining order against him. After their divorce, Berry ran her car in the garage, waiting for the carbon monoxide to kill her, but she stopped herself when she pictured her mother finding her body.

During this time, Berry was fixated on another Black movie star with crossover appeal, an abusive childhood, and an unstable love life: Dorothy Dandridge. In 1965, ten years after her breakthrough Best Actress nomination for *Carmen Jones*, Dandridge was found dead on her bathroom floor, nude, broke, and mostly forgotten at forty-two. Berry had seen *Carmen Jones* on TV when she was eighteen and was so rapt by Dandridge's vixenish turn—in its time, a decisive break from Hattie McDaniel mammy roles—that she went to the local library to research her. Here was someone, like her, who had embodied Black beauty in a white landscape. Years later, Berry met Dandridge's former manager, Earl Mills, and became determined to play Dandridge on-screen. She had competition: Janet Jackson had optioned her autobiography and Mills's memoir, and Whitney Houston had optioned a biography. Cirrincione hounded Mills until his book was freed up again and then pounced on the rights for Berry. They shopped it to studios all over town. "The answer was no, no, no," Berry recalled, "and the very reason that I wanted to make the movie was the very reason they didn't want to make it—and that's because nobody knew who she was."

Finally, HBO picked up *Introducing Dorothy Dandridge* as a TV movie, with Berry starring and executive-producing. A young writer named Shonda Rhimes wrote the first draft of the script. Berry's identification with Dandridge ran deep; Mills had given her Dandridge's elegant blue evening gown, and Berry took it as an omen that it fit her perfectly. To learn more about Dandridge, she arranged a meeting with the aging Sidney Poitier. "He connected to her sense of honesty and vulnerability, said he viewed her as a fawn in need of protection," Berry recalled. Poitier thought that Dandridge had been robbed of an Oscar for *Carmen Jones.* "As Black people," he told Berry, "we must learn to swallow it bitter and spit it sweet."

Berry was haunted by Dandridge's downfall. Some believed that Dandridge's death was an accidental overdose, but Berry wasn't so sure. "It is a mystery, but I am inclined to believe, especially after playing her and looking at some things that have happened in my life, that she was so discouraged that she killed herself," she said. "Even though she had packed her bags, I think, somehow, she had reached the end. She was just tired."

Introducing Dorothy Dandridge premiered in August 1999, seven years after Berry started pursuing the project. "It totally changed [Berry's] esteem in the public," its director, Martha Coolidge, recalls. "I mean, a lot of people didn't consider her an actress." In January 2000, Berry won the Golden Globe. Onstage, she thanked Dandridge, who "never got to stand here and be recognized by her peers, but because she lived, I am able to." That fall, she won the Emmy Award.

Berry vowed not to let the industry chew her up and spit her out as it had Dandridge—or to let Hollywood allow her to destroy herself. "I can't go crazy. I can't. It's not even an option," she told an interviewer. "I value my life too much, and when I read stories in history about the people before me, people who got up every day and some of them had shackles on their feet and they fought the fight, how could I even consider not fighting the fight?"

IN MARGARET MITCHELL'S *GONE WITH THE WIND*, published in 1936, Mammy is described as "a huge old woman, with the small, shrewd eyes of an elephant." Her role, which she accepts with pride and purpose, is to serve her masters at Tara. "She was shining black, pure African," Mitchell wrote, "devoted to her last drop of blood to the O'Haras." And yet, she was quick to speak her mind, which was only proof of her loyalty: "Whom she loved, she chastened."

In other words, she was a natural fit for the sassy, back-talking servant honed by Hattie McDaniel. McDaniel read the novel three times and, by her account, longed to play a character "who was fearless, who cringed before no one, who did not talk in whispers, walk on tiptoe, who criticized a white woman's morals." But that didn't mean the role was hers. There were other contenders, most prominently Louise Beavers. In Atlanta, Mitchell was besieged by white women who wanted the part for their maids. Even Eleanor Roosevelt sent a letter of recommendation for her personal White House cook, who, she promised, was "extremely capable and has a great deal of histrionic ability."

David O. Selznick spent more than a year putting together the financing and the cast for what the gossip columns dubbed "Selznick's Folly." Eventually, he struck a deal with his father-in-law, Louis B. Mayer, that secured half the budget and the services of Clark Gable, as Rhett Butler. The search for Scarlett O'Hara, meanwhile, became a publicity bonanza. Casting Mammy dragged out just as long, and McDaniel had her champions, among them Bing Crosby, who wrote to Selznick in early 1937 suggesting the "little lady" from *Show Boat*. While Beavers showed up to her audition in fancy attire, McDaniel dressed in traditional Mammy rags, and Selznick said he could "smell the magnolias."

By late 1938, Selznick was screen-testing Scarletts and Mammys in pairs, including McDaniel and British ingénue Vivien Leigh. Their chemistry—Leigh's frilly willfulness, McDaniel's side-eye disapproval—must have been obvious from the start, but even Leigh was signed before McDaniel. Finally, on January 27, 1939, McDaniel signed her contract, which promised her to Selznick for $450 a week.

Meanwhile, the Black protests against *Gone with the Wind* had escalated. Walter White, executive secretary of the NAACP, wrote to Selznick warning of "very definite apprehension as to the effect this picture will have." Selznick promised to be "awfully careful that the Negroes come out decidedly on the right side of the ledger." But he couldn't contain the scathing editorials in Black newspapers, including one, by Earl Morris in the *Pittsburgh Courier*, contending that the casting of Mammy "means about $2,000 for Miss McDaniel" but "nothing in racial advancement."

Selznick tried to assuage his critics by subtracting the most objectionable parts of Mitchell's novel, including the liberal use of the N-word. But the bigger problem was lost on him—that the story romanticized antebellum society and left the impression that the Confederacy's loss was bad for whites *and* their former slaves, including Mammy. If McDaniel had any qualms, she didn't show them. "Don't worry," she assured the *Pittsburgh Courier.* "There is nothing in this picture that will injure colored people. If there were, I wouldn't be in it." Selznick International even sent out a photo of McDaniel posing with a group of Black representatives, at least some of whom were studio employees.

As ever, McDaniel was less interested in challenging the system than in succeeding within it, and she was willing to play the role of studio apologist—even if it curdled her reputation in the Black press. Although her Mammy was feisty, she didn't make waves on set. While the white stars got private limos, the Black cast was given a single car to and from work; McDaniel remained good-humored. Her costar Butterfly McQueen wasn't as compliant. After she refused to eat watermelon in one scene, McDaniel warned her, "You'll never come back to Hollywood; you complain too much."

McDaniel's Mammy was the irascible queen of her domain, unafraid of bossing around Miss Scarlett or even Rhett. ("You control yourself," she chides him.) But her back talk never threatens the white hierarchy, and her existence—including her name—is circumscribed by her servitude. McDaniel played a similar role in the studio system, providing comic relief but never defying her white superiors. At least *Gone with the Wind* let her show her dramatic range. In her final scene, after Scarlett's daughter has been killed in a riding accident, Mammy cries with concern to Olivia de Havilland's Melanie. Even then, Mammy's grief is conjoined with Scarlett's; her virtue is her loyalty, even though, in theory, she's free to walk away. Still, there was no denying the charisma of McDaniel's performance. Selznick saw it himself before the film was released, upping McDaniel to a long-term contract and predicting in one memo, "I think she is going to be hailed as the great Negro performer of the decade."

Despite the film's rosy portrait of the Old South ("a civilization gone with the wind . . ."), trouble came when the film scheduled its gala premiere in Atlanta in December 1939. Word got back to Selznick that the city elders would not welcome the Black cast members. They even objected to having the souvenir program include McDaniel's head shot. Selznick acquiesced. And McDaniel, once again choosing compliance, did not object. Instead, two days before the premiere, she wrote to Selznick, "I hope that Mammy when viewed by the masses will be the exact replica of what Miss Mitchell intended her to be." At the opening, Atlanta's mayor, who had helped orchestrate McDaniel's exclusion, mentioned her performance to a burst of cheers. Mitchell telegrammed McDaniel: WISH YOU COULD HAVE HEARD THE APPLAUSE.

Black critics were often complimentary as well, even when they excoriated the film as a whole; the *California Eagle* credited McDaniel's "brilliant work" in a "difficult film." Others were less forgiving, such as playwright Carlton Moss, who published an open letter in the *Daily Worker* condemning, among other noxious tropes, a Mammy who "loves this degrading position in the service of a family that has helped to keep her people enchained for centuries." Even as Black activists picketed the film, McDaniel defended her role in it, claiming that she had drawn on figures like Harriet Tubman and Sojourner Truth. To her, Mammy represented "an opportunity to glorify Negro womanhood" and "the brave efficient type of womanhood which, building a race, mothered Booker T. Washington, George Carver, Robert Moton, and Mary McLeod Bethune."

As the Academy Awards approached, the Black press, despite its misgivings, began to advocate for McDaniel. She received an endorsement from the Black sorority Sigma Gamma Rho, which wrote to Selznick, "We trust that discrimination and prejudice will be wiped away in the selection of the winner of this award, for without Miss McDaniel, there would be no *Gone With the Wind.*" In early February 1940, McDaniel walked into Selznick's office with a file of clippings to show him the support she was getting. Selznick, who had felt personally betrayed by Black objections to the film—"We bent over backward," he groused to the NAACP's Walter White—made sure McDaniel had a place on the ballot.

Gone with the Wind received thirteen nominations, with McDaniel and de Havilland competing for Best Supporting Actress. On February

29, 1940, McDaniel arrived at the Cocoanut Grove—which was being picketed outside—in a white ermine jacket over an aqua-blue evening gown garlanded with a corsage of white gardenias. She was not only the first Black Oscar nominee but also the first Black attendee who wasn't serving the guests. (That year, the Academy also allowed its first Black voting members.) Nevertheless, McDaniel and her date, the Black actor Wonderful Smith, were seated at a segregated table near the stage, along with a white man who was possibly McDaniel's agent.

Variety had described the Best Supporting Actress race as "neck and neck," but by the time McDaniel entered the room, to an ovation, everyone knew she had won—the late edition of the *Los Angeles Times* had leaked the results before the ceremony. After dinner, outgoing Academy president Frank Capra welcomed his successor, Walter Wanger, who spoke about the Academy's future while Alfred Hitchcock snoozed in his seat. Seventeen-year-old Judy Garland, who received the award for Outstanding Juvenile Performance for *The Wizard of Oz*, sang "Over the Rainbow." But the night's emotional high point came when Fay Bainter, the previous year's winner for *Jezebel*, presented Best Supporting Actress. "To me, it seems more than just a plaque of gold," she said. "It opens the doors of this room, moves back the walls, and enables us to embrace the whole of America, an America that we love, an America that almost alone in the world today recognizes and pays tribute to those who give it their best, regardless of creed, race, or color." Bainter's lofty words showed how Hollywood was determined to view itself, in an implicit contrast to Hitler's Germany. When she announced that McDaniel had won, there were shouts of "Hallelujah!"

Selznick International had reportedly written McDaniel's speech for her, although, according to *Variety*, she was so "overcome" that she left the sanctioned speech at her table. Either way, she appeared to speak from the heart. "I sincerely hope," she said, her voice heavy, "I shall always be a credit to my race and to the motion picture industry." But was it possible to do both at once?

As McDaniel returned to her seat, Louella Parsons grabbed her by the arm and said, "See, Hattie, you've made me cry!" De Havilland, still expecting to beat her sister to an Oscar, fled to the hotel kitchen and wept, perhaps the only attendee not to grasp the larger importance. Later, McDaniel reshot her speech for the newsreels, so it could be shown nationwide. "Well," she told the press, "all I have to say is I did my best and God did the rest." A few days later, she expressed her hope that "my winning the award will be inspiration for the youth of my race, that it will encourage them to aim high and work hard, and take the bitter with the sweet."

In part due to McDaniel's Oscar win, the Black protests against *Gone with the Wind* died down. By the time it began a new round of showings in April, it was even more popular than the year before. It remained the highest-grossing film for a quarter century. Rhett, Miss Scarlett, "Frankly, my dear, I don't give a damn," dear old Tara—all of it found a permanent place on the movie screen of America's collective imagination, along with the image of Mammy lacing up her mistress's corset.

At ninety-two pages, William Edmund Barrett's novella *The Lilies of the Field* reads like a modern-day Christian parable. Inspired by the Sisters of Walburga, who fled Hitler's Germany to form an outpost in the wilds of Colorado, it tells the story of a Black itinerant handyman, Homer Smith, who stops near a run-down rural convent. The nuns, believing that God has sent him ("*Gott ist gut*," one cries), enlist him to build a chapel. Reluctant at first, Homer completes his task, bringing together the whole town—and then takes off so quickly that the Spanish locals hail him as a mystic. One claims that a white light encircled him.

Published in 1962, this simple tale of common humanity radiated the idealism of the Kennedy years—and who better to headline the movie version than Sidney Poitier? His position in Hollywood was anomalous, especially after the 1961 release of the film version of *A Raisin in the Sun*. But the import of that fame was bearing down on him. "I was being pushed to change the world as it related to me and mine," he wrote. "I was being pushed to do the impossible."

Those pressures, along with his torrid affair with Diahann Carroll, were deteriorating his marriage to Juanita Hardy, who was back in Pleasantville, New York, raising their four daughters. Everything felt out of sync, including America itself, riven over the civil rights movement.

The Lilies of the Field, with its free-roaming hero, came on the heels of the 1961 Freedom Rides, in which activists traveled on buses through the South in defiance of segregation laws. No sooner was the book published than director Ralph Nelson took it to United Artists. The studio had so little confidence that it offered a budget of just $250,000. Poitier arranged to take a reduced fee and 10 percent of the profits. The shoot, in Tucson, took exactly fourteen days, a schedule so tight that Nelson was said to have planned it with a stopwatch. Like the chapel in the story, the movie was a product of communal faith.

The film, with the shortened title *Lilies of the Field*, wore its politics lightly. Its message was symbiosis: Homer teaches the nuns a Negro spiritual; they give him work and a sense of purpose. Bosley Crowther, in his *New York Times* review, wrote that Poitier's character "could be a white man just as well." But his Blackness gave the film special poignancy, Crowther concluded: "This young man has a special reason to prove himself all around." He could easily have been describing Poitier.

That summer, Poitier attended the March on Washington for Jobs and Freedom among a cadre of movie stars, including Charlton Heston and Marlon Brando. Hollywood, still smarting from the blacklist, had been hesitant to align itself with any left-leaning cause. But pressure came from the NAACP, which accused Hollywood of treating the Negro as "an invisible man," and stars like Gregory Peck were putting their weight behind integration. The industry's embrace of the march was, the *New York Times* observed, an "indication that some creative leaders of the movie industry have decided it is time to rejoin the nation after nearly 16 years of spiritual secession."

United Artists sensed an opportunity to sell *Lilies of the Field* as a parable of tolerance, especially after some southern theaters refused to show it. The movie opened in October 1963 and was a modest success. Its "come together" ethos was made more urgent after the Kennedy assassination, while the film was playing its second month at L.A.'s Egyptian Theatre. It expanded in December, with a "Calling All Churches" campaign geared toward religious and civic clubs. Even so, Poitier refused to return to the coast to campaign for an Oscar nomination, telling columnist Sheilah Graham just before Christmas, "I'm an actor, not a politician."

Nevertheless, in late February 1964, the thirty-seven-year-old Poitier was nominated for Best Actor. No Black actor had won since Hattie McDaniel, twenty-four years prior. Meanwhile, in Washington, President Johnson had taken up the Civil Rights Act. It had just gone to the Senate, where a group of southern legislators launched a filibuster that would last an extraordinary seventy-five days. If there was ever a time for Hollywood to pick a side, it was then. Suddenly, *Lilies of the Field* became, in the words of the *Los Angeles Times*'s Oscar forecast, "a tribute to a Negro in a Negro-conscious world." So strongly did the town's sense of righteousness unite around Poitier that one of his competitors, Paul Newman, who was in New York rehearsing a play, decided to skip the Oscars and support him.

Poitier considered himself a "dark horse, so to speak" and considered not attending. But he decided that showing up would be a good career move, and "Diahann and I felt it would be good for black people to see themselves competing for the top honor." On the afternoon of April 13, 1964, Carroll helped him into his tux, which he had worn eighteen months earlier at the White House, and he left for the Santa Monica Civic Auditorium. Though his marriage to Hardy was disintegrating, he and Carroll decided not to arrive together. The world may have swooned over the endlessly publicized affair between Elizabeth Taylor and Richard Burton, but an adulterous affair between two Black stars was another matter.

As he sat alone in the audience, Poitier felt his palms sweat. He expected the absent Albert Finney to win for *Tom Jones*, and noticed a cameraman walking the aisles, ready to home in on the losers. His anxiety mounting, Poitier looked "too cool for words" but felt "ripped up internally." *I'm never going to put myself through this shit no more*, he thought. Then it occurred to him: What if he actually won? He was seized with the fear of making history and sounding "dumb." He told himself, "Think, Sidney, think, time is of the essence! Whatever I say must be the truth first, and it must be something intelligent and impressive that will leave the people in that room and the millions watching at home—leave them all duly and irrevocably impressed with the intelligence and decorum of one black actor, Sidney Poitier."

As Anne Bancroft read off the nominees, Poitier felt a "volcano" inside him. He froze his smile in place, his mouth dry. When he heard Bancroft say "The winner is Sidney Poitier," he leaped up, feeling faint. Onstage, he blanked on the speech he had just thought up, until the words rushed back to him. He heard himself saying, in a line laden with meaning, "Because it is a long journey to this moment, I am naturally indebted to countless numbers of people . . ."

The unprecedented image of Poitier holding his award beamed across the country. One ten-year-old girl was watching from her linoleum floor in Milwaukee. "Up to the stage came the most elegant man I had ever seen," Oprah Winfrey recalled many years later. "I remember his tie was white, and of course his skin was Black. And I'd never seen a Black man being celebrated like that. And I've tried many, many, many times to explain what a moment like that means to a little girl—a kid watching from the cheap seats, as my mom came through the door bone-tired from cleaning other people's houses."

Poitier was whisked off to the pressroom. Shortly after, Sammy Davis Jr., presenting the music awards, was handed the wrong envelope and quipped, "Wait till the NAACP hears about *this!*" The *New York Times* summed up the historic breakthrough: "The outburst for Mr. Poitier was recognition not only of his talent, but also of the fact that Hollywood has felt guilty about color barriers of the past, some of which still exist here."

But Poitier himself was doubtful. The day after the ceremony, he sat on a hotel sofa and told a reporter, "I like to think it will help someone. But I don't believe my Oscar will be a sort of magic wand that will wipe away the restrictions on job opportunities for Negro actors." Before the awards, he had announced (wrongly, it turned out) that he would no longer act in films centrally about race, saying, "I don't want to die as the most successful Negro actor. It will have circumscribed me terribly." But were the restrictions any looser than before?

In the Bahamas, Nassau held a motorcade in his honor. In New York, the city declined requests for a ticker-tape parade, but Poitier was invited to City Hall to receive a medallion from the mayor. When two reporters kept asking him about civil rights issues, he snapped back, "Why don't you ask me human questions? Why is it everything you guys ask refers to the Negroness of my life and not my acting?" Since the army, he had been careful to cork up any anger or exasperation, but now it had burst to the surface. He immediately added that he had intended no offense.

THE SCRIPT FOR MONSTER'S BALL spent years in development hell before it got to Halle Berry. Milo Addica and Will Rokos were white writing partners who had come from unstable households and were interested, Addica said, in a story about "breaking the cycle of violence" imposed by fathers on sons. They became fascinated by the fact that executioners often pass down their jobs within families, and in 1995 they completed a screenplay about three generations of death row corrections officers in Georgia, white men steeped in racism and machismo. After overseeing the execution of a Black man, one of them crosses paths with his widow, a waitress named Leticia. Not realizing their connection, they begin a grief-fueled interracial romance.

After changing hands several times, the script reached producer Lee Daniels, with Sean Penn attached to direct and Marlon Brando, Robert De Niro, and *American Beauty*'s Wes Bentley playing the male leads. But Penn and De Niro's fees were too high, and that plan fell apart. Oliver Stone showed interest. So did Tommy Lee Jones. Lionsgate agreed to make it, but the deal blew up. Finally, after Daniels had what he described as a nervous breakdown, Lionsgate gave him $2.5 million, and he secured Swiss-German director Marc Forster and actors Peter Boyle, Billy Bob Thornton, and Heath Ledger.

But who would play Leticia, the volatile widow with a crumbling psyche? When Berry read the screenplay, she saw a chance to undercut her glamour girl image and establish herself as a serious actress. "I called my manager and said, say yes, say yes, say yes," she recalled. "He said, 'I'm glad you love it, but they don't want you.' The director thought I was too beautiful or something." Forster was meeting with Whitney Houston and Alfre Woodard. "I kept calling the producer—it was like a dead end," Berry's then-manager Vincent Cirrincione recalls. He got Forster on the phone directly. "I mentioned *Jungle Fever*—he wasn't sure what it was." Cirrincione sent over a package of clips, including Berry's scenes as the "crack ho" in *Jungle Fever*. Daniels says that Berry was "who I wanted for the movie" and that he overruled Forster. According to Forster, Lionsgate vice chairman Michael Burns "asked only two things of me—give me hope at the end of the movie and cast Halle Berry."

Berry was eager to refocus on acting; her public image was getting overwhelmed by gossip. After *Introducing Dorothy Dandridge*, she took a role in the cyber thriller *Swordfish*, which included a topless scene, and the media spread the (false) story that she had been paid an extra $250,000 for each breast. In May 2000, she was fined $13,500 for driving away from a car accident. Her estranged father, whom she hadn't seen in years, sold a story to *The Star* for a six-pack of beer. "I thought, If you're going to sell the damn story, then at least make some real money," the actress said.

Monster's Ball would prove that she was more than Revlon ads and tabloid spreads. It was a "woman brought low" tale, a genre that had given actresses legitimacy at least since Bette Davis's turn in *Of Human Bondage*. Its climactic sequence was a sad, drunken sex scene between Berry and Thornton, playing two lost souls finding connection in sorrow. After the gratuitous nudity in *Swordfish*, Berry would do it only "if Billy Bob agreed to be as naked as I was." They shot for twenty-one days in New Orleans, and each day, Berry, Thornton, and Forster would meet to discuss the sex scene. They agreed that the characters had to make love like animals, like people desperate for air.

Finally, on day nineteen, Forster cleared the room of all but two crew members. Berry felt safe with Thornton, knowing that he was madly in love with Angelina Jolie. Forster asked them to improvise their lines, as Leticia sucks down whiskey and babbles in nervous, manic despair. The line that came out of her mouth was "Make me feel good," a plea that captured the film's theme of connection through trauma.

The film wrapped in the summer of 2001, and Lionsgate scheduled a limited release for the day after Christmas, buying maximal time for postproduction while still qualifying for awards. In between, the 9/11 attacks struck. Like *Lilies of the Field*, *Monster's Ball* played to a shell-shocked country, and its somber tone fit the national mood almost too well. Tom Ortenberg, then Lionsgate's president, recalls, "As a marketer, I always saw the message as the spirit of hope, and that spirit of hope was my mantra that informed everything we did in our promotion." A. O. Scott's *New York Times* review credited Berry's "fearless concentration" for converting "potential sentimentality into honest, complex emotion."

A Best Picture push was a reach. "At the time," Forster says, "Lionsgate was a very small studio, and they didn't have the budget for a big campaign circuit. Instead of focusing on pushing the film, they decided to focus on Halle." Lionsgate was well aware that no Black woman had ever won Best Actress, but to push the point could seem like pandering. Berry's main competition was Sissy Spacek, star of *In the Bedroom*, for which Harvey Weinstein, in his post–*Shakespeare in Love* King of the Jungle mode, was making a full-throttle Oscar push. In the Oscar economy that Weinstein had wrought, spending for newspaper ads was up 20 percent from the year before, and Miramax appeared to be throwing far more money at *In the Bedroom*'s campaign than the film's $1.7 million production budget. "Running a campaign against some of these guys is very, very difficult," Ortenberg complained at the time. "Miramax spends a fortune. And the people over at DreamWorks run a campaign like they've got a candidate in the New Hampshire primary."

Despite the Miramax bucks behind *In the Bedroom*, Ortenberg saw it as the art house choice, while *Monster's Ball* was playing "more broadly," so he decided to position Berry as the populist candidate, especially given that she had been picked as the next Bond girl, in *Die Another Day*. In late January, she lost the Golden Globe to Spacek. Forster recalls, "Halle turned to me and said, 'The race ain't over yet.'" According to Forster, they went over to talk with Warren Beatty, Berry's costar from *Bulworth*, and he "urged Halle to reach out to the African American community and get them behind the movie."

With twelve days before the Oscar nominations, Berry pulled off a coup: a full hour on *The Oprah Winfrey Show*. Between raving about Berry's "raw" performance in *Monster's Ball* (which she claimed to have seen five times) and cooing over photos from Berry's "top-secret" wedding to R&B singer Eric Benét, Winfrey delivered a priceless endorsement. "I sent in my ballot already," she announced after the commercial break. "I put *Halle Berry* in great big, bold letters to nominate you for an Oscar, and I hope everybody else does the same." Then she repeated, "I put it in big, *black*, bold print, so they can't miss it."

Lee Daniels still felt that Berry was the underdog. "We lost everything to Sissy Spacek," he recalls. "We did not think she would win the Academy Award." But at least one Oscar player could tell that Lionsgate's "populist" angle was working. Two days before the awards, Ortenberg had lunch with Weinstein. "Fuck you," Weinstein told him. "You beat us."

"What do you mean?"

"Fuck you. You beat us, Halle won—you know it, I know it." If there was anyone who could checkmate Harvey, it was Oprah.

On March 24, 2002, Berry arrived at the Kodak Theatre in an Elie Saab dress: embroidered see-through mesh on top, shimmering burgundy skirt below. The first post-9/11 Oscars had turned out to be a major night for Black Hollywood; not only was Berry nominated, but both Denzel Washington (*Training Day*) and Will Smith (*Ali*) were in the Best Actor category. Questioned on the red carpet, Berry acknowledged the "special" nature of the evening, but added, "I just hope one day that the fact that we're Black won't be such a big deal." In her opening monologue, Whoopi Goldberg, in her fourth go-round as host, nodded to both the racial breakdown and the Weinstein era: "Can you believe this campaign? So much mud has been thrown this year, all the nominees look Black."

Russell Crowe, the previous year's winner for *Gladiator*, opened the Best Actress envelope. When Berry heard her name, her face contorted with emotion. She had not written a speech. "The only thing I remember," she said later, "is somehow I was up on the stage, and I remember Russell whispering in my ear, 'Breathe, mate. Breathe.'" Her body was shaking, her mouth agape. All she could do, for a moment, was weep. "This moment," she finally said, "is so much bigger than me. This moment is for Dorothy Dandridge, Lena Horne, Diahann Carroll. It's for the women that stand beside me—Jada Pinkett, Angela Bassett, Vivica Fox—and it's for every nameless, faceless woman of color that now has a chance because this door tonight has been opened." Sobbing as violently as she had in her big scene with Billy Bob Thornton, she thanked the Academy "for choosing me to be the vessel through which this blessing might flow."

It was as if the full weight of history had invaded her body. But even as the evening ended, she felt the magic start to fade. "Driving home that night, back to my house, I felt like Cinderella," she recalled. "I said, 'When this night is over, I'm going back to who I was.'"

HATTIE MCDANIEL CELEBRATED HER OSCAR win with a lavish house party, where she treated the guests to her impression of Fanny Brice. Everything pointed to a golden future, and not just for her. "I consider this recognition a step further for the race, rather than personal progress," she told the *Pittsburgh Courier*.

Navigating her new life, though, became complicated immediately. When her agent pushed her to negotiate for a raise from Selznick, who had her under contract, she declined, causing some Black journalists to accuse her of "Tomism." "Big salaries and little work don't interest me," McDaniel reasoned, expecting Selznick to set her up with new and interesting roles. Instead, Selznick wanted to milk her association with her Oscar-winning part, even buying up the rights to the title *Mammy* for potential film and radio projects. In the spring of 1940, he booked McDaniel on an appearance tour to promote the expansion of *Gone with the Wind* to Black movie houses. McDaniel pushed back, asking to play *both* Black and white theaters. Selznick agreed, and she set out on what was to be a twelve-week, nine-city tour. McDaniel's ten-minute act gave her the chance to revive the satirical, subversive persona of her Colorado days. Dressed as Mammy, she parodied scenes from *Gone with the Wind*, playing all the parts (including the white ones), and sang two original songs, "Mammy's Meditation #1" and "Mammy's Meditation #2," which infused her sexless character with bawdiness. ("Things is changin' nowadays," she crooned, "an' Mammy's gettin' bored.")

When McDaniel appeared at Glendale's Roxy theater, Selznick had a deputy in the audience report back. He asked her to tone down the act, writing to his vice president of production, "She will, if we don't watch out, rob herself of stature as a performer by stooping to cheap things." The ticket sales were weak, even with Black crowds, and McDaniel trudged through Baltimore, Washington, New York City, and Cleveland. By Chicago, she wired Selznick's offices saying she wanted to "come home for a rest."

Back in Hollywood, she found few opportunities beyond Selznick's attempts to squeeze her Mammy image for publicity. In a gambit to get her into fan magazines, the studio asked her to supply cooking tips—after all, she'd worked as a cook. McDaniel, who didn't use recipes in her cooking, conjured up instructions for corn bread, icebox cake, and "Mammy's Fried Chicken à la *Maryland*"—a plug for her new film, for which Selznick had loaned her out to Fox to play a cook. It was as if the Oscar had never happened, and she was back in her employer's kitchen, smiling as she worked.

More uninspired roles followed, including in the Bette Davis vehicle *The Great Lie*. Warner Bros. offered McDaniel a contract, then terminated it, then renewed it, giving her little more than run-of-the-mill maid roles. The rare exception was *In This Our Life*, starring Bette Davis and Olivia de Havilland as feuding sisters. When Davis's impulsive character kills a girl in a hit-and-run, she blames it on the family maid's son (Ernest Anderson), a studious young man who dreams of practicing law—a prototype of the "exceptional Negro" that Sidney Poitier would come to embody. The maid, played by McDaniel, knows that her boy is innocent but laments, "He tried to tell them, but they don't listen to no colored boy."

The idea that the police would apply a racial double standard was beyond what most Hollywood movies dared to imply. The film, whose production was interrupted by Pearl Harbor, was shelved as the studios scrambled to adjust to the patriotic new mood. When it was finally released, the Atlanta censorship board cut the parts about racism—McDaniel's best scenes since *Gone with the Wind*—and accused the film of insulting white southerners. After the expurgated version was mysteriously screened in Harlem, McDaniel, taking a rare stand against the studio system, asked to be let out of her Warner Bros. contract. Her Oscar, though, made her a useful tool in the Office of War Information's mission to promote American tolerance, and she was assigned to the Negro Division of the Hollywood Victory Committee to play USO shows. By 1942, she was living in a seventeen-room mansion, with her Oscar standing proud on the mantel. But it increasingly symbolized a summit from which she had dropped.

Instead of blaming her slump on white producers, McDaniel aimed her resentment at the NAACP's Walter White, who was courting studio heads in his campaign to improve Hollywood representation. At the association's annual convention in May 1942, White told a private luncheon crowd, including Selznick, Louis B. Mayer, and Frank Capra, "Restriction of Negroes to roles with rolling eyes, chattering teeth, always scared of ghosts or to portrayals of none-too-bright servants perpetuates a stereotype which is doing the Negro infinite harm." But he neglected to invite the generation of performers who'd made their careers playing these stereotypes, many of whom, including McDaniel, saw him as a direct threat to their livelihoods.

Just as concerning, the changing times brought a new crop of stars. At the convention's mass gathering at the Shrine Auditorium, McDaniel watched from a ten-thousand-person crowd as White stood onstage with Lena Horne, who embodied his vision of a new kind of sophisticated Black star; White wanted a "complete break with the tradition of showing Negroes as menials." McDaniel made her feelings plain. "I naturally resent being completely ignored at the convention after I have struggled for eleven years to open up opportunities to our group in the industry," she told the *Baltimore Afro-American*. "You can imagine my chagrin when the only person called to the platform was a young woman from New York who had just arrived in Hollywood and had not yet made her first picture." She expressed her belief in incremental change to the *Pittsburgh Courier*: "It takes time and I don't believe that we will gain by rushing or attempting to force studios to do anything they are not readily inclined to do."

McDaniel was personally welcoming to Horne, even offering advice. "She was extremely realistic and had no misconceptions of the role she was allowed to play in the white movie world," recalled Horne, who soon found herself stymied in Hollywood as well. McDaniel appeared in only two roles in 1943, four in 1944. Her friend Ruby Berkley Goodwin recalled this period as "bitter years of loneliness and disillusionment when she thought her race did not appreciate her artistry." That bitterness erupted in April 1944, when McDaniel was asked to give the keynote speech at the NAACP's First Annual Motion Picture Unity Award Assembly, held in a Baptist church auditorium. Midway through, she described Horne, one of the honorees, as "a representative of the new type of nigger womanhood." She stopped and insisted, "I said *Negro* womanhood." The audience was scandalized—it seemed like a Freudian slip at best.

More disappointments followed. At the age of fifty-one, McDaniel told Louella Parsons that she was pregnant—it was either a bizarre attempt to change the narrative or a delusion born of despair. Either way, no baby arrived. Her third marriage came to a contentious end in 1945, a year in which she had no movie roles and was preoccupied with a legal battle against a group of white residents of L.A.'s West Adams district, who were suing to expel their Black neighbors, including McDaniel. She continued to feel needled by Walter White, whom she accused of speaking to her "with the tone and manner that a Southern Colonel would use to his favorite slave." But White's campaign was unabating. "What is more important?" he argued. "Jobs for a handful of Negroes playing so-called Uncle Tom roles or the welfare of Negroes as a whole?"

In 1946, McDaniel appeared in *Song of the South*, the notorious Disney film based on Joel Chandler Harris's tales of Uncle Remus. Set in a honeyed version of the Old South, it portrayed the Black plantation workers smiling through their servitude—like *Gone with the Wind* with catchy songs and cartoon critters. McDaniel played yet another iteration of the aproned, opinionated Mammy. At the Academy Awards, where *Song of the South* won Best Original Song for "Zip-A-Dee-Doo-Dah," McDaniel's costar James Baskett received a special bronze honor, for his "heart-warming characterization" of Uncle Remus—the Academy's misconceived idea of a liberal gesture.

Screenings of *Song of the South*, like those of *Gone with the Wind*, drew Black picketers, and Walter White denounced it as "a dangerously glorified picture of slavery." By now, McDaniel was fed up having to justify her choices year after year. In a 1947 guest column for *The Hollywood Reporter*, titled "What Hollywood Means to Me," she vigorously defended her pathbreaking career, writing, "I have never apologized for the roles I play. Several times I have persuaded the directors to omit dialect from modern pictures . . . I have been told that I have kept alive the stereotype of the Negro servant in the minds of theatre-goers. I believe my critics think the public more naïve than it actually is."

That fall, McDaniel made an unlikely comeback, in the CBS Radio series *Beulah*, taking over the role of a wisecracking Black housekeeper previously voiced by white men. With McDaniel, the show became so popular that it was spun into a television sitcom. Yet again, the role drew criticism from Black journalists, and McDaniel argued that she was representing millions of Black domestics: "Why do we as a race deny our heritage? Surely you don't think that the role I portray is obsolete?" If times were changing, McDaniel could not.

By 1950, the year that Poitier starred in *No Way Out*, McDaniel was divorcing her fourth husband and absorbed in the teachings of Mary Baker Eddy. One morning in 1951, her Oscar date, Wonderful Smith, found her passed out at home, having suffered a stroke. The doctors discovered that she also had breast cancer. McDaniel died on October 26, 1952, at the age of fifty-nine, still the only Black actor to have won a competitive Oscar. She had wanted to be buried at Hollywood Memorial Park, alongside the likes of Rudolph Valentino and Douglas Fairbanks, but the cemetery did not allow her to break one last color line.

In her will, McDaniel left her Oscar to Howard University, where the drama department had once warmly welcomed her for a luncheon. There it stood, for a time, under glass. Sometime in the late sixties— likely in the heat of campus protests, as students at the historically Black university agitated for a curriculum that more accurately reflected their history—the award went missing and was never seen again.

IN THE INCREASING TURBULENCE OF the sixties, Sidney Poitier felt the weight of the nation on his shoulders. "I was now viewed as a fixture in the film world," he wrote, "but my fellow black actors, almost to a man, were trapped in a drought of inactivity and unemployment that sapped and embittered whatever satisfaction they may have derived from the success of a single one of us." His affair with Diahann Carroll, which had become public, made him a target of the Black press. He divorced Juanita Hardy and moved into a Riverside Drive apartment with Carroll, but once they were free to be together, the relationship unraveled. He took roles in *The Bedford Incident* and *The Slender Thread* that weren't written specifically for a Black actor, which he considered a sign of progress. But a more typical project was *A Patch of Blue*, about a blind white girl who falls in love with a man she meets in the park—without knowing he's Black. It was the "love is blind" trope made literal, with Poitier embodying a sort of racial stress test for white audiences: If you can't accept *this* one, then whom?

In 1967, as riots spread through Birmingham, Newark, and Detroit, Poitier appeared in three films whose combined box-office receipts made him the number one star in America. In each, he played a "civilized" Black man whose extraordinariness helps enlighten the regressive white characters forced into his company. In *To Sir, with Love*, he was a high school teacher brought in to tame a rowdy class of teens in London's East End. (A fellow teacher tells him to work his "black magic.") In *In the Heat of the Night*, he was Virgil Tibbs, the best homicide detective in Philadelphia, who gets picked up for murder passing through Mississippi and helps the white sheriff, played by Rod Steiger, solve the case. And in Stanley Kramer's *Guess Who's Coming to Dinner*, he was John Prentice, a doctor engaged to a young white woman who brings him home to meet her seemingly liberal parents in San Francisco.

The parents, Mr. and Mrs. Drayton, were played by Spencer Tracy and Katharine Hepburn. Before filming began, Poitier was invited to dine with them at Tracy's house, in what he interpreted as a test. Hepburn cooked dinner. It was a strange echo of the movie, which itself was a metaphor for Poitier's place in Hollywood: a well-behaved guest in a white world, where his primary job was not to offend.

Aside from its warm lesson of cross-racial tolerance, *Guess Who's Coming to Dinner* captured a trickier dynamic: the tension between Black generations. The Draytons' housekeeper, Tillie (Isabel Sanford), casts a wary eye on Dr. Prentice, declaring, "I don't care to see a member of my own race getting above hisself." And in a stirring scene between Poitier and fifty-three-year-old actor Roy Glenn, Prentice pleads with his disapproving father and his "whole lousy generation" to get "off our backs." It was as if Poitier were exorcising the old Hattie McDaniel world once and for all. The future looked more like the young couple at the heart of the movie, which was released a year after the Berry family welcomed their biracial daughter, Halle. Watching the film as a child, Berry said, "I felt seen."

Perhaps no Black celebrity could encompass the cultural crosscurrents of the late sixties, but Poitier, at his height, suddenly found himself ripe for taking down. "Black people particularly disliked *Guess Who's Coming to Dinner*, which I made a point of seeing," James Baldwin observed, "because they felt that Sidney was, in effect, being used against them." In September 1967, between the release of *In the Heat of the Night* and *Guess Who's Coming to Dinner*, the *New York Times* ran an astonishing column by Black writer Clifford Mason, titled "Why Does White America Love Sidney Poitier So?" What followed was a demolishing of Poitier's screen image, which Mason described as "a showcase nigger, who is given a clean suit and a complete purity of motivation." Harking back to Poitier's Oscar-winning role, Mason predicted that "until the day of complete honesty comes, white critics will gladly drag out a double standard and applaud every 'advance' in movies like 'Lilies of the Field' as so much American-style, democratic goodwill. Which is what the road to hell is paved with."

A stunned Poitier called it "the most devastating and unfair piece of journalism I had ever seen." Mason had used not only Poitier's dignity against him but also his peerlessness, which frustrated Poitier as much as anybody. He started calling around town asking questions about his detractor. But his fellow Black actors resented him, too. "I was the perfect target," he said, "and I was aware of it, but there wasn't anything I could do." He could tell them about how hard he had pushed the studios to hire more Black actors, but that had never worked, so what would they care? They knew the "naked truth about Hollywood," he wrote: that "the motion picture industry was not yet ready to entertain more than one minority person at that level. I knew it too, and I couldn't fight that."

At the 1968 Academy Awards, which were postponed two days after the assassination of Martin Luther King Jr., the top acting prizes went to Poitier's white costars Katharine Hepburn in *Guess Who's Coming to Dinner* and Rod Steiger in *In the Heat of the Night*, which also won Best Picture. Poitier, incredibly, wasn't nominated for either film. His days as a bankable leading man were vanishing before his eyes. His one 1969 release, *The Lost Man*, bombed, the only consolation being that his white costar Joanna Shimkus became his second wife. He built a house in Nassau and based himself in the Bahamas for four years. The most popular films on the island were blaxploitation movies: sexed-up, cheaply made action flicks like *Shaft* that traded refinement for roughness. "Generally these black heroes were seen beating up on white Mafia guys; it was a 'get whitey' time," Poitier observed. He watched them with fascination, knowing that he was seeing his obsolescence.

"My own career went into a decline at that point," Poitier recalled, "and I recognized that there would be no reviving it for a while." Though he had intermittent successes in the seventies—including two films he directed and acted in with Bill Cosby, *Uptown Saturday Night* and *Let's Do It Again*—his leading-man status was usurped by his temperamental opposite, Richard Pryor. As always, there seemed to be room for just one.

Poitier watched the seventies pass without any more Oscars for Black actors. There was the breakthrough year of 1973, when Paul Winfield and Cicely Tyson were nominated for *Sounder* and Diana Ross was nominated for *Lady Sings the Blues*. But none of them won. Neither did Diahann Carroll, nominated for *Claudine* two years later. By the time Poitier released his 1980 autobiography, *This Life*, he and Hattie McDaniel were still a club of two, and he lamented that "the present situation is somewhat bleak."

In the eighties, Poitier more or less vanished from the screen, but he took comfort in the rise of a new class of Black talent, like Morgan Freeman and Danny Glover. In 1983, Louis Gossett Jr. became the first Black Best Supporting Actor winner, for *An Officer and a Gentleman*. Denzel Washington won the same category for *Glory* seven years later. "The impact of the black audience is expressing itself," Poitier told an interviewer in 1989. "They look to films to be more expressive of their needs, their lives. Hollywood has gotten that message—finally." But the nineties went by without another Black Best Actor, to say nothing of a Black Best Actress. By the time Poitier released his "spiritual autobiography," *The Measure of a Man*, in 2000, his thirty-six-year-old statuette was less an honor than an indictment. His bio on the book jacket read, "Sidney Poitier was the first—and remains the only—African-American actor to win the Academy Award for Best Actor for his outstanding performance in *Lilies of the Field* in 1963, but he believes that will soon change, given the excellence of African-American talent in the industry today."

Two years later, Poitier, now a graying, seventy-five-year-old eminence, was invited back to receive an honorary Oscar. "Here I am, this evening, at the end of a journey that in 1949 would have been considered almost impossible," he said, citing the year he arrived in Hollywood. Invoking the Hattie McDaniel generation, he continued: "I accept this award in memory of all the African American actors and actresses who went before me, in the difficult years, on whose shoulders I was privileged to stand, to see where I might go."

Moments later, Poitier watched Halle Berry win for *Monster's Ball*. "I was out of my mind, semi-conscious," Berry said later. "But it was almost as if Sidney had a light on his head, because he was in the balcony and I saw him standing up, and I have that very clear memory." Soon after, Poitier watched Denzel Washington become the second Black Best Actor winner, for *Training Day*, after a thirty-eight-year gap. Gazing at Poitier in the balcony, Washington said, "I'll always be chasing you, Sidney. I'll always be following in your footsteps." Poitier rose, and they held their statuettes out to each other.

What did all this "progress" mean? Two days later, in an editorial titled "Hollywood History and Fantasy," the *New York Times* hit a note of skepticism: "It remains to be seen whether the door has been opened wide or merely set ajar only to swing shut again."

HALLE BERRY'S EMOTIONAL ACCEPTANCE SPEECH became the subject of immediate critique and ridicule. When the BBC solicited opinions online, many echoed that of a Londoner who found her display "toe-curlingly embarrassing." In the letters page of the *Los Angeles Times*, where a familiar debate played out over political correctness versus "merit," readers objected to the invocation of race at all. "I think she sold her peers short and left the impression that she was being recognized as a black actress and that Hollywood was making amends for years of racial bias," one "disappointed" El Monte resident wrote. On *Saturday Night Live*, Maya Rudolph played a hysterical Berry, clutching her Oscar and thanking Tootie from *The Facts of Life*.

That June, Berry's Oscar-winning role came under renewed scrutiny when Angela Bassett, who had been nominated for Best Actress in 1994, for *What's Love Got to Do with It*, made scathing remarks to *Newsweek*. She had turned down the role in *Monster's Ball*, she revealed, because "I wasn't going to be a prostitute on film" (even though the character was a waitress) and "it's such a stereotype about black women and sexuality." She didn't "begrudge Halle her success" but said, "I would love to have an Oscar. But it has to be for something I can sleep with it at night."

Bassett's comments sparked a heated debate in the Black community, just as McDaniel's *Gone with the Wind* role had six decades earlier. "After all this time has passed, so many want to stand up and applaud Halle," one Black female TV executive told the *Los Angeles Times*. "But others say, 'Isn't it sad that she had to be the sexual object of a white man?'" Some accused Bassett (whom Lionsgate denied was ever offered the role) of envy. Vanessa Williams, who had been the first Black Miss America, accused the media of pitting Black women against one another to "try to tear a sister down." One male shopper at a Black-owned bookstore in L.A. observed that Washington's corrupt cop role in *Training Day* hadn't drawn the same criticism. "But men have it easier," he said. "We can get away with a lot. And Denzel, he has such a reputation of becoming like a Sidney Poitier."

Berry declined to weigh in, but the impression that she had misused her emotions and her sexuality dented her historic victory. "The moment I won the Oscar, I felt the teardown the very next day," she said later. She focused on the next phase of her career. Shortly after the Oscars, she sat down with her manager to lay out a plan that might establish her as a global box-office commodity. The studios had an unwritten (but often spoken) rule that "Black doesn't travel," meaning that foreign markets wouldn't support Black stars. It was a new version of an idea from Poitier's era, that Black-themed films could never profit because of resistance in the South, which fed a reluctance to make those films in the first place. But the Oscar win and the grosses of *Die Another Day* suggested that Berry could dispel that myth.

Bond producers Barbara Broccoli and Michael G. Wilson thought that her character, Jinx, might be ripe for a spinoff, a possibility that delighted Berry. But MGM thought that the $80 million project was too risky. "Nobody was ready to sink that kind of money into a Black female action star," Berry said later. Fortunately, there was another potential franchise on offer: *Catwoman*. The *Batman* spinoff had been in development since Michelle Pfeiffer played the role in the early nineties. After Nicole Kidman passed, Warner Bros. offered the $90 million project to Berry, who was paid $12.5 million. At the time, the studio's head of production said that the green light was "based on her performance in which she won an Academy Award."

Berry admitted that *Catwoman* was an unconventional move. "People said to me, 'You can't do that. You've just won the Oscar,'" she recalled. "Because I didn't do Jinx, I thought, 'This is a great chance for a woman of color to be a superhero. Why wouldn't I try this?'" As the first big-budget action film headlined by a Black woman, *Catwoman* was a test for Berry and for Black Hollywood. Shortly before its release, in July 2004, the *New York Times* laid out the stakes: "In the zero-sum calculations of the movie industry, Ms. Berry's bankability as a star will be judged largely on . . . whether she can make it a financial winner." But the buzz was already bad. Instead of the long-running comic book character Selina Kyle, the filmmakers had reimagined Catwoman as Patience Phillips, a meek graphic designer who works for a beauty company that, she discovers, is producing toxic skin cream. Once she becomes Catwoman, she actually *acts* feline, rubbing her nose in catnip and slurping the tuna off her sushi.

Catwoman was greeted with near-universal derision, with one critic suggesting that Berry return her Oscar in disgrace. The movie made only half its budget back. Thanks to her midriff-baring dominatrix costume, Berry once again came under fire from Black critics. "When you talk about Halle Berry, it's all about her sexuality," critical studies professor Todd Boyd told the *New York Times*. "That ties into a historical representation of black women as being either a Mammy character or someone like Halle Berry, who is represented as a sexual object."

Like McDaniel and Poitier, Berry found herself representing everyone and pleasing no one. In 2005, just three years after she won the Oscar, she received the Razzie Award for Worst Actress for *Catwoman*. In the ultimate good-sport move, she showed up in person to accept the prize (a spray-painted golf ball), mocking her now-infamous Oscar speech as she wept and thanked Warner Bros. "for casting me in this piece of shit." Not that the real Academy Awards afforded her much more respect; the year after she won, she returned to present the Best Actor prize to Adrien Brody, who shocked her with an unexpected wet kiss. *What the fuck is going on right now?* she thought.

Worse, the Oscar barely affected the offers she received. "I thought, 'Oh, all these great scripts are going to come my way; these great directors are going to be banging on my door,'" she recalled. "It didn't happen." Her role in the X-Men series kept her on-screen, and she eked out a few thrillers and indie dramas, but none had the profile of *Monster's Ball.* "She didn't get the same opportunities the other women got," recalls her former manager Vincent Cirrincione. "She's still a woman of color, so a lot of movies didn't think of her."

She was more visible in supermarket tabloids, as her personal life devolved into a series of high-profile disasters. She divorced Benét in 2005 and had a daughter named Nahla with French Canadian model Gabriel Aubry. After Berry and Aubry split up, the ensuing custody battle provided nonstop gossip fodder that upstaged her acting career. She tried keeping a low profile, but the paparazzi staked out her house. By 2012, she was engaged to French actor Olivier Martinez and longed to move with Nahla to Paris. But a judge denied her request, as the move would have violated her custody agreement with Aubry. The legal battle forced Berry to drop out of a Broadway play, and she worried that her taste in men was cursed by a "broken picker." That November, Aubry and Martinez got into a brawl outside Berry's Hollywood Hills home. She filed a protective order against Aubry. The whole mess was splashed across the tabloids. She married Martinez and had a son, but that marriage broke up as well. In the divorce proceedings, Berry represented herself.

As the chaotic years passed, Berry's feelings about her Oscar changed. After a decade and a half, no other woman of color had won Best Actress. In 2016, she lamented, "When I said 'the door tonight has been opened,' I believed that with every bone in my body, that this was going to incite change, because this door, this barrier, had been broken. And to sit here almost fifteen years later, and knowing that another woman of color has not walked through that door, is heartbreaking. It's heartbreaking, because I thought that moment was bigger than me. And it's heartbreaking to start to think, Maybe it *wasn't* bigger than me."

For McDaniel, for Poitier, for Berry, the Oscar came to symbolize not progress but false promise—a chance for Hollywood to congratulate itself and then go back to business as usual while the winner was left isolated and open to public attack. Each felt the burden of being Hollywood's token, but the Oscar was also a token: a shiny gold-plated man trapped on a pedestal. After nine decades of Academy Awards, being the first and only was no longer enough. Something bigger, something *structural*, had to change.

And then something did.

ELEVEN

The Envelope

2017

How Cheryl Boone Isaacs weathered
#OscarsSoWhite, *Moonlight* faced off against
La La Land, and an eleventh-hour mix-up pushed the
Academy into its future.

At 2:30 a.m. on January 14, 2016, Cheryl Boone Isaacs arrived at Academy headquarters. A soft-spoken woman in her sixties with bangs and chunky glasses, Boone Isaacs had been Academy president since 2013. With some three hours to go before announcing the eighty-eighth annual Oscar nominations, she had arrived early to get camera-ready and to practice saying the names phonetically; the previous year, she had accidentally caused an online sensation when she referred to cinematographer Dick Pope as "Dick Poop."

The mangled name was quickly overshadowed by a bigger scandal. In 2015, all twenty acting nominees had been white, and the civil rights drama *Selma* received no nods for its cast or its director, Ava DuVernay. In response, an activist named April Reign tweeted, "#OscarsSoWhite they asked to touch my hair," launching a hashtag movement that laid

Hollywood's diversity problems at the Academy's feet. This put Boone
Isaacs in a bind: as the Academy's first Black president (and third female
president, after Bette Davis and Fay Kanin), she was the face of an organization that seemed woefully out of step with Barack Obama's America.
She was also a seasoned publicist whose instinct was to deflect. When
a journalist asked her if the Academy had a diversity problem, she said,
"Not at all."

But the Academy's race problem had been under intense scrutiny
since 2012, when the *Los Angeles Times* reported, under the headline
"Unmasking the Academy," that the nearly six-thousand-person membership was 94 percent white and 77 percent male, with a median age
of sixty-two. People under fifty represented just 14 percent of the roster,
African Americans made up 2 percent, and Latinos were less than that.
The executive branch—Hollywood's gatekeepers—was an astonishing
98 percent white. The paper had painstakingly tracked down members,
finding that some hadn't worked in the industry for decades, including
a bookstore owner and a nun. The exposé included stinging assessments
from Black artists, including director Bill Duke, who called the Academy
"an elitist group with no concern or regard for the minority community
and industry."

To Boone Isaacs, who was then the only person of color on the forty-
three-member Board of Governors, none of this was news. The Academy
had done its own demographic accounting and come up with even worse
numbers than the *Times* did. "But when you see it in black and white,"
she recalls, "it's a bit startling." Boone Isaacs was used to being the only
Black person in the room—and not saying anything about it. She had
seen moments of "inclusion" come and go in Hollywood. In the eighties
and nineties, the successes of *Do the Right Thing* and *Boyz n the Hood*
suggested that viewers were eager to watch more diverse movies. But
then the window closed. "It's just how the wheel moves," she'd tell herself.

But did the Academy really deserve blame for the whiteness and
maleness of Hollywood at large? Boone Isaacs's fellow governor Frank
Pierson, who since winning an Oscar for the screenplay for *Dog Day
Afternoon* had served as Academy president, told the *L.A. Times*, "I don't
see any reason why the academy should represent the entire American

population. That's what the People's Choice Awards are for." The Academy had always stood for *merit*, a word that had been used like a cudgel in debates over affirmative action. No doubt expressing the views of many Academy members, white film composer William Goldstein, who had been discovered by Motown founder Berry Gordy in what Goldstein viewed as a looser, more multicultural age, wrote in to the paper to rail against "political correctness" in the arts, asserting, "The demographics of the Academy are not a social injustice."

The Academy's identity rested on exclusivity. In 2004, at the urging of executive director Bruce Davis, who felt that certain branches were getting bloated, the board had narrowed intake to fewer than two hundred new members per year, depending on vacancies due to death or retirement. The tightened admission policies kept the circle limited to people who knew people in the business, or people who got nominated for Oscars, which helped ensure an Academy that remained demographically static.

The Academy was not blind to the growing problem. In 2011, the board brought in Dawn Hudson, an Arkansas-born indie film executive, to be its first CEO, with the mission to drag the sclerotic institution into the future. Hudson was concerned about diversity and urged the executive committees to look beyond their immediate circles for new members. But the *L.A. Times* story put those incremental efforts to shame. In its wake, the Academy brought in a diversity officer and did away with the membership cap. The ascendance of Boone Isaacs, in 2013, echoed Obama's, but as the country had learned from his first term, having a Black figurehead didn't guarantee a "post-racial" transformation—in fact, the backlash could be severe. Months before *12 Years a Slave* won Best Picture, in 2014, a follow-up story in the *L.A. Times* revealed that the Academy's demographic makeup had scarcely budged, and Boone Isaacs was left to give a rosy spin on how the numbers were "moving in the right direction." The 2015 nominations, which gave rise to #OscarsSoWhite, turned up the pressure. At the end of the year, Boone Isaacs welcomed a black-tie audience at the Governors Awards by announcing "A2020," an initiative with the quixotic goal of doubling the number of women and underrepresented groups in the Academy within five years. "Now please enjoy your dinner," she concluded, to modest applause.

The happy talk fizzled when one of the honorees, Spike Lee, took the stage. "We can talk, you know, yabba, yabba, yabba, but we need to have some serious discussion about diversity, and get some *flave* up in this," he scolded. Throwing the industry's hypocrisy in its face, he added, "Everybody in here probably voted for Obama, but when I go to offices, I see no Black folks except for the brother man at security."

So, two months later, as Boone Isaacs sat in the makeup chair at the Academy building, she was hoping for a smoother ride in 2016. The accountants from PricewaterhouseCoopers had dropped off the tabulations, and a staff member handed her the nominations with a grave stare on her face. *Oh, no*, Boone Isaacs thought, opening the packet. Not only were the acting nominees again all white, but *Straight Outta Compton*, about the gangsta rap group N.W.A., was recognized only for the work of its white screenwriters, and the *Rocky* sequel *Creed*, which had a Black director and star, had received a single nomination—for Sylvester Stallone.

Just before 5 a.m., Boone Isaacs took the elevator down to the Academy theater, where she and John Krasinski read off the names to a crowd of bleary-eyed reporters. She kept her tone upbeat, but as she said later, "I just knew it was going to be tough from a PR standpoint."

It was. April Reign immediately revived her #OscarsSoWhite hashtag, which went viral. The *L.A. Times* ran a cover with head shots of the all-white nominees, lined up like mug shots. Jada Pinkett Smith, whose husband, Will Smith, had failed to receive a nomination for *Concussion*, announced on Facebook that she would boycott the ceremony. Spike Lee also vowed to boycott, writing on Instagram, "40 White Actors In 2 Years And No Flava At All. We Can't Act?! WTF!!" Lupita Nyong'o, who had won for *12 Years a Slave*, wrote on Instagram that the "lack of inclusion" had gotten her "thinking about unconscious prejudice and what merits prestige in our culture" and shared a quote from James Baldwin: "Not everything that is faced can be changed. But nothing can be changed until it is faced." Even President Obama weighed in, asking, "Are we making sure that everybody is getting a fair shot?"

Unlike the previous year, the nominations couldn't be explained away by a lack of options. *Creed*'s Michael B. Jordan was an attractive new star. The poor showing for *Straight Outta Compton* suggested that a film about hip-hop, as opposed to civil rights or slavery, just didn't resonate with Academy members. Netflix had pushed for *Beasts of No Nation*'s Idris Elba for Best Actor, but the fact that a streaming platform was nosing into the Oscar game at all unnerved the industry. There was talk that the "fifth slot" that might have gone to Elba had been taken by Bryan Cranston for *Trumbo*, a biopic that cast Dalton Trumbo as a noble freethinker; in an irony that Trumbo would surely have savored, it had taken him six decades to turn from pariah to "safe choice."

With the #OscarsSoWhite fiasco spinning out of control, Boone Isaacs released a lengthy statement saying that she was "heartbroken and frustrated about the lack of inclusion" and promising "big changes." "You don't want the conversation to get away from you," she said later. "That's just PR 101." But talk was cheap. "It became apparent," she recalled, "that doing business as usual wasn't going to be enough."

ON JANUARY 21, THE BOARD of Governors, which included Tom Hanks and Annette Bening, met for an emergency session in the Academy's seventh-floor conference room and unanimously approved a plan to diversify the voting body by aggressively recruiting new members. At the same time, some existing members would be shifted to "emeritus status," which did not include voting for the Oscars. Voting privileges would be granted to those who had been active in the industry in the previous ten years, with the exception of those with credits spanning three decades and anyone who had ever been nominated for an Oscar. In other words, if you had two acting credits in the Carter era, start packing for the ice floe.

The plan was met with praise, including from Ava DuVernay, who tweeted, "Shame is a helluva motivator." The Academy could point to the precedent of Gregory Peck's purge from 1970. "In the '60s and '70s, it was about recruiting younger members to stay vital and relevant," Boone Isaacs wrote to the membership. "In 2016, the mandate is inclusion in all of its facets: gender, race, ethnicity and sexual orientation."

But the pushback came hard. As *Sunset Boulevard* had proven, no anxiety is as pervasive in Hollywood as the fear of obsolescence. Eighty-four-year-old heartthrob Tab Hunter called the policy "bullshit," pronouncing, "Obviously, it's a thinly-veiled ploy to kick out older white contributors—the backbone of the industry—to make way for younger, 'politically-correct' voters." *The Hollywood Reporter* published a series of guest columns by irate Academy veterans. Director Stephen Verona (*The Lords of Flatbush*, 1974) was "flabbergasted and then outraged." Executive David Kirkpatrick (*Terms of Endearment*, 1983) accused the Academy of "exchanging purported racism with ageism." Lesbian screenwriter Patricia Resnick, who wrote the feminist classic *9 to 5*, complained about being potentially "booted into the 'emeritus' status and replaced by younger members" to help the Academy deal with its "publicity nightmare." As the Oscars approached, little bombs kept exploding. Charlotte Rampling, nominated for Best Actress for *45 Years*, told a French interviewer that the boycott was "racist against whites" and mused that "sometimes maybe black actors didn't deserve to make the shortlist." She later expressed regret for the comment, but it likely torpedoed her chances against Brie Larson (*Room*).

The backlash, now noisier than the original outcry, was a funhouse mirror reflection of the political rise of Donald Trump, who was blustering his way through the Republican primaries on a platform of white grievance and ridiculing "political correctness." The undertow of the Obama years was now a familiar dynamic in American life: as marginalized groups attained more influence, others felt threatened and resentful. Of course, the national political divide couldn't be neatly mapped onto Hollywood, which had few out-and-out conservatives. Some of the older members who felt that they were being painted as bigots had marched for civil rights in the sixties. But the wheel had turned, and many of those who had come up in the New Hollywood of *Easy Rider* and *One Flew Over the Cuckoo's Nest* were now old-timers who saw themselves as freethinking McMurphys, with Boone Isaacs in the role of Nurse Ratched. Few seemed interested in examining the structural forces that had homogenized the industry, painting a line between Black movies and the "prestige" films that won Oscars. Hate mail poured into Boone Isaacs's office, including a letter from an older white woman who called the Academy president an "embarrassment." Boone Isaacs watched the drama play out with resignation. "If I had been a white male, they would not have tried to make it look like a race issue," she says. "It's kind of, like, 'Oh, this Black woman's going to say whether or not I can vote?'"

CHERYL BOONE ISAACS WAS BORN in 1949, the youngest daughter of a postal worker and a homemaker in Springfield, Massachusetts. Like many Black parents, hers told her that she would have to be twice as good and work twice as hard to succeed in a white world. Her gateway to show business was her older brother Ashley, who worked for United Artists promoting films like *Tom Jones* and *Lilies of the Field*. Ashley cut a dashing figure. "Just totally cool, with his chinos and the broadcloth in pastel colors, and loafers with no socks," his sister recalls. He would come home to Springfield with a projector and show new releases in the dining room. Cheryl says, "The fact that he was in that world—oh, my gosh, oh, my gosh!"

Ashley moved to the film division at CBS and then to Sidney Poitier's production company. Cheryl was awed by Poitier: "He was the king in the Black community, just the *king*." When Ashley brought her to the Academy Awards in 1970, the year that *Midnight Cowboy* won, she felt like Cinderella at the ball. But Cheryl, naturally shy, knew that her job was to stay quiet and fade into the background.

At Whittier College, she developed an interest in "the international concept" and spent her junior year in Copenhagen. At twenty-one, she became a stewardess for Pan Am, one of two Black women in a class of about thirty. "I had my favorite route, which was to Tokyo, to Hong Kong, to Sydney, to either Fiji or Tahiti, to Hawaii, and then home," she recalls. By the late seventies, Ashley, as 20th Century–Fox's president of distribution and marketing, was the highest-ranking Black executive in Hollywood. Cheryl followed him to Los Angeles, but she wanted to make it on her own, so "we decided he wasn't going to help me." When people saw her résumé, they assumed she was Pat Boone's daughter.

In 1977, while Ashley was working on the rollout for *Star Wars*, Cheryl was hired to work the press junket for Steven Spielberg's *Close Encounters of the Third Kind*. She had no Black coworkers. "I said to myself, *I'm just going to put my head down and work, and I'll look up in ten years and see where I am*." In the eighties, she joined Paramount, at a time when the studio boasted pioneering female executives like Dawn Steel and Sherry Lansing. She eventually rose to executive vice president of worldwide publicity, working on Best Picture winners *Forrest Gump* and *Braveheart*. She got used to directors giving her skeptical looks upon their first meeting. One time, a colleague informed her that "there was a concern that the filmmakers would think they got the B team."

Cheryl was the only relative who knew that Ashley was gay; both were double minorities in an industry when one would have been plenty. "I thought I should have been promoted a little faster a couple of times," she says, but "you didn't really spend a lot of time talking about the obvious." In 1987, the year she worked on *Beverly Hills Cop II*, a friend cajoled her into applying for membership to the Academy. The next year, the same friend convinced her to join the board, "at which point I almost had a heart attack." As the only Black member, she shrank in her chair next to the likes of Lew Wasserman: "I don't think I opened my mouth for the first couple of years." When Gregory Peck rejoined the board, she met him while they were taking a group photo. "Hi, I'm Greg Peck," he boomed, and asked what branch she was from. Knowing that Peck had crusaded against the inclusion of publicists in the Academy, she looked him straight in the eye and, in a rare moment of gumption, said, "Public relations."

Ashley joined the board in 1991, making the Boones the only siblings to serve together. But the fact that the Academy's two Black board members were also related only underscored how anomalous they were in Hollywood. In 1993, Ashley was diagnosed with pancreatic cancer; he died the following May. Few had known he was sick, or that he left behind a male partner. "Ashley was very private," says Boone Isaacs. "We didn't have a memorial service. He didn't want one. Some people got very upset with me."

Left alone to break barriers, in 1997 she became the first Black woman to run a studio marketing department, at New Line, and later formed her own consulting firm for awards campaigning. By 2013, Academy board members were cajoling her to run for president. "I would say, 'Are you kidding? That is such a long shot.' Friends of mine said, 'Well, what do you have to lose?' And I thought, *Embarrassment?*"

For several years, Boone Isaacs had been a member of Soka Gakkai International, a Buddhist sect boasting celebrity adherents like Tina Turner and Orlando Bloom. Every morning and evening, she chanted *nam-myoho-renge-kyo* to the Gohonzon, an enshrined scroll that hung in her living room in Hancock Park. Buddhism had taught her to "look at adversity as an opportunity to improve your fate," and she realized that she had boxed herself in at the Academy. She agreed to run. "The Buddhist community was elated," she recalls. "I would go to meetings, and people would say to me, 'I just want you to know I'm chanting for you.'" She won.

In her new position, people would tell her, "You must be overwhelmed." She wondered if they would have said those same words to a man. As a Black woman, she would tell herself, "I can't get angry." But the barrage of grievances in the wake of #OscarsSoWhite irked her. She tried a charm offensive. When William Goldstein sent another angry missive to the *L.A. Times*, accusing the Academy of "capitulating to the PC police," she invited him to come in and talk to her directly. Goldstein did most of the talking. Boone Isaacs tried explaining to anyone who would listen that no one was being punished for how they voted. She was shocked when disgruntled members would say to her face, "What do they want? We just voted for *12 Years a Slave!*"

"*They* meaning *me?*" she would reply.

At the annual Oscar luncheon in February 2016, she addressed a crowd that included Eddie Redmayne, Matt Damon, and Alicia Vikander, telling them over plates of arctic char, "This year, we all know there's an elephant in the room. I have asked the elephant to leave." But the elephant wasn't moving. Chris Rock, who'd been tapped before the blowup to host the ceremony, rejected calls to pull out. Instead, he rewrote his monologue to gleefully poke the wound. Onstage at that year's Oscars, he welcomed viewers to "the Academy Awards, otherwise known as the White People's Choice Awards." (He also ribbed Jada Pinkett Smith's boycott, which "is like me boycotting Rihanna's panties: I wasn't invited.")

Boone Isaacs struck a nobler tone when she appeared, in a red dress, to praise the Academy's "concrete action" and invoke Martin Luther King Jr.: "The ultimate measure of a man is not where he stands in moments of comfort and convenience, but where he stands at times of challenge and controversy." The night ended, sedately, with a Best Picture win for *Spotlight*. But the next Oscar race was already under way—and already full of land mines.

THE HASHTAG OSCARSSOWHITE WAS STILL trending on Twitter when the Sundance festival, the unofficial starting pistol for awards season, began on January 21, 2016. The throng of movie executives flooding into Park City, Utah, were keenly aware of the pressure they faced to avoid a third #OscarsSoWhite year in a row in 2017. The industry had egg on its face, and change, the decision makers had been told, had to start with them. The festival's first few days were muted when it came to acquisitions, with the exception of *Manchester by the Sea*, Kenneth Lonergan's bleak drama about a janitor, played by Casey Affleck. Amazon bought the domestic rights for ten million dollars, giving it an opening to become the first streaming service to break into the Best Picture race—a prospect that rattled those in the industry who relied on the traditional theatrical model.

By day five of Sundance—just three days after the Academy announced its diversity initiative—buyers still had plenty of money on the table, and a sense of restlessness pervaded the mountain air. That night, some twelve hundred spectators filled up the Eccles Theatre for the premiere of *The Birth of a Nation*, directed by and starring Nate Parker.

Everything about the film signaled the arrival of a major Black auteur. *The Birth of a Nation* depicted the 1831 slave rebellion led by Nat Turner, who preached the Bible to his fellow slaves in Virginia before enlisting them to rise up against their white masters. Parker, a debonair thirty-six-year-old, was playing Turner and making his directorial début. The film resembled nothing so much as *Braveheart*, Mel Gibson's Best Picture winner from twenty years earlier: an actor-director playing a historical rebel-hero, bloody battle scenes set to a sweeping score, and an ending that redounded the hero's Christ-like martyrdom onto the man playing him. (In the final scene, the hanged Turner sees an angel welcoming him to heaven.)

Parker's film promised several potential Oscar narratives rolled into one: it was a Hollywood-style epic with weighty historical themes, it had a telegenic mascot who could compete in both the directing and acting races, and it could head off another all-white nomination slate at the pass. To top it off, Parker had appropriated the title of D. W. Griffith's racist 1915 landmark, the blockbuster that had launched the film industry while inspiring a revival of the Ku Klux Klan. Here was a chance to rewrite that story, giving Hollywood an opportunity to atone for its original sin while anointing a new talent.

Perhaps that's why, when Parker came onstage for his welcome speech, the Sundance crowd gave him a standing ovation before the movie even began. Two hours later, he returned, to another standing ovation. "This has been a passion project of mine for the last seven years," he told the crowd, then brought out a large, mostly Black cast that looked like an #OscarsSoWhite antidote. From the stage, Parker called out his college roommate Jean Celestin, with whom he shared story credit.

From the audience, a woman in a red coat said, "This film carries a lot of responsibility. How can we help you carry it?"

"Talk to people," Parker implored. "I made this film for one reason: with the hope of creating change agents." He added, "There are systems in our life right now, in your environment *right now*. Are you passive, or are you corrupt and complicit?"

Not everyone was breathless. One audience member recalls, "Immediately after that premiere, one of my colleagues texted me, 'How's *Birth of a Nation*?' And I said, 'It's not great, but it's going to go for so much money right now.'" This was correct. No sooner had the credits rolled than buyers, in the heat of "festival fever," burst from the theater to make offers. Six bidders warred into the night, with Netflix offering a whopping $20 million. By 4 a.m., Parker and his producers had struck a deal with Fox Searchlight, which had offered less money but promised a 1,500-screen release and a full-bore marketing campaign, including a road show that would send Parker to churches and colleges. Searchlight paid $17.5 million—a Sundance record by a margin of $5.5 million—positioning the film as the early Best Picture front-runner for 2017.

Among the losing bidders was Harvey Weinstein, who had topped out at $12 million. Weinstein's influence had ebbed since his Miramax glory days. In 2005, amid contentious battles over budgets and autonomy, Bob and Harvey Weinstein had separated from Disney, their corporate parent of twelve years, in an acrimonious divorce. (The turning point came when Michael Eisner forbade Miramax from distributing Michael Moore's political documentary *Fahrenheit 9/11*.) The brothers jettisoned the company they'd named after their parents and set up a new shop, the Weinstein Company. Harvey's Oscar streak returned with back-to-back Best Picture wins for *The King's Speech* and *The Artist*, in 2011 and 2012. For both campaigns, Weinstein had hired Cheryl Boone Isaacs as a consultant, though both were the kind of old-fashioned period films that her diversity push now threatened to undercut. Weinstein, for his part, publicly opposed the "emeritus status" plan, saying, "I just don't think it's fair that people who are in the Academy are penalized."

But he had bigger headaches. Even as Weinstein continued to travel in private jets and town cars, his company was lurching toward financial doom. In 2015, the Weinstein Company had cut its yearly film slate in half and laid off fifty employees. A scuttled $950 million deal to sell its television business to ITV left the studio scrambling and Weinstein forced to live less large. Without Disney's money to throw around anymore, he couldn't outrun his competitors for *The Birth of a Nation*. And both of his 2016 Oscar hopefuls, Quentin Tarantino's *The Hateful Eight* and Todd Haynes's *Carol*, got left off the Best Picture list, Weinstein's first time in eight years without a horse in the race. The morning of the nominations, Weinstein was in his town car, lamenting to an associate, "These are the times that try men's souls."

Facing the prospect of irrelevance in the very Oscar game he had created, Weinstein focused on his best hope for 2017: *Lion*, a based-on-a-true-story tearjerker he had acquired at Cannes, about a small Indian boy adopted by an Australian woman played by Nicole Kidman. But his spotty Oscar record was not the gravest threat to his operation. Weinstein had continued his campaign of sexual assault and coercion, sometimes paying his accusers for their silence with six- or seven-figure settlements. Employees were kept quiet, too, with intimidation tactics and contracts enforcing strict confidentiality.

Lately, though, there had been cracks in the omertà. In 2015, an employee named Lauren O'Connor sent a memo to Weinstein Company executives describing the "toxic environment for women at this company." They offered her a settlement, and she withdrew the complaint. The same year, Italian model Ambra Battilana Gutierrez told the NYPD that Weinstein had groped her in his office, and she agreed to meet him again wearing a wire. The accusations got into the tabloids, which painted Gutierrez as a fame-hungry opportunist, and the DA's office declined to pursue charges. Even at the Oscars, Weinstein's predations were waved away with jokes. In 2013, host Seth MacFarlane had ribbed the Best Supporting Actress nominees, "Congratulations, you five ladies no longer have to pretend to be attracted to Harvey Weinstein."

AT THE ACADEMY, THE CRISIS-LADEN winter of 2016 became an exasperating spring. As each branch vetted new members and Academy librarians worked overtime scrutinizing older members' credits, the board fielded frantic calls from people asking if they were marked for demotion. "There was just a lot of apprehension and fear, and a lack of understanding of what we were going to do," says Lorenza Muñoz, who oversaw member relations. "It was really hard to be in that fire, and it was a daily fire." In April, the Academy sent out a letter to the membership, conceding that the emeritus plan had "unintentionally caused so much confusion and anger." It clarified that no one would be disenfranchised simply for being "over the hill," and pointed out that lifetime voting privileges had not been guaranteed since the Gregory Peck reforms. However, members with credits spanning three decades would now be voters for life—so the new rules actually *favored* people with long careers.

The Academy's critics gleefully cast the "clarification" as backpedaling and, emboldened, vowed to counterattack. There was discussion of a class-action lawsuit for age discrimination. Awards strategist Bruce Feldman slammed the board for "running the Academy as if it's an oligarchy" and declared that "the incumbents should all be displaced." In one of its democratizing efforts, the Academy had recently changed its rules to allow any member to run for the board, instead of the old nomination-by-committee method. That opened the door to an insurgency. In May, a cadre of Boone Isaacs's critics, including Feldman and William Goldstein, ran on a platform of maintaining "excellence" instead of changing the Academy's "standards" for the sake of diversity. They all lost, and Boone Isaacs was reelected—indicating that her critics were louder than they were numerous.

Soon, members began receiving letters from the Academy asking for an updated list of credits and informing them brightly that they might "qualify for emeritus status." Robert Bassing, a screenwriter in his nineties, threatened to sue, angered by Boone Isaacs's clarifications. "She explained it's not about diversity, it's about being 'relevant,' which really pissed me off," he said. "Because I already know that! I mean, when you're ninety, you're not relevant." Mother Dolores Hart, the Academy's only nun, was also demoted. She was inducted in 1960, three years after her film début in the Elvis Presley flick *Loving You*, and three years before she forsook Hollywood for the veil. At the Abbey of Regina Laudis, in Bethlehem, Connecticut, she dutifully watched her screeners every year on a laptop during Lectio Divina, the time for "holy reading." "I'm not going to go down screaming," she said. "But I think if they cut off too much of the elder community, they're going to clip the *wisdom* dimension of the Academy."

Ultimately, the "purge" ended up affecting less than 1 percent of the membership, or about seventy people. In June, the Academy released a list of 683 new invited members—a record number; 46 percent were female and 41 percent were nonwhite, representing 59 different countries. They included actors John Boyega, America Ferrera, Ice Cube, Idris Elba, and Daniel Dae Kim; directors Ryan Coogler, Marjane Satrapi, and the Wachowskis; and three Wayans brothers, Damon, Marlon, and Keenen Ivory. As if to rebut charges of ageism, the oldest new inductee was ninety-one-year-old Mexican actor Ignacio López Tarso.

Also on the list was Nate Parker, who appeared to be coasting toward Oscar glory as Fox Searchlight approached the fall release of *The Birth of a Nation*. Over the summer, posters went up of Parker wearing an American flag as a noose, and cardboard standees showing rioting slaves popped up in multiplexes amid superhero displays. Coming on the heels of Trump's hostile takeover of the Republican primaries, the movie, it was clear, was meant to be a statement, a battle cry, an awards darling, and a hit.

Then, in August, journalists resurfaced a disturbing episode from Parker's past. In 1999, when he was a nineteen-year-old student at Penn State, Parker and his roommate were charged with raping a freshman girl after a night of drinking. The roommate was Jean Celestin, Parker's wrestling teammate and cowriter of *The Birth of a Nation*. Both men maintained that the sex was consensual. Parker was acquitted; Celestin was found guilty and sentenced to a six-month prison term, but the conviction was later overturned. Their accuser, who maintained anonymity, claimed that the university had protected the athletes and that Parker and his friends had posted her photo around campus for students to smear with dirt. The incident was not a secret—it was on Parker's Wikipedia page—but in the frenzied bidding war at Sundance, the studios had apparently been too busy drawing up their release strategies to google him.

Parker tried to get ahead of the story, calling the incident "a very painful moment in my life" and reiterating that he had been cleared of all wrongdoing. "Seventeen years later, I'm a filmmaker," he told *Variety*. "I have a family. I have five beautiful daughters." Then another awful bombshell dropped when the accuser's brother revealed that she had killed herself in 2012, after suffering from severe depression, drug addiction, and delusions that God was talking to her through her car radio. "He's probably going to get an Academy Award," the woman's sister said of Parker. "It eats me up."

Parker, who had been promoting the movie with Spike Lee on Martha's Vineyard, was stunned to learn of his accuser's death. On Facebook, he wrote that he was "filled with profound sorrow," admitting only that he "may not have shown enough empathy even as I fought to clear my name." But the damage was irreversible, and the scandal threw a race-and-gender grenade into an already fraught awards year. "I cannot separate the art and the artist," Roxane Gay wrote in the *New York Times*, "just as I cannot separate my blackness and my continuing desire for more representation of the black experience in film from my womanhood, my feminism, my own history of sexual violence, my humanity."

Months after "festival fever" had worn off, *The Birth of a Nation* itself seemed ham-handed and preening. Against the historical record, Parker had inserted scenes of sexual violence that supposedly sparked the match of Nat Turner's rebellion—an artistic liberty that now seemed repugnant. The face of the movie had become radioactive even before it opened. Overnight, the presumptive Best Picture front-runner all but evaporated, leaving a void that was filled, almost immediately, by *La La Land*.

DAMIEN CHAZELLE WAS AN OLD person's ideal of a young person: mad about jazz, mad about Old Hollywood, bursting with thoughts on Count Basie and Fred Astaire. When producers Jordan Horowitz and Fred Berger first met him, at a restaurant in West Hollywood in 2010, he talked endlessly about Jacques Demy's French New Wave musicals *The Umbrellas of Cherbourg* and *The Young Girls of Rochefort*, the primary influences for the movie he wanted to make: a splashy musical love letter to Los Angeles.

Chazelle, a Rhode Island native with a French father, was twenty-five and had already premiered a movie at the Tribeca Film Festival, a lovelorn, MGM-inspired musical romance called *Guy and Madeline on a Park Bench*, shot in black and white for sixty thousand dollars. It was his senior thesis project at Harvard. Chazelle had spent his college years feeding his brain with Fred and Ginger, Godard, Hitchcock. Golden age movie musicals thrilled him. "Suddenly, I started thinking of them as experimental movies in mainstream garb," he said later. "That was the initial thing where I woke up and went, 'Oh, my God, I've been sleeping on a gold mine.'"

The movie he pitched to Horowitz and Berger was *La La Land*. "It was very much a romantic love story set in Los Angeles, about a guy and a girl," Horowitz recalls. "It had a lot to do with jazz, and she was an actress, and there was definitely a weird *Bonnie and Clyde* thing that happened at one point." The two producers were barely thirty themselves, but they had a deal with Focus Features to develop movies for under a million dollars, and Chazelle had an alluring notion of how to mix the classic and the contemporary. Horowitz says, "Fred and I were like, 'That was great, but we're going to get rid of that crime part.'"

Still, an original jazz musical? Higher-ups pushed Chazelle to change his hero from a jazz pianist to a rocker. "Every one of the contours that felt special and distinctive were the things we were urged to change," Berger said. When Focus Features ultimately passed, they shopped it around, but the budgets they were offered were always three million less than they could stomach. Chazelle told the two producers, "I think I need another movie in order to achieve what we're trying to do with *La La Land.*" He made *Whiplash*, a $3.3 million chamber drama based on his time playing drums in a cutthroat high school jazz band. It was nominated for Best Picture in 2015, and J. K. Simmons, who played the autocratic band leader, won Best Supporting Actor. Now that Chazelle had a hit to his name, Lionsgate picked up *La La Land.*

The road remained rocky. The original leads, Emma Watson and *Whiplash* star Miles Teller, slipped out of reach. "Everything felt like a complete mess and a complete jumble," Chazelle recalled. He landed a new pair, Emma Stone and Ryan Gosling, whom Chazelle saw as a Fred-and-Ginger duo, as they'd costarred in two movies already. The cast spent three months rehearsing, with Gosling learning to play piano and Stone learning choreography. Every Friday night, Chazelle screened his eclectic influences: *Top Hat, Singin' in the Rain, Boogie Nights.* They shot the musical numbers at Hollywood Center Studios, where, as Chazelle knew well, Astaire had filmed *Second Chorus.*

The most complicated feat was the opening number, in which the denizens of Los Angeles, stuck in standstill traffic, emerge from their cars and burst into euphoric dance on the freeway, overlaying the timeless myth of Hollywood onto banal modern-day L.A. Chazelle, shooting in sweeping, nostalgic CinemaScope, had just forty-eight hours on the 105–110 interchange, a stretch of highway that curved a hundred feet off the ground. Both days were over a hundred degrees. Once the movie was in the can, the filmmakers had second thoughts. "For our first test screening, we had cut the freeway number," recalls Horowitz, instead starting with a title sequence and an overture. Then they swapped the freeway scene back in. When the film opened the Venice Film Festival, in August 2016, the number got its own applause. *Deadline* called the film a "romantic fever dream of a musical." Lionsgate, bullish on its awards prospects, had already pushed the release date from July to December.

La La Land was about letting go of cynicism, about hope and romance and living for your art. Most of all, it was about Los Angeles, where people still flocked year after year with nothing but big dreams, as Chazelle had. In other words, it was the kind of movie-obsessed movie that had always cakewalked to the Academy Awards—although, with the changing makeup of the Academy, who knew if the old rules still applied? *La La Land* left Venice walking on air on its way to Telluride, where the world would get its first glimpse of *Moonlight*.

BARRY JENKINS HAD ALL BUT given up on making movies when he read *In Moonlight Black Boys Look Blue*. In 2008, he débuted his first feature, *Medicine for Melancholy*, but then things had stalled. His screenplay about Stevie Wonder and time travel went nowhere. He worked briefly as a carpenter and cofounded an ad company. "I was in this gray area," he recalls. "All of the things I had started after making my first feature— signing with an agency, getting a blind deal with a studio—were kind of evaporating."

Born in 1979, Jenkins began his life in Liberty Square, a public housing project in Liberty City, Miami, known as "the Pork and Beans." When it opened, in 1937, it attracted an upwardly mobile Black middle class. By the eighties, the crack epidemic was rampant, and the Liberty City that Jenkins knew was "underdeveloped and somewhat feral." His mother, a nurse's aide, was addicted by the time he was a toddler, before entering rehab. The man he knew as his father, who denied his paternity, had left when his mother was pregnant and died when Barry was twelve. Jenkins directed his pain inward, "hiding behind athletics and all my jockitude." He went to Florida State University on a scholarship and enrolled in its film school, then made *Medicine for Melancholy* for $13,000.

Now his former classmate Adele Romanski urged him to get back to directing. "Sometimes we just get in a comfortable place, and you need somebody to come and make you feel uncomfortable, and I think that's what I did," she says. They had brainstorming sessions on Google Hangouts, Romanski in L.A., Jenkins in Oakland. They talked about adapting the James Baldwin novel *If Beale Street Could Talk*. One gray day in his studio apartment, Jenkins opened up a script that a Florida friend had sent him months earlier. The writer, Tarell Alvin McCraney, was an accomplished playwright, but *In Moonlight Black Boys Look Blue* wasn't formatted like a play or a screenplay—more like fortyish pages of stream of consciousness. "It seemed like it was kind of caught between two worlds," Jenkins says.

But he felt a jolt of recognition. The script told the story of Chiron, a Black boy living in Liberty Square. The scenes drifted among three time periods, showing Chiron as a child, an adolescent, and a young man, as he grapples with masculinity, his attraction to other men, and his mother's addiction. "I could just see so much about my childhood in it," Jenkins recalls. "I was a very quiet dude. I kind of just kept to myself. It's Tarell's story, for sure, but the mannerisms, the quietude of the character, that was definitely me." Jenkins was straight, but he, too, had been a neglected child who struggled as an adult with the feeling that he was "unworthy of love."

He flew to Florida to meet McCraney. "We had a very awkward sit-down in a dimly lit bar," Jenkins recalls. "But as we began to talk to each other and about each other, the first thing that happened was we realized that we were in two of the same schools at the same time, and probably had passed each other in the hallway." They were born eleven months apart and had shopped at the same mini mart, danced in the same amphitheater. And both had mothers who were sexual assault survivors, crack addicts, and HIV-positive. "Clearly," McCraney said later, "we were seeing the same moon, and yet we just weren't looking at each other." McCraney had written the script after his own mother died, in 2003. As an effete, relentlessly bullied child, he had witnessed her first overdose when he was around seven, not long after Blue, the drug dealer who acted as his surrogate father, was shot and killed. In college, McCraney was given an assignment to write about a happy memory from childhood, and he wrote about the day Blue taught him to ride a bicycle. In *Moonlight*, Blue became the character played by Mahershala Ali.

Jenkins saw McCraney's tale as a way to hide his own story behind someone else's and to put the contradictions of Liberty City on-screen. "Everything was so lush and fertile," he recalls, "and yet, with the crack cocaine epidemic and the destabilization of the working class, there was all this rampant beauty but also this abject poverty." He had never seen that dichotomy reflected on-screen.

Jenkins revised the script at a café in Brussels, dropping in elements from his own life. In one scene, little Chiron boils water on the stove for his bath, as he had. Jenkins made Chiron's mother a nurse-practitioner, as his mother had been after going to AA. "It was a way for me to shrink the distance between myself and Chiron, between Tarell's experience and my experience," Jenkins says. But it wasn't until he was shooting the film in Liberty Square that the distance came to a vanishing point. British actress Naomie Harris had three days to film her scenes as Chiron's mother, and the shoot flung Jenkins back to his mother's darkest days, to the mothering he had lacked in the years before her recovery. Romanski says, "I remember being on set during that part of production and going, *He just realized this is his story.*"

Moonlight was made for $1.5 million in Liberty City, with three unknown actors in the role of Chiron; Jenkins chose them less for their physical resemblance than for the shared ache in their eyes. After overcoming the skepticism of residents who had seen Hollywood crews come and go, the filmmakers were a welcome presence; the bright movie lights gave kids a safe place to play where the streetlights had been shot out. Small as it was, *Moonlight* had powerful connections. New York–based indie distributor A24 had chosen the film as its first production project, and it had backing from Brad Pitt's company, Plan B. Jenkins had met the Plan B executives in 2013, when he moderated a Q&A for its film *12 Years a Slave* at Telluride, the small but influential festival held in a Colorado ski town. Jenkins had worked at the festival for several years, rising from popcorn maker to the "ringleader" of one of its theaters, where he gave the turn-off-your-cell-phones speech and hosted talkbacks. When *Moonlight* was accepted as part of the festival's 2016 slate, he felt both pride and imposter syndrome.

Moonlight was hardly the big attraction. There was a live tribute to Casey Affleck, to herald his star turn in *Manchester by the Sea*, and Damien Chazelle and Emma Stone were on hand to promote *La La Land*; both films were seen as slam-dunk awards favorites. *Moonlight*'s first screening was scheduled at Chuck Jones' Cinema, named for the Looney Tunes animator. The theater was in Mountain Village, on the other side of the mountain from Telluride, and to get there, spectators had to take a gondola lift across a verdant mountainscape and then walk along faux cobblestone roads. On September 2, the festival's first night, some five hundred people took this enchanted route to see the world premiere of *Moonlight*. "No audience had ever seen the movie," Adele Romanski says. "We didn't do tests. We didn't have previews." Jenkins was "probably the most nervous I've been before a screening," he recalls. "These were people who had seen me make popcorn at this festival, Telluride patrons, and for them to realize, *Oh, that guy used to take our tickets*—it was crazy, man."

Like the Academy, Telluride's audiences were overwhelmingly white. Would they embrace a story like Chiron's? *Moonlight* didn't pander to white viewers; it had no white characters at all. But by the end of that screening, Jenkins recalls, "there were fifty-five-year-old dudes in North Face vests who were beside themselves." Afterward, the *Moonlight* team stayed up late drinking wine and waiting for the reviews to come out online. Raves appeared, promising "a film that will strike plangent chords for anyone who has ever struggled with identity, or to find connections in a lonely world." The buzz traveled across the mountain. "The next screening turned into mayhem," festival moderator Noah Cowan recalls. "Every movie star who was there was insisting on going to see it, and any opinion maker, so people were getting shut out by the hundreds." As the conspicuously Black cast left the theater, the people waiting in line for the next screening greeted them with spontaneous applause.

Jenkins met Damien Chazelle at a filmmakers' event. Jenkins opened with a question about *Guy and Madeline on a Park Bench*; Chazelle had also, amazingly, seen Jenkins's *Medicine for Melancholy*. "He immediately accessed my heart," recalled Chazelle. Before the Oscar race engulfed them, the *Moonlight* and *La La Land* teams became friendly after mixing at an Academy function on the mountain, presided over by Cheryl Boone Isaacs. Although Telluride had shown that white audiences would respond to *Moonlight*, Boone Isaacs wondered about its prospects. "It really wasn't the, quote, kind of movie, that Academy members historically would have thought to vote for," she says. "Not that it wasn't good. But they just didn't. It's a world so foreign to them."

Days after Telluride, the action moved to Toronto, where Harvey Weinstein was waiting with *Lion*. Boone Isaacs attended its premiere and the afterparty at Soho House, where the murmurs, even as champagne flutes were passed around, were of Weinstein's well-publicized financial problems. The Oscar buzz was now narrowing in on *La La Land*, *Manchester by the Sea*, and, to everyone's surprise, *Moonlight*, but the film's awards path came with significant hurdles. With three people playing the protagonist, there was no hope for a lead actor campaign. And *Brokeback Mountain*'s loss to *Crash* in 2006 suggested that a gay film might turn off some Academy members. Among the advice offered from award season veterans was to downplay the love story between Chiron and his friend Kevin and emphasize the theme of adversity.

Boone Isaacs had brought in new voters, but not enough to bypass white members who had nothing in common with Chiron. The way to win them over, the seasoned strategists knew, was to make them not only empathize but feel like they were better people for having done so. They needed someone to root for: not just Chiron but, by extension, Barry Jenkins. In more ways than one, *Moonlight* was an underdog story.

THE BIRTH OF A NATION opened on October 7, the same day *Access Hollywood* footage emerged in which Donald Trump boasted about grabbing women "by the pussy." Nate Parker had not done himself any favors in his press tour. Despite pleas from Fox Searchlight, he refused to show any contrition. "I was falsely accused. I was proven innocent. And I'm not going to apologize for that," he said on *Good Morning America*. Even Gabrielle Union, one of the film's stars and a rape survivor herself, had attested to her "stomach-churning confusion" over the accusations. The film drew a lackluster $7 million on its opening weekend.

The Birth of a Nation became a cut-and-dried case of whether a work of art should be embraced despite the apparent sins of the artist. (The answer: no.) But a more ambiguous scenario was emerging around *Manchester by the Sea*'s Casey Affleck. After he directed the 2010 pseudo-documentary *I'm Still Here*, two women, producer Amanda White and cinematographer Magdalena Górka, sued him for sexual harassment. The allegations were nowhere near as extreme as the ones against Parker, but they were still gross: Affleck ordering a crew member to show White his penis, Górka finding Affleck in her bed caressing her back.

Affleck denied the allegations, both lawsuits were settled, and he was barred from speaking about the case. But Oscar observers wondered why Parker's scandal had sunk his movie, while Affleck was now the front-runner for Best Actor. Surely there was an element of racial privilege. And while Parker had cast himself as a righteous hero, Affleck was playing a damaged, emotionally stunted loser, leaving viewers with less cognitive dissonance. Still, Oscar voters, who had just been morally implicated by #OscarsSoWhite, had to ask themselves uncomfortable questions. Did every nominee require an ethical CAT scan? How recent, and how severe, did an infraction have to be before the industry offered "redemption"?

Even as Trump's rank misogyny went free of consequences, Hollywood was reckoning with one case of male toxicity after another. That spring, minutes before Woody Allen's new film débuted at Cannes, his estranged son, Ronan Farrow, released a blistering indictment of the "self-perpetuating spin machine" that had protected Allen from scrutiny over the sexual abuse accusations brought by Farrow's sister Dylan, for which Allen was never prosecuted or charged. Twitter recoiled at an old interview with Bernardo Bertolucci in which he admitted that he and Marlon Brando had surprised teenage actress Maria Schneider with a lubricating stick of butter during the rape scene in Last Tango in Paris. And Mel Gibson, who had spent a decade in the professional wilderness after his "Jews are responsible for all the wars in the world" rant during a DUI arrest, was now back in the Oscar race with the war drama Hacksaw Ridge. At its Los Angeles premiere, at the Academy theater, Gibson received a standing ovation.

In November, Trump won the election, sending an ugly fissure through the American populace. His upset win, fueled by racist backlash toward Obama, was a particular knife wound for Black America. Cheryl Boone Isaacs watched the returns from her bed. "It was surprising," she says. "And yet, in some ways, not. Because we certainly learned in marketing: there's a lot of people between the coasts."

The next night, Moonlight had a long-planned screening in the back-yard of the Underground Museum, a Black arts center in L.A.'s Arlington Heights neighborhood. Jenkins trudged in during the end for a Q&A

and was surprised to find the place packed. Instead of asking questions, audience members made impassioned statements. "It was very clear to me that the film had become a symbol," he recalls. "People were thankful that the movie allowed them to embrace someone like Chiron, who was not going to be embraced by the incoming president."

Trump had cast Hollywood as part of the "coastal elite" that he was running against (despite being a real estate mogul from New York). Now Hollywood faced the possibility that it was out of step with half of the country. The Oscar front-runners mapped out a fragmented America: the northeastern white working class of *Manchester by the Sea*, the southern Black poor of *Moonlight*, and the Californian creative underclass of *La La Land*. Lionsgate had pitched Chazelle's film as a reverie, with the slogan "Here's to the fools who dream." But the country wasn't feeling so dreamy, and the publicity team couldn't lean into its own message. Nor could it pretend that *La La Land* was a serious statement on social issues. Angling for a message that would seem relevant but not desperate, the studio played up the idea of struggling artists sacrificing for their art—a narrative it hoped would still play in Trump's America.

In the postelection haze, the industry zombie-walked through the winter frenzy of screenings, luncheons, and cocktail parties, with Academy members flocking from one function to the next—the vast ecosystem that Harvey Weinstein had created. One night in January, Nicole Kidman wafted into New York City's Monkey Bar in a sleek Louis Vuitton dress, accompanied by an eight-year-old Indian boy in a suit: Sunny Pawar, her costar in *Lion*. After a sea bass dinner, the cast answered questions for Academy members. Pawar, through an interpreter, said that his favorite things about the United States were the Statue of Liberty and Disneyland. In a booth toward the back, Weinstein craned his head to watch. Without Disney cash, he had increasingly relied on what might be called humanitarian campaigns or, less charitably, PR stunts: arranging for the woman who inspired *Philomena* to have a well-publicized meeting with the Pope, or lobbying Parliament to pardon Britons who were charged under the same antigay law as Alan Turing, the subject of *The Imitation Game*. It was the same playbook he'd invented for *My Left Foot*. Now he arranged for *Lion*'s adorable child star to meet

President Obama in the White House days before his administration ended. After the election, with immigration in the news, Pawar had trouble getting a visa to attend the New York premiere, a red-tape hurdle that Weinstein fanned into a headline-grabbing cause célèbre. "He was the Donald Trump of the movie business," says Bruce Feldman, who was now consulting for his old foe from the *Schindler's List* days. "Harvey would do a lot of things that were kind of misguided or shamefully obvious, but the truth is he always made it work for him."

Lion was a long shot for Best Picture, but Weinstein was determined to grab nominations for its stars Kidman and Dev Patel. "Poor Dev was being dragged to an opening of a car wash if an Academy member was there," one producer recalls. At the Weinstein Company offices, Harvey would preside over tense strategy meetings that often left young staffers in tears. "Everybody would, of course, be deferential," Feldman says. "Did he think the movie would win or not? Didn't make any difference. He decided he's going for this and he's going to make it happen, and everybody else better damn well be on that bus."

On the awards circuit, Weinstein no longer loomed as large as he once had, but his influence was everywhere. Many top strategists were Miramax alumni, most prominently Cynthia Swartz, in New York, and Lisa Taback, in L.A. Taback was now working on *La La Land*, and both consulted on *Moonlight*. Strategies from the so-called Weinstein playbook were evident. In December, Chazelle appeared in Paris alongside filmmaker Agnès Varda, Jacques Demy's widow, to play up his French New Wave influences. Chazelle was a valuable presence on the campaign trail, especially with the older generation that felt the Academy was pushing it out to pasture. "If you were a director who had worked in the fifties or sixties," one publicist observed, "there was a good chance Damien would know who you were and everything you had done."

Moonlight was not without star power; Brad Pitt and Julia Roberts hosted a private screening at CAA, and Jenkins was becoming a star in his own right. "I didn't know what campaigning *was*," he says. "So, I was just myself." But the conventional wisdom was that *Moonlight* was a reach for the Academy's conservative wing—too Black, too gay—and that the front-runner was still *La La Land*. At the Golden Globes, *La La*

Land won all seven of its nominations, setting a record for a single film. *Moonlight* had no such luck. The trouble started early, when Mahershala Ali unexpectedly lost the Supporting Actor award. "Brie Larson and Eddie Redmayne were sitting at our table, and they just started pouring us drinks, because it was a cycle all night of us not winning," Jenkins recalls. *Moonlight* won just one Golden Globe, for Best Drama—a big one, but it didn't have to compete with *La La Land*, which won Best Musical or Comedy. By the end of the night, Jenkins was four gin and tonics deep and ready to shrug off awards season: "I thought, I'm still going to go out and talk about the film and meet audiences at the intersection of their experience and Chiron's, but that's it. I made my peace with it."

The most pivotal moment of the Globes, however, was Meryl Streep's acceptance speech for the lifetime achievement award. Streep, who had lost her voice, sounded like a woman who had crawled through a desert, but her speech was a full-throated condemnation of Donald Trump. Recalling with horror his mockery of a disabled reporter at a campaign event, Streep declared, "Disrespect invites disrespect. Violence incites violence. When the powerful use their position to bully others, we all lose."

Predictably, the president-elect responded the next day by tweeting that Streep was "over-rated." But the speech marked a sea change in Hollywood's awkward attempt to position itself in Trump's America. After two timid, uncertain months, Streep—one of the only movie stars with the stature to risk alienating half the country—had unambiguously picked a side. The Oscar race may have been narrowing to *La La Land* vs. *Moonlight*, but a more fundamental question hovered: Was Hollywood really La La Land, a place where dreamers went to forget their troubles? Or was it part of the resistance?

THE OSCAR NOMINATIONS CAME OUT four days after Trump's inauguration, at which the new president darkly opined on "American carnage." The Academy offered an alternative vision. Boone Isaacs showed up at the Academy building that morning to "smiling faces." To everyone's relief, there would be no third consecutive year of #OscarsSoWhite: there were nominees of color in all four acting categories, including Mahershala Ali and Naomie Harris (*Moonlight*), Denzel Washington and Viola Davis (*Fences*), and Dev Patel (*Lion*). "It was a very good morning," Boone Isaacs recalls.

La La Land received fourteen nominations, tying the all-time record with *All About Eve* and *Titanic*. *Moonlight* and the sci-fi drama *Arrival* both got eight, and *Manchester by the Sea* made Amazon Studios the first streaming company to get a Best Picture nomination. The implosion of *The Birth of a Nation* (which got no nominations) had opened up space for a plethora of less bombastic movies about Black lives, not just *Moonlight*, but also *Fences*, *Loving*, and *Hidden Figures*. But the list also included a Best Directing nomination for Mel Gibson, indicating that many voters were willing to go along with the redemption rinse cycle.

Three days later, in one of his first official acts, Trump signed an executive order temporarily banning entry to the United States from seven predominantly Muslim countries and indefinitely blocking Syrian refugees. The ban ricocheted, unexpectedly, through awards season. Asghar Farhadi, the Iranian director of *The Salesman*, which was nominated for Best Foreign Language Film, announced that he would decline to attend the ceremony in protest. United Talent Agency would replace its Oscar weekend party with a rally. At the Producers Guild of America Awards, where the conversation typically tended toward domestic grosses, the specter of Trump hovered like a Marvel supervillain's. John Legend, the only Black lead in *La La Land*, spoke of Los Angeles as "the home of so many immigrants" and said, "Our vision of America is directly antithetical to that of President Trump." The SAG Awards, the next night, were peppered with defiant speeches, none more stirring than the one given by Mahershala Ali, who had converted to Islam seventeen years earlier. "I think what I've learned from working on *Moonlight* is we see what happens when you persecute people: they fold into themselves," he said, quietly choking up.

Not everyone met the moment with such gravitas. Weinstein, smelling an opportunity, ran a cringeworthy ad featuring Pawar's face and the words "It took an extraordinary effort to get 8-year-old actor Sunny Pawar a visa so that he could come to America for the very first time. Next year, that might not be an option." It was typical Weinstein overreach, but it underlined the pitfalls of injecting politics into awards season. In the *Los Angeles Times*, critic Glenn Lovell predicted that the Oscars would be a "referendum on Trump" and that the voters, after the embarrassment of #OscarsSoWhite, might "prefer real-life issues over sentiment or institutionalized nostalgia." But the headline—"Will the political climate deprive 'La La Land' of the best picture Oscar?"—drew backlash, since it implied that *La La Land* was the entitled winner and *Moonlight* the affirmative-action case.

Oscar pundits were now questioning the "unbearable whiteness of *La La Land*," with its "white jazz savior" hero. The *Moonlight* and *La La Land* teams, who had become friendly over months of luncheons and passed crostini, were bewildered to find themselves shoehorned into a political debate. "It didn't occur to me that we were going to be these people who were jockeying for a position, who all these people on Twitter and all these blogs and awards pundits or whatever the hell they call themselves would be arguing about," Jenkins recalls.

La La Land was tearing through a late-season winning streak at the PGAs, the DGAs, and the BAFTAs. But, as with *Saving Private Ryan*, front-runner fatigue was catching up to it, and there were signs of a shift toward *Moonlight*. After all, people whispered, Emma Stone and Ryan Gosling were no Fred and Ginger. Midway through the Academy voting period, *L.A. Times* critic Justin Chang published an impassioned column that began, "'Moonlight' deserves to win the Oscar for best picture." He wrote, "Jenkins' movie strikes me as the wisest possible rejoinder to the bluster and hostility, the blasts of toxic masculinity and racist invective, that have taken the place of grounded, principled discourse in this country." The film, Chang clarified, "doesn't deserve to win the Oscar simply because it would be the most politically resonant choice," but "there absolutely is a political reason to honor 'Moonlight,' and it has nothing to do with being on-message or avoiding another #Oscar[s]SoWhite, and everything to do with that tricky, still-uncharted territory where questions of artistry and representation converge."

A week before the Oscars, the Writers Guild of America held its awards at the Beverly Hilton. While the Academy had put *Moonlight*'s screenplay in the adaptation category, the Writers Guild considered it original, since McCraney's underlying play had never been produced. That gave *Moonlight* and *La La Land* a direct face-off. *Moonlight* won—a surprise that made even Jenkins wonder if the tide was turning. He recalls, "I knew there were still five more days of Academy voting after that award, and I thought, *Oh, shit.*"

THE DECISION TO ASK WARREN Beatty and Faye Dunaway to present Best Picture was an obvious one. It was the fiftieth anniversary of *Bonnie and Clyde*, the film that had helped usher in the New Hollywood. That year's producers, Michael De Luca and Jennifer Todd, were Oscar buffs who loved the tradition of bringing in legends for the final envelope. De Luca called Beatty, who "mulled and wanted to make sure that Faye was on board," he recalls. "She had—not conditions, but some requests. It was a little bit of negotiating."

One point of negotiation was who would announce the winner. It was decided that Dunaway would introduce the nominees and then Beatty would do the honors. Acknowledging the fraught year gone by, he would also make some opening remarks about "the increasing diversity in our community" and how "our goal in politics is the same as our goal in art, and that's to get to the truth."

When they got to rehearsal, though, Dunaway wanted to read out the winner. "I should do this," she kept nudging. Beatty, having experienced half a century of Dunaway's antics, gave her a wry "here we go again" look and went the flirtatious route. "He teased Faye," De Luca says, "wouldn't give her the envelope, and it was a little comic bit." With some gentle diplomacy, the producers kept the original plan intact.

De Luca and Todd had enough to deal with. The host, Jimmy Kimmel, had a plan to sneak in a busload of tourists during the ceremony, a stunt that took weeks of planning. At another point, candy parachutes would rain from the ceiling for the stars to grab at. And in the event that President Trump tweeted about the Oscars during the broadcast, Kimmel would live-tweet back at him from the stage—an idea that proved technically complicated, as his phone screen had to be projected onto the set.

Then there were endless minutiae. The Friday before the show, an

Academy staffer showed Todd and De Luca a prototype of the winner cards, which for the first time weren't printed by the Academy's regular stationery company. Todd, who wears glasses, asked that they be reprinted in a bigger font, so that the presenters wouldn't have to squint. "But," she recalls, "Mike and I never saw the *outside* of the envelope," on which the categories were printed in a gold-on-maroon color scheme that was difficult to read. And instead of a faux-wax seal with an easy-to-pull ribbon, as in past years, the new envelope was sealed with a cumbersome piece of tape.

Another minor irritant was Brian Cullinan, one of two PricewaterhouseCoopers accountants responsible for overseeing the envelopes. The Oscar accountants, each stationed on one side of the stage, were the only people privy to the results, and each memorized the winners beforehand in the event of a problem. That week, Cullinan and his colleague Martha Ruiz gave an interview in which they were asked what would happen if the wrong winner were announced. "We would make sure that the correct person was known very quickly," Cullinan said, adding that they would check with each other and then inform the stage manager. But *was* that the protocol? Before the show, the accountants buttonholed stage managers Gary Natoli and John Esposito to clarify.

"If you know who the winner is, you don't need to check with each other," Natoli recalled telling Cullinan. "You need to immediately go out and rectify the situation, ideally before the wrong winners get to the mic." In any case, such a scenario was absurdly unlikely.

Cullinan, a PwC partner who lived in Malibu and rode a Harley-Davidson, was a dead ringer for Matt Damon. During an onstage bit at the 2015 Oscars, host Neil Patrick Harris had ribbed Cullinan about the resemblance. The next year, Cullinan tweeted a photo of himself and his doppelgänger from the red carpet. In the days before the 2017 ceremony, he asked Jennifer Todd if there was any way for him to do another comedy bit during the show. "I was like, 'I'll let you know if anything comes up. It's really up to Jimmy and the writers,'" she recalls. "And then he followed up via email: 'Hey, did you come up with anything?'" Todd and De Luca asked telecast director Glenn Weiss, "What do we do about the Pricewaterhouse guy?"

"I'll throw him in a bumper," Weiss said, meaning a quick shot before a commercial break.

"Okay," Todd said. "It's off our plate?"

The morning of the show, February 26, 2017, began with multiple crises. Bill Paxton had died the day before and needed to be worked into the "In Memoriam" segment. At the final dress rehearsal, part of the set malfunctioned and knocked over two miniature art deco buildings. "It sounded like a bomb exploded," De Luca recalls. Jimmy Kimmel remembers, "That was a bad omen just to begin." In the writers' room, the comedian's wife thought the building was collapsing and threw their daughter under a desk. Some fifty technicians had to be called in for repairs. "We thought *that* was going to be the big thing of the day," Todd says.

Heading into the show, the *La La Land* team was cautiously steeling for victory. "When we were walking on the red carpet into the Oscars, almost everybody said we were going to win," a *La La Land* publicist recalls. "And yet all of us had a stomachache that night, thinking, *This is definitely not a done deal.*"

Like Snow White before him, Justin Timberlake kicked off the Eighty-Ninth Academy Awards by singing his way down the aisle, but with better results: the audience was up on its feet dancing to the nominated song "Can't Stop the Feeling." Kimmel, in his opening monologue, joked, "I want to say thank you to President Trump. I mean, remember last year, when it seemed like the *Oscars* were racist?"

The first award was Best Supporting Actor, which went to Mahershala Ali. *Hm*, Barry Jenkins thought. *This is interesting.* Later, he and McCraney won Best Adapted Screenplay. In his speech, Jenkins struck a defiant chord: "All you people out there who feel like there's no mirror for you, that your life is not reflected, the Academy has your back, the ACLU has your back, we have your back. And for the next four years, we will not leave you alone. We will not forget you."

La La Land immediately lost a string of categories—Costume Design, Sound Editing—before winning for Production Design. "When those crafts categories didn't go the way that we had hoped they would go, we were like, *Ooh, there may be something amiss for us*," producer Jordan Horowitz recalls. The editing prize, often an indicator for Best

Picture, went to *Hacksaw Ridge*, eliciting flashbacks to Trump winning Pennsylvania early on Election Night. Could the Academy's conservative wing strike back for Mel Gibson? It would have likely unsettled Cheryl Boone Isaacs, who appeared, wearing a strapless black dress, to make a speech about the industry "becoming more inclusive and diverse with each passing day." She had detected a late surge for *Hidden Figures*, about three Black women who had worked in the NASA space program and who, like her, had spent their careers in a white man's world.

Damien Chazelle had passed the week in bed with a 103-degree fever. "I was pumped up with steroids at the ceremony," he recalls. "My fever had just broken. I was already sort of delirious." Toward the end of the night, Halle Berry presented him with the Best Directing award. Then Casey Affleck won Best Actor, after months of carefully calibrated media appearances that downplayed his sexual harassment scandal, apparently with success. On stage left, PwC's Martha Ruiz handed Leonardo DiCaprio the Best Actress envelope. The winner was Emma Stone, a hopeful sign for *La La Land*. Horowitz recalls, "Damien won and then Emma won, and we were like, *Oh, man, maybe this is actually going to work out*."

When it was time for the final award, Brian Cullinan, on stage right, handed the envelope to Warren Beatty. After Dunaway introduced the nominees, as planned, Beatty opened it and looked at the card. Something about it didn't make sense. He looked in the envelope to see if he had missed anything, then glanced at Dunaway. He stammered, "And the Academy Award . . . for Best Picture . . ."

Jimmy Kimmel was sitting in the second row with Matt Damon; he was planning to close the show with a running joke about their mock rivalry. The day before, he had watched Dunaway and Beatty rehearse more times than seemed normal. "It put this idea in my head that maybe they couldn't see the teleprompter," he says. "So, that was in my head throughout the confusion, that maybe Warren couldn't see the card."

Onstage, Dunaway threw up her hands, laughing. "You're impossible," she told Beatty. Surely, she was thinking back to his teasing at the rehearsal. He showed her the card, befuddled. But maybe this was him being chivalrous and *finally* agreeing to let her read the winner. Dunaway glanced at the card and read over a drumroll, "*La La Land.*"

As the music played, Jenkins allowed the speech he'd prepared to slip from his mind. He'd been thinking for months about Chiron, about how a kid like that could never have dreamed of making a film that got eight Academy Award nominations. "It's a dream I never allowed myself to have," he said later. "When we were sitting there, and that dream of winning didn't come true, I took it off the table."

JORDAN HOROWITZ HAD MADE A deal with his coproducers early in awards season: they could speak first at every ceremony where *La La Land* won, but if they won at the Oscars, Horowitz would go first. Then he tried to put the whole thing out of his mind. As Beatty stumbled, he thought, *Oh, what an asshole for delaying it so much.*

When Dunaway finally read out the winner, Horowitz let out a "primal scream." He says, "I had allowed myself fully into the expectations game, and I needed to win. It was really important to me, and I let out this scream. And my wife took me by the shoulders, and she looked at me and said, '*You need to calm down.*'" He took a deep breath.

Onstage, he took the envelope from Beatty and the surprisingly heavy statuette from Dunaway. He made his speech, then turned the mic over to his coproducer Marc Platt. As Platt spoke, Horowitz noticed a commotion. "People are scurrying around, but nobody really knows what's happening. It's very clear that shit's unwinding in some way." A man in a headset—stage manager Gary Natoli—came toward him, saying, "Where's the card? Let me see it."

Horowitz looked down at the card in his hand, which bore the inexplicable words "Emma Stone, *La La Land.*" "My overwhelming feeling at that moment is that time stopped," he recalls. "I knew Emma had her card, because I had *seen* Emma's card, and all of a sudden I was holding Emma's card, and it made absolutely no sense whatsoever, so the only explanation I had for it was like some kind of fucked-up magic, some time-stoppage magic."

Natoli took the card and walked offstage. "And then I realized, *Oh, they fucked up,*" Horowitz says. "We *didn't* win Best Picture. And I'm fairly certain—and you can see this on the tape—the moment that I fully recognize it, I drop my hand, and I remember feeling the weight of the thing that I already thought was heavy got, like, ten times heavier."

MOMENTS EARLIER, ON STAGE RIGHT, Brian Cullinan had pushed through the spectators in the wings and informed stage manager John Esposito that he thought the wrong winner had been announced. "Are you sure?" Esposito said. "I'm positive," the accountant told him. Esposito radioed Natoli, who was crouched in the audience near Kimmel. Natoli sent word to stage left to check with the other accountant, Martha Ruiz, who confirmed that *Moonlight* was the winner. "Get the accountants out there!" Natoli urged over his headset. But neither accountant budged. "We had to push them onstage, which was just shocking to me," Natoli said later. "Brian had led us to believe that Faye had just said it incorrectly. So, I went looking for the envelope."

Oscar producers Michael De Luca and Jennifer Todd were backstage celebrating the end of a successful evening. "We were high-fiving," De Luca says. "I took off my headphones and was drinking a Diet Coke." Emma Stone's speech had ended seconds before midnight, meaning they'd hit their mark for the final commercial break. "So, then we were like, 'Fuck it! *La La Land*, they can talk as long as they want,'" Todd says. "That's when I remember somebody put a glass of champagne in front of me. We were done!"

Todd put her headset on a table. When she heard yelling coming from it, she put it back on. "It was Gary, the stage manager, and Glenn, the director. And they were like, 'We think it's the wrong envelope.'" She shrieked, "*They announced the wrong picture.*"

"The tone in Jenn's voice—it was like out of a Fritz Lang movie," De Luca says. "The hair on the back of my neck stood up, and I couldn't comprehend the sentence. It was one of those surreal moments where the worst thing ever is described to you, and the people responsible for it have said it could never happen."

CHERYL BOONE ISAACS WAS WATCHING from the audience. When *La La Land* was announced, she wasn't surprised, because the movie had heart.

"It's like the year of *Shakespeare in Love*. I kept saying to people, 'That's going to win.' It's that heart thing," she says. After all she had gone through at the Academy, it was a low-key end to a turbulent year.

Then she noticed Natoli coming onstage, with Brian Cullinan trailing behind him. "Brian is always tan, and he wasn't tan, like he'd lost all color in his face," she recalls. "I just thought, *Why is he why is he—are you kidding me?* I felt like Al Pacino: 'Just when I thought I was out . . . !' It was very fast and very slow in my head. It happened very quickly, and yet it took forever."

A few rows ahead of her, Matt Damon leaned over to Kimmel. "He does not remember saying this, but I distinctly remember him telling me, 'They gave the award to the wrong movie,'" Kimmel says. "For a moment, I just felt like a member of the audience watching. And then it occurred to me that I was really the only one with a microphone on and that I should probably go up, because there were no other options."

ONSTAGE, THE THIRD *La La Land* producer, Fred Berger, was thanking Damien Chazelle, who stood behind him watching the commotion in a daze. "It was panic," Chazelle recalls. "The more you could see, the more it looked like someone had died or there'd been some fucking terrorist attack." Ryan Gosling, who assumed there had been a medical emergency, broke into laughter when he realized what was going on. Berger, picking up the chatter behind him, ended his speech, "We lost, by the way."

Jordan Horowitz had regained his focus. "I start to look around, and I'm like, *So, how are we going to solve this?* Whatever was happening, it was taking too long for my taste." He took to the microphone and said, "There's a mistake. *Moonlight*, you guys won Best Picture." There were gasps, and tentative applause. To some, it sounded like Horowitz was just being gallant: *La La Land* may have won, but *Moonlight* had won some larger battle. "*This is not a joke*," Horowitz insisted. "*Moonlight* has won Best Picture."

With millions of eyes on him, he had a split second to think. "It was very clear that nobody had any fucking idea what was happening. You could see it on people's faces, like, *What is this person doing? Is this a mistake? A joke?* And that's when, out of the corner of my eye, I saw Warren standing next to me with the red card, and I suddenly realized they had to see it—they had to *see* the card that said *Moonlight*." Like King Arthur pulling the sword from the stone, he snatched the card from Beatty and held it up, thinking, "I hope this camera operator knows what to do." The audience, stunned, rose to its feet.

Kimmel took the microphone. His foremost thought was that the *La La Land* people would feel terrible. "We gave someone an Oscar and have to take it away from them and give it to somebody else, which is a first," he recalls. "So, you have to handle that very delicately, and I don't typically excel as far as handling things delicately goes." Onstage, he joked to Horowitz, "I would like to see you get an Oscar anyway. Why can't we just give out a whole bunch of them?"

But Kimmel was missing the uncomfortable symbolism, a year after #OscarsSoWhite, of asking a Black movie that had won to share the moment with a white movie that hadn't. Horowitz, though, saw the enormity of the moment. "I was definitely not in the mood for jokes," he says. Cutting off Kimmel, he said decisively, "I'm going to be really proud to hand this to my friends from *Moonlight*."

The *Moonlight* team had registered the chaos with disbelief. "We had to be told to move," producer Adele Romanski recalls. She'd assumed the chaos was some kind of bomb threat. In the aisle, actor Andrew Garfield embraced her. "What's happening?" she asked. Garfield told her, "You have to go on the stage."

The *La La Land* producers handed the statuettes to their counterparts and hugged them. After a year of bitter divides, racial and political, it was a rare image of harmony. Gosling stood on the steps shaking everyone's hands. As the faces onstage changed from mostly white to mostly Black, Beatty stepped in front of the mic. "I want to tell you what happened," he told America, explaining that the card had read "Emma Stone," which is why he had stared at Dunaway so blankly.

Next to him, Kimmel saw Denzel Washington in the audience mouthing a single word at him and pointing. The word was: "BARRY." *Oh, right,* Kimmel thought. The real winners had to speak.

Barry Jenkins now heard himself giving a half-thrilled, half-baffled acceptance speech. "Very clearly, even in my dreams this could not be true," he said. "But to hell with dreams! I'm done with it, 'cause this is true. Oh, my goodness!"

"I'm still not sure this is real," Romanski said next. She turned around to acknowledge the *La La Land* crew, but they had vanished. The cameras cut to the slack-jawed spectators: Octavia Spencer, Samuel L. Jackson. The *Moonlight* team ambled offstage, where their *La La Land* friends were crowded in the wings: two movies that would be forever entwined. No one knew what to feel, except confusion. What the hell had just happened?

IN THE MOMENTS AFTER THE ceremony, the Dolby Theatre was like Dealey Plaza, with a thousand Oscar-caliber Zapruders. Instead of the second gunman, there was talk of a second envelope. On social media, people were posting grainy close-ups of Leonardo DiCaprio holding the Best Actress envelope and then of Beatty walking back onstage with it. In the pressroom, Emma Stone thickened the plot when she said, "I also was holding my Best Actress in a Leading Role card that entire time. So, whatever story—I don't mean to start stuff, but whatever story that was, I had that card." An old Hollywood genre was revived: the whodunit.

Jimmy Kimmel had not even gotten offstage when someone asked him, "Was this a prank?" He was dumbfounded that anyone would assume the envelopes had been switched on purpose, but it was as reasonable as any other explanation. When he saw De Luca and Todd, he joked, referring to the set collapse of hours earlier, "As if World War Two today wasn't enough? We needed *this*?"

Nearby, someone asked Beatty for the envelopes. "I'm not handing this to anyone," he replied. He held them high above his head, so no one could snatch them. Beatty had been famous long enough to know how quickly public perception could crystallize. Already, social media observers were speculating that he and Dunaway were senile. When his wife, Annette Bening, called him to ask what had happened, he said, "I have the envelopes, and I'm not giving them to anyone." As he told Oscar head writer Jon Macks the next day, "I wanted to hold the envelope to preserve the chain of evidence." ("What is this," Macks replied, "*CSI: Oscar*?")

Dunaway had already slipped off to the Governors Ball, after snacking on some backstage cashews. "She headed for the hills," Kimmel says.

Backstage, Kimmel was giving a toast to his writers when someone approached De Luca and Todd and whispered, "Warren's in the green-room and wants to talk to you both." When they found him, Todd recalls, "Warren was very shaken up." Some fifteen minutes after the show ended, the interested parties assembled like suspects from *Clue*: Beatty, who held the murder weapon; the two Oscar producers; Kimmel; Academy CEO Dawn Hudson; communications director Teni Melidonian; Boone Isaacs; ABC vice president of communications Richard Horrmann; stage manager Gary Natoli; and Brian Cullinan, in the role of the suspicious butler. "What happened, dudes?" Boone Isaacs said.

Beatty held up the evidence and said, "This is the envelope some-body gave me, and then this is the envelope someone handed me later." One read, "Emma Stone." The other read, "*Moonlight*."

Cullinan stood in the corner, shaking his head. "He was still try-ing to pretend like Faye had read it wrong, even though he must have known what happened," Todd recalls. But Cullinan hadn't put the pieces together, and he was baffled that Beatty was holding the *Moonlight* en-velope while saying he'd been given the wrong one. Everyone else saw a guilty accountant trying to deflect. De Luca says, "It wasn't exactly a profile in courage."

Kimmel tried to keep the mood light, inviting Beatty on his late-night talk show. "That would be great—for *you*," Beatty retorted. "We were just all asking questions," Kimmel recalls. "And I remember as I was trying to get to the bottom of it, I was thinking, *I have no business being here asking any questions. I'm the host of the show, and it's over!* But I knew I'd have to go on the air the next night and explain what had happened."

After a few minutes, director Glenn Weiss came in. "Look, it's the wrong envelope," he said, opening his iPad to reveal a magnified shot of Beatty holding the Best Actress envelope. It would take several more hours to piece together the rest: both accountants had an entire set of envelopes, one for each side of the stage. When one person handed an envelope to the presenter, the other was supposed to put the unused duplicate in a briefcase and move on to the next. When DiCaprio went out to present, he had taken the Best Actress envelope from Ruiz on stage left. On stage right, Cullinan was concerned that the presenters would futz over the tape on the back of the envelope and was showing each person that it was easier to slip a finger under the flap and pop it open. After Emma Stone won, Cullinan had two envelopes left in his hand: Best Picture on top and the Best Actress duplicate on the bottom. He flipped them over to show Beatty the trick with the tape, which put the Best Actress duplicate on top. He then mistakenly handed the duplicate Best Actress envelope to Beatty and tossed the Best Picture envelope in his briefcase and forgot all about it.

In the greenroom, Dawn Hudson turned to Cullinan. "Your one job was to give Warren the right envelope."

"No," the accountant said, bewildered. Minutes before the screwup, he had tweeted a backstage photo of Emma Stone. "The lesson here is we're too celebrity-obsessed as a culture," De Luca says. "It's even poisoned *accountants*." Cullinan deleted the Emma Stone photo and was gone before anyone noticed. "He basically disappeared," Kimmel says.

Moments later, *Moonlight* producer Adele Romanski got in an elevator to the Governors Ball and found herself standing next to Warren Beatty. "He was gripping the [Best Picture] envelope, and I remember some person who worked at the awards was asking him for it, and he refused, *adamantly* refused to hand it over, and then got up to wherever the elevator took us, and Barry was up there, and at that point he gave it to Barry. And Barry has the envelope, and he has it framed now."

At the ball, as guests lined up for iced octopus tentacles and chocolate Oscar lollipops, the usual air of celebration was more like bewilderment. Some thought the envelope mix-up was great live television, others a historic embarrassment for the Academy in a year of embarrassments. Some speculated that it had been staged to boost ratings. Beatty was on the phone with Bening, who was telling him, "Warren, come home."

"No," Beatty insisted. "I have done nothing wrong."

At Lionsgate's afterparty at Soho House, the *La La Land* crew tried to reconcile the disappointment of losing with the absurdity of having fake-won. "It wasn't happy or sad," Horowitz says. "It was just different.

It was a third thing that nobody could have anticipated, and we were all sort of just processing that in real time."

The *Moonlight* people were also ambivalent. Mahershala Ali said later, "It never quite felt like we won, even though we won, in part because we were so connected with the *La La Land* people. In that moment, I don't think we could be as joyous. It wasn't what it should have been." Barry Jenkins ended the night at 3 a.m. in his suite at the Four Seasons. After sleeping for a few hours, he woke up and watched the clip on his phone, oddly charmed by the way the two films had come together. "It's messy," he told a reporter that morning, "but it's kind of gorgeous."

Boone Isaacs awoke for a day of damage control. She had insisted that PwC put out a late-night statement before the Academy: "I was adamant that they needed to come out first to acknowledge the error." As disastrous as the show's finale had been, she realized that it could have been worse—say, if the broadcast had ended before *Moonlight* got to accept the award, or if the reverse had happened and the statuettes had to be taken from Black hands and given to white ones.

Even so, she felt "sadness for the filmmakers. As beautifully as they acted, did we steal a moment?" Before heading to Academy headquarters, she knelt before her Gohonzon. "I was just chanting, hoping that they all understood that it was purely an accident, this is not malicious, this is not underhanded. This was something that was read incorrectly. Why, I don't know. This is bigger than us."

Nam-myoho-renge-kyo.
Nam-myoho-renge-kyo.
Nam-myoho-renge-kyo.

THE 2017 ACADEMY AWARDS SET multiple benchmarks. There were a record six nominated Black actors, and Ali was the first Muslim actor to win. Damien Chazelle, at thirty-two years and thirty-eight days old, was the youngest Best Directing winner, beating Norman Taurog, who won in 1931, by seven months. (Had Orson Welles won for *Citizen Kane*, he would have lapped them both by six years.) *Moonlight* was the first Best Picture winner with an all-Black cast and—if you don't count *Midnight Cowboy*—an explicitly queer story.

But these milestones were overshadowed by what became known as Envelopegate. Brian Cullinan and Martha Ruiz, who were removed from PwC's Academy account, received so many death threats on social media and had so many paparazzi swarming their homes that the firm hired U.S. Marshals to protect them. Jordan Horowitz was, to his discomfort, hailed as a "hero." Envelopegate immediately superseded Allan Carr's opening number in the annals of Oscar debacles. Even President Trump, who had held his fire during the ceremony, weighed in, "I think they were focused so hard on politics that they didn't get the act together at the end. It was a little sad."

And yet, *Moonlight*'s win, a year after #OscarsSoWhite, signaled that something had changed. It wasn't just that the Academy had welcomed new members, or demoted a minuscule number of old ones. In its un-assuming way, *Moonlight* had scrambled the definition of what a Best Picture looked like. It reflected an America that had never seen itself in a movie, much less on the Oscar stage. "Five or six years earlier, if *Moonlight* had come out, there wouldn't have been a push by the studio," Boone Isaacs says. "It would have mattered if it was a good movie or not, but it just wouldn't have been in the paradigm."

Nevertheless, the Academy, like the industry it represented, still had an enormous imbalance that couldn't be righted overnight. If a single Best Picture win stood for anything, it was a collective willingness to pay attention. "You can't assume that the previous winners and nominees in these categories have been what they are purely based on merit, because to accept that is to accept some very fundamentally horrible things about society," Barry Jenkins says. "When *Moonlight* came along, people *had* to put in the screener, and I think when they did put in the screener, they saw our film for what it truly was. They realized that they could see themselves in a character like Chiron."

Looking back, Jenkins says, "If there was anybody I felt bad for that night, above us, it was Cheryl. All these things she had been building kind of coalesced with the reading of that envelope." That May, the ex-hausted Boone Isaacs announced that she would not seek another term on the Board of Governors, after twenty-four cumulative years. Her tu-multuous tenure had been as transformative as Gregory Peck's. "It was bittersweet," she recalls. "Somebody said, 'Oh, you can continue to be president.' But we're talking about getting new blood in here, and I'm sticking around? No, no, no. I thought, *I'm just going to break from everything right now. Just let my head get all clear.* So, I did."

Harvey Weinstein had spent Oscar weekend negotiating with the family of Trayvon Martin for the rights to their story, along with Jay-Z. *Lion* didn't win any Oscars, but its $140 million haul boosted the Weinstein Company's prospects. Weinstein's staff had noticed that he seemed disengaged as campaign season wore on, as if something graver were pulling at his attention. That spring, Weinstein was reflecting on his "maverick" days of Oscar campaigning. "Those movies that win, like *Moonlight*, are a result of some of the work that we did," he told an interviewer at his TriBeCa office. He even mused about producing the Oscars with his old nemesis Steven Spielberg: "If we could survive each other, we'd do a great job."

In October, less than eight months after *Moonlight* won, the *New York Times* and *The New Yorker* published back-to-back stories exposing Weinstein's decades-long history of sexual abuse, coercion, and cover-ups; Weinstein denied all allegations of nonconsensual sex. Ronan Farrow, who wrote *The New Yorker* story, teed up his blockbuster by noting, "His movies have earned more than three hundred Oscar nominations, and, at the annual awards ceremonies, he has been thanked more than almost anyone else in movie history, ranking just after Steven Spielberg and right before God."

Weinstein's fall had been presaged by the Nate Parker scandal and the misbehavior of other famous men. But Weinstein was the torpedo that blew a hole through Hollywood's membrane of self-protection. As more victims spoke up, roused by the hashtag MeToo, more powerful men fell from grace: Kevin Spacey, Louis CK, Matt Lauer, Les Moonves. So seismic was the quake that it ricocheted backward in time, through the offices of long-dead movie moguls like Louis B. Mayer. A ninety-year-old actress who had been under contract at MGM told *The New Yorker*, "If you were under contract to him, you were like a piece of chattel. You were supposed to bow and scrape and curtsy. Mr. Mayer was, in his own mind, godlike." A story as old as Hollywood.

At 10 a.m. on the Saturday after the Weinstein revelations, the Academy board held an emergency meeting. Over coffee and fruit, it overwhelmingly voted to expel him. "We do so not simply to separate ourselves from someone who does not merit the respect of his colleagues," the board announced, "but also to send a message that the era of willful ignorance and shameful complicity in sexually predatory behavior and workplace harassment in our industry is over." The decision opened up the question of what to do about other problematic members, such as Roman Polanski and Bill Cosby. The Academy announced that it would create an ethical code of conduct—a throwback to the "morality clauses" of the 1920s, when Hollywood had been similarly rocked by scandal and the Academy materialized to help clean up the mess. The Oscars without Weinstein was like Oz without the Wizard. But the world, finally, had seen behind the curtain.

Gettin' Jiggy wit It

The twin hashtags OscarsSoWhite and MeToo pushed Hollywood and, by extension, the Academy into an era of reckoning. Where previous chapters of Oscar history had hinged on labor relations or communism, the awards were increasingly dominated by discussions of race and gender. The expansion of the Academy's membership made the voting body not only less white and less male but also more international; three years after *Moonlight*, *Parasite* became the first non-English film to win Best Picture. The A2020 initiative, which sought to double the Academy membership of women and minorities in five years, had once seemed like a pipe dream. But by 2020, the Academy actually surpassed its goals.

And yet, each milestone only highlighted how homogenous the Oscars had been for so long. In 2018, Rachel Morrison (*Mudbound*) became the first woman ever nominated for Best Cinematography. The next year, *Roma* producer Gabriela Rodriguez became the first Latin American woman nominated for Best Picture. As of this writing, the female nominees for Best Directing can be counted on two hands, and no actresses of color have joined Halle Berry's party of one. In 2020, the Academy unveiled a list of eligibility rules for Best Picture contenders, requiring a minimum level of representation by historically underrepresented groups in front of or behind the camera. The guidelines signaled a return to the regulatory function of the Academy's first decade—albeit toward vastly different ends—and were alternately applauded, derided as "political correctness," and criticized for not going far enough.

Simultaneously, the Academy became the nexus for another existential Hollywood crisis. As with the special award for *The Jazz Singer* in 1929, the year of *Moonlight* and *La La Land* contained the seed of a new upheaval, when Netflix won its first Oscar, for the documentary short *The White Helmets*. The rise of streaming platforms, a change as potentially seismic as the arrival of talkies or television, threw into question what a movie even was, and the century-old studios begun by the likes of Louis B. Mayer had to contend with new players like Apple and Amazon. But Netflix, like Miramax in the nineties, represented a threat to the existing power structure and struggled to land a Best Picture winner of its own. In 2019, it mounted a gargantuan campaign for *Roma*, but the winner was Universal's *Green Book*, which harked back to the crossracial mawkishness of *Driving Miss Daisy* (complete with the driving). The COVID-19 pandemic only hastened the shift away from cinemas, and the legacy studios took the if-you-can't-beat-'em-join-'em route and started streaming services of their own.

The Academy, meanwhile, has faced its own crisis of relevance. As Hollywood has come to rely more and more on mega-franchises like *Star Wars* and Marvel, the gap between popular taste and the kind of movies nominated for Oscars has grown into a chasm, while the ceremony's ratings have steadily declined. The high-water mark was the year of *Titanic*—a world-conquering hit that also won Best Picture—culminating in a ceremony watched by 55.25 million people. But that was an eon ago. In 2009, after *The Dark Knight* failed to make the Best Picture list, the Academy, for the first time since 1944, expanded the category from five movies to as many as ten. If the hope was to create more room for Batman and friends, the plan backfired: the next year, the winner was *The Hurt Locker*, then the lowest-grossing Best Picture winner to date. The expanded category has let in the occasional comic book tentpole like *Black Panther* (itself a breakthrough for Black Hollywood), but more often it has given oxygen to small, worthy films unfamiliar to mass audiences. In 2018, the Academy tried to rectify the situation by announcing a new category, "Outstanding Achievement in Popular Film," but the blowback was so severe that the Academy backtracked into the hedges. In 2021—the "Pandemic Oscars," staged in a pop-up night-club inside a train station—the small-scale *Nomadland* won Best Picture, and the ratings dropped to an all-time low of 10.4 million people. The Academy had to evolve or die, and not for the first time.

Oscar history tends to repeat itself. The characters in this book all wanted something that the Academy and its awards could give them. Louis B. Mayer wanted to consolidate his power. Mary Pickford wanted to keep her image clean. Bette Davis wanted to blaze her own path. Olivia de Havilland and Joan Fontaine wanted to outrun each other. Dalton Trumbo wanted his life back. Gregory Peck wanted to save an institution. Allan Carr wanted his name in lights. Steven Spielberg wanted to honor his father. Harvey Weinstein wanted to gobble up everything in sight. Halle Berry wanted victory to be bigger than her. Cheryl Boone Isaacs wanted to right the ship. And yet, all were players in a history that moved at its own pace, the tectonic plates of show business shifting underfoot. Art would poke the eye of commerce, and then commerce would reassert itself. Tastes, politics, and power would realign. Most often, when change came, the Academy resisted until it couldn't anymore. But you can't fight the future.

The pandemic delayed the opening of the already much-delayed Academy Museum of Motion Pictures, which finally opened to the public in September 2021, in a 300,000-square-foot building designed by Renzo Piano. So strenuously did the museum try to fill the demographic blind spots of the Academy's first century that it got immediate backlash for omitting the Jewish moguls who founded the industry. The organization hatched by Louis B. Mayer seemed to have snubbed him, until it announced that it would add a permanent exhibition about the studio founders. Among the museum's artifacts are the sled from *Citizen Kane* and one of the model sharks from *Jaws*, both movies that the Academy notably *didn't* award its top prize in their time. As the Academy approaches its hundredth year, the eternal question has become more pointed than ever: Are the Oscars relevant?

On March 27, 2022, I was back at the Academy Awards. It had already been one of the rockiest Oscar seasons in recent memory. After years of circling the top prize, Netflix finally had a front-runner, Jane Campion's *The Power of the Dog*. Much like Miramax in 1999, Netflix was no longer the underdog: it was an empire intent on conquering the City of Gold. But *The Power of the Dog*, like *Saving Private Ryan* and *La La Land* before it, suffered from a bout of inevitability fatigue. A week before the Oscars, the feel-good *CODA*, about a deaf family with a hearing daughter, won the Producers Guild award, raising the possibility of a late surge.

Adding to the eleventh-hour oscillation was an Oscar staple: the campaign trail gaffe. On the red carpet for the Directors Guild awards, Campion was asked about actor Sam Elliott's criticisms of her gay-themed Western, which he had called a "piece of shit." "I'm sorry, he was being a little bit of a B-I-T-C-H," Campion said, adding, with an exquisite half grimace, "He's not a cowboy; he's an actor." The next day, she won a Critics Choice Award, and in her speech, she unexpectedly turned to Venus and Serena Williams, the subjects of the film *King Richard*, and cracked, "Venus and Serena, you're such marvels. However, you do not play against the guys, like I have to." It was a gender-imbalance joke that stomped on a racial-imbalance minefield, which is generally not where you want to be late in your Oscar campaign. Campion's social media fortunes rose and fell like a fly ball, and she swiftly issued an apology.

The year's central conflict, though, had less to do with the horse race than with the Academy's announcement that eight categories would not be presented during the live broadcast. Reportedly under pressure from ABC due to the dwindling ratings, the Academy gave in—and received weeks of blowback, its detractors including everyone from Spielberg to the excitable entity known as Film Twitter. In a way, this was a Hollywood sequel. Three years earlier, the Academy had tried to banish some categories to the commercial breaks but reversed itself after a similar outcry. This time, it held firm: those eight categories would be presented during an unaired first hour, and the winners' speeches would be shown in edited form. (Ironically, one of the demoted categories was for editing.)

The category-cutting fracas was a symptom of a deeper identity crisis. The Oscars strive to be two things at once: an industry recognition of the crafts represented by its branches and a splashy television event that must appeal to a mass audience. In the past few years, those two goals had appeared increasingly incompatible. For one thing, mass audiences didn't watch network television as they used to. But moviegoing had changed, too. The kind of films that were supposed to get big audiences *and* win Oscars, such as Spielberg's remake of *West Side Story*, stumbled at the pandemic-depressed box office. Without a sustainable middle, Hollywood was bifurcated: on one side, *Spider-Man: No Way Home*, which grossed more than $1.8 billion worldwide; on the other, *The Power of the Dog*, which got twelve Oscar nominations and some undisclosed amount of Netflix streams.

Instead of embracing the discrepancy—because the Oscars *should* be celebrating merit regardless of profitability, and they *should* be lifting up small movies—the Academy contorted itself in trying to be something it's not. It would recognize an "Oscars Fan Favorite," as calculated by online voting and Twitter. It announced a puzzling slate of presenters, including athletes Shaun White, Tony Hawk, and Kelly Slater. Film lovers griped that the Academy was "self-loathing," aggravating its die-hard followers by pandering to a wider audience. There was talk that the Oscars should leave network TV altogether and join the streaming revolution, where they could be as long and as niche as they wanted to be. In their tenth decade, the Oscars seemed as vulnerable as ever. Could they survive into their second century? Who were they even *for*?

I was contemplating these questions way up in Mezzanine 3, Row F, of the Dolby Theatre when I got the sneaking sense that something was not going as planned. It was hours into the ceremony, and Will Smith had just walked onstage and confronted Chris Rock, who was presenting the Best Documentary Feature award. From the nosebleed section, they looked like two small, famous blobs doing a comic bit. "Wow," Rock said, "Will Smith just smacked the shit out of me." I wondered, *Can people say "shit" on network TV?* But it was the word *fucking* that clued me in. Then I heard it again: "Keep my wife's name out your *fucking mouth*." Smith was unmic'd and palpably angry.

"What just happened?" the woman next to me asked. People murmured and shifted in their seats. The show kept moving. "I'm still in shock," my seatmate said, checking her phone. "They literally muted it on TV." At the commercial break, I sprinted down to the ground-floor lobby. "It looked like it was a joke at first," a guy in a tuxedo said. A man who worked a tech job at the ceremony came by and clarified: "Everything I know from backstage was that that was totally real."

What happened, the attendees (and the world) soon pieced together, was this: Rock made a joke comparing Smith's wife Jada Pinkett Smith to Demi Moore's character in *G.I. Jane*, because both had a shaved head. (Pinkett Smith's was a result of her alopecia.) Then Smith went up and smacked him. On social media, viewers were studying footage and taking sides, deconstructing the moment in terms of race, masculinity, and trauma. But at the Dolby, the mood was mostly bewilderment, like at a bar where a fight between strangers has broken out. It felt chaotic, unpredictable, shocking, alarming—and that was before the realization that Smith was, in all likelihood, about to win Best Actor and give a speech.

When the stars of *Pulp Fiction* reunited to present the Best Actor award, a crowd gathered around the circular bar outside the orchestra section. "Shh!" someone said. "We all want to hear what he got to say. Shut up!" Everyone fell silent as Smith's face filled the bar monitor. In his speech—which had the raw, confused emotion of a man navigating euphoria, rage, shame, pride, and "Shit, what did I just do?"—Smith returned over and over to the word *protect*, the concept that united the character he had won the Oscar for playing, Richard Williams, father of Venus and Serena, and the astonishing action he had just taken on live TV. Tears came to his eyes as he said, "Love will make you do crazy things." But was that any justification for violence?

The night ended with *CODA* winning Best Picture, in a staggering loss for Netflix. Apple Studios had acquired *CODA* for a record-breaking sum after its Sundance premiere, making 2022 the first year that a streamer won Best Picture. In another universe, that would have been the defining story of the Ninety-Fourth Academy Awards. But everyone was too on edge to think about it. At the Governors Ball, where Queen's "Another One Bites the Dust" was blasting, one Academy official wondered aloud if the incident would outrank Envelopegate on the list of craziest Oscar moments. I walked out, following Campion and her

Best Directing Oscar down what remained of the red carpet, and went to the *Vanity Fair* party, where I passed two simultaneous conversations where a different sitcom star was trying to make sense of "the Slap." A famous comedian told me that the fight was a sign of how thin-skinned celebrities had become. "Tonight was the purest example of how much this place has lost its fucking mind," the comedian said. "Los Angeles is like Gotham City right now."

Around one o'clock, I decided to take one last look at the dance floor before leaving. The deejay was playing "He's the Greatest Dancer," by Sister Sledge. I felt a presence behind me and spun around: there was *Will Freaking Smith*, with a huge smile on his face, dancing up a storm. Pinkett Smith stood nearby, raising the roof. A circle of phones flew up and started recording. The deejay, seizing the moment, put on "Gettin' Jiggy wit It," and the newly minted Best Actor gleefully danced and rapped along to his younger self: *na-na, na, na, na-na-na!*

Smith held his glistening statuette in one hand. In a matter of hours, he had assaulted someone on live television, ripped his soul open while winning an Oscar, and written himself a bizarre new chapter in Academy Awards history. Had we witnessed a psychic breakdown? A husband defending his wife? A jerk? A victim? A monster? In a Hollywood ending that seemed too dark and surreal to be true, he appeared to be having the time of his life.

ACKNOWLEDGMENTS

As any Oscar aficionado knows, the business of giving thanks is not to be taken lightly. I began this book in 2018 and got to the finish line only with the help of a small village of people. Firstly, thank you to the many people I interviewed, who helped me piece together a range of stories spanning the decades. My particular gratitude belongs to those who fielded multiple calls or emails. Whether their names appear in these pages or not, the people I spoke to shared invaluable wit, insight, and love of the movies.

I'm indebted to the countless, sometimes nameless journalists who covered Hollywood over the last century, and to the authors whose names appear in the bibliography. Writing this book meant reading some wonderful books, but I'm especially thankful to the authors who personally shared their expertise or pointed me in the right direction: Peter Bart, Peter Biskind, Larry Ceplair, Scott Eyman, Robert Hofler, Nicole LaPorte, and Jan Stuart. I'm deeply thankful to the librarians and archivists who helped me on my scavenger hunt, including those who went the extra mile when the pandemic struck and their jobs (and mine) became infinitely more complicated; thanks to Ned Comstock at USC's Cinematic Arts Library, Jane Klain at the Paley Center for Media, Valerie Yaros at SAG-AFTRA, John Leroy Calhoun and Jeremy Megraw at the New York Public Library for the Performing Arts, and Louise Hilton and Libby Wertin at the Academy's Margaret Herrick Library. For permission to use material, thank you Candice Bergen, Cecilia Peck, Kristen Ray, and Mitzi Trumbo.

Several parts of this book grew out of magazine pieces, and I'm forever grateful to the editors who indulged my interests and shaped what emerged: Susan Morrison and Michael Agger at *The New Yorker* and Claire Howorth at *Vanity Fair*. For most of my adult life, I've had a professional home at *The New Yorker*, and I'm indebted to all my colleagues there, among them Bruce Diones, Sarah Larson, Michael Luo, Shauna Lyon, Fergus McIntosh, David Remnick, and the talented fact-checkers and copy editors who make everyone look good.

I've learned from watching the Oscars that it is imperative to thank one's agent, and I'm delighted to thank David Kuhn, whose taste, counsel, and gumption made this book possible. Thanks to Nate Muscato, Elena Steiert, and everyone at Aevitas. I have David to thank for bringing me to Harper, and to the editor of this book and my previous one, Gail Winston, who encouraged me to think big and then wrangled the bigness into shape; thank you for your enthusiasm, wisdom, patience, and class. Tremendous thanks to Maya Baran, Jonathan Burnham, Hayley Salmon, Beth Silfin, and the entire team at Harper.

My research assistant, Fergus Campbell, emailed me out of the blue in 2020, asking if I wanted a summer intern, and wound up putting in years of hard work and good company—it was a pleasure to share this process with you. Jenna Dolan contributed cheerful and eagle-eyed copy editing, Agata Nowicka the cover of my dreams. The brilliant Dan Fishback gave me more insight, encouragement, and friendship than I can repay. For various indispensable things along the way, thank you Ethan James Green, Daniel Gomez, Teni Melidonian, Catherine Olim, Katherine Rowe, Daniel Smith-Rowsey, Ben Ryan, Jeffrey Schwarz, Rachel Syme, and Sam Wasson. For your friendship, advice, and support, endless thanks to Keith Bunin, Nancy Franklin, Bill Keith, Shira Milikowsky, Laura Millendorf, Jesse Oxfeld, Natalia Payne, Neal Peters, Rhonda Sherman, Rachel Shukert, Jason Zinoman, the Birnbaums, the Donates, and the Theaterists.

Thank you to my parents, who let me stay up and watch the Oscars, and to Alissa, Russell, and their new arrival. Most of all, thank you to my husband, Jaime Donate, who spent innumerable nights listening, with love and endurance, to the quotidian twists and turns of book writing and to an almost unbearable volume of Oscar trivia. I love our life together.

Well, I hear the orchestra playing me off. Thank you to the Academy! Good night!

NOTES

Because this book covers a range of eras, my research methods varied from one time period to the next. They included archival research, primarily at the New York Public Library for the Performing Arts and the Academy's Margaret Herrick Library (abbreviated as "AMPAS" in the notes); contemporary press reports; published books; and more than 150 interviews, both attributed and on background. When quoting directly from sources I interviewed, I use the present tense ("he says," "she recalls," and so on), except for the words of those who died during the writing of this book, Louise Fletcher, Sidney Sheinberg, Leon Vitali, and Bobby Zarem.

Introduction: A Little Too Scared to Hope

xiv   "I cannot think of a case where this has happened": My account of the night first appeared in "Scenes from the Oscar-Night Implosion," *The New Yorker*, Feb. 27, 2017.

xv   "Ego and bragging rights": Author interview with Terry Press for "Oscar Dearest," *The New Yorker*, Feb. 27, 2017.

xv   "There was more excitement": Frances Marion, *Off with Their Heads! A Serio-Comic Tale of Hollywood* (New York: The Macmillan Company, 1972), 161.

One: You Ain't Heard Nothin' Yet, 1927–29

1   "the only card game": Niblo's account of the evening is from his speech at the first Organization Banquet of the Academy of Motion Picture Arts and Sciences, reprinted in Erika J. Fischer, *The Inauguration of "Oscar": Sketches and Documents from the Early Years of the Hollywood Academy of Motion Picture Arts and Sciences* (München and New York: K.G. Saur, 1988), 296–98.

1   Typically, his wife Margaret: Scott Eyman, *Lion of Hollywood: The Life and Legend of Louis B. Mayer* (New York: Simon and Schuster, 2005), 134–35.

2   "When we need a set": Quoted in Christopher Silvester, *The Penguin Book of Hollywood* (London, New York: Viking, 1998), 79.

2 "[E]veryone is moving down": Letter to Jesse Lasky Jr., May 23, 1927, Ref. 1927, Jesse L. Lasky files, Margaret Herrick Library, Beverly Hills, CA (library hereafter cited as "AMPAS").

2 "You are talking about the devil": Quoted in Eyman, *Lion of Hollywood*, 7.

2 "His people respected him": Frederica Sagor Maas, quoted in Eyman, *Lion of Hollywood*, 10.

3 "Lousy Bastard": Eyman, *Lion of Hollywood*, 97.

3 "refined amusement": Quoted in Debra Ann Pawlak, *Bringing Up Oscar: The Story of the Men and Women Who Founded the Academy* (New York: Pegasus Books, 2011), 11.

3 "the business of making idols": Quoted in Eyman, *Lion of Hollywood*, 44.

3 a cadre of Jewish moguls: Neal Gabler, *An Empire of Their Own: How the Jews Invented Hollywood* (New York: Anchor Books, 1998), 3.

3 Each Independence Day: Gabler, *An Empire of Their Own*, 79.

4 "I worship good women": Quoted in Marion, *Off with Their Heads!*, 99.

4 During preproduction for *The Merry Widow*: Eyman, *Lion of Hollywood*, 98.

5 A hundred million people a week: Scott Eyman, *The Speed of Sound: Hollywood and the Talkie Revolution, 1926–1930* (New York: Simon and Schuster, 1997), 16–17.

6 "biggest strike in the history of the film industry": "Studio 'Strike' Situation," *Variety*, Nov. 17, 1926.

6 "on the ground that children": Quoted in William J. Mann, *Tinseltown: Murder, Morphine, and Madness at the Dawn of Hollywood* (New York: Harper, 2014), 33.

6 "the devil and 500 non-Christian Jews": Quoted in Mann, *Tinseltown*, 99–100.

7 The papers breathlessly reported: Mann, *Tinseltown*, 31.

7 "the almost complete submergence": Quoted in Mann, *Tinseltown*, 169.

7 "DEAD DIRECTOR VISITED QUEER PLACES!": Mann, *Tinseltown*, 222.

7 "Censorship of the films": "Censorship," *Los Angeles Times*, July 26, 1929.

8 "we thought maybe at the most": Quoted in Fischer, *The Inauguration of "Oscar,"* 299.

8 "a cinema club": "Cinematic Stars Talk Club Plan," *Los Angeles Times*, Jan. 18, 1927.

8 "who has accomplished distinguished work": *Bulletin*, No. 1 (June 1, 1927), Academy History Archive, AMPAS.

8 "I never in my life": Quoted in Fischer, *The Inauguration of "Oscar,"* 307.

9 "that an actor should head": Letter to Hedda Hopper, Nov. 14, 1941, Folder 72, Hedda Hopper Papers, AMPAS.

9 WE ARE NOW PREPARING: Folder 13, Cecil B. DeMille Collection, AMPAS.

9 "uniting into one body": "The Reasons Why," Organization Banquet, 1927, Academy History Archive, AMPAS.

10 Pickfair was more than their home: Eileen Whitfield, *Pickford: The Woman Who Made Hollywood* (Lexington: University Press of Kentucky, 1997), 206–7.

10 "only the waltz or two-step": Quoted in Whitfield, *Pickford*, 225.

10 "one lousy drop": Quoted in Whitfield, *Pickford*, 226.

11 "demonstrated conclusively": Adolph Zukor, *The Public Is Never Wrong* (New York: G.P. Putnam's Sons, 1953), 173.

11 on a getaway to a friend's mansion: Mary Pickford, *Sunshine and Shadow* (Garden City, NY: Doubleday and Company, 1955), 195–96.

11   "discreet, or thought they were": Zukor, *The Public Is Never Wrong*, 192.

11   "The lunatics have taken charge": Quoted in Whitfield, *Pickford*, 192.

11   "Adela, if I divorce Owen": Quoted in Whitfield, *Pickford*, 196.

11   "I have learned that I do not belong": Quoted in Whitfield, *Pickford*, 199.

11   "a lynch mob": Quoted in Whitfield, *Pickford*, 202.

12   "It was as though Mary": Quoted in Whitfield, *Pickford*, 224–25.

12   "A wild impulse would seize": Pickford, *Sunshine and Shadow*, 252.

13   A heater had burst: "Mary Pickford Speaks for Movie Uplift, Doug Saves Bungalow," *New York Mirror*, May 14, 1927.

13   "Ready, Doug?": Speeches from the banquet appear in full in Fischer, *The Inauguration of "Oscar,"* 295–317.

15   "bring sunshine into the lives": "Mary Pickford on A.M.A.S.," *Variety*, May 18, 1927.

15   "Mary Pickford is tired": "Easy to Purge the Fraternity," *New York Evening World*, May 1927.

15   "AGAINST 'SPANKING'": *Salt Lake City Telegram*, May 13, 1927.

15   "spirit of defiance": "Industry Fashioning Weapon of Defence," *The Film Spectator*, May 28, 1927.

15   "soft as a feather": Zukor, *The Public Is Never Wrong*, 242–43.

16   GREAT WORK BOY: Quoted in William Wellman Jr., *The Man and His "Wings": William A. Wellman and the Making of the First Best Picture* (Westport, CT: Praeger, 2006), 61.

16   "Remember me, Mr. Fairbanks?": Quoted in Wellman, *The Man and His "Wings,"* 63.

17   "You need something solid": Quoted in Wellman, *The Man and His "Wings,"* 118.

17   "Wellman stubbornly refused": Jesse Lasky, *I Blow My Own Horn* (Garden City, NY: Doubleday and Company, 1957), 208.

17   "The people that you see": Quoted in Eyman, *The Speed of Sound*, 100.

17   "too much like a capital-labor conflict": Quoted in King Vidor, *A Tree Is a Tree* (New York: Harcourt, Brace and Company, 1953), 145–51.

18   "Every set would have musicians": Quoted in Kevin Brownlow, *The Parade's Gone By . . .* (Berkeley: University of California Press, 1968), 341.

18   "equipped with comfortable chairs": *Bulletin*, No. 1.

18   "I found that the best way": Quoted in Eyman, *Lion of Hollywood*, 117.

18   "I considered it to be such a touchy subject": Quoted in Peter H. Brown and Jim Pinkston, *Oscar Dearest: Six Decades of Scandal, Politics and Greed Behind Hollywood's Academy Awards, 1927–1986* (New York: Harper and Row, 1987), 20.

19   "one of the most hectic weeks": "Salary Cutting Fluke," *Variety*, July 6, 1927.

19   At one studio café: "'Cold Cuts' Suggestive," *Variety*, July 6, 1927.

19   "Those jerks in charge": Quoted in Brown and Pinkston, *Oscar Dearest*, 18.

19   "The emergency could never": *Bulletin*, No. 4 (Aug. 10, 1927), Academy History Archive, AMPAS.

19   "It is the kind of harmony": "Brilliant Victory for the Producers," *The Film Spectator*, Aug. 20, 1927.

19   Emboldened, Actors' Equity cofounder Frank Gillmore: "Salary Cut Flop May Take Equity into Coast Studios," *Variety*, July 13, 1927.

20   "advance to the attack": "Studios Win over Equity," *Variety*, July 27, 1927.

20 "Don'ts and Be Carefuls": "Mayer's Resolutions and Don'ts; Actors Without Representation," *Variety*, Oct. 12, 1927.

20 "commodious, exclusive and convenient": *Bulletin*, No. 5 (Nov. 25, 1927), Academy History Archive, AMPAS.

20 "throw upon a canvas": Quoted in Eyman, *The Speed of Sound*, 26.

20 "Americans require a restful quiet": Quoted in Eyman, *The Speed of Sound*, 37.

21 "Just a gimmick": Quoted in Eyman, *The Speed of Sound*, 68.

21 "Hiya, honey!": Quoted in Eyman, *The Speed of Sound*, 59.

21 "Sam was the bridge": Quoted in Eyman, *The Speed of Sound*, 61.

21 Weeks later, he asked Harry: Jack L. Warner, *My First Hundred Years in Hollywood: An Autobiography* (New York: Random House, 1965), 167–68.

22 "new era in motion picture presentation": Quoted in Eyman, *The Speed of Sound*, 89.

22 "I said to myself": Quoted in Eyman, *The Speed of Sound*, 92.

22 "The future of this new contrivance": Mordaunt Hall, "Vitaphone Stirs as Talking Movie," *New York Times*, Aug. 7, 1926.

22 "will bring to the motion picture": Quoted in Eyman, *The Speed of Sound*, 94.

22 The crowd was studded: Eyman, *The Speed of Sound*, 103–4.

23 Gobsmacked by his intensity: Eyman, *The Speed of Sound*, 129–31.

23 "insisted on ad-libbing": Quoted in Eyman, *The Speed of Sound*, 13.

24 The next day, *The Jazz Singer* premiered: Eyman, *The Speed of Sound*, 139–40.

24 "A million dollars or not": Warner, *My First Hundred Years in Hollywood*, 181.

24 "terror in all their faces": Quoted in Eyman, *The Speed of Sound*, 160.

24 "We are in a manner": *Bulletin*, No. 6 (Jan. 1, 1928), Academy History Archive, AMPAS.

25 "The Academy is the League of Nations": *Bulletin*, No. 9 (April 2, 1928), Academy History Archive, AMPAS.

25 "breakdowns" or "severe colds": Quoted in Scott Eyman, *Mary Pickford: America's Sweetheart* (New York: Donald L. Fine, 1990), 99.

25 "putting lip rouge": Quoted in Whitfield, *Pickford*, 256.

25 The cause of the trouble: Tracey Goessel, *The First King of Hollywood: The Life of Douglas Fairbanks* (Chicago: Chicago Press Review, 2016), 372–74.

26 "almost my very life": Quoted in Whitfield, *Pickford*, 252.

26 "I was like a wild animal": Pickford, *Sunshine and Shadow*, 303.

27 a simple decision: Pickford, *Sunshine and Shadow*, 293–95.

27 "And what have we got?": Quoted in Eyman, *The Speed of Sound*, 179.

27 "One cannot pick up a daily paper": Quoted in Eyman, *The Speed of Sound*, 177.

27 "Do you have to hear the wind": Quoted in Eyman, *The Speed of Sound*, 145.

27 "We are all groping": *Bulletin*, No. 11 (June 4, 1928), Academy History Archive, AMPAS.

28 In July, some 125 of them: *Bulletin*, No. 12 (July 16, 1928), Academy History Archive, AMPAS.

28 "in the press of other business": *Bulletin*, No. 11.

28 In a letter to Academy secretary: The letter, dated Nov. 7, 1927, is in a restricted folder in the Academy Archives at AMPAS and was paraphrased by a librarian.

29 "a valued ornament": *Bulletin*, No. 12.

29 "Include them, by all means": *Bulletin*, No. 13 (Aug. 11, 1928), Academy History Archive, AMPAS.

29 "Suddenly, with sound": Frank Capra, *The Name Above the Title: An Autobiography* (New York: The Macmillan Company, 1971), 101.

30 "You could not move the camera": Quoted in Eyman, *The Speed of Sound*, 261.

30 "screen actors without stage experience": "No Stage Director or Writer Required for Talkers, but Screen Actors in Them Flop," *Variety*, Oct. 17, 1928.

30 "Sounds too ladylike": Marion, *Off with Their Heads!*, 182.

30 "At the studio gates": Marion, *Off with Their Heads!*, 185.

31 "corny Kansas accent": Quoted in Eyman, *The Speed of Sound*, 182.

31 "All of us in pictures": Quoted in Eyman, *The Speed of Sound*, 182–83.

31 "just fast enough to give": Quoted in Eyman, *The Speed of Sound*, 273.

31 "That's not me!": Quoted in Eyman, *The Speed of Sound*, 181.

32 "He didn't like sound pictures": Quoted in Eyman, *The Speed of Sound*, 273.

32 "Let's go down and have a look": Quoted in Eyman, *The Speed of Sound*, 379–80.

32 "idealized male figure": *Bulletin*, No. 19 (Feb. 23, 1929), Academy History Archive, AMPAS.

32 "an artistic and striking bronze statuette": *Bulletin*, No. 18 (Jan. 17, 1929), Academy History Archive, AMPAS.

33 "Back then, there were five people": King Vidor, *King Vidor: Interviewed by Nancy Dowd and David Shepard* (Metuchen, NJ: Scarecrow Press, 1988), 88.

33 "It was his own picture": Quoted in Charles Higham, "Long Live Vidor, a Hollywood King," *New York Times*, Sept. 3, 1972.

33 "favoritism or friendship": *Bulletin*, No. 19.

34 "smiler with a knife": Quoted in Eyman, *Lion of Hollywood*, 128–29.

34 "This award consists of an artistic statuette": Letter from Woods to Zukor, Feb. 19, 1929, Correspondence 1929, Folder 12, Adolph Zukor Collection, AMPAS.

34 "May we have your assurance": Letter from Woods to Zukor, Feb. 29, 1929, Correspondence 1929, Folder 12, Adolph Zukor Collection, AMPAS.

34 URGENTLY REQUEST: Telegram from Woods to Zukor, May 10, 1929, Correspondence 1929, Folder 12, Adolph Zukor Collection, AMPAS.

35 "I am deeply impressed": Correspondence 1929, Folder 12, Adolph Zukor Collection, AMPAS.

35 "I did not attend the Academy dinner": Gloria Swanson, *Swanson on Swanson* (New York: Pocket Books, 1980), 388.

35 "talking picture entertainment": *Bulletin*, No. 21 (May 12, 1929), Academy History Archive, AMPAS.

35 "soft lantern lights shedding rays": Quoted in Anthony Holden, *Behind the Oscar: The Secret History of the Academy Awards* (New York: Simon and Schuster, 1993), 96.

36 consommé Celestine: Program and menu, 1927/28 (1st) Academy Awards, Academy Awards Collection, AMPAS.

36 "It is now two years": Speeches from *Bulletin*, No. 22 (June 3, 1929), Academy History Archive, AMPAS.

37 "Personally I have not heard much": Quoted in "4,000 Actors for 600 Jobs," *Variety*, May 22, 1929.

37 "I notice they gave *The Jazz Singer*": Quoted in Eyman, *The Speed of Sound*, 283.

37 "It was more like a private party": Quoted in Holden, *Behind the Oscar*, 93–94.

37 "It was nothing then": Quoted in Brown and Pinkston, *Oscar Dearest*, 21.

37 "the little gold-washed statuette": Marion, *Off with Their Heads!*, 162.

38 "Within two years": Quoted in Eyman, *The Speed of Sound*, 378.

38 Frank Gillmore had promised to "invade": "Equity in Coast Drive, Based on Stage Actors' Film Invasion," *Variety*, April 24, 1929.

39 "aggressive intrusion": "Press Against Screen Players Organizing," *Variety*, June 12, 1929.

39 "refutation of statements": "Academy Continues," *Variety*, July 3, 1929.

39 "invaded a healthy, wealthy": Quoted in "Equity Badly Whipped," *Variety*, Aug. 21, 1929.

39 "body of screen actors": "Actors Defy Equity," *Variety*, Oct. 9, 1929.

39 "completely new Douglas": Pickford, *Sunshine and Shadow*, 311–12.

40 Guests at Pickfair now noticed: Whitfield, *Pickford*, 266.

40 "I can make you the biggest star": Eyman, *Lion of Hollywood*, 193–94.

40 "They weren't going to do": Quoted in Eyman, *The Speed of Sound*, 312.

41 His shares of Loew's cratered: Eyman, *Lion of Hollywood*, 146; and Eyman, *The Speed of Sound*, 340.

Two: Rebels, 1933–39

43 "a charming picture of youth": Quoted in James Zeruk Jr., *Peg Entwistle and the Hollywood Sign Suicide: A Biography* (Jefferson, NC: McFarland and Company, 2014), 154.

44 "I am afraid I'm a coward": Quoted in Zeruk, *Peg Entwistle and the Hollywood Sign Suicide*, 184–85.

45 In the first year of the decade: *Bulletin*, No. 38 (March 5, 1931), Academy History Archive, AMPAS.

45 On March 8, a drained-looking Mayer: Eyman, *Lion of Hollywood*, 178–80.

46 "At least it postpones the execution": Quoted in Leonard Mosley, *Zanuck: The Rise and Fall of Hollywood's Last Tycoon* (Boston: Little, Brown, 1984), 124.

46 "magnificent temple to the motion picture": Prospectus for Academy Hollywood Building, 1931, Academy History Archive, AMPAS.

46 "false conceptions of Hollywood": *Bulletin*, No. 43 (March 24, 1932), Academy History Archive, AMPAS.

46 "You'd be surprised how the greatest": Quoted in Holden, *Behind the Oscar*, 116.

47 As he sat at the barber's: Capra, *The Name Above the Title*, 146–47.

47 "SQUAWKS GALORE": "No Production Shut-Down," *Variety*, March 14, 1933.

47 "All hell broke loose": Capra, *The Name Above the Title*, 146.

48 "a horizontal industry salary cut": *Emergency Bulletin*, No. 3 (April 12, 1933), Academy History Archive, AMPAS.

48 "the kind of an organization": *Bulletin*, No. 12 (May 22, 1933), Academy History Archive, AMPAS.

49 Those among them who were members: "New Film-Actor Org.," *Variety*, Oct. 3, 1933.

49 "Some Academy members say": Quoted in "100% Screen Actors' Guild," *Variety*, Oct. 10, 1933.

49 "The Academy of M. P. Arts and Sciences": "Acad's Finale Seems Certain," *Variety*, Jan. 2, 1934.

50   "I wrote and threw away": Capra, *The Name Above the Title*, 153.

50   "old cracked house of stone": Capra, *The Name Above the Title*, 3.

50   "crammed with retching, praying": Capra, *The Name Above the Title*, 5.

50   Capra bluffed: Capra, *The Name Above the Title*, 19.

50   "The nutty little Montague affair": Capra, *The Name Above the Title*, 29.

50   "the unexpected wow": Capra, *The Name Above the Title*, 52.

51   "dreamy love affair": Capra, *The Name Above the Title*, 77.

51   "infested by shacks": Capra, *The Name Above the Title*, 78.

51   "Hey, Dago": Quoted in Capra, *The Name Above the Title*, 83.

51   "My goal, as a youth": Capra, *The Name Above the Title*, 93.

51   "In 1929," he wrote: Capra, *The Name Above the Title*, 105.

52   "The major studios had the votes": Capra, *The Name Above the Title*, 116.

52   "The voting was 'kosher'": Capra, *The Name Above the Title*, 117.

53   "I dreamed about Oscars": Capra, *The Name Above the Title*, 140.

53   "Damn those Academy voters!": Capra, *The Name Above the Title*, 142.

53   "There was a mystique": Capra, *The Name Above the Title*, 144.

53   "You little son-of-a-bitch": Quoted in Capra, *The Name Above the Title*, 152.

53   "I stayed with the Academy": Quoted in Joseph McBride, *Frank Capra: The Catastrophe of Success* (New York: Simon and Schuster, 1992), 186–87.

54   "Day by day I kept persuading": Capra, *The Name Above the Title*, 153.

54   "I applauded like an idiot": Capra, *The Name Above the Title*, 153.

54   "Well, well, well, what do you know!": Quoted in *The Name Above the Title*, 154. Capra's account is legendary, but a *Los Angeles Times* report suggests that Rogers in fact did call Capra and his fellow loser George Cukor up to the stage for a bow. Even if he was invited to the stage, his humiliation was evident.

55   "I do not regret the dust": Bette Davis, *The Lonely Life* (New York: G. P. Putnam's Sons, 1962), 12.

55   "Created in a fury": Davis, *The Lonely Life*, 15.

55   "It was my first serious theatre": Davis, *The Lonely Life*, 49.

56   "Let her become a secretary!": Quoted in Davis, *The Lonely Life*, 50.

56   "I worshiped her": Davis, *The Lonely Life*, 55.

56   "shook with applause and bravos": Davis, *The Lonely Life*, 89.

56   "My legs": Davis, *The Lonely Life*, 101.

56   "I was simply asked to lie": Davis, *The Lonely Life*, 109–10.

56   One of the secretaries advised: Davis, *The Lonely Life*, 113.

57   "sweet, drab sister": Davis, *The Lonely Life*, 136.

57   "Spice in pictures": Quoted in "Accident Saves Bette Davis from Being Just Another Good Girl," *Variety*, March 28, 1933.

57   "such a disagreeable character": Davis, *The Lonely Life*, 141.

57   "THE MENACE OF THE ACADEMY": *The Screen Player*, April 15, 1934.

58   "The Academy's one purpose": Quoted in "Cantor, Re-elected Prez of Screen Guild, Terms Academy a 'Company Union'; Deprecates Strike Idea," *Variety*, May 15, 1934.

58   "There will be no personal": Sidney Sutherland, "An Award that *Means* Something . . . ," *The Screen Guilds' Magazine*, Dec. 1934.

58   "The quietness": Capra, *The Name Above the Title*, 159–60.

59   "Forget bus pictures": Quoted in Capra, *The Name Above the Title*, 161.

59   "I got an actor here": Quoted in Capra, *The Name Above the Title*, 164.

59   "stopped at every bar": Capra, *The Name Above the Title*, 165.

60   "fun-loving, boyish, attractive": Capra, *The Name Above the Title*, 170.

60   "My understanding of Mildred's vileness": Davis, *The Lonely Life*, 142–43.

60   "We pulled no punches": Davis, *The Lonely Life*, 142.

61   "the audience was so wrought": Mordaunt Hall, "The Screen: Leslie Howard and Bette Davis in a Picturization of W. Somerset Maugham's Novel 'Of Human Bondage,'" *New York Times*, June 29, 1934.

61   "Well! RKO knew": Davis, *The Lonely Life*, 145.

61   "a cinch to get": "Hollywood Bunch Has Winners All Guessed for Academy's Awards," *Variety*, Feb. 12, 1935.

61   "a wild burst of indignation": Muriel Babcock, "Prize Vote This Year Wide Open," *Pittsburgh Sun-Telegraph*, Feb. 24, 1935.

61   "near-sighted": "Just as You Say . . . ," *Movie Classic*, June 1935.

62   "was never a sincere expression": "Annual Academy Prizes Become 'Free-for-All,'" *St. Louis Post-Dispatch*, Feb. 24, 1935.

62   "I suppose there was no chance": Quoted in McBride, *Frank Capra*, 325.

62   "It now appears": "What's Doing on the Gold Coast?," *New York Times*, Feb. 24, 1935.

62   "It seemed inevitable": Davis, *The Lonely Life*, 146.

63   "I cannot say I wasn't crushed": Davis, *The Lonely Life*, 146.

63   "Dizzy night": Capra, *The Name Above the Title*, 172.

63   "A little bird tells us": "Live and Learn . . . ," *The Screen Guilds' Magazine*, March 1935.

64   "I was made to trudge": Davis, *The Lonely Life*, 147.

64   "intractable child": Davis, *The Lonely Life*, 149.

64   "she thinks she has found it": Robbin Coons, "In Screenland," *San Pedro News Pilot*, Aug. 23, 1935.

64   "I had scaled the Mount Everest": Capra, *The Name Above the Title*, 172.

64   "secret malingering campaign": Capra, *The Name Above the Title*, 173.

65   "My malingering had maligned": Capra, *The Name Above the Title*, 175.

65   a forebear of the angel: As Joseph McBride points out, the tale bears a strong resemblance to "The Flying Yorkshireman," a 1937 short story to which Capra later bought the rights.

66   "the living symbol": Capra, *The Name Above the Title*, 186.

66   "a thousand tinkling bells": Capra, *The Name Above the Title*, 184.

66   "it would be presiding": Capra, *The Name Above the Title*, 187.

66   "Six months before": Capra, *The Name Above the Title*, 188.

66   "warpath against the Academy": "Acad's Big Brother Bid to Scribes Has Guild Looking Under Woodpile," *Variety*, May 1, 1935.

67   Among their grievances: "H'Wood 100% Closed Shop?," *Variety*, Jan. 22, 1936.

67   "a company of gentlemen": Quoted in McBride, *Frank Capra*, 378.

67   Cecil B. DeMille railed: David Thomson, "The Man Who Would Be King," *DGA Quarterly* (Winter 2011).

68   "exploitation and entertainment": "Manning Steaming Up Acad Awards Banquet," *Variety*, Feb. 19, 1936.

68 "uncharacteristic dither": Richard Schickel, *D. W. Griffith: An American Life* (New York: Simon and Schuster, 1984), 582.

69 "We used him": Quoted in McBride, *Frank Capra*, 339.

69 the boycotts "fizzled": Capra, *The Name Above the Title*, 188.

69 "liberally distributed to secretaries": "Warner Write-ins Almost Wreck Academy Slate; 'Bounty' Voted Best Pic, McLaglen, Davis Tops," *Variety*, March 11, 1936.

69 "a traitor before a firing squad": Davis, *The Lonely Life*, 155.

69 "Dear Bette! What a *lovely* frock": Quoted in Holden, *Behind the Oscar*, 130.

69 "invaluable initiative": "Report: Eighth Annual Awards of Merit," 1936, Academy History Archive, AMPAS.

70 "I stared down at the little gold-plated man": Davis, *The Lonely Life*, 154.

70 "This nagged at me": Davis, *The Lonely Life*, 150.

70 "Hangover Prize": Sidney Skolsky, "Flim-Flam," *Citizen*, undated column from March 1936, Folder 359, Hollywood Columnists' Clippings, AMPAS.

70 "backview was the spit of my husband's": Davis, *The Lonely Life*, 154.

70 "To the profession these statues": Stanley Skolsky, "Films Crown Hepburn, Laughton Year's Best," (New York) *Daily News*, March 17, 1934.

70 "while I had an Uncle Oscar": Quoted in "Who's Who in the Hills," *Canyon Crier*, March 17, 1949.

70 Another theory has it: Bruce Davis, *The Academy and the Award: The Coming of Age of Oscar and the Academy of Motion Picture Arts and Sciences* (Waltham, MA: Brandeis University Press, 2022), 217–20.

71 "When Walt referred to the 'Oscar'": Marion, *Off with Their Heads!*, 242.

71 "storm clouds likely to precipitate": "Demand Change in Acad Award Voting to Frustrate Write-ins," *Variety*, March 25, 1936.

71 "Frank, what the hell": Quoted in McBride, *Frank Capra*, 376.

72 He immersed himself: Capra, *The Name Above the Title*, 192–93.

72 "the Jewish producers": Quoted in McBride, *Frank Capra*, 364.

72 "I didn't wiggle": Quoted in Capra, *The Name Above the Title*, 198.

72 "It was a one-man show": Quoted in McBride, *Frank Capra*, 336.

73 "change its attitude": Quoted in Holden, *Behind the Oscar*, 133.

73 "the lurking suspicion": Douglas W. Churchill, "Hollywood from A to Z," *New York Times*, March 14, 1937.

73 "tables next to each other": Sidney Skolsky column from March 8, 1937, Hollywood Columnists' Clippings, AMPAS.

73 "Well, they all may be": Quoted in McBride, *Frank Capra*, 339.

73 "My hopes were soon shattered": Davis, *The Lonely Life*, 156.

73 "waste of this gifted lady's talents": Bosley Crowther, "At the Strand," *New York Times*, July 23, 1936.

74 "assembly-line actress": Davis, *The Lonely Life*, 157.

74 Her "one-woman strike": Davis, *The Lonely Life*, 158–59.

74 "England and her Magna Charta": Davis, *The Lonely Life*, 160.

75 "Once and for all": Davis, *The Lonely Life*, 161–62.

75 "I think, m'lord": Quoted in Davis, *The Lonely Life*, 163.

75 "was so furious": Davis, *The Lonely Life*, 167.

75 "In a way, my defeat": Davis, *The Lonely Life*, 170.

76 "The trouble was": Quoted in McBride, *Frank Capra*, 366.

76 "Oh, *that*, for crissake": Capra, *The Name Above the Title*, 218.

76 Without his megaphone: Capra, *The Name Above the Title*, 221–23.

77 "All contractual relations": "In Other Words, the Academy's Just Bowing Out," *Variety*, June 23, 1937.

77 "Our Guild's in trouble": Quoted in Capra, *The Name Above the Title*, 267.

77 "What the hell": Quoted in McBride, *Frank Capra*, 376.

78 "Oscar Mob": "Acad May Have to Hire a Hall to Take Care of Oscar Mob," *Variety*, Jan. 19, 1938.

78 "the Academy has absolutely no treasury": Letter from Donald Gledhill, Dec. 9, 1937, Folder 4, Loeb and Loeb files, AMPAS.

78 "accept it or throw it away": Quoted in "Capra Labels Mahin Walkout on Acad Awards 'Injection of Politics,'" *Variety*, Feb. 23, 1938.

78 "I accepted the challenge": Capra, *The Name Above the Title*, 267.

79 "Well, you little dago": Quoted in Capra, *The Name Above the Title*, 232.

79 "a golden opportunity": Capra, *The Name Above the Title*, 241.

80 "He's dead, Frank": Quoted in Capra, *The Name Above the Title*, 252.

80 "Julie Marsden, the Jezebel": Davis, *The Lonely Life*, 174.

80 "It was *he* who helped": Davis, *The Lonely Life*, 175.

80 "burn the place down": Davis, *The Lonely Life*, 177.

81 "to an unnecessary degree": "Divorces Bette Davis," *New York Times*, Dec. 7, 1938.

81 "responsibility in economic": "Okay Academy Revamp," *Variety*, Aug. 17, 1938.

81 "tough sledding": Folder 4, Loeb and Loeb files, AMPAS.

82 "a clash of events": Capra, *The Name Above the Title*, 266–72.

82 "I had to sacrifice": Quoted in McBride, *Frank Capra*, 406.

84 "must have been delighted": Davis, *The Lonely Life*, 178.

84 "I was now a sovereign state": Davis, *The Lonely Life*, 179–80.

84 "alien films": "Foreign Films Eligible for Oscars," *Variety*, Dec. 27, 1939.

85 His wife drove him: Capra, *The Name Above the Title*, 315.

Three: War! 1942

87 *Man your battle stations*: "Navy vet recalls attack on Pearl Harbor," KCRA3, Dec. 7, 2018.

88 "stiff-jawed": "City Springs to Attention," *Los Angeles Times*, Dec. 8, 1941.

88 "They've asked for it": Quoted in "What Do Angelenos Think of War? Roving 'Times' Reporter Finds Out," *Los Angeles Times*, Dec. 8, 1941.

88 "It's the War Department, animal": Quoted in Joseph McBride, *Searching for John Ford* (New York: St. Martin's Press, 2001), 347.

88 "Today, particularly, people are thinking": Norman Corwin, "Between Americans," CBS Radio, broadcast Dec. 7, 1941.

89 "A few days later, I was talking with the President": *The Dick Cavett Show*, ABC, Sept. 14, 1970.

89 the FBI was taking Japanese: "Roundup of Japanese Aliens in Southland Begun by F.B.I.," *Los Angeles Times*, Dec. 8, 1941.

89 Some days later, Joan Fontaine heard a knock: Joan Fontaine, *No Bed of Roses* (New York: William Morrow and Company, 1978), 18.

89 "Nine days later, I would have been classified": Quoted in William Stadiem, "Ol-

ivia de Havilland and the Most Notorious Sibling Rivalry in Hollywood," *Vanity Fair*, May 2016.

89 "When I saw the first rushes": Quoted in Ed Sikov, *Dark Victory: The Life of Bette Davis* (New York: Henry Holt and Company, 2007), 190.

90 With all the papers carrying: "Film Academy Sets Awards Date," *Los Angeles Times*, Dec. 8, 1941.

90 "The word 'genius' was whispered": Quoted in Harlan Lebo, *Citizen Kane: A Filmmaker's Journey* (New York: St. Martin's Press, 2016), 5.

90 "take the mickey": Quoted in Lebo, *Citizen Kane*, 8.

91 "In my case I didn't want money": Quoted in Lebo, *Citizen Kane*, 14.

91 "A genius is a crackpot": Quoted in Lebo, *Citizen Kane*, 18.

91 "I would have hated myself, too": Quoted in Lebo, *Citizen Kane*, 20.

92 "We have terrific income in Germany": Quoted in Ben Urwand, "The Chilling History of How Hollywood Helped Hitler," *The Hollywood Reporter*, July 31, 2013.

92 "the charge is certain to be made": Quoted in Thomas Doherty, *Hollywood and Hitler, 1933–1939* (New York: Columbia University Press, 2013), 58.

93 "If you're thinking of a general run": Quoted in Mark Harris, *Five Came Back: A Story of Hollywood and the Second World War* (New York: Penguin Press, 2014), 18–19.

93 "that certain man": Quoted in Harris, *Five Came Back*, 20.

93 "portentous departure": Quoted in Clayton R. Koppes and Gregory D. Black, *Hollywood Goes to War: How Politics, Profits, and Propaganda Shaped World War II Movies* (New York: Free Press, 1987), 27.

94 "I was always afraid": Quoted in Harris, *Five Came Back*, 54–57.

94 "devoted to arousing America against Germany": Douglas W. Churchill, "The Hollywood Round-Up," *New York Times*, May 18, 1941.

94 "splendid cooperation": Quoted in Koppes and Black, *Hollywood Goes to War*, 36.

95 "for as long as the fish are biting": Quoted in Mason Wiley and Damien Bona, *Inside Oscar: The Unofficial History of the Academy Awards* (New York: Ballantine Books, 1987), 108–9.

95 "Awards are a trivial thing": Quoted in Wiley and Bona, *Inside Oscar*, 111.

95 "From birth we were not encouraged": Fontaine, *No Bed of Roses*, 102.

95 "She seems to need what I have": Quoted in Victoria Amador, *Olivia de Havilland: Lady Triumphant* (Lexington: University Press of Kentucky, 2019), 241.

95 "Perhaps my being a puny child": Fontaine, *No Bed of Roses*, 19.

95 "If she got chickenpox": Quoted in Amador, *Olivia de Havilland*, 240.

96 "would tarry too long": Fontaine, *No Bed of Roses*, 33.

96 "She had never been rambunctious": Quoted in Stadiem, "Olivia de Havilland and the Most Notorious Sibling Rivalry in Hollywood."

96 "I regret that I remember": Fontaine, *No Bed of Roses*, 30.

96 "a fresh young beauty": Quoted in Charles Higham, *Sisters: The Story of Olivia de Havilland and Joan Fontaine* (New York: Coward-McCann, 1984), 41.

96 "Two de Havillands on the marquee": Quoted in Scott Feinberg, "New Details About the Joan Fontaine-Olivia de Havilland Feud Revealed," *The Hollywood Reporter*, Dec. 17, 2013.

96 "the sweet closeness of our relationship": Quoted in Higham, *Sisters*, 64.

97 "Rumors of the 'feuding sisters'": Fontaine, *No Bed of Roses*, 102.

97 "Sparks flew": Fontaine, *No Bed of Roses*, 104.

97 "grave error": Fontaine, *No Bed of Roses*, 113–14.

97 "All I could do": Quoted in Stadiem, "Olivia de Havilland and the Most Notorious Sibling Rivalry in Hollywood."

98 "Would you mind if I take your sister?": Quoted in Stadiem, "Olivia de Havilland and the Most Notorious Sibling Rivalry in Hollywood."

98 "heavyset, bespectacled gentleman": Fontaine, *No Bed of Roses*, 99.

98 "Joan has always seemed": Quoted in Fontaine, *No Bed of Roses*, 114.

98 "Can you imagine": Quoted in Higham, *Sisters*, 15.

98 "For me to have won it": Fontaine, *No Bed of Roses*, 131.

99 "my movie textbook": Quoted in McBride, *Searching for John Ford*, 300.

99 "They are laying bets": Quoted in Lebo, *Citizen Kane*, 30.

99 "in pursuit of a lump sum": Quoted in Sydney Ladensohn Stern, *The Brothers Mankiewicz: Hope, Heartbreak, and Hollywood Classics* (Jackson: University Press of Mississippi, 2019), 5.

99 MILLIONS ARE TO BE GRABBED: Quoted in Lebo, *Citizen Kane*, 30.

100 The next day, Mankiewicz was midway: Ladensohn Stern, *The Brothers Mankiewicz*, 127.

100 "somewhat in the posture": Quoted in Ladensohn Stern, *The Brothers Mankiewicz*, 157.

100 "Nobody was more miserable": Quoted in Lebo, *Citizen Kane*, 32.

100 "The actual writing came": Quoted in Lebo, *Citizen Kane*, 32.

100 "a whirling pagoda": Quoted in Ladensohn Stern, *The Brothers Mankiewicz*, 161.

100 "some big American figure": Quoted in Lebo, *Citizen Kane*, 33–34.

100 "We were going to do *The Life of Dumas*": Quoted in Frank Brady, *Citizen Welles: A Biography of Orson Welles* (New York: Anchor Books, 1989), 235.

101 "You can crush a man with journalism": Quoted in Lebo, *Citizen Kane*, 218.

101 "creating a vehicle": Quoted in Ladensohn Stern, *The Brothers Mankiewicz*, 164.

101 "Herman would rather talk": Quoted in Lebo, *Citizen Kane*, 48.

102 "I wrote 'Citizen Kane'": Quoted in Louella O. Parsons, "Accident Is 'Lucky' for Orson Welles," *San Francisco Examiner*, Aug. 25, 1940.

102 "juvenile delinquent credit stealer": Quoted in Lebo, *Citizen Kane*, 54.

102 "Take the money": Quoted in Ladensohn Stern, *The Brothers Mankiewicz*, 174.

102 "The script is most like me": Quoted in Ladensohn Stern, *The Brothers Mankiewicz*, 165.

102 "I feel it my modest duty": Quoted in Lebo, *Citizen Kane*, 55.

103 "there isn't one single line": Quoted in Ladensohn Stern, *The Brothers Mankiewicz*, 182.

103 "There but for the grace of God": Quoted in Pauline Kael, "Raising Kane—I," *The New Yorker*, Feb. 20, 1971.

103 "Uncle Sam's uniform": Quoted in Theodore Strauss, "Out of the Incubator," *New York Times*, June 29, 1941.

103 "fat little Jew": Quoted in Harris, *Five Came Back*, 84.

103 "story of a hell-raising mountaineer": Quoted in Harris, *Five Came Back*, 86.

104 "Mr. Deeds Goes to War": Harris, *Five Came Back*, 84.

105 "It was Willie's intention": Davis, *The Lonely Life*, 206.

105   "Miss Davis was icy": Quoted in Sikov, *Dark Victory*, 182–83.

105   "an opportunity to, in a small way": Quoted in Harris, *Five Came Back*, 120.

105   "Inopportune to make this film now": Quoted in Harris, *Five Came Back*, 105.

105   "If this is not one of the best pictures": Quoted in Harris, *Five Came Back*, 105.

105   "That autumn morning": Fontaine, *No Bed of Roses*, 112.

106   "little goose": Quoted in Higham, *Sisters*, 113.

106   "It's my birthday": Quoted in Fontaine, *No Bed of Roses*, 136.

106   "She never knows whether to save herself": Sidney Skolsky, "Hollywood," *Cincinnati Inquirer*, Feb. 18, 1942.

107   "How's old snake-in-the-grass Eddie?": Quoted in Lebo, *Citizen Kane*, 101–2.

107   "covers the last 60 years": Quoted in Lebo, *Citizen Kane*, 97.

107   "I walked a narrow tightrope": Fontaine, *No Bed of Roses*, 165.

107   "Take my word for it": Quoted in Louella O. Parsons, *Tell It to Louella* (New York: G.P. Putnam's Sons, 1961), 131.

108   "Come tonight if you must": Quoted in Lebo, *Citizen Kane*, 182.

108   "I was appalled": Hedda Hopper, *From Under My Hat* (Garden City, NY: Doubleday, 1952), 290.

108   "Mr. Hearst, I don't know": Quoted in Parsons, *Tell It to Louella*, 131.

108   "Wait until the woman": Quoted in Lebo, *Citizen Kane*, 180.

108   "vicious lie": Quoted in Lebo, *Citizen Kane*, 184.

108   "a cruel, dishonest caricature": Parsons, *Tell It to Louella*, 131.

108   "everybody but St. Peter": Quoted in Lebo, *Citizen Kane*, 185.

109   "I don't believe in lawsuits": Quoted in Parsons, *Tell It to Louella*, 132.

109   "It looks like my throat has been cut": Quoted in Lebo, *Citizen Kane*, 186.

109   "because of his apparent lack of interest": "Welles, as 25% Owner of 'Kane,' Would 'Force' RKO to Release Pic," *Variety*, Feb. 5, 1941.

109   "Mr. Welles' appearance": Douglas W. Churchill, "Orson Welles Scares Hollywood," *New York Times*, Jan. 19, 1941.

109   "continuous shellfire": "All Film Cos. May Suffer Because of Hearst's Peeve at Welles' 'Kane,'" *Variety*, Jan. 15, 1941.

110   "Such an extraordinary suggestion": Quoted in Lebo, *Citizen Kane*, 197.

110   "Don't go back to your hotel": Quoted in Lebo, *Citizen Kane*, 209.

110   "Why not fight?": Quoted in Lebo, *Citizen Kane*, 230.

110   "If Mr. Hearst had taken his lawyer's advice": Hopper, *From Under My Hat*, 291.

111   "I believe the public is entitled": Quoted in Lebo, *Citizen Kane*, 207–8.

111   "Show it in tents": Quoted in Lebo, *Citizen Kane*, 233.

111   "it can be safely stated": Bosley Crowther, "The Screen in Review," *New York Times*, May 2, 1941.

111   "the boy who was spat upon": Quoted in Lebo, *Citizen Kane*, 236.

111   "Welles can prepare his mantel": Quoted in Kael, "Raising Kane—I."

112   "national unity in this hour": Quoted in "Tennesseans Hail York," *New York Times*, July 3, 1941.

112   "The suggestion of deliberate propaganda": Bosley Crowther, "The Screen in Review," *New York Times*, July 3, 1941.

112   "Hollywood's first solid contribution": Quoted in Harris, *Five Came Back*, 88.

112   "It may be a classic": Quoted in Lebo, *Citizen Kane*, 239.

112   The gala opening night: "Dinners Are Held Before Premiere," *New York Times*,

Oct. 29, 1941.

112   "the beauty which shines": Bosley Crowther, "A Beautiful and Affecting Film Is 'How Green Was My Valley,' at the Rivoli," *New York Times*, Oct. 29, 1941.

113   "designed to drug the reason": Quoted in Harris, *Five Came Back*, 89.

113   "groups interested in involving": Quoted in Harris, *Five Came Back*, 90.

113   "Frankly," he opened: Quoted in Harris, *Five Came Back*, 92.

113   When Nye rattled off: Harris, *Five Came Back*, 93.

113   "greatest danger": "Des Moines Speech: Delivered in Des Moines, Iowa, September 11, 1941," Charles Lindbergh: An American Aviator (website), charleslindbergh.com/americanfirst/speech.asp.

113   "I'm anti-Nazi and proud of it": Quoted in Harris, *Five Came Back*, 96.

114   "In truth," Warner said: Quoted in Harris, *Five Came Back*, 97.

114   "Let's continue to play golf": Hedda Hopper, "Hedda Hopper's Hollywood," *Los Angeles Times*, Dec. 10, 1941.

114   "Much speed will be shown": Edwin Schallert, "'Juke Box' Big Talent Source for Pictures," *Los Angeles Times*, Dec. 10, 1941.

115   "a source of pride": "Annual Reports for Year of 1941," Academy History Archive, AMPAS.

115   "Being a Jeffersonian democrat": Davis, *The Lonely Life*, 204.

115   "It's Miss Davis' talents": Virginia Wright, "Cine Matters," *Los Angeles Daily News*, Nov. 11, 1941.

115   "[T]he Golden Boy of Hollywood": "Call Off Academy Dinner but Oscars to Be Awarded 'in Keeping with Times,'" *Variety*, Dec. 24, 1941.

115   "Bette would be the last": Louella O. Parsons, "Bette Davis Quits When Annual Academy Awards Presentation Dinner Is Dropped," International News Service, *Fresno Bee*, Dec. 29, 1941.

116   This was the version: Davis, *The Lonely Life*, 205.

116   "The more I think": Hedda Hopper, "Hollywood," *Pittsburgh Press*, Dec. 29, 1941.

116   "sans orchidaceous glitter": "Will Hold Academy Dinner After All, but Nix Finery, Hoofing and Glitter," *Variety*, Feb. 4, 1942.

117   "a closely waged contest": "'Citizen Kane' Wins Award of Critics," *New York Times*, Dec. 31, 1941.

117   "This young lady": Bosley Crowther, "The Screen in Review," *New York Times*, Nov. 21, 1941.

117   IN SPITE OF AN OPERATION: Quoted in Higham, *Sisters*, 132.

118   "menace No. 1": Edwin Schallert, "We Nominate for Academy Awards," *Los Angeles Times*, Jan. 25, 1942.

118   "If he gets a substantial block": "Welles and 'Kane' Doped to Win a Flock of Oscars Next Week, but 'Valley' and 'York' (Cooper) Hot Faves Also," *Variety*, Feb. 18, 1942.

118   "worked long, hard and faithfully": Hedda Hopper, "Hollywood," *Pittsburgh Press*, Feb. 13, 1942.

118   "Of course we fight": Quoted in Louella O. Parsons, "On Hollywood," *San Francisco Examiner*, Feb. 22, 1942.

118   "But I haven't anything to wear!": Fontaine, *No Bed of Roses*, 144.

119   military radar picked up: Evan Andrews, "World War II's Bizarre 'Battle of Los Angeles,'" History.com, Feb. 23, 2017, updated May 6, 2020, history.com/news/

world-war-iis-bizarre-battle-of-los-angeles.

119 "Would it break down anyone's morale": Quoted in Jill Gerston, "Win or Lose, It's How You Look that Counts," *New York Times*, March 10, 2002.

120 "the two girls faced each other": Quoted in Wiley and Bona, *Inside Oscar*, 118.

120 "uncomfortably obvious": Quoted in Harris, *Five Came Back*, 123.

120 "We will not win this war": Quoted in "Take War to Foe, Willkie Demands," *New York Times*, Feb. 27, 1942.

120 "I haven't given up yet": Quoted in Wiley and Bona, *Inside Oscar*, 119.

121 "He thought he'd get mad": Quoted in Wiley and Bona, *Inside Oscar*, 119.

121 In his bedroom wearing a bathrobe: Ladensohn Stern, *The Brothers Mankiewicz*, 184–85.

121 "It was Sergeant Alvin York": Quoted in Wiley and Bona, *Inside Oscar*, 120.

122 "Now what had I done!": Fontaine, *No Bed of Roses*, 145–46.

122 "could have learned naturalness": Hedda Hopper, "Hedda Hopper's Hollywood," *Los Angeles Times*, March 4, 1942.

122 "If *Suspicion* had been delayed": Quoted in Wiley and Bona, *Inside Oscar*, 120–21.

122 "That Oscar can be a jinx": Fontaine, *No Bed of Roses*, 146.

123 "The Academy members had made": Kael, "Raising Kane—1."

123 "the chief topic of conversation": "Orson Welles' Near-Washout Rated Biggest Upset in Academy Stakes; 'Valley,' Cooper, Fontaine, Ford Cop," *Variety*, March 4, 1942.

123 "The fact that every mention": Thomas F. Brady, "Hollywood Soiree," *New York Times*, March 8, 1942.

123 "The members of the Academy": Kael, "Raising Kane—1."

124 The *Times* further theorized: Fox Film Corporation's *Cavalcade* won in 1934, the year before the studio's merger with Twentieth Century Pictures.

124 "Everybody was happy": Hedda Hopper, "Hedda Hopper's Hollywood," *Los Angeles Times*, March 4, 1942.

124 "Good to see Darryl": Louella O. Parsons, "Woolley Selects Anne Baxter to Play Waif in 'Pied Piper,'" *San Francisco Examiner*, Feb. 28, 1942.

125 "Will this picture help win the war?": Quoted in Koppes and Black, *Hollywood Goes to War*, 66.

125 By the end of 1943: Harris, *Five Came Back*, 287.

125 "I found the work exhilarating": Davis, *The Lonely Life*, 212.

125 "The Navy is very proud of me": Quoted in Harris, *Five Came Back*, 126.

126 "I want every mother": Quoted in Harris, *Five Came Back*, 158.

126 "turning the tremendous power": Quoted in Harris, *Five Came Back*, 204.

127 "Every contract player owed Olivia": Fontaine, *No Bed of Roses*, 129.

127 "frail, sickly child": "Joan Fontaine Film Surprise," *Oakland Tribune*, March 4, 1942.

127 "Well, it's happened": Quoted in Sidney Carroll, "Joan Wins over Olivia," *Oakland Tribune*, March 8, 1942.

128 "If you don't see us together": Quoted in Amador, *Olivia de Havilland*, 240.

128 "it seemed ridiculous to demand": Quoted in Amador, *Olivia de Havilland*, 240.

128 "It was like two little girls": Author interview with Deborah Dozier Potter, July 6, 2021.

128 "As for Olivia": Fontaine, *No Bed of Roses*, 300.

129   "I got married first": Quoted in Stadiem, "Olivia de Havilland and the Most No-
        torious Sibling Rivalry in Hollywood."

129   "Imagine," Fontaine once said: Quoted in Amador, *Olivia de Havilland*, 242.

129   "Dear Mankie": Quoted in Lebo, *Citizen Kane*, 242.

130   "Showmanship in Place of Genius": Lebo, *Citizen Kane*, 245.

130   "everything about him was oversized": Fontaine, *No Bed of Roses*, 153.

130   "I had luck as no one had": Quoted in Lebo, *Citizen Kane*, 249.

131   "Orson brings these things on himself": Quoted in Ladensohn Stern, *The Brothers
        Mankiewicz*, 187.

Four: The Greatest Star, 1951

133   Wilder's secretary locked: Maurice Zolotow, *Billy Wilder in Hollywood* (New York:
        Putnam, 1977), 156–57.

134   "We needed a passé star": Quoted in Sam Staggs, *Close-up on "Sunset Boulevard":
        Billy Wilder, Norma Desmond, and the Dark Hollywood Dream* (New York: St. Mar-
        tin's Griffin, 2002), 9.

135   "hide behind greasepaint": Quoted in Ed Sikov, *On Sunset Boulevard: The Life and
        Times of Billy Wilder* (Jackson: University Press of Mississippi, 2017), 281–82.

135   "The idea of Mae West": Quoted in Staggs, *Close-up on "Sunset Boulevard,"* 8.

135   "Mr. Brackett and I went to see her": Quoted in Staggs, *Close-up on "Sunset Bou-
        levard,"* 9.

135   "I had pneumonia": Quoted in Gregg Barrios, "Legendary Vamp Takes a Final
        Bow: Pola Negri on Her Hollywood Heydays," *Los Angeles Times*, Aug. 8, 1987.

136   "Actors We Hope to Get": Staggs, *Close-up on "Sunset Boulevard,"* 31.

136   "We knew no time": Quoted in Stanley Frank, "Grandma Gloria Swanson Comes
        Back," *Saturday Evening Post*, July 29, 1950.

136   "that terrible girl": Quoted in Sam Staggs, *All About "All About Eve": The Com-
        plete Behind-the-Scenes Story of the Bitchiest Film Ever Made* (New York: St. Mar-
        tin's Griffin, 2001), 19.

136   When a replacement was needed: Staggs, *All About "All About Eve,"* 22.

137   "It certainly became an obsession": Quoted in Staggs, *All About "All About Eve,"*
        23.

137   "I read the story": Quoted in Staggs, *All About "All About Eve,"* 322.

138   "cockamaimy immortality": Joseph L. Mankiewicz and Gary Carey, *More About
        "All About Eve"* (New York: Random House, 1972), 17.

138   "Superb starring role": Quoted in Staggs, *All About "All About Eve,"* 43.

138   "simply could not visualize": Mankiewicz and Carey, *More About "All About
        Eve,"* 69.

138   "bitch virtuosity": Mankiewicz and Carey, *More About "All About Eve,"* 70.

139   "cold potato": Quoted in Karin J. Fowler, *Anne Baxter: A Bio-Bibliography* (West-
        port, CT: Greenwood Press, 1991), 8.

139   "accompany Miss Lawrence": Mankiewicz and Carey, *More About "All About
        Eve,"* 71. Lawrence's husband Richard Aldrich said that Lawrence declined *All
        About Eve* so that she could focus on being "Mrs. A."

139   When Gloria Swanson got the call: Swanson, *Swanson on Swanson*, 491–94.

140   "cinematic obscurity": Swanson, *Swanson on Swanson*, 483.

140 "Is there anyone who can flaunt": Quoted in Swanson, *Swanson on Swanson*, 164.

140 "On the one hand": Swanson, *Swanson on Swanson*, 460.

141 "Mother, we've had a dreadful Christmas": Swanson, *Swanson on Swanson*, 494–95.

141 "Right away, right away": Davis, *The Lonely Life*, 214.

141 "those woman-you-love-to-hate roles": Bosley Crowther, "The Screen: 3 Films Have Premieres Here," *New York Times*, Feb. 16, 1951.

142 "handsome Greek God": Quoted in Staggs, *All About "All About Eve,"* 69.

142 *What drive the man has!*: Davis, *The Lonely Life*, 217.

142 "I was possessed": Davis, *The Lonely Life*, 218.

143 "resurrected me from the dead": Davis, *The Lonely Life*, 225.

143 Gazing up at the studio gates: Frank, "Grandma Gloria Swanson Comes Back."

144 "the brightest things in Hollywood": Quoted in Swanson, *Swanson on Swanson*, 496.

144 "But women of fifty": Swanson, *Swanson on Swanson*, 497–98.

145 "As inexperienced as I was": Quoted in Staggs, *Close-up on "Sunset Boulevard,"* 123.

145 "But I've got to know more": Quoted in Staggs, *Close-up on "Sunset Boulevard,"* 70.

146 "I grasped with fearful apprehension": Swanson, *Swanson on Swanson*, 498.

146 "spent the first day sitting": Quoted in Staggs, *Close-up on "Sunset Boulevard,"* 123.

146 "On high heels": Swanson, *Swanson on Swanson*, 501.

146 TO PROCLAIM THAT: Frank, "Grandma Gloria Swanson Comes Back."

147 "Oh, what am I going to do": Quoted in Staggs, *All About "All About Eve,"* 79.

147 "We never mentioned her": Quoted in Hedda Hopper, "Life Begins Anew at 40 for Bette Davis," *The Hartford Courant Magazine*, Dec. 3, 1950.

147 "He's a *real* man": Quoted in James Spada, *More than a Woman: An Intimate Biography of Bette Davis* (New York: Bantam Books, 1993), 270.

148 "twirling her around": Gary Merrill, *Bette, Rita, and the Rest of My Life* (Augusta, ME: L. Tapley, 1988), 88.

148 Over the din of the plane's engine: Staggs, *All About "All About Eve,"* 74.

148 "Everybody was showing off": Quoted in Staggs, *All About "All About Eve,"* 78.

148 "You're quite right, Mr. Merrill": Davis, *The Lonely Life*, 226.

148 "sweet bitch": Quoted in Staggs, *All About "All About Eve,"* 102.

148 "Bette upstaged Anne Baxter": Quoted in Staggs, *All About "All About Eve,"* 105.

148 "The studio tried to play": Quoted in Staggs, *All About "All About Eve,"* 104.

149 "Hollywood," she said: Quoted in Staggs, *All About "All About Eve,"* 157.

149 "Bette Davis was so rude": Quoted in Staggs, *All About "All About Eve,"* 73.

149 "I never spoke to her again": Quoted in Staggs, *All About "All About Eve,"* 88.

149 "My first feeling of compassion": Merrill, *Bette, Rita, and the Rest of My Life*, 90.

149 "It was a beautiful, tender, sweet": Quoted in Spada, *More than a Woman*, 275.

150 "In my alcoholic haze": Merrill, *Bette, Rita, and the Rest of My Life*, 91.

150 Fox hired security guards: Staggs, *All About "All About Eve,"* 137–38.

150 Mankiewicz watched closely: Mankiewicz and Carey, *More About "All About Eve,"* 86–88.

150 "Don't be silly": Quoted in Staggs, *All About "All About Eve,"* 6–7.

151 "Mr. Zanuck feels that you may turn": Quoted in Marilyn Monroe, *My Story* (New York: Stein and Day, 1974), 74.

151 "There was a breathlessness": Mankiewicz and Carey, *More About "All About Eve,"* 77.

151 "poor little thing": Quoted in Staggs, *All About "All About Eve,"* 94.

151 "eminently braless": Anne Baxter, *Intermission: A True Story* (New York: Ballantine Books, 1976), 291.

151 "She was very beautiful": George Sanders, *Memoirs of a Professional Cad* (Metuchen, NJ, and London: Scarecrow Press, 1992), 63.

151 "That woman hates every female": Quoted in Staggs, *All About "All About Eve,"* 93–94.

151 "Margo Channing was a woman": Davis, *The Lonely Life*, 227–28.

152 "No one is very happy": Quoted in Staggs, *All About "All About Eve,"* 192.

152 "Anne Baxter had been Gary's first choice": Quoted in Staggs, *All About "All About Eve,"* 118.

152 "An hour after I married him": Quoted in Staggs, *All About "All About Eve,"* 193–94.

152 "proper career": Quoted in Gary Carey, *Judy Holliday: An Intimate Life Story* (New York: Seaview Books, 1982), 133.

153 "I just sat at the switchboard": Quoted in Carey, *Judy Holliday*, 15.

153 "It was truly phenomenal": Quoted in Carey, *Judy Holliday*, 30.

154 She was escorted: Will Holtzman, *Judy Holliday* (New York: G.P. Putnam's Sons, 1982), 99–100.

155 "When do we open?": Quoted in Carey, *Judy Holliday*, 115.

155 "In that space of time": Quoted in Frank Daugherty, "A Judy with Punch," *New York Times*, Sept. 10, 1950.

156 "Judy was a big girl": Merrill, *Bette, Rita, and the Rest of My Life*, 76.

156 "On the stage you can get away": Quoted in Garson Kanin, *Tracy and Hepburn: An Intimate Memoir* (New York: Donald I. Fine, 1988), 156.

157 "I was inconsolable": Quoted in Irving Drutman, "Came the 'Dawn' for Judy Holliday," *New York Times*, Jan. 22, 1950.

157 "Well, I've worked with fat asses": Quoted in Holtzman, *Judy Holliday*, 137.

158 "Gloria made a grand entrance": Edith Head and Paddy Calistro, *Edith Head's Hollywood* (New York: Dutton, 1983), 91.

158 "These affairs are known": Swanson, *Swanson on Swanson*, 501–2.

158 "As everyone watched the film": Head and Calistro, *Edith Head's Hollywood*, 91.

158 "You bastard!": Quoted in Sikov, *On Sunset Boulevard*, 303.

159 "a pretentious slice of Roquefort": Quoted in Staggs, *Close-up on "Sunset Boulevard,"* 158.

159 "Gloria Swanson's Magnificent Comeback": Staggs, *Close-up on "Sunset Boulevard,"* 173.

159 "I was interested in it": Quoted in Hopper, "Life Begins Anew at 40 for Bette Davis."

159 "Too bad there's no way": Quoted in Staggs, *All About "All About Eve,"* 201.

159 "a withering satire": Bosley Crowther, "The Screen in Review," *New York Times*, Oct. 14, 1950.

160 "You know, Charlie": Quoted in Staggs, *Close-up on "Sunset Boulevard,"* 45.

160 "*Sunset Boulevard* and *All About Eve* being squared off": Quoted in Staggs, *Close-up on "Sunset Boulevard,"* 44.

160 "I know I cannot take this grind": Quoted in Staggs, *Close-up on "Sunset Boulevard,"* 171.

160 "Americans everywhere went purple": Swanson, *Swanson on Swanson,* 502.

161 "domination of American broadcasting": American Business Consultants, *Red Channels: The Report of Communist Influence in Radio and Television,* 1–3.

162 "You're not on one of those": Quoted in Staggs, *All About "All About Eve,"* 47.

162 "follow the Communist Party line": American Business Consultants, *Red Channels,* 202.

162 By late summer: "Miss Muir Is Ready to Deny Communism," *New York Times,* Sept. 2, 1950.

162 "There is now under way": Jack Gould, "Case of Jean Muir," *New York Times,* Sept. 3, 1950.

162 "Judy only acts dumb": Quoted in Carey, *Judy Holliday,* 137–38.

163 "Of all those who were harassed": Quoted in Carey, *Judy Holliday,* 138.

163 "It seems to me that kind of thing": Quoted in James Ulmer, "A Guild Divided," *DGA Quarterly* (Spring 2011).

163 "the most dramatic evening": Quoted in Kenneth L. Geist, *Pictures Will Talk: The Life and Films of Joseph L. Mankiewicz* (New York: Charles Scribner's Sons, 1978), 191.

164 "the most diabolically clever": Quoted in Wes D. Gehring, *Movie Comedians of the 1950s* (Jefferson: McFarland and Company, 2016), 18.

164 THE PICTURE GIVES WARMTH: Quoted in "Motion Picture Association Defends Film of 'Born Yesterday' as American in Spirit," *New York Times,* Dec. 2, 1950.

164 "if there are any pink ideas": Louella Parsons, "Stars Cast for Movie About Lotta Crabtree," *San Francisco Examiner,* Dec. 2, 1950.

164 "mass hysteria": Frank Scully, "Scully's Scrapbook," *Variety,* Dec. 20, 1950.

164 "Two films about aging actresses": "14 'Oscar' Rankings to 'All About Eve,'" *New York Times,* Feb. 13, 1951.

165 "The film, after all": Quoted in Fowler, *Anne Baxter,* 11.

165 "I've decided recently": Quoted in Staggs, *All About "All About Eve,"* 215.

166 "as if they wanted Norma Desmond": Swanson, *Swanson on Swanson,* 265.

166 "Dahling, just wait": Quoted in Staggs, *All About "All About Eve,"* 219.

166 "a wide-open race": Bob Thomas, "Oscar Race Contenders," *Baltimore Sun,* March 18, 1951.

166 On a plane bound for Los Angeles: Swanson, *Swanson on Swanson,* 262.

167 Swanson began the morning: Swanson, *Swanson on Swanson,* 264.

167 DEAR GLORIA: Quoted in Staggs, *Close-up on "Sunset Boulevard,"* 178.

167 "one of the most exciting parties": Herb Golden, "Ferrer's Oscar Tabs 3 1/2G; N.Y. Takes Play Away from Coast on Awards," *Variety,* April 4, 1951.

168 After the curtain call: Swanson, *Swanson on Swanson,* 265–66.

168 "Her beauty was so arresting": Stanley Kramer, *A Mad, Mad, Mad, Mad World: A Life in Hollywood* (New York: Harcourt Brace and Company, 1997), 184.

169 "Is it all over?": Swanson, *Swanson on Swanson,* 266.

169 "Shall we dance?": Quoted in Golden, "Ferrer's Oscar Tabs 3 1/2G."

169 "everyone wants an Oscar": Sanders, *Memoirs of a Professional Cad,* 62.

170 "What a sleazy affair": Quoted in Swanson, *Swanson on Swanson*, 267.

170 "It was a tasteless exercise": Swanson, *Swanson on Swanson*, 268.

171 "I don't even get a chance": Quoted in Carey, *Judy Holliday*, 119.

171 "Good. A newcomer got it": Quoted in Staggs, *All About "All About Eve,"* 214.

171 "Bette lost *because* Annie": Quoted in Spada, *More than a Woman*, 286.

171 "Why couldn't you have waited": Quoted in Holzman, *Judy Holliday*, 149.

171 "I hadn't thought I would be greatly affected": Swanson, *Swanson on Swanson*, 269.

171 "Would you care to make a statement": Quoted in Golden, "Ferrer's Oscar Tabs 3 1/2G."

171 "It slowly dawned on me": Swanson, *Swanson on Swanson*, 269–70.

172 "I don't know what it is": Quoted in Eyman, *Lion of Hollywood*, 432.

172 "The nationwide cry": "Good-News Awards," *Variety*, April 4, 1951.

173 "Never forget that a great many": Quoted in Staggs, *Close-up on "Sunset Boulevard,"* 182.

173 "awful imitations": Swanson, *Swanson on Swanson*, 506.

174 "I am sure I have been uncompromising": Davis, *The Lonely Life*, 245.

174 "I couldn't use the same voice": Quoted in Carey, *Judy Holliday*, 125.

174 "She didn't trust an award": Author interview with Jonathan Oppenheim, Aug. 24, 2018.

175 On March 26, 1952: Carey, *Judy Holliday*, 146–47.

Five: Who Is Robert Rich? 1947–60

178 "clear this thing up": Quoted in "'Author' of Movie Deepens Mystery," *New York Times*, April 1, 1957.

178 "trying to locate him": Quoted in "'Author' of Movie Deepens Mystery."

178 "I'd recognize him anywhere": Quoted in "Hollywood Whodunit: An Oscar, Whowonit?," *Life*, April 15, 1957.

178 "But if they used our stuff": Quoted in "Hollywood Whodunit."

179 "To date no clear proof": Quoted in Thomas M. Pryor, "Film Body Rules on 'Oscar' Winner," *New York Times*, April 12, 1957.

179 "Hey, kids, your folks around?": Quoted in Larry Ceplair and Christopher Trumbo, *Dalton Trumbo: Blacklisted Hollywood Radical* (Lexington: University Press of Kentucky, 2015), 188–89.

180 "intellectual terror": Quoted in Ceplair and Trumbo, *Dalton Trumbo*, 187.

180 "My father could be so dominant": Quoted in Ceplair and Trumbo, *Dalton Trumbo*, 4.

180 "I never considered the working class": Quoted in Victor S. Navasky, *Naming Names* (New York: Hill and Wang, 1980), 367.

180 "consanguineous societies": Quoted in Ceplair and Trumbo, *Dalton Trumbo*, 48.

181 "Communist fellow traveler": Quoted in Ceplair and Trumbo, *Dalton Trumbo*, 119.

181 "full of energy and a little drunk": Quoted in Ceplair and Trumbo, *Dalton Trumbo*, 141.

181 "Joining the Communist Party": Quoted in Ceplair and Trumbo, *Dalton Trumbo*,

132.

182 "dull beyond description": Quoted in Ceplair and Trumbo, *Dalton Trumbo*, 140.

182 "transformed Dad into a snarling": Quoted in Larry Ceplair and Steven Englund, *The Inquisition in Hollywood: Politics in the Film Community, 1930–1960* (Berkeley and Los Angeles: University of California Press, 1979), 209–10.

182 "turn off the faucets": Quoted in Ceplair and Englund, *The Inquisition in Hollywood*, 211.

182 "flagrant manner": Quoted in Ceplair and Englund, *The Inquisition in Hollywood*, 212.

182 "ominous word from Washington": Quoted in Ceplair and Trumbo, *Dalton Trumbo*, 181.

182 "There seems to be no way of confirming": Quoted in Ceplair and Trumbo, *Dalton Trumbo*, 166.

183 "Nobody can tell me how to run": Quoted in Ceplair and Englund, *The Inquisition in Hollywood*, 259.

183 "Well, I don't think there's any question": Quoted in Ceplair and Trumbo, *Dalton Trumbo*, 195.

183 Without being asked, he named: Ceplair and Englund, *The Inquisition in Hollywood*, 279–80.

183 When Trumbo's turn came: Ceplair and Trumbo, *Dalton Trumbo*, 198–200.

184 "clear its own house": Quoted in Ceplair and Trumbo, *Dalton Trumbo*, 202.

184 "People got scared": Quoted in Ceplair and Trumbo, *Dalton Trumbo*, 214.

185 "take the loss in silence": Quoted in Ceplair and Trumbo, *Dalton Trumbo*, 224.

185 "As far as I was concerned": Quoted in Ceplair and Trumbo, *Dalton Trumbo*, 228.

185 "It simply requires": Quoted in Ceplair and Trumbo, *Dalton Trumbo*, 238.

186 "a group of marooned sailors": Quoted in Glenn Frankel, *High Noon: The Hollywood Blacklist and the Making of an American Classic* (New York: Bloomsbury, 2017), 161.

186 "It was like a pall that fell over": Quoted in Rebecca Prime, *Hollywood Exiles in Europe: The Blacklist and Cold War Film Culture* (New Brunswick, NJ: Rutgers University Press, 2014), 13.

187 "Who do you suppose": Quoted in Frankel, *High Noon*, 168.

187 "the people's art": Quoted in Frankel, *High Noon*, 21.

187 "If you left the party": Quoted in Frankel, *High Noon*, 32.

187 "brooding aura": Quoted in Frankel, *High Noon*, 25.

188 "Aw, it's like any other business": Quoted in Frankel, *High Noon*, 65.

188 "It was these events": Quoted in Frankel, *High Noon*, 142–43.

189 "a picture of conscience": Quoted in Frankel, *High Noon*, 148.

189 "It was now happening to me": Quoted in Frankel, *High Noon*, 170.

189 "the lukewarm Americans": Quoted in Frankel, *High Noon*, 54.

189 "If you want to leave the picture": Quoted in Frankel, *High Noon*, 170–71.

190 "Freddy, if we let him go": Quoted in Frankel, *High Noon*, 181.

190 "I tried to explain": Quoted in Navasky, *Naming Names*, 158.

190 "depending on how the negotiations": Quoted in Navasky, *Naming Names*, 159–60.

190 "Do what you have to do": Quoted in Frankel, *High Noon*, 196.

190 On September 24, Foreman arrived: Frankel, *High Noon*, 197–99.

191 "They quit right then": Quoted in Frankel, *High Noon*, 202.

191 "My partners, you know": Quoted in Frankel, *High Noon*, 219.

191 "completely liberated": Quoted in Prime, *Hollywood Exiles in Europe*, 36.

191 "When I sat down at the typewriter": Quoted in Frankel, *High Noon*, 221.

191 "'HIGH NOON' LOOKS TO SWEEP OSCARS": Frankel, *High Noon*, 260.

191 Foreman's screenplay nomination: Frankel, *High Noon*, 261–262.

192 "I still believe *High Noon*": Kramer, *A Mad, Mad, Mad, Mad World*, 73.

192 "mortal terror of salvation": Quoted in Joel Gardner, "I Am the Sum of My Actions," Interview of Michael Wilson, UCLA Center for Oral History Research.

192 "world I wanted to shun": Quoted in Gardner, "I Am the Sum of My Actions."

192 "struggles of modern man": Quoted in Larry Ceplair, "A Marxist in Hollywood," *Historical Journal of Film, Radio and Television* 34, No. 2 (2014): 187-207.

192 "I was still a very immature": Quoted in Gardner, "I Am the Sum of My Actions."

193 "He was a positively gorgeous-looking guy": Quoted in Ceplair, "A Marxist in Hollywood."

193 "a secondary art form": Quoted in Gardner, "I Am the Sum of My Actions."

193 "We saw a lot of each other": Quoted in Ceplair and Trumbo, *Dalton Trumbo*, 138.

193 "the most aggressive, dangerous aspect": Quoted in Ceplair, "A Marxist in Hollywood."

193 "I remember him coming home": Quoted in Ceplair, "A Marxist in Hollywood."

194 "how the serenity of Quaker life": Quoted in Ceplair, "A Marxist in Hollywood."

194 "construed as being antiwar": Quoted in Joseph McBride, "A Very Good American," *Written By*, Feb. 2002.

194 "came into conflict": Quoted in Ceplair, "A Marxist in Hollywood."

194 "I have been 'laid off'": Quoted in McBride, "A Very Good American."

194 "Surely, whatever your beliefs": Quoted in McBride, "A Very Good American."

195 "I was bowled over": Quoted in McBride, "A Very Good American."

196 "He was so frightened": Quoted in Navasky, *Naming Names*, 345.

196 "heart of a socialist": Author interview with Becca Wilson and Rosanna Wilson-Farrow, Feb. 5, 2022.

196 "I had been a naughty boy": Quoted in McBride, "A Very Good American."

196 "a decision I regretted": Quoted in McBride, "A Very Good American."

197 "The illogic of the blacklist": Quoted in Joseph Dmohowski, "The 'Friendly Persuasion' (1956) Screenplay Controversy: Michael Wilson, Jessamyn West, and the Hollywood Blacklist," *Historical Journal of Film, Radio and Television* 22, No. 4 (2002).

197 "shall be ineligible": Quoted in Ceplair and Trumbo, *Dalton Trumbo*, 338.

197 "forced to keep Moses' name": Quoted in Wiley and Bona, *Inside Oscar*, 273.

197 "Since I have been released from jail": Quoted in Ceplair and Trumbo, *Dalton Trumbo*, 264.

198 "I dreamed of living in luxurious exile": Quoted in Ceplair and Trumbo, *Dalton Trumbo*, 270.

198 "Never has a man": Quoted in Ceplair and Trumbo, *Dalton Trumbo*, 281.

198 "The Trumbos, who had kept a cow": Quoted in Ceplair and Trumbo, *Dalton Trumbo*, 281.

199 "I needed a name": Quoted in Ceplair and Trumbo, *Dalton Trumbo*, 309.

199 "living out an old truism": Quoted in Ceplair and Trumbo, *Dalton Trumbo*, 282.

199 "totally revolt": Quoted in Ceplair and Trumbo, *Dalton Trumbo*, 337.

200 "defeat the blacklist by outwriting": Ceplair and Trumbo, *Dalton Trumbo*, 299.

200 "pony express": Ceplair and Trumbo, *Dalton Trumbo*, 304.

200 "The horse you refuse to feed": Quoted in Ceplair and Trumbo, *Dalton Trumbo*, 309.

200 "very simple and simply made": Quoted in Ceplair and Trumbo, *Dalton Trumbo*, 309.

200 "It has kept me happily absorbed": Dalton Trumbo, *Additional Dialogue: Letters of Dalton Trumbo, 1942–1962*, ed. Helen Manfull (New York: M. Evans and Company, 1970), 390.

200 "That it should have been voted": Quoted in Ceplair and Trumbo, *Dalton Trumbo*, 339.

200 "The weird part": Author interview with Mitzi Trumbo, Jan. 19, 2022.

201 "You see," Trumbo said later: Quoted in Ceplair and Trumbo, *Dalton Trumbo*, 340.

201 "In that way I am able": Quoted in "Hollywood Whodunit."

201 "The Academy, giddy by now": Quoted in Ceplair and Trumbo, *Dalton Trumbo*, 343–44.

202 "I choose to think of Robert Rich": Quoted in Ceplair and Trumbo, *Dalton Trumbo*, 345–46.

202 "Thereupon," Trumbo wrote his lawyer: Trumbo, *Additional Dialogue*, 408.

202 "in the most public way possible": Quoted in Ceplair and Trumbo, *Dalton Trumbo*, 349.

202 "Carl was kind of a different man": Quoted in Frankel, *High Noon*, 265.

203 When Kirk Douglas passed through town: Frankel, *High Noon*, 267.

203 "That was when I really began": Quoted in Frankel, *High Noon*, 270.

203 "I think he felt at that time": Quoted in Navasky, *Naming Names*, 357.

203 "A writer without a credit": Quoted in Ceplair and Englund, *The Inquisition in Hollywood*, 23.

203 "the Frenchman's cold, detached": Quoted in Frankel, *High Noon*, 278.

203 "magnificent screenplay": Quoted in Kevin Brownlow, *David Lean: A Biography* (London: Faber and Faber, 1996), 348.

204 "tremendous clash of wills": Quoted in Brownlow, *David Lean*, 349–50.

204 "the somewhat built-in antipathy": Quoted in Brownlow, *David Lean*, 352.

204 "it was getting a little wearing": Quoted in Brownlow, *David Lean*, 355–56.

204 "the military mentality": Quoted in Gardner, "I Am the Sum of My Actions."

204 "psychotic barbarian": Quoted in Ceplair, "A Marxist in Hollywood."

204 "a very civilized, good chap": Quoted in Brownlow, *David Lean*, 359.

205 "deal with the devil": Quoted in Frankel, *High Noon*, 271.

205 "I was opposed to the whole thing": Quoted in Navasky, *Naming Names*, 164.

205 On August 8, 1956: Frankel, *High Noon*, 273–74.

205 "Obviously there was corruption": Quoted in Navasky, *Naming Names*, 393.

206 "If anyone's going to get a credit": Quoted in Brownlow, *David Lean*, 384.

206 "very badly about seeing Boulle's name": Quoted in Brownlow, *David Lean*, 390.

206 "wicked name": Quoted in Brownlow, *David Lean*, 387.

206 "Who wrote the screenplay": "Whose 'River Kwai'?," *Newsweek*, March 24, 1958.

207   "had the good taste": Quoted in Navasky, *Naming Names*, 161.

207   "Mr. Lean, who wrote the script": Quoted in Brownlow, *David Lean*, 388.

207   "In the wildness of my distress": Quoted in Joseph Dmohowski, "'Under the Table': Michael Wilson and the Screenplay for 'The Bridge on the River Kwai,'" *Cineaste* (Spring 2009).

207   "a ridiculous scene": Quoted in Brownlow, *David Lean*, 388.

207   "some contributions by David Lean": "'Kwai' Credit Disputed," *New York Times*, March 27, 1958.

207   "All in all": Trumbo, *Additional Dialogue*, 414.

207   "After eleven years of investigation": Trumbo, *Additional Dialogue*, 415.

208   "quietly active in stimulating": Trumbo, *Additional Dialogue*, 414.

208   "totally destroy the subterranean market": Quoted in Ceplair and Trumbo, *Dalton Trumbo*, 341.

208   "the guy was warm and truthful": Quoted in Navasky, *Naming Names*, 159.

209   "I felt it was the Academy's problem": Trumbo, *Additional Dialogue*, 470.

209   "For 3 days": Trumbo, *Additional Dialogue*, 471.

209   "history hurt everybody": Trumbo, *Additional Dialogue*, 472.

209   "blast the hell out of them": Quoted in Ceplair and Trumbo, *Dalton Trumbo*, 357.

209   Trumbo's carefully stage-managed interview: Ceplair and Trumbo, *Dalton Trumbo*, 359–60.

210   "Of course not": Quoted in Ceplair and Trumbo, *Dalton Trumbo*, 361.

210   "It seems to me it will be rather difficult": Trumbo, *Additional Dialogue*, 477–79.

211   "Revocation of the Academy rule": Trumbo, *Additional Dialogue*, 481.

211   "guerrilla warfare": Trumbo, *Additional Dialogue*, 485.

211   "the quickest and most skillful writer": Quoted in Ceplair and Trumbo, *Dalton Trumbo*, 370.

211   "It's a pleasure to finally meet you": Kirk Douglas, *I Am Spartacus!: Making a Film, Breaking the Blacklist* (New York: Open Road Integrated Media, 2012), 50.

211   "The gladiator's revolt": Quoted in Ceplair and Trumbo, *Dalton Trumbo*, 372.

212   "Academy night is probably": Trumbo, *Additional Dialogue*, 428.

212   "If I rock the boat": Douglas, *I Am Spartacus!*, 117.

212   "The theme of the film": Quoted in Ceplair and Trumbo, *Dalton Trumbo*, 394.

212   "not a tragic figure": Quoted in Ceplair and Trumbo, *Dalton Trumbo*, 378.

213   "We're all Spartacus": Quoted in Ceplair and Trumbo, *Dalton Trumbo*, 379.

213   "With a good deal of affection": Quoted in Douglas, *I Am Spartacus!*, 125.

213   Kirk Douglas drove to Trumbo's house: Douglas, *I Am Spartacus!*, 126–28.

214   "had more pleasure working with Otto": Quoted in Ceplair and Trumbo, *Dalton Trumbo*, 398.

214   "naturally will get the credit": Quoted in A. H. Weiler, "Movie Maker Hires Blacklisted Writer," *New York Times*, Jan. 20, 1960.

214   "You've got to hand it to Otto": Douglas, *I Am Spartacus!*, 151.

214   "renewed invasion of American filmdom": American Legion News Service, Feb. 5, 1960.

214   "Written by Dalton Trumbo": Ceplair and Trumbo, *Dalton Trumbo*, 410.

214   "If these films are economically damaged": Trumbo, *Additional Dialogue*, 536.

215   "If Dalton Trumbo gets an Oscar": Quoted in Wiley and Bona, *Inside Oscar*, 321.

215   "Do you think he's Irish?": Quoted in Douglas, *I Am Spartacus!*, 164.

215   Michael Wilson's terms included: Ceplair, "A Marxist in Hollywood."

215   "The contrast between the legendary figure": Quoted in Brownlow, *David Lean*, 408.

216   "masterly job": Quoted in Brownlow, *David Lean*, 409.

216   "On the other hand": Quoted in Ceplair, "A Marxist in Hollywood."

216   "walked off the picture": Quoted in Brownlow, *David Lean*, 424.

216   "For the past eleven years": Quoted in Brownlow, *David Lean*, 477.

217   "get my name up there on the screen": Quoted in Ceplair and Trumbo, *Dalton Trumbo*, 446–47.

217   "one of the most frightful cinematic abortions": Quoted in Ceplair and Trumbo, *Dalton Trumbo*, 451.

218   "Oh, I know all about you": Quoted in Frankel, *High Noon*, 286.

219   "a shadow that was always there": Author interview with Jonathan Foreman, Feb. 1, 2022.

219   "Dear Pierre: Hello there": Quoted in Navasky, *Naming Names*, 328.

219   "only time a Hollywood picture": Quoted in McBride, "A Very Good American."

219   "his estimate of himself": Quoted in Ceplair and Trumbo, *Dalton Trumbo*, 559.

219   "A cold chill ran up my spine": Quoted in Aljean Harmetz, "Oscars Go to Writers for 'Kwai,'" *New York Times*, March 16, 1985.

220   "it was certainly Trumbo's story": Quoted in Ceplair and Trumbo, *Dalton Trumbo*, 570.

220   "one more dark chapter in American history": "Cleo Trumbo AMPAS 1993," ceremony, YouTube, youtube.com/watch?v=poIyAm9tT74.

Six: X, 1970

224   "At a time when the morals": Vincent Canby, "The Importance of Being Oscar," *New York Times*, April 20, 1969.

224   Movie attendance: Peter Biskind, *Easy Riders, Raging Bulls: How the Sex-Drugs-and-Rock 'N' Roll Generation Saved Hollywood* (New York: Simon and Schuster, 1998), 20.

225   "The strongest period in Hollywood": Quoted in Daniel Smith-Rowsey, *Star Actors in the Hollywood Renaissance: Representing Rough Rebels* (London: Palgrave Macmillan, 2013), 19.

225   "At that point it was too disarrayed": Author interview with Peter Bart, April 13, 2020.

226   "It was like the ground": Quoted in Biskind, *Easy Riders, Raging Bulls*, 14.

226   "Nobody had ever seen themselves": Quoted in Biskind, *Easy Riders, Raging Bulls*, 52.

226   "being young and single": Quoted in Smith-Rowsey, *Star Actors in the Hollywood Renaissance*, 19.

227   "a swarthy Pinocchio": Quoted in Smith-Rowsey, *Star Actors in the Hollywood Renaissance*, 22.

227   "It was new. It was not safe": Author interview with Dyan Cannon, April 16, 2020.

227   "a trying ritual": Steven V. Roberts, "Who (and What) Makes Oscar 'Possible'?" *New York Times*, April 14, 1969.

228   "Over-50 demographic age": Quoted in Wiley and Bona, *Inside Oscar*, 421.

228 "Many of the young stars": "The Moonchild and the Fifth Beatle," *Time*, Feb. 7, 1969.

228 "You couldn't go to a party": Quoted in Gary Fishgall, *Gregory Peck: A Biography* (New York: Scribner, 2002), 90.

229 "In that film," Harper Lee said: Quoted in Fishgall, *Gregory Peck*, 237.

230 "Peck is so grave and earnest": Vincent Canby, "Screen: 'Stalking Moon,'" *New York Times*, Jan. 23, 1969.

230 "Film turns young people on": Quoted in "Peck: Films Turning Youth On," *Hollywood Citizen-News*, May 7, 1968.

230 "somewhere in between": Quoted in "Hollywood's Reluctant No. 1 Citizen," *San Jose Mercury-News*, Dec. 7, 1969.

230 "He was very patriotic": Author interview with Stephen Peck, March 24, 2020.

230 "emphatic appeal": Folder 2682, Gregory Peck Papers, AMPAS.

231 "some bruising comments": Folder 2682, Gregory Peck Papers, AMPAS.

231 "This is not only surprising": Folder 2682, Gregory Peck Papers, AMPAS.

231 "the worst that can happen": Folder 2681, Gregory Peck Papers, AMPAS.

231 "Men in pageboy haircuts": Candice Bergen, *Knock Wood* (New York: Simon and Schuster, 1984), 135.

232 "Oh, honestly": Bergen, *Knock Wood*, 136.

232 "This is an *art film*": Bergen, *Knock Wood*, 100.

232 "golden lioness of a girl": Quoted in Bergen, *Knock Wood*, 109.

233 "Evidently the Sweet Bird of Youth": Bergen, *Knock Wood*, 139.

233 "Take that goddamned flower": Bergen, *Knock Wood*, 138.

233 "People were sitting and passing a joint": Author interview with Candice Bergen, March 20, 2020.

233 Bewildered, Bergen found the host: Bergen, *Knock Wood*, 141.

233 "I was *beyond* straight": Bergen, *Knock Wood*, 145.

233 "You waited to find Bambi": Bergen, *Knock Wood*, 146.

234 "cosmic consciousness": Quoted in "Never Put Words in Mouth of Edgar Bergen's Daughter," *Los Angeles Times*, May 5, 1968.

234 "One week it's ducks": Author interview with Bergen.

234 "Your problem is you have no soul": Quoted in Bergen, *Knock Wood*, 156.

235 "Dear Mr. Peck": Folder 2682, Gregory Peck Papers, AMPAS.

236 "a rainbow of Academy Awards": Quoted in Peter M. Brant and Tony Shafrazi, "Dennis Hopper Complete Interview," *Interview*, July 15, 2010.

237 "I come from Kansas": Quoted in Peter L. Winkler, *Dennis Hopper: The Wild Ride of a Hollywood Rebel* (Fort Lee, NJ: Barricade Books, 2011), 48.

237 "Now," Hopper recalled: Quoted in Winkler, *Dennis Hopper*, 5.

237 Hopper felt "cheated": Quoted in Winkler, *Dennis Hopper*, 44.

237 "Man, this is suicide!": Quoted in Winkler, *Dennis Hopper*, 47.

237 "a fucking idiot": Quoted in Winkler, *Dennis Hopper*, 55.

237 "Kid, there's one thing": Quoted in Winkler, *Dennis Hopper*, 57.

238 "Brooke, it's not too late": Quoted in Winkler, *Dennis Hopper*, 68.

238 *This guy is looney tunes*: Quoted in Winkler, *Dennis Hopper*, 67.

238 "We'd go to these parties": Quoted in Winkler, *Dennis Hopper*, 78.

238 "Everyone talks about making": Quoted in Winkler, *Dennis Hopper*, 85.

238 "We've gotta save the movie industry": Quoted in Winkler, *Dennis Hopper*, 87.

238 "I was into peyote": Quoted in Winkler, *Dennis Hopper*, 89.

238 "He had a three-day growth": Quoted in Biskind, *Easy Riders, Raging Bulls*, 44.

239 "You are going after fool's gold": Quoted in Biskind, *Easy Riders, Raging Bulls*, 45.

239 "Suddenly I thought, that's it": Quoted in Winkler, *Dennis Hopper*, 101.

239 Fonda called him in L.A.: Biskind, *Easy Riders, Raging Bulls*, 42.

240 "Peter, how's that motorcycle movie": Quoted in Winkler, *Dennis Hopper*, 110.

240 "This is your test": Quoted in Winkler, *Dennis Hopper*, 111.

240 Driving Hopper to the airport: Biskind, *Easy Riders, Raging Bulls*, 62.

240 "This is *my* fucking movie": Quoted in Biskind, *Easy Riders, Raging Bulls*, 63.

240 "I think you ought to take the children": Quoted in Biskind, *Easy Riders, Raging Bulls*, 64.

241 "Congratulations on the first smart move": Quoted in Winkler, *Dennis Hopper*, 96.

241 Hopper pulled a steak knife: Winkler, *Dennis Hopper*, 107–8. In 1994, Hopper claimed on *The Tonight Show* that it was *Torn* who pulled the knife on *him*. Torn sued him for defamation and won a $475,000 judgment. The judge said that Hopper was not a credible witness.

241 "an indictment of blue-collar America": Quoted in Biskind, *Easy Riders, Raging Bulls*, 68.

241 "C'mon, man": Quoted in Winkler, *Dennis Hopper*, 122.

241 "This one day he arrived": Quoted in Winkler, *Dennis Hopper*, 123.

242 "You've ruined my film": Quoted in Biskind, *Easy Riders, Raging Bulls*, 72.

242 "What's Bert doin'": Quoted in Biskind, *Easy Riders, Raging Bulls*, 73.

242 "This is faggot stuff": Quoted in Peter Biskind, "Midnight Revolution," *Vanity Fair*, March 2005.

243 "infantile need for touch": *Waldo Salt: The Screenwriter's Journey*, dir. Eugene Corr and Robert Hillman (PBS, 1990).

243 "I made you a star": Quoted in Biskind, "Midnight Revolution."

244 "counterculture bandwagon": Author interview with Jennifer Salt, April 7, 2020.

244 "We sat there up in the balcony": Author interview with Bob Balaban, April 10, 2020.

244 "My first film of any consequence": Author interview with Brenda Vaccaro, April 7, 2020.

245 "We had a lot of problems": Author interview with Michael Childers, April 23, 2020.

245 "it hit us": Quoted in Biskind, "Midnight Revolution."

245 "like a six-day bacchanal": Biskind, "Midnight Revolution."

246 "What will they say about this?": BAFTA Los Angeles celebration of John Schlesinger, 2002, from *Midnight Cowboy*, 1969, Criterion edition.

246 "It's America today": Quoted in Joyce Haber, "Peter Fonda Upset over Family Story," *New York Times*, May 12, 1969.

246 "a style of a New Hollywood": Quoted in Biskind, *Easy Riders, Raging Bulls*, 74.

246 "a ballad of joy and sorrow": Vincent Canby, "For Neo-Adults Only," *New York Times*, July 27, 1969.

246 "If there's any justice": Quoted in Kevin Thomas, "Nicholson Leaves Obscurity in Dust," *Los Angeles Times*, Aug. 28, 1969.

246 "We were living in a society": Quoted in Winkler, *Dennis Hopper*, 130.

247   "Bert's father, Abe Schneider": Quoted in Winkler, *Dennis Hopper*, 128.

247   "The quality was there": Quoted in Glenn Frankel, *Shooting "Midnight Cowboy": Art, Sex, Loneliness, Liberation, and the Making of a Dark Classic* (New York: Farrar, Straus and Giroux, 2021), 266.

248   "It's not a movie for the ages": Vincent Canby, "Film: 'Midnight Cowboy,'" *New York Times*, May 26, 1969.

248   "As the old moguls": Quoted in Kevin Thomas, "John Schlesinger—English Film Director Looks at U.S.," *Los Angeles Times*, June 29, 1969.

248   "Candice said, 'While you were all downstairs'": Author interview with Elliott Gould, March 26, 2020.

249   "It could have been *me!*": Bergen, *Knock Wood*, 159–60.

249   "I am most anxious": Folder 2683, Gregory Peck Papers, AMPAS.

249   "He spent a year in almost terror": Author interview with Carey Peck, May 2, 2020.

250   "Dear Mr. Peck": Folder 2684, Gregory Peck Papers, AMPAS.

251   "We have checked all of the sponsorship cards": Folder 2684, Gregory Peck Papers, AMPAS.

251   "I urge you to accept": Folder 2684, Gregory Peck Papers, AMPAS.

252   Peck "stressed the importance": Folder 2722, Gregory Peck Papers, AMPAS.

252   "I used to be able to tell": Quoted in Paul E. Steiger, "Movie Makers No Longer Sure What Sparkle Is," *Los Angeles Times*, Nov. 17, 1969.

252   "The movies entered the 60s": Charles Champlin, "The 1960s: A Revolution in Movie Audiences," *Los Angeles Times*, Jan. 18, 1970.

253   "The Oscars are some sort of masturbatory fantasy": Quoted in Wiley and Bona, *Inside Oscar*, 434.

253   "If I get an Oscar": Quoted in Rex Reed, "The Man Who Walked Off with 'Easy Rider,'" *New York Times*, March 1, 1970.

253   "How in the hell": Quoted in Wiley and Bona, *Inside Oscar*, 435.

254   "*Midnight Cowboy* is a terrific movie": Quoted in Biskind, "Midnight Revolution."

254   seemed "somehow an inadequate reflection": Charles Champlin, "Some Oscars for Oscarless of Filmdom," *Los Angeles Times*, Feb. 24, 1970.

254   "save-the-town sentiment": Quoted in Charles Champlin, "Oscar Awards Ritual: End of an Era," *Los Angeles Times*, April 12, 1970.

254   "sluggish dullard of a film": John Simon, "Oscars: They Shun the Best, Don't They?" *New York Times*, March 1, 1970.

255   "hungry Cassius": "Movie Mailbag: What Makes Simon Snicker?," *New York Times*, April 5, 1970.

255   "no less than four Gregory Peck performances": Vincent Canby, "Films of 1969," *New York Times*, Jan. 4, 1970.

255   high-stakes mission: Marc Eliot, *Cary Grant: A Biography* (New York: Three Rivers Press, 2004), 11–17.

258   "We reached each other in the middle": Quoted in Biskind, "Midnight Revolution."

259   "Never again will Hollywood": *Forty-Second Academy Awards*, Dorothy Chandler Pavilion, Academy of Motion Picture Arts and Sciences, aired April 7, 1970.

259   "The evening," Charles Champlin wrote: Charles Champlin, "Oscar Awards Rit-

ual: End of an Era."

260 "he took one look at me": Quoted in Guy Flatley, ". . . D-e-n-n-i-s H-o-p-p-e-r!" *New York Times*, Oct. 18, 1970.

260 "She didn't have to agree": Quoted in Shirley Eder, "John Wayne Relaxes After Oscar Rites," *Philadelphia Inquirer*, April 13, 1970.

260 "a just determination": Quoted in Charles Champlin, "335 Members Lose Oscar Voting Rights," *Los Angeles Times*, April 11, 1970.

260 As one headline put it: "Stodgy Old Oscar Gets a Facelift," Associated Press, May 27, 1970.

260 "actively engaged": Folder 2736, Gregory Peck Papers, AMPAS.

261 "To be an idol": Quoted in Dorothy Manners, "The New Kind of Stars," *San Francisco Examiner*, Oct. 12, 1970.

262 "blindly American": Quoted in Flatley, ". . . D-e-n-n-i-s H-o-p-p-e-r!"

262 "So I don't know": Quoted in Rex Reed, "Jane: 'Everybody Expected Me to Fall on My Face,'" *New York Times*, Jan. 25, 1970.

262 "If you want to know": Quoted in Guy Flatley, "Henry Fonda Takes Aim at . . . ," *New York Times*, Oct. 18, 1970.

262 "Henry Fonda said I was an idiot?": Quoted in Flatley, ". . . D-e-n-n-i-s H-o-p-p-e-r!"

262 Things went downhill: Alix Jeffry, "A Gigantic Ego Trip for Dennis Hopper?" *New York Times*, May 10, 1970.

263 "Man, the movies are coming": Quoted in Brad Darrach, "The Easy Rider Runs Wild," *Life*, June 19, 1970.

263 "He got a priest defrocked": Quoted in Winkler, *Dennis Hopper*, 146–47.

263 "one long sex-and-drugs orgy": Quoted in Winkler, *Dennis Hopper*, 147.

263 "Florence Nightingale instinct": Quoted in Winkler, *Dennis Hopper*, 166.

263 "after *days* of abuse": Quoted in Winkler, *Dennis Hopper*, 168.

263 "They sure named this movie right": Quoted in Biskind, *Easy Riders, Raging Bulls*, 134.

263 "That sound you hear": Stefan Kanfer, "Cinema: From Adolescent to Puerile," *Time*, Oct. 18, 1971.

263 "I had final cut": Quoted in Winkler, *Dennis Hopper*, 176.

264 "de-condition": Quoted in Maggie Paley, "Activist Actress Candice Bergen," *Life*, July 24, 1970.

264 "that producer fellow": Quoted in Bergen, *Knock Wood*, 216.

264 "The difference between you and me": Quoted in Bergen, *Knock Wood*, 213–14.

265 "bourgeois concept": Quoted in Bergen, *Knock Wood*, 217.

265 "the only realistic base": Quoted in Bergen, *Knock Wood*, 209–10.

266 "The Academy is only two or three years": Quoted in Wiley and Bona, *Inside Oscar*, 453.

266 "mostly as a glum reminder": Charles Champlin, "Peck Plays Ex-Convict in 'Shoot,'" *Los Angeles Times*, Aug. 26, 1971.

266 "It was humiliating": Quoted in Fishgall, *Gregory Peck*, 275.

266 "a bit overage": Quoted in Fishgall, *Gregory Peck*, 278.

267 "This film must be distributed": Quoted in Fishgall, *Gregory Peck*, 280.

267 "All things considered": Quoted in Fishgall, *Gregory Peck*, 280.

Seven: Running the Asylum, 1976

270 Between 1964 and 1974: Pew Research Center, "Trust in Government: 1958–2015," in *Beyond Trust: How Americans View Their Government*, Report, Pew Research Center, Nov. 23, 2015, people-press.org/2015/11/23/1-trust-in-government-1958-2015.

271 "Patients straggled by": Ken Kesey, *One Flew Over the Cuckoo's Nest* (New York: Penguin Classics, 2002), vii.

271 "He began to wonder": "Kesey's 'Cuckoo's Nest' Still Flying At 50," *All Things Considered*, NPR, Feb. 1, 2012.

272 "It was a great character for him": Author interview with Michael Douglas, May 14, 2018. This and other interviews about *Cuckoo's Nest* were originally conducted for "Resident Evil," *Vanity Fair*, Aug. 2018.

272 "I was off on life's great adventure": Author interview with Keith Carradine, Oct. 21, 2018.

273 "bombastic-rebel, bomb-thrower": Quoted in Biskind, *Easy Riders, Raging Bulls*, 88.

273 "A 'through these portals . . .'": Author interview with Alan Rudolph, Nov. 12, 2018.

273 "When I heard them": Quoted in Jan Stuart, *The "Nashville" Chronicles: The Making of Robert Altman's Masterpiece* (New York: Simon and Schuster, 2000), 37.

274 "He fascinates me": Quoted in Vincent LoBrutto, *Stanley Kubrick: A Biography* (New York: Donald L. Fine Books, 1997), 322.

274 "two golden eagles": Quoted in John Baxter, *Stanley Kubrick: A Biography* (New York: Carroll and Graf Publishers, 1997), 236–37.

274 "Most people don't realize": Quoted in Baxter, *Stanley Kubrick*, 238.

274 "This is how Napoléon used to eat": Quoted in Baxter, *Stanley Kubrick*, 236.

274 "a vampire on people's brains": Quoted in Baxter, *Stanley Kubrick*, 238–39.

274 the director "Napoleonized" him: LoBrutto, *Stanley Kubrick*, 332.

275 "I plan to do *Napoleon* next": Quoted in LoBrutto, *Stanley Kubrick*, 332.

275 Shortly before 3 p.m.: Details of the robbery from P. F. Kluge and Thomas Moore, "The Boys in the Bank," *Life*, Sept. 22, 1972; and from *The Dog*, dir., Allison Berg and Frank Keraudren (Drafthouse Films, 2013). The surname of Wojtowicz's accomplice has been reported as both "Naturile" and "Naturale."

277 "vividly dramatized": Miloš Forman and Jan Novák, *Turnaround: A Memoir* (New York: Villard Books, 1994), 204.

277 "Mr. Forman, aren't you a real son of a bitch?": Quoted in Forman and Novák, *Turnaround*, 205.

278 "I thought about her": Author interview with Bo Goldman, Feb. 12, 2018.

278 "He was always very friendly": Forman and Novák, *Turnaround*, 209.

278 "In the book," Forman recalled: Forman and Novák, *Turnaround*, 211.

279 "It was a movie script!": Quoted in Stuart, *The "Nashville" Chronicles*, 39.

279 "Do you know anything": Author interview with Joan Tewkesbury, Oct. 12, 2018.

280 "Nashville to me is like Hollywood": Quoted in Eugene Wyatt, "What I Consider America Is Today," *Tennessean*, June 6, 1975.

280 "Assassination has become acceptable": Quoted in Bruce Williamson, "Playboy Interview: Robert Altman," *Playboy*, Aug. 1976.

280 The two men faced off: Biskind, *Easy Riders, Raging Bulls*, 215.

281 "I want to be the Cecil B. DeMille": Quoted in Joseph McBride, *Steven Spielberg: A Biography* (Jackson: University Press of Mississippi, 2010), 13.

281 It played one night: McBride, *Steven Spielberg*, 12.

281 "wimp in a world of jocks": Quoted in Michael Sragow, "A Conversation with Steven Spielberg," *Rolling Stone*, July 22, 1982.

281 "Every day for three months": Quoted in Molly Haskell, *Steven Spielberg: A Life in Films* (New Haven, CT: Yale University Press, 2017), 37.

281 "I don't want to make films like Antonioni": Quoted in McBride, *Steven Spielberg*, 155.

282 "It was very mature work": Author interview with Sidney Sheinberg, Nov. 16, 2018.

282 "one of the most phenomenal": Pauline Kael, "The Current Cinema: Sugarland and Badlands," *The New Yorker*, March 18, 1974.

282 "I want these people to be people": Quoted in Biskind, *Easy Riders, Raging Bulls*, 262–63.

282 "I can make something of this": Quoted in McBride, *Steven Spielberg*, 230.

283 "Who wants to be known": Quoted in Carl Gottlieb, *The "Jaws" Log* (New York: First Newmarket Press for It Books, 2012), 30.

283 "I wanted to do *Jaws*": Quoted in "Summer of the Shark," *Time*, June 23, 1975.

283 "like having immigrant parents": Author interview with Louise Fletcher, April 20, 2018.

284 "I slowly started to realize": *Completely Cuckoo*, dir. Charles Kiselyak (Quest Productions, Warner Home Video, 1997).

285 "man's folly": Author interview with Leon Vitali, Oct. 25, 2018.

285 a hundred ballrooms: Baxter, *Stanley Kubrick*, 283.

285 "Have the art department": Quoted in LoBrutto, *Stanley Kubrick*, 383.

285 "He was like a very strict headmaster": Author interview with Gay Hamilton, Nov. 15, 2018.

286 "Two men arrived": Author interview with Jan Harlan, Nov. 16, 2018.

287 "If we do our jobs right": Author interview with Carl Gottlieb, Oct. 29, 2018.

287 "my heart bled": Gottlieb, *The "Jaws" Log*, 61.

287 "bears a passing resemblance": Gottlieb, *The "Jaws" Log*, 62.

288 "I'd rather just watch it": *The Making of "Jaws,"* dir. Laurent Bouzereau, (Universal Home Video, 1995).

288 "drinks and dinner and consciousness-raising": Gottlieb, *The "Jaws" Log*, 67.

288 "a boisterous three-hundred-pound child": Gottlieb, *The "Jaws" Log*, 75.

288 "We had all the executives there": Author interview with Joseph Alves, Nov. 18, 2018.

288 "like a wake": Quoted in "Summer of the Shark," *Time*.

288 "What happened in May": Quoted in Nancy Griffin, "In the Grip of 'Jaws,'" *Premiere*, Oct. 1995.

288 "I just went back to Alfred Hitchcock": *The Making of "Jaws."*

289 "More than anything I want": Quoted in Stuart, *The "Nashville" Chronicles*, 25.

289   "All right, I put all my money": Author interview with Michael Murphy, Oct. 19, 2018.

289   "I would try anything": Quoted in Stuart, *The "Nashville" Chronicles*, 216–17.

289   "I admire Kubrick": Quoted in Williamson, "Playboy Interview: Robert Altman."

290   "I don't think Linnea": Quoted in Stuart, *The "Nashville" Chronicles*, 253.

290   "I left the screening early": Quoted in Stuart, *The "Nashville" Chronicles*, 242.

291   "Look at what you've done": Quoted in Stuart, *The "Nashville" Chronicles*, 205.

291   *Jaws* author Peter Benchley: McBride, *Steven Spielberg*, 239.

291   "like a 26-foot turd": Quoted in Griffin, "In the Grip of 'Jaws.'"

291   "Dreyfuss would say, 'What am I doing'": *The Making of "Jaws."*

292   "I would give anything": Quoted in Griffin, "In the Grip of 'Jaws.'"

292   When Universal's Sid Sheinberg visited: McBride, *Steven Spielberg*, 244–45.

292   "I thought my career as a filmmaker": Quoted in McBride, *Steven Spielberg*, 242.

292   "sitting morose and alone": Gottlieb, *The "Jaws" Log*, 153.

292   Out at sea one day: Gottlieb, *The "Jaws" Log*, 165–66.

292   "I feel like an old man": Quoted in William Wolf, "Boy-Wonder Director Sinks His Teeth into Shark-Scare Film 'Jaws,'" *Cue*, Aug. 12, 1974.

293   "I shall *not return!*": Quoted in Gottlieb, *The "Jaws" Log*, 173.

293   "Hell, no. I don't want no movie": *The Dog.*

293   "Love is a very strange thing": *The Dog.*

293   "a guy who imagines": *The Making of "Dog Day Afternoon,"* dir. Laurent Bouzereau (Warner Bros. Entertainment, 2006).

293   "A utopian city": Sidney Lumet, *Sidney Lumet: Interviews*, ed. Joanna E. Rapf. (Jackson: University Press of Mississippi, 2006), 87.

294   "I had just done *Godfather II*": Quoted in Lawrence Grobel, *Al Pacino in Conversation with Lawrence Grobel* (London: Simon and Schuster, 2006), 30.

294   "Freaks are not the freaks": Sidney Lumet, *Making Movies* (New York: Vintage Books, 1995), 14.

294   "A little less Blanche DuBois": Author interview with Chris Sarandon, Nov. 13, 2018.

295   "You two know each other": Lumet, *Making Movies*, 112.

295   "My part of the crowd": Author interview with Lionel Pina, Nov. 2, 2018.

295   "Al was a star": Author interview with Carol Kane, Nov. 9, 2018.

295   "Sidney would tell us stories": Author interview with Marcia Jean Kurtz, Nov. 2, 2018.

296   "The first show was dynamite": Gottlieb, *The "Jaws" Log*, 184.

296   "It was that moment": Quoted in Tom Shone, *Blockbuster: How Hollywood Learned to Stop Worrying and Love the Summer* (New York: Free Press, 2004), 24.

296   "too primitive": Quoted in McBride, *Steven Spielberg*, 253.

296   "I have a four-scream movie": Quoted in McBride, *Steven Spielberg*, 254.

296   After the Long Beach screening: Shone, *Blockbuster*, 26.

297   "the use and misuse of power": *American Icons: "One Flew Over the Cuckoo's Nest,"* Studio 360, WNYC Studios, Sept. 20, 2013.

297   "I would go up to the maximum-security": Author interview with Christopher Lloyd, Feb. 25, 2018.

297   "It was rather striking": Author interview with Brad Dourif, Feb. 22, 2018.

298 "The director had something in mind": Author interview with Bill Butler, Nov. 12, 2018.

298 "Come on, now. Eat up": Quoted in Aljean Harmetz, "The Nurse Who Rules the 'Cuckoo's Nest,'" *New York Times*, Nov. 30, 1975.

298 "At one point, some grip": Author interview with Anjelica Huston, Feb. 16, 2018.

299 "This is my picture": Quoted in Stuart, *The "Nashville" Chronicles*, 277.

299 "I can take things when they are good": Quoted in Stuart, *The "Nashville" Chronicles*, 277.

300 "Mind if I ask you a few questions?": Quoted in Stuart, *The "Nashville" Chronicles*, 278.

300 "My job is to show *him*": Quoted in Brian Kellow, *Pauline Kael: A Life in the Dark* (New York: Penguin, 2011), 91.

300 "After I saw it": Quoted in Stuart, *The "Nashville" Chronicles*, 280.

300 "I've never before seen a movie": Pauline Kael, "The Current Cinema—Coming: 'Nashville,'" *The New Yorker*, March 3, 1975.

300 "If one can review a film": Vincent Canby, "Film View: On Reviewing Films Before They're Finished," *New York Times*, March 9, 1975.

301 "that rarest thing in contemporary movies": Charles Michener with Martin Kasindorf, "Altman's Opry Land Epic," *Newsweek*, June 30, 1975.

301 "I don't think it said the truth": Quoted in "Nashville Watches 'Nashville'—And Comes Away Puzzled," *Tennessean*, Aug. 9, 1975.

301 "I'd rather see *Bambi*": Quoted in George Vecsey, "Nashville Has Mixed Feeling on 'Nashville,'" *New York Times*, Aug. 10, 1975.

301 More than half went to radio: "Ripping Response to Jaws," *The Hollywood Reporter*, June 26, 1975.

301 "hit right in the old collective unconscious": "Summer of the Shark," *Time*.

302 "I'm afraid the movie": Quoted in Bob Lardine, "For Disaster Lovers, the Summer of the Shark," (New York) *Sunday News*, April 6, 1975.

302 "sharklate" and "jawberry": McBride, *Steven Spielberg*, 255.

302 "the compulsory topic at parties": "The Shark Has Pearly False Teeth, Dear," *Christian Science Monitor*, Aug. 18, 1975.

302 "open season for Freudian sleuths": Haskell, *Steven Spielberg*, 63.

302 "my metaphor for America": Michener and Kasindorf, "Altman's Opry Land Epic."

302 "we didn't have King Kong": Quoted in Williamson, "Playboy Interview: Robert Altman."

302 "We talked for about a half hour": Lumet, *Making Movies*, 164.

303 "gaudy street-carnival of a movie": Vincent Canby, "Screen: Lumet's 'Dog Day Afternoon,'" *New York Times*, Sept. 22, 1975.

303 "the picture to beat": Gary Arnold, "A Gritty and Gripping 'Dog Day Afternoon,'" *Washington Post*, Oct. 15, 1975.

303 "one of the most satisfying": Pauline Kael, *When the Lights Go Down* (New York: Holt, Rinehart and Winston, 1980), 198–99.

303 "If you don't show this in the prison": *The Dog*.

303 In a long and self-contradicting letter: The *Times* editor declined to publish the letter, telling Wojtowicz, "I just don't believe you have profoundly come to grips

with the motives for your crime, and the complex relationship between art and reality." It was published instead in the Summer/Fall 1976 issue of *Gay Sunshine: A Journal of Gay Liberation* and reprinted in *Jump Cut* in July 1977, under the headline "Real 'Dog Day' Hero Tells His Story."

304 "a powerful, smashingly effective movie": Pauline Kael, "The Current Cinema: The Bull Goose Loony," *The New Yorker*, Dec. 1, 1975.

304 "breaking our verbal agreement": Les Ledbetter, "Kesey, at Oregon Farm, Mulls over Screen Rights," *New York Times*, March 31, 1976.

304 "go through the roof": Quoted in Baxter, *Stanley Kubrick*, 292.

304 "It would make no sense": Quoted in Martha Duffy and Richard Schickel, "Kubrick's Grandest Gamble," *Time*, Dec. 15, 1975.

305 "a coffee-table movie": Pauline Kael, "The Current Cinema: Kubrick's Gilded Age," *The New Yorker*, Dec. 19, 1975.

305 "an egocentric film": Jerry Oster, "What's Wrong with the Movies," (New York) *Sunday News*, Dec. 21, 1975.

305 *The Harvard Lampoon*: "'Barry Lyndon' Caught on Lampoon's Spear," United Press International, May 20, 1976.

305 "I fucking knew it": Author interview with Christiane Kubrick, Nov. 19, 2018.

305 "luxurious, like sinking": Vincent Canby, "Kubrick's 'Barry Lyndon' Is Brilliant in Its Images," *New York Times*, Dec. 19, 1975.

306 *"Jaws* is about to be nominated": *TVTV Looks at the Academy Awards*, aired April 8, 1976, Top Value Television.

306 "I want to be the first": Quoted in McBride, *Steven Spielberg*, 256.

306 "The odds lengthen": Charles Champlin, "The Oscar Contenders: A Preguessing Game," *Los Angeles Times*, Jan. 11, 1976.

307 "New York primary": Quoted in Williamson, "Playboy Interview: Robert Altman."

307 "the destructive effect": Quoted in Stuart, *The "Nashville" Chronicles*, 302–3.

307 "How fabulous!": *TVTV Looks at the Academy Awards*.

308 "The old rule": Forman and Novák, *Turnaround*, 222.

308 "We'd rather see *Jaws*": *TVTV Looks at the Academy Awards*.

309 "It is not a Hollywood movie": Quoted in Wyatt, "'Nashville' Garners Top Honors in New York Critics' Awards."

309 "True love inspired it": Quoted in Ralph Kaminsky, "Academy Awards Sidelights," *Boxoffice*, April 5, 1976.

310 "We went back to the set": *The Making of "Dog Day Afternoon."*

310 "I don't want to do this anymore": Author interview with Douglas.

310 "I could feel the nerves": Forman and Novák, *Turnaround*, 225.

311 "been out there a while": Quoted in Grobel, *Al Pacino in Conversation with Lawrence Grobel*, 41.

311 "a goulash of impressions": Forman and Novák, *Turnaround*, 224–25.

312 "Any one of them could have thanked me": Quoted in Ledbetter, "Kesey, at Oregon Farm, Mulls over Screen Rights."

313 WELCOME TO THE CLUB: Quoted in Forman and Novák, *Turnaround*, 225.

313 "Well, the Academy is a private club": Quoted in Williamson, "Playboy Interview: Robert Altman."

313 "What do you mean, 'responsible'?": Quoted in Mitchell Zuckoff, *Altman: The Oral Biography* (New York: Alfred A. Knopf, 2009), 289.

313 "I have nothing against Lily Tomlin": Quoted in Guy Flatley, "At the Movies," *New York Times*, Aug. 27, 1976. Altman and Fletcher reconciled in 1992, when he cast her in *The Player*.

314 When a television reporter chided him: *The Dog*.

314 "I think Steven Spielberg will endure": Quoted in Williamson, "Playboy Interview: Robert Altman."

314 "a free ticket for half a dozen rides": Quoted in McBride, *Steven Spielberg*, 259.

Eight: Fiasco, 1989

318 "parched, drab and leaden": Howard Rosenberg, "A Night with All the Excitement of an Envelope Opening," *Los Angeles Times*, April 12, 1988.

318 "a serious identity crisis": Janet Maslin, "An Identity Crisis for the Oscars," *New York Times*, April 13, 1988.

319 "I wish the next guy luck": Quoted in "Academy Awards Regains Its TV Audience," Associated Press, April 13, 1988.

319 "He reveled in the lore": Author interview with Bruce Vilanch, July 8, 2020.

319 "It used to be the laundry room": Author interview with Don Blanton, July 14, 2020.

320 "I want to bring glamour back to Hollywood": Quoted in Robert Hofler, *Party Animals: A Hollywood Tale of Sex, Drugs, and Rock 'N' Roll Starring the Fabulous Allan Carr* (Cambridge, MA: Da Capo Press, 2010), 6.

320 "I went into the kitchen": Author interview with Gary Pudney, July 15, 2020.

321 "Everyone should take their clothes off": Quoted in Hofler, *Party Animals*, 13.

321 "We'd go to Allan's": Quoted in Hofler, *Party Animals*, 8–9.

321 "There was everyone from Rod's band": Author interview with Alana Stewart, July 28, 2020.

321 "This scene, it's hilarious": Author interview with Vilanch.

321 "He named a theater after himself": Quoted in Aljean Harmetz, "'Orchestrating' Academy Awards," *New York Times*, April 1, 1978.

322 "Many stars took part in that show": Quoted in John Culhane, "For Oscar's Producer, the Key Is C," *New York Times*, March 26, 1989.

322 "At home I was secure": Quoted in Hofler, *Party Animals*, 55.

322 "I don't want to be rude": Quoted in Hofler, *Party Animals*, 61.

323 "I was like a career doctor": *The Fabulous Allan Carr*, dir. Jeffrey Schwarz (Automat Pictures, 2017).

323 "I hit California at just the right time": Quoted in Hofler, *Party Animals*, 91.

323 "Columbia doesn't have a clue": Quoted in Hofler, *Party Animals*, 17.

323 "black tie or glitter funk": Hofler, *Party Animals*, 21.

324 "I have more enthusiasm for the Academy Awards": Quoted in Harmetz, "'Orchestrating' Academy Awards."

324 "frankly a little disappointed": Quoted in Paul Rosenfield, "The Oscar Show and the Exercise of Power," *Los Angeles Times*, March 30, 1989.

324 "I want you to keep this six months": Quoted in Hofler, *Party Animals*, 89.

325 "If you can explain to me *Apocalypse Now*": *The Fabulous Allan Carr*.

325 "like I was the president of my class": Quoted in Hofler, *Party Animals*, 73.

325 "I'm thrilled when Gregory Peck and his wife": *The Fabulous Allan Carr*.

325 "tasteful minor extravaganza": Quoted in Hofler, *Party Animals*, 171.

326 "He was just really horrible with the drinking": Author interview with Tony Lutz, July 9, 2020.

326 "my *Gandhi*": Quoted in Hofler, *Party Animals*, 192.

326 "Allan was a showman": Author interview with Richard Kahn, Aug. 3, 2020.

326 "I want to bring glamour back": Quoted in Hofler, *Party Animals*, 200.

326 "But they're coming here to talk business": Quoted in Hofler, *Party Animals*, 206.

327 "What kind of water would you like?": Author interview with Vilanch.

327 "This will be a nice thing to do": Quoted in Hofler, *Party Animals*, 200.

327 "Allan told me that this was a dream come true": Author interview with Jeff Margolis, July 17, 2020.

328 "Women watch the Oscar show": Quoted in Hofler, *Party Animals*, 200.

328 "The fashions have gotten boring": Quoted in Hofler, *Party Animals*, 201.

328 "Edith is dead, and it shows": Quoted in Rosenfield, "The Oscar Show and the Exercise of Power."

328 "The designers weren't eager to loan": Quoted in Hofler, *Party Animals*, 211–12.

328 "has some of the Academy's conservatives edgy": Quoted in Hofler, *Party Animals*, 203.

328 "We don't need a host": Quoted in Hofler, *Party Animals*, 207.

329 There were only three nominated that year: Hofler, *Party Animals*, 207.

329 "We listened to it": Author interview with John Hamlin, July 30, 2020.

330 "The first thing people will see": Quoted in Rosenfield, "The Oscar Show and the Exercise of Power."

331 "Then get her a fucking dog sitter!": Quoted in Hofler, *Party Animals*, 216.

331 "We're on her side": Quoted in Rosenfield, "The Oscar Show and the Exercise of Power."

331 "For some reason, Lana doesn't want to take part": Quoted in Marilyn Beck, "Hollywood: Turner Turns Down Oscar Show," *Press Democrat*, Jan. 5, 1989.

331 "I'm going to shock people": Quoted in "Producer Hopes to Revive Oscar Magic," Associated Press, March 16, 1989.

332 "I'm not doing the show here": Quoted in Steve Pond, *The Big Show: High Times and Dirty Dealings Backstage at the Academy Awards* (New York: Faber and Faber, 2005), 5.

333 "Hooray for Nepotism!": Kevin Koffler, "Carr Puts Oscar Spotlight on the New Hollywood," *Los Angeles Herald-Examiner*, Mar. 22, 1989.

333 "Instinctively, it just felt like something": Author interview with Chad Lowe, July 21, 2020.

333 "We immediately would form little cliques": Author interview with Keith Coogan, July 7, 2020.

333 "He was like Fred Astaire": Author interview with Ricki Lake, Aug. 4, 2020.

333 "I was very new to the business": Author interview with Blair Underwood, July 13, 2020.

333 "This generation sees Oscar in a different way": Quoted in Rosenfield, "The Oscar Show and the Exercise of Power."

334   "CAA's goal": Michael Ovitz, *Who Is Michael Ovitz?* (New York: Portfolio/Penguin, 2018), 10.

334   "The script had no sex": Ovitz, *Who Is Michael Ovitz?*, 11.

334   "was that the project was CAA packaging run amok": Ovitz, *Who Is Michael Ovitz?*, 12.

335   "It will be shorter than *Lawrence of Arabia*": Quoted in "Some Nerves, Some Laughs at Annual Oscars Luncheon," Associated Press, March 22, 1989.

335   "asking me to please see what I could do": Author interview with Nikki Haskell, July 10, 2020.

335   "I don't think he's a member of the Screen Actors Guild": Quoted in Claudia Puig, "Judge Awaits Verdict on Oscar Tickets," *Los Angeles Times*, March 23, 1989.

335   "He called on my car phone": Author interview with Robert Newman, July 11, 2020.

335   "For three weeks you are the most powerful person": Quoted in Rosenfield, "The Oscar Show and the Exercise of Power."

335   "Right now I think the show is a triple": Quoted in Alan Mirabella, "Some Enchanted Evening," (New York) *Daily News*, March 29, 1989.

335   "no more sense of business or money": Quoted in Nancy Churnin, "A Real Cinderella Story for a Real Snow White," *Los Angeles Times*, San Diego Edition, April 5, 1989.

336   "We want to see if you fit into the dress": Quoted in Seth Abramovitch, "'I Was Rob Lowe's Snow White': The Untold Story of Oscar's Nightmare Opening," *The Hollywood Reporter*, Feb. 20, 2013.

336   "At that point, I just stopped asking questions": Author interview with Eileen Bowman, July 14, 2020.

338   "I mean, the phone calls go all night": *Entertainment Tonight* segment provided by Jeanne Wolf.

338   "As you probably know, I'm producing the Oscar telecast": Quoted in Hofler, *Party Animals*, 210.

339   "Without hesitation, I said yes": Rob Lowe, *Stories I Only Tell My Friends: An Autobiography* (New York: Henry Holt and Company, 2011), 237.

339   "We need to let the audience know": Quoted in Hofler, *Party Animals*, 208.

339   "At one point, which was very, very painful": Author interview with Jo Schuman Silver, July 8, 2020.

339   "I was devastated": Email to author from Mayim Bialik, Aug. 25, 2020.

340   "a dress extra": Quoted in Hofler, *Party Animals*, 222.

341   "to show our support for Allan Carr": Quoted in Hofler, *Party Animals*, 225.

341   "Thank you for making my dream come true": Author interview with Newman.

341   "The star of all time will be here soon": Hofler, *Party Animals*, 225.

342   "I empathized with her": Quoted in Abramovitch, "'I Was Rob Lowe's Snow White.'"

342   "The minute that it started": Author interview with Peter Bart, July 7, 2020.

342   "so embarrassed, she couldn't even give me her hand": Quoted in Churnin, "A Real Cinderella Story for a Real Snow White."

342   "I actually got bumped": Author interview with Bruce Davis, March 18, 2022.

343   "that thousand-yard stare": Lowe, *Stories I Only Tell My Friends*, 239.

343 "His mouth is agape": Lowe, *Stories I Only Tell My Friends*, 239.

343 "Oh, my God! Steve, you have a big hit!": Author interview with Silver.

343 "It just wasn't classy enough": Quoted in Hofler, *Party Animals*, 228.

344 "I had no idea you were such a good singer": Quoted in Lowe, *Stories I Only Tell My Friends*, 239.

344 "Don't you think the Snow White opening": Quoted in Hofler, *Party Animals*, 230–31.

345 "I burned a lot of bridges on this one": Author interview with Vilanch.

345 "Oh, my God": Author interview with Margolis.

345 "flatulent gas bag": Bob Wisehart, "Overdone, Overblown and, Mercifully, Over," *Sacramento Bee*, March 30, 1989.

345 "a flaming wreck": Jerry Buck, "Oscar Show Lacked Focus," Associated Press, March 30, 1989.

345 "deserves a permanent place": Janet Maslin, "The Oscars as Home Entertainment," *New York Times*, March 31, 1989.

346 "Dick, we got a problem": Quoted in Hofler, *Party Animals*, 238.

346 "Allan was having lunch": *The Fabulous Allan Carr*.

347 "For its own reasons, however": Quoted in "Oscar Night Snow White Controversy Continues," Associated Press, April 1, 1989.

348 He called Army Archerd: Hofler, *Party Animals*, 240.

348 "vast and artful, top-of-the budget floral arrangements": Charles Champlin, "Allan Carr: 'We Won the Town,'" *Los Angeles Times*, April 4, 1989.

348 "an overstuffed turkey": "For Some, the Oscar Show Was One Big Carr Crash," *Los Angeles Times*, April 9, 1989.

348 "unintentionally creating the impression": Nina J. Easton, "Disney & Oscar Live Happily Ever After . . . ," *Los Angeles Times*, April 7, 1989.

349 "an embarrassment both to the academy": "Actors, Filmmakers Object to Academy Show," *Santa Cruz Sentinel*, April 28, 1989.

349 "I collared the people one by one": Quoted in Pond, *The Big Show*, 9.

349 "What we're responding to": Quoted in Nina J. Easton, "Academy Steps in to Review Oscar Ceremony," *Los Angeles Times*, April 19, 1989.

349 "They just froze him out": Author interview with Jeanne Wolf, July 10, 2020.

349 "Don't ever try to take the piss out of the Oscars": Lowe, *Stories I Only Tell My Friends*, 240.

350 "For the first time, the board of governors": Quoted in Easton, "Academy Steps in to Review Oscar Ceremony."

351 "a black hole for serious film makers": Jack Mathews, "Raiders of the Lost Art," *Los Angeles Times*, Dec. 29, 1989.

352 "Those bastards in Hollywood!": Quoted in Hofler, *Party Animals*, 248.

353 "He had no family at that point": Author interview with Joanne Cimbalo, July 9, 2020.

354 "Carr did a good job": Quoted in Robert Reinhold, "The Trials of Putting on a Show for Academy Awards Night," *New York Times*, March 5, 1990.

Nine: The Harveys, 1999

357 "It's not rocket science": Author interview with Bruce Feldman, Nov. 3, 2020.

358 "He's passionate about films": Quoted in Peter Biskind, *Down and Dirty Pictures:*

Miramax, Sundance, and the Rise of Independent Film (New York: Simon and Schuster, 2004), 355.

359 "Look, you have to keep it interesting": Quoted in David J. Fox, "Playing the Oscar Game Like a 'Piano'?" *Los Angeles Times*, March 11, 1994.

359 "And you guys can accomplish": Quoted in Bob Weinstein, "All Thanks to Max," *Vanity Fair*, April 2003.

360 "Easy! You got a Nobel Prize winner": Quoted in Biskind, *Down and Dirty Pictures*, 47.

360 "I had never seen anything so crass": Reid Rosefelt, "Harvey and Bob Weinstein: The Early Days," personal blog shared with author, Feb. 6, 2011.

360 "Harvey was still not a threat": Author interview with Ira Deutchman, Sept. 1, 2021.

361 "Well, other people do it": Lisa Rose, as told to Georgina Rannard, UGC and Social News team, "What It Was Like to Work for Harvey Weinstein," BBC, Oct. 13, 2017.

362 "In those days the studios": Quoted in Biskind, *Down and Dirty Pictures*, 99.

362 "It is not as cold and calculating": Quoted in Terry Pristin and James Bates, "The Climbing Game," *Los Angeles Times*, March 29, 1993.

362 "Harvey would keep the blinds closed": Author interview with Teri Kane, Aug. 16, 2021.

362 "He just loved the idea": Author interview with Mark Gill, Aug. 17, 2021.

363 "waiting for Godot to come": Quoted in Biskind, *Down and Dirty Pictures*, 111.

364 "the poohbahs of Hollywood": Kenneth Turan, "The Declaration of Independents," *Los Angeles Times*, Feb. 18, 1993.

364 "Commerce has overwhelmed art": Janet Maslin, "Is a Cinematic New Wave Cresting?," *New York Times*, Dec. 13, 1992.

365 "tired of being in the minor leagues": Quoted in Claudia Eller, "On-screen Chemistry," *Los Angeles Times*, Dec. 1, 1995.

365 "cost almost as much": Quoted in Fox, "Playing the Oscar Game Like a 'Piano'?"

365 "There's a pretty giant misunderstanding": Description of the press conference from Nicole LaPorte, *The Men Who Would Be King: An Almost Epic Tale of Moguls, Movies, and a Company Called DreamWorks* (New York: Mariner Books, 2010), 31–32.

366 "You never knew if he was gonna hug": LaPorte, *The Men Who Would Be King*, 10.

366 Spielberg was vacationing: LaPorte, *The Men Who Would Be King*, 15.

367 "This is as if Babe Ruth": Quoted in Alan Citron and Claudia Eller, "'Dream Team' Trio Outline Plans for Studio," *Los Angeles Times*, Oct. 13, 1994.

367 "the prototype plugged-in multimedia company": Richard Corliss, "Hey, Let's Put on a Show!," *Time*, March 27, 1995.

368 "Next time I see you in a tie": Quoted in LaPorte, *The Men Who Would Be King*, 86.

368 "The snack thing was big": Author interview with Mike Gottberg, Aug. 31, 2021.

368 "I guarantee that, when their first film premieres": Quoted in Corliss, "Hey, Let's Put on a Show!"

368 re-create her nude horseback scene: Lauren David Peden, "Big Little Movies Stand Up to Summer's Blockbusters," *New York Times*, Aug. 22, 1993.

369 "So, how do you justify": Quoted in Biskind, *Down and Dirty Pictures*, 120.

369 "I didn't make it for your wife!": Quoted in Biskind, *Down and Dirty Pictures*, 135.

369 "The first scene is *fucking brilliant*": Quoted in Mark Seal, "Cinema Tarantino: The Making of *Pulp Fiction*," *Vanity Fair*, Feb. 13, 2013.

370 "Quentin brought back": Author interview with Bumble Ward, Sept. 14, 2021.

370 "*Pulp Fiction* is shit!": Quoted in Seal, "Cinema Tarantino: The Making of *Pulp Fiction*."

370 "It could not have been a bigger": Author interview with Liz Manne, Sept. 1, 2021.

370 "The hero ain't the hero": Quoted in Betsy Sharkey, "Cover Your Eyes, Quick," *New York Times*, Oct. 30, 1994.

370 "I'm their Mickey Mouse": Quoted in Lynn Hirschberg, "The Man Who Changed Everything," *New York Times*, Nov. 16, 1997.

370 "I'm drinking sweet vintage champagne": Quoted in Judy Brennan, "Oscar Nods Mark Independents' Day," *Los Angeles Times*, Feb. 15, 1995.

371 "have lunch with little old ladies": Quoted in Seal, "Cinema Tarantino: The Making of *Pulp Fiction*."

371 "tread dangerously close": Quoted in Aljean Harmetz, "Bear Hunting in Oscar Season: Five Strategies," *New York Times*, Jan. 29, 1995.

371 "I'm always going up against": Quoted in Biskind, *Down and Dirty Pictures*, 206.

371 "It was heated": Author interview with Cheryl Boone Isaacs, Oct. 8, 2020.

371 "Monday night, we'll be the fucking homeless people": Quoted in Frank DiGiacomo, "Lusty 'Pulp' Crew's Oscar Night Frolic: Weinstein Brothers Close Down Chasen's," *New York Observer*, April 3, 1995.

372 "What about mediocrity?": Quoted in DiGiacomo, "Lusty 'Pulp' Crew's Oscar Night Frolic."

372 "If she had killed you with an Oscar": Author interview with Lynn Hirschberg, Sept. 23, 2021.

372 "At 4 a.m., we're going": Quoted in DiGiacomo, "Lusty 'Pulp' Crew's Oscar Night Frolic."

372 "He pushed me down": Quoted in Maureen Dowd, "This Is Why Uma Thurman Is Angry," *New York Times*, Feb. 3, 2018.

374 "I don't want to cause Disney": Quoted in Bernard Weinraub, "Mavericks Adapting to Power of Studios," *New York Times*, June 24, 1996.

374 "We worked like crazy": Author interview with Amy Hart, Aug. 31, 2021.

374 "What *was* that?": Author interview with Donna Gigliotti, Sept. 22, 2021.

374 "I reported the incident": Quoted in Megan Twohey, Jodi Kantor, Susan Dominus, Jim Rutenberg, and Steve Eder, "Weinstein's Complicity Machine," *New York Times*, Dec. 5, 2017.

376 "nearly a Neruda scholar": Quoted in Dinitia Smith, "A Little Film with Amazingly Sturdy Legs," *New York Times*, Jan. 21, 1996.

376 "polite indifference": Quoted in Biskind, *Down and Dirty Pictures*, 243.

376 "I regarded them as angels": Quoted in Elaine Dutka and John Clark, "Miramax Finds Success Breeds Admiration, Envy," *Los Angeles Times*, Jan. 30, 1997.

376 "This is a terrific vindication": Quoted in James Bates and Claudia Puig, "Independent Films Dominate Oscar Picks," *Los Angeles Times*, Feb. 12, 1997.

377 "They were so dialed in to the voters": Author interview with Paul Zaentz, Aug. 19, 2021.

378 John Ericson, a retired actor: Mark Lander, "How Miramax Sets Its Sights on Oscar," *New York Times*, March 23, 1997.

378 "We wanted people to think": Quoted in Claudia Eller, "Miramax's 'Patient' Approach," *Los Angeles Times*, March 21, 1997.

378 The honeymoon wouldn't last: Biskind, *Down and Dirty Pictures*, 274–76.

379 "so rumpled his monkey suit": Frank DiGiacomo, "The Night Miramax Owned Los Angeles," *New York Observer*, March 31, 1997.

379 "shocking similarities": Quoted in LaPorte, *The Men Who Would Be King*, 152.

379 "reparations": Quoted in LaPorte, *The Men Who Would Be King*, 154.

379 "splendid piece of work": Quoted in Bernard Weinraub, "Plagiarism Suit over 'Amistad' Is Withdrawn," *New York Times*, Feb. 10, 1998.

379 "the spinach movie": LaPorte, *The Men Who Would Be King*, 151.

380 "When you have a vagina": Quoted in LaPorte, *The Men Who Would Be King*, 385.

380 "*Titanic* has great special effects": Quoted in Bernard Weinraub, "The Oscar Chase: Power and Dollars," *New York Times*, March 6, 1998.

380 "Harvey didn't get crazy about winning": Author interview with Cynthia Swartz, Aug. 25, 2021.

380 "whoring for Oscars": Quoted in Biskind, *Down and Dirty Pictures*, 312.

380 "I offered Sean Connery": Quoted in Frank DiGiacomo, "Oscars MCMXCVIII," *New York Observer*, March 29, 1998.

380 "We would often walk": Quoted in Denis Hamill, "Hallowed Be Their Names: Mystic Cords of Memory Bind 'Saving Private Ryan' Scripter to the Joes Who Won the War," (New York) *Daily News*, Aug. 2, 1998.

381 "I said, 'That's the greatest fucking story'": Author interview with Mark Gordon, Sept. 21, 2021.

381 They made a deal with Don Granger: Details of *Saving Private Ryan's* development from LaPorte, *The Men Who Would Be King*, 164–68; and Peter Bart, *The Gross: The Hits, the Flops—the Summer That Ate Hollywood* (New York: St. Martin's Press, 1999), 145–53.

382 "You bet he's got to die": Quoted in LaPorte, *The Men Who Would Be King*, 169.

382 "We had different iterations": Author interview with Gary Levinsohn, Aug. 27, 2021.

383 "One of Steven's gifts": Author interview with Walter Parkes, Sept. 14, 2021.

383 "So, between my father's stories": *Into the Breach: "Saving Private Ryan,"* featurette (DreamWorks, 1998).

383 "I didn't want to shoot the picture": *Into the Breach.*

383 "In my heart, I loved my dad": Quoted in McBride, *Steven Spielberg*, 462.

383 "He wanted to be like those young men": Author interview with Ian Bryce, Aug. 30, 2021.

383 "laboring to get it accurate": *Into the Breach: "Saving Private Ryan."*

384 "I thought that the actual idea": Author interview with Terry Press, Sept. 22, 2021.

384 strict new fruit-and-vegetable diet: Bart, *The Gross*, 253–54.

384 "quite possibly the greatest combat sequence": Richard Schickel, "Steven Spielberg: Reel War," *Time*, July 27, 1998.

385 "We don't have to take any shit": Quoted in LaPorte, *The Men Who Would Be King*, 174.

385 "He held—and still holds": Author interview with Mitch Kreindel, Oct. 6, 2021.

385 "Houston, we have a problem": Quoted in Scott Feinberg, "'Harvey Always Wanted More': Weinstein, Spielberg and the Oral History of the Nastiest Oscar Campaign Ever," *The Hollywood Reporter*, Feb. 20, 2019.

385 "I'd written a bunch of screenplays": Author interview with Marc Norman, Aug. 27, 2021.

386 "Couldn't she have waited": Quoted in Biskind, *Down and Dirty Pictures*, 327.

386 "All of a sudden, Universal pulls the plug": Author interview with Ed Zwick, Aug. 25, 2021.

387 "He was obsessed with her": Author interview with Matthew Cohen, Aug. 27, 2021.

387 Shortly before *Emma* filmed: Jodi Kantor and Rachel Abrams, "Big-Name Actresses Say They Were Harassed by Weinstein," *New York Times*, Oct. 11, 2017.

388 "Let us have pirates": Quoted in Hermione Lee, *Tom Stoppard: A Life* (New York: Alfred A. Knopf, 2021), 449.

389 "It literally was presented wet": Author interview with Tony Angellotti, Aug. 12, 2021.

389 "my friend Harvey": Quoted in Alex Kuczynski, "The First Lady Strikes a Pose for the Media Elite," *New York Times*, Dec. 7, 1998.

389 "exhilarating cleverness": Janet Maslin, "Film Review: Shakespeare Saw a Therapist?" *New York Times*, Dec. 11, 1998.

390 "very colorful and fun": Author interview with David Brooks, Sept. 14, 2021.

390 "Has Red Buttons seen the movie?": Author interview with Gigliotti.

390 "Harvey made the Academy feel": Quoted in LaPorte, *The Men Who Would Be King*, 199.

391 "This is thirty-six hours before the supper": Author interview with Bobby Zarem, Aug. 20, 2021.

391 "the first feel-good Holocaust weepie": Owen Gleiberman, "'Life Is Beautiful,'" *Entertainment Weekly*, Oct. 30, 1998.

391 At the Directors Guild of America Awards: Robert W. Welkos, "Benigni Rising Has Hollywood Gushing," *Los Angeles Times*, March 19, 1999.

391 "the Pope's Oscars": Bernard Weinraub, "Using the Hard Sell to Grab the Gold," *New York Times*, March 7, 1999.

392 Incensed, she marched into Spielberg's office: Feinberg, "'Harvey Always Wanted More.'"

393 "You don't have to campaign": Quoted in LaPorte, *The Men Who Would Be King*, 201.

393 "I called Steven to congratulate him": Quoted in Bernard Weinraub, "Just a Couple of Old Pals Wrestling for an Oscar," March 15, 1999.

393 "She was always pissed off": Author interview with Peter Bart, Aug. 13, 2021.

394 "virtually anointed": Weinraub, "Using the Hard Sell to Grab the Gold."

394 "one of the most contentious ceremonies": Nikki Finke, "Much Ado About Oscar," *New York*, March 15, 1999.

394 "DreamWorks was having a conversation": Author interview with Marcy Granata, Aug. 17, 2021.

394 "We don't want to be Big Brother": Quoted in Finke, "Much Ado About Oscar."

396 "My legs are hurting": Quoted in Weinraub, "Using the Hard Sell to Grab the Gold."

396 "I believe the award is for achievement": Quoted in John Lippman, "Studio's Oscar Mission Is to Save 'Saving Private Ryan,'" *Wall Street Journal*, Feb. 10, 1999.

398 "I felt," she said later: Quoted in Feinberg, "'Harvey Always Wanted More.'"

399 "I don't think I spoke to any press": Author interview with David Parfitt, Aug. 26, 2021.

399 "I will *never* take the high road": Quoted in Feinberg, "'Harvey Always Wanted More.'"

399 "pale, haunted look": William Booth and Sharon Waxman, "After the Ceremonies, All Decked Out in Tinseltown," *Washington Post*, March 23, 1999.

400 "Just wait and see": Quoted in Frank DiGiacomo, "A Tense Best-Picture Victory for the Miramax Mogul Who Stormed Oscar Beach," *New York Observer*, March 28, 1999.

400 "Steven was no longer naïve": Quoted in Feinberg, "'Harvey Always Wanted More.'"

400 "with tense pleasure": DiGiacomo, "A Tense Best-Picture Victory for the Miramax Mogul Who Stormed Oscar Beach."

401 "It's no longer about the material": Quoted in Bernard Weinraub, "Morning After Complaints Follow Miramax Mogul's Big Night," *New York Times*, March 23, 1999.

401 the newly formed Lionsgate: Originally called Lions Gate Films, the company, formed in 1997, bears no relation to Robert Altman's Lion's Gate Films.

401 "They're distorting the process": Quoted in Amy Wallace, "'Shakespeare' Hit by Snipers," *Los Angeles Times*, March 23, 1999.

401 "The movie itself is about putting on a show": Quoted in Wallace, "'Shakespeare' Hit by Snipers."

401 "The newspapers report the town": Quoted in DiGiacomo, "A Tense Best-Picture Victory for the Miramax Mogul Who Stormed Oscar Beach."

401 "There's still nothing quite as exhilarating": Vincent Canby, "Hollywood's Shocked and Appalled by Miramax? Oh, Please!" *New York Times*, March 25, 1999.

402 "We figured five, ten or twenty-five": Quoted in Amy Wallace, "Studio Built Victory 'One Brick at a Time,'" *Los Angeles Times*, March 27, 2000.

402 "couldn't afford the embarrassment": Quoted in Wallace, "Studio Built Victory 'One Brick at a Time.'"

403 "never hid the darkness": Quoted in Wallace, "Studio Built Victory 'One Brick at a Time.'"

403 "Congratulations. You saw the playbook": Quoted in Wallace, "Studio Built Victory 'One Brick at a Time.'"

403 vases of five red roses: LaPorte, *The Men Who Would Be King*, 249.

403 "I would be invited to private screenings": Author interview with Tom O'Neil, Aug. 25, 2021.

404 After it got six Golden Globe nominations: "Matt Drudge's 'Exclusive' Report on 'A Beautiful Mind' Challenged," *Advocate*, Dec. 22, 2001.

404 "discovering shocking Jew-bashing passages": Quoted in Biskind, *Down and Dirty Pictures*, 440.

404 "You're going down for this!": Quoted in Biskind, *Down and Dirty Pictures*, 440–41.

404 "You can't work this way": Quoted in Biskind, *Down and Dirty Pictures*, 441.

405   "This is a town that smells blood": Quoted in Ken Auletta, "Beauty and the Beast," *The New Yorker*, Dec. 16, 2002.

405   "Three months ago they were saying": Quoted in Rick Lyman, "It's Harvey Weinstein's Turn to Gloat," *New York Times*, Feb. 12, 2003.

405   In its headline the next morning: Robert W. Welkos and Susan King, "The Harveys," *Los Angeles Times*, Feb. 12, 2003.

Ten: Tokens, 1940, 1964, 2002

407   Its reporters started calling: Esther Breger, "The 'Hollywood Blackout' at the 1996 Academy Awards," *The New Republic*, Jan. 29, 2016.

407   "shocking level of minority exclusion": Pam Lambert, "What's Wrong with This Picture?," *People*, March 18, 1996.

407   "It doesn't stand to reason": Quoted in Greg Braxton, "Jackson Plans to Organize Grass-Roots Oscar Protest," *Los Angeles Times*, March 17, 1996.

408   "The Academy is probably": Quoted in Braxton, "Jackson Plans to Organize Grass-Roots Oscar Protest."

408   "the wonderful performances": Quoted in Breger, "The 'Hollywood Blackout' at the 1996 Academy Awards."

408   "thirty-five years too late": Quoted in Pond, *The Big Show*, 110.

408   "open up the consciousness of Hollywood": Quoted in Greg Braxton, "Protest of Oscars Is Taking Shape, Jesse Jackson Says," *Los Angeles Times*, March 22, 1996.

408   The press called the action: Breger, "The 'Hollywood Blackout' at the 1996 Academy Awards."

408   "a living repository": Sidney Poitier, *The Measure of a Man: A Spiritual Autobiography* (New York: HarperCollins, 2000), 232.

409   Hattie McDaniel knew the truth: Details of Henry McDaniel's biography from Jill Watts, *Hattie McDaniel: Black Ambition, White Hollywood* (New York: Amistad, 2005), 1–24.

410   "I knew that I could sing and dance": Quoted in Watts, *Hattie McDaniel*, 31.

410   "cactus hair": Quoted in Watts, *Hattie McDaniel*, 40.

410   "different nationalities in their native brogue": Quoted in Watts, *Hattie McDaniel*, 44.

411   "put my drill in your cavity": Quoted in Watts, *Hattie McDaniel*, 72.

411   "ups and downs": Quoted in Watts, *Hattie McDaniel*, 63.

412   "There is a colored woman": Quoted in Watts, *Hattie McDaniel*, 103–4.

412   "But of course, the Academy": Quoted in Watts, *Hattie McDaniel*, 110.

412   "surpass Louise Beavers in prominence": Quoted in Watts, *Hattie McDaniel*, 120.

413   "smart tailored gowns": Quoted in Watts, *Hattie McDaniel*, 132.

413   "handkerchief head roles": Quoted in Watts, *Hattie McDaniel*, 133.

413   "I can be a maid": Quoted in Watts, *Hattie McDaniel*, 139. Watts traces this line only to sources appearing after McDaniel's death.

413   "Unless the propaganda": Quoted in Watts, *Hattie McDaniel*, 148.

413   One morning in 1944: Sidney Poitier, *This Life* (New York: Ballantine Books, 1980), 69.

414   "He helped me to understand": Poitier, *This Life*, 74.

414   "He will walk with kings": Quoted in Poitier, *This Life*, 3.

414 "free of the crushing negative self-image": Poitier, *This Life*, 40.

415 "But I'm here": Poitier, *This Life*, 39.

415 "From the moment I got off": Poitier, *This Life*, 75.

415 "enormous effort at being likable": Poitier, *This Life*, 75.

415 "Just go on and get out": Quoted in Poitier, *This Life*, 82.

416 "I soon found that living": Poitier, *This Life*, 127.

416 Because of his association: Poitier, *This Life*, 169.

417 "*Porgy and Bess* is an insult": Poitier, *This Life*, 202.

417 "I understand how you feel": Quoted in Poitier, *This Life*, 204.

417 "As smart as I thought I was": Poitier, *This Life*, 207.

417 "deep and powerful strain": Bosley Crowther, "Screen: A Forceful Social Drama," *New York Times*, Sept. 25, 1958.

417 "When Sidney jumps off the train": James Baldwin, "Sidney Poitier," *Look*, July 23, 1968.

418 "they weren't going to give an Oscar": Tony Curtis, *American Prince: A Memoir* (New York: Harmony Books, 2008), 195.

418 "As I see myself": Quoted in Thomas M. Pryor, "A 'Defiant One' Becomes a Star," *New York Times*, Jan. 25, 1959.

418 "I had worked so hard to be accepted": Quoted in Jill Gerston, "Halle Berry: The Prom's Co-Queen Finally Gets Her Revenge," *New York Times*, March 12, 1995.

418 "flawless cafe au lait skin": Gerston, "Halle Berry: The Prom's Co-Queen Finally Gets Her Revenge."

419 "I felt a lot of guilt": Quoted in Dana Kennedy, "Halle Berry, Bruised and Beautiful, Is on a Mission," *New York Times*, March 10, 2002.

419 "She said if I fight it": Quoted in Kennedy, "Halle Berry, Bruised and Beautiful, Is on a Mission."

419 "secret society": Quoted in Joyce Maynard, "Roles of a Lifetime," *T Magazine*, Oct. 18, 2012.

419 "show who I was": Quoted in Maynard, "Roles of a Lifetime."

419 "My mother tried hard": Quoted in Maynard, "Roles of a Lifetime."

419 "America's advancement in space": "Foreign Intrigue," *Miami Herald*, Nov. 8, 1986.

419 "It makes me very proud": Quoted in "Miss United States Is in the Finals of Miss World," Associated Press, Nov. 13, 1986.

419 "Well, there goes your commercial career": Quoted in Karen S. Schneider, "Hurts So Bad," *People*, May 13, 1996.

420 "I left so fast": Quoted in Schneider, "Hurts So Bad."

420 "I convinced him that in this day": Quoted in Kennedy, "Halle Berry, Bruised and Beautiful, Is on a Mission."

420 "It was important to me": Quoted in Gerston, "Halle Berry: The Prom's Co-Queen Finally Gets Her Revenge."

420 "Some executive explained it": Quoted in Kennedy, "Halle Berry, Bruised and Beautiful, Is on a Mission."

420 She wanted the part of a park ranger: Gerston, "Halle Berry: The Prom's Co-Queen Finally Gets Her Revenge."

420 "I identify with being a black woman": Quoted in Lynn Hirschberg, "The Beautiful and the Damned," *New York Times*, Dec. 23, 2001.

421 "The answer was no, no, no": Quoted in Hirschberg, "The Beautiful and the Damned."

422 "He connected to her sense": Halle Berry, "Halle Berry Pens Tribute to Sidney Poitier: 'An Angel Watching over All of Us,'" *Variety*, Jan. 12, 2022.

422 "It is a mystery": Quoted in Bernard Weinraub, "Hollywood's First Black Goddess and Casualty," *New York Times*, Aug. 15, 1999.

422 "It totally changed [Berry's] esteem": Author interview with Martha Coolidge, Feb. 5, 2021.

422 "I can't go crazy": Quoted in Weinraub, "Hollywood's First Black Goddess and Casualty."

422 "a huge old woman": Margaret Mitchell, *Gone with the Wind* (New York: Simon and Schuster, 2008), 30.

423 "who was fearless": Quoted in Carlton Jackson, *Hattie: The Life of Hattie McDaniel* (Lanham, MD: Madison Books, 1990), 54.

423 "extremely capable": Quoted in Jackson, *Hattie*, 34.

423 "little lady": Quoted in Jackson, *Hattie*, 36.

423 "smell the magnolias": Quoted in Jackson, *Hattie*, 35.

423 "very definite apprehension": Quoted in Watts, *Hattie McDaniel*, 153.

423 "awfully careful that the Negroes": Quoted in Watts, *Hattie McDaniel*, 154.

423 "means about $2,000": Quoted in Watts, *Hattie McDaniel*, 156.

424 "Don't worry": Quoted in Watts, *Hattie McDaniel*, 159.

424 "You'll never come back to Hollywood": Quoted in Watts, *Hattie McDaniel*, 163.

424 "I think she is going to be hailed": Quoted in Watts, *Hattie McDaniel*, 167.

425 "I hope that Mammy": Quoted in Watts, *Hattie McDaniel*, 169.

425 WISH YOU COULD HAVE HEARD: Quoted in Watts, *Hattie McDaniel*, 172.

425 "brilliant work": Quoted in Watts, *Hattie McDaniel*, 174.

425 "loves this degrading position": Quoted in Watts, *Hattie McDaniel*, 176.

425 "an opportunity to glorify": Quoted in Watts, *Hattie McDaniel*, 177.

425 "We trust that discrimination": Quoted in Jackson, *Hattie*, 51.

425 "We bent over backward": Quoted in Watts, *Hattie McDaniel*, 175.

426 *Variety* had described: Ceremony details from Wiley and Bona, *Inside Oscar*, 100.

426 Selznick International had reportedly: Watts, *Hattie McDaniel*, 179.

426 "See, Hattie, you've made me cry": Quoted in Jackson, *Hattie*, 52.

427 "Well," she told the press: Quoted in Jackson, *Hattie*, 54.

427 "*Gott ist gut*": William E. Barrett, *The Lilies of the Field* (New York: Grand Central Publishing, 1982), 12.

427 "I was being pushed to change the world": Poitier, *This Life*, 195.

428 "could be a white man": Bosley Crowther, "Screen: A Disarming Modern Parable," *New York Times*, Oct. 2, 1963.

428 "indication that some creative leaders": Murray Schumach, "Hollywood Cause," *New York Times*, Aug. 25, 1963.

428 "I'm an actor, not a politician": Quoted in Sheilah Graham, "Van Johnson Is Still Wearing Ring," *Los Angeles Evening Citizen News*, Dec. 23, 1963.

429 "a tribute to a Negro": Philip K. Scheuer, "Tipster's Guide to the Oscar Race," *Los Angeles Times*, April 12, 1963.

429   "Diahann and I felt": Poitier, *This Life*, 245.

429   As he sat alone: Poitier's description of the ceremony from Poitier, *This Life*, 248–49.

430   "Up to the stage came": Oprah Winfrey's acceptance speech for the Cecil B. DeMille Award, *Golden Globe Awards*, NBC, aired Jan. 7, 2018.

430   "The outburst for Mr. Poitier": Murray Schumach, "Poitier Wins Oscar as Best Film Actor," *New York Times*, April 14, 1964.

430   "I like to think it will help": Quoted in Murray Schumach, "Poitier Reflects on Oscar Victory," *New York Times*, April 15, 1964.

430   "I don't want to die": Quoted in Joseph Finnigan, "Sidney Poitier Seeks New Roles," *Oakland Tribune*, April 5, 1964.

430   "Why don't you ask me": Quoted in "City Awards Poitier Cultural Prize," *New York Times*, April 21, 1964.

431   "breaking the cycle of violence": Quoted in Robert W. Welkos, "A Death Row Tale Finally Gets a Reprieve," *Los Angeles Times*, Aug. 12, 2001.

431   "I called my manager": Quoted in Hirschberg, "The Beautiful and the Damned."

431   "I kept calling the producer": Author interview with Vincent Cirrincione, Feb. 11, 2021.

431   "who I wanted for the movie": Author interview with Lee Daniels, Feb. 10, 2021.

432   "asked only two things of me": Author interview with Marc Forster, Feb. 22, 2021.

432   "I thought, If you're going to sell the damn story": Quoted in Hirschberg, "The Beautiful and the Damned."

432   "if Billy Bob agreed": Quoted in Hirschberg, "The Beautiful and the Damned."

432   "As a marketer": Author interview with Tom Ortenberg, Feb. 24, 2021.

433   "fearless concentration": A. O. Scott, "Film Review: Courtesy and Decency Play Sneaky with a Tough Guy," *New York Times*, Dec. 26, 2001.

433   "Running a campaign against some of these guys": Quoted in Rick Lyman, "What Price Buzz? Hollywood Breaks Bank for Oscar Race," *New York Times*, Feb. 3, 2002.

433   "I sent in my ballot already": *The Oprah Winfrey Show*, Harpo Productions, aired Feb. 1, 2002.

434   "We lost everything to Sissy Spacek": Author interview with Daniels.

434   Two days before the awards: Author interview with Ortenberg.

434   "The only thing I remember": Quoted in Ramin Setoodeh, "How Halle Berry Fought Her Way to the Director's Chair," *Variety*, Sept. 9, 2020.

435   "Driving home that night": Quoted in Maynard, "Roles of a Lifetime."

435   "I consider this recognition": Quoted in Watts, *Hattie McDaniel*, 180.

435   "Big salaries and little work": Quoted in Watts, *Hattie McDaniel*, 182.

435   "Things is changin' nowadays": Quoted in Watts, *Hattie McDaniel*, 187.

435   "She will, if we don't watch out": Quoted in Watts, *Hattie McDaniel*, 189.

435   "come home for a rest": Quoted in Watts, *Hattie McDaniel*, 194.

437   "Restriction of Negroes": Quoted in Watts, *Hattie McDaniel*, 217.

437   "complete break with the tradition": Quoted Watts, *Hattie McDaniel*, 227.

437   McDaniel made her feelings plain: Watts, *Hattie McDaniel*, 220.

437   "She was extremely realistic": Quoted in Watts, *Hattie McDaniel*, 224.

437   "bitter years of loneliness": Quoted in Watts, *Hattie McDaniel*, 229–30.

437   Midway through, she described Horne: Watts, *Hattie McDaniel*, 231.

438 "with the tone and manner": Quoted in Watts, *Hattie McDaniel*, 242.

438 "What is more important?": Quoted in Watts, *Hattie McDaniel*, 243.

438 "a dangerously glorified picture": Quoted in Watts, *Hattie McDaniel*, 248.

438 "I have never apologized": Hattie McDaniel, "What Hollywood Means to Me," *The Hollywood Reporter*, Sept. 29, 1947.

439 "Why do we as a race": Quoted in Watts, *Hattie McDaniel*, 257.

439 "I was now viewed": Poitier, *This Life*, 265.

440 "I felt seen": Berry, "Halle Berry Pens Tribute to Sidney Poitier: 'An Angel Watching over All of Us.'"

441 "Black people particularly disliked": Baldwin, "Sidney Poitier."

441 "a showcase nigger": Clifford Mason, "Why Does White America Love Sidney Poitier So?," *New York Times*, Sept. 10, 1967.

441 "the most devastating and unfair": Poitier, *This Life*, 331.

441 "I was the perfect target": Poitier, *This Life*, 330.

442 "Generally these black heroes": Poitier, *This Life*, 335.

442 "My own career went into a decline": Poitier, *This Life*, 336.

442 "the present situation is somewhat bleak": Poitier, *This Life*, 341.

442 "The impact of the black audience": Quoted in Michael E. Ross, "Sidney Poitier on 40 Years of Change," *New York Times*, Feb. 28, 1989.

442 "Sidney Poitier was the first": Poitier, *The Measure of a Man*, jacket.

443 "I was out of my mind": Noela Hueso, "Sidney Poitier and Halle Berry," *The Hollywood Reporter*, Dec. 16, 2010.

443 "It remains to be seen": "Hollywood History and Fantasy," *New York Times*, March 26, 2002.

443 "toe-curlingly embarrassing": "Halle Berry: Your Thoughts on Her Speech?," BBC News, March 27, 2002.

443 "I think she sold her peers short": "Best Acting Oscars Spark Debate About Political Correctness, Merit," *Los Angeles Times*, March 27, 2002.

444 "I wasn't going to be a prostitute": Quoted in Allison Samuels, "Angela's Fire," *Newsweek*, June 30, 2002.

444 "After all this time": Quoted in Greg Braxton and Anne Valdespino, "Dust-up Over an Oscar Role," *Los Angeles Times*, July 1, 2002.

444 "The moment I won the Oscar": Quoted in Jonathan Van Meter, "Halle Berry: Halle's Hollywood," *Vogue*, Aug. 20, 2010.

445 "Nobody was ready to sink": Quoted in Setoodeh, "How Halle Berry Fought Her Way to the Director's Chair."

445 "based on her performance": Quoted in Sharon Waxman, "Making Her Leap into an Arena of Action; Halle Berry Mixes Sexiness with Strength," *New York Times*, July 21, 2004.

445 "People said to me, 'You can't do that'": Quoted in Setoodeh, "How Halle Berry Fought Her Way to the Director's Chair."

445 "In the zero-sum calculations": Waxman, "Making Her Leap into an Arena of Action."

445 "When you talk about Halle Berry": Quoted in Waxman, "Making Her Leap into an Arena of Action."

446 "for casting me in this piece of shit": Quoted in Xan Brooks, "Razzie Berry Gives a Fruity Performance," *Guardian*, Feb. 26, 2005.

446 *What the fuck is going on right now?* she thought: *Watch What Happens Live with Andy Cohen*, Bravo, aired Aug. 3, 2017.

446 "I thought, 'Oh, all these great scripts'": Quoted in Setoodeh, "How Halle Berry Fought Her Way to the Director's Chair."

446 "broken picker": Quoted in Maynard, "Roles of a Lifetime."

446 "When I said 'the door tonight has been opened'": Remarks at the Makers Conference, Feb. 2, 2016, Rancho Palos Verdes, CA.

Eleven: The Envelope, 2017

450 "Not at all": Quoted in Kara Warner, "Academy President Cheryl Boone Isaacs on 'Selma' Snubs, Lack of Diversity," *Vulture*, Jan. 15, 2015.

450 94 percent white and 77 percent male: John Horn, Nicole Sperling, and Doug Smith, "Unmasking the Academy: Oscar Voters Overwhelmingly White, Male," *Los Angeles Times*, Feb. 19, 2012.

450 "But when you see it in black and white": Author interview with Boone Isaacs.

450 "It's just how the wheel moves": Author interview with Cheryl Boone Isaacs for "Oscar Dearest." Boone Isaacs's quotations throughout come from interviews both for *The New Yorker* piece and for this book; other material is drawn from *The New Yorker* piece, as noted.

451 "political correctness": William Goldstein, "Academy Awards: It's About Art, Not Political Correctness," *Los Angeles Times*, Feb. 21, 2012.

451 "moving in the right direction": Quoted in John Horn and Doug Smith, "Diversity Efforts Slow to Change the Face of Oscar Voters," *Los Angeles Times*, Dec. 21, 2013.

451 "Now please enjoy your dinner": Quoted in Michael Cieply and Brooks Barnes, "For Spike Lee, an Honorary Oscar, but Diversity Takes Center Stage," *New York Times*, Nov. 15, 2015.

452 "We can talk, you know, yabba, yabba, yabba": Quoted in Cara Buckley, "Oscars 2016: It's a Nearly All-White Nominees' List—Again," *New York Times*, Jan. 14, 2016.

452 "Are we making sure": Quoted in "President Obama Responds to #OscarsSoWhite Controversy," Associated Press, Jan. 27, 2016.

454 "Obviously, it's a thinly-veiled ploy": Quoted in Scott Feinberg, "Academy's New Voting Rules Raise Questions, Concerns and Anger Among Members," *The Hollywood Reporter*, Jan. 23, 2016.

454 "flabbergasted and then outraged": Stephen Verona, "Oscar Voter Rips Diversity Plan: 'Try Telling the NBA to Hire More White, Latino, Chinese or Eskimo Players,'" *The Hollywood Reporter*, Jan. 25, 2016.

454 "exchanging purported racism": David Kirkpatrick, "Oscar Voter Who Once Ran Studios Chides Academy for 'Exchanging Purported Racism with Ageism,'" *The Hollywood Reporter*, Jan. 28, 2016.

454 "booted into the 'emeritus' status": "Gay Female Oscar Voter to Academy: Don't Kick Me out 'to Help You Deal with a Publicity Nightmare,'" *The Hollywood Reporter*, Jan. 28, 2016.

454 "racist against whites": Quoted in Rachel Donadio, "Charlotte Rampling Says Oscars 'Boycott' Is 'Racist Against Whites,'" *New York Times*, Jan. 22, 2016.

457 "capitulating to the PC police": William Goldstein, "I'd Like to Thank the Academy . . . for Capitulating to the PC Police," *Los Angeles Times*, Jan. 26, 2016.

457 "This year, we all know there's an elephant": Quoted in Michael Cieply, "Despite Diversity Controversy, Oscars Ceremony Remains Intact," *New York Times*, Feb. 8, 2016.

459 "This has been a passion project": "'The Birth of a Nation' Premiere—Complete, Uncut Q&A @ The Sundance Film Festival 1–25–16," YouTube, youtube.com/watch?v=SM3BDY_bwUQ.

459 No sooner had the credits rolled: Matt Donnelly and Sharon Waxman, "Inside Historic Sundance Bidding War for 'Birth of a Nation': Why Netflix Offered More but Still Lost," *The Wrap*, Jan. 27, 2016.

460 "I just don't think it's fair": Scott Feinstein, "Oscars: Harvey Weinstein Discourages Boycott, Predicts Chris Rock Will 'Annihilate' Hollywood," *The Hollywood Reporter*, Feb. 25, 2016.

460 Even as Weinstein continued: Brent Lang and Ramin Setoodeh, "Harvey Weinstein to Release Fewer Indie Films," *Variety*, Nov. 24, 2015.

461 "toxic environment for women": Quoted in Jodi Kantor and Megan Twohey, "Sexual Misconduct Claims Trail a Hollywood Mogul," *New York Times*, Oct. 6, 2017.

461 "There was just a lot of apprehension": Author interview with Lorenza Muñoz, Dec. 8, 2020.

461 "unintentionally caused so much confusion": Quoted in Gregg Kilday, "Academy Clarifies Its Rules Determining Members' Voting Rights," *The Hollywood Reporter*, April 18, 2016.

461 "running the Academy as if it's an oligarchy": Quoted in Scott Feinberg, "After #OscarsSoWhite, the Academy Struggles with Diversity, Age and 'Relevance,'" *The Hollywood Reporter*, April 27, 2016.

462 "She explained it's not about diversity": Author interview with Robert Bassing for "Oscar Dearest."

462 "I'm not going to go down screaming": Author interview with Dolores Hart for "Oscar Dearest."

463 Their accuser, who maintained anonymity: Kate Briquelet and M. L. Nestel, "Inside the Nate Parker Rape Case," *The Daily Beast*, Aug. 16, 2016.

463 "a very painful moment in my life": Quoted in Ramin Setoodeh, "'The Birth of a Nation' Star Nate Parker Addresses College Rape Trial," *Variety*, Aug. 12, 2016.

463 "He's probably going to get": Quoted in Briquelet and Nestel, "Inside the Nate Parker Rape Case."

463 "filled with profound sorrow": Quoted in Kate Erbland, "Nate Parker Writes 'Devastated' Facebook Response to College Rape Trial and Accuser's Suicide," *IndieWire*, Aug. 17, 2016.

463 "I cannot separate the art and the artist": Roxane Gay, "Nate Parker and the Limits of Empathy," *New York Times*, Aug. 19, 2016.

464 "Suddenly, I started thinking": Quoted in Manohla Dargis, "'La La Land' Makes Musicals Matter Again," *New York Times*, Nov. 23, 2016.

464 "It was very much a romantic love story": Author interview with Jordan Horowitz, Oct. 16, 2020.

464 "Every one of the contours": Quoted in Rebecca Ford, "How 'La La Land' Went

from First-Screening Stumbles to Hollywood Ending," *The Hollywood Reporter*, Nov. 3, 2016.

465 "Everything felt like a complete mess": Quoted in Ford, "How 'La La Land' Went from First-Screening Stumbles to Hollywood Ending."

465 "romantic fever dream": Pete Hammond, "'La La Land' Review: A Gorgeous Musical Romance for This Age—and the Ages," *Deadline*, Aug. 31, 2016.

466 "I was in this gray area": Author interview with Barry Jenkins, Nov. 5, 2020.

466 "hiding behind athletics": Quoted in "'Moonlight' Director Barry Jenkins and Playwright Tarell Alvin McCraney," *Fresh Air*, NPR, Oct. 19, 2016.

466 "Sometimes we just get in a comfortable place": Author interview with Adele Romanski, Nov. 17, 2020.

467 "unworthy of love": "'Moonlight' Director Barry Jenkins and Playwright Tarell Alvin McCraney."

467 "Clearly," McCraney said later: Quoted in E. Alex Jung, "*Moonlight*'s Tarell Alvin McCraney on Writing the Original Source Material, Taking Inspiration from Myths, and Creating Heroes with Black Skin," *Vulture*, Nov. 29, 2016.

469 "a film that will strike plangent chords": David Rooney, "'Moonlight': Telluride Review," *The Hollywood Reporter*, Sept. 2, 2016.

469 "The next screening turned into mayhem": Author interview with Noah Cowan, Nov. 9, 2020.

469 "He immediately accessed my heart": Quoted in Kristopher Tapley, "Damien Chazelle and Barry Jenkins on That Oscar Shocker: The Morning-After Interview," *Variety*, March 1, 2017.

470 "I was falsely accused": *Good Morning America*, ABC, aired Oct. 3, 2016.

470 "stomach-churning confusion": Gabrielle Union, "Op-Ed: 'Birth of a Nation' Actress Gabrielle Union: I Cannot Take Nate Parker Rape Allegations Lightly," *Los Angeles Times*, Sept. 2, 2016.

471 "self-perpetuating spin machine": Ronan Farrow, "My Father, Woody Allen, and the Danger of Questions Unasked," *Hollywood Reporter*, May 11, 2016.

473 "He was the Donald Trump": Author interview with Bruce Feldman, Nov. 13, 2020.

475 "the home of so many immigrants": Quoted in "John Legend Slams Trump at PGA Awards, Mark Burnett Booed," *Hollywood Reporter*, Jan. 28, 2017.

476 "referendum on Trump": Glenn Lovell, "Op-Ed: Will the Political Climate Deprive 'La La Land' of the Best Picture Oscar?," *Los Angeles Times*, Feb. 6, 2017.

476 "unbearable whiteness of *La La Land*": Geoff Nelson, "The Unbearable Whiteness of *La La Land*," *Paste*, Jan. 6, 2017.

476 "'Moonlight' deserves to win the Oscar": Justin Chang, "The Quiet Storm," *Los Angeles Times*, Feb. 18, 2017.

477 "mulled and wanted to make sure": Author interview with Michael De Luca and Jennifer Todd, Nov. 9, 2020.

478 "We would make sure that the correct person": Quoted in Matthew Jacobs, "What Would Happen If A Presenter Announced the Wrong Winner at the Oscars?," *Huffington Post*, Feb. 24, 2017.

478 "If you know who the winner is": Quoted in Steve Pond, "Oscars Stage Manager Details PwC Accountants' Incompetence: 'They Froze,'" *The Wrap*, March 1, 2017.

479 "That was a bad omen": Author interview with Jimmy Kimmel, Dec. 15, 2020.

480 "I was pumped up with steroids": Author interview with Damien Chazelle for "Moonwalkers," *The New Yorker*, Oct. 22, 2018.

481 "It's a dream I never allowed": Quoted in Tapley, "Damien Chazelle and Barry Jenkins on That Oscar Shocker: The Morning-After Interview."

482 "We had to push them": Quoted in Pond, "Oscars Stage Manager Details PwC Accountants' Incompetence: 'They Froze.'"

485 "I have the envelopes": Quoted in Scott Feinberg, "'They Got the Wrong Envelope!': The Oral History of Oscar's Epic Best Picture Fiasco," *The Hollywood Reporter*, Feb. 26, 2018.

485 "I wanted to hold the envelope": Author interview with Jon Macks, Nov. 12, 2020.

486 "What happened, dudes?": Quoted in Feinberg, "'They Got the Wrong Envelope!': The Oral History of Oscar's Epic Best Picture Fiasco."

486 "That would be great—for *you*": Quoted in Feinberg, "'They Got the Wrong Envelope!': The Oral History of Oscar's Epic Best Picture Fiasco."

487 "Your one job": Quoted in Feinberg, "'They Got the Wrong Envelope!': The Oral History of Oscar's Epic Best Picture Fiasco."

487 "Warren, come home": Quoted in Peggy Siegal, "Serious Moonlight," *Avenue*, April/May 2017.

488 "It never quite felt like we won": Quoted in Feinberg, "'They Got the Wrong Envelope!': The Oral History of Oscar's Epic Best Picture Fiasco."

488 "It's messy": Quoted in Tapley, "Damien Chazelle and Barry Jenkins on That Oscar Shocker: The Morning-After Interview."

489 "I think they were focused": Quoted in Gregg Kilday and Kim Masters, "Oscars Producer Michael De Luca Breaks Silence on Backstage Chaos: 'It Was Like the Hindenburg,'" *The Hollywood Reporter*, March 1, 2017.

490 "Those movies that win": Quoted in Lacey Rose, "Harvey Weinstein on Jay Z, Trump and His Dream to Produce the Oscars (with Spielberg)," *The Hollywood Reporter*, April 17, 2017.

490 "His movies have earned": Ronan Farrow, "Abuses of Power," *The New Yorker*, Oct. 23, 2017.

490 "If you were under contract": Quoted in Dana Goodyear, "Exposure," *The New Yorker*, Jan. 8, 2018.

491 "We do so not simply": Quoted in Brooks Barnes, "Harvey Weinstein Ousted from Motion Picture Academy," *New York Times*, Oct. 14, 2017.

Afterword: Gettin' Jiggy wit It

497 I was contemplating these questions: My account of the night first appeared in "What It Felt Like in the Room When Will Smith Slapped Chris Rock at the Oscars," *The New Yorker*, March 28, 2022.

BIBLIOGRAPHY

Amador, Victoria. *Olivia de Havilland: Lady Triumphant*. Lexington: University Press of Kentucky, 2019.

American Business Consultants. *Red Channels: The Report of Communist Influence in Radio and Television*. New York: Counterattack, 1950.

Barrett, William E. *The Lilies of the Field*. New York: Grand Central Publishing, 1982.

Bart, Peter. *The Gross: The Hits, the Flops—the Summer that Ate Hollywood*. New York: St. Martin's Press, 1999.

Baxter, Anne. *Intermission: A True Story*. New York: Ballantine Books, 1976.

Baxter, John. *Stanley Kubrick: A Biography*. New York: Carroll and Graf Publishers, 1997.

Bergen, Candice. *Knock Wood*. New York: Simon and Schuster, 1984.

Biskind, Peter. *Down and Dirty Pictures: Miramax, Sundance, and the Rise of Independent Film*. New York: Simon and Schuster, 2004.

——————. *Easy Riders, Raging Bulls: How the Sex-Drugs-and-Rock 'N' Roll Generation Saved Hollywood*. New York: Simon and Schuster, 1998.

Brady, Frank. *Citizen Welles: A Biography of Orson Welles*. New York: Anchor Books, 1989.

Brown, Peter H., and Jim Pinkston. *Oscar Dearest: Six Decades of Scandal, Politics and Greed Behind Hollywood's Academy Awards, 1927–1986*. New York: Harper and Row, 1987.

Brownlow, Kevin. *David Lean: A Biography*. London: Faber and Faber, 1996.

——————. *The Parade's Gone By . . .* Berkeley: University of California Press, 1968.

Capra, Frank. *The Name Above the Title: An Autobiography*. New York: The Macmillan Company, 1971.

Carey, Gary. *Judy Holliday: An Intimate Life Story*. New York: Seaview Books, 1982.

Ceplair, Larry, and Steven Englund. *The Inquisition in Hollywood: Politics in the Film Community, 1930–1960*. Berkeley and Los Angeles: University of California Press, 1979.

Ceplair, Larry, and Christopher Trumbo. *Dalton Trumbo: Blacklisted Hollywood Radical*. Lexington: University Press of Kentucky, 2015.

Curtis, Tony. *American Prince: A Memoir*. New York: Harmony Books, 2008.

Davis, Bette. *The Lonely Life*. New York, G. P. Putnam's Sons, 1962.

Davis, Bruce. *The Academy and the Award: The Coming of Age of Oscar and the Academy of Motion Picture Arts and Sciences.* Waltham, MA: Brandeis University Press, 2022.

Doherty, Thomas. *Hollywood and Hitler, 1933–1939.* New York: Columbia University Press, 2013.

Douglas, Kirk. *I Am Spartacus! Making a Film, Breaking the Blacklist.* New York: Open Road Integrated Media, 2012.

Eliot, Marc. *Cary Grant: A Biography.* New York: Three Rivers Press, 2004.

Eyman, Scott. *Lion of Hollywood: The Life and Legend of Louis B. Mayer.* New York: Simon and Schuster, 2005.

————. *Mary Pickford: America's Sweetheart.* New York: Donald L. Fine, 1990.

————. *The Speed of Sound: Hollywood and the Talkie Revolution, 1926–1930.* New York: Simon and Schuster, 1997.

Fischer, Erika J. *The Inauguration of "Oscar": Sketches and Documents from the Early Years of the Hollywood Academy of Motion Picture Arts and Sciences.* München and New York: K.G. Saur, 1988.

Fishgall, Gary. *Gregory Peck: A Biography.* New York: Scribner, 2002.

Fontaine, Joan. *No Bed of Roses.* New York: William Morrow and Company, 1978.

Forman, Miloš, and Jan Novák. *Turnaround: A Memoir.* New York: Villard Books, 1994.

Fowler, Karin J. *Anne Baxter: A Bio-Bibliography.* Westport, CT: Greenwood Press, 1991.

Frankel, Glenn. *High Noon: The Hollywood Blacklist and the Making of an American Classic.* New York: Bloomsbury, 2017.

————. *Shooting "Midnight Cowboy": Art, Sex, Loneliness, Liberation, and the Making of a Dark Classic.* New York: Farrar, Straus and Giroux, 2021.

Gabler, Neal. *An Empire of Their Own: How the Jews Invented Hollywood.* New York: Anchor Books, 1998.

Gehring, Wes D. *Movie Comedians of the 1950s.* Jefferson: McFarland and Company, 2016.

Geist, Kenneth L. *Pictures Will Talk: The Life and Films of Joseph L. Mankiewicz.* New York: Charles Scribner's Sons, 1978.

Goessel, Tracey. *The First King of Hollywood: The Life of Douglas Fairbanks.* Chicago: Chicago Press Review, 2016.

Gottlieb, Carl. *The "Jaws" Log.* New York: First Newmarket Press for It Books, 2012.

Grobel, Lawrence. *Al Pacino in Conversation with Lawrence Grobel.* London: Simon and Schuster, 2006.

Harris, Mark. *Five Came Back: A Story of Hollywood and the Second World War.* New York: Penguin Press, 2014.

————. *Pictures at a Revolution: Five Movies and the Birth of the New Hollywood.* New York: Penguin Books, 2008.

Haskell, Molly. *Steven Spielberg: A Life in Films.* New Haven, CT: Yale University Press, 2017.

Head, Edith, and Paddy Calistro. *Edith Head's Hollywood.* New York: Dutton, 1983.

Higham, Charles. *Sisters: The Story of Olivia de Havilland and Joan Fontaine.* New York: Coward-McCann, 1984.

Hofler, Robert. *Party Animals: A Hollywood Tale of Sex, Drugs, and Rock 'N' Roll Starring the Fabulous Allan Carr.* Cambridge, MA: Da Capo Press, 2010.

Holden, Anthony. *Behind the Oscar: The Secret History of the Academy Awards.* New York: Simon and Schuster, 1993.

Holtzman, Will. *Judy Holliday: A Biography*. New York: G.P. Putnam's Sons, 1982.

Hopper, Hedda. *From Under My Hat*. Garden City, NY: Doubleday, 1952.

Jackson, Carlton. *Hattie: The Life of Hattie McDaniel*. Lanham, MD: Madison Books, 1990.

Kael, Pauline. *When the Lights Go Down*. New York: Holt, Rinehart and Winston, 1980.

Kanin, Garson. *Tracy and Hepburn: An Intimate Memoir*. New York: Donald I. Fine, 1988.

Kellow, Brian. *Pauline Kael: A Life in the Dark*. New York: Penguin, 2011.

Kesey, Ken. *One Flew Over the Cuckoo's Nest*. New York: Penguin Classics, 2002.

Koppes, Clayton R., and Gregory D. Black. *Hollywood Goes to War: How Politics, Profits, and Propaganda Shaped World War II Movies*. New York: Free Press, 1987.

Kramer, Stanley. *A Mad, Mad, Mad, Mad World: A Life in Hollywood*. New York: Harcourt Brace and Company, 1997.

Ladensohn Stern, Sydney. *The Brothers Mankiewicz: Hope, Heartbreak, and Hollywood Classics*. Jackson: University Press of Mississippi, 2019.

LaPorte, Nicole. *The Men Who Would Be King: An Almost Epic Tale of Moguls, Movies, and a Company Called DreamWorks*. New York: Mariner Books, 2010.

Lasky, Jesse. *I Blow My Own Horn*. Garden City, NY: Doubleday and Company, 1957.

Lebo, Harlan. *Citizen Kane: A Filmmaker's Journey*. New York: St. Martin's Press, 2016.

Lee, Hermione. *Tom Stoppard: A Life*. New York: Alfred A. Knopf, 2021.

LoBrutto, Vincent. *Stanley Kubrick: A Biography*. New York: Donald L. Fine Books, 1997.

Lowe, Rob. *Stories I Only Tell My Friends: An Autobiography*. New York: Henry Holt and Company, 2011.

Lumet, Sidney. *Making Movies*. New York: Vintage Books, 1995.

————. *Sidney Lumet: Interviews*. Ed. Joanna E. Rapf. Jackson: University Press of Mississippi, 2006.

Mankiewicz, Joseph L., and Gary Carey. *More About "All About Eve": A Colloquy with Joseph L. Mankiewicz*. New York: Random House, 1972.

Mann, William J. *Tinseltown: Murder, Morphine, and Madness at the Dawn of Hollywood*. New York: Harper, 2014.

Marion, Frances. *Off with Their Heads! A Serio-Comic Tale of Hollywood*. New York: The Macmillan Company, 1972.

McBride, Joseph. *Frank Capra: The Catastrophe of Success*. New York: Simon and Schuster, 1992.

————. *Searching for John Ford: A Life*. New York: St. Martin's Press, 2001.

————. *Steven Spielberg: A Biography*. Jackson: University Press of Mississippi, 2010.

Merrill, Gary. *Bette, Rita, and the Rest of My Life*. Augusta, ME: L. Tapley, 1988.

Mitchell, Margaret. *Gone with the Wind*. New York: Simon and Schuster, 2008.

Monroe, Marilyn. *My Story*. New York: Stein and Day, 1974.

Mosley, Leonard. *Zanuck: The Rise and Fall of Hollywood's Last Tycoon*. Boston: Little, Brown, 1984.

Navasky, Victor S. *Naming Names*. New York: Hill and Wang, 1980.

Ovitz, Michael. *Who Is Michael Ovitz?* New York: Portfolio/Penguin, 2018.

Parsons, Louella O. *Tell It to Louella*. New York: G.P. Putnam's Sons, 1961.

Pawlak, Debra Ann. *Bringing Up Oscar: The Story of the Men and Women Who Founded the Academy*. New York: Pegasus Books, 2011.

Pickford, Mary. *Sunshine and Shadow*. Garden City, NY: Doubleday and Company, 1955.

Poitier, Sidney. *The Measure of a Man: A Spiritual Autobiography*. New York: HarperCollins, 2000.

—————. *This Life*. New York: Ballantine Books, 1980.

Pond, Steve. *The Big Show: High Times and Dirty Dealings Backstage at the Academy Awards*. New York: Faber and Faber, 2005.

Prime, Rebecca. *Hollywood Exiles in Europe: The Blacklist and Cold War Film Culture*. New Brunswick, NJ: Rutgers University Press, 2014.

Sanders, George. *Memoirs of a Professional Cad*. Metuchen, NJ, and London: Scarecrow Press, 1992.

Schickel, Richard. *D. W. Griffith: An American Life*. New York: Simon and Schuster, 1984.

Shone, Tom. *Blockbuster: How Hollywood Learned to Stop Worrying and Love the Summer*. New York: Free Press, 2004.

Sikov, Ed. *Dark Victory: The Life of Bette Davis*. New York: Henry Holt and Company, 2007.

—————. *On Sunset Boulevard: The Life and Times of Billy Wilder*. Jackson: University Press of Mississippi, 2017.

Silvester, Christopher, ed. *The Penguin Book of Hollywood*. London, New York: Viking, 1998.

Smith-Rowsey, Daniel. *Star Actors in the Hollywood Renaissance: Representing Rough Rebels*. London: Palgrave Macmillan, 2013.

Spada, James. *More than a Woman: An Intimate Biography of Bette Davis*. New York: Bantam Books, 1993.

Staggs, Sam. *All About "All About Eve": The Complete Behind-the-Scenes Story of the Bitchiest Film Ever Made*. New York: St. Martin's Griffin, 2001.

—————. *Close-up on "Sunset Boulevard": Billy Wilder, Norma Desmond, and the Dark Hollywood Dream*. New York: St. Martin's Griffin, 2002.

Stuart, Jan. *The "Nashville" Chronicles: The Making of Robert Altman's Masterpiece*. New York: Simon and Schuster, 2000.

Swanson, Gloria. *Swanson on Swanson: An Autobiography*. New York: Pocket Books, 1980.

Trumbo, Dalton. *Additional Dialogue: Letters of Dalton Trumbo, 1942–1962*. Ed. Helen Manfull. New York: M. Evans and Company, 1970.

Vidor, King. *King Vidor: Interviewed by Nancy Dowd and David Shepard*. Metuchen, NJ: Scarecrow Press, 1988.

—————. *A Tree Is a Tree*. New York: Harcourt, Brace and Company, 1953.

Warner, Jack L. *My First Hundred Years in Hollywood: An Autobiography*. New York: Random House, 1965.

Watts, Jill. *Hattie McDaniel: Black Ambition, White Hollywood*. New York: Amistad, 2005.

Wellman, William, Jr. *The Man and His "Wings": William A. Wellman and the Making of the First Best Picture*. Westport, CT: Praeger, 2006.

Whitfield, Eileen. *Pickford: The Woman Who Made Hollywood*. Lexington: University Press of Kentucky, 1997.

Wiley, Mason, and Damien Bona. *Inside Oscar: The Unofficial History of the Academy Awards*. New York: Ballantine Books, 1987.

Winkler, Peter L. *Dennis Hopper: The Wild Ride of a Hollywood Rebel*. Fort Lee, NJ: Barricade Books, 2011.

Zeruk, James, Jr. *Peg Entwistle and the Hollywood Sign Suicide: A Biography*. Jefferson, NC: McFarland and Company, 2014.

Zolotow, Maurice. *Billy Wilder in Hollywood*. New York: Putnam, 1977.

Zuckoff, Mitchell. *Altman: The Oral Biography*. New York: Alfred A. Knopf, 2009.

Zukor, Adolph. *The Public Is Never Wrong*. New York: G.P. Putnam's Sons, 1953.

PHOTOGRAPH
CREDITS

INDEX

Note: Italic page numbers refer to photographs.

ABOUT THE AUTHOR

MICHAEL SCHULMAN is the author of the *New York Times* bestseller *Her Again: Becoming Meryl Streep* and a staff writer at *The New Yorker*, where he has contributed since 2006. His work has also appeared in the *New York Times* and *Vanity Fair*, among other publications. He lives in New York City.